THE ILLUSTRATED ENCYCLOPEDIA OF
TREES
OF THE WORLD

THE ILLUSTRATED ENCYCLOPEDIA OF
TREES
OF THE WORLD

The ultimate reference and identification guide to more than 1300 of the most spectacular, best-loved and unusual trees around the globe, with 3000 specially commissioned watercolors, maps and photographs

TONY RUSSELL • CATHERINE CUTLER • MARTIN WALTERS

HERMES
HOUSE

CONTENTS

Introduction   8

HOW TREES LIVE   10

WORLD DIRECTORY OF TREES   88

How to Identify a Tree   90
How to use the Directories   94

TREES OF TEMPERATE AMERICA   96

TREES OF TROPICAL AMERICA   208

TREES OF BRITAIN AND EUROPE   280

TREES OF AFRICA, ASIA AND AUSTRALASIA 438

INTRODUCTION

Trees are the most complex and successful plants on earth. They have been around for 370 million years and quite likely will be around for many millions of years to come. Today, they cover almost a third of the earth's dry land and comprise more than 80,000 different species ranging from small Arctic willows that are just a few inches high to the lofty giant redwoods, which stand at an amazing 113m/368ft.

Trees are the oldest living organisms on earth. In California, there are Bristlecone pines which are known to be over 4,500 years old and in the United Kingdom there are yew trees of a similar age. Ever since the first primates appeared in the Palaeocene epoch, 65 million years ago, trees have played an integral part in human development, providing food, shelter, safety, medicines, timber and fuel among other things.

Trees are indeed essential to all life. They reduce pollution by absorbing vast amounts of carbon dioxide from the atmosphere while at the same time replacing it with "clean" oxygen. Each day 0.4ha/

Above: Giant redwoods, Sequoiadendron giganteum, *can reach heights in excess of 100m/325ft.*

1 acre of trees will produce enough oxygen to keep 18 people alive. Forests of trees help to regulate water flow and can reduce the effects of flooding and soil erosion. They even influence weather patterns by increasing humidity and generating rainfall.

With their myriad shades of green, trees make our cities and towns more colourful. They increase wildlife diversity, and create a more pleasant living and working environment. They provide shade in summer and shelter in winter. It is also a fact that post-operative hospital stays are shortened when patients are in rooms with views of trees.

For centuries, poets, writers and artists have been inspired by the beauty of trees. Works such as Wordsworth's *Borrowdale Yews* and John Constable's

Left: Robinia pseudoacacia *trees have been used to create avenues for at least 400 years. Pollarding keeps the shape neat and even.*

Above: Ancient trees are important points of reference in our towns and the countryside, and help determine the character of an area.

majestic elms in *The Hay Wain* will live on long after the original trees depicted have died. Trees help to bring beauty to our gardens and parks. Chosen well, they will provide stunning flowers, foliage, fruit and bark every day of the year. Nothing brings structure and maturity to a garden as successfully as a tree.

With so many obvious values it should be safe to assume that trees are venerated the world over. Unfortunately that is not the case. More than ten per cent of the world's tree species are endangered. More than 8,750 species are threatened with extinction – some are down to their last one or two specimens. Across the world we are losing at least 40ha/100 acres of trees every minute.

This book is a celebration of trees in all their forms, from hardy evergreens and deciduous broadleaves, to desert survivors and tropical palms. It reveals what incredible organisms trees are, and describes the diversity that exists throughout the world and how they each contribute to the planet. The first section describes the origins of trees, how they have evolved, how they live, grow, reproduce and why they die. It looks in detail at their leaves, bark, fruit, flowers, buds, cones and seeds, and

details the fascinating role each plays in the life of the tree. Trees inhabit many natural landscapes, from the highest mountain ridges all the way down to sea level, and have adapted to different circumstances. The heat of the tropics, the biting cold of northern lands, the salt and wind of the sea and the pollution of the city have all contributed to the evolution of the tree.

The second section of this book features a comprehensive encyclopedia of the most well-known, unusual, or economically and ecologically important species that thrive around the world. Each entry provides a detailed description of the tree, its height, habit, colour and leaf shape, and whether it produces flowers, fruit or cones. Its habitat and most interesting features are described to aid identification, and a map helps to locate wild populations for each entry.

This book aims to bring a greater understanding and appreciation of trees to a wider audience. It should encourage you to look more closely at the diversity of trees in your own locality and, if you have the opportunity to visit far-flung regions, to appreciate the diversity that exists in the world.

Below: The monkey puzzle tree, Araucaria araucana, *has a distinctive and instantly recognizable silhouette.*

HOW TREES LIVE

Trees have three obvious features that together distinguish them from all other living plants. First, they produce a woody stem, roots and branches which do not die back each winter but continue to grow year upon year. This means that from the time a tree begins to germinate until the time it dies it is always visible. Be it the smallest garden apple tree or the largest English oak, this basic principle of growth remains the same.

Second, trees live longer than any other living organism on the planet. It is not exceptional to find living trees that are more than 1,000 years old and many are considerably older. Third, trees are the largest living organisms on the planet. Around the world there are trees in excess of 100m/328ft tall or 1,500 tonnes in weight.

Trees have been growing on earth for 370 million years and today can be found growing almost everywhere from the Arctic Circle to the Sahara Desert. For much of the world, trees are the climax species of all plants – which in simple terms means if land is left untended long enough it will eventually become colonized by trees.

So why are trees so successful? Well, as with all plants, trees need light to survive. Without light, photosynthesis cannot take place and food for growth cannot be made. Trees are superb competitors for light; their woody stem enables them to hold their leaves way above the leaves of any other plant. This means they can absorb vast quantities of light while shading out other plants in the process.

Such is the extensive nature of a tree's root system that it can access moisture from deep in the subsoil – something few other plants can do. As such, trees are well equipped to survive periods of drought, particularly as their structure and size allows them to store food and water for times of deficiency. All in all trees are an incredibly competitive and successful group of plants – which is why they have been around so long. They are also a fascinating group of plants, as the following pages will clearly show.

Left: Cedars of Lebanon, Cedrus libani, *in the remnants of a forest in the Bcharre Valley, in Lebanon. This species is known to live for over 2,000 years.*

THE EVOLUTION OF TREES

The first trees evolved more than 300 million years ago. By 200 million years ago they were the most successful land plants on earth, growing in all but the most inhospitable places, such as the Polar regions. Their ability to produce vast amounts of oxygen has enabled other life forms, including humans, to evolve.

The first living organisms appeared on earth 3,800 million years ago. These primitive, single-celled life forms were followed 500 million years later by the earliest cyanobacteria or blue-green algae. Also single-celled, these were the first organisms able to harness the sun's energy to produce food. This process, known as photosynthesis, had an important by-product – oxygen, which gradually began to accumulate in the earth's atmosphere.

Archaeopteris: the first tree

The first known land plant, which was called *Cooksonia*, evolved around 430 million years ago. *Cooksonia* was erect and green-stemmed with a simple underground root system. It was followed about 60 million years later by *Archaeopteris*, the first real tree.

Below: The timeline below shows the evolution of life forms from the first ammonites of the Devonian period, 417–360 million years ago, through to the development of flowering trees such as magnolias during the Cretaceous period, 144–65 million years ago.

With a woody trunk up to 40cm/16in across, *Archaeopteris* had branches and a large root system. It also had the ability to produce buds and continue growing year after year. Fossils of *Archaeopteris* found recently suggest that it may have been able to live for as long as 50 years. As forests of *Archaeopteris* spread across the earth, the amount of oxygen in the atmosphere rapidly increased, paving the way for an explosion in the evolution of new land animals.

The Carboniferous period

During the Carboniferous period, the earth's climate was warm and humid. Great forests and swamps of trees, ferns and mosses covered the land. One of the most common trees was *Lepidodendron*. Known as the scale tree, it reached heights of 30m/98ft and had a trunk more than 3m/10ft across. It looked like a palm tree, but instead of fans of long, thin leaves it had fern-like fronds, each ending with cone-shaped structures containing spores for reproduction.

At the close of this period, the first primitive conifers, or gymnosperms, began to appear. These plants protected their seeds in cones and had a much more efficient reproductive system than their predecessors. None of these early conifers survives today. Their nearest relatives are species of *Araucaria* (monkey puzzle), *Podocarpus* and *Taxus* (yew).

Pangaea

A vast supercontinent that existed 280–193 million years ago was known as Pangaea. The northern part, called Laurasia, comprised the landmasses of North America, Europe and Asia all joined together. The southern part, Gondwanaland, was made up of South America, Africa, Arabia, India, Australia and Antarctica.

Since they were part of Pangaea the continents have moved. Fossil evidence taken from samples of ice deep in the Antarctic ice cap shows that relatives of *Nothofagus moorei*, the Antarctic beech, grew in that region more than 200 million years ago.

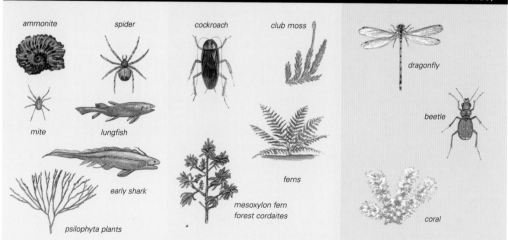

| DEVONIAN (417–360M YEARS AGO) | CARBONIFEROUS (360–286M YEARS AGO) | PERMIAN (286–245M YEARS AGO) |

ammonite spider

cockroach club moss

dragonfly

mite lungfish

beetle

early shark

ferns

psilophyta plants

mesoxylon fern
forest cordaites

coral

Above: One very early tree that is still around today is the deciduous Ginkgo biloba, or maidenhair tree. It is the last surviving member of a family of trees called the ginkgos; along with conifers, they dominated the land for 250 million years.

The Mesozoic era

This era lasted from 245–65 million years ago. It was the age of dinosaurs and saw dramatic fluctuations in world climate. Conifers adapted to these changes so successfully that different species evolved for almost every environment. Today they survive in some of the coldest and hottest parts of the planet.

Ginkgos were also successful: fossils show that they grew throughout the Northern Hemisphere, from the Arctic Circle to the Mediterranean and from North America to China. Fossils of the Jurassic period (208–144 million years ago) also show the dawn redwood, *Metasequoia glyptostroboides*. Previously thought to have been

extinct since that time, the dawn redwood was discovered growing in China in 1941. During the Cretaceous period (144–65 million years ago) flowering plants (angiosperms) evolved and began to exert their dominance over conifers. Among the earliest were magnolias, which are common today.

The Tertiary era

Many of the trees that grew during the Tertiary era (65–2 million years ago) still grow today. The main difference between the Tertiary and the present was the scale of the forests. During the early Tertiary era the planet was warmer than it is today. Europe and North America had a similar climate to that of present-day South-east Asia and vast swathes of forest covered virtually every available piece of land. Oak, beech, magnolia, hemlock, cedar, maple, chestnut, lime and elm occurred alongside tropical trees such as the nypa palm. As the era progressed however, the climate began to cool.

The ice ages

By 1.5 million years ago the climate had cooled so much that the first of four ice ages began. Trees that we now regard as tropical began to die at the far north and south of their ranges. As the temperature dropped further so more temperate species succumbed.

Only those trees close enough to the Equator were able to survive. Each glaciation was interspersed with warmer inter-glacial periods lasting anything up to 60,000 years. During these warmer periods, many trees recolonized their previous ranges. Every continent suffered; however, some fared better than others because of differences in topography. In North America, for example, the mountain ranges all run from north to south. Heat-loving trees were able to spread south as the ice sheets advanced, using the valleys between mountain ranges to reach refuges nearer the Equator. The trees were able to recolonize their old ranges back along these same routes. In Europe, however, recolonization was impossible. The Pyrenees and the Alps, which stretch from east to west, meant that many trees were unable to move south ahead of the ice. Once trapped they perished, leaving Europe with a far less diverse tree flora than that of North America or Asia.

The modern era

Since the last ice age began to wane 14,000 years ago, the temperature of the earth has gradually increased and trees have begun to recolonize temperate areas of the world. Today there are over 80,000 different species of trees on earth.

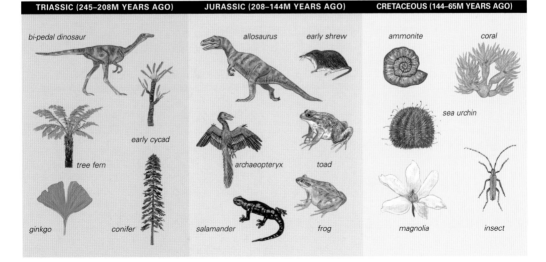

TRIASSIC (245–208M YEARS AGO)

bi-pedal dinosaur

early cycad

tree fern

ginkgo

conifer

JURASSIC (208–144M YEARS AGO)

allosaurus

early shrew

archaeopteryx

toad

salamander

frog

CRETACEOUS (144–65M YEARS AGO)

ammonite

coral

sea urchin

magnolia

insect

CLASSIFICATION OF TREES

Classification is the process by which plants or animals are grouped and named according to their specific similarities. The theory and practice of classification is called taxonomy and those that work in this field are known as taxonomists.

There are over 300,000 different species of flowering plants and gymnosperms or conifers in the world. Botanists have classified them in order to try and make sense of the way that they are related to each other. Rudimentary grouping of trees has occurred for centuries, not always with great accuracy. For example the English oak, *Quercus robur*, and the holm (evergreen) oak, *Q. ilex*, have always been regarded as being closely related because of the fruit they produce. However, the sweet chestnut, *Castanea sativa*, and the horse chestnut, *Aesculus hippocastanum*, which were also once classified on the basis of their fruit, are now thought to belong to two quite different families.

The science of classification starts to become ever more complex as botanists study trees more closely. Where once trees were classified on the basis of just one or perhaps two characteristics, now many more of their features are compared before a degree of relatedness is decided.

Below: The horse chestnut (left) and sweet chestnut (right) were once thought to be related.

Carl Von Linné (1707–78)

Ever since the time of the Greek philosopher Aristotle (384–322BC) it had been recognized that, both in the plant and animal world, there was a natural order where everything had its place and was linked to other species by a common thread. However, it was not until the 18th century that the Swedish botanist Carl Von Linné (also known as Linnaeus – the Latin name that he gave himself) made the first attempt to link all plants by one specific feature. He classified them by the way they reproduced themselves and the make-up of their reproductive systems – in the case of flowering plants, their flowers. As he admitted, his choice of feature for classification was artificial. Linnaeus had not found the common thread, the natural order of all living things. Nevertheless, he did create a system of classification that is still in use today.

Linnaeus invented the principle of using two Latin words to name a species. He chose Latin because it was the language of scholarship, and was understood across the world but no longer used as a spoken language, so

Above: Trees often have common names that refer to their place of origin, colouring, or use.

the meaning of its words would not change over time. The first of the two words is known as the generic (genus) name and the second the specific (species) name. The generic name gives a clue to the species' relationship with others. Closely related species are given the same generic name but different specific names. For example, the English oak is called *Quercus robur* and the closely related turkey oak is called *Quercus cerris*. All species with the same generic name are said to belong to the same genus.

Similar genera (the plural of genus) are combined into larger groups known as families. For example the oak genus, *Quercus*, belongs to the same family as the beech genus, *Fagus*. This family is called Fagaceae, and is commonly known as the beech family. Similar families are gathered together in turn into larger groups called orders. The beech family, Fagaceae, combines with the birch family, Betulaceae, to make the beech tree

order Fagales. Similar orders are then combined into subclasses. The beech order is part of the hazel subclass, which is called Hamamelidae. In turn, Hamamelidae is combined with all of the other plant subclasses that are characterized by embryos that contain two seed leaves, to form a group that is known as the dicotyledons. This group is then joined together with all plants that have an embryo that contains only one seed leaf (monocotyledons) into one group that contains all flowering plants – the Magnoliophytina. Finally, this is gathered together with all of the other groups of seed-producing plants and then combined with the non seed-producing plants, such as ferns, into the Plant Kingdom.

Charles Darwin (1809–82)

The "common thread" or natural order of all living things was left for Charles Darwin to discover. Darwin recognized that plants, or animals for that matter, were usually alike because of their common ancestry.

Trees alive today can be classified in terms of their relatedness because they have all evolved over time from a single common ancestor that existed millions of years ago. The science of the ancestry of all living things is called phylogeny and it goes hand in glove with taxonomy.

Once the interrelatedness of all plants was understood, scientists began to trace back the evolution of trees. In many ways this process is similar to tracing back one's own family tree. The major difference is that fossil records are used. The different characteristics of trees living today compared to fossils of those from the past reflect the evolutionary changes that have occurred to the common ancestral line over millions of years. Each evolutionary change has been in response to a different environmental condition and has resulted in a different tree.

For most of us, classification only becomes pertinent when we are trying to identify a species.

Below: The cork oak (left) and common beech (right) look different, but in fact they are both members of the beech family, Fagaceae.

Above: It is possible to recognize trees that belong to the same family by certain obvious characteristics. For example hazel (above left), alder (above centre), birch (above right), and hornbeam (not shown) all belong to the birch family, Betulaceae, and all produce catkins.

For botanists and taxonomists however, classification is an everyday procedure and a frequent cause of disagreement. It is now more than 200 years since Linnaeus developed his system of classification and 150 years since Darwin announced his theory of evolution. Nevertheless taxonomists still move species from one genus to another and some botanists cast doubt on whether plant classification should be based upon the evolutionary process at all.

ROOTS

Tree roots provide anchorage, ensuring that the tree does not fall over. They obtain water, the lifeblood of any tree, by sucking it from the soil. Roots provide the tree with minerals, which are essential for growth. They also store food, such as starch produced by the leaves, for later use.

Roots have the ability to influence the size of a tree. Around 60 per cent of the total mass of any tree is made up by its trunk. The remaining 40 per cent is split evenly between the branches and the root system, each having a direct relationship with the other. If there are not enough roots, the canopy and leaves will not be able to obtain enough water and branches will start to die back. In turn, if branches are damaged or removed and there are fewer leaves to produce food, a tree's roots will begin to die back.

A shallow existence

Contrary to popular belief, tree roots do not penetrate deep into the soil. In most cases the roots of even the tallest tree seldom reach down more than 3m/10ft. The overall shape of a tree is like a wine glass, with the roots forming a shallow but spreading base.

More than three-quarters of most trees' roots can be found within 60cm/24in of the surface. They seldom need to go deeper: the top layers of the soil are normally rich in organic material, minerals and moisture, which are just the ingredients that roots require.

However, roots do spread outwards considerably within the upper layers of the soil. The bulk of a root system will be found within 3–4m/10–13ft of a tree's trunk. However, very fine roots may spread anything up to twice the radius of the canopy, which in a large tree can mean anything up to 30m/98ft away from the trunk.

Tap root

Tap roots

The first root that every tree grows from its seed is called a tap root. Tap roots grow straight down and from day one have the ability to extract moisture and minerals from the soil. Within days of the tap root emerging from a seed, side roots (known as laterals) grow off the tap root and begin to move horizontally through the top layers of the soil. On some trees, such as oak, the tap root persists for several years. In most species, it withers and the lateral roots take over.

Lateral roots

Lateral roots

Most lateral roots stay close to the surface for the whole of a tree's life. Sometimes they may develop from the tap root or grow directly from the base of the trunk; in the latter case they can be more than 30cm/12in wide. Within 1m/3ft of the trunk they taper to around 10cm/4in across, and at 4m/13ft away they are usually under 5cm/2in in diameter and far more soft and pliable.

Stilt roots

Stilt roots

Mangroves grow throughout the tropics on coastal mudflats. Many species have stilt-like roots that arch from the main stem down into the mud. Once these have taken root, they help to anchor the tree so that it remains stable in the constantly moving mudflat silt. The roots graft together, creating a three-dimensional framework that holds and supports the mangrove tree clear of the mud.

Pillar roots

The weeping fig, *Ficus benjamina*, and the banyan, *F. benghalensis*, have roots that grow and hang down from the

Left: Few trees can survive indefinitely in waterlogged conditions such as these. In swampy or boggy ground most trees will survive for a time until their roots become waterlogged. Many trees will happily grow alongside watercourses though. Willow, ash and poplar all thrive near water.

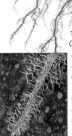

Left: The farther they are from the trunk, the finer roots become. Growing from these fine roots are millions of tiny hairs, each one made up of a single cell. It is these root hairs that collect the necessary ingredients, such as nitrogen and potassium, for a tree to grow. Each is in contact with the soil particles around it and is able to absorb both the moisture and the diluted minerals that surround each particle. Root hairs have a lifespan of no more than a few weeks, but as they die, new ones are formed.

Pillar roots

branches. These roots grow quickly – up to 1cm/½ in a day – and once anchored in the soil they form prop-like pillars, capable of bearing the weight of the spreading branches they grew from originally. This system enables the tree to continue to grow outwards almost indefinitely. A banyan tree planted in the Royal Botanic Garden of Calcutta in 1782, for example, now covers an area of 1.2ha/3 acres and has 1,775 pillar roots.

Symbiotic associations

Within the soil, tree roots come into contact with the living threads, or *hyphae*, of numerous fungi. Quite often this association is beneficial to both the tree and the fungus. Usually the tree acquires hard-to-obtain nutrients such as phosphorus from the fungus and the fungus gets carbohydrates from the tree. The structures formed between tree roots and fungi in these mutually beneficial associations are known as mycorrhiza. Sometimes, however, contact with fungus can be damaging for a tree.

Roots and water

Tree roots require water to survive but they also need to obtain a supply of oxygen. It is important that they have water readily available, but roots will not do well if they are continually submerged. In constantly waterlogged conditions roots will not be able to obtain enough oxygen and a tree will effectively drown.

Roots and oxygen

The swamp cypress thrives in wet conditions. To counter the lack of soil oxygen, its roots have developed strange knobbly growths, called knees. These grow out of the water or wet

Below: The breathing roots of this mangrove protrude through the sand on Mafia Island, near Tanzania.

ground to gain access to the air, and therefore to a supply of oxygen. Swamp cypress knees can reach a height of 4m/13ft. They not only absorb oxygen, but also provide support to the tree, making it less likely to blow over in strong wind.

Below: Honey fungus, Armillariella mellea, is one of the biggest killers of trees in the temperate world. Once it has made contact with a tree's roots, it rapidly spreads through the entire vascular system of the tree, killing tissue as it goes.

TRUNK AND BARK

*What makes a tree different from all other plants is the tough, woody framework it raises above the
ground: a framework, made up of a trunk and branches, that lasts for the entire life of the tree. As each
year passes, this framework gets bigger as the trunk and branches expand upwards and outwards.*

The main purpose of the trunk is to
position the leaves as far as possible
from the ground. The higher they are,
the less competition there is from other
plants for light. Without light trees die.
The trunk supports the branches and
the branches support the leaves.

The trunk and branches have two
other functions. They transport water,
which has been collected by the roots,
up through the tree to the leaves.
Second, they move food, which is
produced in the leaves, to every other
part of the tree, including the roots.

Considering the importance of the
functions that the trunk and branches
perform, it is extraordinary that more
than 80 per cent of their mass are
made up of dead cells. The only living
cells in a tree's trunk and branches are
those in the area immediately beneath
the bark. It is here that all of the
activity takes place.

The inner tree

A tree's bark is like a skin. It is a corky
waterproof layer that protects the all-
important inner cells from disease,
animal attack and, in the case of
redwoods and eucalyptus, forest fires.

Some barks, such as that of the ubber
tree, exude latex to 'gum up' the
mouths of feeding predators. Pine trees
have a similar defence mechanism,
exuding a sticky resin which can
literally engulf a whole insect. Some
trees, such as the South American
quinine tree, *Cinchona corymbosa*,
produce chemicals in their bark which
are poisonous to attackers.

Bark is perforated with millions of
tiny breathing pores called lenticels,
which pass oxygen from the outside
atmosphere through to the living cells
beneath. In cities and along busy roads
these lenticels get clogged up with dirt
and carbon. Some trees, such as the
London plane, *Platanus* x *hispanica*,
have adapted by regularly shedding
their old bark. All trees are constantly
growing and their girth expanding.
This is reflected in the cracks and
crevices that appear in the bark of
many trees. As bark splits, new corky
cells are produced to plug the gap.

Beneath the outer bark is the inner
bark, or phloem. This is a soft spongy
layer of living tissue that transports
sap – sugary liquid food – from the
leaves to the rest of the tree.

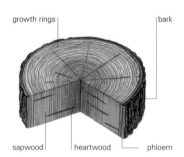

*Above: A section through the trunk of a larch
tree showing the darker heartwood and the
lighter sapwood.*

Beneath the phloem is a thin tissue
known as the cambium. Although it is
only one cell thick, the cambium is
extremely important. It is here that all
tree growth takes place. Cambium cells
are constantly dividing, producing
phloem cells on the outside and on the
inside wood cells, or xylem.

Xylem has two parts: the sapwood,
made up of living cells, and the
heartwood, composed of dead cells.
The sapwood transports water and
minerals from the roots to the leaves.
Most of these are carried in sapwood
made by the cambium during that year.
The heartwood forms the dense central
core of the trunk, supporting the tree
and giving the trunk rigidity. The two
main constituents of xylem are
cellulose and lignin. Cellulose, a
glucose-based carbohydrate, makes up
three-quarters of the xylem and is used
in the construction of cell walls. Lignin
comprises most of the remaining
quarter and is a complex organic
polymer. It is lignin that gives wood its
structural strength. If water and air
reach the heartwood as a result of
damage to the outer layers of the
trunk, decay will occur and in time the
tree may become hollow.

*Left: Most trees over 500 years old are hollow.
Eight people sitting around a table can fit
inside the trunk of this tree.*

| Banyan tree | Cola nut | Kapok | Papaya | Flame of the forest | Tembusu |

Bark invaders

While bark exists to provide a protective barrier over the living tissue of a tree's trunk and branches, there are plenty of creatures capable of penetrating that barrier. Bark beetles and wood-boring insects eat cellulose and excavate breeding chambers and galleries for egg-laying purposes. Often the damage inflicted by insects is much greater than just the physical effects of their mining. Insects may carry fungal diseases. Beetles that bore into infected trees become coated with fungal spores, which they carry to other, healthy trees. Once underneath the bark, the fungus quickly blocks the cells transporting food and water, leading to the tree's demise.

How we use bark

Bark not only forms protection for trees, it can also be incredibly useful to

Below: Trees grow from terminal and lateral buds positioned towards the tip of the branches.

us. Much of the wine that we drink is sealed in bottles with bark from the cork oak tree, *Quercus suber*. In Mediterranean regions, cork oaks are grown in orchards. Every ten years or so, the outer corky bark is carefully removed, leaving the cambium layer intact. The cambium then produces more cork cells to replace the bark that has been harvested. Bark also provides us with food and medicine. The spice cinnamon is made from the dried and ground bark of the Sri Lankan cinnamon tree, *Cinnamomum ceylanicum*, while the bark of the Pacific Yew, *Taxus brevifolia*, contains a substance called taxol, which has been highly effective in the treatment of some forms of cancer. Some trees have very attractive bark, making them ideal ornamental plants for parks and gardens. The Tibetan cherry, *Prunus tibetica*, has highly polished mahogany-red bark, for example, and the Himalayan birch, *Betula utilis*, has bark the colour of freshly fallen snow.

| Himalayan cherry | Indian horse chestnut | Floss silk tree | Eucalyptus | Paperbark maple | Birch 'Snow Queen' |

BUDS

Buds act as protective sheaths for the growing tips of trees during the coldest months of the year.
In winter, even though deciduous trees will have shed their leaves, they can still be readily
identified by their buds.

For trees to grow they need water, minerals, nutrients and the right growing conditions, namely sunlight and warmth. In parts of the world where there is little seasonal variation, such as the tropics, favourable climatic conditions may allow growth to continue all year round. However, even in tropical rainforests very few trees grow non-stop. The normal pattern for most trees, particularly those in temperate regions, is for a period of growth followed by a period of rest. The period of rest coincides with the time of year when the climate is least favourable to growth. Across Britain, Europe and North America this is during the cold and dark of winter.

Throughout the winter resting period, the growing tips of a tree, known as the meristem, are vulnerable to cold winds and frost. Prolonged low temperatures can very easily damage or even kill the meristem. Trees have therefore evolved ways to protect this all-important tissue.

Protective sheath

During early autumn, as the growing season approaches its end, the last few leaves to be produced by the tree are turned into much thicker but smaller bud leaves, known as scales. These

Above: A lime tree breaking bud.

Above: A sycamore breaking bud.

toughened leaves stay on the tree after all of the other leaves have fallen off and form a protective sheath around the meristem. This sheath is known as a leaf-bud. Its thick scales are waterproof and overlap each other, creating a defence system able to withstand the onslaught of winter. Often a coating of wax, resin or gum is used to strengthen these defences.

Inside the bud

Winter buds contain all that the tree will need to resume growing once the days lengthen and the temperature increases in spring. Inside is a miniature shoot, miniature leaves all carefully folded over one another and, in some species, such as the horse chestnut, *Aesculus hippocastanum*, miniature flowers.

Trees without buds

Not all trees produce buds, even in temperate regions. Some, such as the wayfaring tree, *Viburnum lantana*, have "naked buds" with no bud scales. At the end of the growing season in this species, the last leaves to be formed stop growing before they are

fully developed. A dense layer of hair then forms on them to protect them from the cold and they proceed to wrap themselves around the meristem. When spring arrives the protective leaves simply start growing again from where they left off.

Eucalyptus trees also have "naked buds" but as back-up they produce tiny concealed buds beneath the leaf base. These are only activated if the growing tip gets damaged.

Below: An Indian horse chestnut bud opening to reveal long, thin, down-covered leaves.

Below: Some buds contain all of the cells needed for the whole of the following year's growth. Others contain just enough to start growing in spring and then produce more growth cells once the leaves have emerged from the bud.

Some conifers, such as western red cedar, *Thuja plicata*, and lawson cypress, *Chamaecyparis lawsoniana*, have no distinct buds at all; instead they produce little packets of meristematic cells, which are hidden beneath the surface of each frond of needles.

The growing season

As spring arrives, buds open and the leaves begin to emerge. For all trees the trigger for this to happen is increasing warmth and light. Individual species each have their own trigger point, which is determined by their geographical origins. Species that originated in colder regions, such as birch or willow, burst bud earlier than those such as horse chestnut or sweet chestnut, which evolved in warmer parts of the world. Birch instinctively knows that northern European summers are relatively short affairs, and that it needs to get going as quickly as possible to make the most of the growing season. Sweet chestnut, on the other hand, instinctively expects a long, Mediterranean summer, so is in less of a rush to get started.

Horse chestnut bud

Day one

Left: The sticky buds of horse chestnut will open over a period of three days in springtime.

Day two

Day three

BUD ARRANGEMENTS

Even in winter, when deciduous trees display bare branches, trees can still be identified by the shape, size, colour and arrangement of the buds on the twigs.

Opposite buds

The buds of trees such as sycamore and ash are said to be opposite – that is, in pairs on each side of the twig, exactly opposite each other. Ash buds are easily recognizable by their distinctive black colouring.

Alternate buds

The buds of trees such as beech and willow are arranged alternately on different sides of the twig. Willow buds are generally longer and more slender than those of beech.

Hairy buds

Magnolia buds are very distinctive and easily recognized by their covering of thick grey fur. Magnolia buds are some of the largest found on any tree.

Clustered buds

Oak buds appear almost randomly on the twig, but always with a cluster of buds at the tip. Cherries also adopt this clustered approach.

Whiskered buds

As well as being clustered, some oaks, such as the turkey oak, also have thin whiskers surrounding the buds.

Naked buds

The wayfaring tree does not have a true bud. Instead it has immature hairy leaves which surround the growing tip to protect it from the cold.

Trees that have everything for the coming year's growth pre-packaged inside the bud tend to have a single growth spurt immediately after their leaves emerge. This can mean that they achieve virtually all their growth for the whole year within the first four weeks of spring. Those trees that over-winter with just enough growth cells in the bud to aid emergence in spring grow more slowly but grow for a longer period of time. In some instances these species may continue growing for more than 100 days. However, by the end of the season the overall growth of each will be similar.

Below: Sweet cherry buds.

Below: Magnolia bud.

Below: Wingnut bud.

Below: Horse chestnut bud.

LEAVES

Each leaf on a tree is a mini power station, generating food, which the tree uses to provide the necessary energy for living and growing. The process by which leaves produce food is called photosynthesis. During this process the leaves absorb carbon dioxide and emit oxygen.

Leaves contain a green pigment called chlorophyll, which absorbs light energy from the sun. This energy is used to combine carbon dioxide, which the leaf absorbs from the atmosphere, with water taken from the soil. The resulting products are glucose and oxygen. Glucose provides the energy to run the tree and can be turned into starch for storage or cellulose, which forms the tree's cell walls. The oxygen is released by the leaf back into the atmosphere. A mature tree can produce the same amount of oxygen every year as that used by ten people.

Leaf structure

Each leaf is covered by a skin of tightly packed cells known as the epidermis. This skin is coated by a waxy covering called the cuticle. The cuticle acts as waterproofing, preventing the leaf from losing any more water than is necessary. The transfer of oxygen and carbon dioxide to and from the atmosphere takes place through tiny holes in the cuticle known as stomata. Stomata are concentrated on the underside of the leaf away from the direct heat of the sun to minimize water loss. The cells around the stomata have the ability to enlarge and decrease the size of the hole. Despite this, water is lost from the leaf through the stomata. This loss of water is known as transpiration. Even though stomata normally

Left: Tiny breathing holes in the leaf are known as stomata.

cover less than one per cent of a leaf's total area, a large amount of water is lost in this way. A large deciduous tree can lose up to 300 litres/66 gallons per day in summer. The lost water is usually replaced by water drawn from its roots. In times of drought however, the amount of water lost may exceed that available to the roots. When this happens the leaves wilt and die, stopping the tree from producing food.

Inside the leaf cells, the chlorophyll is contained in millions of tiny cell-like vessels called chloroplasts. Most of these are found in the upper part of the leaf, which receives the most light. Beneath the chloroplasts are the vascular tissues that make up the xylem, and which transport the raw ingredients for photosynthesis, such as water and minerals, all the way from

Below: Cross section of a leaf.

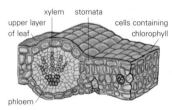

upper layer of leaf — xylem   stomata — cells containing chlorophyll

phloem

Above: When chlorophyll production stops and any residue decays, other pigments are seen.

Life cycle of leaves

Above: In spring new leaves form.

Above: Summer.

Below: The changing tones of autumn.

Above: Winter profile.

the roots to the leaf. Alongside the xylem is the phloem, which transports the sugary products of photosynthesis from the leaf to all other parts of the tree. Both vascular systems rely on a process called osmosis to move liquid. Osmosis is a process whereby liquid moves from one cell to another. The catalyst for this to happen is the fullness, or turgidity, of each cell. As one cell becomes full, so the liquid within it permeates through the cell wall into a neighbouring cell that is less turgid. Once this cell is full, liquid starts to permeate from it into the next empty cell and so on.

Leaf size and shape
One of the most interesting things about leaves is the incredible range of shapes and sizes. The smallest so-called broad leaf is produced by the Arctic willow, *Salix nivalis*. This tundra species has leaves less than 5mm/¼in long. Some conifers have needles that are even smaller.

All broad-leaved tree leaves have one thing in common: a network of visible veins, which spread out across the leaf from its base. It is within these veins that the xylem and phloem are found. The veins join together at the leaf base to form the stalk, or petiole.

Simple leaves
These come in a wide variety of shapes. At their most basic they may be entirely round or heart-shaped, or have no

indentation around the leaf edge. Many leaves, such as those of cherry trees, are oval in shape and have small serrations around the edge. On others the serrations may be more pronounced, as with the sweet chestnut, *Castanea sativa*. Some trees, such as the oak, produce leaves with distinctive lobing. These lobes may be rounded, or more angular.

Compound leaves

At first glance the leaflets of compound leaves look like separate leaves growing off the same stalk. However, closer inspection of a new compound leaf reveals that the whole stalk and its leaflets all emerge from the same leaf bud. It is in essence all one leaf. Many of the trees in our cities have compound leaves. One of the most easily recognized is the horse chestnut, which has seven or nine large leaflets all attached to the same point of the main leaf stalk. The golden-leaved robinia, *Robinia pseudoacacia* 'Frisia', has paired leaflets that come off the leaf stalk opposite each other (pinnate leaflets), as does the European ash, *Fraxinus excelsior*. Occasionally the leaf stalk to which the leaflets are attached may sub-divide, producing side stalks and a bipinnate leaf. One of the best examples of a tree with bipinnate leaves is the Japanese angelica tree, *Aralia elata*, which has leaves in excess of 50cm/20in long.

Evergreen leaves
A deciduous tree keeps its leaves for only part of the year; they grow in the spring and fall off in the autumn. By contrast, evergreen trees, which include most conifers and trees such as holly, box and laurel, have leaves all year round. This does not mean the same leaves stay on the tree for the whole of its life. Evergreen leaves fall from trees and are replaced throughout the year. The real difference between evergreen and deciduous trees is that the leaves of deciduous trees all fall at around the same time, while those of evergreens do not. On average, evergreens keep their leaves for between three and five years, although on some firs and spruces the needles may be retained for up to ten years.

Needles
Pines, firs, larches, spruces and cedars all have needles, as do yews and redwoods. Although visually quite unlike other leaves, needles are in fact just compact versions of simple leaves, and do the same job of producing food for the tree. Needles lose far less water than the leaves of broadleaf trees. They are therefore better equipped to survive in areas where water is in short supply, such as northern temperate regions where the ground is frozen for months at a time.

Below: The soft, feathery needles of the western red cedar.

Below: The 1m/3ft-long leaves of the tropical breadfruit tree.

Below: The fine pencil-like leaves of Eucalyptus champmaniana.

FLOWERS

Flowers contain the tree's reproductive organs. Some trees, such as cherry, have both male and female reproductive organs within the same flower. Others, such as hazel, have separate male and female flowers on the same tree. Some trees only produce flowers of one sex.

Flowers are the sex organs of a tree. What happens in them determines the ability of the tree to reproduce itself. Trees are passive organisms; they cannot actively go out and search for a mate, so they have to engage in sex by proxy. Each tree needs a go-between to get its pollen either to another tree or from the male to the female part of its own flowers. Depending on the species of tree, this go-between may be wind, water or an animal, such as a bird or insect. Over countless generations each species has developed its own flower to suit a specific go-between. The African baobab tree, *Adansonia digitata*, for example, has developed large flowers that produce vast quantities of nectar at night. These flowers attract bats, which feed on the nectar and in the process get covered in pollen. The bats transfer that pollen from flower to flower and tree to tree.

Inside the flower

There are almost as many different forms of tree flower as there are trees. Indeed the whole classification system for trees (and other flowering plants) is built around the design of the flowers. Although outwardly tree flowers may look very different, their basic components are all the same. Most flowers have four main parts: the stamen, which is the male reproductive organ and produces the pollen; the stigma, which receives the pollen; the

style, which links the stigma to the ovary; and the ovary, which contains ovules that, after fertilization, develop into seeds. A few tree flowers have only male or female parts.

If both male and female components are present in the same flower, then the flower is said to be "perfect". The tree is then capable of self-pollination and it is known as an hermaphrodite. Self-pollination is far from ideal, and can lead to genetic weaknesses in the same way as inbreeding does in animals. Cross-pollination with another tree is better because it enables different genes to mix. Trees that are hermaphrodites include cherry, laburnum and lime.

To avoid self-pollination, some trees have developed separate male and female flowers. Such trees are known as monoecious and are particularly common where the main vector for pollination is the wind. Monoecious trees include beech, birch and hazel.

Some species only produce male or female flowers on any one tree. These species are "dioecious". This division of trees into sexes overcomes the problem of self-pollination but raises a new problem. Trees of opposite sexes must be relatively close together to have any chance of breeding at all. Trees that are dioecious include yew, holly and the New Zealand kauri pine. Holly berries are found only on female trees and then only when there is a male tree not too far away.

Life cycle of a flower from bud

Left: In winter the flowers are protected within buds.

Left: The flowers emerge as the temperature rises in spring.

Right: Once fully open the flowers are pollinated by insects.

Left: Fertilized flowers produce berries in summer.

Right: Birds eat the berries and the seeds they contain are dispersed within the birds' droppings.

Welcoming guests

Tree flowers come in all manner of sizes, shapes and colours. Much of this diversity is linked to the pollinator. In general, flowers that are pollinated by animals tend to be larger and showier then those that are pollinated by wind. The wind is indiscriminate but animals need to be attracted. Some animal pollinators are attracted to flowers of certain colours and a few trees actually

Below: Magnolias are insect-pollinated.

Below: Italian alders are wind-pollinated.

alter the colour of flowers once they have been pollinated to discourage further visitors. For example the colour of the markings inside the flowers of the horse chestnut, *Aesculus hippocastanum*, changes from yellow to red after pollination. To a bee, red looks black and very unattractive, so it visits a flower that has yet to be pollinated instead.

Sometimes tree flowers themselves may be quite inconspicuous but are surrounded by showy sterile flowers or leaf bracts to draw pollinators to them. The pocket handkerchief tree, *Davidia involucrata*, from China, for example, has large white bracts that guide pollinating moths to its flowers.

Gone with the wind

Most wind-pollinated trees evolved in places where there was a shortage of insects. Wind pollination is common in the colder northern temperate regions of the world. All conifers are wind pollinated and most produce such large amounts of tiny-grained pollen that on breezy days, clouds of the stuff may fill the air around them. Conifer stamens are positioned at the tips of the branches to aid dispersal. Those of pine trees are bright yellow and stand upright from the needles like candles.

Alder, birch and hazel are also wind pollinated. Rather than having erect

Below: Burmese fish tail palm is pollinated by insect and by wind.

stamens like those of pines they have drooping catkins, each containing millions of pollen grains. In many places, these catkins are one of the first signs of spring. They are made all the more conspicuous by the fact that they appear before the tree comes into leaf. Oak also has pollen-bearing catkins but these are hardly ever seen because they open in late spring after the tree's leaves have emerged.

Insect pollinators

Pollination by insects is by far the most common method of reproducing among trees. More than 60 per cent of tree species in equatorial regions are pollinated by some kind of insect. Trees that use insects as pollinators tend to produce flowers with copious amounts of sugar-rich nectar. Their pollen grains are larger than those of wind-pollinated species and also quite sticky so that they adhere to insects' bodies.

Below: The flowers of the persimmon tree.

Above: Magnolia grandiflora has some of the largest flowers borne by any tree.

Birds and mammals

In the tropics, birds are important pollinators of tree flowers. Flowers that are pollinated by birds tend to be tubular in shape (to keep the nectar out of reach of other animals), brightly coloured and unscented, since most birds have a poor sense of smell. Hummingbirds use their long beaks to reach inside the flowers of trees such as the angel's trumpet, *Brugmansia*, from Brazil. In Australia and South Africa, bottle-brush trees, *Banksia*, have masses of protruding pollen-covered stamens, which brush against birds' feathers as they collect nectar. Few temperate trees are pollinated by birds. The giraffe is the most unique pollinator of all. It transfers pollen between the flowers of the knobthorn acacia, *Acacia nigrescens*, which grow high up in the tree's branches.

Below: The flowers of Prunus x yedoensis.

SEEDS

Seeds are the next generation of tree. They contain all that is necessary for the creation of a mature tree virtually identical to its parents. Seeds come in a variety of forms; they may be contained within nuts, fruit or berries, or have "wings" to aid dispersal by the wind.

Every tree seed has the potential to develop to become part of the next generation. "From little acorns mighty oak trees grow" is a well-known and accurate saying, although it has to be said that a tiny proportion of all acorns will ever have the opportunity to become mighty oaks. A mature oak tree can produce up to 90,000 acorns in a good year, but fewer than 0.01 per cent will grow to become anything like as mighty as their parent. Most acorns will be eaten by mammals or birds (a wood pigeon can eat up to 120 acorns a day), or simply land in a spot where germination and growth are impossible. It is because of this low success rate that the oak produces so many acorns. In terms of seed production 90,000 is actually quite modest; alder trees will produce around 250,000 seeds a year.

Different seed types

Seeds are produced from the female part of the flower once it has been pollinated and one or more of its ovules fertilized. Just as tree flowers have evolved over millions of years in their quest to find the most effective method of pollen dispersal, so tree seeds also take on many different forms. The fundamental problem facing pollen is exactly the same as that for seeds; trees cannot move, so they have to find other ways of distributing what they produce.

Some trees wrap their seeds inside brightly coloured, sweet tasting fruits or berries. The fruit or berry has two

Left: Apple seeds are contained within an edible, fleshy, protective fruit.

Left: The first year's growth from an acorn.

roles; firstly to protect the seed and secondly to tempt animals to take it away from the tree. After a fruit or berry is eaten, the seed passes through the animal's digestive system and is excreted, often far from the parent tree, in its own ready-made package of fertilizer.

Other trees enclose their seeds within tough outer casings as nuts. Once again, these casings help to protect the seed, but in this case it is the actual seed inside that is the attraction. Squirrels will collect and hoard the nuts, eating some in the process, but many of the nuts are never eaten and wherever the squirrel has stored them they will proceed to germinate and grow.

Conifer seed is known as "naked seed" because each individual seed is produced without a protective coat or cover. Conifer seeds are encased together in a cone but the scales of each cone can be bent back to reveal the unprotected seed inside. Each seed is often equipped with light, papery wings, which enable it to "fly" away from the parent tree on the wind.

Below: Crab apples contain seeds.

Other seeds, such as those of alder, are contained in cones, but rely on water for their distribution.

Whatever the method of dispersal there is always one aim: to get the seed as far away from the parent plant as possible. There is no point competing for living space with one's own progeny. Dispersal also reduces the risk of cross-pollination between parent and offspring in years to come.

Matters of time

Most ovules are fertilized within days of pollen landing on the stigma. How long seed takes to ripen varies from tree to tree. Elm seed can be ready for dispersal less than ten weeks after fertilization.

Most temperate broad-leaved trees disperse their seed in the autumn of the year in which their flowers were fertilized. In many conifers, on the other hand, seed takes two years to develop. This is because fertilization is delayed for a year after pollination. Some conifers will hold seed in a sealed cone for many years after it has ripened, waiting for a special event to trigger its release. For the giant redwood this trigger is forest fire, which kills off all competing vegetation and provides a thick bed of nutrient-rich ash for its seeds.

Below: Douglas fir seeds are paper-thin.

Above: Tamarind pods grow to 18cm/7in long and contain a soft pulp.

Right: The seeds of sweet chestnut are contained within a spiny casing to protect them from predation.

Berries and fruit

Most fruit and berries are brightly coloured to attract birds. Bright red rowan berries are loved by starlings, while red holly berries attract waxwings and fieldfares. The berries of hawthorn provide a vital source of food for many different birds in winter.

Normally, the flesh of berries is digested but the seed is not, and it gets passed out in the bird's droppings.

Fruits range in size from large tropical varieties, such as mango and papaya, to the small, glossy, black berry of the European elder tree. Many fruits are eaten by humans, and some trees, such as apple and olive, are farmed specifically for their fruit. Some fruits only become good for human consumption as they begin to rot, such as the fruit of the medlar tree, *Mespilus germanica*.

Nuts and other seeds

Essentially, nuts are edible seeds. Some, such as hazelnuts, are encased in a

Above: Seeds such as this of the sycamore are attached to wings to aid dispersal.

Right: Walnut seeds are protected within a hard wooden casing.

Above: The nuts or seeds of the cream nut tree are edible, but difficult to find because they are also irresistible to monkeys.

woody shell. Others, like chestnuts, are surrounded by an inedible but more fleshy outer coating. They are distributed by birds and mammals. Squirrels and jays bury those nuts that they are unable to eat straight away. Some of the store is never returned to and these may germinate. Some seed casings are impenetrable to all but the most determined of foragers. The Brazil nut has one of the toughest cases of all but it is staple food for the agouti, a cat-sized rodent. Agoutis collect Brazil nuts and bury them, just as squirrels do in temperate forests.

Many dry seeds rely on wind for their dispersal. Eucalyptus seed is like fine dust and can be borne considerable distances on the wind. Some heavier seeds also ride on the wind. Those of maple and ash trees have extended wings known as keys, which help to keep the seed airborne. Sycamore seeds have paired keys.

Alder trees grow alongside rivers and watercourses. Each of their seeds is attached to a droplet of oil, which acts like a tiny buoyancy aid. After falling from the tree into the water, the seed floats downstream until it is washed ashore. Wherever it lands it will attempt to grow.

Above: Some seed heads are incredibly attractive, such as these remarkable magnolia seed capsules.

The world's largest seed comes from the coco de mer palm, *Lodoicea maldivica*, which is found in the Seychelles. It looks like an enormous double coconut and takes ten years to ripen. The heaviest of these seeds can weigh up to 20kg/45lb.

Germination

Inside every ripe tree seed are the beginnings of a root, a shoot and two specialized leaves, which are known as cotyledons. If a seed arrives in a suitable location it will germinate straight away or wait until conditions become right for it to do so. In temperate areas this is in spring, when air and soil temperatures begin to rise.

Germination to seedling

Below: The first thing to emerge from the seed is the root. No matter which way the seed is lying, the root will instinctively grow downwards into the soil. Once the root has become established and is providing additional food and moisture, the two cotyledons emerge and begin the process of photosynthesis. Shortly afterwards, true leaves appear from a bud between the cotyledons and the tree begins to grow.

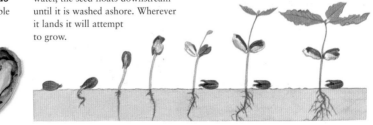

LIFE CYCLE OF TREES

*The life cycle of a tree is a fascinating, and in many cases very long, process of change and development.
The initial struggle is coupled with rapid growth, while a sapling establishes itself. It then goes through a
middle period of relative inactivity, to an eventual slow decline into old age and death.*

There is a saying that "an oak tree spends 300 years growing, 300 years resting and 300 years dying". Although these time spans may be optimistic for some oaks and very optimistic for most other tree species, there are, in fact, several important truths within this statement.

There is no doubt that trees have the potential to live for a very long time. They include by far the oldest living organisms on earth. The oldest tree in the world is a bristlecone pine, *Pinus longaeva*, which is growing 3,050m/10,000ft up in the White Mountains of California and has been verified as 4,700 years old. Close on its heels is Scotland's Fortingall yew, which is estimated to be somewhere between 3,000 and 5,000 years old.

Trees go through various stages of growth in much the same way as humans. In our early years we develop and grow at a relatively fast rate. By the end of our teens, growth slows down and stops and our bodies stay pretty much the same for the next 40 years or so. Then, as our three score years and ten approaches, we begin our decline into old age and eventual demise. This is similar to a tree's life cycle, the only real difference being the amount of time that it takes.

So how do trees grow?

As with any living organism, it all begins with a birth. In the case of trees it is the germination of a seed. However, it can also occur naturally when a piece of an older tree breaks away, develops its own root system and grows as a completely new tree. This frequently happens with willows growing along riverbanks. When the river floods, a lower branch may be broken off by the force of the water and swept downstream. Eventually this branch will come to rest and from it roots will develop, grow down into the mud and a new willow tree will grow. A tree grown in this way is known as a

Above: In old age some trees need help to retain their branches.

cutting. Cuttings have the same DNA as the tree they were once part of.

Seeds do not have the same DNA as the tree that produces them. A seedling tree will develop its own genetic identity, taking on characteristics from both its male and female parent or, in the case of a self-fertilized tree, the characteristics contained in the genes of the male and female sex cell that initially produced it.

Once a seed or cutting has put down roots and sprouted its first leaves, the process of growth begins. The first few years, known as the establishment years, are critical in the life of any tree and the odds are stacked against survival. A young tree is vulnerable to being eaten or trampled by animals, its root system may not be able to withstand drought and it is far more vulnerable to forest fire than a larger tree. Other major threats include long periods of frost or waterlogging, which a fully grown tree would survive more easily.

The growing years

Once a tree is established, it can get down to some serious growing. Trees grow upwards, downwards and outwards. The rate of growth will be determined by many factors, including the availability of water, light levels and climatic conditions.

Below: This sweet chestnut is in the final stages of its life cycle. It is still alive even though its trunk is hollow.

Upward growth

There is a popular misconception that trees grow from the bottom up and are continually moving skywards. In other words, if you were to go to any tree and paint a ring around it 2m/6½ft above the ground and then return to it five years later when the tree was 2m/6½ft taller then the ring would be 4m/13ft above the ground. Well, this is not the case; the tree may well be 2m/6½ft taller but the painted ring will still be 2m/6½ft above the ground. Growth occurs year on year only from the tips of the previous year's growth.

At the tip of each branch are growing cells. As these divide, they make the branch grow longer, so the tree becomes taller and wider. How fast these cells divide will depend on the species and many other external factors, such as the availability of water and light. Some plants, such as bamboo, can grow more than 50cm/20in a day, but there are no trees that grow at anywhere near this rate. The fastest-growing trees come from tropical parts of the world, simply because there are no seasonal changes and so growing conditions remain good throughout the year. One species of tropical eucalyptus from New

Below: Tree growth is determined by the amount of sunlight the leaves can absorb and the uptake of water through the roots.

Guinea, *Eucalyptus deglupta*, can grow 10m/33ft in just over a year, as can *Albizia falcata*, another tropical tree, from Malaysia. Willow is one of the fastest growing temperate trees. When it is coppiced (the stem is cut back down to the stump) it can grow more than 3m/10ft in a year.

Growth in any tree is affected by age; as trees get older their growth rate decreases until they eventually stop growing altogether.

Downward growth

There is a direct relationship between growth put on above ground by the branches and that achieved below ground by the roots. This relationship is known as the root:shoot ratio. The leaves on the branches provide food for the roots and in turn the roots provide water and minerals for the leaves. As a tree grows, it produces more leaves. These require more water and minerals, so the root system needs to grow in order to provide these minerals. To do that it needs more food from the leaves. All parts of the tree must work in harmony in order to continue the growth of the tree. The tree roots must develop to provide sufficient anchorage for the tree. The balance is a fine one; if leaves or roots fail, the tree will suffer and may die.

Outward growth

As the branches grow longer, so the trunk, branches and roots become thicker. In temperate regions a mature tree trunk increases in diameter by about 2.5cm/1in every year. This growth is a result of the need for the tree to be able to transport increasing amounts of water and food to and from its branches. This process occurs immediately below the bark surface in the vascular system, which contains the phloem and xylem. Throughout a tree's life, the cambium constantly produces new phloem and xylem cells, which cover the inner wood. As these cells are added, so the tree's girth expands. In tropical regions this growth continues throughout the year. In temperate areas, growth only occurs in the spring and summer.

Above: Without competition for light, saplings will establish much more quickly than those trying to grow in another tree's shade.

Growth rings

The cycle of growth in a temperate tree can be clearly seen when the tree is cut down. Each year the new cells that are produced under the bark create a new ring of tissue, visible in a cross section of the trunk. Each ring has light and dark sections. The light tissue is less dense and is made up of cells produced in the spring when the tree is growing fastest. The dark part of the ring is composed of cells laid down in the summer when the rate of growth has slowed. These rings are known as growth rings. By counting them it is possible to work out the age of a tree.

Old age

As a tree gets older, so its rate of growth slows down and eventually it stops. In theory, provided that the root:shoot ratio remains stable the tree should live for many years. However, as a tree ages and its growth slows, so it also loses the ability to defend itself from attack. Opportunistic fungi will exploit this and eventually disease and decay upset the root:shoot ratio and the tree starts to decline.

Rejuvenation

Some trees respond to hard pruning or coppicing. The re-growth is effectively young wood and displays all the characteristics of a young tree. Coppicing carried out on a regular basis can extend a tree's life almost indefinitely. In England, there is a coppiced small-leafed lime, *Tilia cordata*, at least 2,000 years old, which is still growing as a juvenile.

TREES AND WEATHER

Climate is the main controlling influence over where and how trees grow. Throughout time, climate changes have dictated the pattern of tree distribution and evolution across the world. In times of intense cold, such as the ice ages, billions of trees perished.

The relatively settled climate of the last 12,000 years has resulted in fairly static patterns of tree distribution over that time. However, even minor changes in the earth's climate now, perhaps due to the greenhouse effect, could have a dramatic effect on future patterns of tree distribution and growth. An increase in the mean temperatures of just 2°C/35°F would result in a significant northward migration of temperate trees in the Northern Hemisphere. Thousands of acres of sugar maple plantations in New England would disappear as the climate became too warm for them. Spruce would have difficulty surviving in the United States, Great Britain and central Europe for the same reason. Deserts would expand into the Mediterranean regions of the world, threatening the natural diversity of trees in California, Spain and France. In the Southern Hemisphere more than half of the rainforest of northern

Australia would disappear, along with vast areas of rainforest in central Africa and South America.

Influencing weather patterns

Whereas the climate controls tree distribution on a global scale, trees actually influence weather patterns on a regional or local level. The process of photosynthesis raises humidity in the air. Where trees are found in large numbers, such as in equatorial rainforests, this humidity has an effect on daily rainfall. In the morning the sun warms up the forest and warm, moist air rises from the trees. As the air rises, it cools and condenses into water droplets, causing clouds to form, and it begins to rain. This process is repeated daily throughout the year all around the world's equatorial regions.

Reducing the effects of weather

Ever since man evolved, trees have been used to reduce the effects of cold and wind exposure. Forests and woodlands provided natural shelter, and many original human settlements

Above: Palm trees are well equipped to cope with the heat and drought of the tropics.

were created in clearings cut from the forest. Trees were also used to shelter stock. The practice of "wood pasture", grazing cattle or sheep within a forest, has been going on in Britain since the 2nd century. Timber from trees has been used to build shelters and dwellings for thousands of years and early man discovered that wood from trees could be burnt to provide heat.

Today, our use of trees to control the extreme effects of the weather has become far more sophisticated. We now know which are the best species to include within wind shelter belts, for example. We know how tall, how wide and how dense the belt should be. We also know how far away it should be from the area we wish to shelter. On average, a shelter belt 20m/66ft wide and 20m/66ft tall will provide wind protection on the leeward side for a distance of 400m/1,312ft. Such protection can increase cereal crop production by as much as 20 per cent.

Trees also help reduce the effects of frost. If tree shelter belts are planted across a hillside, cool air descending the slope will become "trapped" by

Below: In areas of severe exposure trees will grow away from the direction of the prevailing wind.

the trees. Frost "ponds up" above the trees rather than travelling farther down the hillside or into the valley bottom. The same principle applies to snow. Strategic planting of trees on lower mountain slopes dramatically reduces the chance of avalanches occurring and their effects if and when they do occur.

Another important function trees have is the stabilization of soil and prevention of erosion. Tree roots help bind soil to the ground and soak up rainfall, while leaves and branches reduce the effects of wind on the ground. The latter is particularly important in areas of low rainfall where soil is often dry and loose. One of the biggest causes of soil erosion is deforestation. Once trees have been felled, fragile topsoil becomes exposed to both wind and rain, and is soon washed or blown away. Once the soil

Above: Reducing temperatures in autumn will trigger an explosion of colour as the leaves begin to die.

Below: Many conifers have adapted to regular heavy snowfall by developing weeping branches, which are able to shed snow.

Above: Welwitschia mirabilis has adapted successfully to the Namibia Desert.

has gone so has the opportunity to grow food crops. Trees are now being re-planted in the Sahel region of Africa to try to reduce the effects of soil erosion and also the expansion of the Sahara Desert.

Trees also help protect against the effects of heavy rainfall and flooding. Those planted in water catchment areas soak up excessive amounts of rain, enabling the soil to release smaller volumes of water into the watercourses gradually, thus reducing the possibility of flash-flooding farther downstream. Trees such as willow, planted alongside riverbanks, reduce the effects of riverbank erosion when water levels are high.

Indicators of climate change

In many parts of the world where there are seasonal differences in rainfall and temperature, trees form clear annual growth rings in their trunks. The width of these rings varies depending on the growing conditions in any one year. In cold, dry years, tree growth is slow, producing a narrow ring. In warm, wet years, tree growth is faster and the ring produced wider. As tree rings build up, they provide a year-by-year record of changes in climate. Because trees live for such a long time, these records may cover hundreds or thousands of years.

TREES AND POLLUTION

Trees are the air filters of the world. They absorb carbon dioxide from the air and replace it with oxygen. They also trap airborne particle pollutants, which are one of the main causes of asthma and other respiratory problems in humans.

The process by which trees produce food and thereby harness energy for growth is called photosynthesis. As part of the process, trees absorb vast amounts of carbon dioxide from the atmosphere and break it down. The carbon is effectively locked up within the trees' woody structures of roots, trunk and branches. A healthy tree can store about 6kg/13lb of carbon a year. On average, 0.4ha/1 acre of trees will store 2.5 tonnes of carbon per year. Trees are the most effective way of removing carbon dioxide from the atmosphere and thereby reducing the effects of global warming.

When trees die naturally, the carbon they contain is gradually released back into the atmosphere as carbon dioxide. This happens so slowly that the gas can be reabsorbed by the next generation of trees growing alongside. However, when trees, or coal (fossilized wood), are burnt, the carbon they contain is released much more quickly. Living trees and other plants are only able to reabsorb some of it – the remainder stays in the atmosphere. Continual burning means a continual build-up of carbon dioxide.

The practice of "slash and burn" agriculture, carried out in tropical rainforests to create agricultural land,

Below: Across the world 40ha/100 acres of forest are felled every minute.

Above: An ongoing threat to the tropical rainforests is the expansion of agriculture.

releases hundreds of thousands of tonnes of carbon dioxide back into the atmosphere. Even more serious is the large-scale burning of fossil fuels, such as coal and oil, in the West. The carbon dioxide produced traps more of the sun's energy than normal inside the atmosphere and so contributes to global warming.

During the photosynthesis process trees not only remove carbon dioxide from the atmosphere, they also replace it with oxygen, effectively producing clean air. Every day 0.4ha/1 acre of trees produces enough oxygen to keep 18 people alive.

Biological filters

As well as removing carbon dioxide from the atmosphere, trees absorb sulphur dioxide produced by the burning of coal; hydrogen fluoride and tetrafluoride released in steel and phosphate fertilizer production; and chlorofluorocarbons, which are produced by air-conditioning units and refrigerators. Trees also trap other particle pollutants, many of which are by-products of the internal combustion engines in cars. These particles are one

of the main reasons for the increasing incidence of asthma and other respiratory illness in people across the world. Research has shown that trees act as excellent biological filters, removing up to 234 tonnes of particle pollutants every year in cities the size of Chicago.

Trees cause pollution

Some trees emit large amounts of certain volatile organic compounds (VOC), which react with nitrogen oxides and sunlight to form ozone – a significant ground-level air pollutant. Volatile organic compounds exist in fossil fuels, such as petrol. Most petrol nozzles are fitted with filters to stop the VOC from escaping into the atmosphere. It is of course impossible to stop trees from emitting high rates of VOC, but some tree species produce more than others. Scientists suggest that these trees should not be grown in large quantities where high levels of nitrogen oxides already exist, such as in and around towns and cities.

Trees that produce high levels of VOC include eucalyptus, oaks and poplars. The blue haze often seen over the Blue Mountains near Sydney, Australia, is in part caused by the release of VOC by eucalyptus trees. Ten thousand eucalyptus trees will emit about 10kg/22lb of VOC an hour, which is equivalent to that released by the spilling of 54 litres/12 gallons of petrol an hour.

There is evidence to suggest that certain tree species, particularly conifers such as spruce and fir, increase acidification of streams, rivers and lakes. This increased acidification can cause the decline of freshwater flora and deplete stocks of freshwater fish. The evidence for this effect is not clear-cut however. Acid deposition from the atmosphere (acid rain) can increase acidification in freshwater, and therefore the decline of freshwater flora and fauna may be attributable to that. There is much debate over whether conifer plantations in water-catchment areas actually do increase the level of acidification. Long-term studies are currently underway in

North America, Great Britain and Scandinavia to establish the truth. In the meantime, forest policy in Great Britain at least has been revised so that coniferous tree species are no longer being planted directly adjacent to lakes and rivers.

Trees are subject to pollution

Although trees can act as natural "air filters", ideally they need clean air to live and grow. Photosynthesis becomes more difficult for trees in areas of high air pollution. In highly polluted cities such as Mexico City, it is estimated that less than ten per cent of the tree population is healthy. Some trees, such as the London plane, *Platanus* x *hispanica*, are able to cope with relatively high levels of air pollution, but it is estimated that more than half of the trees in large cities are in decline due to air pollution. In New York City the average lifespan of trees is less than 40 years.

In many parts of the world the air is now highly polluted. Pollutants such as sulphur dioxide reach high into the atmosphere where they vaporize and

mix with other chemicals and moisture to form acid rain. The damage caused by acid rain affects both coniferous and broad-leaved trees. The effects are more obvious on evergreen trees than deciduous ones because their needles or leaves are replaced less often. Discoloration of foliage is the first sign of acid rain damage. This is followed in extreme cases by defoliation and death. Nutrients are stripped from the leaves as acid rain falls through the canopy and the roots are slowly killed as the acid soaks into the soil.

There are a range of other sources of pollution that affect trees. Too much ozone disrupts the process of photosynthesis and can sterilize pollen, so reducing seed production. Particles of soot are also harmful because they coat leaves and thus prevent vital sunlight getting through. Even salt that is spread to de-ice roads can affect the chemistry of the soil around the roots of roadside trees.

Below: Views of greenery make travelling by road less stressful for motorists, but the pollution emitted by vehicles is ultimately damaging to the trees.

GIANT TREES

Trees are by far the largest living organisms on earth. Some of the tallest specimens would dwarf the Leaning Tower of Pisa in Italy, or Big Ben in London. A single banyan tree in India covers an area that is larger than a football pitch.

Not only are trees the oldest living things on earth, they are also the largest. The world's biggest trees include the most famous individual trees of all. Some of these arboreal giants are local celebrities, others nationally famous and a few known about around the world.

Almost every country has its dendrologists (tree experts) and tree measurers, who can always be readily identified by their measuring tapes and skyward gaze. Countries such as Britain and the United States even have their own tree registers, which detail the largest specimen of just about every tree species that grows in that country. Books are written about the biggest trees and photographs taken. Champion trees are big news and interest in them is growing.

What is a champion tree?

A champion tree is the tallest or fattest living example of a species. In order to be proclaimed champion it must have been accurately measured and those measurements recorded in an agreed way. The height is taken to be the distance from the ground to the top of the tallest living part of the tree. Girth is considered to be the distance around the trunk, and is read at 1.3m/4ft 3in from the ground.

Right: Compare the height of trees to the Leaning Tower of Pisa, which stands 58m/190ft tall. From the left: Montezuma cypress, 35m/115ft; New Zealand kauri, 51m/167ft; giant redwood, 83m/272ft.

Tropical giants

The tallest tropical tree, which is called *Araucaria hunsteinii*, is a relative of the monkey puzzle and grows in New Guinea. When last measured the largest specimen was 89m/293ft tall. In Africa, Dr David Livingstone (1813–73), camped under a baobab tree, *Adansonia digitata*, which had a girth of 26m/85ft. This tree appears not to exist now and the largest baobab alive today is 13.7m/45ft in circumference.

One of the largest trees in the world is found in the Calcutta Botanic Garden in India. It is a banyan tree, *Ficus benghalensis*, that was planted in 1782. In not much over 200 years it has grown into an arboreal titan with vital statistics that are simply astounding. The tree covers an area of about 1.2ha/3 acres and can provide shade for more than 20,000 people. It has 1,775 "trunks" (pillar roots) and an average diameter of more than 131m/430ft.

Temperate giants

For sheer volume, the largest single living thing on earth is a giant redwood, *Sequoiadendron giganteum*, called

Above: One of the largest trees in South America is this Fitzroya cupressoides.

General Sherman. The tree, which stands in the Sequoia National Park, California, has a diameter of 17.6m/58ft, is 95m/311ft tall and weighs 1,200 tonnes.

General Sherman is not the tallest tree in the world, however. This accolade belongs to a specimen of its cousin, a coastal redwood, *Sequoia sempervirens*, which goes by the simple but appropriate name of "Tall Tree". It grows on the Californian coast and when last measured, in October 1996, was 112.2m/368ft tall. If transported to London and placed next to the Houses of Parliament, this tree would be more than 14m/46ft taller than Big Ben.

General Sherman is not the fattest tree in the world either. That title is held by a Montezuma cypress,

Taxodium mucronatum, growing in the grounds of a church at Santa Maria del Tule, near Oaxaca in southern Mexico. This enormous tree is made even more impressive by its very close proximity to the church and other buildings, which take on toy-town proportions in its shade. The Santa Maria del Tule Montezuma cypress has a girth of 36.3m/119ft, outstripping even the mighty African baobabs.

Two trees from New Zealand also deserve a mention. They are the kauri, *Agathis australis*, which grows in the north of the North Island, and the totara, *Podocarpus totara*, which grows on both the North and South Islands. Both trees are antipodean giants, reaching ages approaching 2,000 years, girths of 13m/43ft and heights approaching 60m/197ft. They hold great religious significance for the Maori people, who believe that important spirits live within the trees.

Both species have suffered at the hands of the loggers over the last 200 years and many of the biggest specimens have gone. Those that remain are protected within special sanctuaries, such as Waipoua State Forest, north of Auckland.

The tallest tree ever recorded was an Australian eucalyptus called the mountain ash, *Eucalyptus regnans*, measured in 1872 in Victoria. Unfortunately it never qualified as a champion tree because when it was measured it was already on the ground. It was 132.6m/435ft tall at the time, and thought to have been over 150m/500ft tall when it was at its peak. At one time giant mountain ash clothed the valleys that run from Melbourne to Tasmania. Today, only remnants of this mighty forest remain. There are still some big eucalyptuses in Australia, but nothing approaching these dimensions. There are now no trees over 100m/328ft tall.

There are no world-record-breaking trees in Britain but there is plenty of time for that situation to change. Britain has a good climate for tree growth. It is moist with few extremes of temperature as a result of its proximity to the Gulf Stream. A large number of exotic trees have been introduced into Britain in the last 200 years and many of them are world-beaters in their native habitats. The British examples are still babies but their growth rates so far suggest that some have the potential to develop into record-breaking giants. The title of tallest tree in Britain is currently shared between two Douglas firs, *Pseudotsuga menziesii*, both growing in Scotland. Each measures 62m/203ft tall – taller than the Leaning Tower of Pisa, which stands at 58m/190ft.

Below: Giant redwoods can attain heights in excess of 100m/328ft.

THE FOLKLORE OF TREES

Trees have been worshipped by people since at least the beginning of recorded time and most likely long before that. Like all ancient cultures in different parts of the world, the first inhabitants of Britain and Europe depended on trees for shelter, fuel, food and to cure their ills.

Trees were by far the largest living things ancient people encountered and, as such, inspired awe and admiration and acquired great spiritual importance. They were believed to hold mystical powers, to be able to foretell the future and even to bestow everlasting life. We may dismiss such extravagant ancient beliefs as superstitious nonsense, but much tree folklore is based upon a deep factual understanding of how trees grow and respond to the changing seasons.

The mystical yew

Out of all the native trees of Europe it is the yew, *Taxus baccata*, that attracts the most folklore. It has long been associated with darkness and death. In 1664 Robert Turner wrote: "*If the yew be set in a place subject to poisonous vapours, the very branches will draw and imbibe them, hence... the judicious in former times planted it in churchyards on the west side, because those places were... fuller of*

Below: Druids believed that the evergreen foliage of the yew represented eternal life.

putrefaction and gross oleaginous vapours exhaled out of the graves by the setting sun." Such ideas seem extreme, but there are actually some strands of fact here. Yew trees are commonly found in churchyards and of those that are newly planted many are on the west side of the church.

So why are there so many yew trees in churchyards, particularly in Britain? Several explanations (including that of yew trees collecting bad air) have been given. A central ready supply of yew wood in the village could be quickly turned into long bows in time of strife by the parishioners, and that the walls around most churchyards would stop roaming stock from eating the yew's poisonous foliage, are two of the more plausible ones. However, the most likely reason and the one most tree experts agree on is that the trees predated the churches. The yew was not always associated with death. The Druids believed that its evergreen foliage represented eternal life, a sacred gift that would pass to anyone who slept beneath its boughs. So the locations where yew trees grew became

Above: The rowan's red berries symbolized Christ's blood.

sites of worship, places where people congregated. Centuries later, when Christianity arrived, Christians chose to build their churches on these sacred sites, symbolically linking the tree to Christ's resurrection. Slowly but surely the original reason for the yew's presence in early churchyards faded and it was simply accepted that yew trees would be planted alongside new churches as they were built.

A protective rowan

The rowan or mountain ash, *Sorbus aucuparia*, is also found near churches and quite often around dwellings, especially in regions of Europe inhabited by the Celts. It is said that the wood was used to make the cross upon which Christ was crucified – its bright red berries symbolizing Christ's blood. It was also believed that the presence of a rowan in a churchyard would prevent the "slumbers of the dead from being disturbed". Rowans were widely believed to have protective powers, particularly against witchcraft. A rowan planted by a house door would prevent evil spirits entering.

Other trees were considered to have the opposite effect. At one time many people believed that if the white flowers of hawthorn, *Crataegus*

monogyna, were taken into the house, a death would surely follow. The same was believed of the elder, *Sambucus nigra*. If a sleeper inhaled the scent of elderflowers, the unlucky person would drift into a deep coma and death would eventually follow.

Above: The Druids followed their rites in groves of oak.

A mighty oak
The oak, *Quercus robur* or *Q. petraea*, has always been considered the king of the forest, the greatest and noblest of trees. It measures its lifespan in centuries and produces hard, strong timber, which has been used to build everything from churches and houses to ships. In Roman Europe citizens who had achieved some great deed were crowned with oak wreaths, and even today, oak leaves are still included in the design of military decorations.

Oak leaves always feature in depictions of the mythical Green Man, who is in essence the spirit of all trees, but in particular of oak, and an ancient fertility symbol. In ancient British belief, people were the children of the oak, and so the Green Man was seen as the source of humankind. Carvings of the Green Man can be found in churches across Europe, often placed high in the roof, so as not to be in conflict with Biblical references.

It is widely documented that King Charles II of England hid in an oak tree in an attempt to avoid capture after his defeat at the Battle of Worcester in September 1651. His father, Charles I, had a similar adventure in an oak tree in 1646. Henry VI, head of the House of Lancastrians, sought shelter under an oak tree before fleeing to Muncaster in northern England in 1464 during the course of the War of the Roses. In Britain, 29 May was once widely celebrated as Oak Apple Day, marking the anniversary of Charles II's triumphal return to London on his restoration in 1660. Anyone not wearing a sprig of oak leaves on that day traditionally risked having their legs whipped with stinging nettles.

Prediction and country lore
Many trees were believed to predict the future. Ash, *Fraxinus excelsior*, was thought to be helpful in romantic predictions. Ash leaves placed beneath the pillow of sleeping unmarried girls would offer them a glimpse in a dream of their future husbands. In parts of Europe, girls gathered crab apples on Michaelmas Day (29 September) and arranged them on the ground to form the initials of the one they wished to marry. On 10 October the apples were checked and the girl whose initials were best preserved was deemed most likely to achieve her aim.

Some old sayings reflect the deep understanding that farmers and others who worked the land had of their environment. "When the elmen (elm) leaves are as large as a farden (farthing, an old English coin), It's time to plant kidney beans in the garden," is an example of how trees were used as a natural calendar, indicating the gradual warming of the soil in spring by their response to the changing seasons and weather conditions.

"When the oak is out before the ash…we are in for a splash; when the ash is out before the oak we are in for a soak" is an old country way of forecasting the British summer weather. There is some confusion over just what is "out". Some consider it to be the flowers, and yet oak flowers are almost invariably produced up to two months after ash flowers. Others consider it to be the leaves, yet oak leaves are almost always well formed long before the bare branches of ash even begin to green up.

Some folklore shows what now seems an astute understanding of the healing properties of trees. Those suffering from aches and pains – or hangovers – were often advised to eat willow bark. This is not as strange as it may seem, for the bark of white willow, *Salix alba*, contains salicylic acid, which is a natural pain-reliever and a component of the drug aspirin.

Below: Historically ash has been associated with healing and protective properties.

ANCIENT TREES

The oldest living things in the world are trees. The life span of most is measured in centuries rather than years and there are some that have existed for millennia. Temperate trees generally live longer than tropical trees; although there are baobabs in South Africa said to be more than 3,000 years old.

Until recently we knew more about the ages of trees in temperate than tropical regions (because there are no annual growth rings to count in tropical trees), but now evidence suggests that tropical trees can live just as long as their temperate counterparts. For many years it was thought that the rapid growth and decay that occurs in tropical rainforests meant that tropical trees rarely lived for more than 200–300 years. However, recent advances in carbon-dating have clearly shown that many tropical trees are capable of living for more than 1,000 years.

Ancient tropical trees

There is speculation that some tropical trees may be more than 1,500 years old. The oldest tropical tree recorded with any certainty is a *castanha de macaco* (monkey nut), *Cariniana micrantha*, which is related to the Brazil nut. One specimen of this

Below: Africa's oldest known tree is a baobab growing in Sagole, South Africa. It could be over 5,000 years old.

Amazonian rainforest tree is known to be 1,400 years old. The cumaru tree, *Dipteryx odorata*, from Brazil, is also known to live for more than 1,000 years. One of the best known and largest of all tropical rainforest trees, the Brazil nut, *Bertholletia excelsa*, regularly attains heights in excess of 50m/164ft, but none of those carbon-dated so far has been found to be more than 500 years old.

Africa's oldest known tree is a baobab, *Adansonia digitata*, growing in Sagole, in South Africa's Northern Province. Near its base it is 13.7m/45ft in diameter, and it is thought to be more than 5,000 years old.

The oldest tree in the world with a known and authenticated planting date is a fig tree, *Ficus religiosa*. It grows in the temple gardens in Anuradhapura, Sri Lanka, and was planted as a cutting taken from another fig tree given to King Tissa in 288BC. King Tissa planted it and prophesied that it would live forever: over 2,000 years later it is still going strong.

Above: English oaks, Quercus robur, *have been known to live for more than 1,000 years.*

The world's oldest?

People have a fascination for the oldest and biggest. Over the years ancient trees have grabbed their fair share of the headlines. An 11,700-year-old creosote bush, *Larrea tridentata*, was said to grow in California's Mojave Desert. A 10,000-year-old huon pine, *Dacrydium franklinii*, was "discovered" in Tasmania. The most incredible is a king's holly, *Lomatia tasmania*, also from Tasmania, which was reported to be up to 40,000 years old. These are all great stories, but are they true?

Close scrutiny reveals that these are all clones that have grown from plants that were on the same site before. In terms of the age of the growth that can be seen above ground today, none is any older than 2,000 years. Whether or not they qualify for the title of oldest living trees is debatable. They have the same genetic material as the seedlings that first grew on the same spot all those millennia ago, but then all living things that reproduce asexually have the same genetic make-

up as their ancestors. We would not consider a female aphid produced asexually to be the same animal as its mother. No doubt the veracity of these claims will continue to be debated for some time to come.

Ancient temperate trees

The oldest living tree in the temperate world is the bristlecone pine, *Pinus longaeva*. Bristlecone pines originated in the White Mountains of eastern

Below: Olive trees will live for centuries; the oldest is believed to be 2,000 years old.

California. The oldest are found in an area known as Schulman Grove, named after Dr Edward Schulman, who spent more than 20 years studying the trees there. In 1957 he discovered that many of them were over 4,000 years old and one of them, which he christened Methuselah, was considerably older. These trees all have solid centres, so Schulman was able to bore right into the centre of each tree and take out pencil-thick radial cores, from which he was able to count the growth rings. Carbon-dating since then has confirmed Dr Schulman's original age for these trees and Methuselah is verified as being 4,700 years old.

For many years the giant redwoods, *Sequoiadendron giganteum*, were assumed to be the oldest trees because they were the biggest. We now know that isn't the case. The oldest redwood is a giant known as General Sherman, which stands in the Sequoia National Park, California, and is approximately 2,700 years old.

The oldest tree in Europe is believed to be the Fortingall Yew, which stands

Above: Methuselah, the world's oldest bristlecone pine.

in a churchyard in Perthshire, Scotland. Although much of its trunk has rotted away, its girth suggests that it is at least 4,000 years old. There are many contenders for the oldest oak tree, *Quercus robur*, and in truth we will probably never know for certain which is the oldest. Oaks have a habit of looking more ancient than they actually are. England and Wales have possibly the best collection of ancient oaks in western Europe. There are several oaks in Britain and across Europe that are believed to be up to 1,000 years old, but their exact age is anyone's guess. Three oaks are locally proclaimed as being 1,500 years old: one in Brittany, France, another one in Raesfeld, Germany, and a third in Nordskoven, Denmark. The oldest olive tree, *Olea europaea*, grows in the Garden of Gethsemane, at the foot of the Mount of Olives in Jerusalem. It is said to have been planted at the time of Christ.

UNDERSTANDING BOTANICAL NAMES

Botanical names offer an international language, understood by gardeners, botanists, horticulturalists and foresters all over the world. Although they may appear confusing and difficult to remember, botanical names can tell us much about a plant once we understand the basics of plant nomenclature.

Botanical names are sometimes referred to as "scientific names" or "Latin names", even though some are derived from Greek, Arabic and other languages. It was the Swedish botanist Carl von Linné (1707–78), who published his work under the Latinized form of his name, Carolus Linnaeus, who created a referable system of nomenclature that became the foundation of the system used today. He classified organisms by the way they reproduced themselves and the make-up of their reproductive systems.

The binomial system of nomenclature

Linnaeus employed what is known as the "binomial" system of nomenclature, which gives each organism a two-word name. The first word is the generic (genus) name, which is always a noun. Most generic names are derived from older Latin, Greek or Arabic names. Some are based on characters in Greek mythology, such as Daphne, the nymph who was turned into a laurel tree by Apollo, while others commemorate people such as botanists; *Buddleia*, for

example, is named after the Reverend Adam Buddle, who described it in the early 18th century. The generic name gives a clue to the relationships between organisms, because closely related species are given the same generic name but different specific names. For example, the English oak is called *Quercus robur* and the closely related Turkey oak is called *Quercus cerris*. All the species with the same generic name are said to belong to the same genus.

The second part of the name is the specific (species) epithet and is normally a qualifying adjective. The same descriptive word may be applied to quite different plants in many different genera: for example in the names *Magnolia sinensis*, *Camellia sinensis* and *Nyssa sinensis*, *sinensis* means "from China", and quite often specific names indicate the geographical origin of a plant in this way. Others describe a particular feature, such as leaf colour. *Quercus alnifolia*, for example, means "golden-leaved oak". Specific epithets also commemorate people, and many

species, such as *Magnolia wilsonii* or *Pterocarya forrestii*, are named in honour of the prolific plant hunters (in these cases the Englishman Ernest Wilson and the Scotsman George Forrest) who brought the first propagating material to Europe.

Each two-word name, known as the binomial, can only ever represent one plant. The advantage of using old languages such as Latin or ancient Greek is that they are recognized universally but are no longer used as a spoken language, so that the meanings of the words should not change over time. If a continually evolving language, such as English, were used, there is every chance that names would be corrupted or changed over time and cause confusion. We all think we know what we mean by "dandelion", for instance, but across Europe this name represents over 1,000 different plants.

Subspecies, varieties and cultivars

Occasionally, other words and names follow the binomial name. These reflect the fact that the plant is not exactly the same as the named species. A subspecies, such as *Magnolia campbellii* subsp. *mollicomata*, occurs when a regionally isolated population of a species shows distinct and regular characteristic differences to the species as a whole. This may be because it is growing on an island, on the other side of a mountain range, or in another part of the world, and the difference may result from climatic or physical changes in the environment. In evolutionary terms, a subspecies may be on its way to becoming a different species, but the differences are such that reclassification is not justified.

A variety is a plant that occurs naturally in the wild and regularly displays different characteristics to those that are normal for the species,

Above: The English oak, Quercus robur, is known all over Europe, but is one of many species in the Quercus genus. All species of oak have common features.

Quercus dentata

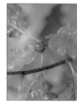

Quercus petraea

Quercus suber

Quercus frainetto

Above: Sorbus americana.

Above: Tilia americana.

Above: Fraxinus americana.

but not across whole populations, or not great enough to warrant it being named as a different species. For example the Christmas box, *Sarcococca hookeriana* var. *digyna*, is the same as the species, *S. hookeriana*, except that it regularly produces narrower leaves and two stigmas in each flower, whereas the species has three stigmas.

A cultivar exhibits a difference that does not occur regularly in the wild but is maintained only through horticultural techniques such as continual selection or grafting. An example is *Quercus rubra* 'Aurea': the species, *Q. rubra*, has deep green

Above: Taxus baccata, the original species.

Below: Taxus baccata 'Semperaurea', a variety of the original species.

leaves, whereas the cultivar 'Aurea' has bright yellow leaves in spring, which gradually turn green. It is the result of a chance mutation, which was noted and propagated; once its reproduction was perfected it was made commercially available.

Name changes

The natural conclusion from all of this is that once a plant is named under the binomial system that name will remain

the same for ever, and everyone will have a clear understanding of what plant that name represents. Most of the time this is true, but for botanists and taxonomists, some botanical names are a subject of constant disagreement. Taxonomists are still regularly moving species from one genus to another, and when this happens the consequence is that the generic name changes, and quite possibly the specific name does too.

What do they mean?

It can be useful to learn the meanings of some of the most commonly used specific names. Many provide information about a tree's origins, habit or appearance, and can be helpful clues to the conditions they will need in order to grow well.

Geographical
atlantica = of the Atlas mountains of North Africa (*Cedrus atlantica*)
europaeus = of Europe (*Euonymus europaeus*)
lusitanica = of Portugal (*Prunus lusitanica*)
orientalis = eastern (*Thuja orientalis*)
sinensis = of China (*Nyssa sinensis*)

Habitat
aquatica = growing by water (*Nyssa aquatica*)
campestre = of the fields (*Acer campestre*)
maritima = by the sea (*Prunus maritima*)
montana = of the mountains (*Clematis montana*)
sylvatica = of the woods (*Fagus sylvatica*)

Habit
arboreum = tree-like (*Rhododendron arboreum*)
fastigiata = erect, upright (*Taxus baccata* 'Fastigiata')
nana = dwarf (*Betula nana*)
pendula = weeping, pendulous (*Betula pendula*)
procera = very tall, high (*Abies procera*)
repens = creeping (*Salix repens*)

Leaves
cordata = heart-shaped (*Tilia cordata*)
decidua = dropping its leaves, deciduous (*Larix decidua*)
incana = grey and/or downy (*Alnus incana*)
latifolia = broad-leaved (*Ilex latifolia*)
macrophyllum = large-leaved (*Acer macrophyllum*)

Flowers
floribunda = free-flowering (*Dipelta floribunda*)
paniculata = flowers in panicles (*Koelreuteria paniculata*)
parviflora = small-flowered (*Aesculus parviflora*)
racemosa = flowers in racemes (*Sambucus racemosa*)
stellata = star-like flowers (*Magnolia stellata*)

Colours
alba = white (*Populus alba*)
aurea = golden (*Pinus sylvestris* 'Aurea')
bicolor = two-coloured (*Picea bicolor*)
carnea = flesh pink (*Aesculus* x *carnea*)
nigra = black (*Pinus nigra*)
rubra = red (*Quercus rubra*)

THE PLANT HUNTERS

For centuries man has sought out new tree species; firstly for food, medicine and timber and latterly for ornamental purposes. Over the last 200 years plant hunters have scoured the world in search of previously unknown species to introduce to gardens and arboreta.

Ever since they first appeared on earth, trees have spread to new places by natural means. Sometimes their movements have been the result of large-scale geological events, such as the break up of the supercontinent Pangaea, which began to occur around 193 million years ago. Sometimes they have been in response to changes in global climate. For example successive ice ages saw a migration of plants away from the poles and towards the Equator. Interglacial warm periods saw a movement back towards the poles but also away from low-lying land, which became flooded as the polar caps melted and sea levels rose. These movements occurred over many plant generations and sometimes took tens of thousands of years.

Later, the development of human civilization brought an accompanying quickening in the rate at which trees migrated and species settled in entirely new areas. Humans quickly realized that trees were useful. They could be used to make basic tools, produce food and provide shelter and fuel. As humans moved around the earth, they

started using the trees that surrounded them and took parts of other trees with them, sometimes in the form of their fruits and berries. Inadvertently to begin with, but then consciously, humans became the vehicle for seed distribution and then, ultimately, moving trees. Trees took on new importance, becoming symbols for pagan worship. As time passed, their medicinal properties became better understood too.

The early plant hunters

The first record of plant hunting and tree collecting dates from 1495BC. Queen Hatshepsut of ancient Egypt sent out expeditions to Somalia to collect the incense tree, *Commiphora myrrha*, which produced a resin that was burned in Egyptian temples.

The Romans sped up the process of distribution, taking many trees with them as their empire expanded. Later, during medieval times, monks were also responsible for moving trees right across Europe, as they developed a network of monasteries from Russia to Portugal.

As civilization developed, so did the aesthetic appreciation of trees. Trees were considered an integral part of

Above: The Oriental plane was introduced to much of Europe by the Romans.

garden creation and from the 16th century onwards, European plant hunters started to look outside their own continent for new introductions. One of the first trees to be brought in was the horse chestnut, *Aesculus hippocastanum*, which was introduced into Vienna and then into France and England from Constantinople by the Austrian botanist Clusius in 1576. It was followed shortly afterwards by the Oriental plane, *Platanus orientalis*, introduced into Britain from Greece in the late 1590s.

It was in the early 1600s, as the exploration of North America began, that plant hunting really started to take off. Stories of amazing new trees swept through Europe and everyone with influence and money wanted their own collection. John Tradescant, (1570–1638) and his son, also called John (1608–62), were the first organized plant hunters. After starting out as gardeners for the rich and famous (including King Charles I), they introduced a phenomenal range of plants including dogwoods, *Cornus* species; lilac, *Syringa* species; red maple, *Acer rubrum*; the tulip tree,

Below: The Royal Botanic Gardens at Kew, England, has a fine ornamental tree collection.

Liriodendron tulipifera; and the false acacia, *Robinia pseudoacacia*, from North America into Britain.

The past 200 years

As travel became easier, European plant hunters ventured farther and farther afield in search of ever more exotic and wonderful trees. North America, South America, the Himalayas, China, Japan, Australia and New Zealand all contained huge, largely unexplored tracts of land, ripe for discovery. Expeditions were funded by wealthy landowners or botanical institutions such as London's Kew Gardens, keen to build up their collections of botanical rarities. Arboreta sprang up all over Europe. Among the first was the magnificent Westonbirt Arboretum in England, created by Robert Holford in 1829.

David Douglas (1799–1834)

Born in Perthshire, Scotland, David Douglas was probably one of the greatest tree collectors of all time. From an early age he displayed a great interest in all things horticultural. By the time he was ten he was apprentice gardener to the Earl of Mansfield at Scone Palace. In his early twenties he was commissioned by the Horticultural Society in London (later to become the Royal Horticultural Society) to collect for them in North America. Over the

Below: Liriodendron tulipifera *was introduced into Europe by John Tradescant (junior) in 1650.*

next ten years Douglas walked almost 10,000 miles, exploring the Pacific coast of North America. Along the way he collected over 200 species never seen in Europe before, which included the Monterey pine, *Pinus radiata*, from Southern California; the noble fir, *Abies procera*; the grand fir, *Abies grandis*; and perhaps the finest tree of them all, the Douglas fir, *Pseudotsuga menziesii*.

William Lobb (1809–64)

A Cornishman, William Lobb was the first plant hunter employed by Veitch and Sons, nurserymen of London and Exeter. His first journey for the company in 1840 took him to the South American Andes, where, among other things, he collected more than 3,000 seeds from the monkey puzzle tree, *Araucaria araucana*. The seed was dispatched to Veitch and Sons, and by 1843 the first seedlings were on sale. In 1849 Lobb was sent on his second trip, this time to North America, with the aim of picking up from where Douglas had left off 20 years before. It was on this trip that he discovered the western red cedar, *Thuja plicata*, and collected seed from the coastal redwood, *Sequoia sempervirens*. Lobb's third trip in 1852, again to North America, was the one for which he is best remembered. It was on this trip that he discovered the largest tree in the world, the giant redwood, *Sequoiadendron giganteum*. Lobb arrived back at Veitch and Sons with seed from this remarkable tree just before Christmas in 1853. The tree was immediately named 'Wellingtonia' in honour of the Duke of Wellington, who had recently died. The Victorians fell in love with Wellingtonia and virtually overnight it became the most sought-after tree for estates across the British Isles.

Ernest Wilson (1876–1930)

Another employee of Veitch and Sons, Ernest Wilson was sent to China in 1899 to find what had been described as "the most beautiful tree in the world" – the pocket handkerchief tree, *Davidia involucrata*. When he

Above: The giant redwood species was introduced to Europe by William Lobb.

arrived in China, he was presented with a scruffy piece of paper with a map on it. The map covered an area of roughly 51,200km²/20,000 miles². On it was marked the rough position of a single pocket handkerchief tree. Amazingly Wilson found the tree's location, but all that was left was a stump. The tree had been cut down and its timber used to build a house. Undaunted, Wilson continued to search the area and eventually found another pocket handkerchief tree, from which he collected seed to send back to England. In 1906 Wilson left the employment of Veitch and Sons to become a plant hunter for the Arnold Arboretum in Boston, USA. From there he carried out further trips to China and to Japan. During his plant-hunting career Wilson introduced more than 1,000 new species to the western world.

Charles Sargent (1841–1927)

Born in Boston, USA, Sargent created the Arnold Arboretum. A botanist and plant hunter, he collected mainly in North America and Japan. Sargent had several plants named after him. Perhaps the best-known is the Chinese rowan, *Sorbus sargentiana*.

TREE CULTIVATION

People grow trees for several reasons. Foresters plant on a large scale to produce trees for timber, while farmers and landowners cultivate them for their fruit. Many trees are grown for pure ornament, to brighten up parks or add structure to gardens.

Ever since people first appeared on earth they have lived in a world dominated by trees. When modern humans finally arrived 35,000 years ago, trees covered more than two-thirds of all dry land on the planet. The other third was covered by ice or occupied by grassland or desert.

Modern humans have grown up alongside trees and forests. People have used them for shelter, as a source of food, fuel and all the necessary implements for life. In the beginning,

Above: Fruit trees have been cultivated in orchards for more than 2,000 years.

Below: The first roadside tree planting was carried out by the Romans, to provide shade for their marching legions.

they would have used whatever tree happened to be near to them. Gradually, however, awareness grew that certain tree species were better used for specific purposes. Harvesting trees from the wild had one serious disadvantage however – the more that were taken, the farther people had to travel from home to find the right tree for the job.

Semi-natural forests

Eventually people learnt that trees could be "managed". Seed could be collected, seedlings grown and trees planted in more convenient locations closer to human settlement. These were the first artificial plantations. At the same time, people realized that some trees did not die once they had been cut down, but re-grew from the stump. They learned that regular cutting (coppicing) provided a ready supply of thin, straight sticks, which could be used for a variety of purposes. The trees were all native to the area, and had been part of the original natural forest, but now that people were managing them in these ways, the forest had become semi-natural.

Above: The para rubber tree is grown in plantations throughout South-east Asia, where it is widely cultivated for its harvest.

Early plantations

The idea of growing specific trees together in one place for a clearly defined purpose dates back almost to prehistory. Ancient Egyptians grew plantations of sandalwood so that they could have a ready supply of incense, for example. Both the ancient Greeks and Romans planted groves of olives, as well as orchards of cork oak. Fruit, such as apples and pears, has been grown in orchards in much of western Europe since early medieval times. In Britain from the 16th century, forests of oak were planted to supply timber to build wooden ships for the navy. One large warship could consume as many as 3,000 trees.

With the advent of the Industrial Revolution came the need for vast quantities of raw materials, many of which came from trees. One tree that typifies this change is the para rubber tree, *Hevea brasiliensis*, which originated in the Amazon rainforest. As early as the 15th century, rubber

was being extracted from this tree to make shoes, clothes and balls. In 1823, Charles Macintosh, a Scottish inventor, coated cloth with rubber and invented the raincoat we now know as the mackintosh. Just 16 years later, an American, Charles Goodyear, discovered that heating rubber with sulphur caused the rubber to stabilize. This led to many new uses for rubber, including the manufacture of tyres. In 1872, Joseph Hooker, director of the Royal Botanic Gardens at Kew in England, sent plant hunter James Wickham to Brazil to collect seed from the para rubber tree. There, Wickham collected more than 70,000 seeds. Out of these seeds, 9,000 grew into young saplings, which were then shipped to Sri Lanka and Singapore. These saplings began rubber growing on an entirely new continent and formed the basis for plantations that now cover more than a million ha/2,500,000 acres across South-east Asia.

Plantation forestry

The form of tree cultivation that we are most familiar with is the growing of trees in man-made forests for timber. Around 1.2 billion ha/3 billion acres of the temperate world are now covered with commercial timber plantations. More than 80 per cent of

Below: In many areas, timber-producing, fast-growing conifers have replaced traditional broad-leaved woodlands.

these are plantations of softwood trees – fast-growing conifers, such as the Monterey pine, *Pinus radiata*, which is widely planted in New Zealand, Australia and South Africa, and sitka spruce, *Picea sitchensis*, which is grown in the Northern Hemisphere. Both of these species have the potential to grow more than 1m/3ft in height per year. They are both harvested at 20–60 years of age, depending on growth rates, for use in construction or to create pulp for papermaking. Once harvested the forest is re-planted and the whole process begins again.

This "sustainable" forestry has far less impact on the environment than the wholesale destruction of natural forests, such as that which occurs in many parts of the tropics. Even so, it does have its disadvantages. Conifer plantations are normally made up of just one species, often not native to the country it is being grown in. The trees are planted close together in rows, thus creating poor habitats for wildlife. Some organizations have begun to acknowledge that this is unacceptable, and have taken steps to remedy the problem. In Britain, the Forestry Commission, for example, now ensures that at least 20 per cent of the ground is left unplanted and that other, native tree species are also grown within the conifer plantation.

Plantation forestry is not restricted to temperate countries, though. Large

Above: There are more than 20 different varieties of fir which are now cultivated for Christmas trees.

areas of Java are now planted with teak, for instance, to provide wood for furniture-making. Like the softwoods from conifer plantations, this timber is sustainably produced – the trees are replaced with new saplings immediately after they are cut down. Sustainable forestry is now being developed all over the world and is actively encouraged by organizations such as the Forestry Stewardship Council (FSC), based in Oaxaca, Mexico. Consumers are also better informed about where wood comes from – most products made from timber grown in certified sustainable forests now carry an FSC label.

Christmas trees

Growing Christmas trees is now big business, with thousands of acres being devoted to their cultivation. These are "short rotation crops" being harvested normally in less than ten years from planting. Traditional Christmas trees, such as the Norway spruce, *Picea abies*, now have competition from many other species, such as the Nordman fir, *Abies nordmanniana*, which has citrus-scented needles that remain on the tree for longer after it has been felled.

TREES FOR TIMBER

Wood is humanity's oldest natural resource. It has provided us with food, fuel, weapons, shelter and tools for thousands of years. Wood can be easily shaped, it has great strength and is durable, hard-wearing and naturally beautiful.

If you look around any room, you will see several things that are made of wood. Furniture, panelling, doors and window frames are the most obvious, but even the paint on the doors, the paper this book is printed on and the photographic film the photographs were taken with, all have a proportion of wood in them.

Wood is unique because it is the one basic natural resource that mankind can renew. When all of the world's oil, gas and coal has been exhausted, there will still be trees and we will still have wood – that is, as long as we manage our forests and woodlands properly.

What is wood?

Wood is a type of tissue produced within trees by a specialized cell layer known as the cambium. Cambium encircles a tree, producing on its outside phloem cells, which transport food manufactured in the leaves to other parts of the tree, and on its inside xylem cells, or living sapwood, which transport water and minerals from the roots to the leaves. This sapwood is constantly being renewed,

Below: Teak produces a strong, durable timber.

overlaying the existing sapwood and so enlarging the core of the tree. As each growing season passes, so the core of the tree gets larger. Only the xylem cells in the current year's sapwood are able to transport water and minerals; the cells beneath gradually die. As they die the old cells undergo a chemical change, turning drier, harder and normally darker. It is this change that creates the visually distinctive banding in a sawn log, demarcating the boundary between the young, soft sapwood and the older, harder inner wood, or heartwood.

Is there a difference between wood and timber?

No, both refer to the woody cells that make up the structure of a tree. The difference between the two words is a matter of timing. When a tree is standing and growing, its bulk is referred to as wood. Once the tree has been cut down and sawn up, that bulk becomes timber. We buy planks from a timber merchant, but once the planks have been turned into something, the object that they have been turned into is generally referred to as being made of wood, rather than timber.

A global business

Timber is produced by almost every country in the world. In general, softwood timber, such as spruce, larch and pine, is more likely to have been grown in temperate regions, whereas hardwood timber, such as teak, mahogany and ebony, is more likely to have come from the tropics. Some countries, such as Canada and Brazil, are virtually self-sufficient in timber supplies. Others, such as Great Britain and Japan, must import up to 90 per cent of their timber requirements. Over the last 100 years or so, the global trade in timber has increased dramatically. For many developing

countries, timber is financially by far their single most important export. Unfortunately, this reliance on timber has resulted in the destruction of millions of hectares of natural forest. It is estimated that 80–200 million hectares/200–500 million acres of natural forest were destroyed in the last ten years of the 20th century.

Timbers of the world

The world's most famous types of timber are household names. But, perhaps surprisingly, not every type is sourced from trees of just one species. Ebony, for instance, may come from any one of five different trees.

Mahogany

Ever since the 16th century, when it was first brought to Europe by the Spanish, mahogany has been the most prized wood for cabinet- and furniture-making in the world. Mahogany is the collective name for the timber of several species of tree in the genus *Swietenia*, which originate from Central and South America. The most

Below: The red-brown colouring of mahogany timber is valued for furniture production.

Above: Pine is used for construction work and was traditionally used for economy furniture.

favoured species is *S. mahoganii*, but because this tree is now very rare most commercial supplies of mahogany now come from *S. macrophylla*. Mahogany has distinctive, rich red-brown colouring, complemented by dark figuring. As well as being beautiful, it is also very durable and is quite impervious to rot and woodworm.

Teak
Indigenous to India, Burma and Indonesia, teak, *Tectona grandis*, has been introduced to Central America, where it is widely planted. Its timber has beautiful golden brown heartwood and is extremely strong and durable. Teak timber is used to make all manner of things, including furniture, boats, staircases and sea defences.

Ebony
Certain species of *Diospyros* provide the timber known as ebony. There are two main types: African ebony, produced by trees that originated in West Africa and Madagascar, and East Indian ebony, produced by trees from Sri Lanka and southern India. Both types have a distinctive almost jet-black colouring. Ebony has always been used for furniture and sculpture, but it is best known as the timber used to make the black keys of pianos.

Oak
There are more than 450 species of oak, most of which occur in temperate regions. The most important group for timber production is known as the "white oaks" and includes the English oaks, *Quercus robur* and *Q. petraea*; the American oak, *Q. alba*; and the Japanese oak, *Q. mongolica*. Timber from white oak has a creamy fawn sapwood and yellow-brown heartwood with silver-grey veining. It is one of the world's most popular timbers. Oak beams were used in the construction of many of the most important old buildings in western Europe, including the majority of tithe barns, churches and cathedrals.

Spruce
This is a group of 20 evergreen conifers found growing naturally in most of the cool temperate regions of the Northern Hemisphere. Of those, only two are commercially important: Norway spruce or 'whitewood', *Picea abies*; and sitka spruce, *Picea sitchensis*. Norway spruce occurs in the wild throughout much of northern Europe, while sitka spruce originates from the Pacific coast of North America. Both timbers are widely used for interior building work, general joinery and the manufacture of pallets. Sitka spruce produces a significant amount of the world's virgin pulp supply for newspapers.

Pine
European redwood, red deal and Scots pine are just three of the names given to the timber of *Pinus sylvestris*, a tree that occurs right across Eurasia from Spain to Siberia. Pine is one of the heaviest softwoods and has attractive pale red-brown heartwood. It is often used in the manufacture of economy furniture, as well as for general building work. In Britain, pine has been used for many years for making railway sleepers (railroad ties).

Elm
The elm occurs naturally throughout northern temperate regions of North America, Europe and Asia. Although different species grow in different regions, the characteristics of the timber are broadly similar. The heartwood is dull brown with a reddish tinge and has prominent, irregular growth rings, which give an attractive figuring. Elm is very water-resistant – in Roman times it was used as a conduit for water, the heartwood being bored out to create a basic drainpipe. The Rialto bridge in Venice stands on elm piles. Sadly, because of Dutch elm disease, elm timber is in short supply across much of Europe and elm trees are much rarer than they once were.

Below: Oak was once used for building ships. It has a straight grain and is very durable.

GENERAL USES OF TREES

It is easy to take wood for granted because it features in almost every area of life. Humans have had a long association with trees and consequently there is an impressively wide range of useful products that can be obtained from trees.

Over the centuries and to the present day, tree products have found their way into the larder, medicine cupboard, wine cellar, paint store, garage, garden shed, wardrobe, bathroom, library and jewellery box.

Medicinal uses

Although the bark and wood of trees is seldom edible, extracts from them have given rise to some of the world's most important medicines. Malaria is said to have killed more people than all of the wars and plagues in history combined. Oliver Cromwell and Alexander the Great are two of the better-known people to have died at its hands. For centuries the only known treatment was quinine, an alkaloid found in the bark of the evergreen cinchona tree, which grows in the tropical forests of Peru and Bolivia. Quinine was first used to treat malaria by the Quechua Indians and in the 16th century the Spanish Conquistadors realized its potential. Called the "miracle cure" when it finally arrived in Europe, it was used to cure King Charles II, King Louis XIV and the Queen of Spain, among countless others. Quinine has been chemically reproduced since the 1940s; however, in recent years some forms of malaria have developed resistance to synthetic quinine and the

Below: Aspirin was originally derived from the bark of the white willow, Salix alba.

Above: Extracts of the leaves of Ginkgo biloba *have been used to improve memory loss.*

cinchona tree has once again become the centre of attention.

If you have ever had a headache then the chances are that you will have reached for a bottle of aspirin, the world's most widely used drug. Before aspirin came in bottles, aches and pains could be cured by walking to the nearest river and finding a piece of willow bark to chew on. Aspirin is a derivative of salicylic acid, which comes from the bark of the white willow, *Salix alba*. Nowadays aspirin is produced synthetically.

The last remaining member of a family that existed when dinosaurs roamed the earth, the maidenhair tree, *Ginkgo biloba*, has long been used for medicinal purposes. The leaves have traditionally been a staple of Chinese herbal medicine and used to treat everything from asthma to haemorrhoids. Now maidenhair tree leaves have found their way into western medicine and are used to treat memory loss and coronary conditions. Fluid extracted from the leaves helps

to improve blood circulation. It relaxes blood vessels, enhancing blood flow throughout the body but in particular that going to the brain.

More than 2,000 different trees are currently used for medicinal purposes. Many, such as the Pacific yew, *Taxus brevifolia*, are helping in the fight against cancer. *Castanospermum australe,* the Australian Moreton Bay chestnut, contains an unusual alkaloid called castanospermine, which is able to help neutralize the Aids virus HIV. Witch hazel, *Hamamelis virginiana*, is a tree with strong antiseptic qualities. Native American tribes such as the Cherokee made a "tea" of the leaves, which they used to wash sores and wounds. Another important medicinal tree species is *Eucalyptus globulus*. Its leaves contain the oil cineol, which is very effective in the treatment of coughs, sore throats, bronchitis and asthma.

Trees in the home

One of the world's favourite drinks – coffee – is made from the seeds (beans) of three small evergreen trees, *Coffea arabica*, *C. canephora* and *C. liberica*. Now cultivated extensively throughout the tropical world, they originate from the montane forests of Ethiopia, where they grow to approximately 6m/20ft tall.

Products made from the Amazonian tree *Hevea brasiliensis* have found their way into just about every home in the world. Better known as the para rubber tree, its cultivation accounts for about 90 per cent of the world's raw rubber supply. *Hevea brasiliensis* produces a gummy, milky white sap beneath its bark as a natural defence against attack from wood-boring insects. This sap, known as latex, is tapped and collected once the tree reaches seven years old. An experienced tapper can harvest about

Above: A mature cork oak may produce up to 4,000 bottle stoppers per harvest.

Above: Olive trees provide an important crop of fruit for many Mediterranean regions.

450 trees a day. *Hevea brasiliensis* is cultivated on more than 7 million ha/17 million acres of land across the tropics. These plantations yield about 6.5 million tonnes of natural rubber every year.

Cork comes from the outer bark of the cork oak tree, *Quercus suber*. An evergreen tree, the cork oak is grown in Mediterranean countries, such as Portugal, Spain and Italy. Cork is a great insulator and it protects the tree's inner bark from forest fires and hot dry summer winds. It is also resistant to moisture and liquid penetration. The Romans used cork to insulate their houses and beehives, as soles for their shoes, stoppers for bottles, jugs and vases, floats for fishing nets and buoys for navigation purposes. Today its main use is in the wine industry. The cork oak is not stripped of its bark until it reaches 25 years old. After that, the cork is harvested every nine to twelve years, giving the tree time to grow a new "skin". Cork oaks are long-lived trees, regularly exceeding 200 years old. A mature tree provides enough cork to make 4,000 bottle stoppers per harvest.

Much of the food that stocks our supermarket shelves comes from trees. Citrus fruits, such as oranges and lemons, are produced by evergreen trees of the *Citrus* genus, originally from South-east Asia. The species that yields Seville oranges, *Citrus aurantium*, was introduced to Spain in the 12th century and its fruit became a valuable provision on long sea voyages, helping to prevent scurvy among the sailors. Today the orange is the most widely grown fruit in the world – every year more than 70 million tonnes are harvested.

Olive trees, *Olea* species, have been grown for their fruit for more than 5,000 years. Originally from Europe's Mediterranean region, they are now cultivated across the world, from Australia to California. The fruit is either eaten whole or pressed for its oil, which has significant health benefits. A ripe olive is about 20 per cent oil.

Even when we brush our teeth we are using products from trees. Toothpaste contains carboxymethal cellulose, which is basically pulped up wood. In Africa, small sticks made from the wood of a tropical tree called *Diospyros usambarensis* are chewed to clean teeth. The wood contains anti-fungal bacteria, which help to combat gum disease and tooth decay.

Below: Timber has been used for boat building.

CHOOSING AND PLANTING TREES

"The right tree for the right spot" may sound rather simplistic, but time spent researching just what is the right tree for a location is likely to yield dividends both in terms of maintenance and the tree's survival. Simple actions can help give a tree a good start in life and maintain its health.

Although trees are generally more resilient than other plant forms, most still require specific conditions of soil, shelter and light to thrive. Climatic changes may also affect a tree's ability to establish and grow satisfactorily. It is therefore important to ascertain the key facts about a location before selecting, obtaining and planting a tree. For example, trees such as the Japanese maples, *Acer* spp, prefer to be grown in dappled shade, while others such as the Judas tree, *Cercis siliquastrum*, thrive only in full sun. Most willows, *Salix* spp, prefer moist soil, and some tender trees such as the Loquat, *Eriobotrya japonica*, require a sheltered warm location to survive.

The golden rule is to identify the conditions of your location first and then find a tree to suit it. Acquiring the tree first and then trying to find a suitable spot may lead to compromise and ultimately to growing difficulties. An important point on species choice: find out the maximum height of any

Above: Bare-rooted plants need planting immediately so that they do not dry out or become damaged. This is the most economical method of buying hedging.

Above: Buying small and established trees that have a protected root ball is a good idea, as long as the soil around the root doesn't become deficient in nutrients.

Right: Nurseries and garden centres stock a whole array of trees to choose from, and should offer advice about the suitability of the purchase for its intended site, as well as aftercare instructions.

Below: Electronic meters are one way of indicating the acidity and alkalinity of soil. Garden centres also sell inexpensive soil-testing kits.

tree you are considering and check that you have room to plant at least that distance away from any buildings.

Soil type

It is important to discover the alkalinity or acidity of the soil – measured on the "pH scale", which runs from 1–14. Soil-testing kits are available from garden centres and nurseries. Neutral soil gives a reading of around 7, below 7 indicates that the soil is on the acid side, and from 7–14 indicates an alkaline soil. Once you

have this information you can begin to identify suitable trees for the site. There are some general rules that apply to choosing trees: for example, cherry trees and other fruit trees, such as plums, thrive in alkaline soil, while most conifers and tree rhododendrons require acid soil to grow well. Observation and identification of the trees that are already growing well in the locality is also helpful. Changing the soil to suit the tree is not really an option for most gardens and it is better to work with the soil that you have.

Purchasing trees

Trees can usually be obtained from nurseries, garden centres, do-it-yourself stores and even supermarkets. They can also be purchased by mail order and over the internet. Your objective should be to obtain the best quality tree, wherever it comes from. Even when you cannot see the actual tree before purchasing there are certain questions worth asking: Has the tree been container-grown or is it bare-rooted? Container-grown trees can be planted at almost any time of year, except in high summer or when the ground is frozen. Bare-rooted trees should ideally be planted in the period from mid-autumn to early winter or, failing this, from late winter to mid-spring. Bare-rooted trees are likely to be cheaper.

Avoid "pot-bound" trees. These have been grown for too long in a pot that is too small for the root system. A telltale sign is roots growing out of the drainage holes in the bottom of the pot. Moss or other plant material growing on the soil surface is also an indication that the tree has been in the pot for a long period. It is perfectly in order for you to lift the tree from the pot to examine the root system. As well as identifying pot-bound trees, this can also be helpful in establishing if the tree has been containerized – that is dug up from the soil and simply placed in a pot for sale. If this is the case the soil may simply fall from the root system as you lift it from the pot.

It is recognized that smaller trees, below 1m/3ft in height, generally survive and establish more easily than larger, more developed, trees. They are also less likely to require staking and are less costly to purchase.

Tree planting

1 Choose your site away from buildings and other trees. Strip off the surface vegetation or turf over an area of about 1m/3ft diameter.

2 Dig a hole in the centre of the stripped area at least 15cm/6in wider and deeper than the root system of the tree or the container holding it. Heap the soil you dig out on a plastic sheet. Break up the walls and bottom of the planting hole to ensure that the roots can penetrate the surrounding soil.

3 Apply water to the hole, the soil heap and the roots of the tree. In soils that have either a high clay content or are extremely free-draining, mix some well-rotted organic material, such as leaf mould or garden compost, into the soil to improve its quality.

4 If you have chosen a container-grown tree, remove it from the pot and gently tease the roots on the outside and bottom of the root-ball away from the compost. Place the tree in the centre of the hole, ensuring that the top of the root-ball is level with the surrounding ground level.

5 Replace the heaped soil around the roots in the pit, firming gently with your heel as you proceed. Fork over the soil lightly and water well.

AFTERCARE

It is worth considering introducing a short length of plastic pipe, such as kitchen waste pipe, into the hole before planting. This should be at a 45 degree angle, with the lower end positioned directly beneath where the root system will be, and the upper end just above the ground surface, approximately 60–90cm/24–36in from where the stem of the tree will be. Once planted, the tree can be watered through this pipe, ensuring that the water gets to where it is most easily absorbed by the roots with minimal waste or evaporation.

Place a 1m/3ft diameter mulch mat (a piece of carpet underlay or thick blanket will do) around the tree. Finally, apply a mulch of treated pulverized or chipped bark over the matting to a depth of 5cm/2in. This will suppress weed growth and help to retain moisture in the soil.

BEST TREES FOR ALKALINE SOIL

Alkaline soils normally overlie limestone or chalk. They are quite often shallow, stony soils but have the advantage of being free-draining and warm quickly in the spring. Several trees originating from the Mediterranean region thrive in these conditions including the Judas tree, Cercis siliquastrum.

The acidity or alkalinity of soil is reflected by its pH reading, which basically measures the level of calcium in the soil. Calcium is an alkaline mineral that can be leached from soil through rainwater percolation, but where the soil overlies calcium-rich chalk or limestone the levels of calcium will remain high. Alkaline soil is often shallow and stony, but has the advantages that it is free-draining and warms up quickly. Alkaline soils will normally dry out more quickly in times of drought. Many of the trees that grow well in these conditions originate from the Mediterranean region and other warm countries with similar climates and free-draining soils. They therefore thrive in sunny positions, where the warmth helps to ripen the wood, producing more flowers.

Below: Olive trees are found on shallow, stony, alkaline soils. Trees that are hundreds of years old still produce good crops of olives.

Above: In warmer temperate regions Albizia julibrissin grows into a beautiful 'mimosa-like' tree with clusters of salmon-pink flowers.

Silk tree *Albizia julibrissin*
Also known as pink siris, this broadly spreading Asian tree is sometimes confused with mimosa, *Acacia dealbata*, because of its finely divided, delicate, fern-like leaves. However, when in flower it is easily distinguished from mimosa by its clusters of beautiful, fluffy flowers with salmon-pink stamens, which are borne on the tree from late summer to early autumn. The flowers are slightly fragrant with a scent of freshly cut hay. The tree enjoys long warm summers and is best grown in a sheltered sunny position. In autumn the leaves turn yellow and orange before falling.

Japanese crab apple *Malus floribunda*
This is one of the most popular of all the flowering crab apples and one of the most floriferous, producing masses of flowers over its small, rounded crown in mid- to late spring – usually a full two weeks before most other flowering crabs. When in bud, each flower is a deep rich pink, opening to pale pink and then white flushed pink as it matures. It was introduced into Europe and the USA from Japan in 1862, but intriguingly there is no known wild population in

Above: Japanese crab apple produces masses of pale pink flowers in mid- to late spring.

Japan. After flowering, small pea-sized, rounded fruits, yellow flecked with red, are borne from late summer to autumn.

Variegated box elder *Acer negundo* 'Flamingo'
This sparsely branched, fast-growing maple, also known as ash-leaf maple because of its pinnate, ash-like foliage, is one of relatively few maples that actively thrive in alkaline soil. 'Flamingo' is a Dutch clone developed in the 1970s. It has soft leaves that are pink in bud and open pale green, with creamy-white to pale pink variegation around the margin, which may extend in places to the midrib of the leaf. The shoots have a blue-green bloom.

Right: The tall candle-like spikes of horse chestnut flowers are a familiar sight in parks and gardens in spring.

Below: The variegated box elder Acer negundo *'Flamingo' is one of very few maples that thrives in alkaline soil.*

Common horse chestnut
Aesculus hippocastanum
Horse chestnuts thrive in any soil, including alkaline, and are common in cultivation in parks and gardens. They are among the most ornamental of all spring-flowering trees. A large specimen grown in an open position is a spectacular sight, especially when covered with a profusion of erect, candle-like spikes of flowers, white with blotches of red and yellow, in late spring.

Horse chestnut fruits contain an oil which was once used to make horses hooves and fetlocks shine: this is one explanation for the common name.

BEST TREES FOR ACID SOIL

Calcium is an alkaline mineral which is found in all soils. It can be lost from soil through rainwater percolation. Where the soil overlies sandstone or granite, the level of calcium falls and the soil becomes acidic. The trees detailed below cannot grow in calcium-rich soil because they become chlorotic.

The acidity or alkalinity of soil is reflected by its pH reading, which measures the level of calcium in the soil. Neutral soil (a balanced mix of calcium and other minerals) has a pH reading of seven. A pH level below seven indicates an acid soil with less calcium. The trees described here will thrive in soil with pH less than seven.

Red oak *Quercus rubra*
This common North American oak provides spectacular autumn leaf-colour, particularly in New England. It has been widely grown in Britain and Europe since its introduction in 1724 and will grow well (and quickly) on both acid and alkaline soils. However, it will produce vibrant red autumn leaf colour only on acid soils – elsewhere the colour tends to be a dull yellow or brown. Even on acid soil red oak rarely colours well in milder regions of

Above: One of the most recognized "acid loving" genera is Rhododendron.

Europe. This is because the tree needs the dramatic night-time temperature reductions, which occur as autumn approaches in the mountains of North America and in northern Europe, to stimulate the leaf colour change.

Below: In the right conditions the red oak will produce stunning autumn leaf colour displays.

Sweet gum *Liquidambar styraciflua*
Originating in North America, this large deciduous tree has yet to exceed 30m/100ft in Europe, even though it has been grown there since the 17th century. It thrives on moist, acid soils, where it produces autumn leaves of

Below: The leaves of the sweet gum produce a vibrant autumn colour on acid soils.

every hue from orange to deep plum purple, whereas on shallow alkaline soils it seldom colours well. Two of the best cultivars for autumn colour are 'Lane Roberts' and 'Worplesdon'.

Sassafras albidum

This is an attractive tree with distinctive variable-shaped leaves that may be heavily lobed and similar in outline to leaves of the common fig. It belongs to the same family as cinnamon, *Cinnamomum* spp., and bay, *Laurus nobilis*, and has aromatic bark. It was long used to flavour non-alcoholic root beer and in Creole cooking in its native south-eastern United States, until sassafras oil was found to be carcinogenic in the 1960s (most sassafras flavouring is now produced synthetically). The tree grows well only on acid soils and has leaves that turn yellow, orange or purple in autumn.

Eucryphia glutinosa

In cultivation in Europe and North-west America this beautiful small tree is deciduous to semi-evergreen, but in its native Chile it is evergreen. It grows best in a sheltered position with dappled shade and in moist acid loam.

Below: Rhododendron arboreum is one of the largest of all the tree rhododendrons.

Given these conditions it will produce masses of fragrant white flowers with rose-pink stamens throughout the late summer months, followed by beautiful autumn leaf colours.

Tree rhododendron

Rhododendron arboreum
Sometimes known as Cornish red, this magnificent rhododendron is known to reach heights in excess of 15m/50ft in its native habitat in the Himalayas. It is widely grown in temperate northern and western regions of Europe and North America. Like most rhododendrons it will not tolerate lime in the soil and grows best in moist but well-drained acid loam.

Japanese stewartia *Stewartia pseudocamellia*

This is one of the most beautiful trees for growing on acid soil. It has red-brown flaking bark and a graceful spreading habit. Its white camellia-like flowers have bright orange stamens and appear in late summer, when few other trees are in flower. It also has excellent autumn leaf colour, which varies from bright orange to deep wine-purple. Originally from Japan, it has been cultivated in the West since

Below: The beautiful camellia-like flowers of the Japanese stewartia are borne in summer.

Above: The evergreen Chilean fire bush is one of the most beautiful small trees.

the 1870s but despite its beauty it is not widely grown possibly because it doesn't tolerate drought and wind.

Rauli *Nothofagus nervosa*

This fast-growing attractive tree from Chile and Argentina is known as southern beech because its leaves are reminiscent of European beech. In fact they show more resemblance to common hornbeam because of their prominent leaf veins. On moist acid soils the new leaves emerge in spring a warm bronze and in autumn turn a rich orange-marmalade colour.

Chilean firebush *Embothrium coccineum*

The Chilean fire bush grows wild from the Pacific Coast to high in the Andes Mountains in Chile and southern Argentina. It is a beautiful small evergreen tree that will thrive only in moist acid soil and prefers to be grown in dappled shade. In spring it produces clusters of large brilliant orange-red flowers that look like glowing red embers along the branches.

Red maple *Acer rubrum*

This is one of the most striking of all American maples. It produces bright red showy flowers before the leaves emerge in early spring and, on acid soil, scarlet-red autumn leaf colours. It is a fast-growing, handsome large tree, ultimately reaching 30m/100ft in its native eastern North America. It will grow on neutral to slightly alkaline soils but seldom thrives and rarely produces vibrant autumn colour.

BEST GARDEN TREES

*Such is the diversity of trees around the world that it doesn't matter how big or small the plot,
how acid or alkaline the soil, or how sheltered or exposed the location, there is bound to be at
least one tree that is exactly right for a site.*

In addition to their beauty, trees bring
structure, height and permanency to a
garden. They provide welcome shade
on hot summer days. They screen us
from views we would rather not look
at and shelter other garden plants
from cold wind and torrential rain.
Trees produce oxygen, help to clean
the air and lock up carbon, and can
even reduce the effects of flooding and
soil erosion.

Trees are a prominent part of the
permanent structure of a garden, and
isolated specimens are often planted as
focal points of the design. The most
popular choices put on a show-
stopping performance at some time in
the year, such as spectacular blossom
or vivid autumn colour. They also need
to be able to look good in all seasons
to earn their place in the garden.

For garden planting close to
buildings there are certain trees that
are best avoided because their invasive
roots can cause structural damage.
These include some species of poplar,
willow and oak. It is difficult to give a
rule-of-thumb, "no go" distance when
planting trees near to buildings because
there are so many factors to be
considered, such as the species, soil
type and fluctuations in the water
table. The answer is to research each
location and potential species carefully.

There are trees for every season,
such as cherries for spring, dogwoods
for summer, maples for autumn and
golden pines for winter. Some trees,
such as the Asian birches, have it all:
great bark, stunning autumn colour,
graceful weeping form and delightful
catkin flowers.

Mount Fuji cherry *Prunus
'Shirotae'*
The Japanese name 'Shirotae' roughly
translates as "snow white" and is said
to be a reference to the way that this
tree's pure white pendulous flowers
hang – looking like drifts of snow in
the deep gullies that surround Mount
Fuji. It is a beautiful tree and one of
the finest cherries for spring flowering
in any garden. The Mount Fuji cherry
has a fresh look to it: the flowers are
well set off against bright apple green
leaves, which emerge at the same time
as the flowers. It has been cultivated
outside Japan since the early 20th
century and is sometimes sold as
Prunus 'Mount Fuji'.

*Below: As well as adding height, colour, fruit,
scent and definition to the garden, trees help
reduce sound and pollution.*

Above: The Mount Fuji cherry, Prunus *'Shirotae', has long been considered one of the best flowering cherries for cultivation.*

Willow-leaved pear *Pyrus salicifolia* 'Pendula'

This small tree can withstand long periods of ice and snow, prolonged drought and temperatures in excess of 32°C/90°F. It is also extremely attractive. The tree is fairly dense and slightly mounded, with the main branches more or less horizontal and younger branchlets drooping from them. In ideal growing conditions it

Below: In late spring the leaves of the willow-leaved pear tree are joined by pure white, closely packed lightly scented flowerheads.

may reach a height of 9m/30ft; more commonly 6–7m/20–23ft is a good size. The narrow silver-grey leaves are willow-like (hence the name) and emerge in mid-spring, covered in a beautiful soft white down that extends to the young branches and buds. These are followed in mid-summer by small brown, pear-shaped fruits.

Wedding-cake tree *Cornus controversa* 'Variegata'

For unadulterated flamboyancy, one small tree is outstanding: the wedding-cake tree brightens even the dullest spring day, bringing to a garden a sense of light and sustained ornamentation that is rarely achieved

by other trees. Each branch grows away from the main stem in an ordered, horizontal plane, reducing in length towards the top of the tree. The result is perfectly symmetrical and reminiscent of the tiers of a wedding cake, hence the name.

The icing on this particular cake is the leaves, which are bright fresh green bordered by a rich cream margin. In spring the leaves are joined by clusters of cream flowers, and in autumn mall purple-black berries shine out among purple-red leaves. This variegated form was cultivated in Japan in the mid-1800s.

Himalayan birch *Betula utilis* var. *jacquemontii*

The bark colour of this beautiful Asian birch is very variable and, depending on the location from which seed is collected, may vary from copper-brown through pink to pure white. The variety *jacquemontii* has stunning white bark flecked with orange-brown lenticels. Although attractive all year round, it is in winter that this tree really stands out: when planted against an evergreen backdrop the effect is sensational. It is a graceful medium-sized tree, eventually reaching 15–20m/50–65ft.

Below: This beautiful wedding-cake tree is a variegated cultivar of the dogwood, C. controversa, *which originated in Japan, China and the Himalayas.*

TREES FOR SPRING

More trees flower in spring than at any other time of year. Magnolias and cherries predominate, but unusual and dramatic trees such as the handkerchief tree are well worth seeking out. Many public gardens are renowned for their springtime flowering displays of trees and shrubs.

As lengthening days and rising temperatures encourage their plump buds to open, deciduous trees usher in the spring with an explosion of fresh colour that makes them the centre of attention, both in the wild and in parks and gardens. Before they have come fully into leaf the trees allow sunshine to filter through their young foliage, creating dappled, luminous effects. The absence of a heavy leafy canopy also means that early-flowering bulbs and herbaceous plants can flourish on the ground beneath, completing the seasonal picture.

Some of the world's finest ornamental trees flower in springtime. Catkins are an endearing feature of

Below: Along with cherries, one of the first small trees to flower in spring is the snowy mespilus, Amelanchier lamarckii.

trees such as willow, hazel and alder early in the year, and the flowers of many species open before the leaves appear, or while they are still very small. From the large flamboyant flowers of the Asian magnolias to more delicate blossoms such as those of the North American snowy mespilus, *Amelanchier lamarckii*, trees herald the spring with a remarkable variety of floral colour and form.

Flowers are not the only spring attraction trees have to offer. Some species have richly coloured new leaves, creating a display that can be just as striking as a covering of blossom, and many cultivars have been bred to accentuate such features. One of the loveliest springtime displays is that of *Sorbus aria* 'Lutescens', whose new leaves open in globular buds of

Above: Some of the earliest magnolias flower in mid-winter and continue until late spring.

shining silvery white. Unusual leaf colour may be spectacular yet fleeting, as in the sunrise horse chestnut, *Aesculus* x *neglecta* 'Erythroblastos', with bright salmon-pink leaves, or a more lasting feature, such as the soft yellow foliage of the golden false acacia, *Robinia pseudoacacia* 'Frisia'.

Snowy mespilus
Amelanchier lamarckii
The snowy mespilus has a rather spreading habit, quite often with several stems growing from the base, which adds to its attractiveness. The overall form is light and airy, with plenty of space between the slender branches. In spring it produces masses of small, white star-shaped flowers in open, spreading racemes, which contrast superbly with the warm copper-bronze of the newly emerging leaves. First described in 1783 from a plant cultivated in France, the snowy mespilus is believed to be native to Canada, from where it was introduced into France in the 17th century. It has been widely cultivated in the West as a garden ornamental since the 1800s and has naturalized in parts of southern England, as well as in Belgium, Holland and north-west Germany.

Judas tree *Cercis siliquastrum*

The Judas tree is one of the loveliest of all spring-flowering trees. It is also one of the most curious, because it produces lilac-pink, pea-shaped flowers, as if by magic, from every twig and branch, and even growing straight out of the main stem. In a good spring the whole tree is covered in a lilac-pink cloud of blossom. Attractive, delicate, blue-green heart-shaped leaves emerge just as the flowers are fading in late spring. It has been cultivated in western Europe for more than 350 years, but originates from the eastern Mediterranean and western Asia. It is widely planted in gardens and parks in southern USA.

Voss's laburnum *Laburnum* x *watereri* 'Vossii'

This beautiful small tree makes a spectacular garden feature in late spring. It is sometimes known as the golden chain tree, and when fully in flower there is really nothing quite like it. It has weeping chains, up to 30cm/12in long, of large, fragrant, bright yellow pea-flowers, which drip from every spreading branch. Raised in Holland late in the 19th century, it has superseded all other forms of cultivated laburnum.

Below: Voss's laburnum is one of the most popular garden trees. It produces beautiful long chain-like racemes of fragrant, golden-yellow pea-flowers in late spring.

Above: Magnolia campbellii is one of the earliest magnolias to come into flower.

Great white cherry *Prunus* 'Tai Haku'

The great white cherry is one of the most beautiful flowering cherries in cultivation. It also has one of the most curious stories. 'Tai Haku' was an old Japanese cultivar, grown in the Kyoto region until the 1700s. It was thought to be extinct until, in 1923, the English plantsman Collingwood Ingram found a moribund specimen in a garden in England, and progeny from the original tree was taken back to Japan and planted in the Kyoto Botanical Gardens. Today it is widely cultivated in Japan and throughout Europe and North America. In mid-spring it produces a profusion of delightful, pure white single flowers, with dusky pink central stamens. These flowers, which drip from every branch and twig, are accompanied by bronze young leaves newly emerged from their winter buds.

Handkerchief tree *Davidia involucrata*

This large, stately tree is one of the highlights of spring. Its flower clusters are small, but each one is guarded by a pair of long white, or creamy-white, bracts, which hang in profusion from every bough, like miniature sails. The whole effect is dramatic, particularly when a slight breeze sets the bracts fluttering. The tree is native to Sichuan and Hubei provinces in western China, where the French Jesuit Missionary Abbé Armand David discovered it in 1869. When Ernest Wilson, the English plant collector, went to find it in 1903, he described finding a grove of around 20 mature trees "growing on a precipitous slope…their crowns one mass of white…and most conspicuous as the shades of night close in".

Campbell's magnolia *Magnolia campbellii*

One of the most remarkable of all flowering trees, this magnificent large magnolia is covered in pale pink to deep rose-pink flowers, which may be up to 30cm/12in across, in early spring. The flowers resemble large pink water lilies: the inner tepals are closed in bud-like formation while the outer tepals become wide-spreading as they mature, creating a cup-and-saucer shape. After its introduction into Europe around 1865 from its native Himalayas, the tree is believed to have flowered first in County Cork, Ireland, in 1885. It grows well in the warmer states of the USA.

TREES FOR SUMMER

Trees appear to dominate the landscape in summer more than at any other time of the year, with their broad canopies adding a rich tapestry of colour and texture to town and countryside. When foliage abounds, trees are at their most easy to identify.

As the leaves expand to create a canopy, deciduous trees take on their characteristic silhouettes and create strong blocks of colour and texture. Trees are a valuable addition to the summer garden, forming excellent backdrops for other, smaller plants as well as providing much-needed shade and shelter.

Although not so numerous as spring-flowering trees, those species that flower in summer can be just as attractive. The early summer flowers of the horse chestnuts, *Aesculus* spp, are held above the leaves in spectacular white, pink or red spikes, or "candles", effectively set off by the dark green foliage behind them. While the spring-flowering magnolias bear their flowers before the leaves, their summer-flowering cousins, such as *Magnolia grandiflora*, benefit from the beautiful contrast between their huge waxy white blooms and glossy dark foliage. The cup-shaped flowers of *M. wilsonii* hang face-down, so that they can be enjoyed from under the tree. The starry flowers of the Japanese snowbell tree, *Styrax japonica*, also hang under the branches so that they are not lost among the neat, bright green leaves.

The fragrance of summer-flowering trees travels far on a breeze or in the still air of warm evenings. Limes, *Tilia cordata* and *T. tomentosa*, have abundant, richly scented flowers, which are much visited by honeybees. Aromatic leaves such as those of the myrtle, *Myrtus luma*, are also at their most powerful in hot weather.

Golden-leaved robinia *Robinia pseudoacacia* 'Frisia'

The pinnate leaves of this graceful, wide-spreading tree are a bright, intense, almost glowing, golden yellow. The tree looks its very best when the early morning or late evening summer sun shines through its translucent

Above: Robinia pseudoacacia 'Frisia' holds its yellow colour into summer.

foliage. The vibrancy of the leaves is at its most intense in early summer, when the tree's beauty is heightened by clusters of white pea-like flowers interspersed with the foliage. 'Frisia' is a cultivated form of the American black locust tree, *R. pseudoacacia*. It was raised in 1935 and has become one of the most popular trees for ornamental planting.

Golden rain tree *Koelreuteria paniculata*

This is one of the most stunning of all summer-flowering trees. Each flower is made up of four small bright yellow petals, around a central cluster of orange-red stamens. Individually they are not particularly striking, but as there are about a hundred on each long panicle, with several hundred panicles distributed throughout the tree's canopy, the effect is stunning. The abundant flowers, coupled with the attractive bright green pinnate leaves, make it easy to see why this tree has become a firm favourite for planting in the summer garden. Native to northern China and southern

Above: Koelreuteria paniculata produces a spectacular display of flowers in summer.

Mongolia, it was introduced to Europe as long ago as 1763 and is believed to have been cultivated at Croome Park, Worcestershire, England. It is planted as an ornamental species in parks, gardens and streets throughout the USA.

Snowdrop tree *Halesia carolina*
This is a beautiful, early summer-flowering tree. In a good year every branch is laden with pendulous, creamy-white, snowdrop-shaped flowers, the centres of which are filled with a mass of bright orange stamens. It has oval pointed leaves which, when they first emerge in early summer, are covered in soft white down. They make the perfect landing strips for bees, which love to forage for the sweet nectar within the flowers. This

Below: The small bell-shaped, white flowers of Halesia carolina are resistant to pests and diseases making it a good garden tree.

spreading, medium-sized tree originates from south-eastern United States and was introduced into Europe in 1756, having been identified by Stephen Hales, an English clergyman and amateur botanist for whom the genus was named, but it is still surprisingly uncommon in cultivation.

Honey locust *Gleditsia triacanthos* 'Sunburst'
As its name suggests, the frond-like, almost feathery, new leaves of this attractive small tree are bright golden-yellow, and contrast superbly with the older dark green foliage. The effect is carried right through summer as fresh leaves are produced. This is the ideal tree to brighten up a dull corner in the garden. The honey locust is native to central and south-eastern United States and had arrived in Europe by 1700, when Bishop Henry Compton planted a specimen from Virginia in his garden at Fulham Palace in London. The cultivar 'Sunburst' originated in 1953 as a sport of the American form, *G. triacanthos inermis*.

Tulip tree *Liriodendron tulipifera*
This is one of the finest and largest of all summer-flowering trees. A mature specimen is truly majestic and never more so than in summer, when its broad shapely crown is covered with tulip-like flowers. Each cup-shaped flower is bright yellow-green with

orange markings on the inside. *Liriodendron tulipifera* is native to eastern North America and is believed to have been introduced into Europe by John Tradescant, gardener to King Charles I of England, in the 1640s. By 1688 specimens were being grown in the grounds of Fulham Palace, London.

Manna ash *Fraxinus ornus*
Ash trees are not renowned for their flowers, as most are small, inconspicuous and borne in early spring, but the manna ash produces very attractive, large pendulous panicles of creamy-white fragrant flowers, which hang in numerous fluffy clusters from each branch in late spring and early summer. This beautiful flowering ash grows wild in south-western Asia and southern Europe and has been widely cultivated as an ornamental in Western parks and gardens since 1700.

Golden-leaved Indian bean tree *Catalpa bignonioides* 'Aurea'
There can be no better tree to have in the garden in summer than the golden-leaved Indian bean tree, sometimes called the golden catalpa. It has just about the most radiant golden leaves of any tree. The leaves are slightly translucent and appear to intensify the light, so that even on cloudy days walking beneath the canopy makes it feel as if the sun has come out. *Catalpa bignonioides* 'Aurea' is a distinct form of the Indian bean tree, native to the eastern United States from Mississippi to Florida. It was cultivated in Europe in 1877 and has been maintained in cultivation by propagation ever since.

Below: Fraxinus ornus is a small compact tree with a showy display of stunning white flowers in summer.

TREES FOR AUTUMN

There are few trees that flower in autumn. Instead an incredible kaleidoscope of colour is produced by the leaves of many tree species. The myriad shades of green foliage fade in many species to leave pigments in a startling array of colours such as red, scarlet, orange and yellow.

Above: Acer species are renowned for their spectacular autumn foliage.

Autumn is the time of year when trees really do take centre stage, bringing a hundred different shades of fiery colour to the countryside and the garden. During spring and summer, leaves contain a green pigment known as chlorophyll, which absorbs light energy from the sun. The energy is used to carry out the process called photosynthesis, which produces the food trees require to live and grow, and this is stored in leaves in the form of starches and sugars. In autumn, as day length reduces and night-time temperatures begin to fall, most trees begin a period of dormancy when they do not need food. Any remaining chlorophyll gradually breaks down and the green pigment begins to disappear,

so that other pigments, which have been present in the leaves all the time, are revealed. These range from purple through red and orange to gold and yellow, representing the varying levels of starches and sugars that have been stored in the leaves.

Many trees also produce fruits that ripen to beautiful, glowing colours in autumn. Some, such as apples, pears and walnuts, are edible straight from the trees; others can be turned into jams or wine, while many provide food for birds and other creatures. The red and orange berries of many species harmonize with the autumn tints of the surrounding foliage, but some autumn fruits are truly spectacular. The berries of the Kashmir rowan, *Sorbus*

cashmiriana, are pure white, in startling contrast to the orange leaves. The fruits of the spindle trees, *Euonymus* spp, are even more dramatic, as their lipstick pink lobes split open to reveal vivid orange seeds inside.

Japanese maple *Acer palmatum*
One of the finest small trees for autumn leaf colour is the Japanese maple, *Acer palmatum*, which, despite its name, is also native to China and Korea. It has been a favourite for cultivation in western parks and gardens since its introduction in the

1820s from Japan, where it was grown in temple gardens. Today, literally hundreds of cultivars of *A. palmatum* are available. They vary according to the colour and vibrancy of their autumn foliage, as well as the shape and size of their palmate leaves. The cultivar 'Osakazuki' is one of the most reliable for autumn colour, turning brilliant red every year. 'Burgundy Lace' has fine, dissected purple palmate leaves.

Katsura tree *Cercidiphyllum japonicum*
The Katsura tree is one of the most beautiful of all autumn trees. It has been described as the "queen of the forest" and the title is quite apt, for there are few trees that can match its regal splendour in autumn. It has delicate heart-shaped leaves that turn a clear butter yellow in mid-autumn. When seen against a blue autumnal sky the effect is stunning. As a bonus, the leaves also emit a sweet caramel-like fragrance as they turn colour. The tree is native to China and Japan and was introduced into the West in 1881. Today, it is frequently found planted in parks, gardens and arboreta right across the Western hemisphere.

Persian ironwood *Parrotia persica*
This medium-sized tree is remarkable in autumn for the way its leaves have the ability to turn almost any colour, from deep purple to bright orange, sometimes within the same leaf. In a good year the whole effect is reminiscent of a giant, sprawling bonfire. Persian ironwood is one of the few autumn-colouring trees that perform well in soil with high lime content. In its native habitat, from northern Iran to the Caucasus, it has a relatively upright habit, whereas in cultivation in Europe and the USA it tends to be broad and spreading.

Chinese mountain ash
Sorbus vilmorinii
The fruits are unequalled for their beauty and make this graceful small tree worthy of growing in any garden. The fruits are pea-sized, at first deep pink, then gradually fading to blush-white. They are borne in open pendulous clusters from mid-autumn, while the pinnate leaves become plum-coloured. The fruits persist on the tree well into winter.

Rowan *Sorbus aucuparia*
Otherwise known as mountain ash, this small tree, which is native to most of northern and western Europe, is widely grown for its fruits, which are prominent from early autumn onwards. They are glossy bright orange-red, about the size and shape of a pea, and are borne in large pendulous clusters. The sight of a rowan covered in berries is unforgettable. However, these fruits are short-lived once ripe because they are loved by birds, who will strip a tree of its fruit overnight in their quest for the sweet fleshy pulp inside. The mountain ash is a common tree of the uplands and, as its alternative name suggests, can often be found growing high on mountain slopes where few other trees would survive. It is, however, a popular tree for planting in urban areas and brings colour to the streets in autumn.

Below: A typical autumnal parkland scene includes leaf fall and different fading foliage colours.

TREES FOR WINTER

It is in winter that conifers and other evergreen trees come to the fore, retaining their solid presence and form in the landscape when deciduous species are bare and skeletal. It is also the best time of year to enjoy some of the beautiful bark that many trees, such as the Tibetan cherry, produce.

The elegant form of many large conifers makes them ideal for planting as isolated specimens in key locations, where they become even more prominent in winter. Their foliage contributes texture and colour to the winter scene, and as hedges and screens they provide formal structure and shelter from wind. Their sculptural forms look particularly effective in frosty or snowy weather.

Some deciduous species also have much to offer in winter. Those that retain their fruits, such as the crab apples, *Malus* spp, and the strawberry tree, *Arbutus unedo*, look ornamental and are of value to visiting birds. Some, such as witch hazel, *Hamamelis*

Below: With their evergreen foliage conifers add so much to the winter landscape.

spp, and Persian ironwood, *Parrotia persica*, produce flowers in winter, though these are few and far between. Once stripped of their leaves it is the trunks and branches of deciduous trees that are visually important, and there are a number that have interesting contorted or weeping branches, such as the corkscrew hazel, *Corylus avellana* 'Contorta'. These are at their best in winter, when their unusual forms are not obscured by foliage. Among the cherries, maples and birches, there are several species with interesting and unusual bark, polished and glowing in the winter sun, or peeling to reveal fresh new colours beneath. Of course the bark is there all year round, but it is in winter that it really comes into its own.

Tibetan cherry *Prunus serrula*
This popular Asian cherry, which has been in cultivation in the West for almost 100 years, seldom grows more than 10m/33ft tall. It is grown mainly for its beautiful bark, which resembles highly polished mahogany, particularly when seen as the waning late afternoon sunshine burns deep into its gleaming surface, lending a warmth and depth to its red-brown colouring that is unique in nature. As the tree matures, horizontal fawn banding develops on the trunk, separating and adding contrast to the bark in a way that seems to intensify its rich colour.

Below: Even in late winter, when deciduous trees are stripped of their foliage, their trunks and branches add height and structure to the surrounding landscape.

Above: The smooth bark of Prunus serrula *is this tree species' most identifiable feature.*

Corkscrew hazel *Corylus avellana* 'Contorta'

This small European tree has a twirling, twisted habit, which extends from the main stem to the tips of the uppermost branches. It is what might be called a "structural tree", as it provides interesting form and outline. It is at its most visually striking in winter when the foliage has fallen to reveal its remarkable corkscrew-like skeleton. It is best seen in sunshine on a cold frosty winter morning, against an azure sky. In late winter the tree drips with butter-cream catkins. These are the male flowers, known as "heralds of spring", which will soon release copious amounts of pollen into the air. A closer look reveals the female flowers – tiny ruby-red stars waiting for the males to perform.

Kilmarnock willow *Salix caprea* 'Pendula' (*S. caprea* 'Kilmarnock')

The Kilmarnock willow is a weeping form of the European native goat willow, which grows alongside rivers and in wet soils throughout western

Right: The corkscrew hazel has incredible twisted branches, which are at their most visible in winter.

Europe. It is a neat, umbrella- or mushroom-shaped small tree with attractive silver-grey weeping branches, which may reach to the ground on mature trees. The effect is best seen in winter, when there are no leaves to obscure its sculptural shape. Towards the end of winter each bare weeping branch becomes covered with beautiful silver-grey "pussy-willow" catkins that gradually turn golden yellow.

Paperbark maple *Acer griseum*

This popular Chinese tree, cultivated in the West since its introduction in 1901, has the finest bark of all the maples. It is a striking, vibrant cinnamon colour, very smooth to the touch and wafer thin; it flakes away in papery strips to reveal fresh bright orange bark beneath. It is seen to best advantage when low winter sunlight backlights each translucent flake. The paperbark maple is occasionally planted alongside some of the white-barked birches, and the striking contrast between them can be the highlight of a winter garden.

Koster's blue spruce *Picea pungens* 'Koster'

No winter garden is complete without conifers, and one of the finest for winter colour is Koster's blue spruce. It

Above: The bark of Acer griseum *invites touch. It appears rough, though its texture is thin and papery, shedding easily.*

is a cultivar of the North American Colorado blue spruce, and was raised in Holland in 1901. It is now a popular tree in parks throughout Europe and the USA, where it is planted for its striking silvery-blue needles, which look as if a layer of frosted icing has been laid upon them when viewed from a distance.

Golden Scots pine *Pinus sylvestris* 'Aurea'

Scots pine is native to all of Europe, and is widely planted in the USA. It is cultivated for its straight-grained timber from its long trunk, as well as for its ornamental warm red bark. In 1876 a yellow-needled variety, *P. sylvestris* 'Aurea', was raised, and is now one of the best conifers for the larger winter garden. For nine months of the year the foliage is very similar to that of ordinary Scots pine, *P. sylvestris*, but in response to reducing temperatures and light levels, the previous year's growth turns a beautiful bright golden-yellow almost overnight. The effect is remarkable, as the bright young foliage is offset by the darker, older needles.

GLOBAL DISTRIBUTION OF TREES

The natural distribution of trees around the world is influenced by the weather. Over millions of years each tree species has adapted to a particular set of climatic conditions and so their distribution is limited to where those conditions exist.

Trees in different parts of the world all function in much the same way. They all require the same things to survive, namely water, minerals, air and light. They all have leaves, roots and a persistent woody stem containing a vascular transport system, which takes water and minerals from the roots to the leaves and food from the leaves to the rest of the tree. That, however, is where the similarity ends.

Throughout the world, trees have adapted to the climate that surrounds them. The amount of rainfall, the temperatures they have to endure, the number of daylight hours and the angle of the sun all influence both the behavioural patterns of trees and their natural distribution across the planet.

Trees growing in the tropics look very different to those found in temperate parts of the world. In a large number of cases they represent very different groups of plants. In general, conifers dominate the colder and drier areas of the world, and broad-leaved trees are more common in warmer and wetter regions.

Below: The world is broken up into zones that experience different climatic conditions. Individual tree species seldom occur within more than one zone.

Equatorial rainforest

Five degrees latitude north and south of the Equator is the area where Equatorial rainforest exists. The conditions in these rainforest areas are perfect for tree growth: the morning sun heats up the vegetation, causing water to evaporate from the leaves. Warm, wet air rises from the trees, forms clouds and produces rain in the afternoon. This happens on every day of the year and there are no major seasonal changes. Numerous trees thrive here, among them rosewood, *Dalbergia nigra*, and the gaboon, *Aucoumea klaineana*.

Monsoon forest

Moving away from the Equator, the climate becomes drier. Within 5 and 25 degrees north and south of the equator there is a marked dry season during the winter months when the air is colder and clouds do not form. Trees can only grow during the summer months when warm air allows clouds to form and causes rain to fall. This seasonal change is known as monsoon and the forest that grows in these regions is monsoon forest. Monsoon forest covers a vast proportion of the Indian subcontinent, parts of Central America, East Africa, Madagascar and south-eastern China. Trees of the monsoon forest include Indian rosewood, *Dalbergia latifolia*, and East Indian ebonys, among them *Diospyrus melanoxylon*.

Savannah and desert

Between 25 and 35 degrees of latitude, clouds seldom form, rain rarely falls and the climate becomes progressively drier. Savannah grassland, which borders the monsoon areas, eventually gives way to desert. Few trees can survive in this harsh environment. Those that do include the giant saguaro cactus, *Carnegiea gigantea*, from North America, and the dragon's blood tree, *Dracaena cinnabari*, from Yemen.

Mediterranean forest

Beyond latitudes of 35 degrees, the conditions for tree growth gradually improve. At 40 degrees from the Equator, the Mediterranean forest region begins. This region contains most European Mediterranean countries, California, Chile and parts of Australia. Typically, the climate is characterized by hot, dry summers, and winters with moderate rainfall. Mediterranean trees include the holm oak, *Quercus ilex*, and the olive tree, *Olea europaea*.

Temperate forest

Between 40 and 50 degrees of latitude the climate becomes damp and windy, with cold temperatures in winter months restricting tree growth. This temperate region covers central and western Europe (including the British Isles), central North America, New Zealand, Japan and parts of China. The natural tree cover of this area is primarily broad-leaved. Trees that thrive here include oak, beech, ash, birch and maple.

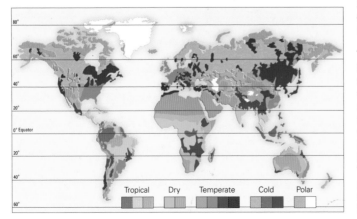

Tropical Dry Temperate Cold Polar

Above: Conifers are particularly well adapted to cold conditions.

Boreal forest

From 50 to 70 degrees of latitude, the length of the tree growing season diminishes and winter lengthens. Known as the boreal region, this area covers by far the greatest landmass of all the forest regions. It includes most of central Canada, northern Europe and Russia, right across to the Pacific coast. The natural tree cover of this region is primarily conifer and includes Scots pine, *Pinus sylvestris*, and sitka spruce, *Picea sitchensis*. The tree density of this region is greater than in temperate or Mediterranean regions, but less than both Monsoon and the Equatorial regions.

Tundra

Above 70 degrees, winter lasts almost all year and very few trees are able to survive. Known as tundra, this area includes northern Canada, Iceland, Greenland and the far north of Europe and Russia. One tree that does survive is the dwarf willow, *Salix reticulata*.

Micro climates

There is always some blurring at the edges of every climatic forest region. Land that is close to the sea will generally be warmer than that which is landlocked. Consequently a greater diversity of tree species will grow here

than for the same latitude inland. The west coasts of Britain and Ireland benefit from the Gulf Stream, which brings warm, moist air from the Caribbean. This allows trees that grow naturally in the Mediterranean forest region to survive and sometimes to flourish. One Mediterranean forest tree that tends to grow well in gardens in Cornwall, the Isles of Scilly and the west coast of Scotland is the Chilean azara, *Azara lanceolata*.

Montane forest

In mountainous areas, trees typical of regions farther from the Equator thrive. Because of their latitudes, both the Alps of central Europe and the

Rocky Mountains of North America are technically within the temperate region. But because of their high altitude, which decreases average temperatures and effectively shortens the summers, the tree cover is more typical of boreal forest. In the Alps, Norway spruce, *Picea abies*, is the dominant species.

Tree zoning

Whether or not a tree will survive in any region, given its basic requirements of water, minerals, air and light, depends on the lowest temperatures it will have to endure. Over the years, through trial and error, botanists and horticulturalists have identified the average annual minimum temperatures that individual tree species can withstand. Maps of the world have been produced that put countries or regions into zones, according to the average annual minimum temperatures that occur in them. Most of Britain is suitable for tree species rated at zone eight – trees that are capable of surviving average annual minimum temperatures of around 5°C/41°F. Tree species rated at zone nine would find this average fairly chilly. They prefer the average temperatures not to fall below 10°C/50°F.

Below: Savannah grassland is the harsh intermediate zone between Mediterranean forest and desert. The closer conditions are to a desert, the fewer trees exist.

TEMPERATE TREES

Temperate trees are found in the bands 40 to 50 degrees north and south of the Equator. These areas include most of North America, Britain and Europe, southern Russia, northern China, Japan, New Zealand, Tasmania, southern Argentina and Chile.

In temperate regions the climate is suitable for tree growth for six months of the year, when temperatures average more than 10°C/50°F. There are well-defined seasons but few extremes in either temperature or rainfall.

Although the temperate regions are suitable for both deciduous and evergreen trees, it is deciduous broad-leaved trees, such as oak, which predominate. Many trees that live in the windy conditions of the world's temperate regions are wind pollinated.

Temperate diversity

There is far less tree diversity within temperate regions than in the tropics. This is partly because the climate is less favourable and partly due to historical climatic changes.

Temperate trees have been forced to migrate towards the Equator and back again several times during the last two million years because of successive ice ages. Inevitably these mass movements had casualties. Some tree species perished as they were unable to successfully disperse their seeds with enough speed to escape the freezing conditions expanding outwards from the polar regions. Other species became extinct because their escape routes were blocked by high mountain ranges, such as the Alps and Pyrenees.

Temperate pioneers

The density of temperate woodlands is such that light is rarely in short supply and there are few other plants, such as climbers, that have the ability to stifle tree growth. Temperate pioneer trees have large canopies and their branches

and leaves are free to grow right down the trunk. Their wood is light in colour. Birch is one of the most successful temperate pioneer tree species. It will colonize land far more readily than any other species and is quite often found growing on disused industrial sites, spoil heaps, landfills and railway embankments. Willow, poplar and pine are also early colonizers of inhospitable land.

Other temperate species

The temperate tree species that has been around longer than any other is the maidenhair tree, *Ginkgo biloba*. Today it grows wild in a small area of Chekiang province, China, although it has been widely planted elsewhere.

There are more than 450 species of oak tree across the temperate world. In Europe the two main species are the English oak, *Quercus robur*, and the

1 Oak
2 Beech

Above: Oak is the predominant tree species in temperate regions of the world.

Below: Species such as oak and beech are slow to establish on new sites and move in only after pioneer species, such as birch, willow, pine and poplar, have improved soil conditions with their fallen leaves. Oak and beech are the predominant woodland species of Great Britain.

One of the most recognizable temperate trees is the monkey puzzle or Chile pine, *Araucaria araucana*. This hardy evergreen grows up to the snow line in its native Andes Mountains. It has rigid, spiny and prickly leaves.

One temperate tree that looks like it belongs in the tropics is the tree fern, *Dicksonia antarctica*. Native to Tasmania, it grows well in warm, moist temperate regions, such as southern Ireland, where frosts are not too severe. *D. antarctica* is a very exotic-looking tree with a fibrous trunk and large fern-like fronds, which can reach over 3m/10ft long. In Tasmania there are tree fern forests with specimens growing to more than 10m/33ft tall.

Perhaps the most beautiful of all temperate trees is the tulip tree, *Liriodendron tulipifera*. It is native to North America, where it grows from Nova Scotia to Florida. The tulip tree is a large species, growing to heights in excess of 40m/131ft. It has flowers that resemble greenish-orange tulips. Quite often a mature tree will be covered with a stunning spectacle of flowers.

sessile oak, *Q. petraea*. The holm or evergreen oak, *Q. ilex*, originates from the Mediterranean but also grows well in southern temperate regions of Europe and America.

Close to 80 species of oak are native to North America, including the red oak, *Q. rubra*, which has large, sharply pointed leaves that turn red in autumn.

TROPICAL TREES

Tropical trees are found in three main parts of the world: central Africa, Amazonia in South America, and South-east Asia. The total area they cover amounts to about 9 million square kilometres (3½ million square miles) and represents 7 per cent of the earth's land surface.

In the rainforest, levels of rainfall, warmth and sunlight are constant, creating ideal conditions for tree growth throughout the year. Most tropical trees have evergreen leaves with pointed tips. These "drip tips" help the trees to keep their leaves dry, shedding excess water during tropical rainstorms. Tropical trees include the fastest growing trees in the world; 5m/16½ft of vertical growth per year is commonplace. Fast growth means a fast metabolism; consequently everything happens at a fast rate, including the advent of senility. Very few of the tropical trees live beyond 500 years of age, whereas many temperate trees are much older.

Tropical diversity
The range of tropical species is amazing – there are over 2,000 tree species in Madagascar alone.

The reason for so many different species is not fully understood. However, the fact that today's tropical rainforests have existed for millions of years means that there has been plenty of time for new species to evolve. Evolution takes place primarily as a response to outside influence. It is possible there are so many tropical tree species because there are so many potential killers of trees in tropical forests. The climate is ideal for tree growth and for insects, fungi and viruses. New tree species may have evolved specifically to repel attackers.

Despite their great species diversity, most tropical rainforest trees look very similar to one another; they have tall, thin trunks supported by roots with prominent buttresses. The crowns of these trees are comparatively small and bear large, thick, evergreen leaves not dissimilar to those of laurel. Most tropical trees have thin bark because there is no need to provide protection against frost or water loss.

Often, however, the wood of tropical trees is stained dark with chemicals for protection against fungal attack.

Tropical pioneers
Such is the competition for space and light in a tropical rainforest that only those trees that can react quickly to changes in the density of the canopy survive. If a gap opens up in the canopy when a mature tree dies, light reaches the forest floor and there is a scramble by other plants to fill that gap. The first species to colonize gaps are herbaceous plants and climbers. These plants do their best to smother the ground to prevent another tree from filling the gap because they need the light to survive. Eventually a branchless, umbrella-like tree shoot

Below: Rainforests are characterized by layers of planting. At the top are the tallest trees, usually with large leaves to take any moisture and light, and buttress roots to anchor them into the ground. Below these are smaller trees with glorious flowers and luscious fruit to attract pollinators.

1 Kapok
2 Palm tree
3 Brazil nut

with a thick, slippery trunk will emerge from the ground. At the top of this trunk a huge canopy of leaves unfolds, desperate to capture as much light as possible. The thick, slippery trunk provides nothing for climbing plants to grip on to and the tree's leaves are held well out of reach of grasping tendrils. These pioneer trees can grow up to 10m/33ft tall in their first year, quickly filling the space left by the fallen tree.

Tropical species

Outside the tropics most tropical trees are known for their products. Brazil nut, *Bertholletia excelsa*, is probably one of the best-known tropical trees because of the nuts it produces. It grows wild in Brazil and throughout Peru, Columbia, Venezuela and Ecuador. The Brazil nut is among the largest tropical trees, reaching heights in excess of 40m/131ft. It has thick, leathery, oval-shaped leaves up to 20cm/8in long. Brazil nuts flower in November, producing fruit pods at the end of thick branches the following June. Up to 25 individual nuts can be found in each large, spherical, woody fruit pod. Each tree can produce up to 300 fruit pods a year and

Above: Such is the diversity of the Amazon rainforest that over 500 different species have been found within a single hectare (2½ acres).

thousands of tons of Brazil nuts are exported from South America each year. In economic terms, the Brazil nut is second only to rubber in importance to Brazil as an export cash crop.

The weeping fig, *Ficus benjamina*, originates from the tropical forests of South-east Asia and today is grown from India through to northern Australia. It is an attractive tree with narrow, leathery leaves, which can be up to 12cm/4¾in long. Mature weeping figs can have dramatic twisting branches. In temperate areas this species is grown as a conservatory or house plant. In the warmer tropical regions it produces small red figs in pairs along its twisting branches.

Palm trees have different leaf shapes from both Brazil nuts and weeping figs. Long, narrow and strap-like, the leaves branch out from the tree top. There are around 3,000 species of palm in the world, and the vast majority of them grow in the tropics.

DESERT TREES

There are few places on earth, other than the polar regions, where plants will not grow. Even in the harsh environment of the desert, plants – including trees – somehow manage to cling to life. Deserts are very inhospitable places for trees.

Trees that survive in the desert have developed unique ways of coping with the day-to-day difficulties of survival. The main problems facing desert trees relate to water – or lack of it. Hot sun, drying winds and low, erratic rainfall make it difficult for tree roots to supply enough water to make up for that lost by transpiration from the leaves. Desert trees have adapted to the extremes of heat and aridity by using physical and behavioural mechanisms.

Plants that have adapted by altering their physical structure are called either xerophytes or phreatophytes. Xerophytes, such as cacti, usually have special means of storing and conserving water. They often have few or no leaves, which helps them to reduce transpiration. Phreatophytes are plants, such as the African acacias, that have adapted to parched conditions by growing extremely long

roots, allowing them to acquire moisture from the water table.

Other plants have altered their behaviour to cope. They have to make the most of the times of greatest moisture and coolest temperatures, remaining dormant in dry periods and springing to life when water is available. Many germinate after heavy seasonal rain and then complete their reproductive cycle very quickly. These plants produce heat- and drought-resistant seeds that remain dormant in the soil until rain eventually arrives.

The Joshua tree

The *Yucca brevifolia*, or Joshua tree, grows in the Mojave Desert of California, Nevada, Utah and Arizona. It has spiky, leathery, evergreen leaves at the tips of the branches, thus reducing the effects of transpiration. The leaves have a hard, waxy coating

that also helps to reduce water loss. Originally considered a member of the agave family, the Joshua tree is now known to be the largest yucca in the world. It can grow up to 12m/40ft tall with a trunk diameter of 1m/3ft.

Welwitschia

A dwarf species from Africa, *Welwitschia mirabilis* is one of the strangest trees on earth. It grows on the dry gravel plains of the Namib Desert in southern Angola and is a throwback to the prehistoric flora that existed on the supercontinent of Gondwanaland millions of years ago. Its shape and growing characteristics are so unusual that there is no comparable living plant. It is a unique species occupying its own genus.

The bulk of *Welwitschia's* "trunk" grows under the sand like a giant carrot. Its girth can be up to 1.5m/5ft

1 Baobab
2 Date palm
3 *Welwitschia mirabilis*

and its height (or in this case length) up to 4m/13ft, less than a third of which appears above ground. Its subterranean trunk is a water storage organ made of hard wood and covered with a cork-like bark. Broad, leathery leaves emerge from the part of the trunk that appears above ground. The leaves, which can reach 2m/6½ft long, sprawl across the desert floor. They have specially adapted pores to trap any moisture that condenses on the leaves during the night when the temperature falls. As rain falls about once in four years in the Namib Desert this method of moisture collection is vital. Recent carbon-dating has established that some of these trees are more than 2,000 years old.

Other desert trees

The acacias and tamarisks, which grow in African deserts, are phreatophytes – they have developed incredibly long root systems to cope with the absence of surface water. These roots take water from the permanent water table, which may be anything up to 50m/164ft below the desert surface. Once mature, they have little

trouble combating harsh desert conditions – the difficulty is in establishing themselves, as the roots have to first grow through great depths of bone-dry soil before they reach the water. Phreatophytes grow in places where the soil is occasionally wet, such as dried-up riverbeds, as these are the only spots where they can get started.

Perhaps the most successful desert plants are cacti. The giant saguaro cactus, *Carnegiea gigantea*, is the ultimate desert tree. It has no leaves at all but does have a thick green trunk, which is capable of photosynthesis and storing water. The giant saguaro can grow to heights in excess of 10m/33ft.

The Socotran desert-rose tree, *Adenium obesum*, grows in desert conditions on the Indian Ocean island of Socotra, Yemen. It has a swollen grey trunk, which looks like a sack of potatoes. This trunk has the ability to expand in size on the rare occasions that rain falls, enabling it to store huge quantities of water for the drought period to follow.

MOUNTAIN TREES

*Mountains tend to be covered with conifers and most are members of the Pinaceae family –
pines, spruces, hemlocks and firs. The higher the elevation, the slower the trees grow. The point beyond
which no trees will survive is known as the tree line.*

In many ways mountains have the same climate as subarctic regions, having short summers, cold winters and a mean temperature that rarely rises above 10°C/50°F. Wind speeds tend to be greater at high altitudes. These drying winds and shallow soils, often frozen for long periods of time, mean that only those trees that are protected against water loss and frost damage will survive.

Conifers and evergreens

A characteristic that conifers and broad-leaved evergreens share is leaves that are resistant to water loss and cold. Broad-leaved evergreens often have thick, leathery leaves with a waxy coating.

Conifers further reduce water loss by having fine, rolled, needle-like leaves, that expose a small surface area to the elements.

Conifers and other evergreens are efficient at functioning in low light and temperature conditions. Once deciduous trees have lost their leaves in autumn they cannot produce food or grow until the next year's leaves grow – anything up to six months. Yet, during this time there are periods when the temperature and light is sufficient for photosynthesis to occur. Evergreens and conifers take advantage of this. Deciduous trees are also vulnerable when their young leaves are bursting from the bud in spring. These new leaves are sensitive to frost and can easily be damaged. Evergreens have tough leathery leaves that are never so vulnerable.

Mountain characteristics

Trees become progressively shorter as they approach the tree line. The reason for their shortness is not cold but increasing wind –

constant stem movement stunts a tree's growth. High winds can also damage trees and to avoid this some species have evolved a low-growing, almost sprawling habit.

Many mountain trees have adopted characteristics to cope with this harsh environment. They are conical or spire-shaped with branches and twigs that point downwards. This prevents snow from building up on the branches and breaking them. Instead it simply slides off the tree to the ground.

Mountain trees will also grow away from the direction of the prevailing wind, giving them a windswept appearance. The reason for this is that the waxy coating on the leaves or needles on the windward side gets worn away by the sandpaper effect of harsh winds carrying ice particles. Once the coating has gone the leaves and shoots are open to dehydration,

1 Sitka spruce
2 Brewer spruce

Above: As trees approach the elevation beyond which they will not grow (known as the tree line), they become stunted and eventually prostrate.

Below: Most of the conifers found in mountainous regions are members of the Pinaceae family – pines, spruces, hemlocks and firs. Such trees have adapted to cope with the harsh and extreme conditions of the weather, from freezing snow to fierce winds, driving rain, and the blistering heat of the summer sun.

moves slowly downwind. Research has shown that the average movement of these clumps is 2–7m/6½–23ft per century.

Often the branches at the bottom of mountain trees grow much better than those at the top, giving a skirted effect around the tree's base. This is because in the depths of winter these lower branches are protected from the ravages of the wind by snowdrifts.

Mountain species

The dwarf mountain pine, *Pinus mugo*, is native to the mountains of central Europe, the Carpathians, the Balkans and the Italian Apennines. It is a low-growing, shrubby tree with twisting, snake-like stems and branches that form dense, impenetrable entanglements (known in Germany as *krummholz*).

Brewer's spruce, *Picea breweriana*, is a tree that originates from the Siskiyou Mountains of California and Oregon, where it grows at elevations of up to 2,100m/7,000ft. In Scotland the rowan or mountain ash, *Sorbus aucuparia*, will grow at altitudes in excess of 700m/2,300ft.

and slowly die. The tree compensates for the lack of leaves and shoots on the windward side of the crown by producing more on the leeward side.

In exposed mountain regions, young trees can only grow in the shelter of other trees. This leads to clumps of trees scattered across the mountainsides. As trees die on the windward side and new ones grow on the leeward side, the whole clump

COASTAL TREES

Coastal conditions differ radically around the world. It is one of the most difficult environments for trees to grow in. Those that survive have adapted to the strong winds and salt-laden water by growing additional roots on their windward sides to improve anchorage, and their habit becomes low and squat.

Only the toughest tree species can survive a combination of strong winds and salt spray. Exposure to ocean storms, with winds in excess of 160km/h or 100mph, is only part of the problem. Strong wind alone is something that many trees are able to withstand. However, if those winds are laden with huge quantities of sea salt, most trees will simply die.

Salt damage

Trees can be damaged by salt in two ways: through direct contact with the foliage and by absorption from the soil through the roots. Direct and prolonged contact with salt will cause leaf-burn, branch die-back and defoliation. This in turn will reduce the ability of the tree to photosynthesize and produce its own food, so eventually it dies. Salt can also

dramatically reduce the amount of seed and fruit produced.

The most common cause of tree death by salt is through its uptake from the soil. When salt-laden winds that have travelled across the ocean reach land they condense, producing rain or dense sea mists. The salt precipitation from these mists and rain soaks into the soil. The highest salt concentrations are deposited closest to the coast.

Salt causes the soil structure to deteriorate, leading to a decrease in soil fertility. Natural calcium in the soil is replaced by sodium chloride. This increases soil alkalinity, making it dramatically harder for trees to survive. Salt also makes the soil less permeable and reduces the moisture content, causing its root systems to dehydrate and die back. The moisture

that is absorbed by the roots can literally poison the tree. It takes only half a per cent of a tree's living tissue to contain salt before the tree starts to die. This process is also what damages trees planted on roadsides, where the road is regularly covered with salt to clear it of ice.

Mangroves

One genus of trees has adapted so well to life alongside the coast that its members can actually grow with their roots in salt water. Called mangroves, they are found throughout the tropics,

Below: New Zealand is home to a diverse collection of trees. The kanuka and puriri trees and the nikau palms all thrive here. The kanuka tree is a pioneer tree, endemic to the area. The nikau palm is New Zealand's only native palm tree and thrives in coastal areas and warmer, inland regions.

1 Nikau palm
2 Puriri tree
3 Kanuka tree

particularly in shallow, muddy estuarine and coastal situations. They have to cope not only with waterlogging but also with the high salinity of seawater.

The most notable feature of mangroves is their roots. Many species are anchored in the soft mud by prop roots, which grow from the trunk, or drop roots, which grow from the branches. Oxygen is piped from the roots above ground to those below the water line. This aeration is particularly important to mangroves because they need oxygen to carry out the process of ultra-filtration, which they use to exclude salt from the tree. Each root cell works like a mini desalination plant, screening out the salt and allowing only fresh water to flow into the root system and on through the rest of the tree.

Mangroves display several other adaptations to their situation. They have leathery, evergreen leaves, which are able to conserve the fresh water within them but keep out salt-laden water that lands on them. They also

Above: Mangroves have a root system that copes with continual immersion in water.

have wind-pollinated flowers, which are able to take full advantage of sea breezes, and spear-shaped seed pods, which can stab into the mud or float away from the mother tree, coming to rest elsewhere.

Monterey cypress

At the Monterey Peninsula in San Francisco, clinging to life and the cliff edge, are two groves of Monterey Cypress, *Cupressus macrocarpa*.

The trees grow on the shore cliffs and, being undermined by the waves, occasionally fall into the sea. There are fewer than 300 trees left, ancestors of a species that covered great swathes of the temperate world at the start of the glacial cool-down a million years ago. Monterey cypress, along with other American giants, such as the Douglas fir and the giant redwood, retreated to the Pacific coast to escape the worst of the cold. When the climate warmed up 12,000 years ago and the glaciers withdrew, the trees moved back to the land they had occupied before the ice ages – all, that is, except the Monterey cypress, which remained on the Californian coast, where it has been growing in decreasing numbers since.

The trees that are left are stunted and gnarled, seldom reaching more than 15m/50ft tall. Collect seed from any of them and sow it anywhere else in the temperate world however and it grows into a magnificent giant. Wherever there is the need for shelter from the wind and salt spray off the sea, this is the tree to plant.

TROPICAL ISLAND TREES

Islands often contain a diversity of plant life that is very different to that of the nearest mainland. This is because evolution on islands occurs in isolation. Some islands, such as New Caledonia in the Pacific Ocean, still have a range of trees which evolved during the Jurassic period.

The reason for the often unique plant life on individual islands lies in the earth's history and how each island was first formed. Islands are normally formed as a result of continental drift or volcanic activity on the seabed.

About 200 million years ago, most of the world's land was clumped together in a single supercontinent, known as Pangaea. Pangaea began to

Below: Islands have unique eco-systems. The weather they receive, their landmass and the vegetation that thrives on them can differ dramatically to that of the nearest mainland.

break up about 190 million years ago. First it split in two. The northern part, Laurasia, contained what are now North America, Europe and Asia, while the southern part, Gondwanaland, consisted of present-day South America, Africa, India, Antarctica and Australasia. Gradually Laurasia and Gondwanaland also broke up to form the continents we recognize today.

This fragmentation process created the major continents, and thousands of islands. When these islands broke away from the continents, they carried with them a collection of the flora and fauna that existed on the larger land-masses at that time. Over the following millions of years, plants and animals on these isolated fragments of land adapted to their new environments, and often evolved in different ways to those on the mainland.

In some cases, evolution has continued on the continents, while little has changed on some of the islands. The island of New Caledonia off the east coast of Australia is home to an amazing collection of ancient trees no longer found anywhere else on earth. So primeval is its landscape that it has been used as a backdrop for films on dinosaurs. In other cases the reverse has been true, with island life forms changing quite dramatically.

Not all of the world's islands were created by the break-up of the continents. Many were formed more recently by undersea volcanic activity and have never been attached to the continents at all. At first these islands had no plants of their own.

The Hawaiian Islands

Archipelagos such as the Hawaiian Islands began as barren outcrops of rock. Hawaii's native trees are all descendants of the few plants whose seeds washed up on its shores or were carried there by birds.

Tarweed is a daisy-like plant from California. Fragments of this plant floated across the ocean to Hawaii millions of years ago. Tarweed gradually colonized the island and then began to evolve into new plants, filling the empty niches. Today Hawaii has 28 species whose ancestry can

1 Coco-de-mer
2 Palm tree

Above: Coconut palms have large seeds that can float for hundreds of miles across the ocean.

be traced back to tarweed. One, *Dubautia reticulata*, is a tree that can grow to more than 10m/33ft tall.

The Galapagos Islands

Like the Hawaiian Islands, the Galapagos Islands formed in volcanic activity after the break-up of the continents. Mangroves were among the first and most successful tree colonizers of the Galapagos Islands. Four species exist there today: the black mangrove, *Avicennia germinans*; the red mangrove, *Rhizophora mangle*; the button mangrove, *Conocarpus erecta*; and the white mangrove, *Laguncularia racemosa*. Mangroves are able to live in shallow seawater and grow on the shores of almost all the islands. They are a vital part of the coastal ecosystem, as fallen leaves and branches provide nutrients and shelter for a wide variety of sea creatures, and their tangled roots protect the coastline from erosion and storm damage. The Galapagos Islands' mangroves are thought to have established themselves from plants and seeds that floated from the Far East across the Pacific Ocean.

The Virgin Islands

The warm, moist climate on the northern coasts of the Virgin Islands in the West Indies supports an amazing array of tree species. Growing wild here are West Indian locust, bay rum, sandbox, kapok and hog plum. To the south and east the climate becomes much drier, creating ideal growing conditions for the turpentine tree, acacia, white cedar and the poisonous manchineel tree.

The Seychelles

More than 80 species of tree grow on the Seychelles in the Indian Ocean that grow nowhere else on earth. Among them is the record-breaking coco de mer palm with its 20kg/45lb nut. This is the largest seed of any plant in the world and it has been found washed ashore in places as far away as

Africa, India and Indonesia. Before the islands were discovered the coco-de-mer seed was thought to have grown on the seabed, hence its name.

New Caledonia

Situated off Australia's east coast, this island has been described as having "one of the richest and most beautiful flora in the world". The island is home to trees that are remnants of families that became extinct elsewhere millions of years ago, some as far back as the Jurassic period. *Araucaria columnaris* is a rocket-shaped relative of the monkey puzzle tree which grows wild in Chile and Argentina. Of the 19 living species of *Araucaria*, 13 are found in New Caledonia and nowhere else. The island also has unique members of the podocarp family, to which most of New Zealand conifers belong, and proteas, which only occur otherwise in South Africa.

New Caledonia is also home to some of the tallest tree ferns in the world, many of them over 30m/98ft tall. The island's rarest tree is a small evergreen called *Xeronema moorei*; this unique tree grows in isolated pockets high in the mountains and is found nowhere else on earth.

URBAN TREES

Trees have become a vital part of urban areas around the world. From plane tree avenues of Europe, the leafy avenues of downtown Manhattan to the cherry-covered walkways of Tokyo, they bring beauty and environmental benefits right to the heart of our cities.

Trees have been planted in large numbers in our towns and cities ever since the 18th century. Before that time, urban trees were the privilege of royal palaces, cathedrals, churches, monasteries and universities. Some of the earliest town plantings were in specially landscaped town gardens, squares and crescents, such as Berkeley Square in London, which was planted with London plane trees in 1789. These trees still exist today, tall spreading giants bringing shade and cool in summer.

Quite often these early plantings only took place in the more affluent areas of towns and were for the private enjoyment of those who lived there. The poorer residential and industrial areas were left largely devoid of trees.

Below: The London plane tree, Platanus x hispanica, *is popular in urban settings throughout the temperate world. It grows quickly, is hardy and tolerates the pollution of modern cities.*

It wasn't until the Victorian era that municipal parks were laid out for the benefit of all town dwellers. At this time, the idea of parks as the "green lungs" of towns and cities developed, improving citizens' health as well as giving them opportunities to walk, meet and relax. Public parks began to appear in North America and all over the British Empire, and trees were seen as an integral part of them. Today some of the finest tree collections in the world are found in city parks.

Urban street planting also became prevalent during this time, although the planting of trees along roadsides between towns had been going on for centuries. Plane and poplar trees were planted by the Roman troops to provide shade and shelter for their legions as they marched back and forth across southern Europe. This tradition was repeated by Napoleon for his armies and many Napoleonic roadside trees can still be seen today in France, Germany and Spain.

The environmental benefits of trees in towns and cities were recognized towards the end of the Victorian era by Ebenezer Howard, whose book *Garden Cities of Tomorrow* inspired the early landscaping of suburbs and new towns that were being built outside the cities to house rapidly increasing populations. These new towns were built on "green field" sites and the inclusion of street trees, park trees and areas of woodland between housing were drawn into landscape plans long before the houses were even built. Howard's ideas quickly spread and were used by town planners across Europe and the Americas.

Urban trees today

Trees have become an integral part of cities around the world. In terms of planning, they have become almost as important a feature of the urban landscape as the buildings themselves. Trees have a higher priority in our towns and cities now than at any time previously.

Above: Urban trees provide shade in summer and shelter in winter.

The architectural value of trees and the health benefits they offer are now well-recognized and some cities have instigated massive tree-planting campaigns. By 2010, one million more trees will be planted in the centre of London.

Benefits of urban trees

Trees reduce air pollution. They help to trap particle pollutants such as dust, ash and smoke, which can damage human lungs, and they absorb carbon dioxide and other dangerous gases, releasing vital oxygen in their place.

In a year, 0.4ha/1 acre of trees in a city park absorbs the same amount of carbon dioxide as is produced by 41,850km/26,000 miles of car driving.

Urban trees conserve water and reduce flooding. They lessen surface runoff from storms as their roots increase soil permeability. Reduced overloading of drainage systems, the main cause of localized flooding, occurs in towns with a high tree population.

Trees modify local climates as they help to cool the "heat island" effect in inner cities caused by the storage of thermal energy in concrete, steel and tarmac. They also provide a more

pleasant living and working environment. They reduce wind speed around high-rise buildings, increase humidity in dry climates and offer cooling shade on hot, sunny days.

Without trees, towns and cities are sterile landscapes. Trees add natural character; they provide colour, flowers, fragrance, and beautiful shapes and textures. They screen unsightly buildings and soften the outline of masonry, mortar and glass.

Trees for urban environments

One of the finest large trees for planting in towns and cities is the London plane, *Platanus* x *hispanica*. Most trees suffer in urban areas as their bark's "breathing pores", known as lenticels, get clogged with soot and grime. The London plane frequently sheds its old bark, revealing fresh, clean bark beneath.

The maidenhair tree, *Ginkgo biloba*, native to China, is also tolerant of air pollution. Its slow growth and narrow habit make it an ideal tree for street planting. Other trees suitable for the urban environment include laburnum, *Laburnum* x *watereri* 'Vossii'; black locust, *Robinia pseudoacacia*; hawthorn, *Crataegus laevigata* 'Paul's Scarlet'; Indian bean tree, *Catalpa bignonioides*; and cherry, *Prunus* species.

HEDGEROW TREES

Hedges are live fences or barriers consisting of trees and shrubs, which are used to contain livestock, act as boundary markers or provide shelter. Most hedges are thought to have been created in the last 200 years, as a result of Enclosure Acts passed in Britain and other European countries.

There are three ways of producing a hedge. The first and most obvious is by planting. Second, hedges may be the remnants of woodland that was cleared for farming, leaving only narrow strips to stand as field boundaries. Finally, hedges can develop naturally by seeding into uncultivated land at the edges of fields, where banks, fences, or ditches exist or once existed.

Early hedges

The Romans are known to have planted hedges right across their empire. These early hedges were established to contain livestock and also as defensive, impenetrable barriers against attack. At the very least they would slow down an invading force.

The Anglo-Saxons introduced the concept of villages and marked out many of today's parish boundaries. Natural markers such as old trees, large rocks, cliffs and streams were used to denote boundaries; on open ground where no such features existed, marker trees were planted, which over the years seeded and developed into hedges. Words such as "*hegeraewe*", "*hege*", "hazel-rows", "willow rows", "*hagaporn* (hawthorn) rows" and "hedge-sparrow" regularly occur in charters of this time.

Fields and Boundaries

In Britain in the 18th and 19th centuries, various Acts of Parliament brought the ancient open field system to an end, dividing the countryside into smaller, more manageable fields – normally around 4ha/10 acres in size. The new fields were enclosed by hedges, except in areas where stone was readily available to create dry-stone wall boundaries. The most popular tree for planting was hawthorn, *Crataegus monogyna*.

Below: A familiar landscape of the British countryside with fields bounded by hedgerows.

Above: Trees are a natural feature of hedgerows and field boundaries.

The best hedgerow trees

Hedges differ in content from region to region and reflect the local soil, topographical and climatic conditions, and their original purpose. A hedge planted to contain livestock may contain different tree species from one planted to create shelter. The local natural tree population should feature within the hedge, and sometimes the region's economic past will have a bearing on the content too: for example in some regions blackthorn, *Prunus spinosa*, was planted in hedgerows because the berry was used to make dye for wool.

The best trees, most commonly used for stockproof hedging, are those that naturally develop a thick, impenetrable framework of branches, ideally protected by an armoury of thorns. They should be tough, able to withstand constant browsing by livestock, and respond readily to pruning. The tree's natural response to browsing and pruning should thicken and strengthen the hedge.

Hawthorn, *Crataegus monogyna*, and blackthorn offer all the qualities described above and are widely planted in hedgerows across Europe. They are invaluable to wildlife, particularly insects and birds, as they produce flowers for pollen in spring and edible fruits in late summer and autumn. Their thick, dense foliage also provides ideal shelter and nesting habitat for birds. Other trees regularly found in hedgerows include beech, *Fagus sylvatica*, which provides an effective screen right through winter by retaining its dead leaves; hazel, *Corylus avellana*, which was once valued for supplying the wood needed to make sheep hurdles; holly, *Ilex aquifolium*, which produces spiny dense evergreen foliage; and elm, *Ulmus* spp., the leaves of which provide a browse for livestock.

6

3

4

5

1 Laid beech (trained horizontalll)y)
2 Beech
3 Hawthorn
4 Oak
5 Oak grown from laid hedge
6 Ash

WETLAND TREES

All trees require water to survive and grow. Some, such as palm trees, can manage with very little moisture while others require a constant supply of fresh water and are therefore commonly found growing alongside rivers and streams, and on flood plains.

The banks of rivers and streams provide ideal growing conditions for trees. In a forest or woodland situation the river itself provides a gap in the overhead canopy, allowing the trees plenty of natural light. Waterways are also rich in minerals and nutrients flushed from the soil further upstream. Flooding and constant fluctuations in water levels ensure regular deposits of minerals and nutrients to keep riverside soils fertile. The riverside soils are also normally deep and moist.

There are times, however, when this environment may become inhospitable to trees. During prolonged flooding the soil will become waterlogged, preventing oxygen getting to the roots. Very bad floods may cause soil erosion: the bank may be undermined or in extreme cases even washed away. Parts of the tree's root system may become exposed or broken off, and the force of the water may even wash whole trees away.

How wetland trees survive

Wetland trees survive flooding by absorbing air through the lenticels (pores) in their bark and trunk. This

Below: Where willows thrive, there will be a large supply of water nearby.

air is piped down to the roots immersed in water, where it is stored in large air pockets called aerenchyma. Some trees can survive being submerged in water for over six months of the year. Willows and alders are particularly good at doing this.

The root systems of wetland trees tend to be much larger than those of other trees. Not only does this help to stabilize the riverbank and reduce soil erosion, it also helps the tree cope with physical adaptations that may be required in this environment. Often, tree trunks are not vertical but grow or lean out across the water – this helps them exploit the extra light in that direction. To counteract the strain this

Above: Willow trees are a good indicator of the presence of water, and are frequently to be found along riverbanks.

leaning growth habit puts on the tree, and the root system in particular, long "anchor roots" develop, growing deep into the soil on the opposite side of the tree. Having evolved the leaning habit, such species grow this way even when they are planted away from rivers and in full light.

Wetland tree dispersal

Some wetland trees take advantage of their proximity to flowing water and flooding to aid their dispersal and population advancement. Crack willow, *Salix fragilis*, is particularly adept at this technique. Its twigs readily break off and float downstream, eventually being washed up on a new bank where they grow roots and develop into new trees. Another tree that increases its population in this way is the common alder, *Alnus glutinosa*. It produces cone-like seed capsules with inbuilt air pockets to aid buoyancy. They fall from the tree into the water and float downstream, releasing seeds as they go. Eventually the seeds float to shore, where many germinate in the damp, muddy conditions.

Drying out waterlogged soil

Trees such as willow, alder and poplar are often planted in wetland areas to help dry out the soil and improve drainage (a specific need if housing is nearby). Depending on its species and size, during the growing season one tree may suck more than 1,000 litres/ 220 gallons of water from the soil each day. If trees are removed from an area that is prone to waterlogging, the water table will rise and anaerobic conditions will be produced, thereby preventing other plants from colonizing the area. In extreme cases water run-off and soil erosion may occur. Planting trees in wetland water-catchment areas substantially reduces the risk of flash flooding. Waterlogged soil is very likely to have low nitrogen levels, which means it has low fertility. Trees such as alders not only help to dry out the soil but can also improve its fertility.

1 Weeping willow
2 Goat willow
3 Pollarded willow
4 Alder
5 White poplar

ENDANGERED TREES

Trees are one of the most successful groups of plants on earth, but despite their proliferation, some trees are increasingly under threat. Ten per cent of the world's tree species are currently threatened with extinction. Across the world more than 40ha/100 acres of forest are felled every minute.

One third of the land on earth is covered by trees. But that figure is set to decrease. As the human population expands, so ever larger areas of the world are changed to meet people's needs. One of the first things to be decimated is forest; the timber is used for industry and the land for housing.

Ten per cent threatened with extinction

There are more than 80,000 species of tree in the world. Around 8,750 of them are threatened with extinction. Almost 1,000 of those are critically endangered and some species are literally down to just one or two trees.

The threats to tree species are many and varied. They include felling of woodlands and forests for timber and fuel, agricultural development, expansion of human settlements, uncontrolled forest fires and the introduction of invasive alien tree species. Across the world we are losing at least 40ha/100 acres of forest every

minute. At the same time we are planting only 4ha/10 acres.

Can we live in a world without trees?

The simple answer is no. Trees are essential to all life and incredibly important to the planet as a whole. They provide services of incalculable value to humans, including climate control, production of oxygen, pollution control and flood prevention. They also prevent soil erosion and provide food, medicine, shelter and timber. Forests are also extremely important from an ecological point of view – tropical forests contain almost 90 per cent of the world's land-based plant species, for example.

Trees in danger

The monkey puzzle tree, *Araucaria araucana*, has become one of the most familiar trees in the temperate world. As an ornamental species, it is grown in virtually every botanical garden in

Europe. Yet, in its native homeland, high in the Andes Mountains of Chile and southern Argentina, the monkey puzzle is threatened with extinction. Thanks to its tall, straight trunk, its timber is highly sought after and the land it once stood on claimed for new uses. Monkey puzzle forests have been felled on a massive scale and it is thought there are now more monkey puzzle trees growing in Britain than there are in South America.

Another native of Chile and Argentina, the alerce tree, *Fitzroya cupressoides*, is a magnificent slow-growing conifer. Its Latin name was given in honour of Captain Robert Fitzroy, who captained HMS *Beagle* on Charles Darwin's epic voyage around the world in the 1830s. Even back then alerce was being felled for timber. Today it is one of the world's rarest

Below: Destruction of woodland and unsustainable forestry have contributed to the rarity of some of the world's trees.

conifers, with only 15 per cent of the original trees remaining. Although international trade in alerce timber is banned, illegal felling still continues.

Wilmott's whitebeam, *Sorbus wilmottiana*, grows in only one place in the entire world and that is the Avon Gorge, which passes through the west of the city of Bristol in England. This beautiful little tree, which produces clusters of attractive creamy white flowers in June and bunches of red berries in September, is critically endangered. There are only about 20 trees now remaining in the wild.

The Australian wollemi pine, *Wollemia nobilis*, was thought to be extinct until 40 survivors were found in a remote canyon in the Blue Mountains of New South Wales in 1994. A distant relative of the monkey puzzle tree, the wollemi pine has existed unchanged for almost 200 million years.

The Pacific yew, *Taxus brevifolia*, hit the headlines in the 1990s when it was found to contain a toxin called

Below: Fitzroya cupressoides is one of the world's rarest conifers.

Above: Lawson cypress has become an endangered species since felling for timber and disease have taken their toll.

taxol, which, when administered to humans, helped in the treatment of breast, ovarian and lung cancer. The greatest concentrations of taxol were found to exist in the tree's bark and for a while wholesale bark stripping took place, threatening the survival of what was already a rare species of tree. Bark from ten trees is needed to produce enough taxol to treat a single patient but steps have now been taken to protect the tree in the wild. Pacific yew plantations have been established and this, together with the recent chemical synthesis of taxol, has taken the pressure off the species in the wild.

Madagascar has some of the world's most extraordinary flora, including six different species of baobab, three of which are found nowhere else in the world. *Adansonia grandidieri*, named after Grandidier, is the grandest of them all. It is also the rarest. Although recognized by botanists the world over as a tree that must be conserved, numbers continue to dwindle. The problem here is not logging but human overpopulation. As Madagascar's people continue to increase in number more and more of the island's wilderness is turned into agricultural land.

Hope for the future

The problem with man's exploitation of trees is that it is very often done in an unsustainable way. Areas of forest are felled and cleared, often with little regard to replanting. Once the tree cover is removed, the animals, insects and birds that populated the area move away or die and soil erosion occurs, making it very difficult for trees to recolonize the felled area.

In some parts of the world, notably western Europe, sustainable silviculture is now practised with excellent results. Large areas of forest or woodland are never felled; trees are selectively thinned and removed one at a time, or in small clearings. These trees are then replaced by young seedlings that thrive naturally in the gaps once the light is allowed in. If this sustainable method of management could be adopted in other parts of the world then the future for some of the world's endangered trees might not be so bleak.

Below: The monkey puzzle tree is now threatened with extinction in the wild.

WORLD DIRECTORY OF TREES

Identifying trees can be an absorbing, rewarding and fascinating pastime to involve the whole family. Recognizing trees in their natural habitat helps create a stronger sense of familiarity with the area in which you live. In each locality, certain trees will thrive. This is because the soil conditions, weather and geography of the area are beneficial to the survival of the tree.

Each tree has specific characteristics making exact identification possible. It may be the overall profile, the flowers, fruit, shape of the cones, size of the leaves or even the bark that helps identify each tree with the family to which it belongs.

The fact boxes provide general information of interest about each tree. Not every tree species is included, but those that feature on the following pages are a good representative sample of some of the most beautiful, culturally significant and ecologically important trees in the world today. Within each of the directories there are species that have originated in that continent, but also others that have naturalized there, after being cultivated by plant hunters of the past.

Left: Swamp cypress, Taxodium distichum, *displaying their distinctive "knee-like roots", which allow them to grow in waterlogged conditions.*

HOW TO IDENTIFY A TREE

Looking at and identifying trees can be an immensely enjoyable and fascinating pastime, but, unless you know what to look for, it can be confusing. The following information should help to reduce the confusion and provide a clear route to tree identification.

Whether growing in a woodland or forest, lining the hedgerows of our fields, bringing green to our city streets or standing in defiant isolation on some windswept hillside, trees form an integral part of the landscape. They are the most diverse group of plants on the planet, providing variation in shape, size, colour and texture, and in the detail of their leaves, flowers, fruit and bark.

What to look for

There are many clues to a tree's identity, primarily built around seven main features. These features will generally not all be visible at the same time, flowers and berries normally only being present during certain seasons, for example, but some features are constant. The colour and texture of bark changes little throughout the lives of most trees.

Shape and size – Is the tree tall and spire-like or low and wide-spreading?
Evergreen or deciduous – Are there leaves on the tree all year round or does the tree lose its leaves in the autumn?
Leaves – Are they long and needle-like or broad and flat?

Below: It is quite often possible to identify a tree from a distance by its overall shape.

Flowers – Are flowers (or flower buds) present? If so, what colour and shape are they?
Fruit – Does the tree have any fruit, berries, seeds, nuts or cones on it, and if so what are they like?
Bark – Does the bark have distinctive colouring or patterning?
Buds – In winter, buds can be a tremendous help in identifying temperate trees. What colour and shape are they, and how are they positioned on the twig?

By working through these features step by step, it should be possible to identify any tree.

There are other points to consider that relate to the tree's location and the environment surrounding the tree, which may yield some clues. The acidity of the soil will dictate what species will grow successfully, for example. Some trees, such as the red oak, *Quercus rubra*, will only grow well on acidic soil (low pH), while others, such as whitebeam, *Sorbus aria*, prefer chalky, alkaline soil (high pH). The position of wild trees should also be taken into account. Some trees grow well alongside, or even in, water, for instance. Willow or alder enjoy damp conditions and grow naturally

Above: In winter the buds and bark are important clues to identification.

next to rivers; hawthorn on the other hand does not. Some trees, such as beech, will grow well in dense shade; others, such as the Judas tree, will only thrive in full sun.

It is generally easier to identify trees in the wild than in a park or arboretum. This is simply because the pool of species is likely to be greater in a park or arboretum than in a natural setting. Most hedgerows will contain fewer than ten tree species, for example, and the majority of those will be common native species. At the other extreme, an arboretum may contain up to 4,000 species, brought together from various habitats in different countries all over the world.

Shape and size

Some trees have such a distinctive shape that it becomes almost unnecessary to continue down the identification trail, other than to confirm the initial assumption. The Lombardy poplar, *Populus nigra*

'Italica', is particularly distinctive with its remarkable narrow shape and upright habit. This shape is known as "fastigiate". Another very distinctive tree is the monkey puzzle, *Araucaria araucana*. No other tree has such sharply toothed evergreen foliage and stiff branching. Once a tree has been identified, stand well back from it and try to commit its overall shape to memory. Then look for other trees with similar shape and confirm their identity. After a while you will find that certain species become instantly recognizable.

Evergreen or deciduous

In winter, in temperate regions, this is a fairly obvious feature to substantiate; at other times of year, or in the tropics, it may require a little more detective work. Most evergreen leaves fall into two categories. They will either be long, thin and needle-like, which will suggest that they belong to a conifer, or they will be thick and leathery, quite often with a shiny surface. In most temperate countries the latter are few and far between, making identification relatively easy. A non-conifer evergreen in Britain is quite likely to be either holly, *Ilex aquifolium*, or holm oak, *Quercus ilex*, for example. In the tropics, you may well need to look at the leaves more closely and take other features of the tree into account before its identity becomes clear.

Below: Palm trees are clearly identifiable by their frond-like leaves and single trunk.

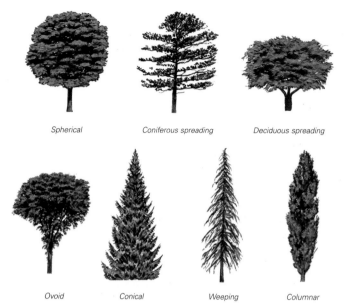

Spherical *Coniferous spreading* *Deciduous spreading*

Ovoid *Conical* *Weeping* *Columnar*

Above: Tree shape or form is the first step in identifying trees.

Leaves

For most trees, the leaves are probably the most important aid to identification. There are many different leaf shapes but almost all of them fall into the following six categories. Leaves may be "entire", which means that they are undivided and have no serrations around the edge, such as those of magnolia. They may be "serrated" with sharp serrations around the edge, as with the leaves of sweet chestnut, or be "lobed", curving

Below: Deciduous trees are easier to identify when in full leaf in summer.

in toward the centre of the leaf and then back out again, as in oak. They may be "palmate", which means hand or palm-like – maple leaves are palmate. On some leaves the indentations may go right down to the petiole (leaf-stalk) as with horse chestnut, then the leaf is called a "compound palmate" leaf. Sometimes the leaf is subdivided into smaller leaflets, the leaf is then called "pinnate".

Below: Evergreen trees can be identified by their cones or flowers.

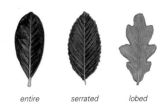

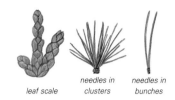

| entire | serrated | lobed | | palmate | compound palmate | pinnate | | leaf scale | needles in clusters | needles in bunches |

Temperate trees with pinnate leaves include ash and rowan. Many tropical trees have pinnate leaves.

Flowers

Most trees produce flowers in spring, although some, such as the Indian bean tree, *Catalpa bignonioides*, which is native to the USA, wait for summer. Relatively few temperate trees flower in autumn or winter although some tropical trees flower all year round. Tree identification can be much easier when flowers are evident. Knowing whether a tree produces flowers in early or late spring, for example, can also help to identify it. Cherries are instantly recognizable by their flowers, as are magnolias. The difficulty arises when individual species or varieties of cherry or magnolia are required. Here again the flower can help. Ask yourself the following questions. What colour is it? Does it have double or single

petals? How long are the flower stalks? Close examination of flowers will always enable trees to be separated. The way that flowers are held on the tree is also important. Where do they appear, on the ends of twigs or in the leaf axils? Are they individual or do they appear in clusters? If they are held in clusters, what are those clusters like?

Fruit

Late summer to autumn is the best time to identify trees by their fruit. Some fruit or seeds are instantly recognizable – acorns will immediately

Below: Fruit and seeds appear in a variety of forms to attract a wide range of pollinators.

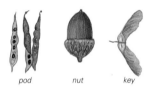

| pod | nut | key |

Above: There are hundreds of different leaf shapes, colours and arrangements to help identify trees. Needles too are quite distinct, and like leaves, are arranged differently on different trees.

identify an oak tree and conkers a horse chestnut tree. Fallen fruit are particularly useful indicators for tropical trees, which may be too tall for flowers or leaves to be visible. Some fruit are particularly distinctive, such as those of spindle trees, *Euonymus* species. The casing is normally bright pink and opens very much like a parasol to reveal orange seeds, which hang on tiny threads.

Bark

Some trees are probably better known by their bark than any other feature. Silver birch, for example, has striking silvery white bark, while the Tibetan cherry, *Prunus serrula*, has bark that is polished, peeling and mahogany red.

Below: Indian bean tree flower clusters help identify the tree in summer.

Below: Simpoh air has distinctive yellow flowers that form in racemes.

Below: Buds and flowers can help identify a willow tree that is not in leaf.

Above: Breadfruit are instantly recognizable in their native West Indies.

Above: The cones of the Likiang spruce age to become almost purple in colour.

Above: The sweet chestnut tree can be identified by its distinctive fruit in the autumn.

Other trees may not have such striking bark colour but bark may still be a useful feature to aid identification. For instance, beech has smooth light gray bark, cherry has distinctive horizontal banding and plane trees have buff-coloured bark which is constantly "flaking" to reveal fresh, light fawn bark beneath. Bark can vary between young and mature trees.

Buds

Winter is the time when tree identification can be most difficult. However, close inspection of the buds can be of considerable help. Ash has very distinctive black buds, for example, while those of magnolias tend to be large and covered with a dense coating of light-grey hairs. Horse chestnut buds are large and sticky, sycamore buds lime-green in colour. The positioning of buds can also help identify a tree. They may be in pairs on opposite sides of the twig, or they may be alternately positioned with one on the left followed by one on the

Right: In winter the overall shape of a tree and its bark, twigs and buds will all help towards identification. Quite often, in managed woodlands, the task of identification will be made simpler by the fact that many trees of the same species will be planted together.

right. Some buds hug the twig, such as those of willow, while others, such as oak buds, appear in clusters.

Equipment

When identifying trees, a good field guide is essential. It is worth getting one that fits inside your pocket and preferably has a waterproof cover. A pair of binoculars can be useful to look at leaves, flowers or buds, which may be at the top of the tree. A notepad and pencil will allow you to sketch relevant features and make notes on locations. Finally, sealable plastic bags are useful. They enable you to collect specimen leaves, fruit or seeds and take them home for closer examination.

HOW TO USE THE DIRECTORIES

The directories will help you to identify the most popular and best-known trees in different locations throughout the world. The associated descriptions will clarify how each tree can be identified at all times of the year, even in winter when deciduous trees only have bare branches, bark and twigs to show.

There are four directory sections: Trees of Temperate America, Trees of Tropical America, Trees of Britain and Europe, and Trees of Asia, Africa and Australasia. Within each directory, trees are subdivided using the Cronquist system for classification of flowering plants, as developed by Arthur Cronquist in 1981. Each main group of trees is divided into families,

then genus and finally species. Each main entry discusses the primary characteristics of the tree plus the uses to which it is put. There is a detailed description to aid identification plus an accurate watercolour illustration of the tree in leaf and also in winter profile, where appropriate. Additional boxes on the page describe other trees of interest within the same family group.

As the distribution of trees can cross continents, some of the most widely planted trees are included in more than one of the directories. Where the tree is featured as an additional box entry in one section, a cross-reference points the reader to its main illustrated entry elsewhere in the book. Colour maps of all the featured trees show at a glance the natural distribution of the tree.

Other Common Names(s)
Occasionally some trees have different common names in other countries to the UK. These are listed underneath its UK common name.

Common Name
This is the popular, non-scientific name of the tree entry.

Genus Name
This is the internationally accepted botanical name for the tree entry.

Tree Introduction
This provides a general introduction to the tree and may include information on usage, preferred conditions, and other general information of interest about each tree.

Identification
This description will enable the reader to properly identify the tree in any season. It gives information on leaf shape, size, colour and arrangement, type of flower, type of bark, number of buds and type of fruit.

Ash-leaved Maple
Box elder *Acer negundo*

This variable small to medium-size maple is found growing wild across North America, particularly alongside rivers and in moist soils. The leaves do not resemble those on the Canadian flag, but are pinnate with up to seven leaflets that individually resemble the leaves of elder, *Sambucus*. The name "box" is derived from the timber, which is white and dense, like boxwood.

Identification: The bark is brown to silver-grey, thin and smooth. The leaves are pinnate, with each leaflet approximately 10cm (4in) long and sometimes lobed. Leaflets are arranged opposite in pairs, with a terminal leaflet that is usually slightly bigger than the rest. They are rich green above and lighter green with some hair beneath. Both male and female flowers are small, yellow-green and borne on separate trees in spring, just as the leaves are emerging. The male flowers are tassel-like with long drooping stamens; the females soon develop the familiar seed wings. The fruit is the classic, downward-pointing, two-winged seed.

Flower Illustration
A watercolour illustration shows the colour and shape of the tree's flowers.

Leaf Illustration
A watercolour illustration shows the colour, size, shape and arrangement of leaf.

Summer Profile
A watercolour illustration of the tree in full leaf is given for each entry.

Winter Profile
Where appropriate, there is a watercolour illustration showing the branch outline of the tree during the winter months.

1 Map
A map shows the area of natural distribution of the featured tree. The relevant area is shaded in yellow.

2 Distribution
Describes the tree's natural distribution throughout the world.

3 (7/8)
Plant hardiness zones have been given in the American temperate and tropical tree sections for those trees originating from elsewhere in the world.

4 Height
Describes the average height of the tree given optimal growing conditions.

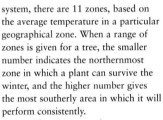

- **Distribution**: North America
- USA zones 7-8
- **Height**: 20m (66ft)
- **Shape**: Broadly columnar
- **Deciduous**
- **Pollinated**: Insect
- **Leaf shape**: Pinnate

5 Shape
Describes the overall shape of the tree. For more information on tree shapes, turn to the section "How to Identify a Tree" on page 90.

6 Deciduous
Trees are either deciduous or evergreen.

7 Pollinated
Describes the method of pollination.

8 Leaf Shape
Describes the shape of the leaf. For more information on leaf shapes, turn to the section "How to Identify a Tree" on page 90.

Plant Hardiness Zones

Within each of the directories some non-native entries have been included because they have been introduced into the region and are popular garden or park plants. Where this is the case in the temperate and tropical trees of the Americas directories, a plant hardiness zone has been indicated. The zonal system, developed by the Agricultural Research Service of the US Department of Agriculture. According to this system, there are 11 zones, based on the average temperature in a particular geographical zone. When a range of zones is given for a tree, the smaller number indicates the northernmost zone in which a plant can survive the winter, and the higher number gives the most southerly area in which it will perform consistently.

As with any system, the temperature rating is not hard and fast. It is simply a rough indicator, as many factors other than temperature also play an important part where hardiness is concerned. These factors include altitude, wind exposure, proximity to water, soil type, the presence of snow or existence of shade, night temperature, and the amount of water received by a tree. These kinds of factors can easily alter a tree's hardiness by as much as two zones.

Zone 1	Below -45˚C (-50˚F)
Zone 2	-45 to -40˚C (-50 to -40˚F)
Zone 3	-40 to -34˚C (-40 to -30˚F)
Zone 4	-34 to -29˚C (-30 to -20˚F)
Zone 5	-29 to -23˚C (-20 to -10˚F)
Zone 6	-23 to -18˚C (-10 to 0˚F)
Zone 7	-18 to -12˚C (0 to 10˚F)
Zone 8	-12 to -7˚C (10 to 20˚F)
Zone 9	-7 to -1˚C (20 to 30˚F)
Zone 10	-1 to 4˚C (30 to 40˚F)
Zone 11	Above 4˚C (40˚F)

TREES OF TEMPERATE AMERICA

Temperate America roughly equates to an area from Alaska to Mexico and from southern Argentina to Patagonia. Within these regions there are vast differences in temperature and landscapes, ranging from cold northern tundra, and high mountain ranges, to arid deserts, and exposed coastlines. This has resulted in the evolution of a large, diverse and fascinating population of native tree species. Within the following pages you will find representatives of great diversity, including northern tundra dwarf willows, west-coast giant conifers, swamp species of the Everglades and the amazing drought-tolerant Joshua tree of the Mojave Desert. In addition to native tree species, the Americas contain vast numbers of cultivated ornamental species that have their origins in other parts of the world, many of which are included here.

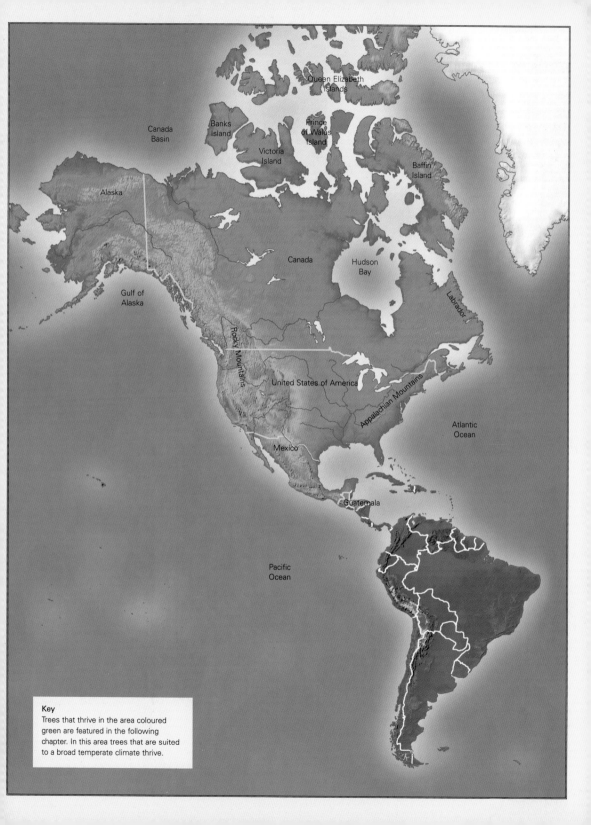

Queen Elizabeth
Islands

Canada
Basin

Banks
Island

Prince
of Wales
Island

Victoria
Island

Baffin
Island

Alaska

Gulf of
Alaska

Canada

Hudson
Bay

Labrador

Rocky Mountains

United States of America

Appalachian Mountains

Atlantic
Ocean

Mexico

Guatemala

Pacific
Ocean

Key
Trees that thrive in the area coloured
green are featured in the following
chapter. In this area trees that are suited
to a broad temperate climate thrive.

PODOCARPS

The podocarps are predominantly forest trees from the Southern Hemisphere. They are all coniferous evergreens with linear or scale-like leaves. The most extensive genus is Podocarpus, with over 70 species that range from southern temperate regions through all the tropics to the West Indies and Japan. Many can be grown in a temperate environment and are a major component of temperate rainforests.

Japanese Podocarp

Podocarpus nagi

This tender, slow-growing tree was described by Charles Sprague Sargent, one-time director of the Arnold Arboretum, Boston, as "one of the most strikingly beautiful of all evergreen trees". It has wider leaves than most other podocarps, and was originally mistaken by the Dutch botanist Kaempfer for a species of laurel. It is popular as a street tree in the Bay Area and around San Diego.

Identification: The bark is at first smooth and purple-brown, flaking into large scales in maturity. The leaves are opposite, dark glossy green and leathery with pronounced veins running down their length; they are pointed at the tip and tapered at the base and 5cm (2in) long. Male flowers are catkin-like spikes clustered along the shoot and are up to 2.5cm (1in) long. Female flowers are solitary or in pairs and develop into a globular fruit about 1cm (½in) wide, which is covered in a plum-like bloom.

Distribution: Southern Japan, Taiwan and China, and widely planted in south-west USA from California to Arizona.
Height: 25m (80ft)
Shape: Broadly conical
Evergreen
Pollinated: Wind
Leaf shape: Ovate

Left: The male flowers are catkin-like spikes, up to 2.5cm (1in) long, and are clustered along the shoot.

Bigleaf Podocarp

Podocarpus macrophyllus

An attractive, formal-shaped tree, which is extremely hardy, and able to withstand severe and prolonged frost. It is a prominent feature in many Japanese temple gardens. There is a magnificent specimen at the entrance to the Kyoto Botanic Gardens, Japan. In the USA it is found from Sacramento to California, and is commonly grown against walls, and occasionally clipped and shaped into hedging and screening. It grows particularly well on moist acid soils.

Identification: The bark is red-brown, smooth on juvenile trees becoming heavily fissured in maturity and shredding vertically. The leaves are dark green and glossy above, and a lighter pea-green beneath. They are arranged spirally around the shoots in clusters. The fruit appears in late summer and is purple-green, about 1cm (½in) long, and held in a fleshy bowl not dissimilar to an acorn cup.

Left: The pointed linear leaves are leathery, dark green and glossy.

Far left: The fruit is globular, purple-green and contained in a fleshy bowl.

Distribution: Japan and China. It is widely planted in Los Angeles, in Phoenix, Arizona, and in southern California.
Height: 20m (70ft)
Shape: Broadly conical
Evergreen
Pollinated: Wind
Leaf shape: Linear

Right: The leathery leaves are pointed, up to 1cm (⅓in) wide and up to 15cm (6in) long.

Totara

Podocarpus totara

The totara is a slow-growing evergreen tree that is noted for its longevity (it usually lives between 800 and 1,000 years). It grows in milder regions of the USA. Growing up to 30m (100ft), it has a straight, deeply grooved trunk that often reaches nearly two-thirds of its overall height. The bark peels off in long strips to reveal a beautiful golden-brown hue. Its timber is valued for general construction. Montane totara, *P. cunninghamii*, is a similar species, which has thinner, papery bark.

Above right: The cherry-like fruit contains two round seeds.

Identification: The crown develops from conical to a more broadly ovoid shape as it matures. It is noted for its massive trunk, which can be up to 2m (6½ft) in diameter, and for the huge strips of bark that peel away in a curtain-like fashion until finally falling from the tree's trunk.

Distribution: Throughout the North Island of New Zealand and into the north-eastern regions of the South Island. Hardy to zone 9.
Height: 30m (100ft)
Shape: Broadly conical
Evergreen
Pollinated: Wind
Leaf shape: Linear

Left: The dull green needles are stiff and leathery with a sharp point at the tip.

OTHER PODOCARPS OF NOTE
Plum-fruited Yew *Podocarpus andina* (*Prumnopitys andina*)
This tree has foliage similar to the common yew. It produces fruit 2cm (¾in) long, which is yellow in colour and similar to a plum with an edible fleshy covering. The seed is noted for not having a resinous odour. The tree is cultivated throughout the warmer temperate regions as an ornamental specimen. Canelo, a yellow hardwood obtained from this podocarp, is used in the production of furniture.

Below: The foliage is similar to common yew.

Manio *Podocarpus salignus*
Native to Chile, this tree is commonly referred to as the willowleaf podocarp, as its leaves are linear and sickle-shaped, resembling those of a willow. It can grow to 20m (66ft) tall, forming an attractive tree with gently pendulous branching and graceful foliage.

Prince Albert's Yew

Saxegothaea conspicua

The genus *Saxegothaea* is monotypic, meaning there is only one tree in the genus. *S. conspicua* is an evergreen tree forming part of the temperate rainforests of southern Chile and adjacent Argentina. It is found growing in association with other forest species, such as *Nothofagus dombeyi*, *Drimys winteri* and *Podocarpus nubigena*, all prized for timber. It is cultivated throughout warmer regions of the Northern Hemisphere as an ornamental tree. The generic and common names are in commemoration of the husband of Queen Victoria of the United Kingdom.

Above: Needles of Prince Albert's yew are slightly curved with a sharp tip and are up to 3cm (1¼in) long.

Distribution: Along lowland areas at the base of the west Andean slopes, from Chile (Biobio to the Chiloé province), and into south-west Argentina.
Height: 15m (50ft)
Shape: Broadly conical
Evergreen
Pollinated: Wind
Leaf shape: Linear

Identification: Grows to a height of 15m (50ft) or more, developing a slender, conical crown in its native environment and a more bushy habit in cultivation. The foliage is similar in appearance to the genus *Taxus*. The fruit is thick, round and composed of fleshy scales.

Right: The leaf on the right shows the topside view, and that on the left shows the underside colouring.

PLUM YEWS AND CHILE PINES

The plum yews, or Cephalotaxus, are very similar to the podocarps in that they produce cones or fruit that are drupe-like. This is a characteristic also shared by the false nutmegs, or Torreya species. Of much greater difference is the Chile pine, belonging to the unique Southern Hemisphere family Araucariaceae. It shares the characteristics of this family, being an evergreen, long-lived coniferous tree.

Plum Yew

Cephalotaxus harringtonia

The plum yew is the most widely cultivated of the four species of *Cephalotaxus*. It is a useful landscape plant in southern USA. It forms a small evergreen tree up to 10m (33ft) tall with foliage similar to that of yew, but with much broader and drupe-like fruit that resembles a plum. When crushed, the foliage is pungent. In cultivation it is useful for tolerating shade, where it can develop an impressive, mound-like appearance.

Identification: Leaves are broader and longer than yew. The upper surface is pale green and glossy, and the underside is slightly grey in colour with two distinctive green bands. The leaf apex is acute and often spine-tipped.

Above: Needles are up to 5cm (2in) long, glossy dark green above with two light bands of stomata beneath.

Distribution: Japan and Korea. In the USA it survives in hardiness zones 6–9.
Height: 10m (33ft)
Shape: Spreading
Evergreen
Pollinated: Wind
Leaf shape: Linear

Left: The fruit has distinctive pale banding and browns as it matures.

Chile Pine

Monkey puzzle *Araucaria araucana*

This is a uniquely bizarre tree for its triangular, very sharp, pointed leaves and distinctive whorls of long branches. It was introduced into cultivation in the late 18th century. It is widely admired for its architectural habit, but often looks misplaced. Even in its native Andean forest it is an impressive oddity. Female trees of the Chile pine produce cones 15cm (6in) in length, which take over two years to ripen. The seed is edible.

Identification: As a young tree it has a slightly rounded conical outline, with foliage to ground level. As it matures, the crown broadens and the lower branches fall away. This reveals an impressive trunk with horizontal folds of grey bark, similar in appearance to elephant hide.

Above: The distinctive bark of the Chile pine.

Right: Male cones are borne in clusters at the tips of each shoot.

Distribution: Forms groves in the Andean forests of Chile and south-western Argentina.
Height: 50m (164ft)
Shape: Broadly conical, becoming domed in maturity
Evergreen
Pollinated: Wind
Leaf shape: Linear to triangular

Left: The female ovoid cone is 15cm (6in) long.

Right: The leaves.

Stinking Cedar

Torreya taxifolia

This tree is very similar in foliage to the yew, *Taxus*, but differs in having incredibly sharp, spine-like tips to the needles. When crushed, the needles release a pungent, disagreeable odour, hence the common name. In outline this tree forms a broad-based pyramid, rarely growing taller than 15m (50ft) in height. As is the case with other *Torreya* species, it is commonly found in moist woodland areas. Its timber has been used for fencing, but it is not an abundant tree in its native Florida and is now considered to be under threat in the wild. It has been widely planted in ornamental collections worldwide.

Right: The fruit is a purple-green berry containing one seed.

Far right: Needles are sharply pointed, glossy dark green above and light green beneath.

Identification: This evergreen tree differs from the Californian nutmeg in having much shorter, convex needles, which can be up to 3cm (1¼in) long and sharply pointed. The needles are simple and linear in shape, and arranged alternately. The bark is grey-brown in colour and furrows as the tree ages. The fleshy seed is poisonous if eaten. It is cultivated as an ornamental tree.

Distribution: Restricted to the Apalichicola River in north-west Florida, and then moves northwards into Georgia.
Height: 15m (50ft)
Shape: Broadly conical
Evergreen
Pollinated: Wind
Leaf shape: Linear

OTHER SPECIES OF NOTE

Kaya Nut *Torreya nucifera*
This *Torreya* originates from the lowland valley areas of Honshu, Shikoku and Kyushu in Japan. A similar species to the Californian nutmeg, it develops a rather more open crown and has much shorter leaves. It survives in USA hardiness zones 7–9.

Below: Kaya nut needles.

Fortune Plum Yew
Cephalotaxus fortunei
Native of east and central China, where it forms a tree up to 15m (50ft) tall. It develops an open habit, largely as a result of its long needles, which can be 15cm (6in) long. Survives in USA hardiness zone 7. See also page 282.

Californian Nutmeg

Torreya californica

The Californian nutmeg is very similar to some of the podocarps and plum yews in having drupe-like fruit and linear foliage. It is distinctive in producing very sharp spines at the tips of its leaves. Beneath the resinous, fleshy fruit the seed is grooved and resembles commercial nutmeg, but has no similarity in use. It is largely grown as an ornamental tree in gardens and arboreta, as the crown forms a very attractive conical outline, and the branching develops in open whorls.

Identification: An evergreen to 20m (66ft) tall. The leaves are thin and short (up to 5cm (2in)). They are deep yellowish-green and have a shiny upper surface. Their underside has two distinctive ranks of white stomatal bands. The bark is reddish-brown and flaky.

Above: There is no botanical connection between the fruit of the Californian nutmeg (above) and the spice nutmeg, Myristica fragrans.

Distribution: Restricted to forested areas of California.
Height: 30m (100ft)
Shape: Broadly conical
Evergreen
Pollinated: Wind
Leaf shape: Linear

Below: Needles are reminiscent of some of the silver fir species, Abies. They are up to 5cm (2in) long and sharply pointed.

GINKGO, YEWS AND INCENSE CEDAR

The maidenhair tree is the only surviving representative of the Ginkgoaceae family, the other members being known solely from fossil records. The genus Taxus is present in three continents across the Northern Hemisphere and has related characteristics to the Torreya species. Incense cedar is one of only three species belonging to the genus Calocedrus.

Maidenhair Tree

Ginkgo biloba

Distribution: Originating from China, thought to be from the provinces of Anhwei and Kiangsu. It is widely cultivated throughout the Northern Hemisphere including Japan and USA.
Height: 40m (130ft)
Shape: Broadly conical
Deciduous
Pollinated: Wind
Leaf shape: Fan

Fossil records show that *Ginkgo biloba* existed over 200 million years ago. It was introduced to general cultivation in 1754. It produces male and female flowers on separate trees. When ripe, the fruit has a rancid odour; the seed beneath this pungent flesh is edible if roasted. *Ginkgo* has an attractive outline.

Identification: A deciduous tree, unique in producing fan-shaped leaves that resemble those of the maidenhair fern, *Adiantum*, hence its common name. The foliage is produced on characteristic short shoots, most apparent in winter. The bark is a pale grey.

Above: The foliage turns golden-yellow in autumn.

Right: The foliage is tolerant of the urban landscape.

Left: The fruit is orange-brown when ripe and has a single edible kernel.

Common Yew

Taxus baccata

The common yew develops a very dense, evergreen canopy. It has become associated, over recent centuries, with churchyards. In the USA it is a popular hedging tree. Yew wood is extremely durable, and is valued in the production of furniture and decorative veneers used in cabinet-making. It was commonly used for making bow staves. A number of cultivars have been created. One of the most striking is 'Standishii', which has an upright habit and golden-yellow foliage.

Distribution: Europe, including Britain, eastwards to northern Iran and the Atlas mountains of North Africa. It survives in USA zones 5–7.
Height: 20m (66ft)
Shape: Broadly conical
Evergreen
Pollinated: Wind
Leaf shape: Linear

Identification: Common yew develops a broad and loosely conical outline. The leaves are glossy above with a central groove. The bark is rich brown with a purple hue. In spring the male cones shed pollen with cloud-like abundance. The fruit is a red fleshy aril, turning red at maturity, around an olive-green seed.

Below: Yew leaves are needle-like in appearance. The canopy-like foliage creates a sombre feel.

Right: Poisonous yew berries are not digested by birds.

Incense Cedar

Calocedrus decurrens

Incense cedar is native to western North America. The natural habit of this tree is unusual in that it develops a columnar, almost fastigiate, form. Shiny, mid-green leaves develop in flattened sprays produced on branches that are almost horizontal to the main stem. It has a very attractive, exfoliating grey to reddish-brown bark. There are only two other species of tree in this genus, *C. macrolepis* from China and *C. formosana* from Taiwan.

Identification: The foliage of the incense cedar is dense, dark green and usually present to the base of the tree with only a short, exposed bole. The male and female flowers are produced on the same tree. Often, abundant quantities of oblong cones are produced, and become pendulous with their own weight.

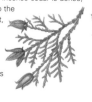

Above: The red-brown bark of the incense cedar is similar to that of the giant redwood.

Far left: The yellow-brown cones have six overlapping scales.

Distribution: Western North America from mid-Oregon southwards to Baja California in northern Mexico.
Height: 40m (130ft)
Shape: Narrowly columnar
Evergreen
Pollinated: Wind
Leaf shape: Linear scale-like

OTHER SPECIES OF NOTE

Above: Japanese yew is a wide-spreading, open-growing tree.

Japanese Yew *Taxus cuspidata*
Occurring naturally throughout Japan and most of north-east Asia. It can survive in USA hardiness zones 8–10. It reaches 20m (66ft) high in the wild, but is more shrub-like in cultivation. It has spine-tipped leaf apices. This is one of the parents, together with the common yew, of a hybrid *Taxus x media*, the most common form of which is the fastigiate 'Hicksii'.
See also page 284.

Canadian Yew *Taxus canadensis*
This small tree or large shrub is native to eastern North America from Newfoundland to Virginia. It is the hardiest yew and the only one with male and female flowers on the same tree. The leaves are more pointed than on the English yew and the foliage is not so poisonous.

Pacific Yew

Taxus brevifolia

The Pacific yew is endemic to the rainforests of western North America. It is a small tree, which grows in the shade of larger trees, often beside streams and gullies. Ever since its bark was found to contain an alkaloid called taxol, which inhibits the growth of some forms of cancer, it has become increasingly rare in the wild. It takes about ten Pacific yew trees to yield enough bark for the 2g of taxol needed to treat a single patient. Consequently thousands of yews have been felled and stripped of their bark in the quest for taxol.

Distribution: Western North America from British Columbia to California.
Height: 20m (70ft)
Shape: Broadly conical
Evergreen
Pollinated: Wind
Leaf shape: Linear

Identification: This small to medium-size tree has thin reddish-brown bark not dissimilar to that of the English yew. The branches are slender and slightly pendulous, and the winter buds are covered with golden scales. The leaves are needle-like, dark green above and sage-green beneath. The needles are arranged on the shoot in two opposite horizontally spreading rows.

Above: The seed is contained in a red fleshy fruit known as an aril.

Right: The needles are approximately 2.5cm (1in) long.

FALSE CYPRESSES

Trees belonging to the genus Chamaecyparis, *or false cypress, have a number of obvious characteristics in common. All are evergreen, and their leaves are arranged in flattened sprays and have a pungent aroma when crushed. The habitats from which they originate are generally wet and they all produce very durable timber. The genus is present in western North America, Taiwan and Japan.*

Leyland Cypress

x *Cupressocyparis leylandii*

This fast-growing conifer is a hybrid between two American species: Monterey cypress, *Cupressus macrocarpa*, and Alaska cedar, *Chamaecyparis nootkatensis*. The hybrid cross has never naturally occurred in the USA because the natural ranges of the two parents do not overlap. It originated in 1888 at Leighton Hall, Powys, Wales, where the two parents were growing close to each other in a garden. Since then, Leyland cypress has become one of the most popular trees for hedging and screening. It is extremely fast growing, quite often exceeding 2m (6ft) growth in one year.

Right: The fruit is a small brown cone.
Far right: The leaves are scale-like.

Identification: The bark is red-brown developing shallow fissures as it matures. The leaves are small, with pointed tips. They are dark green above, lighter green beneath and borne in flattened sprays. Male and female flowers are found on the same tree. The male flowers are yellow, the female's green; both appear in early spring at the tips of the shoots. The fruit is a globular woody brown cone approximately 2cm (¾in) in diameter.

Distribution: Of garden origin. Originated as a hybrid in the United Kingdom. Widely planted throughout the USA.
Height: 30m (100ft)
Shape: Narrowly columnar
Evergreen
Pollinated: Wind
Leaf shape: Scale-like

Alaska Cedar

Nootka cypress, *Chamaecyparis nootkatensis*

The nootka cypress is common throughout the coastal forests of western North America, where there are living examples many thousands of years old. It is distinctively conical in outline; the branches are flexible and develop a weeping appearance that distinguishes it from other *Chamaecyparis* species. There is an elegant naturally occurring form called 'Pendula', which produces elongated sprays of foliage that hang from pendulous branches. Referred to as yellow cedar, the wood is noted for being fine textured, straight grained and yellow.

Identification: Up to 30m (100ft) tall. The bark resembles the western red cedar in that it produces thin strips when peeled. It is brown in colour with a pinkish hue. Both male and female flowers are produced on the same tree. The cones, which take two years to develop, are about 1cm (½in) across and a deep plum colour.

Below: The foliage has pale green margins.

Right: Each cone scale has a sharp spike.

Below: The branches have a graceful upward sweep towards the tip.

Distribution: From Alaska, south towards northern California. At varying altitudes, from sea level to above the tree line, where competition is reduced. Found in the Olympic Mountains, the Cascades of Washington and Oregon, and east to the Blue Mountains.
Height: 30m (100ft)
Shape: Narrowly conical
Evergreen
Pollinated: Wind
Leaf shape: Linear scale-like

Henry's Cypress

Chamaecyparis henryae

Henry's cypress is named after the North American traveller and plant collector Mrs J. Norman Henry, who first collected it in the 1960s. It is closely related to the American white cypress, *Chamaecyparis thyoides*, with which it shares many characteristics. However, in maturity it more closely resembles *C. nootkatensis*. Despite originating from south-eastern USA, it is perfectly hardy and grows well in Virginia and in the United Kingdom.

Identification: This medium-size tree has red-brown smooth bark, which becomes finely fissured with age. On young trees the foliage is a bright yellow-green colour, but as the tree matures it gradually turns dull green. The scale-like leaves are borne on flattened fan-shaped sprays, and give off a citrus, fruity aroma when crushed. The cones are small, 1cm (½in) across, ovoid, green ripening to brown. When they first appear in summer they are covered with a soft glaucous bloom.

Below: Each cone is at first almost spherical, but then ripens to an irregular, angular woody structure.

Distribution: Coastal plains of Florida, Alabama and Mississippi.
Height: 20m (70ft)
Shape: Narrowly conical
Evergreen
Pollinated: Wind
Leaf shape: Scale-like

Left: Scale-like leaves are borne on flattened fan-shaped sprays.

OTHER SPECIES OF NOTE

Hinoki Cypress *Chamaecyparis obtusa*
Native to the southern islands of Japan, Hinoki cypress is cultivated as an ornamental tree and is highly prized for its beauty, surviving in USA hardiness zone 4. It produces valuable timber that is used for making furniture, wood panelling and veneers. The crown develops to a medium, broad, conical shape. Bark is soft, stringy and more grey than other *Chamaecyparis* species. Bright stomatal banding on the underside of the leaves gives the foliage a variegated appearance.

Southern White Cedar
Chamaecyparis thyoides
Height 15m (50ft). The southern white cedar originates from eastern North America along the Atlantic coast of New England, south towards Georgia. Its fine foliage has white undersides, hence its common name. A hardy tree. Cultivars include 'Glauca' and 'Variegata'.

Sawara Cypress *Chamaecyparis pisifera*
Native to Japan, this medium-size tree is planted as an ornamental. In the USA it survives in zone 5. Its branches are arranged in two opposite, horizontally spreading rows, giving the tree a neat uniform appearance. The scale-like leaves, which are borne in flattened sprays, have two distinctive white bands of stomata on the underside. The tree is an attractive green-blue colour.

Port Orford Cedar

Lawson cypress, Oregon cedar

Chamaecyparis lawsoniana

It originates from North America and develops into a tall, columnar tree, to 40m (130ft), with reddish-brown fibrous bark. The scented foliage has distinctive stomatal markings on the underside of the leaves. In Pacific north-western America it is a very important source of timber with many uses, from boat-building to cabinet-making. An incredible diversity of cultivars has been produced, which vary in form, foliage and colour.

Identification: Young trees have smooth, brown-green and shiny bark, with a pendulous dominant shoot that is distinct from the mature trees. It produces globular cones on the foliage tips, which begin fleshy with a bluish-purple bloom and become woody and wrinkled.

Below: The cones are globular, 7mm (¹⁄₃in) in diameter, purple-brown and remain on the tree long after the seed has been shed.

Distribution: North-western USA from south-west Oregon to north-west California. Present in the Klamath and Siskiyou Mountains to an altitude that approaches 2,000m (6,561ft).
Height: 40m (130ft)
Shape: Narrowly conical
Evergreen
Pollinated: Wind
Leaf shape: Linear scale-like

Below: The top side of the foliage is dark green to blue, and when crushed smells of parsley.

TRUE CYPRESSES

These trees are closely related to the genus Chamaecyparis, *since their leaves are scale-like and produced in sprays. Unlike the false cypresses, the foliage is not flattened. Their cones are composed of fewer scales, between six and eight, and are twice the diameter, but contain less seed. True cypresses are distributed throughout regions of North America, Europe and Asia.*

Santa Cruz Cypress

Cupressus abramsiana

Distribution: Santa Cruz Mountains in California.
Height: 20m (70ft)
Shape: Columnar
Evergreen
Pollinated: Wind
Leaf shape: Scale-like

This fast-growing, dense-foliaged, symmetrical tree grows in only a few locations in the Santa Cruz Mountains of California. It was not named until 1948 and is very closely related to Californian cypress, *Cupressus goveniana*. At one stage it was considered to be just a variation of that species. However, the cones are larger and the foliage a brighter green than the Californian cypress. On young trees the branches are strongly ascending.

Right: Seeds of the Santa Cruz cypress are contained within globular cones that may be up to 2.5cm (1in) across.

Identification: The bark is red-brown with a silver sheen when young, becoming fissured in maturity. The stem has a tendency to fork low down. Each strongly ascending branch is covered with finely divided sprays of bright, rich green, scale-like foliage. Cones are large and appear from a very early age, sometimes when the tree is less than 1m (3ft) tall. They are irregularly globular, 2.5cm (1in) across with a slight beak to each scale. The seeds within are glaucous dull brown.

Arizona Cypress

Cupressus arizonica

The Arizona cypress belongs to a group of cypresses that are found in south-western USA along the northern border with Mexico. They are distinguished from each other largely by their geographical distribution through this region. All have blue-grey glaucous foliage composed of scale-like leaves, and tolerate the dry, sun-drenched conditions. Other cypresses in this group include the smooth cypress, *C. glabra*; San Pedro cypress, *C. montana*; Piute cypress, *C. nevadensis;* and the Cayamaca cypress, *C. stephensonii.*

Identification: Develops a conical habit to a height of 20m (66ft). Has a textured, finely fissured bark. The foliage is dull grey-green, often lacking the white, resin-secreting glands common to other cypresses in this group.

Above and right: The rounded cones are 2.5cm (1in) across with six large scales and a short stalk.

Right: The scale-like needles closely overlap, and are pale to grey-green with a sharp point.

Distribution: From the central region of Arizona south towards the northern border of Mexico.
Height: 20m (66ft)
Shape: Narrowly conical
Evergreen
Pollinated: Wind
Leaf shape: Linear scale-like

Right: The scales are arranged irregularly along the shoot.

Monterey Cypress

Cupressus macrocarpa

With an incredible ability to withstand exposure to salt-laden winds, this tree has become as common a sight along the exposed coastal habitats of Europe as in its native California. It can attain a height of 40m (130ft), but individual trees are often stunted by the extreme conditions. In cultivation it is best known for being the female parent of the leyland cypress, × *Cupressocyparis leylandii*. Since cypress timber is strong and durable, it is often used for structural work.

Right: Juvenile trees are pyramidal to columnar.

Left: Mature trees become flat-topped with widespread horizontal branches.

Identification: Mature trees display a great variability in habit, from a dense crown of ascending branches to a more horizontal cedar-like form. Leaves are arranged in loose, circular sprays around the shoots. When crushed, its foliage releases an aromatic odour.

Distribution: Known from two sites along the coastline near Monterey, California: at Cypress Point and Point Lobos.
Height: 40m (130ft)
Shape: Broadly conical
Evergreen
Pollinated: Wind
Leaf shape: Linear scale-like

Above: Cones are up to 4cm (1½in) across.

OTHER SPECIES OF NOTE
Guadelupe Cypress *Cupressus guadelupensis*
Grows to a height of 20m (66ft) in the wild. This cypress is restricted in natural distribution to Guadelupe off the coast of Baja California. The island is part of a series of ridges once connected to the mainland. The tree is seldom seen in cultivation.

Mexican Cypress *Cupressus lusitanica*
Height 30m (100ft). The Mexican cypress was first named in Portugal, having been brought over from Mexico and cultivated there. It was also believed to have been of Asiatic origin, hence its other common name, cedar of Goa. *See also page 292.*

Sargent's Cypress *Cupressus sargentii*
This bushy small tree occurs on dry mountain slopes up to elevations of 670m (2,200ft) throughout the coastal range of California. This species is closely related to *C. goveniana*, but is distinguishable by its short trunk, spreading branches and handsome open crown. The branches are covered with attractive smooth bark, which is at first orange, becoming bright red-brown, and on maturity, purple-brown.

Modoc Cypress *Cupressus bakeri*
The Modoc cypress is native to the dry hills and low slopes in the Siskiyou Mountains of California and Oregon, particularly in Shasta County and south-east Siskiyou County. It is a tree that grows to 15m (50ft) tall with smooth red-brown bark that matures to grey but with minimum fissuring. The scale-like, dark grey-green leaves are arranged all around the shoot.

Californian Cypress

Cupressus goveniana

Otherwise known as Gowen's cypress, after James Gowen, the renowned British rhododendron nurseryman, this multi-stemmed tree has small natural populations on Point Pinos Ridge, 3.2km (2 miles) west of Monterey, and along a narrow coastal strip in Mendocino county. In the wild it is more often a large shrub, but in cultivation elsewhere it attains heights around 20m (66ft). It appears to be a short-lived tree, regularly dying back after 50 years or so.

Identification: The Californian cypress has bright red-brown thin bark with shallow, linear fissures, which separate the surface into long thread-like scales. The leaves are acutely pointed, dark green and scale-like. The cones are smaller than *C. abramsiana*, about 2cm (¾in) across, more oval than spherical with six to ten scales. The seed they contain is almost black.

Distribution: Monterey peninsula, Southern California.
Height: 20m (66ft)
Shape: Broadly columnar
Evergreen
Pollinated: Wind
Leaf shape: Scale-like

Above right and below: The needles are arranged in four ranks, which are flattened to the rather long and slender branches.

PATAGONIAN CYPRESS AND ARBORVITAE

A common characteristic of Fitzroya *is the three-whorled arrangements of the leaves, which distinguish it from the closely related* Cupressus. *The arborvitae, or* Thuja *species, are similar to Lawson cypress, but have much larger and broader leaves, and* Thujopsis, *or hiba, differs from* Thuja *in having thick white markings on the underside of its leaves.*

Patagonian Cypress

Fitzroya cupressoides

This unique genus of tree has a restricted distribution and is one of the world's oldest trees, recorded at over 3,500 years. It is often referred to as the redwood of South America. Its reddish, lightweight and straight-grained timber, commonly used for shingles, furniture and masts, has been highly prized for centuries.

Identification: It has reddish brown, deeply ridged bark that peels off in strips. The foliage is produced in pendulous sprays and is blue-green with distinctive white markings on both surfaces. In cultivation it is slow-growing and forms a multi-branched, shrub-like habit.

Above: The cones develop at the end of each spiky shoot.

Left: Needles are bright blue-green with two white stomatal bands.

Distribution: South America: from southern Chile to Argentina. It is now restricted to higher-altitude rainforests along the coastal ranges from south of Valdira, including Chiloe Island, to the Andean slopes.
Height: 50m (165ft)
Shape: Broadly columnar
Evergreen
Pollinated: Wind
Leaf shape: Linear scale-like

Left: The angular cones have nine woody scales.

White Cedar

Thuja occidentalis

This slow-growing evergreen tree's origins are in eastern Canada and south-eastern USA, where it is predominantly a tree of upper forest levels, surviving in rocky outcrops as well as sites with high moisture content. Similar to its more westerly cousin, it is valued commercially as a timber that has good resistance to decay and tolerates contact with moisture. Many cultivars have been developed, mostly from dwarf forms. 'Rheingold' has attractive golden-yellow foliage.

Identification: Twisted sprays of foliage give this tree a distinctive outline. During autumn and winter, the foliage has attractive hints of orange and brown. The bark is brown with a golden-orange hue and shreds with age. Yellow cones develop from as early as six years.

Right: Needle scales are dark green above, yellow green below.
Below: When crushed, the foliage smells of fresh apples.

Left: The upright cones are 1cm (½ in) across. Yellow-green at first, they ripen to brown.

Distribution: South-eastern Canada and USA: from Nova Scotia and New Brunswick, west to Quebec and northern Ontario; through Michigan, Illinois and Indiana to the states of New England.
Height: 20m (66ft)
Shape: Narrowly conical
Evergreen
Pollinated: Wind
Leaf shape: Linear scale-like

Western Red Cedar

Thuja plicata

Also known as giant arborvitae, this evergreen tree originates from the northwestern Pacific coastline of America, where it is a major component of the moist, lowland coniferous forests. Some trees have been recorded at over 1,000 years old. The timber has been utilized for centuries. Native American Indians used to burn out the trunks to make canoes. It has become an economically important timber, being straight-grained, soft and easily worked. It has been widely used to make roofing shingles. Many cultivars have been produced, including a distinctive variegated form called 'Zebrina'.

Identification: A very tall, narrow, conical evergreen tree up to 50m (165ft). Individual specimen trees with low branching can layer to form a secondary ring of vigorous, upright trunks. The foliage is dark green and glossy above, with a sweetly aromatic scent when crushed. The bark is reddish-brown, forming plates with maturity. It is fibrous and ridged.

Distribution: Originating from the Pacific coastline of North America, it grows from southern Alaska, through British Columbia, south to Washington and Oregon to the giant coastal redwood forests of California.
Height: 50m (165ft)
Shape: Narrowly conical
Evergreen
Pollinated: Wind
Leaf shape: Linear scale-like

Left: The shoots are coppery brown with sprays of deep glossy green, scale-like needles that are flattened in one plane.

Oriental Arborvitae

Thuja orientalis

Distribution: China and Korea.
Height: 15m (50ft)
Shape: Columnar
Evergreen
Pollinated: Wind
Leaf shape: Scale-like

Below: When crushed, the needles emit a strong "pine" aroma.

Otherwise known as Chinese thuja, this medium-size tree is frequently planted from Texas to California and north to Nevada. It is common in parks and cemeteries, and is quite often seen planted on each side of the front door of houses. It is different to all other thujas in having distinctive erect or upward-curving branches, which bear the foliage in vertical sprays. It has given rise to several popular cultivars including 'Aurea Nana', 'Conspicua' and 'Elegantissima'.

Identification: The oriental arborvitae is frequently multi-stemmed, forming a dense crown of foliage virtually to ground level, which obscures the copper-red bark of the trunk. The dark green colouring of the leaves is virtually identical on both the upper and lower surfaces. The cones are an irregular shape, about 2cm (¾in) long with approximately six scales each with a protuberance shaped like a rhino's horn. The seeds inside are dark red-purple and without wings.

OTHER SPECIES OF NOTE

Japanese Thuja *Thuja standishii*
Native of Japan, from Honshu and Shikoku. An evergreen tree, to 25m (80ft), with very deep, rich red-brown bark that peels off in square plates. It is similar in form to hiba, in having branches that curve sharply upwards, and foliage that is hard and irregular in outline. The young, growing leaf tips are blue-grey. When crushed, the foliage has a lemon scent. *See also page 298.*

Hiba *Thujopsis dolabrata*
A monotypic genus and single species, this broadly conical, evergreen tree originates from Japan. It is distinguished from thuja by its broader scale-like leaves, which have strong bands of white stomata on their underside. Hiba is a slow-growing tree, reaching 20m (66ft) high. It has bark that is red-brown to grey, peeling with maturity into fine strips. *See also page 299.*

Korean Thuja *Thuja koraiensis*
Native to Korea and the Jilin province of China, this is a small tree, to 10m (33ft). A similar species to the Japanese thuja, it has blue-green foliage that is unique in having silvery undersides to the leaves. *See also page 298.*

Right: In spring, the new growth is vivid lime-green. As it matures, so its appearance becomes progressively darker.

JUNIPERS

The junipers are similar to the true cypresses, Cupressus, *in that they have two types of leaves on the same plant, both juvenile and scale-like. Unlike cypresses, the fruit consists of a cone in which the scales have fused together to give a berry-like appearance. The common juniper is probably found in more regions of the world than any other tree.*

Western Juniper

Sierra juniper *Juniperus occidentalis*

This tough, medium-size tree is a common species in western USA where it inhabits rocky slopes and dry hillsides, quite often in conjunction with the Western yellow pine, *Pinus ponderosa*. In the Sierra Nevada 2,000-year-old specimens with huge trunks can be seen growing out of what appears to be solid rock. It was first identified and introduced into cultivation by plant collector David Douglas in 1829.

Identification: The bark is red-brown and smooth, becoming fissured and flaky in maturity. The leaves are scale-like, small, silver-grey-green and held closely to the shoot. Individual, stiff, spiny leaves are quite often found towards the ends of growing tips. Male flowers are yellow and the female's green. They are normally produced on separate trees in spring. The fruit is an egg-shaped, blue-black cone, 1cm (½in) long, and covered with a glaucous bloom.

Right: The leaves are scale-like and silver-grey-green.

Distribution: West coast USA from Washington to California.
Height: 20m (70ft)
Shape: Broadly conical
Evergreen
Pollinated: Wind
Leaf shape: Scale-like

Eastern Red Cedar

Juniperus virginiana

The most widely distributed conifer through central and eastern North America, the eastern red cedar is tolerant of dry, exposed and elevated sites – a characteristic that has made it a useful tree for screening and wind protection. The heartwood is a beautiful reddish-brown and has a typical cedar scent, which is retained through drying. The wood has moth-repellent properties and is commonly used to make blanket boxes and chests. The oil is extracted from the fruit and leaves for use in soaps and fragrances.

Identification: An evergreen tree up to 30m (100ft). Eastern red cedar develops a dense pyramidal to columnar habit, with two types of foliage. It has red-brown bark, which exfoliates in long strips. The fruit is berry-like, light green in spring and dark blue when mature.

Above: The dense scale-like foliage is 6mm (¼in) long, sage-green above and grey-green beneath.

Left: The small cones have a blue-grey bloom when ripe.

Distribution: Eastern and central USA Great Plains eastwards. South-west Maine to southern Minnesota into the Dakotas and southwards to Nebraska and central Texas. East to Florida and Georgia.
Height: 30m (100ft)
Shape: Narrowly conical
Evergreen
Pollinated: Wind
Leaf shape: Linear scale-like

Common Juniper

Juniperus communis

The common juniper is believed to be the most widespread tree in the world, growing naturally from Alaska, Greenland, Iceland and Siberia, south through most of Europe, temperate Asia and North America. It is a hardy tree, tolerating intense cold, exposed coastal locations and high mountain ranges. In North America it seldom attains heights in excess of 5m (16ft) tall.

Below: The whorls of three needles can be clearly seen below.

Identification: Depending on its location, the overall shape of common juniper may be thin and tree-like or wide-spreading and shrub-like. It has thin, dark red-brown bark that peels in vertical papery strips. The leaves are needle-like, sharply pointed and up to 1cm (½in) long. They are grey-green and carried in whorls of three along the shoot. The yellow male, and green female, flowers are borne on separate trees in clusters within the leaf axils. The fruit is a green, berry-like cone that takes between two and three years to ripen. When ripe it turns a glaucous, purple-black. The fruit is used to give gin its characteristic flavour.

Distribution: Europe, Asia and North America.
Height: 6m (20ft)
Shape: Narrowly conical
Evergreen
Pollinated: Wind
Leaf shape: Needle-like

OTHER SPECIES OF NOTE

Chinese Juniper
Juniperus chinensis
This erect, narrow juniper, native to China and Japan, is commonly used for bonsai. It has been in cultivation for centuries, and many cultivars have been developed including 'Keteleeri', 'Pfitzeriana' and 'Hetzii'. It has grey through to reddish-brown bark, which naturally peels off in long strips. The scale-like leaves are dark green on the outer surface and have a broad green stripe on the inner, which is separated by two white stomatal bands. In the wild it can attain heights up to 25m (80ft) tall. *See also page 295.*

Mexican Juniper *Juniperus flaccida*
The Mexican juniper has a weeping habit that resembles that of *Chamaecyparis,* or the false cypress. It is found throughout northern and central Mexico.

Himalayan Juniper
Juniperus recurva
The attractive weeping habit of this tree's foliage gives rise to its name. The foliage is bluish-grey, and is dry to the touch and making a rasping sound in the wind. It originates in the Himalayas from Afghanistan to south-western China and northern Burma. *See also page 295.*

Utah Juniper

Juniperus osteosperma

This small, candelabra-shape tree makes a distinctive feature in deserts from Wyoming and Utah to California and Arizona around the Grand Canyon, where some arid slopes are clothed in dense, almost pure forests of Utah juniper. It is a hardy tree withstanding long periods of drought and dramatic changes of temperature. It has been recorded at altitudes in excess of 2,500m (8,000ft).

Identification: The Utah juniper has ash-grey to silverywhite, fibrous bark that peels into long thin scales in maturity. It has bright yellow-green, blunt, scale-like leaves, which are held either opposite or in threes on the shoot. Male flowers are yellow and the female's green, and they are borne on separate trees in spring. The fruits are rounded, 1cm (½in) across, reddish-brown, with a thick, firm skin covered with a glaucous bloom. Each fruit contains up to two seeds. The fruit used to be ground into flour and made into cakes by Native Americans.

Distribution: From Wyoming to California.
Heigh: 6m (20ft)
Shape: Conical
Evergreen
Pollinated: Wind
Leaf shape: Scale-like

Above: True to its name, the Utah juniper is the most abundant species of juniper in Utah state.

REDWOODS AND BALD CYPRESS

This group of conifers are all members of the Taxodiaceae family and are found in the Northern Hemisphere. The group includes some of the biggest, tallest and oldest trees in the world. The coast and giant redwoods are evergreens originating from California. The dawn redwood and swamp cypress are deciduous conifers. All have distinctive, fibrous, reddish-brown bark.

Coast Redwood

Sequoia sempervirens

The *Sequoia* takes its name from a native American Cherokee called Sequoiah. This majestic tree attains heights in excess of 100m (328ft). The current champion, known as the "Stratosphere Giant", is 114m (374ft). The trunk is quite often branchless for two-thirds of the height.

Left: The cones are 2–3cm (¾–1¼ in) long.

Identification: Young trees have a cone-like form with widely spaced, level, slender branches, upcurved at the tips. Old trees become columnar with flat tops and branches that sweep down. Leading shoots have small pinkish-green needles arranged spirally. Needles on main and side shoots are arranged in two flat rows, 1–2cm (½–¾ in) long, dark green above, and speckled with two bands of white stomata on the underside. Male flowers are yellowish-brown; female flowers are green, in separate clusters on the same tree.

Distribution: Found in a narrow coastal band running for approximately 800km (500 miles) from Monterey, California, to the Oregon border.
Height: 100m (328ft)
Shape: Narrowly conical
Evergreen
Pollinated: Wind
Leaf shape: Linear

Left: The fissured, reddish-brown thick, spongy bark acts as a fire-resistant blanket.

Giant Redwood

Sequoiadendron giganteum

The largest living thing in the world is a giant redwood called "General Sherman", which is estimated to weigh 5,440 tonnes. Some giant redwoods live up to 3,500 years. They thrive in any soil, site or exposure with a moderate supply of moisture, but do not grow well in heavy shade. The bark is red-brown, soft, thick and fibrous.

Left: Needles and cones.

Distribution: Restricted to 72 groves on the western slopes of the Sierra Nevada, California.
Height: 80m (262ft)
Shape: Narrowly conical
Evergreen
Pollinated: Wind
Leaf shape: Linear

Right: The trunk of a redwood may grow to more than 3m (10ft) in diameter.

Identification: The crown of the tree is conical, becoming broad in old age. The leaves grow to 8mm (⅓in), and are sharp-pointed with spreading tips. They are matt grey-green at first, covered with stomata, and turn a dark, shiny green after three years. When crushed, the foliage emits a fragrance of aniseed. The male flowers are yellowish-white and ovoid, held at the end of minor shoots, and shed pollen in early spring. The female flowers are green, and develop into bunches of green ovoid cones, which ripen to brown in their second year.

Swamp Cypress

Bald cypress *Taxodium distichum*

Also known as the bald cypress because of its deciduous habit, this tree grows naturally in wet conditions and can tolerate having its roots submerged for several months. In these conditions it will produce aerial roots known as "knees" or "pneumatophores", which provide oxygen to the roots. An excellent tree for colour: the leaves turn from old gold to brick-red in early to mid-autumn.

Right: Autumn needles.

Left: Cones are borne on the same trees as male flowers.

Identification: Bark is a dull reddish-brown and frequently fluted. The crown is typically conical, although some trees develop a rather domed appearance in maturity, with heavy, low, upswept branches. Shoots are pale green, up to 10cm (4in) long, with soft, flattened 2cm- (¾in-) long leaves arranged alternately along the shoot, emerging late in the season. The male flowers, to 5–6cm (2–2½in), are prominent throughout the winter as three or four catkins held at the end of each shoot. These lengthen to 10–30cm (4–12in) when pollen is shed in early spring. Female cones are on a short stalk, globular and light green until ripe.

Right: The deciduous, needle-like foliage turns red in autumn.

Distribution: South-eastern USA: from Delaware to Texas and Missouri.
Height: 40m (130ft)
Shape: Broadly conical
Deciduous
Pollinated: Wind
Leaf shape: Linear

Pond Cypress
Taxodium ascendens
This broadly conical tree from the south-eastern USA reaches 40m (130ft) tall. It has linear leaves 1cm (½in) long, which are closely pressed around upright, deciduous shoots. The bark is red-brown, thick and heavily fluted. Male flowers are yellow-green, and held in catkins up to 20cm (8in) long. Female flowers are green and appear in clusters at the base of the male catkins. The fruit is a green globular cone, which is unlikely to exceed 3cm (1¼in) across.

Chinese Swamp Cypress
Glyptostrobus pensilis
This small tree seldom reaches more than 10m (33ft). It originates from south-east China and grows wild in swamps and along riverbanks. It is rare in the wild. It has linear, scale-like leaves, 1.5cm (⅝in) long, arranged spirally on deciduous side shoots. The bark is grey-brown and the flowers insignificant. The fruit is an egg-shape green cone, to 2.5cm (1in) long. This tender tree does not thrive in northern Europe, where the temperature dives too low.

Dawn Redwood

Metasequoia glyptostroboides

Until this beautiful tree was discovered growing in east Szechwan by Chinese botanist T. Kan in 1941, it had only been seen as a fossil and was deemed extinct. It was introduced to the West in 1948. Since then it has become a popular species for ornamental planting. It has bright orange-brown stringy bark, and the trunk is quite often fluted.

Identification: The crown is conical in most trees. When grown in the open, the crown is dense, but in shade it becomes sparse. The leaves are down-curved at the tips, 2cm (¾in) long, bright green above with a pale band each side of the midrib below. Male flowers are ovoid, and set on panicles, which are up to 25cm (10in) long. The female cone is green ripening to brown, and 2cm (¾in) across with stalks 2cm (¾in) long.

Distribution China: the Shui-sha valley, in the north-west part of Hueph Province and into Szechwan Province. USA zone 4.
Height: 40m (130ft)
Shape: Narrowly conical
Deciduous
Pollinated: Wind
Leaf shape: Linear

Below: The leaves are positioned opposite each other on the shoot.

TRUE CEDARS AND HEMLOCKS

Although there are only four true cedars, they are without doubt the real stars of the coniferous world.
Nothing can touch them for sheer majesty and dignity. Three are clustered around the Mediterranean
and the fourth makes it a little further east into the Himalayas. The hemlocks, on the other hand, are all
to be found in either North America or Asia.

Eastern Hemlock

Tsuga canadensis

Otherwise known as the Canada hemlock, this beautiful, tall, fast-growing tree is common in parks and gardens throughout North America. On the northern plains it makes a broad and strongly branched tree, but in the mountain valleys to the south it is far more slender and conical. There is an ancient wood of eastern hemlocks on one of the hills in the Arnold Arboretum near Boston, Massachusetts. Some of the trees in the wood have girths over 3m (10ft).

Identification: The bark is purple-grey, smooth when juvenile becoming fissured with scaly ridges in maturity. The male flowers are yellow, and the female flowers small green cones, which are borne at the shoot tip. Both are found on the same tree. The fruit is a small, pale fawn, oval hanging cone, up to 2.5cm (1in) long.

Left: The fruit is a cone, to 2.5cm (1in) long, and may contain up to 50 tiny winged seeds.

Right: The linear leaves are 1cm (½in) long, dark glossy green above, with two white stomatal bands on the underside.

Distribution: Eastern USA from Nova Scotia south to Alabama and Georgia.
Height: 30m (100ft)
Shape: Broadly conical
Evergreen
Pollinated: Wind
Leaf shape: Linear

Cedar of Lebanon

Cedrus libani

This large, stately tree is probably the best known of all the cedars. It has been revered for thousands of years. In biblical times it stood as a symbol for fertility. King Solomon is believed to have built his temple out of its timber. On Mount Lebanon it grows at altitudes up to 2,140m (7,021ft). Although numbers are decreasing in the wild, it has been widely planted as an ornamental tree in parks, gardens and arboreta in Britain and North America.

Identification: The bark is dull brown with even, shallow fissures. For the first 40 years of its life, cedar of Lebanon is a narrow, conical tree; thereafter it broadens rapidly with long, level branches that seem, in some cases, to defy gravity, such is their length. The needles are grey-blue to dark green (depending on the provenance of the individual tree), 3cm (1¼in) long and grow in dense whorls on side shoots and singly on fast-growing main shoots. The cone is barrel-shaped, erect, grey-green and matures to purplish-brown.

Distribution: Mount Lebanon, Syria and the Taurus Mountains in south-east Turkey. USA zones 6–8.
Height: 40m (130ft)
Shape: Broadly columnar
Evergreen
Pollinated: Wind
Leaf shape: Linear

Right: Cones are 12cm (4¾in) long.

Atlantic Cedar
Cedrus atlantica
Also known as the
Atlas cedar after the
mountain range
where it originates. It
is the fastest growing
of all the cedars,
reaching 3m (10ft) in
less than seven years.
It is also the straightest, maintaining its leading
stem into old age. The form 'Glauca' is far more
widely planted, in arboreta, than the true species
because of its strikingly beautiful silvery blue
foliage. *See also page 291.*

Cyprus Cedar *Cedrus brevifolia*
The tree is confined to forests surrounding Mount
Paphos in Cyprus. At one time considered a
form of Lebanon cedar, it is now treated as a
separate species. It does not look much like
Lebanon cedar as it maintains a single stem, has
shorter needles, a more open habit and, from a
distance, has a yellow-green crown. In the USA
it grows in arboreta and parks.

Deodar *Cedrus deodara*
This beautiful large ornamental tree is planted
along the Gulf Coast into Texas and along the
Mississippi Valley. It is grown in the west around
Vancouver and in California. It has blue-grey
foliage, which turns dark green with age. The
overall shape is narrowly conicalm becoming
broad in maturity. It is easily distinguished from
other cedars by the way in which the ends of
the branches droop down. *See also page 290.*

Western Hemlock

Tsuga heterophylla

This tall, elegant tree has weeping branches
and soft pendulous foliage. However, this
softness is deceptive: western hemlock is as
hardy as any conifer. It thrives in the
Rockies up to 1,830m (6,000ft) above sea
level and is extremely shade-tolerant,
out-growing its competitors in the
thickest forest.

Identification: Bark is reddish-purple in young trees,
becoming dark purple-brown with
age. The tree has a narrow
conical shape, with ascending
branches that arch gently
downwards towards the tip. The
leading shoot is always lax.
Needles are 2cm (¾in) long,
deep dark green above
with two broad blue-
white stomatal bands
beneath. New growth
is bright lime-green
in spring, contrasting
dramatically against
the rather sombre
mature foliage. Male and
female flowers are red.
Much pollen is shed in
late spring. Cones are
pendulous, egg-
shaped, 2.5cm (1in)
long, with few scales,
and are pale brown
ripening to deep brown.

Distribution: West coast USA
from Alaska to California.
Height: 60m (200ft)
Shape: Narrowly conical
Evergreen
Pollinated: Wind
Leaf shape: Linear

*Left and
below: Small egg-
shaped cones appear
in late summer at the
tips of branches.*

Mountain Hemlock

Tsuga mertensiana

Native to the west coast of America from
Alaska to California, this handsome tree
has a columnar crown of grey pendulous
foliage. The mountain hemlock is sometimes
mistaken for *Cedrus atlantica* 'Glauca', as it
has thick blue-grey needles, which radiate
all around the shoot.

Identification: The bark is dark orange-brown,
becoming vertically fissured into rectangular flakes in
maturity. The branches are slightly drooping with
weeping branchlets hanging from them. The shoot
is a shiny pale brown colour. The needles are similar
to a cedar's, 2cm (¾in) long, dark grey-green to blue-
grey, and are borne radially all over the shoot. The
cone is spruce-like, 7cm (2¾ in) long, cylindrical and
buff-pink maturing to brown.
Male flowers are violet-purple and borne on slender
drooping stems. The female flowers are erect and
have dark purple and yellow-green bracts.

*Below: Cones
before and after
opening.*

Distribution: Alaska to
California.
Height: 30m (100ft)
Shape: Columnar
Evergreen
Pollinated: Wind
Leaf shape: Linear

*Left: The needles have a definite
bluish tinge to them and radiate
out from the twigs. From their
ends, shoots appear star-like.*

TRUE FIRS

The term "fir" has become a general description for anything vaguely coniferous-looking. In reality this is erroneous: the true, or silver, firs are a select band of conifers botanically linked within the genus Abies. They include some of the finest conifers and nine of the best are found in North America. They range across the continent, from the balsam firs of Canada to the Santa Lucia firs of California.

Noble Fir

Abies procera

This is a superb species that truly deserves its name. It has a stately, noble appearance with a long, straight stem and large cones that stand proudly above the surrounding foliage. It is particularly hardy, growing at up to 1,500m (4,921ft) in the Cascade Mountains, USA. Noble fir has been planted widely outside its natural range for its timber, which is light brown, close-grained and very strong.

Identification: The bark is silvery grey, smooth and has occasional resin blisters. Young trees are conical, with widely spaced whorls of branches. Older trees become flat-topped, with characteristic twisted, dead branches. Needles are grey-green above with two distinct white stomata bands on the underside. They are strongly parted on the shoot, curving upwards and then down. Needles on top of the shoot are 1cm (½in) long; beneath the shoot, they are 4cm (1½in) long. When crushed, they emit a pungent smell, like cat's urine. Cones are broad cylinders up to 25cm (10in) long, and are held erect from the branch.

Above: Cones are normally confined to the topmost branches.

Below: Male flowers are clustered beneath the shoot in spring.

Distribution: Cascade Mountains of Oregon, Washington State and northern California.
Height: 80m (262ft)
Shape: Narrowly conical
Evergreen
Pollinated: Wind
Leaf shape: Linear

Right: Female flowers are upright on the shoot.

Santa Lucia Fir

Bristlecone fir *Abies bracteata*

Sometimes known as the bristlecone fir because of the long bristle attached to each cone scale, this west-coast species is the rarest native North American fir. It is found growing naturally only in the bottom of a few rocky canyons. It is rare in the wild and in cultivation.

Although relatively hardy, it has not been widely planted. In 1852 it was introduced to Europe by William Lobb.

Identification: Bark on young trees is dark grey with wrinkles and black lines around branch knots. Older trees develop black or purple-black bark with deep cracks. The shape is broad at the base, narrowing rapidly to a long, conical crown. Branches tend to fan out and droop towards their tips. Needles are strongly parted each side of the shoot. They are forward pointing, up to 5cm (2in) long with a sharp tip, dull green above and have two bright white bands beneath. Cones are found on the topmost branches, like candles. Each cone scale has a long bristle, giving it a very distinctive appearance. Cones normally disintegrate on the tree.

Above: New needles often have a purple tinge to them.

Distribution: Santa Lucia Mountains, southern California.
Height: 35m (115ft)
Shape: Narrowly conical
Evergreen
Pollinated: Wind
Leaf shape: Linear

Left: The cone has hair-like protrusions, giving it a very scruffy appearance.

Grand Fir

Giant fir *Abies grandis*

This silver fir is one of the true giants of North American coniferous forests. Before deforestation took its toll, many grand firs exceeded 90m (300ft) in height. It is an extremely fast-growing tree, attaining 50m (160ft) within 100 years. It was first discovered by the plant collector Douglas on the Columbia River in 1825.

Identification: When young the bark is olive-brown, smooth but pockmarked with resin blisters. In maturity the bark fades to silver-grey and the base of the trunk become fissured. The needle-like leaves are 5cm (2in) long, glossy deep green above and silver-grey beneath. They are parted uniformly at each side of the shoot, and when crushed have a scent of oranges. The male flowers are reddish-yellow, and the female greenish-yellow, borne in clusters on the same tree in spring.

Distribution: North of Vancouver Island, through British Columbia and south to Navarro River, California.
Height: 60m (200ft)
Shape: Narrowly conical
Evergreen
Pollinated: Wind
Leaf Shape: Linear

Right: Female flowers.

Below: The light brown cone, which is 10cm (4in) and cylindrical, stands upright towards the top of the tree.

Red Fir

Abies magnifica

This is a tree of the high mountains, where snow lies for months on end before being followed by long periods of summer drought. It is named after the red colour of its bark, but the botanical name *magnifica* is more appropriate, because this truly is a magnificent species. Its short, regularly spaced, horizontal branches create perfect symmetry.

Identification: Bark, even on relatively young trees, is thick, corky and has deep fissures. Overall, red fir has a very regular shape, keeping its neat, conical appearance into old age. The needles are almost round in cross-section, 3.5cm (1⅛in) long, wide-spreading and curving back in towards the shoot at the tips. They are dark grey-green in colour with two lighter bands of stomata on both the upper and lower surfaces. The upright cones are seldom seen, growing right at the top of the tree and disintegrating *in situ*. They grow up to 20cm (8in) long, are barrel-shaped, smooth and golden-green.

Above: Upright cones are borne at the top of the tree.

Distribution: Cascade Mountains of Oregon, Mount Shasta and Sierra Nevada, California.
Height: 40m (130ft)
Shape: Narrowly conical
Evergreen
Pollinated: Wind
Leaf shape: Linear

Left: Male cones are purple-red and appear in spring.

Balsam Fir

Abies balsamea

A common tree in North America and one of the most important in northern USA and Canada. It is probably the most resinous of all the silver firs and a popular choice for Christmas trees. It has an average lifespan of 200 years. Large blisters of resin occur under the bark, and the foliage needs only to be touched to release its fragrant balsam scent, which is valued by aromatherapists. This tree is the main source of Canada balsam, which is used for mounting microscopic specimens. It is a hardy tree, growing well inside the Arctic Circle, and at altitudes in excess of 1,220m (4,000ft).

Below: Upright purple-brown cones are normally covered with sticky white resin.

Identification: The bark is dark grey, smooth at first except for resin blisters, but becoming heavily and vertically fissured in maturity. The narrow needle-like leaves are 2.5cm (1in) long, dark green above, with a triangular, white patch of stomata near the tip, and two silver-grey bands beneath. They are parted on the shoot. The upright, purple-brown, pointed cones are up to 10cm (4in) long. They are normally coated in sticky silver resin, and borne on the topmost branches, from where they disintegrate upon ripening.

Distribution: Eastern Canada and USA from Newfoundland to Virginia.
Height: 20m (65ft)
Shape: Narrowly conical
Evergreen
Pollinated: Wind
Leaf shape: Linear

Right: The branches of balsam fir are dense, and the needles are dark green. At ground level in open spaces, live branches may thrive. In forests low branches die back.

Fraser's Fir

Abies fraseri

Distribution: Virginia, North Carolina and East Tennessee, USA.
Height: 20m (65ft)
Shape: Narrowly conical
Evergreen
Pollinated: Wind
Leaf Shape: Linear

Right: Narrow, needle-like leaves are dark green above and banded silver-grey beneath. The needles spread out on each side of the shoot in two distinct ranks.

This hardy, handsome, symmetrical tree is common in the Great Smoky Mountains, where it grows at altitudes in excess of 2,000m (6,500ft), but has a limited natural range elsewhere. It is planted widely as an ornamental in parks and arboreta, and in recent years has found favour in the UK as a Christmas tree. It was identified by John Fraser in 1811 and named in his honour in 1817.

Identification: The bark is a rich brown colour when young, becoming pink-grey in maturity and covered in resin-blisters. The needle-like leaves are dark green above and silvery white beneath, spreading out in two distinct ranks at each side of the shoot. They are 2cm (¾in) long and broadest near the blunt notched tip. The upright cylindrical cones are 5.5cm (2¼in) long, dark purple, with pale brown bracts between each scale. The winter buds are distinctive, being a deep chocolate-brown colour and covered in thick resin.

Above: Each cylindrical cone has pale brown bracts between each scale.

Vejar Fir

Abies vejari

In the wild this is a rare mountain species, found mainly in the Mexican state of Tamaulipas, where it grows up to elevations around 3,000m (10,000ft), in mixed forests, with *Pinus hartwegii* and *P. rudis*. It is closely related to sacred fir, *Abies religiosa*, but differs in having irregularly arranged leaves, and shorter, squatter cones. Vejar fir was identified and named by Martinez in 1942. It is infrequently found in cultivation in arboreta and botanic gardens.

Identification: The needle-like leaves are forward-pointing, and borne all around the pale orange shoots. They are 1in (2.5cm) long, slightly grooved down the centre and tapering to a fine yellow point. They are dark blue-green above, with two lines of blue-white stomata beneath. As they twist forward some of the leaf underside points upwards. The barrel-shape cones are purple-black and covered in specks of hard white resin. On individual trees cone size may vary from 5 to 15cm (2 to 6in) in length.

Left: The barrel-shape cone stands upright.

Distribution: North-east Mexico, USA.
Height: 30m (100ft)
Shape: Broadly conical
Evergreen
Pollinated: Wind
Leaf shape: Linear

Below: Each needle-like leaf is forward-pointing and borne on pale orange shoots.

OTHER SPECIES OF NOTE
European Silver Fir *Abies alba*
This is the native silver fir of central Europe, particularly France, Switzerland and Germany, where it can attain heights in excess of 50m (165ft). It is a handsome tree, with glossy dark green needles, which have two distinctive white bands of stomata beneath. It is planted in parks and gardens right across temperate regions of the world, including North America. The silver fir is commonly used as a Christmas tree in many parts of Europe. See also page 304.

Abies oaxacana
This rare Mexican species is found in only a few locations in the western Sierra Madre Mountains of central Mexico, where it grows up to elevations of 2,000m (6,500ft). It is fairly tender, and consequently is found as an ornamental species in only botanical collections in California, Texas, and other southern states through to Florida. It is a medium-size tree, with conspicuous orange shoots, which contrast well with its dark green, needle-like leaves.

Corkbark Fir *Abies lasiocarpa* var. *arizonica*
This beautiful, narrow, spire-shape tree is a variety of the alpine fir, *A. lasiocarpa*. It grows wild in the Colorado Rocky Mountains, south into Arizona. It grows at high altitudes above the snowline, and has adapted to these conditions by producing a spire-like crown that does not allow snow to lie heavily upon the branches and break them – it simply slides off the sides to the ground. It appropriately takes its name from the fawn-coloured, thick corky bark.

Sacred Fir

Mexican fir *Abies religiosa*

Otherwise known as the Mexican fir, this tender species is common in the mountains of central Mexico, up to altitudes around 3,000m (10,000ft). In Mexico, its branches are used during religious festivals as decoration around mission halls. Outside Central America the sacred fir is relatively uncommon in cultivation. It has foliage and buds that look similar to the Douglas fir, *Pseudotsuga menziesii*, and the lower branches have a tendency to sweep down to the ground.

Identification: The bark is smooth and grey when young, becoming rough and scaly in maturity. The 2.5cm (1in) needles have two silver bands of stomata beneath. Leaves on the lower side of the shoot spread horizontally; those on the upper side point up and forward. The cones are 10–15cm (4–6in) long, barrel-shaped, purple-black, with distinctive reflexed tips to each cone scale, from which blue-black bracts protrude.

Distribution: Central and southern Mexico, northern Guatemala, USA.
Height: 30m (100ft)
Shape: Broadly conical
Evergreen
Pollinated: Wind
Leaf shape: Linear

Right: The needle-like leaves are dark glossy green above.

Below: As the cone ripens it turns chestnut-brown.

FALSE FIRS AND CEDARS

A group of ancient conifers belonging to the Pinaceae and Taxodiaceae families. The origins of all lay in the Jurassic period, 208–144 million years ago. Today, the Douglas fir and the Japanese red cedar are planted in their millions around the world for timber production. The others are scarcely seen outside botanical collections.

Japanese Red Cedar

Cryptomeria japonica

Distribution: Found in Japan in Honshu, Shikuka and Kyushu. It also grows in Chekiang and Fukien provinces in China. USA hardiness zones 5–9.
Height: 30m (100ft)
Shape: Broadly conical
Evergreen
Pollinated: Wind
Leaf shape: Linear

This stately conifer produces a large, straight trunk, which tapers quickly from a broad base above the roots. It has reddish-brown bark, which is soft, fibrous and peels off, hanging in long strips from the trunk. This tree has been extensively planted throughout Japan and China for its timber, which is strong, light and pink-brown. In the USA it grows at heights of 1,100–2,500m (3,600–8,200ft).

Identification: The crown is narrow when young, broadening with age. Often the heavy branches sweep downwards before ascending at the tips. The foliage consists of bright green branchlets covered with hard, forward-facing needles 1.5cm (⅝in) long. Male flowers are yellowish-brown, ovoid, and clustered along the final 1cm (⅜in) of each branchlet. They are bright yellow when ripe. Female flowers are green rosettes and are on the same tree as male flowers. Cones are globular, 2cm (¾in) across, and held on upright, stiff stalks.

Above: Branches occasionally touch the ground, causing layering.

Right: At the base of each needle is a protruding keel that runs down the branchlet.

Rocky Mountain Fir

Pseudotsuga menziesii var. *glauca*

This medium-size tree is the form of Douglas fir that grows away from the coast in the Rocky Mountains up to altitudes around 3,000m (10,000ft). It is hardier than the species, and more tolerant on soils with a high lime content. It is easily distinguished from the species by its glaucous-blue foliage, and the fact that when the foliage is crushed it emits the odour of paint thinner. The Rocky Mountain fir is widely grown as an ornamental in parks and gardens across the USA.

Above: Rocky Mountain fir has rigid blue needles, which are held at right angles to the shoot.

Distribution: Eastern crests of the Rocky Mountains from Montana to New Mexico.
Height: 25m (80ft)
Shape: Narrowly conical
Evergreen
Pollinated: Wind
Leaf shape: Linear

Identification: The bark is black-brown and extremely rough, even when young. The blue needle-like leaves are shorter and stouter than the species, up to 2.5cm (1in) long, and stand proud from the shoot. The female flowers are bright red, while those of the Douglas fir are greenish-pink. The copper-coloured cones are smaller than the species, less than 7.5cm (3in) long, with trident-shape, protruding bracts, which curve outwards from the cone.

Right: The cones are distinctive by their trident-shaped bracts, which protrude from beneath each cone scale.

Bigcone Douglas Fir

Pseudotsuga macrocarpa

This is the only Douglas fir with sharp, rigid, spine-tipped leaves. It grows wild on steep, rocky mountain slopes, up to altitudes around 2,000m (6,500ft), from the Santa Inez Mountains to the San Bernardino Mountains, and south to the Mexican border. It has a broad crown with sparse, long horizontal branches from which the foliage weeps. There are many forest fires in this part of the world and this tree has adapted to this by producing thick corky bark that is reasonably fire-resistant.

Left: The winged seed is contained beneath each large rounded cone scale and released when the cone matures in late winter.

Identification: The bark is heavily fissured, with the old bark showing grey, and that more recently exposed, pinky-brown. The needle-like leaves are dark blue-grey, up to 7.5cm (3in) long, and arranged in two neat ranks on each side of the reddish-brown shoot. Male flowers are orange-red, female's green-red, and both appear in spring on the same tree. The trident-shaped bract is present, as with all Douglas fir's, but not so obvious on this species.

Right: As the name suggests the cone is large – the largest in the genus – up to 18cm (7in) long.

Distribution: Southern California.
Height: 25m (80ft)
Shape: Broadly conical
Evergreen
Pollinated: Wind
Leaf shape: Linear

Douglas Fir

Pseudotsuga menziesii

Distribution: North-west Pacific Seaboard, from Mexico through USA to Canada including Vancouver Island.
Height: 75m (250ft)
Shape: Narrowly conical
Evergreen
Pollinated: Wind
Leaf shape: Linear

Below: Cones have bracts that project from each scale.

Douglas fir is commercially one of the most important timber-producing trees in the world. It has been planted throughout North America, Europe, Australia and New Zealand. It is a huge tree, attaining heights in excess of 75m (250ft). Quite often there is no branching for the first 33m (110ft). The bark is corky and deeply fissured in maturity; young trees have smooth, shiny grey-brown bark that is pockmarked with resin blisters.

Identification: When young this majestic tree is slender, regularly conical, with whorls of light, ascending branches. In old age it becomes flat-topped with heavy branches high up in the crown. Needles are linear to 3cm (1¼in) long, rounded at the tip. They are rich green with distinctive white banding beneath, and arranged spirally on the shoot. When crushed the foliage emits a sweet citrus aroma. Male flowers are yellow, and grow on the underside of the shoot. Female flowers are green, flushed pink to purple at the tip, and grow in separate clusters on the same tree. The fruit is a hanging cone up to 10cm (4in) long, green, ripening to orange-brown, with distinctive three-pronged bracts.

OTHER SPECIES OF NOTE
Japanese Douglas Fir
Pseudotsuga japonica
Native to Japan. This is the only Douglas fir from east Asia. It grows in the USA, Canada, Mexico, Japan and China. It is a small tree, to 20m (70ft). The linear leaves are soft, rounded at the tip and 2.5cm (1in) long. They are light green above, with two white bands of stomata beneath. The cones are ovoid, to 5cm (2in) long with 15–20 broad, rounded scales.

Chinese Fir *Cunninghamia lanceolata*
This hardy tree, has a domed crown of short, drooping branches that are covered with glossy, dark green, prickly, lance-shaped needles. It is an excellent ornamental species, the attractive foliage contrasting well with its chestnut-brown bark. It has the same range as Japanese Douglas fir. *See also page 302.*

Japanese Umbrella Pine
Sciadopitys verticillata
This tree grows at elevations up to 1,500m (5,000ft) on rocky slopes and ridges. It has been widely planted in North America as an ornamental due to its unusual leaf formation and its regular shape. It has whorls (spirals) of shiny green needles, which are deeply grooved up to 12cm (4½in) long and borne on pale brown shoots. *See also page 302.*

TWO- AND THREE-NEEDLED PINES

There are over 100 different pine species in the world, and almost half are native to North America and Mexico. They naturally divide into west-coast pines, central and east-coast pines, and southern pines North American pines include the oldest and some of the biggest trees in the world. Many are important timber-producing trees, and some have provided food for Native Americans for centuries.

Monterey Pine

Pinus radiata

Distribution: Californian coast around the Monterey Peninsula.
Height: 30m (100ft)
Shape: Broadly conical
Evergreen
Pollinated: Wind
Leaf shape: Linear

Right: Needles are held in threes, are shining dark green and are 10–15cm (4–6in) long.

The Monterey pine is a Californian coastal species with a very limited range. It is seldom found growing wild more than 10km (6 miles) from the coast. Discovered by the plant collector David Douglas in 1833, it has become one of the most widely planted trees for timber production in the world. In New Zealand it makes up more than 60 per cent of all conifers growing there, and covers more than 400,000ha (1 million acres).

Above: Cones may persist on the tree for up to 30 years.

Identification: The bark is dark grey and deeply fissured in old age. Young trees are conical, with sharply ascending branches. Older trees develop a large domed crown, which looks black from a distance. The male flowers are bright yellow and shed copious amounts of pollen in early spring. The cone is reddish-brown with dark grey scale centres. It is roughly ovoid in shape, up to 10cm (4in) across and held on a curved stalk 1cm (½in) long. Large, irregular scales tend to distort its overall shape.

Western Yellow Pine

Pinus ponderosa

The natural range of this pine is vast, stretching from the Pacific coast to elevations of 2,750m (9,000ft) in the Rocky Mountains in Colorado. It is planted as an ornamental species in large parks and gardens because of its attractive bark, fast growth and yellow leading shoots.

Identification: The bark is pale purple-grey, flaking to reveal attractive yellow, red and cinnamon-coloured bark beneath. As a young tree, it is narrow with strongly ascending branches. Older trees develop an irregular crown with several large, horizontal branches and dense foliage. The shoot is stout, bright yellow-brown and has clusters of needles, held in threes, along its length. The needles are up to 25cm (10in) long, dark grey-green and all face forward. Male flowers are dark purple and female flowers red. Both occur on the same tree. The cone is egg-shaped, up to 10cm (4in) long, glossy reddish-brown and has a hard spiny tip to each scale.

Above: Older trees often have an irregular clumped crown.

Distribution: North America, from British Columbia to Mexico.
Height: 50m (165ft)
Shape: Broadly conical
Evergreen
Pollinated: Wind
Leaf shape: Linear

Left: The needles are extremely long, each measuring up to 25cm (10in) from base to tip.

Lodgepole pine

Shore pine, Beach pine *Pinus contorta* var. *latifolia*

The lodgepole pine is so called because it was used by Native Americans to support their lodges. This prolific pine is not only common in the wild but has also been extensively planted in forests as a timber-producing tree. There are four different varieties of lodgepole pine. *Latifolia* is the true lodgepole pine, and is the pine of the Yellowstone Park geyser-basins and gorge. The natural range of the coastal form, *P. contorta* var. *contorta*, is along the Pacific coast in a belt about 160km (100 miles) broad, from the Alaska Panhandle to Point Arena in California.

Left: Each cone scale bears a blunt spine up to 6mm (¼in) long.

Identification: The bark is dark reddish-brown and deeply fissured into dark plates. Young trees have a broad bushy base with upswept branches and quite often swept stems. The needle-like, twisted leaves are held in twos and are 5cm (2in) long. Needle colour varies along its natural range, from dull, deep green in Oregon and California, to bright yellow-green further north. The cone is pale brown, 5cm (2in) long and points backwards along the shoot.

Distribution: Rocky Mountains from Alaska to California.
Height: 30m (100ft)
Shape: Broadly conical
Evergreen
Pollinated: Wind
Leaf shape: Linear

OTHER SPECIES OF NOTE

Scots Pine *Pinus sylvestris*
Although not native to North America, Scots pine is commonly planted from Quebec to Virginia, and from Saskatchewan to Iowa. It is popular as a Christmas tree. It has bright orange-red bark in maturity, which extends to the branches, where it peels and flakes. The needle-like leaves are borne in twos. They are stiff, twisted, bluish-green, set in an orange-brown basal sheath, and up to 7cm (2¾in) long. Although relatively slow growing it can attain heights around 35m (115ft). *See also page 315.*

Jack Pine *Pinus banksiana*
This tree, to 27m (90ft), has a natural range, which extends from the Yukon to Nova Scotia and south to New Hampshire. It grows further north than any other North American conifer. Jack pine grows extremely well on poor, impoverished soils and will be one of the first tree species to colonize sites of forest fires. The rigid, dark green, twisted, needle-like leaves are borne in twos and are 4cm (1½in) long. The 5cm- (2in-) long cones have a characteristic sweep at the tip and point forward along the shoot.

Knobcone Pine *Pinus attenuata*
Native from Oregon south through California to the Mexican state of Baja California, this medium-size tree, to 20m (65ft), has bright grass-green, needle-like leaves, which are borne in threes and are up to 15cm (6in) long. It has upward sweeping branches, which are covered in slender, conical, grey-brown cones that are up to 15cm (6in) long and can remain on the tree for years.

Big-Cone Pine

Pinus coulteri

As the name suggests, this pine produces just about the biggest cone of any pine. They may be up to 30cm (12in) long and weigh over 2kg (4½lb). Once mature and having released their seed, they may remain on the tree for up to ten years. The seeds are edible and were once considered a delicacy by Native Americans. The botanical name refers to Dr Coulter, who in 1831 identified big-cone pine.

Above: The needles are in clusters of three.

Below: The large cones have hooked spines to the ends of each scale.

Distribution: Southern California and north-western Mexico.
Height: 25m (80ft)
Shape: Broadly spreading
Evergreen
Pollinated: Wind
Leaf shape: Linear

Identification: This tree has a straight stem with sparse, stout branching, and foliage at the extremities. The bark is purple-brown becoming deeply fissured with scales in maturity. The needles are up to 25cm (10in) long, grey-green and stiff, and appear at the ends of light brown shoots. On the same tree the male flowers are purple opening yellow, the female's red. They are borne in separate clusters in late spring.

Slash Pine

Swamp pine *Pinus elliottii*

Otherwise known as the swamp pine, this broad, columnar, dark tree inhabits low-lying country on the coastal plains of the Florida Keys. It is also native to the Bahamas, Honduras and eastern Guatemala. It has a tall, tapering trunk, heavy, horizontal branches and, in maturity, a handsome round-topped head. It is much favoured for its timber, which is extremely hard and durable, being used in construction, and for railway sleepers.

Identification: The bark is smooth orange-brown when young, separating into large, thin scales in maturity. The needle-like leaves are dark green, lustrous, with several bands of silver stomata on both sides. They are 20–30cm (8–12in) long and borne in clusters of three (occasionally two). When crushed, they emit a strong lemon scent. The male flowers are dark purple, the female's pink. Both appear in early spring in separate, short, crowded clusters on the same tree. The ovoid, lustrous rich brown cone is up to 15cm (6in). Each cone scale carries a hard spine.

Distribution: Coast of South Carolina, through Florida to Louisiana.
Height: 30m (100ft)
Shape: Broadly columnar
Evergreen
Pollinated: Wind
Leaf shape: Linear

Left: The slash pine has an open crown.

Right: Large shiny-brown cones carry a hard spine on each scale.

Shortleaf Pine

Pinus echinata

This valuable timber tree is native to 21 American states. It is immediately recognizable by the way the needle-like leaves seem to sprout from everywhere on the tree, including the main branches, and sometimes the trunk. It is rarely seen planted in parks and gardens in North America or elsewhere in the world, for that matter, even though it was introduced to Europe as early as 1720.

Identification: The bark is a grey pinkish-orange, becoming scaly and shaggy in maturity. The young shoots (which are brittle) are covered in a distinctive blue-white bloom. Ironically, considering its name, the shortleaf pine has needle-like leaves, which can be up to 10cm (4in) long; they are fresh green above, paler beneath, with light bands of stomata. The 5cm- (2in-) long, light brown, almost oblong, cones are borne on a short stalk. Each cone scale bears a short prickly spine – the name *echinata* means "hedgehog-like".

Distribution: Eastern USA from New York state south to Florida and east Texas.
Height: 30m (100ft)
Shape: Broadly conical
Evergreen
Pollinated: Wind
Leaf shape: Linear

Right: The shortleaf pine has needle-like leaves which are seldom more than 10cm (4in) long.

Left: Each oblong-shaped cone is covered with short prickly spines.

Mexican Pinyon Pine

Pinus cembroides

Distribution: Mexico, Texas, Arizona and California.
Height: 15m (50ft)
Shape: Broadly columnar
Evergreen
Pollinated: Wind
Leaf shape: Linear

Above right: The male flowers are yellow and clustered together towards the tip of the shoot.

Right: As they ripen, the cones turn sandy-brown

This small bushy tree with a short, quite often twisted trunk, inhabits hot, dry, rocky slopes, particularly in the mountain ranges of central and southern Arizona, where it grows above altitudes of 2,000m (6,550ft). It is probably best known for its edible and tasty seeds, which are sold in Mexican markets as "pinones" and elsewhere as "pinyon nuts". It is rare in cultivation.

Identification: The bark is light gray, becoming grey-brown, and rough, in maturity. Both the trunk and main branches tend to twist and run horizontally. The dark green needle-like leaves, which are in threes, are 5cm (2in) long, and tightly packed along the shoots. The 5cm- (2in-) diameter, globular cones are olive-green and covered in resin when young. In maturity, the scales open to release wingless seed.

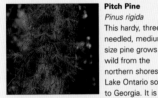

OTHER SPECIES OF NOTE

Pitch Pine
Pinus rigida
This hardy, three-needled, medium-size pine grows wild from the northern shores of Lake Ontario south to Georgia. It is distinctive because not only does it have thick, dark yellow-green, 10cm- (4in-) long, rigid needle-like leaves in the main crown, it also has tufts of much finer foliage sprouting from the stem and main branches. The resin of this tree was originally used to make pitch and paint thinner.

Digger Pine *Pinus sabiniana*
Native to the foothills around the Central Valley of California, this light-demanding, medium-size tree has curious, sparse, thin foliage, which gives an almost transparent effect to woodland it grows in. The needle-like leaves are borne in threes, up to 30cm (12in) long, and a pale greenish-grey colour.

Gregg Pine *Pinus greggii*
This beautiful rare pine is native to northeast Mexico where it attains heights of up to 30m (100ft). It has bright grass-green, needle-like leaves up to 15cm (6in) long, which are borne in threes, and have a very slight serration along the margins. They feel slightly rough to the skin. Gregg pine has clusters of shiny creamy-brown cones, also up to 15cm (6in) long, which persist on the tree for many years.

Loblolly Pine

Pinus taeda

The loblolly pine is a common tree in south-eastern USA, and is quite often seen as a roadside tree. Its timber is valued for construction work and interior joinery, so it is also widely grown in forestry plantations. It is an attractive tree with spreading lower branches, and ascending higher branches, which form a compact, round-topped head. It is sometimes called old field pine because it colonizes disused farmland.

Identification: The bark is bright red-brown and irregularly divided by linear fissures, which become scaly in maturity. The shoots are red-brown to pink-yellow, very slender, and covered with pale green to glaucous, stiff, needle-like leaves, up to 15cm (6in) long. The needles are borne in threes and are finely marked on both the upper and lower sides with fine white bands of stomata. Each scale of the cone is armed with a sharp spine.

Distribution: Virginia to Texas and south to Florida.
Height: 25m (80ft)
Shape: Broadly conical
Evergreen
Pollinated: Wind
Leaf shape: Linear

Below: The grey-brown cones are ovoid, 5–15cm (2–6in) long, and held by short stalks.

FIVE-NEEDLED PINES

*Of the 100 different pine species in the world, approximately twenty are five-needled pines
and among them are some of the most ornamental of all pines, including the beautiful
Mexican white pine,* Pinus ayacahuite, *and the Montezuma pine,* Pinus montezumae,
also from Mexico.

Sugar Pine

Pinus lambertiana

This is the largest pine in the world. It is
known, in the past, to have attained heights
in excess of 92m (300ft) tall with trunks
6m (20ft) across. It has massive cones,
which can be up to 60cm (24in) long.
The sugar pine gets its name because of its
edible, sugary sap, which was highly
prized by Native Americans. It has a
natural range from the Cascade
Mountains down the Sierra Nevada, and
across the border into lower California. It thrives
in mixed conifer forests. It was discovered in 1826
by David Douglas.

Distribution: From Oregon to
Baja California.
Height: 73m (235ft)
Shape: Broadly conical
Evergreen
Pollinated: Wind
Leaf shape:
Linear

Identification: Young bark is thin, smooth and brown-grey, maturing
to orange-pink, with fine fissures. Dried white resin trails are often a
feature of the bark. The needle-like leaves are borne in clusters of
fives, they are up to 10cm (4in) long, bluish-green and faintly serrated
at the margins. Magnificent golden-brown cones hang down from the
ends of the uppermost branches. They contain 2.5cm- (1in-) long
winged seeds, which are edible.

*Left: This is the largest pine in
the world, reaching heights in
excess of 92m (300ft).*

*Right: Each cone may
be up to 60cm
(24in) long and
contains large,
edible seeds.*

Eastern White Pine

Weymouth pine *Pinus strobus*

Distribution: Eastern North
America from Newfoundland
south to Georgia.
Height: 70m (225ft)
Shape: Narrowly conical
Evergreen
Pollinated: Wind
Leaf shape: Linear

*Right: Weymouth Pine cones
are pale brown and up to 15cm
(6in) long.*

Known elsewhere as the Weymouth pine, this is the largest
conifer, and the only five-needled pine to grow east of the
Rocky Mountains. It was, for many years, one of the USA's
main timber-producing trees, reliably producing long,
straight stems, which were originally used to make ships'
masts. It is prone to attack by a fungus that causes the fatal
disease known as white pine blister rust.

Identification: The bark is dark grey and smooth,
becoming deeply fissured in maturity. The slender,
needle-like leaves are up to 12cm (4¾in) long, borne in
clusters of fives, blue-green above and silver-
grey beneath. Male flowers are yellow, the female's
pink, borne in separate clusters on the same tree in late
spring. The eastern white pine has pale brown, hanging,
cylindrical cones, which are up to 15cm (6in) long, often
curved like a banana, and covered with a sticky white resin.

*Left: Slender needles, clustered in fives,
may be up to 12cm (4¾in) long.*

Montezuma Pine

Pinus montezumae

This pine is named after the early sixteenth-century Aztec emperor, Montezuma II. It is a very variable tree with several different forms, all extremely attractive, mainly because of its long, distinctive foliage. It is a fairly tender species, only surviving in the mildest regions of North America and Great Britain.

Identification: The Montezuma pine has pinkish-grey, rough bark with wide, brownish, vertical fissures, leaving ridges, which are cracked horizontally. The juvenile crown is gaunt, with a few ascending branches; however, as it matures, it develops a huge, low dome, with upturned shoots covered with long, lax, brush-like foliage. Male flowers are purple, ripening to yellow; female flowers are red. The cone is conical and up to 15cm (6in) long.

Distribution: North-east Mexico and south into Guatemala.
Height: 20m (66ft)
Shape: Broadly spreading
Evergreen
Pollinated: Wind
Leaf shape: Linear

Left: The blue-green needles are up to 30cm (12in) long.

Ancient Pine

Pinus longaeva

This species, allied to the bristlecone pine, *P. aristata*, contains some of the oldest living trees on earth. The oldest tree is reliably recorded at being more than 4,700 years old and is affectionately known as Methuselah. It is found growing 3,475m (11,400ft) up in the White Mountains of California.

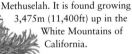

Left: Both needles and cones have a scruffy, feather-like appearance.

Distribution: From the White Mountains, eastern California, through central Utah and southern Nevada.
Height: 15m (50ft)
Shape: Broadly conical
Evergreen
Pollinated: Wind
Leaf shape: Linear

Identification: This species has scaly, black-grey bark. Young trees are conical in habit, but old trees become gnarled and spreading. The shoot is red-brown and hairy, with needles tightly clustered in fives along its length. Needles are approximately 3cm (1¼in) long, and shiny grey-green on top, with white stomata, and resin canals visible as two grooves on the underside. They persist on the tree for anything up to 30 years. Cones are ovoid, rounded at the base, up to 10cm (4in) long and a rich chestnut-red. This species is particularly hardy, being able to withstand prolonged winter periods with temperatures well below freezing, and long summer periods of drought.

OTHER SPECIES OF NOTE
Mexican White Pine *Pinus ayacahuite*
This beautiful tree attains heights of up to 35m (115ft) in its native Mexico and northern Guatemala. It is extremely hardy and grows high on mountain slopes. It has graceful, drooping foliage with blue-green, slender, lax needles, up to 15cm (6in) long. The cone can grow up to 45cm (18in) long and is normally covered with sticky white resin.

Western White Pine *Pinus monticola*
This distinctive, handsome tree is native to the eastern Rocky Mountains, from Alberta to Montana, and down the west coast, from British Columbia to California. It has similar features to its close relative, the eastern white pine, *Pinus strobus*; they are both large trees with a slender pyramidal shape, and they both have needles in clusters of five. The needles of the western white pine are stiffer and shorter, 7.5cm (3in), and the shoot is covered in dense short hairs.

Bristlecone Pine *Pinus aristata*
This tree is closely related to the ancient pine, *Pinus longaeva*, which is confusingly quite often called bristlecone pine. However, they are two distinctly different species. *P. aristata* is a small tree with thick, hairy, red-brown shoots. The needle-like leaves are in fives, to 5cm (2in) long and spotted with white resin, which is not the case on *P. longaeva*. It also has longer bristle-like spines on the tip of each cone scale than *P. longaeva*.

SPRUCES

The spruces, Picea, *are a group of hardy evergreen conifers that grow throughout much of the colder regions of the Northern Hemisphere. They are different to firs,* Abies, *in one significant way. On all spruces there is a peg-like stump at the base of every needle. When the needles fall this peg remains, creating a rough texture to the shoot. Firs have smooth shoots.*

Brewer Spruce

Picea breweriana

Although relatively rare in the wild, the Brewer spruce has been widely cultivated in parks, gardens and arboreta. Trusses of ribbon-like foliage hang from downward-arching, evenly spaced, slender branches. This tree comes from a region of high snowfall, and has adapted this weeping habit so that snow can be easily shed, thus protecting the branches from breakage.

Above: The cone is a narrow cylinder, 10–12cm (4–4¾in) long and light red-brown.

Identification: Dull, dark grey-pink bark when young, maturing to purple-grey with prominent roughly circular plates of bark, which curl away from the trunk at the edges. Male flowers are yellow and red, positioned on the ends of hanging shoots. Female flowers are dark red, cylindrical and found only on topmost shoots. Needles are soft, positioned all around the shoot, point forwards, and up to 3cm (1¼in) long. Their upper surface is glossy dark green and dulls with age. The lower surface has prominent, bright white, linear stomatal bands.

Distribution: The Siskiyou and Shasta Mountains bordering Oregon and California.
Height: 35m (15ft)
Shape: Narrowly weeping
Evergreen
Pollinated: Wind
Leaf shape: Linear

Left: Brewer spruce is one of the most beautiful conifers. It has a very graceful, weeping habit.

Sitka Spruce

Picea sitchensis

Distribution: Narrow coastal strip from Kodiak Island, Alaska, to Mendocino County, California, USA.
Height: 50m (165ft)
Shape: Narrowly conical
Evergreen
Pollinated: Wind
Leaf shape: Linear

The largest of the North American spruces, this is a major species within northwest American forests. Valued for its timber, Sitka spruce has been widely planted across the Northern Hemisphere in forestry plantations. The timber is pale pinkish-brown and very strong for its light weight. Originally used for aircraft framing, it is now the major species used in pulp for paper manufacture.

Far left: Male flower.

Left: Female flower.

Right: Cones are pale buff, 10cm (4in) long, have thin papery scales and are pendulous in habit.

Identification: Bark in young trees is a deep purple-brown colour. Older trees have large, curving cracks, which develop into plates of lifting bark. The overall shape is an open, narrow cone, with widely spaced, slender, ascending branches. Sitka spruce can easily grow more than 1m (3ft) a year when young. Needles are stiff with a sharp point, blue-green above with two white stomatal bands beneath, and up to 3cm (1¼in) long. They are arranged all around the pale, buff-coloured shoot. Male flowers are reddish and occur in small quantities on each tree, shedding pollen in late spring. Female's are greenish-red, appearing only on the topmost shoots.

Engelmann's Spruce *Picea engelmannii*
This tall tree grows up to 40m (130ft) in height, and is native to the Rocky Mountains, from Alberta to New Mexico. It is a natural survivor, being very hardy, and growing on exposed sites in impoverished soils. It has red-brown bark and a narrow crown with dense, level branching. The needles are bluish-green, 2cm (¾in) long, and when crushed, emit a strong menthol fragrance.

Blue Engelmann's Spruce
Picea engelmannii 'Glauca'
This is a slender, attractive cultivar, which has orange flaking bark and bright glaucous, blue-grey, soft needles, with vibrant white stomatal banding. It has a pendulous cone, which is up to 6cm (2½in) long, thin, papery and found mostly in clusters at the top of the tree.

Likiang Spruce *Picea likiangensis*
A beautiful Chinese spruce widely cultivated as an ornamental species across North America. It has a graceful form with widely spaced horizontal branches. However, its most attractive feature is its bright red male and female flowers.

In spring are produced in such profusion that, from a distance, it looks as if the tree is covered with burning embers. *See also page 311.*

Colorado Spruce

Blue spruce *Picea pungens*

Otherwise known as the blue spruce (because of its blue-green needles), the Colorado spruce grows in the Rocky Mountains at altitudes up to 3,000m (10,000ft). It is often found growing as a solitary specimen on dry slopes and beside dried-up stream beds. It was discovered in 1862 on Pike's Peak, Colorado, by Dr C. C. Parry, who sent seeds to Harvard University.

Distribution: Montana, Colorado, Utah, Arizona, New Mexico.
Height: 35m (115ft)
Shape: Narrowly conical
Evergreen
Pollinated: Wind
Leaf shape: Linear

Above: The cone is a pale brown to cream, pendulous cylinder, up to 10cm (4in) long, with thin scales wrinkled at the margins.

Identification: The dark red-brown bark is rough with scales. The tree has a narrow conical form with short, level branches. It has shiny, pale yellow-brown shoots that are slightly hairy, but it is best identified by its foliage. The needles are an attractive blue-grey to grey-green, with a slight glaucous bloom, up to 3cm (1¼in) long, and arranged all around the shoot. Male flowers are red and the female's green. They appear in separate clusters on the same tree in late spring.

Red Spruce

Picea rubens

This widespread tree is found in north-eastern North America from Newfoundland down the Appalachian Mountains to northern Georgia, where it thrives on wet, acid soils. The red spruce is a long-lived species, easily reaching 150 years old. It is able to tolerate low light levels, and will grow in shady forest conditions.

Identification: When young, the bark is a rich purplish-red colour, peeling away in flakes. In older trees the bark is a dark purple-grey, cracking into irregular concave plates. The crown remains narrowly conical throughout the life of the tree. It has a rather dense form that tapers to a clear spire. The needles are thin, wiry, up to 1.5cm (⅝in) long and lie forwards on the shoot but curve inwards. They are glossy, grassy green and when crushed, emit a fragrance reminiscent of apples or camphor. Male flowers are bright crimson. The cones are 4–5cm (1½–2in) long, pale orange-brown with convex scales, which are crinkled and finely toothed.

Above: Young needles are a rich light green.

Below: The cones hang from the shoots.

Distribution: Nova Scotia to North Carolina.
Height: 25m (82ft)
Shape: Narrowly conical
Evergreen
Pollinated: Wind
Leaf shape: Linear

Left: A female flower.

Right: The distinctive red male flowers gave rise to this tree's common name.

Black Spruce

Picea mariana

This extremely hardy spruce occurs right across the north of North America, where it survives in subarctic tundra conditions at the northerly limit for any trees. It is a slow-growing tree, particularly in the far north, and so the leading shoots are always short. This gives the tree a dense, neat appearance, with short branches and short, tightly packed needles. It is this density of foliage, particularly when young, that gives the tree its black appearance, and therefore its name.

Identification: The bark is grey-brown and flaking. The needle-like leaves are slender, to 1.5cm (½in) long, dark blue-green above, blue-white beneath and borne all around pink-brown shoots. When crushed the needles emit the scent of menthol cough drops. Male and female flowers are both red, the male's are carried at the ends of the shoots, and the female's are clustered on the topmost branches. The cones are egg-shaped, shiny red-brown, and less than 5cm (2in) long.

Distribution: Pennsylvania north to Newfoundland and across Canada to Alaska.
Height: 20m (70ft)
Shape: Narrowly conical
Evergreen
Pollinated: Wind
Leaf shape: Linear

Left: The foliage of this tree is dense.

Above: Short needle-like leaves are blue-green above and blue-white beneath.

Above: The cone is a shiny red-brown egg shape and up to 5cm (2in) long. It matures in one year.

White Spruce

Picea glauca

This tough medium-size tree inhabits land with much the same inhospitable growing conditions as the black spruce, *Picea mariana*. In 1905 Charles Sargent of The Arnold Arboretum, Boston, suggested that the white spruce reached higher latitudes than any other evergreen tree, nearly to the Artic Sea, on ground that thawed for only three to four months each summer. It is not particularly ornamental, but has been widely planted in exposed areas to provide shelter.

Identification: The bark is grey-brown, becoming finely fissured and scaly in maturity. The needle-like leaves are positioned mostly on the upper side of the whitish-fawn shoots. They are greenish blue-grey with white bands of stomata on each surface, 1cm (½in) long, pointed but not prickly. Male flowers are red opening yellow, and the female's are purple. Both appear in separate clusters on the same tree in spring. The cone is cylindrical, up to 5cm (2in) long, pale, shiny brown with thin and flexible scales.

Distribution: Across Canada from Alaska to Labrador.
Height: 20m (70ft)
Shape: Narrowly conical
Evergreen
Pollinated: Wind
Leaf shape: Linear

Left: The leaves are mostly on the top of the shoot.

Right: The cone is cylindrical, shiny brown, up to 5cm (2in) and covered with thin papery scales.

Norway Spruce

Picea abies

The Norway spruce has a regular, symmetrical form with horizontal branching at low levels, gradually becoming upswept towards the top of the tree. It grows naturally in northern Europe up to altitudes of around 1,500m (4,921ft). In America it has been cultivated for its timber, especially in the north-eastern USA, south-eastern Canada, the Pacific Coast states and the Rocky Mountain states. It is traditionally used to make the bellies of violins and other stringed instruments.

Left: Cones hang downwards.

Identification: The bark in young trees is deep coppery-pink; on older trees it becomes dark purple, with shallow, round or oval plates, which lift away from the trunk. The needles are rich dark green with a faint sheen, and are up to 2cm (¾in) long. When crushed, they emit a citrus fragrance, which has become synonymous with Christmas. Male flowers are a golden color, shedding copious amounts of pollen in late spring. Female flowers are purple-red, and frequently confined to the top of the tree. Cones are pendulous, cylindrical, slightly curved and up to 15cm (6in) long.

Left: Male flowers occur in groups at shoot tips.

Right: A female flower.

Distribution: Most of northern Europe (excluding UK), from the Pyrenees to western Russia.
Height: 50m (165ft)
Shape: Narrowly conical
Evergreen
Pollinated: Wind
Leaf shape: Linear

OTHER SPECIES OF NOTE

Oriental Spruce *Picea orientalis*
Also called the Caucasian spruce, this attractive tree originates from the Caucasus Mountains and on into Turkey, where it grows on mountainsides up to 2,140m (7,021ft). In maturity it has a dense, columnar form with short, shiny, green needles 1cm (½in) long. Cones have a distinct ash-brown colour. *See also page 308.*

Hybrid American Spruce *Picea x lutzii*
This medium-size hybrid tree was identified in Alaska in 1950, and recognized as a natural cross between Sitka spruce and white spruce. It has the potential to become a major tree within timber plantations because it takes important characteristics from both parents. It has inherited the strength and durability found in Sitka spruce timber, and the hardiness of white spruce, which means it can grow in colder regions of North America, which have not yet been colonized by good timber-producing trees.

Tiger-tail Spruce *Picea polita*
This ornamental, pyramidal-shaped, medium-size spruce originates from central and southern Japan. It is one of the most striking and attractive spruces. Consequently, it has been widely planted in parks and gardens across North America. The needle-like leaves are up to 5cm (2in) long; rigid and spine-tipped – probably the sharpest of any spruce – they are flattened and stand out at right angles to the chestnut-brown shoot. The name "tiger-tail" is derived from the appearance of the foliage-covered branch ends, which are pendulous, much like a tiger's tail.

Serbian Spruce

Picea omorika

The Serbian spruce has a very small natural population and because of this is considered to be endangered in the wild. It is a beautiful, slender, spire-like tree with branches that sweep elegantly downwards, only to arch upwards at their tip. This habit means that it is able to resist damage by efficiently shedding snow rather than collecting it. It is also the most resistant spruce to atmospheric pollution.

Identification: The bark is orange-brown to copper, and broken into irregular to square plates. The shoot is a similar colour to the bark and quite hairy. The needles are short with a blunt tip, less than 2cm (¾in) long, glossy dark green above, with two broad, white stomatal bands underneath. The male flowers are crimson and held below new shoots; the female flowers are also red, but confined to the topmost branches. The Serbian spruce's most distinctive characteristic is its spire-like form.

Distribution: Europe: confined to the Drina Valley in south-west Serbia. In the USA it grows in hardiness zone 3.
Height: 30m (100ft)
Shape: Very narrowly conical
Evergreen
Pollinated: Wind
Leaf shape: Linear

Above: The cone is pendulous, held on a thick curved stalk, tear-shaped, 6cm (2½in) long and purple-brown in colour.

DECIDUOUS LARCHES

This small genus of fewer than a dozen species is confined to temperate regions of the Northern Hemisphere. Deciduous larches are fast-growing conifers, and several species have been widely planted for forestry purposes. Larches are some of the most seasonally attractive conifers. Their needles turn gold and drop in the autumn, to be renewed every spring with a flush of lime-green foliage.

European Larch

Larix decidua

This attractive, hardy tree grows naturally at altitudes up to 2,500m (8,200ft) above sea level. It is a long-lived conifer, with some trees in the Alps recorded at over 700 years old. European larch has been widely planted throughout Europe and North America for both forestry and ornamental reasons.

Identification: Bark on young trees is pale grey and smooth. Old trees have heavily fissured, dark pink bark. Whorls of upswept branches are well spaced. Needles are soft, 4cm (1½in) long and bright green, becoming yellow before dropping in autumn. They are carried singly on main shoots and in dense whorls on side shoots. The shoots are pendulous and straw coloured. Male flowers are pink-yellow rounded discs, normally on the underside of the shoots. Female flowers appear before the leaves in early spring. They are purple-pink, upright and develop quickly into an immature cone.

Right and left: Cones are 4.5cm (1¾in) long.

Distribution: From the Alps through Switzerland, Austria and Germany to the Carpathian Mountains of Slovakia and Romania. USA zone 3.
Height: 40m (130ft)
Shape: Narrowly conical
Deciduous
Pollinated: Wind
Leaf shape: Linear

Western Larch

Hackmatack *Larix occidentalis*

Distribution: From British Columbia south to Oregon and east to Montana.
Height: 50m (164ft)
Shape: Narrowly conical
Deciduous
Pollinated: Wind
Leaf shape: Linear

This magnificent tree, otherwise known as hackmatack, is the largest of all the larches reaching, in some instances, 60m (200ft) tall. It grows at elevations up to 2,000m (7,000ft) in both the Rockies and the Cascade Mountains. It is most prevalent around the Flat Head Lake area of northern Montana, which is where the tallest trees are found. It is fast growing, sometimes forming pure forests, although it is more often found growing alongside lodgepole pine, *Pinus contorta* var. *latifolia*. Seedlings will germinate prolifically on bare ground cleared of other vegetation by forest fires.

Identification: The bark is reddish-brown, thick and deeply fissured into large scales in maturity. The needle-like leaves are bright green and soft, to 4cm (1½in) long, borne in dense whorls on slow-growing side shoots and singly on leading shoots. In autumn they turn golden-yellow. The male flowers are yellow, the female flowers are red, and both are produced on the same tree in separate clusters in early spring. The cone is ovoid, borne in an upright fashion on the branch, about 2cm (¾in) long, with thin scales from which a papery fawn-coloured, tongue-like bract protrudes.

Right: Soft needle-like leaves emerge from winter buds in early spring.

Subalpine Larch

Larix lyallii

Subalpine larch is a tree of the mountains, growing naturally in the northern Rockies and Cascades up to elevations around 2,500m (8,000ft). It quite often demarcates the tree line between bare rock and scree, and the upper limits of tree cover. Its appearance is rather like a short, stunted, drooping western larch, *Larix occidentalis*. It is slow growing, and develops a gnarled windswept appearance from a relatively early age. *L. lyallii* was discovered in 1858 by Scots surgeon David Lyall.

Identification: The bark is thin, smooth and pale grey when young, maturing red-brown with fissures and loosely attached scales. The needle-like leaves are four-angled, pale blue-green, 2.5cm (1in) long, and tufted along densely felted young shoots. Both male and female flowers are dark red to purple, appearing separately on the same tree in early spring. The ovoid, 5cm- (2in-) long cones have a ragged appearance because of the long, twisted bract that curls out from beneath each scale.

Right: The deciduous needle-like leaves are pale blue-green and borne in clusters along young shoots, which are covered with pubescence.

Distribution: Alberta, British Columbia, Idaho, Montana and Washington.
Height: 20m (65ft)
Shape: Narrowly conical
Deciduous
Pollinated: Wind
Leaf shape: Linear

Right: Female flowers are dark red to purple and appear on the tree slightly before the leaves appear in early spring.

OTHER SPECIES OF NOTE

Hybrid Larch *Larix x eurolepis*
The is a hybrid between the European larch, *L. decidua*, and the Japanese larch, *L. kaempferi*. Both species were planted in close proximity to each other at Dunkeld House, Scotland. In 1897 seed was collected from these trees and propagated; the resulting seedlings were identified as hybrids in 1919. They differ from each parent, being more vigorous, and having a deep orange-brown shoot. *See also page 313.*

Japanese Larch *Larix kaempferi*
In the wild this tree grows on the volcanic mountains of the island of Honshu, at heights up to 2,750m (9,000ft). It is an attractive, deciduous conifer, with bright purple-red young shoots, bedecked with fresh green needles, and upward-sweeping branches, especially when young. It is widely grown as an ornamental tree across the USA. *See also page 312.*

Golden Larch *Pseudolarix amabilis*
This slow-growing, deciduous conifer has many characteristics of true larches. It has bright green, deciduous, needle-like leaves, which turn golden in autumn, and pinky-fawn to straw-colour shoots. Unlike true larches in having cones like small globe artichokes, which disintegrate on the tree once ripe and release the seeds. *See also page 313.*

Tamarack

American Larch, Hackmatack *Larix laricina*

This hardy tree is just as much at home on an exposed mountainside as in a boggy swamp. Although widespread in the wild, it is rare in cultivation. A short-lived tree, it is very slow growing, and colonizes inhospitable ground long before other trees.

Identification: Tamarack is a narrow, thin tree with short, level branches. The branches have a characteristic curled tip, which curls upwards and inwards back towards the crown. Young shoots are pink, turning brown as they mature. Needles are soft, blue-green, 2.5cm (1in) long and have two grey stomatal bands beneath. Male flowers are numerous, small and yellow, growing beneath the shoot. Female flowers are red and held upright on the shoot.

Distribution: Alaska and Canada south to New Jersey and Maryland.
Height: 20m (66ft)
Shape: Narrowly conical
Deciduous
Pollinated: Wind
Leaf shape: Linear

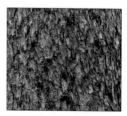

Above: The bark is pinkish-orange, flaking into small circular scales.

Left: Cones have few scales and are pale brown, ovoid, erect and up to 2cm (¾in) long.

TULIP TREES AND MAGNOLIAS

The Magnoliaceae family contains 12 genera and just over 200 species. The majority of species are native to North America or Asia. They include some of the most beautiful of all flowering trees. Magnolias are planted in gardens the world over and countless cultivars have been developed. There are magnolias to suit all locations – some are giants, others little more than large shrubs.

Tulip Tree

Yellow poplar *Liriodendron tulipifera*

This magnificent tree is one of the largest and fastest-growing deciduous trees in North America. It stands out from the crowd for several reasons, including its size, its flower, its leaf shape and its ability to withstand atmospheric pollution. It is an adaptable tree, growing in extreme climatic conditions, from severe Canadian winters to subtropical Florida summers.

Identification: The bark is grey-brown and smooth, becoming fissured with age. In maturity, tulip trees have clear, straight stems with broad crowns. The dark green leaves are up to 15cm (6in) long, being lobed on each side with a cut-off, indented leaf tip. The underside of the leaf is almost bluish-white. In autumn the leaves turn a butter-yellow colour before dropping. Flowers are produced in summer once the tree reaches 12–15 years old. They are upright, 6cm (2½in) long, tulip-shaped and have nine petals: some are green; some are light green to yellowy-orange at the base. Inside each flower is a bright cluster of orange-yellow stamens. Unfortunately, because of the ranchless stem of older trees, the flowers are often positioned at the top of the tree, so it is difficult to admire their beauty.

Distribution: Eastern North America from Ontario to New York in the north, to Florida in the south.
Height: 50m (165ft)
Shape: Broadly columnar
Deciduous
Pollinated: Bee
Leaf shape: Simple

Left: As the flowers fade on the tree, the leaves change colour giving Liriodendron tulipifera *a second flourish of beauty.*

Cucumber Tree

Mountain magnolia *Magnolia acuminata*

Sometimes called the mountain magnolia because it has the ability to grow at altitudes up to 1,220m (4,000ft) in the Smoky Mountains, this is the largest of the seven magnolias native to North America. The common name "cucumber" is derived from the unripe seed pods, which are up to 18cm (7in) long, green and fleshy.

Identification: The brown-grey bark is unlike that of any other North American magnolia; it is rough and divided into narrow ridges with vertical fissures. The overall form is of a tall, broad tree with a conical crown of mainly upswept branches. The leaf is elliptical to ovate, 25cm (10in) long and 15cm (6in) across, rich green above, blue-green and slightly hairy below. The flowers appear in early to mid-summer; they are blue-green to yellow-green, bell-shaped, 9cm (3½in) long and quite often lost among the foliage. The seed pod ripens from a cucumber-like fruit into an erect, bright red cylinder 7.5cm (3in) long, containing as many as 50 seeds.

Left: The flowers appear in summer but are often difficult to see among the leaves.

Distribution: Eastern North America from Ontario to Alabama.
Height: 30m (100ft)
Shape: Broadly conical
Deciduous
Pollinated: Insect
Leaf shape: Simple ovate

Left: Red cylindrical seed pods appear from the middle of summer onwards.

Bull Bay

Magnolia grandiflora

This magnificent, evergreen, flowering tree is more often than not grown as a wall shrub. However, given a warm, sheltered, sunny position it will develop into a broad-canopied, short-stemmed tree. *Magnolia grandiflora* grows best close to the coast and at low altitudes; it rarely thrives above 150m (500ft). The combination of glossy, dark green, leathery leaves and creamy white flowers makes it a very popular garden tree.

Identification: The bark is grey-brown, cracking into irregular small plates. The leaves, which grow up to 25cm (10in) long and 10cm (4in) across, are thick, rigid, glossy dark green above, and either pale green, or covered in copper hairs beneath. Flowers will begin to appear when the tree is only ten years old; they are wide-brimmed and cup-shaped, creamy white to pale lemon and deliciously scented. They can be up to 30cm (12in) across and stand out splendidly against the dark foliage.

Above: The spectacular flowers are like dinner plates, measuring up to 30cm (12in) across.

Left: In the wild, flowers are produced in spring.

Distribution: North American south-east coastal strip from north Carolina to Florida and west along the gulf to south-east Texas.
Height: 25m (82ft)
Shape: Broadly conical
Evergreen
Pollinated: Insect
Leaf shape: Elliptic to ovate

Right: These red seed pods will first appear in midsummer.

OTHER SPECIES OF NOTE

Magnolia 'Charles Raffill'
This is a hybrid between *M. campbellii* and the subspecies *M. campbellii mollicomata*. It is a vigorous, deciduous tree, easily reaching 25m (82ft) in height and, once established, grows up to 60cm (24in) a year. It produces large, deep pink, goblet-shaped flowers in early spring.

Magnolia 'Elizabeth'
This hybrid between *M. acuminata* and *M. denudata* is a small, deciduous, conical tree. It produces pale primrose-yellow, fragrant, cup-shaped flowers in early to mid-spring before the leaves emerge from their winter bud. It was raised at the Brooklyn Botanic Garden, and named after Elizabeth Scholtz, director in 1978.

Magnolia 'Samuel Somner'
This magnificent form of *M. grandiflora* produces probably the largest flowers of any magnolia. They are creamy white, very fragrant, saucer-shaped and up to 35cm (14in) across. The leaves are evergreen, thick, leathery, glossy dark green on the top side and deep brown and hairy beneath. This form is very hardy and wind-resistant and can be grown in the open.

Magnolia 'Wada's Memory'
This lovely deciduous hybrid between *M. kobus* and *M. salicifolia* is broadly conical and grows to about 10m (33ft) tall. It produces white, fragrant flowers, which are cylinder-like as they emerge from the bud in early spring, opening to a lax, saucer shape, approximately 15cm (6in) across. The flowers are held horizontally on the branch.

Sweet Bay

Swampbay *Magnolia virginiana*

This large shrub, or small tree, thrives on coastal plains and in wet swampy conditions. It was the earliest North American magnolia to be introduced to Europe, arriving in Great Britain in 1688. In the wild, the tallest trees tend to grow in the Carolinas and Florida, where heights of 25m (82ft) have been recorded. Elsewhere it seldom achieves 10m (33ft).

Identification: The bark of sweet bay is smooth and grey. The overall form is normally shrubby, with branching low on the stem. Leaves are ovate in shape, up to 12cm (4¾in) long and 6cm (2½in) wide. They are deep lustrous green above, and blue-white and downy beneath, especially when young. The flowers are creamy white, maturing quickly to pale yellow. They are cup-shaped at first, opening to a broad saucer. The flowers are short-lived, but produced over a long period, from early to late summer, and are highly scented. The sweet bay rarely sets seed in Europe. This tree used to be known as the beaver tree because early American colonists used its sweet fleshy roots to bait beaver traps.

Distribution: Eastern United States from Massachusetts to Florida.
Height: 25m (82ft)
Shape: Broadly spreading
Semi-evergreen
Pollinated: Insect
Leaf shape: Ovate

Left: Flowers are produced throughout the summer.

Umbrella Magnolia

Magnolia tripetala

This small, hardy tree is native to mountain valleys throughout eastern USA. It grows in woodland shade and quite often beside streams in valley bottoms. It has fragrant flowers and striking foliage, making it an extremely popular ornamental tree in gardens across the USA. It was identified by American plant collector John Bartram in the 18th century, and since then, has been widely cultivated across the western world. It requires acid soil to grow well.

Identification: The bark is pale grey and smooth. The heavily veined leaves are huge, and not dissimilar to a tobacco leaf. They can be up to 50cm (20in) long and 25cm (10in) wide, rich green above, and sage-green below with soft down. They are borne in large whorls at the tips of the shoots, which look like umbrellas. The loose goblet-shaped flowers appear in late spring; they are 20cm (8in) across, creamy white, very fragrant, with up to 12 narrow, waxy, spreading petals (tepals). The fruit is a squat banana-shaped cone, up to 10cm (4in) long, and covered with crimson seeds.

Distribution: Eastern USA from Pennsylvania to Georgia.
Height: 12m (40ft)
Shape: Broadly spreading
Deciduous
Pollinated: Insect
Leaf shape: Obovate to elliptic

Above: After dropping in October, the large leaves take a long time to decompose and skeletal leaf remains will still be evident beneath the tree the following spring.

Campbell's Magnolia

Magnolia campbellii

This majestic tree is capable of attaining heights up to 30m (100ft) in less than 60 years. It is a hardy tree, growing up to 3,000m (9,850ft) above sea level in the Himalayas. It grows well in the warmer states of the USA. It is grown for its dramatic flowers, which appear only after 20 years. They appear as early as mid-winter and are prone to frost damage.

Below: The flowers are up to 30cm (12in) across.

Identification: The bark is smooth and grey, even in old age. The leaves are up to 30cm (12in) long, with a pronounced point, medium green above, sometimes faintly hairy beneath. The flower buds are large, ovoid and covered in grey hairs. They stand out dramatically on the bare branches in late winter. The flowers are even more dramatic, beginning goblet-shaped, but opening to a lax cup-and-saucer shape, up to 30cm (12in) across. The colour can vary from deep pink to pale pinkish-white. There is a slight fragrance to the flower. Each flower is held upright on a smooth green stalk. The fruit is a cylindrical, cone-like pod, up to 15cm (6in) long, containing bright red seed.

Right: The huge flowers often appear in profusion, both on cultivated and wild trees.

Distribution: Himalayas from Nepal to Assam and on into south-west China.
Height: 30m (100ft)
Shape: Broadly conical
Deciduous
Pollinated: Insect
Leaf shape: Obovate

Ashe's Magnolia

Magnolia ashei

This small tree, or large shrub, is a woodland plant requiring dappled shade. It inhabits deep sandy soils near streams in woodlands in north-western Florida. It was identified by American botanist Ashe, in 1928. It is closely related to the large-leaved magnolia, *M. macrophylla*. It is rare in the wild, but is becoming increasingly common in cultivation.

Distribution: North-west Florida.
Height: 10m (33ft)
Shape: Broadly columnar
Deciduous
Pollinated: Insect
Leaf shape: Elliptic

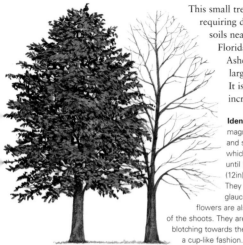

Identification: In common with most magnolias, the bark of *M. ashei* is pale grey and smooth, even in maturity. The leaves, which quite often do not emerge from bud until late spring, are broadly elliptic, up to 30cm (12in) long and 20cm (8in) broad. They are bright green above, glaucous beneath. The fragrant flowers are also borne at the ends of the shoots. They are white with purple blotching towards the base, and arranged in a cup-like fashion.

Left: The leaves are borne in whorls at the ends of the shoots.

Left: The outer petals (tepals) sometimes have a greenish hue. The flowers appear towards the end of spring into early summer.

OTHER SPECIES OF NOTE

Hybrid Magnolia *Magnolia* x *soulangeana*
A hybrid between *M. denudata* and *M. liliiflora*, this is the most widely planted ornamental magnolia. The deciduous, obovate leaves are up to 20cm (8in) long and 12cm (4¾in) wide. The flowers become cup-and-saucer-like with age. They are creamy white, with a pink tinge to the base of each thick petal. *See also page 324.*

Star Magnolia *Magnolia stellata*
This slow-growing, compact Japanese tree, or large shrub, seldom reaches more than 3m (10ft) in height. Its flowers appear on bare branches in late winter and early spring. The flowers are fragrant, pure white, maturing to pale pink, star-shaped, and have 12–18 petals. In the 1860s it was introduced to the USA. *See also page 324.*

Lily Tree *Magnolia denudata*
Also known as "yulan", this is one of the most beautiful flowering trees. It has been cultivated in Buddhist temple gardens, and around imperial palaces, for 1,300 years. The "water lily-like" flowers are pure white and faintly scented of lemons. It was introduced to the west in 1789 and has become very popular. *See also page 322.*

Magnolia dealbata
This medium-size Mexican magnolia is related to the *M. macrophylla*. It has large, papery, bright green leaves borne in whorls at the ends of the shoots. The parchment-colour, wide-spreading, cup-shaped flowers, which appear in early summer, have a distinctive purple blotch at the base of each petal (tepal).

Large-leaved Magnolia

Magnolia macrophylla

This tree, as the name suggests, has the largest leaves of any magnolia, and possibly the largest entire leaf of any American tree. It is native to south-eastern United States, and was discovered in 1759 in the mountains of South Carolina, where it inhabits rich, moist soils, in woodland. Two magnificent specimens grow in front of the museum of the Arnold Arboretum, Boston.

Distribution: South-east United States.
Height: 15m (50ft)
Shape: Broadly columnar
Deciduous
Pollinated: Insect
Leaf shape: Elliptic to oblong

Identification: The bark is pale grey and smooth. The leaves, up to 90cm (36in) long and 30cm (12in) wide, have pronounced veins, and are smooth, bright green above, and almost white underneath. They are borne in large whorls at the tips of stout olive-green shoots. Large, fragrant creamy yellow flowers are borne at the ends of the shoots in early to mid-summer. Distinctive, bright red seeds, in irregular clusters, 7.5cm (3in) long, appear in late summer.

Above: The leaves are papery thin.

Below: The flowers are 30cm (12in).

EVERGREEN LAURELS

The Lauraceae family contains more than 40 genera and 2,000 different species, most of which are tropical, originating from Asia and South America. Those that are hardier, and can survive in temperate regions of the world, tend to have several things in common, including aromatic foliage or bark, and evergreen leaves.

Sassafras

Sassafras albidum

Both the leaves and bark of sassafras are pleasingly aromatic. In the past, both have been used for medicinal purposes. The bark of the root is often used to make a drink not dissimilar to beer. Although fairly widespread in the wild, sassafras has never been widely cultivated in parks and gardens. The leaves, which can be heavily lobed, are similar in outline to those of the common fig.

Identification: A medium-size suckering tree, with wavy or zig-zag branching, which is particularly noticeable when the leaves have fallen in winter. The leaves are 15cm (6in) long, 10cm (4in) across, and variable in shape, sometimes having a pronounced lobe on one or both sides. They are grass-green above and blue-green below. In autumn they turn orange-yellow before dropping. The fruit is a dark blue, egg-shape berry, 1cm (½in) across.

Distribution: Eastern North America from Canada to Florida and westwards to Kansas and Texas.
Height: 25m (82ft)
Shape: Broadly columnar
Deciduous
Pollinated: Insect
Leaf shape: Ovate to elliptic

Left: Male and female flowers are held on separate trees and produced in late spring. Both are inconspicuous and greenish-yellow.

Sorrel Tree

California bay, California olive, Oregon myrtle *Umbellularia californica*

This tree resembles the bay tree in everything but size, being extremely vigorous and capable of reaching 30m (100ft) in height in sheltered, moist valley bottoms. It has a dense, leafy habit, and foliage that, when crushed, emits a very powerful odour, which can induce nausea, headaches and in some cases unconsciousness. It may also cause skin allergies in some people.

Identification: The bark is dark grey and smooth when young, cracking into regular plates as the tree matures. The leaves are up to 12cm (4½in) long, alternately placed on sage-green shoots, elliptic in shape but tapering at both ends, leathery, glossy dark green above and pale beneath. The flowers are inconspicuous, 6mm (¼in) across and yellowy green. They are produced on sage-green upright stalks, 2.5cm (1in) long, in late winter and early spring. The fruit is a pear-shaped berry, 2.5cm (1in) long, green at first, then changing to purple. The timber of Californian laurel is highly prized for veneers and cabinet-making; also known as "pepperwood", it has pale brown figuring and can be polished to a fine finish.

Distribution: North America, California north to Oregon.
Height: 30m (100ft)
Shape: Broadly spreading
Evergreen
Pollinated: Insect
Leaf shape: Elliptic to oblanceolate

Left: Flowers appear in winter and early spring.

Right: The leaves resemble those of bay.

Bay Laurel

Sweet bay *Laurus nobilis*

This is the laurel used by the Greeks and Romans as a ceremonial symbol of victory; it was usually woven into crowns to be worn by champions. Fruiting sprays were also made into wreaths and given to acclaimed poets, hence the term "poet laureate". Where hardy, it is grown in the USA as a specimen shrub, or in woodland gardens. It may need protecting from winter winds.

Identification: A dense, evergreen small tree or shrub, with aromatic leaves that are commonly used as food flavouring. The bark is dark grey and smooth, even in old age. Leaves are leathery, alternate, dark glossy green above with a central lighter vein, and pale green beneath. They are 10cm (4in) long, 4cm (1½in) across and pointed at the tip. Male flowers appear in late winter; they are greenish-yellow, 1cm (½in) across, with yellow stamens, positioned in the axils of the previous year's leaves.

Above: The small male flowers open during late winter. Bay leaves are commonly harvested for use in cooking.

Distribution: Throughout Mediterranean regions. USA zones 8–10.
Height: 15m (50ft)
Shape: Broadly conical
Evergreen
Pollinated: Insect
Leaf shape: Elliptic

Left: The fruit is a rounded berry, 1cm (½in) across, green ripening to a glossy black.

OTHER SPECIES OF NOTE

Wheel Tree *Trochodendron aralioides*
This attractive, evergreen Japanese tree is the sole species in the only genus within the family Trochodendraceae. Its nearest relative is believed to be *Drimys winteri*. It has dark green, shiny, narrow, elliptical, leathery leaves and aromatic bark. Its most interesting feature by far is its wheel-like flowers, which are bright green, 2cm (¾in) across and have exposed stamens radiating outwards from a central disc, rather like the spokes on a cartwheel. They appear on upright slender stalks from early spring to early summer. It survives in USA hardiness zones 8–10.

Gutta Percha *Eucommia ulmoides*
This Chinese tree is the only member of the Eucommiaceae family. It is the only temperate tree that produces rubber, and is also known as the hardy rubber tree. If the leaf is gently torn in half, the two halves will still hang together, held by thin strands of sticky latex. In China, it has been cultivated for hundreds of years and used

for medicinal purposes. Since it has never actually been found growing in the wild, its origins are unknown. It survives in the USA in hardiness zones 4–8.

Mountain Laurel

Calico bush *Kalmia latifolia*

Sometimes known as the calico bush, this multistemmed small tree or large shrub is probably one of the most beautiful evergreens of eastern North America. It grows naturally in the shade of taller trees in woodland, often forming dense impenetrable thickets. It is very popular and cultivated throughout the USA in parks and gardens as an early summer-flowering ornamental. It grows best on acid soils.

Identification: The bark is a dark red-brown becoming fissured into narrow longitudinal ridges in maturity. Mountain laurel has alternate, glossy, dark green leathery leaves with a distinctive light yellow-green central midrib. They are up to 13cm (5in) long, less than half that broad and tapered at both ends. The dark-green leaves make an excellent foil for the saucer-shaped flowers which are borne in tight clusters in late spring.

Right: The flowers are deep rose-pink in bud opening to bright pink.

Distribution: Eastern USA from Lake Erie south to Florida and west to Louisiana.
Height: 6m (20ft)
Shape: Broadly spreading
Evergreen
Pollinated: Insect
Leaf shape: Elliptic to lanceolate

Above: Leaf veins are very distinctive, particularly the central midrib vein.

ELMS AND HACKBERRIES

This Ulmaceae family contains about 15 genera and 140 different species of mainly deciduous trees.
They thrive in all but the poorest of soils and are widespread throughout most temperate regions of the
Northern Hemisphere, including Europe, North America and Asia, except where they have been affected
by the fungus Ophiostoma novo-ulmi, which causes Dutch elm disease.

American Elm

White elm *Ulmus americana*

Known as white elm because of the timber colour, this tree has a wide-spreading crown of pendulous branches. It has been widely planted across eastern USA for ornament and as a shelter belt tree. Since the 1930s the population has been affected by Dutch elm disease.

Distribution: Saskatchewan south to Florida and Texas.
Height: 35m (115ft)
Shape: Broadly spreading
Deciduous
Pollinated: Wind
Leaf shape: Ovate to obovate

Identification: The bark is ash-grey becoming cracked and fissured in maturity. The leaves taper at the tip to a long slender point and are distinctly unequal at the base where they join the leaf stalk (petiole). They are dark green above, lighter green with some pubescence beneath, and rough to the touch.

Right: The leaves are ovate, up to 15cm (6in) long and doubly toothed around the margins.

Hackberry

Nettle tree *Celtis occidentalis*

This medium-size tree, which is closely related to elm, grows naturally right across North America from the Atlantic seaboard to the Rocky Mountains and north into Canada. It produces a profusion of purple, edible, sweet-tasting berries that are an important food source for birds.

Distribution: North America.
Height: 25m (82ft)
Shape: Broadly columnar
Deciduous
Pollinated: Wind
Leaf shape: Ovate

Identification: The bark is light grey, smooth when the tree is young, becoming rough and corky with warty blemishes in maturity. The leaves are ovate, up to 12cm (4½in) long and 5cm (2in) across, pointed, toothed at the tip and rounded at the base, where there are three pronounced veins. They are glossy rich green and smooth on top; lighter green and slightly hairy on the veining underneath. Both the male and female flowers are held separately on the same tree. In spring the flowers are small and green, without petals and appear in the leaf axils. The fruit is a purple-black, rounded berry, approximately 1cm (½in) across and borne on a thin green stalk, 2.5cm (1in) long.

Right: The hackberry's other common name seems more appropriate: it is named after its leaves, which resemble those of the stinging nettle.

Keaki

Zelkova serrata

This large, elm-like Asian tree grows best in its native lands in low-lying river valleys where the soil is deep and rich. It grows at altitudes of 1,220m (4,000ft). Many old Japanese temples are built of its timber, which is strong and extremely durable. In the USA it is a good replacement for the American elm, *U. americana*, and is strong in urban conditions.

Identification: The bark is pale grey and smooth, like beech. In maturity it peels or flakes, leaving light, fawn-grey patches. Lower branching is light and sweeps upwards, ending in thin, straight twigs. Leaves are ovate, 12cm (4½in) long and 5cm (2in) broad, with 6–13 sharp teeth on each side. Small, green male and female flowers appear on each tree in spring. The fruit is round and small, 5mm (¼in) in diameter.

Distribution: China, Japan and Korea. USA zone 5–8.
Height: 40m (130ft)
Shape: Broadly spreading
Deciduous
Pollinated: Wind
Leaf shape: Ovate

Right and far right: The leaves are dark green and slightly rough above; pale green with pubescence beneath. In autumn they turn an orange-red colour.

OTHER SPECIES OF NOTE

English Elm *Ulmus minor* var. *vulgaris*
This large tree, formerly known as *U. procera*, may have been introduced to the USA from England and Spain. It was once one of the most characteristic features of the English countryside, but in the 1960s, Dutch elm disease wiped out almost the entire population. *See also page 337.*

Sugarberry *Celtis laevigata*
This handsome, large tree, also known as the Mississippi hackberry, is often planted as a shade and street tree, and is common throughout central and eastern USA It is often cut back into hedging. It has pale grey bark that sometimes develops a pink tinge with fissured ridges, and narrowly ovate leaves up to 10cm (4in) long. The fruit is a small, rounded orange-red berry, which is sweetly edible.

Cedar Elm *Ulmus crassifolia*
This elm is a slow-growing, round-headed, small tree with a short bole and stiff arching branches. It has ovate to oblong leaves, which are hard, and so firmly fixed to the branches that they hardly move. The bark is pinkish-grey, becoming very fissured and corky in maturity. Cedar elm is native to southern USA.

Rock Elm *Ulmus thomasii*
A slow-growing, small to medium-size tree, native to east and central North America from Montreal, around the south of the Great Lakes, and south to Missouri. It looks similar to the *U. rubra*, except that the branches develop corky wings and the leaves are up to 13cm (5in) long. It is prized for its strong, water-repellent timber.

Slippery Elm

Ulmus rubra

The common name refers to the wet inner bark, which, if sucked, is believed to have medicinal qualities that help to cure throat infections. The leaves of this elm were considered the best to eat by the early settlers of New England. Like American elm, *Ulmus americana* (which has a similar natural distribution across eastern North America), slippery elm is susceptible to attack by Dutch elm disease.

Identification: The bark is sooty-grey to brown and vertically fissured into coarse ridges in maturity. In a young tree the overall shape is upright; as it matures it develops a more rounded crown. The rough textured leaves are dark green, up to 20cm (8in) long, heavily serrated around the margin with a long point at the tip. They are borne in profusion on the tree, creating a dense, dark canopy when viewed from a distance.

Distribution: From Quebec to South Carolina and west to Texas.
Height: 20m (71ft)
Shape: Broadly spreading
Deciduous
Pollinated: Wind
Leaf shape: Oblong-ovate

Above: Individual seeds are centrally carried within their own oval-shaped winged membrane.

WALNUTS AND MULBERRIES

One of the main characteristics of these two families is that they both contain trees that produce edible fruits. The mulberry or Moraceae family includes both mulberries and figs, while the walnut or Juglandaceae family includes the common walnut. There are about 800 different species of fig; the majority of them are found in tropical and subtropical regions.

Black Walnut

Juglans nigra

With its pyramidal habit and large pinnate leaves this is a splendid, ornamental large tree. It has long been grown for its timber and its edible fruit. The timber is of high quality and has a distinctive deep chocolate-brown colour to the heartwood, which is prized for cabinet-making. The fruit, an edible nut, is not as large as an English walnut, *Juglans regia*, but has the same distinctive flavour.

Distribution: Eastern and central USA.
Height: 30m (100ft)
Shape: Broadly spreading
Deciduous
Pollinated: Wind
Leaf shape: Pinnate

Identification: The bark is dark grey-brown to sooty-ash coloured, smooth at first, becoming fissured and ridged in maturity. The leaves are 10cm (4in) long, glossy dark green above, slightly hairy beneath. In autumn they turn a clear butter-yellow before dropping. Both the male and female flowers are catkin-like, yellow-green, and up to 10cm (4in) long when ripe. They are borne separately on the same tree in late spring, early summer. Walnut is late to come into leaf, holding on to bare branches until late May before the leaves appear.

Right: The leaves are pinnate, with up to 17 toothed, pointed leaflets.

Butternut

White walnut *Juglans cinerea*

Distribution: From Quebec south to Tennessee.
Height: 25m (80ft)
Shape: Broadly spreading
Deciduous
Pollinated: Wind
Leaf shape: Pinnate

Right: The fruit is a large, sweet, edible nut, contained within a sticky, angular shell.

This handsome, fast-growing tree is common in forests in the Alleghenies, where it stands out in autumn as the leaves turn colour earlier than most other trees. The fruit, which gives the tree its name, is a large, sweet and very oily nut encased in a thick shell with four distinct ridges and protected by a pointed, shiny, sticky green husk. The botanical name *cinerea* refers to the fact that the bark is an ash-grey colour.

Identification: The leaves are pinnate, with up to 17 toothed and pointed leaflets, up to 13cm (5in) long. They are all attached directly to the midrib of the main leaf except for the terminal leaflet, which is on a short stalk. They are dark grass-green above, paler beneath and covered with slight pubescence. The male and female flowers are borne in pendulous green catkins, up to 10cm (4in) long, and appear on the same tree in late spring.

Southern Californian Walnut

Juglans californica

Distribution: California.
Height: 15m (50ft)
Shape: Broadly spreading
Deciduous
Pollinated: Wind
Leaf shape: Pinnate

Native to the southern Californian coastal region from Santa Barbara to the San Bernardino Mountains, this scrubby, round-headed tree inhabits banks of streams and valley bottoms. Since it is not particularly hardy or attractive, it is rarely found outside its natural region. It was identified in 1899 and plants were sent to Kew Gardens, England, but it never thrived in the damp, cool climate found in that region.

Identification: The trunk of this tree is always short and scrubby with pale grey bark. The leaves are finely serrated around the margin, dull green and attached to the midrib of the main leaf by a short hairy petiole. The flowers are green-yellow and borne in catkins, up to 7.5cm (3in) long, in late spring.

Right: The nut has deep, vertical grooves.

Left: The leaves are made up of 11–15 oblong-lanceolate leaflets, each leaflet up to 5cm (2in) long.

OTHER SPECIES OF NOTE

Common Fig *Ficus carica*
Originally from south-western Asia, this large shrub, or small spreading tree, is now cultivated for its fruit throughout the temperate world. It has smooth, grey bark and distinctive, heavily lobed leaves. The male and female flowers, which are fertilized by wasps, are small and green and borne on separate trees. The delicious fruit is heart-shaped and green, becoming purple-brown when ripe.

Paper Mulberry *Broussonetia papyrifera*
This medium-size, broadly spreading tree is a close relative of the true mulberries and comes from eastern Asia. The paper mulberry has attractive, coarsely toothed, hairy, purple-green leaves, which vary in shape from ovate to rounded, and are deeply lobed. In Japan the tree's inner bark was traditionally used to make paper, hence the common name.

Common Walnut *Juglans regia*
Otherwise known as English walnut, this beautiful tree is native to an area from the Black Sea to China and possibly Japan. It was first introduced into western Europe by the Romans around 2,000 years ago. It has been widely cultivated for its edible fruits ever since. It was brought to America by the early settlers and is found in the east from Massachusetts to Ohio and in the west from British Columbia to New Mexico. It is the only walnut not to have serrated edges to its leaves. *See also page 340.*

Osage Orange

Maclura pomifera

Found primarily in wet areas alongside rivers, this tree is best known for its showy orange-like fruit. The fruit is in fact inedible and, when fresh, full of a sour milky juice. The fruit is not always present because the tree is dioecious (male and female flowers are on separate trees) and therefore both sexes are required to be in close proximity for pollination to occur.

Identification: The bark is orange-brown, while the branches are often twisted, and when broken exude a milky sap. The leaves are a glossy rich green above, and pale green beneath. They are ovate, pointed at both ends, untoothed, 10cm (4in) long and 5cm (2in) wide. Sometimes a sharp green spine is present at the base of the petiole. Male and female flowers are yellow-green, 1cm (½in) long and appear in clusters on separate trees in early summer. The fruit is orange-like, green, ripening to yellow and up to 10cm (4in) across. It is actually a cluster of smaller fruits that have fused together.

Below: The fruit of the osage orange looks remarkably like a real orange.

Distribution: Central and southern America.
Height: 15m (50ft)
Shape: Broadly spreading
Deciduous
Pollinated: Insect
Leaf shape: Ovate

PECANS, HICKORIES AND WING NUTS

The Juglandaceae family contains seven genera and over sixty species of tree, which grow throughout temperate regions of North America, Europe and Asia. They include some of the fastest-growing deciduous trees. The leaves of all species are pinnate and the flowers are all catkins. Many of these trees produce edible fruit in the form of a nut.

Mockernut

Big-bud hickory *Carya tomentosa*

Distribution: East of a line from Minnesota to Texas.
Height: 30m (100ft)
Shape: Broadly columnar
Deciduous
Pollinated: Wind
Leaf shape: Pinnate

This North American hickory, sometimes called big-bud hickory, is highly prized for its timber, which has several uses. Its strength and ability to withstand impact has made it the ideal material for making tool handles all over the world. It is also used to make sports equipment such as hockey sticks. When the wood is burnt it emits a fragrance used to smoke meats. The pinnate leaves give off a pleasing aroma when crushed.

Identification: The bark is silver-grey and smooth, becoming slightly fissured in maturity. The leaves are 30cm (12in) long with up to nine obovate leaflets, the terminal one of which may be up to 20cm (8in) long and 10cm (4in) wide. The upper surfaces of the leaves are dark green. Both the shoots and the leaf stalks are covered in dense short hairs.

Right: The lower surface of the leaves is yellow-green and covered with a fine pubescence.

Right: Mockernut leaves taper towards the tip and are toothed around the margin.

Bitternut Hickory

Carya cordiformis

As the name suggests, the nuts are not palatable. They do however have a high oil content and were valued because they could be crushed to produce lamp oil. The name hickory comes from the native American *pawcohiccora*, meaning nut oil. The species has a similar natural range to that of mockernut, *Carya tomentosa*, but is easily distinguished by its slender, bright yellow winter buds. It is not commonly planted outside its natural range.

Distribution: Similar to Mockernut, east of a line from Minnesota to Texas.
Height: 30m (100ft)
Shape: Broadly columnar
Deciduous
Pollinated: Wind
Leaf shape: Pinnate

Identification: The bark is grey and smooth, becoming thick and heavily ridged in maturity. The pinnate leaves have up to nine heavily serrated leaflets, which may be up to 15cm (6in) long. They are deep green above and yellow-green beneath. In autumn they turn a rich golden-yellow. Both the male and female flowers are carried on catkins: the males in threes, and up to 7.5cm (3in) long, which appear separately on the same tree in late spring. The thin-shelled fruit is an inedible bitter nut.

Right: Bitternut hickory has pinnate leaves that normally bare four pairs of leaflets plus one terminal leaflet. In autumn they turn bright yellow.

Pecan

Carya illinoinensis

This tall tree is known around the world for its delicious nuts. In southern USA it is extensively cultivated within orchards, and is of great commercial value. The pecan grows naturally in damp soils in forests and river valleys, for example by the Mississippi.

Identification: The bark is grey, corky and deeply fissured and ridged. The leaves are pinnate with up to 17 dark green leaflets, 15cm (6in) long. Each leaflet has a serrated margin and curves slightly backwards at the tip. In autumn the foliage can turn a butter-yellow colour. Male flowers are yellow-green, small and clustered on pendulous catkins hanging in threes. They appear in late spring and early summer. The nut is thin-shelled and brown.

Distribution: South-east and central North America.
Height: 30m (100ft)
Shape: Broadly columnar
Deciduous
Pollinated: Wind
Leaf shape: Pinnate

Left: The pecan nut grows inside a husk 5cm (2in) long. Nuts are harvested in autumn.

OTHER SPECIES OF NOTE

Hybrid Wing Nut
Pterocarya x rehderiana
This hybrid, raised at the Arnold Arboretum in 1879, is more vigorous than either of its parents, *P. fraxinifolia* and *P. stenoptera*. It has pinnate leaves, with up to 21 leaflets. The bark is purple-brown, and obliquely fissured. The pendulous catkins are 45cm (18in) long, and contain winged seeds in summer.

Pignut *Carya glabra*
This medium-size, North American hickory has smooth grey bark, which gradually becomes vertically fissured in old age. It has pinnate leaves composed of five to seven smooth, sharply toothed, taper-pointed leaflets. The nut was traditionally used to feed pigs.

Caucasian Wing Nut
Pterocarya fraxinifolia
This fast-growing, large tree regularly achieves 3m (10ft) growth in one year. As the name suggests it is native to the Caucasus, and the shores of both the Black and Caspian seas. At first glance, it looks similar to black walnut, *Juglans nigra*, however, the fruit is nut-like with semicircular wings and carried in a long hanging "necklace", up to 50cm (20in) long. It is grown in botanic gardens in the USA. *See also page 342.*

Shagbark Hickory

Carya ovata

Distribution: Eastern North America from Quebec to Texas.
Height: 30m (100ft)
Shape: Broadly columnar
Deciduous
Pollinated: Wind
Leaf shape: Pinnate

This large, vigorous tree differs from other hickories in having flaking, grey-brown bark, which curls away from the trunk in thin strips up to 30cm (12in) long, but stays attached to the tree at the centre point. This gives the whole trunk a shaggy, untidy but attractive appearance.

Identification: The leaves are pinnate, with five to seven leaflets on each leaf. Each leaflet is up to 25cm (10in) long, yellowish-green and has a serrated edge for the top two-thirds. In autumn the leaves turn brilliant yellow. In winter, the bud scales curve away from the bud at the tip. Both the male and female flowers are small, yellowish-green and borne on pendulous catkins clustered in threes in late spring. In North America, the tree produces a profusion of nuts most years. Elsewhere, crops are not so prolific. The white, sweet-tasting kernel is contained in a green husk.

Right: Fruit occurs at twig ends.

Below: The husk has four ridges.

Right: Leaves appear finger-like before they fill out.

BEECHES

The Fagaceae family contains ten species of true beech, which all occur in temperate regions of the world. They can be found in Asia, North America and Europe, including Great Britain. Beeches are some of the most majestic deciduous trees. They typically have smooth, thin, silver-grey bark and can attain heights in excess of 40m (130ft).

European Beech

Fagus sylvatica

The name "beech" comes from the Anglo-Saxon *boc* and the Germanic word *Buche*, both of which gave rise to the English word "book". In northern Europe early manuscripts were written on thin tablets of beech wood and bound in beech boards. Beech is widely used for hedging because it retains its dead leaves in winter, providing extra wind protection. It is a popular specimen tree in the USA.

Distribution: Europe from the Pyrenees to the Caucasus and north to Russia and Denmark. USA zone 4–7.
Height: 40m (130ft)
Shape: Broadly spreading
Deciduous
Pollinated: Wind
Leaf shape: Ovate to obovate

Identification: The bark is silver-grey and remains smooth even in maturity. The leaves are up to 10cm (4in) long and 5cm (2in) wide. They have a wavy, but normally untoothed, margin and a rather blunt point at the tip. In spring, juvenile leaves have a covering of hairs and are edible, having a nutty flavour. Older leaves become tough and bitter. Beech flowers are small; female flowers are green and the male's are yellow. Both are borne in separate clusters on the same tree in spring. The fruit is an edible nut, with up to three nuts being contained within a woody husk, covered in coarse bristles.

Right: The husks open in early autumn.

Far right: Mature leaves are smooth and have a rich colour.

Copper Beech

Fagus sylvatica 'Purpurea'

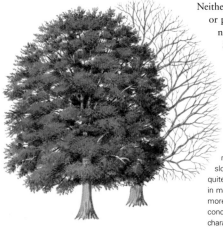

Neither a true species nor of garden origin, copper or purple beeches are "sports" or "quirks" of nature. Their presence was noted near Buchs, Switzerland, and in the Darney forest, Vosges, eastern France in the 1600s.

Identification: Similar to the European beech, but with the most obvious difference being the purple leaves, which are also more oval. Copper beech may grow more slowly and is not quite as spreading in maturity, but this is more a result of local conditions than a distinct characteristic of the tree.

Distribution: Switzerland and Vosges, eastern France. North-east North America from Maine to Wisconsin and from Maryland to Missouri.
Height: 40m (130ft)
Shape: Broadly spreading
Deciduous
Pollinated: Wind
Leaf shape: Ovate to obovate

Left: One in 1,000 seedlings collected from European beech may have purple leaves.

American Beech

Fagus grandiflora

This tree is prolific in North America but has never been much of a success elsewhere. In Britain it never really thrives, developing into a rather shrubby-looking tree. Its one distinctive feature is that it can regenerate very easily from root suckers, particularly when coppiced, or badly damaged.

Identification: The bark is slate-grey, thin and smooth, even in old age. The glossy leaves are ovate to elliptic, up to 12cm (4½in) long and 5cm (2in) wide. They are sharply toothed and taper to a pointed tip. On the underside, they are pale green with tufts of white hair along the midrib and in the vein axils beneath. Young shoots are also covered with fine hair. There are up to 15 pairs of leaf veins as opposed to up to 10 on common beech. Male flowers are yellow; female are green. Both are small and borne in clusters on the same tree in late spring. Fruits are 2cm (¾in) long bristly husks with up to three angular nuts.

Right: American beech nuts (or masts) are held in bristly husks. The leaves are dark green.

Distribution: North America from Nova Scotia to Florida.
Height: 25m (82ft)
Shape: Broadly spreading
Deciduous
Pollinated: Wind
Leaf shape: Ovate to elliptic

OTHER SPECIES OF NOTE

Oriental Beech *Fagus orientalis*
The Oriental beech is native to the forests of the Caspian Sea, the Caucasus, Asia Minor, Bulgaria and Iran. It is similar to common beech, and there is, without doubt, some hybridization between the two species on its western boundary. Oriental beech has larger leaves with more pairs of veining than common beech and will, in good growing conditions, develop into a larger tree. It survives in USA zones 4–7. *See also page 345.*

Pendulous Beech *Fagus sylvatica* 'Pendula'
Several cultivars of common beech have weeping foliage, but 'Pendula' is the best. It grows into a large tree with enormous pendulous branches, which droop from the main stem like elephants' trunks. Where they touch the ground they sometimes take root, sending up another stem that will in turn begin to weep. Over time a large tent-like canopy can develop around the original tree. It is one of the finest specimen trees available in North America.

Dawyck Beech *Fagus sylvatica* 'Dawyck'
This delightful, narrowly columnar "Lombardy poplar"-shape tree was discovered on the Dawyck Estate in the Tweed Valley, southern Scotland, in 1860. It became an "overnight success" with gardeners and nurserymen, providing the perfect solution for those who wanted a beech tree but did not have the room for the much larger-growing kind. It has been widely planted as an ornamental tree right across north-eastern North America.

Japanese Beech

Siebold's beech *Fagus crenata*

This species is sometimes called Siebold's beech after the German doctor who was physician to the Governor of the Dutch East India Company's Deshima trading post. It was Siebold who identified the tree in Japan, where it forms considerable forests from sea level to 1,500m (4,921ft). It was first introduced to the West in 1892 and is grown as a specimen tree in the USA.

Identification: Similar to common beech, it differs mainly in its more obovate leaf shape and a small leaf-like structure found at the base of each seed husk in early autumn. The bark is silver-grey and smooth, even in older trees. The leaves are up to 10cm (4in) long and 5cm (2in) wide with a wavy, finely pubescent margin and blunt teeth. Leaf veins occur in seven to eleven pairs. The leaf stalk is 1cm (½in) long. Leaves turn an "old-gold" colour in autumn. The seed husk is 1.5cm (⅝in) long and covered in long bristles.

Right: A Japanese beech leaf and mast.

Distribution: Japan. USA zones 4–7
Height: 30m (100ft)
Shape: Broadly spreading
Deciduous
Pollinated: Wind
Leaf shape: Ovate to obovate

FALSE BEECHES

This relatively little-known group of trees is from temperate regions of the Southern Hemisphere, and is known by the botanical genus Nothofagus. Nothos *comes from the ancient Greek for "spurious" or "false" and* fagus *means "beech"; so the name can be translated as "false beeches". Although these trees are similar to beech there are some differences. Many Nothofagus are evergreen and have smaller leaves.*

Antarctic Beech

Nothofagus antarctica

A fast-growing, small to medium-size tree that is extremely elegant, especially when young. It has leaves that, when crushed, or on hot days, emit a sweet, honey-like fragrance. Also known as *nirre* in Chile, it inhabits mountainsides from Cape Horn to northern Chile. In autumn, the leaves turn into a range of glorious colours from scarlet through orange to butter-yellow.

Identification: The bark is dark grey, becoming scaly in maturity. The leaves are up to 4cm (1½in) long, broadly ovate, rounded at the tip and finely toothed around the margin. They are set in two neat rows along the shoot and have a crinkly, shell-like appearance. The flowers are small and pendulous, and appear in late spring, the male borne singly or in twos or threes in the leaf axils. The fruit is a four-valved husk approximately 5mm (¼in) long, each valve containing three nuts.

Distribution: South America: southern Argentina and Chile.
Height: 15m (50ft)
Shape: Broadly columnar
Deciduous
Pollinated: Insect
Leaf shape: Ovate

Left: A flower and fruit.

Right: Leaves are finely toothed.

Rauli

Raoul *Nothofagus nervosa*

Also known as *N. procera*, this large, deciduous forest tree has upswept branches and heavily veined leaves. The name was given by early Spanish settlers who saw its grey, smooth bark and called it after the Spanish word for beech. It is a fast-growing tree, which produces good quality timber and is being planted in temperate regions of the Northern Hemisphere for forestry.

Identification: The bark is dark grey and becomes heavily fissured as the tree matures. The leaves are ovate to oblong, up to 10cm (4in) long and 5cm (2in) across. They are easily distinguished from other *Nothofagus* because they have 14–18 pairs of deep veins, but could at first glance be mistaken for hornbeam. The leaves are positioned alternately along the shoot; they are bronze-green above and paler beneath, with some pubescence on the midrib and veins. The fruit is a four-valved husk about 1cm (½in) long, containing three small nuts.

Distribution: Central Chile and western Argentina.
Height: 25m (82ft)
Shape: Broadly conical
Deciduous
Pollinated: Insect
Leaf shape: Oblong to ovate

Left and right: The long, elegant leaves hang heavily. Unlike those of other members of this genus, they have up to 18 pairs of deep veins.

Dombey's Southern Beech

Nothofagus dombeyi

This large, fast-growing, elegant evergreen tree develops a graceful, broad-spreading habit, not dissimilar to *Cedrus libanii*. It is common in Chilean forests, ranging high into the Andes. In severe winters it may shed its evergreen leaves, replacing them the following spring.

Above: The bark is ash-grey, flaking and cracking in maturity.

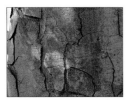

Identification: The stiff leaves are narrowly ovate, rich dark green above and pale beneath and carrying a sheen on both surfaces. The leaves have pronounced veins, and small dark warts on the underside; they are 4cm (1½in) long, with a blunt point at the tip. Both the male and female flowers are red and small and borne in clusters of three in spring. The fruit is a bristly husk, similar to beech and containing three small nuts.

Distribution: Chile and Argentina.
Height: 40m (130ft)
Shape: Broadly columnar
Evergreen
Pollinated: Insect
    Leaf shape: Ovate

Right: The small husks are visible between the leaves.

OTHER SPECIES OF NOTE

Black Beech *Nothofagus solandri*
Native to lowland and mountain regions of New Zealand, black beech is a tall, slender, evergreen tree, to 25m (82ft) in the wild. It has small, elliptic, dark green leaves, which are heavily pubescent beneath, and densely borne on wiry shoots, which develop into ascending fan-like branches. It grows in parks across the USA.

Silver Beech *Nothofagus menziesii*
Native to New Zealand, where it grows up to 1,000m (3,280ft) above sea level, this evergreen tree reaches 30m (100ft) high. It has a silvery white trunk, which dulls to grey in maturity. The leaves are ovate to diamond shape, doubly round-toothed and 1cm (½in) long. The petiole and the shoot are covered in a yellowish-brown hair. It grows in parks in the USA. *See also page 349.*

Myrtle Tree *Nothofagus cunninghamii*
This medium-size, evergreen Australian tree grows thousands of miles from the majority of the *Nothofagus* genus in South America. It has distinctive, small, diamond-shape leaves that are bluntly toothed in the upper half.

Red Beech *Nothofagus fusca*
This beautiful evergreen tree is native to New Zealand from 37 degrees latitude south. It reaches large proportions in the wild, but in cultivation, in the Northern Hemisphere, it seldom exceeds 25m (82ft). The leaves are distinctive with their sharply toothed margin. When the old leaves eventually fall they turn coppery red; hence the common name. *See also page 349.*

Roble Beech

Nothofagus obliqua

Roble is Spanish for oak and in some respects this large South American tree does resemble a European deciduous oak. It also bears oak-like timber, which is tough, durable and over the years has been used for shipbuilding, interior joinery and furniture. It is the most warm-loving of all southern, or false, beeches and thrives in the Mediterranean climate of southern California.

Identification: Roble has grey bark, which becomes cracked and fissured with age. It has dark green, ovate to oval leaves, which are blue-green on the underside, roundly toothed, up to 7.5cm (3in) long, with between eight and eleven pairs of distinct leaf veins. In autumn, the leaves turn golden-yellow. Both the male and female flowers are small and green; the males are borne singly and the females in threes, both in late spring.

Distribution: Argentina and Chile.
Height: 35m (115ft)
Shape: Broadly columnar
Deciduous
Pollinated: Insect
    Leaf shape: Ovate

Above: The fruit is a bristly brown husk, containing three nuts.

CHINKAPINS AND CHESTNUTS

The chestnut genus Castanea *contains just twelve deciduous trees, all of which grow wild in temperate regions of the Northern Hemisphere. They are closely related to both the beech,* Fagus, *and oak,* Quercus, *genera. The majority are long-lived, large trees, which are drought resistant and thrive on dry, shallow soils. All have strongly serrated leaves and edible fruit in the form of a nut.*

American Chestnut

Castanea dentata

This majestic tree was once widespread throughout North America, but since the 1930s its population has been devastated by the effects of chestnut blight, *Endothia parasitica*. Today it is rare in the wild, with the species likely to become endangered in the next 20 years. The disease entered North America from east Asia at the end of the 19th century.

Distribution: Eastern North America.
Height: 30m (100ft)
Shape: Broadly columnar
Deciduous
Pollinated: Insect
Leaf shape: Oblong

Identification: The trunk and form of American chestnut is similar to that of sweet chestnut; it has dark grey-brown bark, which becomes spirally fissured with age. Male and female flowers are found in the same yellow, upright catkin. Catkins are up to 20cm (8in) long and ripen in early summer. Fruit is a spiny green (ripening to yellow) husk, up to 6cm (2½in) across.

Right: The oblong leaves are up to 25cm (10in) long and have a margin edged with sharp-toothed serrations. The nuts can be eaten.

Allegheny Chinkapin

Castanea pumila

This small, deciduous American tree is distinguished from other chinkapins by its ability to throw up suckers from the root system. Quite often they will result in a dense thicket around the base of the tree. It is a hardy tree growing up to 1,400m (4,500ft) on dry sandy ridges in the Appalachian Mountains. It produces sweet-tasting nuts, which are sold in the markets of the western and southern States. It is sometimes confused with the trailing chinkapin, *C. alnifolia*, which is a shrub seldom reaching more than 2m (6ft).

Identification: The bark is light brown tinged with red, slightly furrowed and splitting into plate-like scales. The oblong leaves are up to 13cm (5in) long, coarsely serrated around the margin, and taper to a fine point. When the leaves unfold in spring they are tinged with red and covered in a white pubescence, which remains on the underside of the leaf throughout the summer. In autumn they turn bright yellow. The fruit is a bristly, spined husk surrounding a dark chestnut-brown nut.

Distribution: New Jersey to Florida and west to Texas.
Height: 15m (50ft)
Shape: Broadly spreading
Deciduous
Pollinated: Insect
Leaf shape: Oblong

Right: The leaves may be up to 13cm (5in) long and carry a white pubescence on the underside.

Sweet Chestnut
Castanea sativa

This fast-growing ornamental is native to warm, temperate areas of the Mediterranean and into south-western Asia. It has been widely cultivated elsewhere. The Romans introduced it to Europe as a source of food. It is believed to have been introduced into North America in the early 17th century. *See also page 350.*

Castanopsis cuspidata
This is a large, elegant evergreen tree in its native homelands of southern Japan, China and Korea. In cultivation elsewhere, it seldom becomes more than a small, bushy tree. It is hardy to USA zone 7. The leaves are oval, glossy, dark green and leathery. The fruit is an acorn, borne on a stalk with up to ten others, all encased within rows of downy scales. *See also page 351.*

Japanese Chestnut *Castanea crenata*
This small tree is native to Japan, but cultivated

elsewhere in botanic gardens. In Japan it is a valuable food source, and the tree is grown for its small, edible nuts. It is cultivated in the USA because of its resistance to blight. *See also page 350.*

Golden Chestnut

Golden chinkapin *Chrysolepis chrysophylla*

This evergreen tree is quite often referred to as the golden chinkapin, and botanically as *Castanopsis chrysophylla*, although this is incorrect because the flowers on *Castanopsis* are borne on separate catkins, whereas on this tree they are on the same catkin. The name "golden" refers to the underside of the leaf, which is covered with a bright golden pubescence, a feature that quickly distinguishes it from just about any other member of the Fagaceae family.

Identification: The bark is grey, smooth when young, becoming fissured in old age. The leaves are evergreen, lanceolate to oblong, broad in the centre tapering to a point at each end, up to 10cm (4in) long and 2.5cm (1in) wide. Glossy dark, almost black-green above and with a rich golden pubescence beneath, they are held on a green petiole 1cm (½in) long. Both male and female flowers are fragrant, creamy yellow and borne on the same erect, 4cm- (1½in-) long catkin in summer.

Distribution: Oregon and California.
Height: 30m (100ft)
Shape: Broadly conical
Evergreen
Pollinated: Insect
Leaf shape: Lanceolate to oblong

Below: The fruit is a spiny husk, very similar to sweet chestnut, containing up to three glossy brown nuts.

Tanbark Oak

Lithocarpus densiflorus

This evergreen tree is closely related to an oak, but several of the characteristics relating to its flowers are very different from oak. It is native to California and Oregon, where it grows into a pyramidal-shape tree up to 25m (82ft) tall. The leaves are sharply toothed, dark glossy green above and covered with white pubescence beneath. The fruit is an acorn, 2.5cm (1in) long, set in a shallow, pubescent cup with reflexed scales.

Identification: This tender, small tree has smooth grey-brown bark that becomes uniformly fissured with age. The bark is an excellent source of tannin. It has stiff leathery leaves. Both the underside of the leaf and the young shoots are covered with thick grey-white wool. The male and female flowers are creamy yellow and small. They are held in erect, thin spikes, up to 10cm (4in) long, in May.

Distribution: Oregon and California.
Height: 25m (82ft)
Shape: Broadly pyramidal
Evergreen
Pollinated: Insect
Leaf shape: Oval to oblong

Left: Both male and female flowers are long, upright spikes.

Right: The fruit is a small pointed acorn, in a shallow cup.

AMERICAN OAKS

There are almost 600 different species of oak, Quercus, in the world, the majority of which grow in the Northern Hemisphere. Almost 80 of these grow in North America and at least 60 are large trees. There are oaks native to every region of the North American continent from Alaska to New Mexico. Some play an integral part in the leaf-colour spectacle every autumn in New England.

Northern Red Oak

Quercus rubra

Distribution: Nova Scotia and Quebec south to Alabama.
Height: 25m (80ft)
Shape: Broadly spreading
Deciduous
Pollinated: Wind
Leaf shape: Elliptic to obovate

The northern red oak grows further north in eastern North America than any other oak. It is very common in New England and the Allegheny Mountains, and has been widely planted on the west coast from British Columbia to Oregon. It provides spectacular autumn leaf colour, particularly in New England. Its leaves are similar to scarlet oak, but not so glossy on the upper surface.

Identification: The bark is grey and smooth, becoming deeply fissured in maturity. The leaves are elliptic to obovate, up to 20cm (8in) long, with distinctive narrow lobes, which run to fine points. They are dull matt green above, and pale green beneath, with tufts of fine brown hair in the vein axils. Male flowers are green-yellow catkins, appearing in late spring.

Left: The fruit is a squat acorn, to 3cm (1¼in) long and seated in a shallow cup.

Pin Oak

Quercus palustris

The pin oak, *Quercus palustris*, grows wild from Vermont to Oklahoma, where it grows in valley bottoms and lowland areas that are quite often subject to flooding. It is one of the best oaks for growing in wet conditions, and has developed a shallow rooting system to compensate for waterlogging. Due to its straight, clean stem and narrow, spire-like shape, it is commonly planted in cities across the USA. both as a street tree and in parks such as Central Park in New York.

Identification: The bark is dark grey and smooth, becoming darker grey in maturity. The leaves are elliptic to obovate, up to 15cm (6in) long and 12cm (4½in) across, with up to four pairs of angular lobes each tipped with a sharp pin-like bristle. They are bright glossy green above, paler beneath, with tufts of fawn-coloured hair in the vein axils. The name comes from the pin-like spurs that sometimes appear on vigorous young shoots.

Right: The male flowers are green-yellow hanging catkins, up to 5cm (2in) long.

Distribution: From Rhode Island and Vermont to Tennessee.
Height: 30m (100ft)
Shape: Broadly conical
Deciduous
Pollinated: Wind
Leaf shape: Elliptic to obovate

Scarlet Oak

Quercus coccinea

Scarlet oak is one of the most ornamental trees of eastern North America, contributing greatly to the leaf-colour spectacular. The leaves stay on the trees far longer than those of any of the other autumn-colour trees. It grows on poor sandy soils up to elevations of 1,520m (5,000ft) in the Appalachian Mountains. It does not grow well in shade.

Identification: The bark is slate-grey and smooth, becoming slightly fissured in maturity. Although the leaves are roughly elliptical in shape they are eaten into by several angular lobes, some cutting almost to the midrib. Each lobe point is tipped with a sharp bristle. The upper leaf surface is dark green and glossy, the underside is pale green with tufts of pubescence in the vein axils. Male flowers are borne in yellow, drooping catkins in late spring; the female flowers are inconspicuous, but borne on the same tree. The acorn is 2–3cm (¾–1¼in) long. Half of it is enclosed in a deep, shiny cup. Although very often confused with red oak, *Q. rubra*, the scarlet oak is a narrower and more open tree, with a rounder and deeper acorn cup.

Distribution: Eastern North America from Ontario to Missouri, but not Florida.
Height: 25m (82ft)
Shape: Broadly spreading
Deciduous
Pollinated: Wind
Leaf shape: Elliptic

Left: The leaves, which have a very ragged appearance for an oak, stay on the tree later than its relatives.

OTHER SPECIES OF NOTE

Shingle Oak
Quercus imbricaria
Shingle oak is native to central and eastern USA from Pennsylvania to North Carolina. The name refers to the fact that early colonial settlers made roofing shingles from its wood. Shingle oak has deciduous, oblong to lanceolate, untoothed leaves, up to 15cm (6in) long with a wavy margin. The flat acorn cup is covered with overlapping woody scales.

Swamp White Oak *Quercus bicolor*
The swamp white oak is native to eastern North America from Quebec to Missouri. It is a medium-size tree up to 25m (82ft) tall. As the common name suggests, it grows best in deep, damp soils and alongside rivers. The species name *bicolor* refers to the fact that the leaf is dark glossy green above, and silvery grey and covered in soft down beneath.

Willow Oak *Quercus phellos*
This oak is easily recognized by its narrow, willow-like leaves, which are late unfurling from bud, and have a yellow and red tinted centre that becomes sage-green as the summer progresses. Willow oak is native to an area that extends from Delaware to Texas. This broadly spreading tree is also widely planted in cities, such as New York, as a street tree.

White Oak

Stave oak *Quercus alba*

A large tree, common throughout its range. It grows largest on the lower western slopes of the Alleghany Mountains, and reaches altitudes of 1,400m (4,500ft) in the southern Appalachian Mountains. It is an important timber tree, widely used in cooperage; the close-grained, water-resistant wood is used for making barrel staves.

Identification: The bark is slate-grey, smooth at first, becoming scaly and fissured with age. The leaves are extremely variable, even on the same tree, but on average they are obovate, up to 20cm (8in) long and 10cm (4in) wide, with between two and four narrow lobes on each side of the leaf, which tapers towards the base. They emerge from winter bud pink and covered in a fine pubescence.

Distribution: From Quebec to Texas and across to the Atlantic coast.
Height: 35m (115ft)
Shape: Broadly spreading
Deciduous
Pollinated: Wind
Leaf shape: Obovate

Left: By midsummer the leaves are bright green above and pale green-grey beneath. In autumn the leaves turn deep purple-red before dropping.

Chestnut Oak

Quercus prinus

The bark of this large American oak, which has chestnut-like leaves, was once used for tanning leather by the early settlers. It grows on mountain slopes and in rocky places, particularly in the Appalachian Mountains, where it is found at elevations up to 1,500m (4,800ft) above sea level. It has been widely planted on the Atlantic coastal plain as an ornamental species in parks and gardens.

Identification: The bark is dark grey, thick, with close, broad ridges and deep fissures in maturity. The leaves are up to 20cm (8in) long and 4in (10cm) wide, with 10–15 pairs of prominent, parallel veins, which run out to the tip of a rounded tooth. They are dark, glossy green above with a yellow midrib and sage-green beneath. The fruit is a shining rich red-brown acorn, which is held in a deep cup that encloses up to one half of the acorn.

Distribution: From Maine southeast to Alabama.
Height: 30m (100ft)
Shape: Broadly spreading
Deciduous
Pollinated: Wind
Leaf shape: Oblong to obovate

Left: The acorns of chestnut oak are borne on the tree either singly or in pairs and attached by a short stout stalk, which is seldom more than 1cm (½in) long.

Swamp Chestnut Oak

Basket oak, Cow oak *Quercus michauxii*

Also called basket oak because the wood easily splits into thin strips, which were once used to make baskets for carrying cotton. This tree is a close relative of the chestnut oak, *Quercus prinus*, taking over in the south where chestnut oak leaves off. It grows well in wet areas, and is commonly found in valley bottoms and on flood plains. It was also called cow oak because its sweet acorns became a staple food for the cattle of the early settlers.

Distribution: Atlantic coastal plain to the Mississippi basin.
Height: 25m (80ft)
Shape: Broadly spreading
Deciduous
Pollinated: Wind
Leaf shape: Obovate

Identification: The bark differs from chestnut oak in being much lighter and thinner. It is almost creamy grey and much less ridged and fissured. The leaves are also wider, being up to 25cm (10in) long with 10–14 rounded teeth on each side of the leaf. The leaves are dark green above and almost silver beneath. The fruit is a light brown acorn, up to 3cm (1¼in) long and held in a stout cup.

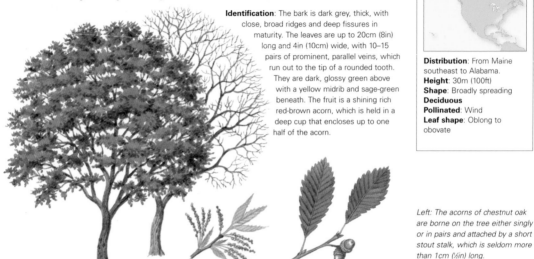

Above: Swamp chestnut oak is a large round-topped tree with distinctive ascending branches.

Left: When the leaves emerge from bud in spring they are bright yellow-green.

Black Oak

Yellow-bark oak *Quercus velutina*

This large oak is native to dry, gravelly uplands and ridges throughout eastern and central North America. It attains its highest elevations in the southern Appalachian Mountains, where it grows up to 1,200m (4,000ft) above sea level. It is also known as yellow-bark oak, a reference to the inner bark, which is a deep yellow-orange colour. It is full of tannic acid and was once used in the tanning of leather and as a yellow dye.

Identification: The outer bark is dark brown and ridged. The leaves, which are tough like parchment, are ovate to elliptic, up to 25cm (10in) long and 15cm (6in) wide. They mostly have seven pointed lobes and a distinct yellow central midrib. They are glossy dark green above and pea-green beneath with tufts of copper-coloured hair in the leaf vein axils. The fruit is enclosed in a bowl-shaped cup, which covers about half of the acorn.

Distribution: From Maine to Georgia in the east and Wisconsin to Texas in the west.
Height: 30m (100ft)
Shape: Broadly spreading
Deciduous
Pollinated: Wind
Leaf shape: Ovate to elliptic

Left: The acorn is red-brown and up to 2.5cm (1in) long.

OTHER SPECIES OF NOTE

Oregon White Oak *Quercus garryana*
The only oak that is native to British Columbia and Washington. Its range extends south along the Coast Range through Oregon into California. It is a broadly spreading, medium-size tree, to 25m (80ft). It has dark green, obovate leaves, with two or three deep, rounded lobes on each side.

Post Oak *Quercus stellata*
Widely spread throughout eastern and central USA, this round-headed, medium-size oak has foliage so dark that the tree appears nearly black in the landscape. It has heavily lobed leaves; the lobes are arranged in a way that gives a cross-like appearance to the leaf. Fence posts were once made from the timber, hence its name.

Blackjack Oak *Quercus marilandica*
A medium-size tree native to south-eastern USA, from Long Island to Texas and Arkansas, where it grows in dry uplands and on the edge of prairies, and may be little more than a tall, spreading shrub. It has distinctive leaves, which are thick and stiff, almost triangular in shape, and up to 15cm (6in) long and 10cm (4in) wide.

Northern Pin Oak *Quercus ellipsoidalis*
A medium-size tree, which usually has a short trunk and a large spreading crown. It grows naturally from northern Indiana northwards to Minnesota, particularly around the Great Lakes region. The leaves, which are deeply lobed almost to the red midrib, unfurl from bud a pale crimson colour, turn shiny dark green in summer and then deep red in autumn.

Valley Oak

Californian white oak *Quercus lobata*

This large, attractive tree, otherwise known as the Californian white oak, grows naturally in the valleys of western California between the Sierra Nevada and the Pacific coast. The oldest trees are to be found in Mendocino county, where there are specimens over 600 years old. It has the deepest-lobed leaves of any oak, hence the species name *lobata*; the lobes penetrate deep into the leaf almost to the midrib.

Identification: The bark is light grey, thick and divided into vertical fissures, becoming tinged with orange or brown in maturity. The leaves are up to 10cm (4in) long, deep green above and pale green with some pubescence beneath. They have between five and eleven rounded lobes on each side of the leaf. The acorn is held in a shallow cup, which encloses less than a third of the acorn.

Right: The fruit is a pointed, slender acorn, up to 6cm (2½in) long.

Distribution: California from Trinity River to Los Angeles.
Height: 30m (100ft)
Shape: Broadly spreading
Deciduous
Pollinated: Wind
Leaf shape: Oblong to obovate

EVERGREEN OAKS

There are over 30 evergreen oaks that are either native, or commonly cultivated, within North America.
Most are medium-size, slow-growing trees and in some cases of great age. They are generally hardy, quite
often found growing high up in mountain ranges or on exposed coastline. Their tolerance of exposure
and salt spray means they are often used to provide shelter from onshore winds.

Live Oak

Quercus virginiana

Distribution: South-east USA.
Height: 15m (50ft)
Shape: Broadly spreading
Evergreen
Pollinated: Wind
Leaf shape: Variable from oblong to elliptic

Right: The acorns are borne in groups of three to five.

This dense, round-topped tree, typically more broad than tall, is native to a coastal belt that runs from Virginia round to southern Texas. In South Carolina it is widely planted as an avenue tree for the long drives leading to the plantation mansions. It is extremely tolerant of salt spray, and is quite often used to provide shelter from onshore winds in coastal areas.

Identification: The bark is dark brown sometimes tinged with red, lightly fissured and separating into small scales in maturity. The evergreen leaves are extremely variable. They may be lobed and toothed around the margin, or entirely smooth and they can vary in length from 5 to 12.5cm (2 to 5in). They are dark green and lustrous above, and pale green and pubescent beneath. The shoots and young branchlets are also covered in a grey down. The fruit is a stout chestnut-brown acorn, which is held in a light brown cup to one third of its length.

Canyon Live Oak

Quercus chrysolepis

The canyon live oak is a squat tree with a short trunk, and long, horizontal-spreading branches forming a broad canopy, sometimes 46m (150ft) across. It occurs naturally from Oregon south to the Mexican border, down both the Coast Range and the Sierra Nevada mountains, where it reaches elevations of 2,750m (9,000ft) above sea level. It was identified by Charles Sargent of the Arnold Arboretum, Boston.

Distribution: West Coast USA.
Height: 15m (50ft)
Shape: Broadly spreading
Evergreen
Pollinated: Wind
Leaf shape: Oblong to ovate to elliptic

Identification: The bark is up to 5cm (2in) thick, ash-grey, sometimes tinged with red, and covered with small scales in maturity. The leaves are similar to the live oak, *Quercus virginiana*, varying from entire and smooth to lobed and spiny, sometimes on the same tree. They are a bright yellow-green above, and pale green beneath with some pubescence. It has distinctive acorns, which are up to 5cm (2in) long and held in a flat cup, which is as wide as the acorn is tall.

Right: The acorns are usually borne singly and held in a flat cup, which is marked with triangular scales.

Arizona White Oak

Quercus arizonica

This long-lived, slow-growing tree has small, thick, hard evergreen leaves, which normally last only one year, falling in spring to be immediately replaced by new ones. It is the most common white oak of southern New Mexico and Arizona and its range extends south to northern Mexico. It grows on hot, sandy hillsides and dry, rocky canyons, up to 3,000m (10,000ft) above sea level. It tends to be a low-spreading tree, with large twisted branches.

Identification: The bark is ash-grey and covered in long, scaly ridges. The leaves may vary from oblong to lanceolate, normally pointed at the tip, but sometimes rounded. They emerge light red in colour, quickly turning dull, dark blue-green above, and pale green below and covered in fine pubescence. The fruit is a dark chestnut-brown, oval acorn, which is up to 2.5cm (1in) long, and enclosed for half its length in a light brown cup covered with pointed, tipped scales.

Right: The leaves can be entire or toothed.

Distribution: Texas, New Mexico and Arizona.
Height: 20m (65ft)
Shape: Broadly spreading
Evergreen
Pollinated: Wind
Leaf shape: Oblong-lanceolate

OTHER SPECIES OF NOTE

Holm Oak
Quercus ilex
This domed, densely branched oak tree is one of the most important trees for shelter in coastal areas throughout Europe.

In the wild in Italy, France and Spain, it grows from sea level to altitudes above 1,500m (5,000ft). It grows across the USA. The bark is charcoal-grey, smooth at first, but quickly developing shallow fissures, which crack into small and irregular plates. In more mature trees the narrow, evergreen leaf normally has an entire margin with no serrations. *See also page 353.*

Turkey Oak *Quercus cerris*
This is a tall, vigorous, deciduous tree with a straight stem, and deeply fissured, grey-brown bark. It is native to central and southern Europe, although its exact range is unknown because it has been planted across Europe for centuries and naturalizes easily. The elliptic leaves are up to 12cm (4¾in) long, with irregular lobing, particularly on young trees. The acorn cups are covered in whiskers. It grows in USA zones 4–7. *See also page 352.*

Californian Live Oak

Quercus agrifolia

There is a suggestion that the botanical name of this tree should be *aquifolia*, which means "holly-like", rather than *agrifolia*, which means "growing wild on arable land". The leaf is holly-like, and the tree does grow naturally in coastal areas, in some cases directly above the high water mark. This dense foliaged, evergreen tree is an attractive feature of the Pacific seaboard.

Identification: On young trees the bark is smooth and light grey; on older trees it becomes almost black and divided into broad, rounded ridges. The leaves vary from narrow lanceolate to almost round and may taper to a fine point or a blunt end. They are a dark, dull green above and pale sage-green below and sometimes covered with a thick coating of rusty colour down in the leaf axils. The acorn is held in a light fawn-coloured cup, which extends over a third of the acorn.

Below: The fruit is a light chestnut-brown acorn, approximately 3cm (1¼in) long .

Distribution: South-western USA.
Height: 25m (80ft)
Shape: Broadly spreading
Evergreen
Pollinated: Wind
Leaf shape: Oval to oblong

BIRCHES

The birches, Betula, *are a group of catkin-bearing, alternate-leaved, deciduous trees, native to northern temperate regions of the world. There are more than 60 species in total, spread right across the region, from Japan to Spain and across North America. They are particularly well known for their attractive bark, which, depending on species, can vary from pure white to red.*

Yellow Birch

Betula alleghaniensis

Distribution: Eastern North America.
Height: 30m (100ft)
Shape: Broadly columnar
Deciduous
Pollinated: Wind
Leaf shape: Ovate to oblong

Previously known as *B. lutea*, this large, handsome birch has long been a valued timber tree to the US Forest Service. The name is well chosen, for it has several yellow characteristics, including the bark. It has been widely planted as an ornamental species elsewhere in the temperate world.

Identification: The bark is yellowish-brown, peeling in horizontal flakes to reveal more vibrant, yellow-coloured bark beneath. The leaves are ovate-oblong, up to 10cm (4in) long and 5cm (2in) across, finely toothed along the margin, tapering to a point, grass-green above, paler beneath. In autumn, they turn golden-yellow. The male flowers are borne in drooping yellow catkins, 10cm (4in) long; female flowers are borne in shorter, red-brown erect catkins.

Above: Male and female flowers occur on the same tree.

Below: Yellow birch fruit.

River Birch

Black birch *Betula nigra*

Distribution: Central and eastern USA from Maine in the east to Minnesota in the west and south to Texas.
Height: 30m (100ft)
Shape: Broadly spreading
Deciduous
Pollinated: Wind
Leaf shape: Ovate

The river birch, or black birch, as it is sometimes known, lives up to its name by growing beside creeks and in low-lying, swampy ground. It has been planted extensively to help control erosion caused by flooding. River birch is one of the few birches to regenerate well from cut stumps and is often coppiced to encourage multiple stems, which display attractive, pink-brown, peeling bark.

Identification: The bark is pink-brown and peeling when young, becoming dark black-purple with orange fissures in maturity. The 10cm- (4in-) long, ovate leaves are edged with sharp, double teeth, which give the leaf a slightly lobed appearance. The leaves are deep green above and blue-green beneath with silver-grey pubescence on the leaf veins. Both the male and female flowers are catkins, up to 7.5cm (3in) long. The male catkins are yellow and hang down; while the female catkins are green and upright. Both appear on the same tree in early spring.

Above: Female flowers are upright green catkins, which are borne on the tree before the leaves emerge in early spring.

Cherry Birch

Sweet birch *Betula lenta*

This attractive tree is common across central and eastern North America. Its alternative common name refers to the fragrance that the shoots and leaves emit when crushed. Winter-green oil was distilled from its wood. It has distinctive, dark red bark with purple flakes. In autumn its leaves fleetingly turn vibrant gold.

Identification: The leaves are ovate, to 13cm (5in) long and 6cm (2½in) across. They are edged with small, sharp teeth, and have distinct leaf veins. They are glossy dark green above, and pale green with fine pubescence below, especially when young. The reddish bark is lined with pale horizontal bands of lenticels.

Left: Male and female catkins are borne separately on the same tree in early spring.

Left and right: The leaves taper to a short point.

Distribution: North America from Quebec to Alabama.
Height: 25m (80ft)
Shape: Broadly spreading
Deciduous
Pollinated: Wind
Leaf shape: Ovate

OTHER SPECIES OF NOTE

European White Birch *Betula pendula*
Also known as silver birch, this hardy ornamental tree has long been planted across North America. It is easily distinguished by its white bark, which is marked by black diamond-like patches, and the lax, rather warty, pendulous shoots at the tips of the branches. European white birch is a prolific seeder, and one of the first trees to colonize cleared ground. *See also page 358.*

Himalayan Birch *Betula utilis*
This Asian birch is one of the most attractive deciduous trees, and has long been planted in parks, gardens and botanical collections across North America. The colour of its bark varies from white to pink-brown or orange-red. The bark is paper thin and peels off in long, ribbon-like horizontal strips. *See also page 359.*

Chinese Red-barked Birch *Betula albo-sinensis*
Discovered in western China in 1901, this birch was first planted at the Arnold Arboretum, Boston, in 1905. It has attractive coppery to orange-red bark, which peels to reveal creamy pink bark beneath. *See also page 359.*

Gray Birch *Betula populifolia*
This North American birch grows wild on the east coast from Nova Scotia and New Brunswick, south to Pennsylvania and Ohio. It is a fast-growing, small species, which seldom reaches 10m (33ft) in height. It has dark green, long, tapering leaves and white bark, which does not peel. It is a common roadside tree throughout its natural range.

Paper Birch

Canoe birch *Betula papyrifera*

Native Americans used the tough, durable bark of this beautiful tree to cover their canoes, having discovered it is impervious to water. It is an extremely hardy tree, growing as far north as Alaska and Labrador. The light, close-grained timber is also used as wood-pulp for paper making. Its peeling bark is one of its most attractive features, varying in colour from pure white to pale pink.

Below: The male and female flowers are catkins, which are borne separately on the same tree in early spring.

Distribution: Coast to coast northern North America.
Height: 20m (65ft)
Shape: Broadly conical
Deciduous
Pollinated: Wind
Leaf shape: Ovate

Identification: The leaves are ovate, up to 10cm (4in) long, and 7.5cm (3in) wide, with shallow teeth around the margin. Each leaf ends in a tapered point and is dark green and smooth on top, and pale green and pubescent along the veins below. In autumn the leaves turn bright marmalade-orange. Male catkins are up to 10cm (4in) long, drooping and bright yellow. Female catkins are green and slightly shorter. Both ripen and disintegrate on the tree in summer, releasing thousands of seeds, dispersed by the wind.

ALDERS

Alders are a group of 36 species of deciduous trees within the Betulaceae family. They are native primarily to northern temperate regions of the world, where they grow in damp conditions, quite often alongside rivers and watercourses. They are easily recognized by their fruit, which is an egg-shaped, pendulous, woody cone containing numerous tiny winged seeds.

Common Alder

Alnus glutinosa

This tree has always been associated with water. It thrives in damp, waterlogged conditions close to rivers and marshy ground, where it creates its own oxygen supply. Alder timber is waterproof, and has been used to make products such as boats and water pipes. It also forms the foundations of many of the buildings in Venice, and is used to make wooden clogs. It was introduced into the USA and has naturalized, growing alongside streams.

Identification: The bark is dark grey-brown and fissured from an early age. The leaves are obovate to orbicular, finely toothed with up to ten pairs of pronounced leaf veins, and a strong central midrib. Up to 10cm (4in) long and 7.5cm (3in) wide, the leaves are dark green and shiny above and pale grey-green beneath, with tufts of pubescence in the leaf axils. Male and female flowers are catkins: the male is greenish-yellow, drooping and up to 10cm (4in) long; the female is a much smaller, red, upright catkin, which, after fertilization, ripens into a distinctive small brown cone. Spent cones persist until the following spring.

Distribution: Whole of Europe into western Asia and south to North Africa. USA zones 3–7.
Height: 25m (82ft)
Shape: Broadly conical
Deciduous
Pollinated: Wind
Leaf shape: Obovate

Left: Catkins appear before the leaves in spring. The cones grow in summer, by which time the rounded leaves are thick on the branches.

Red Alder

Oregon alder *Alnus rubra*

Otherwise known as the Oregon alder, this common, medium-size tree is most prominent in the Coast Mountain and Cascade Valleys regions, where it grows in dense groups alongside roads. As with all alders, it thrives in damp, rich soils, especially alongside creeks and rivers. It has distinctive pale grey to white bark, which from a distance resembles some of the white-barked birches.

Right: The overall outline of red alder is of a conical almost "conifer-shape" tree.

Identification: The leaves are ovate to elliptic, up to 10cm (4in) long and 7.5cm (3in) broad, with a slight point at the tip. They are dark green and smooth above, and pale green with rusty red hairs along the pronounced, straight parallel leaf veins beneath. Both the male and female flowers are catkins, which are borne separately on the same tree in early spring. The male flowers are drooping, orange and up to 15cm (6in) long. The female flowers are much smaller, bright red and borne upright. These ripen into 2.5cm- (1in-) long, egg-shaped woody cones containing numerous seeds.

Distribution: West coast from Alaska to southern California.
Height: 15m (50ft)
Shape: Broadly conical
Deciduous
Pollinated: Wind
Leaf shape: Ovate

Speckled Alder

Alnus rugosa

Native of North America from Newfoundland to Alaska and ranging south on the east coast to West Virginia, Ohio and Minnesota. It is a hardy small tree, or large shrub, which thrives in cold, wet conditions where other trees would struggle. It is a close relative of the European grey alder, *Alnus incana*. Speckled alder has light, soft, close-grained, fawn-coloured wood, which was at one time used for smoking salmon.

Identification: The whole tree has a rather shrubby appearance, with branching from ground level intertwining with branches further up the stem. The bark is dark grey and smooth. The leaves are oval to ovate, up to 10cm (4in) long, and may be either rounded or slightly pointed at the tip. They are sharply and unevenly toothed around the leaf margin, bright green and smooth above and pale green with some pubescence beneath. The fruit is a small green cone-like structure that ripens to woody brown and persists on the tree long after leaf fall.

Distribution: Coast to coast from Newfoundland to Alaska.
Height: 9m (30ft)
Shape: Broadly spreading
Deciduous
Pollinated: Wind
Leaf Shape: Ovate

Left: The male catkins are up to 10cm (4in) long and appear before the tree comes into leaf in early spring.

OTHER SPECIES OF NOTE

Grey Alder *Alnus incana*
Native to the Caucasus Mountains of central Europe, this medium-size tree grows up to elevations of 1,000m (3,280ft). It gets its name from the dense covering of grey hairs on the underside of the leaf. The leaves are ovate, up to 10cm (4in) long, double-toothed and have a pointed tip. The bark is grey and smooth in maturity. See also page 362.

Sitka Alder *Alnus sinuata*
This small, hardy tree is native to western North America from Alaska to California. It grows well at high altitudes and can withstand intense cold and frost. Sitka alder has distinctive yellow male catkins, which can be up to 15cm (6in) long and are borne in great profusion in early spring.

Italian Alder *Alnus cordata*
This handsome, broadly conical tree originates from southern Italy and Corsica, where it grows at up to 1,000m (3,280ft) on dry mountain slopes. It is the largest alder, easily reaching in excess of 30m (100ft) tall. Italian alder has large obovate, glossy, dark green leaves, each up to 10cm (4in) across. It has been widely planted in parks, gardens and arboreta across North America since its introduction in the mid-19th century. It is the only alder that will tolerate dry conditions. See also page 363.

White Alder

Alnus rhombifolia

The white alder grows by running streams and watercourses in canyons in the Rocky Mountains from Idaho and Montana south to southern California. To the early settlers its presence was a good indicator of running water. Its botanical name is derived from the almost diamond shape of the leaves; however, they are more commonly ovate or oval to round. It is a rare tree in cultivation.

Identification: The bark of young trees is smooth and pale grey, becoming dark brown, heavily fissured and scale-like in maturity. The leaves may be up to 10cm (4in) long and 7.5cm (3in) wide. They are unevenly toothed around the edges, dark shiny green above and pale yellow beneath, with some pubescence. Both the male and female flowers are catkins, which are borne separately on the same tree in early spring, before the leaves appear. The male catkins are reddish-yellow and up to 12.5cm (5in) long.

Distribution: Western USA.
Height: 30m (100ft)
Shape: Broadly conical
Deciduous
Pollinated: Wind
Leaf shape: Ovate

Below: When the leaves unfold from the bud they are covered in dense white hair.

Above: The seeds are contained within an oval woody cone.

HORNBEAMS, HOP HORNBEAMS AND HAZELS

Hornbeams and hazels are members of the Betulaceae family. They have a strong association with rural communities, although their economic importance has lessened.

American Hornbeam

Blue beech, water beech and ironwood *Carpinus caroliniana*

American hornbeam has an interesting natural distribution, growing wild down the east coast of North America and then in southern Mexico, Guatemala and Honduras. It is not widely planted, yet it has more attractive foliage and superior autumn colour than the more common European hornbeam.

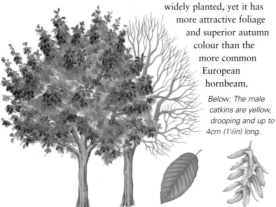

Below: The male catkins are yellow, drooping and up to 4cm (1½in) long.

Identification: The bark is steel-grey and smooth, becoming fluted in maturity. The leaves are dark green all over and turn a mixture of orange, purple and red in autumn. Male and female flowers are catkins borne separately on the same tree in spring. The female catkins are green, smaller and borne at the shoot tips. The fruit is a nut attached to two or three bracts; these fruits cluster together in pendulous catkins.

Distribution: From Quebec southwards to Florida and then west to Texas – then a gap and then southern Mexico, Guatemala and Honduras.
Height: 10m (33ft)
Shape: Broadly spreading
Deciduous
Pollinated: Wind
Leaf shape: Ovate

Left: The leaves are ovate, to 10cm (4in) long, edged with coarse double teeth, taper pointed and carry pronounced parallel veins.

Hornbeam

Carpinus betulus

Distribution: Central Europe, including southern Britain to south-west Asia. USA hardiness zones 4–7.
Height: 30m (100ft)
Shape: Broadly spreading
Deciduous
Pollinated: Wind
Leaf shape: Ovate

Left: The fruit is a ribbed nut.

Hornbeam is sometimes confused with beech because of its silver-grey bark and similar leaf. However, hornbeam bark is far more angular than beech bark. Hornbeam leaves also have obvious serrations around the margin, which are not present on beech. Its timber is dense and hard, and has a clean, white, crisp appearance. It has been introduced into the USA and is a good shade tree for large lawns.

Identification: The leaves are oval to ovate, up to 10cm (4in) long and 5cm (2in) across, double-toothed around the margin and tapering to a long point. There are normally 10–13 pairs of leaf veins. The upper leaf surface of the leaves is dark green, the underside a paler green. In autumn the leaf turns rich yellow before dropping. Both catkins are borne separately in spring on the same tree. The fruit is a distinctive three-lobed bract with a small, ribbed, brown nut at the base of the centre bract. The bract is green in summer, ripening to fawn in autumn and persisting on the tree through to the following spring.

Right: Male catkins are up to 5cm (2in) long. Female catkins (not shown) are smaller.

Hop Hornbeam

Ostrya carpinifolia

This distinctive ornamental tree is primarily known for its hop-like fruit, which, when ripe, hangs in clusters of buff-coloured, overlapping papery scales, enclosing a small brown nut. Mature trees have long, low, horizontal branches, which seem to defy gravity. It is planted as a street tree in the USA.

Identification: The bark of hop hornbeam is smooth and brown-grey when young, becoming flaky, rather like Persian ironwood, in maturity. The ovate to oblong leaves are up to 10cm (4in) long and 5cm (2in) across. They are sharply pointed and have forward-pointing, double teeth around the margin. They are dark green above and paler beneath, with slight pubescence on both sides. Each leaf has 12–15 pairs of parallel leaf veins and a pronounced midrib. The flowers are catkins: the male's are yellow, drooping and up to 10cm (4in) long; the female's are much smaller and green. The shape in maturity is broadly spreading, with the width quite often exceeding the height.

Distribution: Southern Europe to Iran. USA zones 6–9.
Height: 20m (66ft)
Shape: Broadly spreading
Deciduous
Pollinated: Wind
Leaf shape: Ovate

Left and above: The hop-like fruit develops in summer from long, drooping catkins.

OTHER SPECIES OF NOTE
American Hazel *Corylus americana*
This large shrub, or small tree, is native to eastern North America, where it grows in canyons and on the lower slopes of the Appalachian Mountain range. It is instantly recognizable in spring by its long, creamy yellow, male, catkin-like flowers, which release clouds of pollen, to be dispersed by the wind.

Common Hazel *Corylus avellana* This European and Asian hazel is distinguished from its American cousin by the shorter green calyx that encases the seed (nut) in autumn. It is much the same size as the American hazel, *Corylus americana*, seldom reaching more than 6m (20ft) tall, and is widely planted in parks and arboreta across North America. *See also page 367.*

Turkish Hazel *Corylus colurna*
Native to south-east Europe, this hazel has been widely planted as an ornamental tree in parks and gardens across the USA. It is a large, handsome tree, sometimes reaching 25m (80ft) tall. It has a neat conical habit and is valued for street planting and is popular for planting in formal avenues. It is prized for its timber, which is dense, pinkish-brown, and used for cabinet-making. *See also page 367.*

Eastern Hop Hornbeam

American hop hornbeam, Ironwood *Ostrya virginiana*

This medium-size tree has much the same native range as the American hornbeam, *Carpinus caroliniana*, including southern Mexico. It does not have such a distinctive hop-like flower as the European hop hornbeam, *Ostrya carpinifolia*, but makes up for this with a very distinctive leaf, which has variable teeth around the margin. As one of its other names suggests, the American hop hornbeam has very strong, hard timber, which is used to make handles of tools, such as mallets.

Identification: The bark is grey-brown, smooth at first, becoming scaly in maturity. The pointed leaves are ovate, to 12cm (5in) long and 5cm (2in) across, with 12 pairs of distinctive leaf veins, and irregular serrations around the leaf margin. They are dark green and smooth above, and slightly paler green with some pubescence in the vein axils beneath. The flowers are catkins, and the fruit is a nut, which is enclosed in a cream, bladder-like husk, which is borne in hanging clusters of up to 20 husks at a time.

Distribution: Eastern North America.
Height: 20m (65ft)
Shape: Broadly conical
Deciduous
Pollinated: Wind
Leaf shape: Ovate

Left: Male and female flowers are borne on the same tree.

Right: The dark green leaves look like those of the birch tree.

BASSWOODS AND LIMES

There are about 45 different species of lime within the Tilia genus. They are all deciduous and all found in northern temperate regions. Limes are handsome trees, many growing into large, ornamental specimens. Several have been used for urban tree planting, as they respond well to pollarding and hard pruning in residential areas. Limes look good planted in avenues, and within formal vistas.

American Basswood

Tilia americana

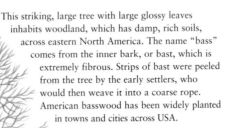

This striking, large tree with large glossy leaves inhabits woodland, which has damp, rich soils, across eastern North America. The name "bass" comes from the inner bark, or bast, which is extremely fibrous. Strips of bast were peeled from the tree by the early settlers, who would then weave it into a coarse rope. American basswood has been widely planted in towns and cities across USA.

Identification: The bark is a greyish-brown, becoming corky, and cracked into long horizontal, scaly ridges, in maturity. American basswood has broadly ovate leaves, which can be up to 25cm (10in) long and 20cm (8in) wide, and taper to a fine point at the tip. The leaves have coarse, forward-pointing teeth, are deep green and shiny on top, paler beneath with tufts of fawn pubescence in the vein axils. In winter the buds are a distinctive light green colour.

Distribution: From New Brunswick to Manitoba and south to Arkansas and Tennessee.
Height: 25m (80ft)
Shape: Broadly columnar
Deciduous
Pollinated: Insect
Leaf shape: Ovate to round

Right: Clusters of pale yellow, fragrant flowers appear in summer.

White Basswood

Beetree linden *Tilia heterophylla*

White basswood has a similar range to American basswood, *Tilia americana*, and is found growing at its best in the Appalachian Mountains. It differs from American basswood in having many more flowers in each cluster, up to 25, and a white underside to the leaf (caused by a covering of short, white hairs, hence the name white basswood). It is also known as beetree linden, a reference to the thousands of bees that descend on the trees' flowers to collect nectar in summer.

Identification: The bark is silver-grey becoming fissured in maturity. It has silver-backed leaves, variable in shape, and coarsely toothed, with a less pronounced tip than American basswood. The leaves are up to 15cm (6in) long and 10cm (4in) wide. The top side is matt, rather dull, green. The flowers are pale yellow, extremely fragrant, pendulous and borne in clusters of up to 25. The winter buds and shoots are pale green.

Distribution: From New Brunswick to Manitoba and south to Arkansas and Tennessee.
Height: 25m (80ft)
Shape: Broadly columnar
Deciduous
Pollinated: Insect
Leaf shape: Ovate

Left: Each leaf is silver-white on the underside.

Right: Globular fruits are attached to a papery husk.

Silver Linden

Silver lime *Tilia tomentosa*

This ornamental tree has been widely planted across eastern USA, although it is rarely found in the west. Its richly scented, pale lemon flowers, which emerge later from bud than on most other limes, are a magnet for bees in summer. The bees become intoxicated by the nectar and fall to the ground, where they perish by the thousand.

Identification: The bark is grey with shallow ridges even in maturity. The leaves are almost rounded, up to 13cm (5in) long and 10cm (4in) broad. They are deep green above, silver below and flutter in the slightest breeze. The overall form is slightly broader than other limes with pendulous branching. This pendulous habit has been cultivated to produce an attractive weeping form, *Tilia tomentosa* 'Petiolaris'.

Above: The fruit is attached to a pendulous papery bract.

Right: The leaf colour creates a silver shimmery effect from a distance.

Distribution: South-west Asia and south-east Europe.
Height: 30m (97ft)
Shape: Broadly columnar
Deciduous
Pollinated: Insect
Leaf shape: Rounded

OTHER SPECIES OF NOTE

Small-leaf Linden
Tilia cordata
Native to most of Europe, this tall, columnar tree has small, cordate leaves. In Britain its presence in woodland indicates that the site is ancient. It grows in USA zone 4. The inner bark, or "bast", was once used to make rope. Some coppiced trees are believed to be over 2,000 years old. *See also page 368.*

Broadleaf Linden *Tilia platyphyllos*
This splendid, large, domed-top tree has a clean, straight trunk and graceful arching branches. It is native to Europe and south-west Asia, where it reaches heights in excess of 30m (100ft). It flowers before any other basswood, with pale lemon flowers appearing from late May, in clusters of three to five. It is grown as an ornamental sporadically throughout North America from Ontario to British Columbia and south to Ohio. *See also page 369.*

Common Lime *Tilia x europaea*
Also known as the European linden, this is a hybrid between *T. platyphyllos* and *T. cordata*, which, although vigorous, has none of the grace of either parent. It is distinguished by the untidy suckering that appears around the base of the trunk. It is common throughout the USA. *See also page 369.*

Carolina Basswood

Tilia caroliniana

Carolina basswood is smaller than the other basswoods and also more tender, rarely surviving to any size further north than the Carolinas. It is at its most prevalent in New Hanover County around Wilmington and the Wrightsville Beach area. It was first discovered here by Mark Catesby in 1726. Its most distinguishing feature is its slender red-brown slightly pendulous shoots.

Identification: The bark is silver-grey to brown, becoming cracked vertically in maturity. The leaves, up to 10cm (4in) long and wide, have a long point at the tip. They are acutely serrated around the margin, dark green above and covered in a pale rusty colour pubescence beneath. The creamy yellow, fragrant flowers appear in June, in clusters of up to 15. After flowering, globular green fruits form.

Distribution: South-eastern USA from North Carolina to Florida and west to Texas.
Height: 20m (65ft)
Shape: Broadly columnar
Deciduous
Pollinated: Insect
Leaf shape: Ovate

Above: Globular green fruits ripen to brown.

Below: The leaves are ovate to slightly heart-shape.

TUPELOS AND MYRTLES

Tupelos are members of the Nyssaceae family, which also includes the dove tree, Davidia involucrata. *They are particularly popular in cultivation because of their brilliant displays of autumn-leaf colour, which may vary from purple through red to bright orange. All Nyssas grow best in moist, lime-free soil.*

Water Tupelo

Cotton gum *Nyssa aquatica*

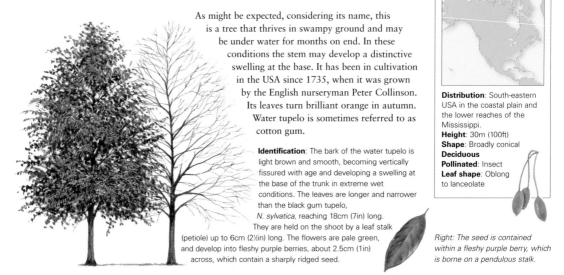

As might be expected, considering its name, this is a tree that thrives in swampy ground and may be under water for months on end. In these conditions the stem may develop a distinctive swelling at the base. It has been in cultivation in the USA since 1735, when it was grown by the English nurseryman Peter Collinson. Its leaves turn brilliant orange in autumn. Water tupelo is sometimes referred to as cotton gum.

Identification: The bark of the water tupelo is light brown and smooth, becoming vertically fissured with age and developing a swelling at the base of the trunk in extreme wet conditions. The leaves are longer and narrower than the black gum tupelo, *N. sylvatica*, reaching 18cm (7in) long. They are held on the shoot by a leaf stalk (petiole) up to 6cm (2½in) long. The flowers are pale green, and develop into fleshy purple berries, about 2.5cm (1in) across, which contain a sharply ridged seed.

Distribution: South-eastern USA in the coastal plain and the lower reaches of the Mississippi.
Height: 30m (100ft)
Shape: Broadly conical
Deciduous
Pollinated: Insect
Leaf shape: Oblong to lanceolate

Right: The seed is contained within a fleshy purple berry, which is borne on a pendulous stalk.

Tupelo

Black gum, Sour gum *Nyssa sylvatica*

Distribution: Eastern North America.
Height: 25m (82ft)
Shape: Broadly columnar
Deciduous
Pollinated: Insect
Leaf shape: Obovate

Right: Tupelo flowers are green and hard to see against the leaves. The fruit usually appears in pairs.

This slow-growing, medium-size tree has a huge range in North America, stretching from Ontario in the north to Mexico in the south. It has been extensively cultivated elsewhere, primarily for its spectacular autumn-leaf colouring, which ranges from yellow and orange through to red and burgundy. Tupelo was introduced into Europe in 1750.

Identification: The bark is dark grey and smooth when young, becoming cracked and fissured into square plates in maturity. The leaves are obovate to elliptic, up to 15cm (6in) long and 3in (7.5cm) across, and have an entire margin and a blunt tip. They are lustrous grass-green above, and glaucous beneath. Both the male and female flowers are small, green and inconspicuous. They are borne in long-stalked clusters on the same tree in summer. The fruit is a blueberry-coloured, egg-shaped glossy berry, up to 1.5cm (⅝in) long. It is edible but not particularly palatable, being rather sour.

Chinese Tupelo

Nyssa sinensis

Distribution: Central China. USA zones 7–9.
Height: 15m (50ft)
Shape: Broadly conical
Deciduous
Pollinated: Insect
Leaf shape: Oblong to lanceolate

Right: The leaves are pointed.

Closely related to both the black gum and water tupelo, this attractive small tree grows in woodland and beside streams in central China. It is comparatively rare in cultivation, although under the right conditions, it produces superb autumn-leaf colours ranging from red to yellow. It was introduced into the USA in 1902 by English plant collector E. H. Wilson, working on behalf of the Arnold Arboretum, Boston.

Identification: The bark is grey-brown, smooth, becoming cracked and flaking with age. The leaves are oblong-lanceolate in shape, up to 20cm (8in) long and 6cm (2½in) wide. They emerge from bud a greenish-red colour, but quickly fade to deep green. They are shiny above, and paler and matt beneath. Both the male and female flowers are small and green. They are borne in separate clusters in leaf axils on the same tree in summer.

Left: The fruit is a purple-blue berry about 2.5cm (1in) long.

See also page 333.

OTHER SPECIES OF NOTE

Swamp Tupelo
Nyssa sylvatica var. *biflora*
This distinctive variety may be considered a separate species. As the name suggests, this tree occupies wetter conditions than the black gum tupelo, *N. sylvatica*, and is found in the coastal plains of south-eastern USA from North Carolina to eastern Florida. Botanically it has a longer leaf, up to 18cm (7in) long, and has female flowers, which cluster in pairs rather than in fours.

Myrtus chequen
This South American, evergreen myrtle is native to Chile. It is usually found growing in wet conditions. It is related to the Chilean myrtle, *Myrtus luma*, but does not have the brilliant cinnamon-coloured bark. It is also a smaller tree, seldom reaching heights in excess of 4m (13ft). It has a brown felt-like stem, which when young is covered in soft white down. *See also page 333.*

Myrtus lechleriana
This small evergreen tree has a bushy habit and grows high in the Andes in Chile, South America. Unlike most myrtles this one flowers in spring rather than late summer. The flowers are creamy white with yellow anthers. It is hardy and because of its bushy habit it is quite often clipped to create a dense screen or hedge.

Chilean Myrtle

Luma apiculata

This beautiful small tree, which is also known as *Myrtus apiculata*, or *Luma apiculata*, has superb cinnamon-orange coloured, thin, felt-like bark, which peels in maturity to reveal cream-coloured patches beneath. Curiously, no matter how hot the weather, the bark of this tree always feels cold to the touch. The tree is particularly prevalent in the Argentinian tourist resort of Bariloche. It is widely grown in botanic gardens and arboreta across southern states of the USA.

Identification: The leaves are broadly elliptic, up to 2.5cm (1in) long, untoothed with a short point, bronze-purple when young, quickly becoming dark green and glossy above and sage-green beneath. When crushed they emit a strong aromatic fragrance. Chilean myrtle has fragrant, creamy white flowers with orange-yellow stamens, which are borne singly in the leaf axils of young shoots, in late summer. The fruit is a small round berry that is red when young, ripening to purple-black in winter.

Distribution: Chile and Argentina.
Height: 12m (40ft)
Shape: Broadly spreading
Evergreen
Pollinated: Insect
Leaf shape: Elliptic

Below: The dark evergreen leaves of the Chilean myrtle are the perfect backdrop for its creamy white flowers.

POPLARS

The poplars, Salicaceae, are a genus of over 35 species of deciduous trees found throughout northern temperate regions of the world. They produce small male and female flowers, which are borne in catkins on separate trees and pollinated by wind. Poplars are fast-growing trees, many of which can withstand atmospheric pollution and salt spray from the sea.

Eastern Cottonwood

American black poplar *Populus deltoides*

This fine tree with its long, clean bole is one of the parents of the most widely planted poplars, *Populus* x *canadensis*, the other parent being *P. nigra*. The botanical name *deltoides* refers to the fact that the leaves are almost triangular.

Identification: When young, the shape of this tree is columnar with a domed top. In maturity, it becomes broad and heavily branched. The bark is pale greenish-yellow on young trees, becoming grey and deeply fissured in maturity. The triangular leaves are up to 13cm (5in) long and wide, running to an acute point at the tip. They are medium green and glossy above, and pale green beneath.

Distribution: Across North America east of the Rocky Mountains from Quebec to Texas.
Height: 30m (100ft)
Shape: Broadly columnar
Deciduous
Pollinated: Wind
Leaf shape: Deltoid (triangular)

Left: Male and female flowers are on separate trees.

Black Cottonwood

Western balsam poplar *Populus trichocarpa*

This large, vigorous North American tree is the fastest-growing balsam poplar. The first black cottonwood to be planted at the Royal Botanic Gardens, in London, in 1896, reached 17m (56ft) tall in just 13 years. Many fast-growing clones and hybrids of this species have been developed for forestry purposes and are now quite widely planted.

Identification: The bark is smooth and yellow-grey, becoming vertically fissured with age. The young shoots and winter buds are golden-yellow, and covered in a sticky, fragrant balsamic gum. In spring, as the buds open and the leaves unfurl, they emit a delicious balsam fragrance. The leaves are ovate and slightly heart-shaped at the base, up to 25cm (10in) long and 13cm (5in) wide, dark, glossy green above and light sage-green beneath, displaying a network of tiny leaf veins. The male catkins are 5cm (2in) long and the female catkins 15cm (6in). Both are carried on separate trees in early spring.

Left: The elegant leaves have a glossy upper surface.

Distribution: Western North America from Alaska to California.
Height: 40m (130ft)
Shape: Broadly columnar
Deciduous
Pollinated: Wind
Leaf shape: Ovate

Right: Male and (far right) female catkins are produced in early spring on separate trees. Female catkins are three times as long as the male ones.

Balsam Poplar

Tacamahacca *Populus balsamifera*

Until fairly recently this tree was known by the Native American name of *tacamahacca*. It is without doubt one of the most distinctive of all American poplars. In spring, woodlands where this tree grows are filled with a heady balsam fragrance, as the leaves unfurl from their long, sticky winter buds. Balsam poplar grows naturally in moist woodlands across northern USA and Canada. This tree has a tendency to throw up suckers from the roots around its base.

Identification: The bark is grey, smooth at first, becoming vertically fissured in maturity. The leaves are ovate, to 13cm (5in) long and 10cm (4in) wide, taper-pointed and finely toothed. When crushed they emit a balsam scent. Both the male and female flowers are in catkins, which are borne on separate trees. The male catkins are 5cm (2in) long and orange-brown when ripe; the female's are 7.5cm (3in) long and yellow-green.

Distribution: From Labrador to Alaska, and south to northern USA from the east to the west coast.
Height: 30m (100ft)
Shape: Broadly columnar
Deciduous
Pollinated: Wind
Leaf shape: Ovate

Right: The leaves are deep glossy green with a network of white veins.

OTHER SPECIES OF NOTE

Black Poplar *Populus nigra*
Native to western Asia and Europe, the western European subspecies of black poplar differs from the species in having a pubescent covering to the petiole, shoot, leaf midrib and flower stalk. It is endangered in the wild, mainly because much of the remaining population is male. It is planted as an ornamental and a windbreak across the USA. *See also page 372.*

Lombardy Poplar *Populus nigra* 'Italica'
This is an upright form of the European black poplar, which has been widely planted as an ornamental species. It is recognizable by its slender, columnar outline and upright branching. Lombardy poplars are predominantly male and are propagated by cuttings. *See also page 373.*

European Aspen *Populus tremula*
This small, ornamental tree, up to 20m (65ft), is native to Europe, from the Atlantic to the Pacific, and south to North Africa. It has grey, smooth bark, broadly ovate leaves up to 7.5cm (3in) long and wide, flowers that are borne in catkins and seeds that are covered in cotton wool-like hairs. *See also page 373.*

Chinese Necklace Poplar *Populus lasiocarpa*
This striking tree has the largest and thickest leaves of any poplar. The word "necklace" in the name refers to the long, pendulous, green seed capsules that appear in midsummer. These ripen, shedding seed, wrapped in a white cotton wool-like covering, over a wide area. It is widely grown across the USA. *See also page 372.*

Quaking Aspen

Populus tremuloides

Probably the most widely distributed tree of North America. Quaking aspen has leaves that appear to be in perpetual motion. They flutter or quake in any breeze, and the sound is audible. This motion is caused by slender leaf stalks, which are inappropriate for the size of the leaves, and cause them to flap together. The leaves are one of the easiest ways to identify this species, although this tree can be mistaken for the European aspen, *P. tremula*. It is distinguished by the pale, yellowish bark, which is found only on the American species.

Identification: The leaves are 5cm (2in) long and broad. They can be more round than ovate, with a short, abrupt tip, and a broad, almost flat base. They are finely toothed, dark glossy green above, pale and dull below. The young shoots are reddish-brown. The flowers are in pendulous catkins on separate trees and appear in spring.

Distribution: Across northern USA and Canada, from Newfoundland to Delaware, and from Alaska south to British Columbia, and down the Rockies.
Height: 30m (100ft)
Shape: Broadly columnar
Deciduous
Pollinated: Wind
Leaf shape: Ovate

Above: The quaking aspen has smaller leaves than its cousin the European aspen.

WILLOWS

*There are more than 300 different species of willows in the world, varying from large, spreading
ornamental specimens, to diminutive, creeping, tundra-based alpines. The majority are native to northern
temperate regions of the world. Willows are mainly deciduous, although one or two subtropical species
have leaves that persist into winter. The male and female flowers are normally borne on separate trees.*

Weeping Willow

Salix x sepulcralis 'Chrysocoma'

Weeping willow is a hybrid between
white willow and Chinese weeping
willow, and developed naturally where
the ranges of these two species met in
western Asia. The form 'Chrysocoma'
has been selected and cultivated from
the hybrid for its golden shoot and
more graceful weeping habit.
It is the familiar weeping form seen
alongside European riverbanks.

Identification: A large, spreading tree with ascending
primary branches, supporting long secondary branches, which
reach to the ground. The bark is pale grey-brown with shallow, corky
fissures. The shoot and young wood is a glorious golden-yellow colour,
as are the long, slender winter buds that hug the
shoot. The leaves are up to 13cm (5in) long and
up to 2.5cm (1in) wide. Male and female flowers
appear as the leaves emerge in early spring.

Distribution: A hybrid, so not
native to anywhere, but
widely cultivated throughout
temperate regions of the
USA as an ornamental.
Height: 20m (66ft)
Shape: Broadly weeping
Deciduous
Pollinated: Insect, and
occasionally wind
Leaf shape: Narrowly
lanceolate

*Below: The hanging branches
make for an unmistakeable form.*

*Left: Catkins grow
upwards.*

*Right: Leaves are
long and slender.*

Black Willow

Salix nigra

This is the largest and probably most frequently seen of all the American willows. It is felled
for timber in the Mississippi delta region, where heights up to 40m (130ft) have been
recorded. Along the coastal plain it is abundant in roadside swamps, where it grows
alongside the coastal plain willow *Salix caroliniana*.

Identification: It has dark, almost
black, bark, which becomes
deeply furrowed in maturity. The
young shoots are yellow at first,
gradually turning reddish-brown.
The pale green leaves are
lanceolate, rounded at the base
and narrowing gradually to a
long, fine point. They are
13cm (5in) long and finely
serrated. The
fruit is a small,
green capsule
that ripens to
release large
quantities of
fluffy seed,
dispersed by
the wind.

Distribution: Eastern and
central North America
extending into north-east
Mexico.
Height: 30m (100ft)
Shape: Broadly columnar
Deciduous
Pollinated: Insect
and occasionally
wind
Leaf shape:
Lanceolate

*Right: Both the male
and female flowers
appear in catkins on
the same tree in early spring.*

Peachleaf Willow

Almond willow *Salix amygdaloides*

Otherwise known as the almond willow, this medium-size tree is native from Michigan to Alberta and eastern Oregon, Colorado and Ohio, with outliers stretching along the St Lawrence River. It is commonly found beside creeks, and is the biggest willow west of the prairie states. It has light, soft, close-grained wood that has light brown heartwood, and nearly white sapwood.

Identification: The lanceolate leaves narrow to a long, slender point at the tip and are rounded at the base. They are up to 10cm (4in) long and 2.5cm (1in) wide, light green and lustrous above, pale and glaucous beneath, with a stout yellow or orange midrib. The overall appearance of this tree is broadly spreading, quite often with several stems growing from the base rather than one single bole. Both the male and female flowers are greeny yellow upright catkins.

Distribution: Eastern and central USA.
Height: 20m (65ft)
Shape: Broadly spreading
Deciduous
Pollinated: Insect and wind
Leaf shape: Lanceolate

Right: The male and female flowers appear on the same tree in the spring.

OTHER SPECIES OF NOTE

Contorted Willow
Salix babylonica 'Tortuosa'
A peculiar, deformed-looking tree, otherwise known as the dragon's claw willow, or corkscrew willow. It has twisted and contorted branches and shoots, and has become widely cultivated as a garden ornamental. It forms a tangled tree up to 10–15m (33–50ft) high. It originates from China, where it was first cultivated more than 100 years ago. Today, cut branches are very popular in flower arrangements. *See also page 379.*

Coastal Plain Willow *Salix caroliniana*
As the name suggests, this small tree, or large shrub, is native to the coastal plain from Virginia to Texas. It is often seen growing alongside the roads, which are like causeways, with ditches of swampland on each side. It has narrow, lanceolate leaves, which are a distinctive yellow-green on the top side, sage-green beneath, and up to 10cm (4in) long.

Pacific Willow *Salix lasiandra*
Otherwise known as the yellow willow, because of its bright yellow new shoots, this medium-size tree, to 20m (65ft) tall, grows naturally from central Alaska south to southern California. It has lanceolate leaves up to 7.5cm (3in) long and 1cm (½in) wide, which are dark green and lustrous above and pale green beneath.

Shining Willow

Salix lucida

This very hardy, tough tree grows further north than any other American willow. It grows beside streams and swamps, where it forms a short trunk with erect branches and a broad, round-topped, symmetrical head. The new shoots are a distinctive shiny, dark orange, gradually becoming darker and tinged with red in the second year. The common name is derived from the high-gloss upper surface of the leaves and the shiny young shoots.

Identification: The bark is thin, smooth and dark brown but tinged with red. The leaves have a long point at the tip and are rounded at the base. They are a smooth, shiny dark green above and paler beneath, with a pronounced broad yellow midrib. The leaf stalk (petiole) is short, thick and also yellow. Both the male and female flowers are borne in erect, pubescent, greenish-yellow catkins, which persist on the tree from early spring through until early summer.

Below: The 13cm- (5in-) long leaves vary from ovate-lanceolate to narrowly lanceolate.

Distribution: From Newfoundland to the shores of Hudson Bay, west to Saskatchewan, and south to Ohio and Pennsylvania.
Height: 10m (33ft)
Shape: Broadly spreading
Deciduous
Pollinated: Insect and wind
Leaf shape: Ovate-lanceolate

PLANES, SYCAMORES AND WITCH HAZELS

The planes are one of the most majestic groups of trees in the world. Their sheer size, form and bark colour make them an essential part of any large-scale ornamental landscape. They are able to cope successfully with the rigours of urban city life and provide welcome shade and shelter in return.

Sycamore

Buttonwood *Platanus occidentalis*

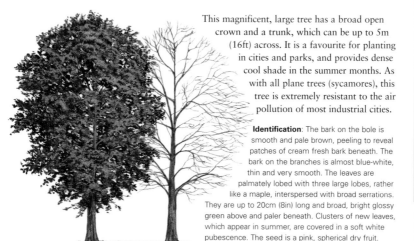

This magnificent, large tree has a broad open crown and a trunk, which can be up to 5m (16ft) across. It is a favourite for planting in cities and parks, and provides dense cool shade in the summer months. As with all plane trees (sycamores), this tree is extremely resistant to the air pollution of most industrial cities.

Identification: The bark on the bole is smooth and pale brown, peeling to reveal patches of cream fresh bark beneath. The bark on the branches is almost blue-white, thin and very smooth. The leaves are palmately lobed with three large lobes, rather like a maple, interspersed with broad serrations. They are up to 20cm (8in) long and broad, bright glossy green above and paler beneath. Clusters of new leaves, which appear in summer, are covered in a soft white pubescence. The seed is a pink, spherical dry fruit.

Distribution: Eastern North America.
Height: 35m (115ft)
Shape: Broadly columnar
Deciduous
Pollinated: Insect
Leaf shape: Palmate

Right: The 2.5cm (1in) fruits hang singly on thread-like stalks.

Oriental Plane

Platanus orientalis

The Oriental plane is a majestic tree. Hippocrates, the ancient Greek "father of medicine", is said to have taught his medical scholars under the great Oriental plane tree that still exists on the island of Kos. Another large Oriental plane on the Bosporus, near Büyükdere, is known as "the plane of Godfrey de Bouillon", because tradition states that he and his knights camped under it during the first crusade in 1096. It was introduced to the USA in the 17th century.

Identification: One of the largest of all deciduous temperate trees. It can reach heights in excess of 30m (100ft) tall, with a great spreading canopy and a trunk girth of 6m (20ft). It has attractive, buff-grey bark, which flakes to reveal creamy pink patches. The leaves are palmate, 20cm (8in) long and 25cm (10in) across, deeply cut into five narrow lobes, shiny green above, pale green below with brown tufts of hair along the veins. The leaves are attached alternately to the shoot. In autumn the leaves turn from clear yellow to old gold. The fruit is globular and mace-like, 2.5cm (1in) across, and attached in clusters of two to six on a pendulous stalk.

Right: Fruit remains on the tree throughout the winter.

Distribution: Albania, Israel, Greece, Cyprus, Lebanon, Syria, Crete. USA zones 7–9.
Height: 30m (100ft)
Shape: Broadly spreading
Deciduous
Pollinated: Insect
Leaf shape: Palmate lobed

Californian Sycamore

Platanus racemosa

The Californian sycamore grows from the upper Sacramento River, where it grows naturally alongside streams and river banks, along the lower Sierra Nevada, up to altitudes of 1,220m (4,000ft), and into the coastal ranges from Monterey southwards to Mexico.

Identification: The bark at the base of old trees is dark brown, deeply fissured and up to 10cm (4in) thick. Elsewhere, and on younger trees, the bark is thin, smooth and pale brown, becoming almost white on upper branches. This tree is often forked with thick, heavy, spreading branches, which form an open, irregular round-topped head. Young twigs and shoots are reddish.

Distribution: Western California from Sacramento to Mexico.
Height: 30m (100ft)
Shape: Broadly spreading
Deciduous
Pollinated: Insect
Leaf shape: Palmate

Left: The leaves are palmate with three to five deeply cut main lobes and shallow, blunt serrations in between.

OTHER SPECIES OF NOTE

London Plane *Platanus x hispanica*
This tree is a hybrid between the Oriental plane, *P. orientalis*, and the American sycamore, *P. occidentalis*. It is widely planted in cities across the world (including London) because of its ability to withstand atmospheric pollution and severe pruning. The London plane differs from each

parent in being more vigorous, and having leaves with shallower lobes and a lighter-coloured bark, which peels to reveal cream patches. *See also page 380.*

Large-leaved Witch Hazel
Hamamelis macrophylla
This is a rare species, which is closely allied to the American witch hazel, *Hamamelis virginiana*. It is native to south-eastern USA and grows in rich soils by streams or along the borders of forests. It has large, 13cm- (5in-) long, obovate leaves, which are bright green, becoming butter-yellow in autumn. Pale lemon-yellow flowers appear in mid-winter.

Ozark Witch Hazel *Hamamelis vernalis*
A small tree, or large shrub, which is found growing naturally only in the Ozark Mountains of Oklahoma and Arkansas, although it has been cultivated in parks and gardens elsewhere in the USA. The flowers, which appear in January and February, are the smallest of any witch hazel, and also the most fragrant. They vary from pale yellow to red, but are more usually pale orange.

American Witch Hazel

Hamamelis virginiana

This large shrub, or small, spreading tree, grows as an understorey to bigger, deciduous trees in forests from Nova Scotia south to central Georgia. It prefers rich, moist soils and is often found on the banks of streams. Outside its native habitat it has been widely cultivated as an ornamental plant in parks and gardens, where winter colour and attraction is required. Witch hazel contains an astringent fluid, which is extracted from both the bark and leaves, and used to bring relief from bruising.

Distribution: Eastern North America.
Height: 7m (22ft)
Shape: Broadly spreading
Deciduous
Pollinated: Insect
Leaf shape: Oval to obovate

Identification: The bark is thick, light brown, generally smooth with some flaking that reveals dark reddish-purple inner bark. The leaves are oval to obovate, occasionally pointed at the tip, but more often rounded and unequal at the base. They are bright green, becoming clear yellow in autumn. This tree's most distinctive feature is its sulphur-yellow, fragrant, spidery-like flowers, which appear in autumn.

Above: A witch hazel leaf.

Right: The flowers appear as the leaves begin to fall and persist well into winter.

SWEET GUMS AND AUTUMN COLOUR

Although these trees belong to different families, they have two things in common: they are deciduous, dropping their leaves in autumn before producing replacements the following spring, and, before they lose their leaves, they produce spectacular leaf colour. Because of their beauty, many are planted as ornamental trees.

Katsura Tree

Cercidiphyllum japonicum

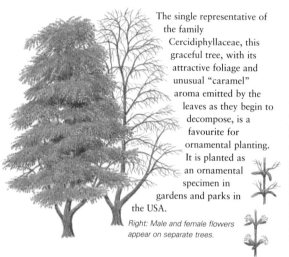

The single representative of the family Cercidiphyllaceae, this graceful tree, with its attractive foliage and unusual "caramel" aroma emitted by the leaves as they begin to decompose, is a favourite for ornamental planting. It is planted as an ornamental specimen in gardens and parks in the USA.

Right: Male and female flowers appear on separate trees.

Identification: The bark is grey-brown, freckled with lenticels and becomes fissured and flaking in maturity. The thin leaves are heart-shaped, slightly toothed around the margin, up to 8cm (3in) long and wide, turning a bronzy pink in autumn. The male flowers are bright red, appearing on side shoots before the leaves appear in early spring. Female flowers develop in late spring in clusters of four to six.

Distribution: Western China and Hokkaido and Honshu in Japan. USA to zone 4.
Height: 30m (100ft)
Shape: Broadly spreading
Deciduous
Pollinated: Insect
Leaf shape: Cordate

Left: Leaves fade to blue-green in summer, and appear in vibrant shades of butter-yellow to purple-pink in the spring.

Oriental Sweet Gum

Liquidambar orientalis

Distribution: South-west Turkey. USA zones 7–9.
Height: 25m (80ft)
Shape: Broadly conical
Deciduous
Pollinated: Insect
Leaf shape: Palmate

Along with its American cousin the sweet gum, *Liquidambar styraciflua*, the oriental sweet gum is widely planted in parks, gardens and arboreta across the USA for its magnificent leaf colour in autumn. It was discovered, and introduced to Europe around 1750, but it wasn't until the late 19th century that it was cultivated in the USA. Its leaves are more deeply cut into three to five lobes than the sweet gum.

Identification: The bark is orange-brown and thick, cracking in maturity into small plates. The leaves are palmately lobed, to 8cm (3in) long and broad, deep matt green above and paler beneath, turning a brilliant marmalade-orange in autumn. Both the male and female flowers are yellow-green and very small. They are borne separately, on the same tree, in spring, at the same time as the leaves emerge from winter bud.

Right: The seed is borne in a 2.5cm (1in), soft, spiky, rounded, hanging fruit.

Sweet Gum

Liquidambar styraciflua

This giant of a tree is known to have reached 45m (150ft) in height and is one of the main constituents of the deciduous hardwood forests of eastern North America. In autumn its leaves turn every shade from orange through red to purple.

Identification: The bark is a dark brown-grey colour becoming fissured into long vertical ridges with age. The leaves are up to 15cm (6in) long and broad, normally with five tapering lobes (sometimes seven), the centre one of which is normally largest. The margin of the leaf is slightly toothed. The leaf shape sometimes leads to identification confusion with maples; however, maple leaves are in opposite pairs on a smooth shoot, whereas *Liquidambar* leaves are alternately positioned on a corky shoot.

Above: Male and female flowers are both small and round, greeny yellow in colour and appear in late spring.

Distribution: North America from Connecticut in the north to Florida and Texas in the south. Also found in Central America.
Height: 40m (130ft)
Shape: Broadly conical
Deciduous
Pollinated: Insect
Leaf shape: Palmate lobed

Left: The seed is contained in clusters of round, brown hanging pods approximately 4cm (1½in) across.

Persian Ironwood

Parrotia persica

A member of the Hamamelidaceae family, it is planted as a specimen tree in the USA because of its autumn colour, which turns from copper to burgundy in mid-season. In the wild it tends to be a broad, upright tree, but in cultivation it becomes a sprawling mass, seldom attaining a height in excess of 15m (50ft). It is named after the climber F. W. Parrot, who conquered Mount Ararat in 1829.

Identification: Quite often seen in large gardens and arboreta as a dense low-spreading mound, which is quite difficult to penetrate because of criss-cross branching. The bark is dark brown, flaking to reveal light brown patches. The leaves are obovate, sometimes elliptic, 12cm (4¾in) long and 6cm (2½in) wide, becoming progressively shallow-toothed and wavy towards the top of each leaf. They are bright glossy green above, and dull green with slight pubescence beneath. The flowers are tiny, clothed in a soft velvet-brown casing, but emerging a startling ruby-red colour, which looks dramatic on the bare branches in midwinter. The fruit is a nut-like brown capsule, 1cm (½in) across.

Above: Small ruby-red flowers appear in winter.

Below: Leaves are darker and glossier on the tops and lighter beneath.

Distribution: Mount Ararat, Eastern Caucasus to northern Iran. USA zones 4–8.
Height: 20m (66ft)
Shape: Broadly spreading
Deciduous
Pollinated: Insect
Leaf shape: Obovate

OTHER SPECIES OF NOTE
Chinese Sweet Gum
Liquidambar formosana
This tender, beautiful small tree was introduced to the USA in 1911 by plant collector Ernest Wilson, during the time he was working for the Arnold Arboretum, Boston. It has grey-white bark that darkens and becomes fissured in maturity, and palmately lobed leaves, which are distinctly heart-shaped at the base. *See also page 383.*

Chittamwood
Cotinus obovatus
This small, rare, American tree is otherwise known as the smoke tree because of its smoky grey, plume-like flowers, which encircle the tree in late summer. It is one of the most brilliantly coloured autumn trees, with large oval-shape translucent leaves, which turn to all shades of orange, red and purple in October.

Weeping Katsura
Cercidiphyllum japonicum 'Pendulum'
This is a beautiful and unusual tree with long pendulous branches that arch gracefully towards the ground. It has long been cultivated in Japan, particularly in temple gardens, but it has been cultivated elsewhere comparatively recently. It is found in botanic gardens across the USA, but should be more widely planted.

MADRONES, PERSIMMONS AND SNOWBELLS

These trees form part of the camellia subclass known as Dilleniidae. They are a mixture of deciduous and evergreen, acid-loving and lime-tolerant species. They have an ornamental appeal that has secured their place in gardens and arboreta across the temperate world.

Pacific Madrone

Arbutus menziesii

The madrones are the biggest plants of the Heath family, which includes heathers and rhododendrons. The Pacific madrone is the biggest of all, and grows naturally from British Columbia (including Vancouver Island) south to California. It is an attractive, ornamental tree that is widely cultivated in botanic gardens and arboreta across temperate regions of the world.

Above: The fruit in early autumn.

Left: The flowers open in March in California, and in May in British Columbia.

Identification: The bark is red-brown, smooth and peels in papery flakes to reveal fresh, green bark beneath. The thick, leathery, evergreen leaves are elliptic, up to 15cm (6in) long and 7.5cm (3in) broad. They are glossy, dark green above and pale blue-white beneath. The flowers are creamy white and small but borne in large, vertical clusters, which may contain in excess of 100 flowers. The Pacific madrone has 1cm (½in) rounded, strawberry-like fruits, which change from green through orange to red in late summer to early autumn.

Distribution: West coast North America.
Height: 40m (130ft)
Shape: Broadly columnar
Evergreen
Pollinated: Insect
Leaf shape: Elliptic

Persimmon

Possum wood *Diospyrus virginiana*

Also known as possum wood, this large, deciduous, North American tree is one of only three truly hardy members of the ebony family, Ebenaceae. The wood resembles that of ebony, being black, dense and very tough. Traditionally it has been used to make golf clubs. In autumn, persimmon leaves put on a spectacular display, turning rich orange-yellow before dropping from the branches.

Identification: A wide-spreading tree with black-brown rugged bark, cracking in maturity into rough, square plates. The leaves are commonly ovate, up to 13cm (5in) long and 7.5cm (3in) across, deep glossy green above and light sage-green beneath with an untoothed margin. By far the most distinctive feature of this tree is the fruit, which is quite often described as orange-like but is more akin in looks and size to a small orange tomato. Measuring 4cm (1½in) across, it ripens on the tree in late summer to early autumn and contains up to eight brown seeds. The fruit is edible but too sharp for most palates.

Right: Both male and female flowers are pale yellow, bell-shaped and borne on separate trees in summer.

Distribution: Central-southern United States from Connecticut to Texas.
Height: 30m (100ft)
Shape: Broadly spreading
Deciduous
Pollinated: Insect
Leaf shape: Ovate to oblong

Arizona Madrone

Arbutus arizonica

The Arizona madrone is much smaller than the Pacific madrone, *Arbutus menziesii*, and has thinner, slender leaves. It is native to dry gravel areas in the Santa Catalina and Santa Rita Mountains in southern Arizona, where it grows up to elevations of 2,500m (8,000ft), and in the San Luis and Animas Mountains of New Mexico. It is cultivated in botanic gardens and arboreta across the southern USA.

Left: The small, orange-red, strawberry-like fruits are sweet tasting and edible.

Identification: The bark on young trees is thin, smooth, dark red, and peeling in long, thin strips. Mature trees tend to have thicker bark with vertical fissures and light grey and red patches. The lanceolate, evergreen leaves are thick, leathery, pointed at the tip and rounded at the base, light green above and sage-green beneath. New leaves emerge from the bud with a reddish tinge. The flowers, which appear in May, are very similar to those of the Pacific madrone, *Arbutus menziesii*, except that the clusters are rather looser in their formation. The fruit, which ripens in October, is dark orange-red and strawberry-like with a sweet, edible flesh.

Distribution: Arizona and south-west New Mexico.
Height: 15m (50ft)
Shape: Broadly columnar
Evergreen
Pollinated: Insect
Leaf shape: Lanceolate

Right: The flowers are small, creamy white and borne in loose clusters.

OTHER SPECIES OF NOTE

Mountain Snowdrop Tree *Halesia monticola*
This magnificent spreading tree differs from the silver bell tree, *H. carolina*, in its greater size (up to 25m (80ft) tall), and its larger flowers. As the name suggests, it grows wild in upland areas, reaching altitudes in excess of 1,230m (4,000ft) in North Carolina, Tennessee and western Georgia. Due to its beauty, it is widely cultivated including in the Arnold Arboretum, Boston, and in Rochester, New York.

Sour Wood *Oxydendron arboreum*
Otherwise known as the sorrel tree, this eastern USA, medium-size tree has leaves that have a bitter taste, similar to that of the herbaceous plant sorrel. They were used by the early American settlers as both a tonic and a cure for fever. It has elliptic 20cm- (8in-) long deciduous leaves that turn scarlet in autumn.

Japanese Snowbell Tree *Styrax japonica*
This is a beautiful, small, spreading tree, which was introduced into North America from Japan in the late 19th century. Since then it has been widely planted as an ornamental in parks,

gardens and arboreta across the USA. It has creamy white, fragrant, open bell-shaped flowers that hang from the tree on long slender stalks in early summer. *See also page 385.*

Silver Bell Tree

Snowdrop tree *Halesia carolina*

This beautiful small tree, otherwise known as the snowdrop tree, is native to southeast USA, from Virginia south to Florida, and west to Illinois. It is widely cultivated as an ornamental tree in parks and gardens elsewhere in the USA. It favours rich, moist soil and is quite often found growing alongside streams. The botanical name *Halesia* commemorates the English clergyman and botanical author D. Stephen Hales (1677–1761).

Identification: The juvenile bark is pale brown and smooth, becoming darker and scaly in maturity. The leaves are ovate to oblong, 20cm (8in) long and 10cm (4in) wide, finely toothed around the margin and running to a long thin tapered point. They are grass-green above and pale green beneath with some pubescence. In autumn they turn clear butter-yellow before dropping. The flowers are bell-shaped, white, sometimes flushed pink, and have clusters of bright orange stamens at their centre. They are borne in loose clusters and hang from the twig on long stalks.

Distribution: South-east USA.
Height: 20m (65ft)
Shape: Broadly conical
Deciduous
Pollinated: Insect
Leaf shape: Ovate to oblong

Above: Husks containing seed.

Below: The flowers appear in spring.

REDBUDS AND LABURNUMS

*These two species, redbuds and laburnums, are both members of the Leguminosae (pea) family
and as such have beautiful pea-like flowers in springtime. They are popular small trees for
cultivation in parks and gardens right across North America. They grow best in full sun
with good drainage.*

Eastern Redbud

Cercis canadensis

This beautiful small tree is commonly found growing in moist woodlands right across its
natural range from New York to Texas. It is also widely cultivated in parks, gardens and as
a street tree. Eastern redbud is prone to canker, which can cause leaves to brown and die in
summer. An attractive form of this species known as
'Forest Pansy' has deep, purple-red foliage
throughout summer and is widely available from
nurseries and garden centres.

Identification: The bark is quite distinctive, being
dark charcoal-brown to almost black. Quite often
bright pink flowers will grow directly from the trunk.
Eastern redbud has rounded, heart-shape leaves,
which are up to 10cm (4in) long
and 13cm (5in) wide. There
are no serrations around the
leaf margin and they emerge
bronze-coloured from winter bud
before quickly turning bright green. They
are smooth and papery thin. In autumn the
leaves turn bright golden-yellow. The distinctive pea-like
pink flowers, 1cm (½in) long, are borne on slender
stalks in clusters along old wood in spring to
early summer.

Distribution: Central and
south USA.
Height: 10m (33ft)
Shape: Broadly spreading
Deciduous
Pollinated: Insect
Leaf shape: Cordate

*Left: The seed is contained within
a flattened green pod, which
ripens to brown.*

*Left: The small pink flowers are
borne in clusters.*

California Redbud

Western redbud *Cercis occidentalis*

Otherwise known as western redbud, this small tree, or
large shrub, is found growing wild in south Utah and
Nevada and through Arizona and California. It is fairly
uncommon throughout this region and
has never been widely cultivated in
parks and gardens like its
eastern cousin. It has
distinctive red-purple shoots,
which are particularly
prominent in spring, just
before the tree comes
into leaf.

Identification: This redbud is
smaller than the eastern redbud,
Cercis canadensis, and quite
often attains only shrub-like
proportions. It also
has smaller
leaves, which
are more
rounded and
leathery, with
a distinctive
notch at the
tip. It has pea-
like flowers that
are rose-
coloured. They are
held on short stalks
and are produced in
clusters on old wood
right back to the main stem
in spring, just before the leaves
emerge from bud.

Distribution: South-western
USA.
Height: 6m (20ft)
Shape: Broadly spreading
Deciduous
Pollinated: Insect
Leaf shape: Cordate

*Right: The fruit
is a pointed "pea-
pod" containing
up to 20 seeds.*

Voss's Golden Chain Tree

Laburnum x *watereri* 'Vossii'

This stunningly beautiful tree is cultivated in parks and gardens right across North America. It is a form of the hybrid, which is a cross between the common laburnum, *Laburnum anagyroides*, and the Scotch laburnum, *L. alpinum*, both of which originate from central and southern Europe. The hybrid was developed at Waterer's nursery, England, before 1864. The form 'Vossii' was raised in Holland late in the 19th century and has superseded all other forms of cultivated laburnum.

Identification: The bark is dark grey and smooth, becoming shallowly fissured in maturity. The leaves are borne in three elliptic leaflets, each 7.5cm (3in) long. They are grass-green above, slightly paler beneath and covered in fine silver pubescence. The flowers, which appear in late spring, are golden-yellow, pea-like, 2.5cm (1in) long and borne in dense, hanging racemes, which can be more than 30cm (12in) long. The fruit is a brown, flat seed pod, up to 7.5cm (3in) long, normally containing just a few seeds. All parts of this tree are poisonous.

Above: The flowers appear in mid- to late spring.

Above: Laburnum seeds should not be eaten.

OTHER SPECIES OF NOTE

Texas Redbud *Cercis canadensis* var. *texensis*
This small, shrubby tree is native to Oklahoma and Texas, where it is found on the limestone hills and ridges in Dallas County, and in the valley of the upper Colorado River. It differs from the eastern redbud, *C. canadensis*, in having rich, glossy leaves that are blunt at the tip and shoots, and are smooth with no pubescence.

Judas Tree *Cercis siliquastrum*
Native to western Asia and south-east Europe but has been widely planted in gardens, parks and arboreta in southern USA. It is similar to eastern redbud, *C. canadensis*, except the bark colour is lighter, and the lilac-pink flowers bigger. This is allegedly the tree from which Judas Iscariot hung himself after betraying Christ. *See also page 386.*

Common Laburnum *Laburnum anagyroides*
This beautiful, small tree, which originates from central and southern Europe, is one of the parents of the hybrid form *Laburnum* x *watereri* 'Vossii', which is widely planted across the USA in parks, gardens and streets. It differs from the form in having shorter, less showy flowers. This tree is poisonous. *See also page 387.*

Chinaberry *Melia azedarach*
Also known as the bead tree because of its yellow, bony, bead-like seeds, which appear in autumn, this attractive, small tree originates from India and China. It is commonly planted in small gardens from Georgia to Texas, and north to Tennessee. It has large, bipinnate leaves and small, fragrant, lilac flowers. *See also page 477.*

Silk Tree

Albizia julibrissin

Sometimes mistakenly called mimosa, this Asian species is extremely popular in areas of the USA where winters are not too severe. It grows from Long Island, south to Texas, and north to Seattle in the west. As a street tree it develops a wide-spreading, flat-topped shape, and reaches 8m (25ft) tall. When in flower it is a beautiful sight and fills the air with the scent of newly cut hay.

Identification: The bark is dark brown and smooth. The dark green leaves give the tree a "feathery" appearance. They are bipinnate up to 50cm (20in) long, with numerous small, taper-pointed, soft, needle-like, untoothed leaflets about 1cm (½in) long. In autumn the leaves turn yellow and orange before dropping. The fragrant flowers are small but borne in dense, fluffy clusters. They have long salmon-pink stamens evident in summer.

Below: The seed is borne in a brown pea-like pod up to 15cm (6in) long.

CHERRIES

The cherry genus, Prunus, *contains over 400 different species of tree, the majority of which are deciduous and native to northern temperate regions of the world. They include some of the most beautiful spring-flowering trees, many of which have been cultivated in parks, gardens and arboreta for centuries. The genus is distinguished by having fruit that is always a drupe surrounding a single seed.*

Sargent's Cherry

Prunus sargentii

Sargent's cherry is one of the loveliest of all cherries, producing a profusion of rich pink, single flowers coupled with bronze-coloured emerging leaves in spring, and brilliant orange-red leaf colours in autumn. It is named after Charles Sargent, of the Arnold Arboretum, Boston, who obtained a supply of the tree's seed from Japan in 1892.

Identification: The bark is a deep mahogany-red, freckled with horizontal pale fawn lenticels. The leaves are elliptic to obovate, up to 13cm (5in) long and 5cm (2in) across, with a leaf margin cut by shallow but sharp serrations. The tip of the leaf is drawn out into a long point. Leaves emerge from the bud in mid-spring a copper-bronze colour, then gradually turn a deep grass-green. The single pink flowers, which are normally produced in profusion, have five petals and are up to 4cm (1½in) across. They appear just before the leaves emerge. The fruit is a black, egg-shaped drupe.

Distribution: Northern Japan, Korea and Sakhalin island. USA zones 4–7.
Height: 20m (66ft)
Shape: Broadly spreading
Deciduous
Pollinated: Insect
Leaf shape: Elliptic to obovate

Above left: The blossom of Sargent's cherry is a rich pink colour.

Above right: Autumn leaves turn glorious shades of orange.

Black Cherry

Rum cherry *Prunus serotina*

Also known as rum cherry because its fruits were once used to flavour rum, this willow leaf-like tree has bark that emits a distinctive odour if scratched. It is a member of the birdcherry group and therefore has its flowers borne in spike-like racemes. It is common in woods throughout a region south of Nova Scotia to Mexico.

Distribution: Eastern and central North America, south to Mexico and Guatemala.
Height: 25m (80ft)
Shape: Broadly columnar
Deciduous
Pollinated: Insect
Leaf shape: Elliptic to lanceolate

Identification: The bark is dark grey and smooth, becoming horizontally fissured in maturity. The leaves are elliptic to lanceolate, 12cm (4½in) long and 5cm (2in) wide, glossy dark green and smooth above, paler beneath with some pubescence along the midrib. They taper to a slight point and are finely toothed around the margin. In autumn they turn bright yellow before dropping. The flowers are white, 1cm (½in) across and grouped in racemes, which may be up to 15cm (6in) long.

Above: The fruit is a black, round, edible cherry up to 1cm (⅖in) across.

Below: The flowers are white.

Pin Cherry

Prunus pensylvanica

A hardy, shrubby tree, which reaches 10m (33ft) in height in the wild, but seldom in cultivation. It is able to withstand cold and exposure and is often used to make shelterbelts. It is not widely cultivated because of the sheer number of alternative, more free-flowering, cherries that are readily available. Its most distinctive feature is bright red shoots, which are particularly evident in late winter and early spring.

Identification: The bark is dark brown, smooth but becoming pockmarked with pronounced lenticels in maturity. The leaves are lanceolate and willow-like, up to 7.5cm (3in) long, narrow and tapering to a long, fine point. They are glossy mid-green above and slightly paler beneath, with a bright red leaf stalk coming off red shoots. The flowers are small, 1cm (½in) across, white, sometimes with a pink blush, and borne on short racemes in clusters of between four and eight. The fruits are black, pea-sized and quite often borne in profusion.

Below: The fruit has sour flesh.

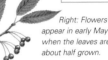

Distribution: All of Canada south to Georgia and Colorado.
Height: 10m (33ft)
Shape: Broadly columnar
Deciduous
Pollinated: Insect
Leaf shape: Lanceolate

Right: Flowers appear in early May when the leaves are about half grown.

OTHER SPECIES OF NOTE
Tibetan Cherry *Prunus serrula*
A small, spreading cherry, popular throughout North America for its striking, highly polished, deep mahogany-red bark, which is a feature in winter. It originates from western China and may attain heights around 15m (50ft), but more often 10m (33ft). The white flowers are inconspicuous and are produced after the lanceolate leaves appear in mid-spring.

Japanese 'Sato' Cherry *Prunus* 'Kanzan'
This colourful cherry, of Japanese garden origin, may be the commonest cherry in cultivation in North America. It produces masses of bright pink, double flowers, borne in dense clusters throughout the crown. Mature trees develop arching branches that rise strongly from the stem and then droop towards the tip, probably because of the weight of the flowers. *See also page 389.*

Mazzard *Prunus avium*
Also known as the gean or wild cherry, this tree originates from Europe, but has long been cultivated in America. It has naturalized in many regions, and is common in southern British Columbia, Vancouver and Seattle. It produces white, single flowers in late spring, and orange and red leaves in autumn. *See also page 388.*

Pissard's Purple Plum *Prunus cerasifera* 'Pissardii'
This is a common variety of the myrobalan plum and is grown in suburbs in western USA and British Columbia. It is grown for its shiny, distinctive, deep purple leaves. It has delicate, small white flowers, which are pink in bud and open before the leaves emerge.

The Great White Cherry

Prunus 'Tai Haku'

This beautiful tree was cultivated in Japan until the 1700s, when it fell from favour and was thought to have become extinct. That was until 1923 when a dying specimen was discovered in a garden in England. The owner had purchased it, along with several other unnamed cherries, from Japan in 1900. Today it has become one of the most widely planted cherries across the world.

Identification: The bark is a warm chestnut-brown, becoming fissured in maturity. It has low spreading branches, which in spring are filled with clusters of large, up to 7.5cm (3in) across, pure white, single flowers with central pink stamens. At the same time, bronze-red leaves begin to unfurl from bud. The combination of leaf and flower is spectacular. The elliptic, taper-pointed and finely toothed leaves rapidly turn mid-green and then orange in autumn.

Distribution: Of garden origin. USA zones 4–7.
Height: 10m (33ft)
Shape: Broadly spreading
Deciduous
Pollinated: Insect
Leaf shape: Elliptic

Left: The leaves are bronze in spring, turning green in summer.

Above and below: 'Tai Haku' has the best snow-white flowers of any cherry tree.

HAWTHORNS

Hawthorns are members of the Rosaceae family and one of the most numerous genera in North America. There are at least 200 different species and countless hybrids and varieties. They are among the most adaptable of all trees, tolerating both waterlogged and excessively dry soils, industrial pollution and coastal salt spray.

Downy Hawthorn

Red haw *Crataegus mollis*

Distribution: Eastern and central North America.
Height: 12m (40ft)
Shape: Broadly columnar
Deciduous
Pollinated: Insect
Leaf shape: Ovate

Otherwise known as the red haw, the downy hawthorn grows wild from Nova Scotia and Quebec south to Texas and west to Nevada. It is also commonly found in city parks in eastern USA. It is a small tree seldom reaching 10m (33ft) and very tolerant of air pollution, making it an ideal tree for urban areas. There is a specific form of this tree known as the Arnold hawthorn, *Crataegus arnoldiana*, which was developed at the Arnold Arboretum, Boston.

Identification: The bark is red-brown, cracking into vertical plates in maturity. The dark green leaves are broadly ovate, approximately 10cm (4in) long, with up to five shallow lobes on each side. The entire leaf margin is sharply toothed, and the texture of the leaf is rough due to hairs on each side. The shoots carry 5cm- (2in-) long spines. The flowers are white with yellow anthers, 2.5cm (1in) across, borne in clusters in late spring. The fruits, which appear towards the end of the summer, are bright red and up to 2.5cm (1in) across.

Right: The leaves are covered with pubescence.

Left: The red fruits are known as haws.

Cockspur Hawthorn

Crataegus crus-galli

One of the most spectacular of all hawthorns because of its long, ferociously sharp spines, which may be up to 10cm (4in) long. It is found growing wild on the edge of woodland, and within open woodland from Quebec south to Florida and west to Texas. It is also planted in towns and cities outside this region. In autumn the leaves turn a fine marmalade-orange colour.

Identification: The bark is dark brown and scaly, peeling to reveal fresh orange bark beneath. The obovate leaves are glossy dark green above, paler beneath, with no pubescence. They are 10cm (4in) long and 5cm (2in) across, tapering at the base and rounded at the tip with some serration around the upper half of the leaf margin. The flowers are creamy white with pink anthers, 1cm (½in) across, and carried in dense, rounded heads in late spring and early summer. The fruits are pea-size, bright red and quite often persist on the tree long after leaf fall.

Distribution: Eastern and central North America.
Height: 8m (26ft)
Shape: Broadly spreading
Deciduous
Pollinated: Insect
Leaf shape: Obovate

Right: The glossy scarlet haws may still be on the tree in mid-winter.

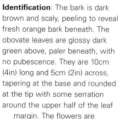

Above: The sharp spine of this species gives the tree its name "Cockspur".

Washington Hawthorn

Crataegus phaenopyrum

An attractive small tree, which grows wild on the banks of streams, in rich soil in woods and thickets, from Virginia to Florida, and is cultivated elsewhere in towns and cities, particularly in the eastern states. It is not common either in the wild or in cultivation and deserves to be better known. It certainly has one of the most attractive forms of hawthorn, with a neat, round-headed canopy and glossy, maple-like leaves.

Identification: The bark is red-brown to grey-brown, rather thin, becoming shallowly fissured and scaly in maturity. The leaves are broadly ovate and almost maple-like, with three to five sharply toothed lobes, glossy dark green above and sage-green and smooth beneath. The shoots carry long glossy spines up to 5cm (2in) long. In early summer, creamy white fragrant flowers, up to 1cm (½in) across, are produced in lax clusters. They are followed by a show of dark crimson, pea-size fruit, which appears in profusion.

Distribution: Eastern North America.
Height: 12m (40ft)
Shape: Broadly spreading
Deciduous
Pollinated: Insect
Leaf shape: Ovate

Right: The glossy round haws are some of the latest to ripen.

Right: The glossy maple-like leaves are a distinctive feature of this tree.

OTHER SPECIES OF NOTE

Black Hawthorn *Crataegus douglasii*
This small, hardy tree, with long drooping branches, grows naturally from Alaska and British Columbia southward to California, and grows at heights in excess of 1,800m (6,000ft) above sea level in the Rocky Mountains. David Douglas, who identified the tree, recorded that its thorns were used for fish hooks.

One-seed Hawthorn *Craetagus monogyna*
This European tree has been cultivated across North America since its introduction by the early settlers, who used it to create hedges to contain their stock. It has now naturalized across wide areas of North America from Quebec to North Carolina and in the west across Oregon and British Columbia. *See also page 395.*

Arkansas Thorn *Crataegus arkansana*
An elegant, small tree, up to 6m (20ft) tall, which grows wild in the White River area near Newport, Jackson County. It has relatively few thorns on its orange-brown, lustrous shoots, and is cultivated as far north as eastern Massachusetts for its large, bright red fruits, which can be up to 2.5cm (1in) across, and persist on the tree well into early winter.

Crataegus arnoldiana
A beautiful small tree with large red fruits the size of cherries, and shallowly lobed leaves. It was found growing wild in the area of the Arnold Arboretum, Boston, and is cultivated in parks and gardens in eastern USA and recognized in winter by its upright "zigzag" branches.

Paul's Scarlet Thorn

Crataegus laevigata 'Paul's Scarlet'

This lovely tree is a cultivar of the Midland hawthorn, *Crataegus laevigata*, which gets its name from the English Midlands, where it is common and a good indicator of ancient woodland. The cultivar 'Paul's Scarlet' was produced as long ago as 1858, and since then has become a favourite ornamental species for parks and gardens.

Distribution: Of garden origin.
Height: 10m (33ft)
Shape: Broadly spreading
Deciduous
Pollinated: Insect
Leaf shape: Ovate to obovate

Identification: The bark is grey and smooth, becoming shallowly fissured in maturity. It has ovate to obovate glossy dark green leaves that are 5cm (2in) long and wide, with shallow lobes around the upper half of the leaf. The double, almost rose-like, flowers are its main feature, being a bright, deep pink colour and produced in dense clusters all over the tree in late spring and early summer. These are followed in late summer by bright red, oval-shaped fruits, up to 2.5cm (1in) long, which persist long into autumn.

Right: Beautiful clusters of rose-like vibrant pink flowers are borne from late spring into early summer.

Right: The ovate leaves are dark green above and pale green beneath.

FLOWERING CRAB APPLES

The flowering crab genus, Malus, contains over 25 species, native mainly to northern temperate regions. They are hardy, small to medium-size deciduous trees, widely grown as garden ornamentals for their profusion of spring flowers and late summer fruit. The flowers are similar to a cherry's, but have five styles presenting the female stigma for pollination instead of just one.

Sweet Crab Apple

Malus coronaria

The sweet crab apple grows wild along streams and woodland edges from New York and Illinois south to Arkansas and Georgia. Although cultivated in parks and gardens elsewhere, the form 'Charlottae', which has strong violet-scented, double flowers, is planted in preference to the true species. It has easy to work, soft, decorative timber, with pink-red heartwood and yellow sapwood.

Identification: The sweet crab apple has red-brown bark, which is shallowly fissured into broad, scaly ridges that flake to reveal lighter-coloured bark beneath. The deep green lobed leaves are ovate, up to 10cm (4in) long and 5cm (2in) broad. They are sharply and sometimes double-toothed around the leaf margin, at first covered in a fine pubescence but soon becoming smooth. The flowers are single, pink, up to 5cm (2in) across and produced in fragrant clusters in late spring. These are followed by rounded, edible fruits 4cm (1½in) across, which gradually ripen from green to yellow.

Distribution: Eastern North America.
Height: 9m (30ft)
Shape: Broadly spreading
Deciduous
Pollinated: Insect
Leaf shape: Ovate

Right: Hard, bitter fruits are borne on short stalks.

Prairie Crab Apple

Malus ioensis

Distribution: Central USA.
Height: 8m (26ft)
Shape: Broadly spreading
Deciduous
Pollinated: Insect
Leaf shape: Ovate

This is the Midwestern sweet crab apple, which grows wild from Indiana and Wisconsin south to Oklahoma and Arkansas, where it inhabits moist stream banks and wood margins. The form of this tree known as 'Bechtel's Crab' is more popular than the species, because it reliably produces a profusion of semi-double pink, fading to white, flowers every spring.

Left: The pink-white flowers are borne in clusters of up to six but more commonly three to four.

Identification: The prairie crab apple is a low, bushy tree with level branches, which have grey bark, unlike the bark on the stem, which is purplish-brown and flakes in long narrow strips. The leaves are broadly ovate and borne on dark red shoots covered in grey pubescence. The single flowers are pink fading to white, each with five petals and borne in clusters of three to four. They are followed by round, smooth fruit, which is pale green, or green flushed with red. It is up to 5cm (2in), very hard and bitter to taste.

Malus 'Dartmouth'
This North American cultivar was raised in New Hampshire before 1883. It bears pure white, single flowers, 2.5cm (1in) across, in profusion in mid-spring against a backdrop of fresh green leaves. These are followed in autumn by deep crimson, slightly angular fruits, up to 5cm (2in) across, which are covered in a purple bloom and persist long after the leaves have fallen.

Hupeh Crab Malus hupehensis
This hardy Chinese tree is one of the most beautiful of all small deciduous trees. It grows wild in the mountains of central China, where local people use the leaves to make a drink called "red tea". Since 1900, when it was introduced to America, it has become increasingly popular for planting in parks and gardens, and in spring it produces a mass of white flowers that are flushed with soft pink. See also page 399.

Willow-leaved pear Pyrus salicifolia
This eastern European and Asian tree is the most ornamental of all the pears. It is a firm favourite for planting where a small tree with silver foliage is required. It was introduced into North America over 150 years ago and has been widely planted since. It makes a very good centrepiece for a lawn and is easily recognizable by its long, narrow, silver-grey leaves and creamy white flowers. The fruit is a small, hard green pear 3cm (1¼in) long. See also page 399.

Japanese Crab Apple

Malus floribunda

Believed to be a hybrid, but cultivated in Japan for centuries. It was introduced into America in 1862. Since then it has become popular and is now commonly found from Ontario to California. It is one of the first crab apples to come into leaf, and the whole crown is smothered in flowers in May. It has an extremely spreading habit and will quite often be wider than it is tall.

Identification: The bark is purple-brown, flaking into thin, vertical plates in maturity. The dark green leaves are elliptic, 10cm (4in) long and 5cm (2in) broad, sharply toothed around the margin and running to a long tapered tip. They are smooth on top, but carry some pubescence beneath. The flowers are followed by pea-size, rounded yellow fruits that are clustered together on long slender stalks.

Above: Fruit.

Right: The flowers are 2.5cm (1in) across, deep red in bud, gradually opening pale pink, and then fading to white.

Distribution: Japan. USA zones 4–8.
Height: 5m (17ft)
Shape: Broadly spreading
Deciduous
Pollinated: Insect
Leaf shape: Elliptic

Pillar Apple

Malus tschonoskii

This slender Japanese tree has become extremely popular for planting in streets and town squares across America (hardiness zones 4–8) because of its narrow, fastigiate form and its ability to grow on impoverished soils. In Japan it grows on shallow, rocky soils that have little nutrient content. It hardly has any fruit, which is a bonus in streets. It does, however, produce stunning leaf colour in autumn.

Distribution: Japan.
Height: 15m (50ft)
Shape: Broadly conical
Deciduous
Pollinated: Insect
Leaf shape: Ovate

Identification: The bark is at first purple-brown and smooth, but becomes increasingly fissured and rough in maturity. The leaves are broadly ovate, up to 13cm (5in) long and 7.5cm (3in) across, sharply toothed and running to a tapered point at the tip. They are grass-green, smooth and glossy above and slightly hairy beneath. The flowers are 2.5cm (1in) across, white, flushed pink with yellow anthers and produced in clusters in mid-spring. The fruit is rounded, green flushed with red, and covered with brown lenticels.

Right: When the leaves emerge from bud they are covered with grey hair.

Right: The fruit is speckled with light brown lenticels.

ROWANS, SERVICEBERRIES AND LOQUATS

*The rose family, Rosaceae, is one of the largest plant families. It encompasses an incredibly diverse range
of plants, including cherries, apples, quinces, loquats, cotoneasters, rowans and roses.
It is also one of the most commonly seen families within cultivation, because of the excellent flowers and
beautiful fruit. The Rosaceae include the following diverse and beautiful group of trees.*

American Mountain Ash

Roundwood *Sorbus americana*

This small tree, or large shrub, grows into a round-topped, spreading, low tree, which
seldom exceeds 10m (33ft). It has a natural distribution that extends from Newfoundland
south to Georgia, and westward into Michigan and Wisconsin. It is not widely planted as an
ornamental, preference in parks and gardens
being given to its European cousin
Sorbus aucuparia, which has creamy
white spring flowers.

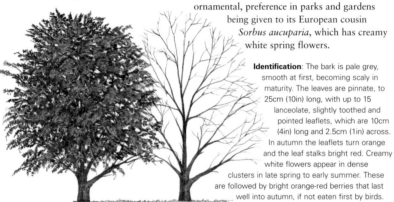

Identification: The bark is pale grey,
smooth at first, becoming scaly in
maturity. The leaves are pinnate, to
25cm (10in) long, with up to 15
lanceolate, slightly toothed and
pointed leaflets, which are 10cm
(4in) long and 2.5cm (1in) across.
In autumn the leaflets turn orange
and the leaf stalks bright red. Creamy
white flowers appear in dense
clusters in late spring to early summer. These
are followed by bright orange-red berries that last
well into autumn, if not eaten first by birds.

Distribution: Eastern North
America.
Height: 10m (33ft)
Shape: Broadly spreading
Deciduous
Pollinated: Insect
Leaf shape: Pinnate

Showy Mountain Ash

Sorbus decora

The showy mountain ash is a northern and high-altitude form of the American mountain-
ash, *Sorbus americana*, and may be of hybrid origin. It gets its name from its large showy
bunches of bright red berries, which first appear in late summer, and may last well into
winter. It covers much of the same range as the
American mountain ash, but occurs further north
in Quebec, Ontario and Labrador.

Identification: The bark is pale grey and
smooth, becoming slightly fissured
and scaly in maturity. The flowers are
creamy white and borne in early summer
in dense, pungent-smelling
clusters. The flowers are
followed by berries in large
heads of up to 15cm (6in)
across, orange at first,
maturing to deep red.

*Right: The leaves are pinnate,
up to 25cm (10in) long, with up to
17 lanceolate, sea green-colour
leaflets, each 7.5cm (3in) wide.*

Right: Each berry is up to 6mm (¼in) across.

Distribution: North-east
North America.
Height: 10m (33ft)
Shape: Broadly spreading
Deciduous
Pollinated: Insect
Leaf shape: Pinnate

American Serviceberry

Amelanchier laevis

Quite often known simply as serviceberry, this small, round-topped tree is native to northeastern North America, from Newfoundland west to Wisconsin, and south along the Appalachian Mountains to northern Georgia, where it occurs naturally in cool ravines and hillside woodlands. It is beautiful in early May, when masses of white fragrant flowers appear alongside emerging leaves that are the colour of light bronze.

Identification: The bark is grey-brown and smooth even in maturity. The leaves are elliptic to ovate or sometimes obovate; up to 6cm (2½in) long and 2.5cm (1in) across. They are finely serrated around the leaf margin and run to a point at the tip. Initially bronze-red, they turn deep green in summer and then bright orange-red in autumn. The flowers are pure white, with five narrow petals and are held in upright, spreading racemes up to 7.5cm (3in) long.

Distribution: Eastern North America.
Height: 12m (40ft)
Shape: Broadly spreading
Deciduous
Pollinated: Insect
Leaf shape: Elliptic to ovate

Left and right: The spring flowers are followed by small, round, purple-black berries.

OTHER SPECIES OF NOTE

Rowan
Sorbus aucuparia
This small, hardy tree is native right across Europe and temperate Asia. It survives in USA hardiness zone 4. It is also known as the mountain ash: appropriate, because it does have bright green, ash-like leaves and is found growing high up on mountainsides: sometimes it seems to be growing out of bare rock. The flowers, which are creamy white and slightly pungent, emerge in mid-spring, and clusters of bright red berries appear in summer. *See also page 400.*

Chinese Rowan *Sorbus hupehensis*
This is a beautiful small tree, native to much of temperate China and cultivated throughout the temperate world as a garden ornamental. It has ash-like, deep green leaves and a display of delightful white berries, slightly flushed with pink. *See also page 401.*

Snowy Mespilus *Amelanchier lamarckii*
Otherwise known as *Amelanchier canadensis*, this beautiful small tree is believed to have originated in north-eastern North America, from where it was introduced into Europe as early as the 17th century. It is widely planted as an ornamental species because of its attractive white star-shaped flowers. They appear in spring alongside leaves that emerge from the bud a warm copper-bronze colour. These are followed by purple-black, sweet-tasting, globular fruits, which are quite often used as a pie filling.

Loquat

Eriobotrya japonica

This magnificent large shrub, or small tree, has probably the most distinctive leaves of any ornamental species grown in America. They are thick, leathery, glossy dark green, with a corrugated appearance and deeply veined. It is grown as a popular ornamental throughout warm, frost-free areas of the USA, from Charleston to California, where it is frequently seen in small gardens, courtyards and growing up walls. It produces round, golden-yellow, edible fruits in spring.

Distribution: China and Japan.
Height: 9m (30ft)
Shape: Broadly spreading
Evergreen
Pollinated: Insect
Leaf shape: Elliptic to ovate

Identification: The bark is grey-brown and smooth, becoming heavily fissured in maturity. The shoots are stout and covered in a slight pubescence. Each shoot carries several large leaves from 13–30cm (5–12in) long, which are dark glossy green above, with some pubescence beneath. Loquat has small white hawthorn-like flowers, which carry the scent of almonds, and are borne in dense flowerheads up to 15cm (6in) across. These are followed by golden-yellow, round fruits that contain several glossy brown seeds.

Left: The leaves are rigid, thick, leathery and up to 30cm (12in) long.

Left: The golden-yellow fruits of the loquat are sweet and edible.

LOCUST TREES AND PAGODA TREES

The pea family, Leguminosae, contains more than 15,000 species of trees, shrubs and herbaceous plants in 700 genera. They are found growing wild throughout the world in both temperate and tropical conditions. Most have compound leaves, pea-like flowers and seed pods, and root systems that have the ability to use bacteria to absorb nitrogen from the soil.

Pagoda Tree

Sophora japonica

Despite its botanical name *japonica*, the pagoda tree is not thought to be a native of Japan. However, it has been widely cultivated there for centuries, particularly in temple gardens and places of learning. In China the flower buds were used to make a yellow dye, and all parts of the tree, if taken internally, create a strong purgative effect. In the USA it is grown as a lawn tree. On trees grown from seed the flowers can take 30 years to appear.

Identification: The bark is greenish-brown, becoming vertically fissured and ridged in maturity. The overall shape is rounded, with branching starting low on the stem. The leaves are pinnate and up to 25cm (10in) long, with up to 15 opposite, untoothed, ovate, pointed leaflets, which are dark green above and glaucous with some pubescence beneath. The flowers are white, pea-like, fragrant and borne in terminal panicles in summer. The fruit is a seed pod up to 7.5cm (3in) long, containing up to six seeds. It ripens from green to brown.

Distribution: Northern China but could be more widespread. It survives to USA hardiness zone 5.
Height: 20m (66ft)
Shape: Broadly spreading
Deciduous
Pollinated: Insect
Leaf shape: Pinnate

Left: The white flowers of the pagoda tree are produced in summer in open sprays.

Black Locust

Robinia pseudoacacia

This locust tree originates from the Appalachian Mountains from Pennsylvania to Georgia; however, it is now naturalized over most of the USA. It was once valued for ships' masts because of its strong, durable timber, and clean straight trunk. Native Americans used the timber to make bows. Black locust has the habit of suckering from the root system and on mature trees suckers can be found up to 10m (33ft) away from the base of the tree.

Identification: The leaves are pinnate, up to 30cm (12in) long, with 11–21 ovate to elliptic untoothed, thin leaflets, each 5cm (2in) long and ending in a sharp point at the tip. They are grass-green above and blue-green below. Quite often there are two sharp spines at the base of each leaf. The fragrant flowers are pea-like, white, with a pea-green blotch in the throat.

Distribution: Eastern USA.
Height: 25m (80ft)
Shape: Broadly columnar
Deciduous
Pollinated: Insect
Leaf shape: Pinnate

Left: The fruit is a dark brown bean pod up to 10cm (4in) long.

Honeylocust

Gleditsia triacanthos

This remarkable tree is probably best known for its armoury of ferocious thorns that cover its trunk and main branches; this could be considered a reason for not planting it. However, honeylocust is widely planted in city streets because it is able to withstand heat, dust, drought and airborne pollutants. Unlike other members of the pea family, it does not have the ordinary "wing and keel" pea flower.

Identification: The bark is dark gray, smooth at first, becoming vertically fissured in maturity with clusters of sharply pointed spines. The leaves are pinnate, or bipinnate, with numerous small leaflets. Each leaflet may be up to 4cm (1½in) long. Leaf shoots are bright green and carry brown spines. In autumn the leaves turn golden-yellow. The flowers are yellow-green and small, and borne in small, upright racemes up to 5cm (2in) long.

Distribution: From New England to Texas, USA.
Height: 30m (100ft)
Shape: Broadly spreading
Deciduous
Pollinated: Insect
Leaf shape: Pinnate

Right: The seed is contained in a large, up to 45cm (18in) long, often twisted, brown hanging pod, in late summer.

Kentucky Coffee Tree

Gymnocladus dioica

This tree is widely planted in parks and gardens as an ornamental tree even outside its natural range, which extends from New York and Pennsylvania to Nebraska. It is said that the seeds of this tree were roasted to make into a type of coffee by early European settlers in North America. Raw seeds of this species are poisonous. It is easily distinguished by its huge bipinnate leaves, which may be up to 1m (40in) long and carry up to 140 leaflets.

Distribution: Central and eastern USA.
Height: 25m (80ft)
Shape: Broadly columnar
Deciduous
Pollinated: Insect
Leaf shape: Bipinnate

Identification: The bipinnate leaves have ovate leaflets, each up to 7.5cm (3in) long, which are thin, untoothed and emerge from winter bud a bronze colour, before turning dark green above and sea-green beneath. The flowers are greenish-white and fragrant, 2.5cm (1in) across, and borne in conical panicles up to 10cm (4in) long.

EUCALYPTUS

There are more than 400 species of eucalyptus, or gum tree, native to the Southern Hemisphere. They are abundant in Australia, Tasmania, New Guinea, the Philippines and Java. Most eucalyptus are evergreen and fast-growing, with attractive bark, luxuriant foliage and white flowers. They have been widely cultivated for their ornamental qualities and timber, in other warm temperate regions.

Cider Gum

Eucalyptus gunnii

The cider gum is native to the island of Tasmania, where it grows in moist mountain forests up to 1,300m (4,265ft) above sea level. It is one of the hardiest of all eucalyptus species and one of the most widely planted around the world. Cider gum has attractive glaucous-coloured, round, juvenile foliage, which is prized by flower arrangers and florists. Trees that are regularly coppiced maintain juvenile foliage. Wild trees grow up to 30m (98ft) tall.

Right: If left to mature, cider gum leaves become long and slender, and hang from the branches.

Identification: This potentially large, fast-growing tree has smooth, grey-green to orange bark, peeling to reveal creamy fawn patches. The juvenile leaves are round, 4cm (1½in) across, glaucous to silver-blue and borne opposite in pairs. Mature leaves are lanceolate, up to 10cm (4in) long, sage-green to silver-coloured and borne alternately on the twig. Flowers are white with numerous yellow stamens, borne in clusters of three in the leaf axils during summer. The fruit is a green, woody capsule, open at one end, and contains several seeds.

Right: After pollination in summer, the flowers develop into woody fruit.

Distribution: Tasmania. Thrives in the Pacific Northwest. USA zones 8–10.
Height: 30m (100ft)
Shape: Broadly columnar
Evergreen
Pollinated: Insect
Leaf shape: Juvenile leaves are rounded, and the mature leaves are lanceolate

Tasmanian Blue Gum

Eucalyptus globulus

This fast-growing, but rather tender Australasian tree, is the floral emblem of Tasmania. It was introduced into the San Francisco area of the USA as a timber-producing species in 1875, but since then it has escaped from cultivation and taken over extensive areas in the hills to the south, where it grows at elevations in excess of 600m (2,000ft). In good growing conditions the blue gum will grow more than 2.5m (8ft) in one year.

Left: Mature leaves are lanceolate, glossy green and up to 40cm (16in) long.

Identification: The bark is a patchwork of blue-grey, yellow and brown, at first smooth, but becoming shaggy in maturity, and peeling in long ribbons. The juvenile leaves are an attractive glaucous grey-green colour and rounded. Quite often trees are pruned back hard to encourage juvenile foliage, which is used in floral arrangements. The adult leaves are ovate to lanceolate, waxy to the touch, glossy green and up to 40cm (16in) long. The flowers are creamy white with golden-yellow stamens. They grow singly in the leaf axils in spring.

Right: The leaves are arranged opposite each other on the twigs.

Distribution: Tasmania and the State of Victoria, Australia. USA zones 8–10.
Height: 60m (195ft)
Shape: Broadly columnar
Evergreen
Pollinated: Insect
Leaf shape: Lanceolate

Longbeak Eucalyptus

Eucalyptus camaldulensis

The longbeak eucalyptus has a natural range that extends right across northern Australia. Consequently it is not as hardy as the blue gum, *Eucalyptus globulus*, and has not become naturalized in the wild, in California, to such an extent. It is found in profusion in the Bay area and further east into Arizona, where it is common in towns and cities as an ornamental species. Elsewhere, further northward, it is kept in check by winter frost. The longbeak eucalyptus has a much more open crown than that of the blue gum.

Identification: The bark is a mixture of light fawn, yellow and grey-red, smooth at first, becoming straggly, and peeling in narrow strips in maturity. The adult leaves are pale green with a white midrib, 15cm (6in) long and 2.5cm (1in) across. At first glance there is a similarity in the leaf with weeping willow, *Salix babylonica*. The hard seed capsules ripen to a five-pointed star shape.

Distribution: Northern Australia. USA zones 8–10.
Height: 25m (80ft)
Shape: Broadly columnar
Evergreen
Pollinated: Insect
Leaf shape: Lanceolate

Left: The white flowers grow in clusters of five to six. The flower buds have a distinctive, stout, beak-like tip, hence the name.

OTHER SPECIES OF NOTE

Mountain Gum *Eucalyptus dalrympleana*
This handsome tree is native to Tasmania, New South Wales and Victoria in Australia. It is also known as the broad-leaved kindling bark because it sheds large, dry patches of pale cream bark. It grows on steep, rocky slopes at elevations of up to 1,500m (4,921ft) above sea level. It has grey-green lanceolate leaves that are bronze-coloured when juvenile. *See also page 407.*

Small-leaved Gum
Eucalyptus parviflora
This hardy, medium-size gum tree originates from New South Wales, but has been grown as an ornamental in parks, and arboreta across southern states of the USA since the 1930s. It has smooth, grey, peeling bark, grey-green ovate juvenile leaves, and blue-green, ovate, mature leaves up to 5cm (2in) long. *See also page 408.*

Alpine Ash *Eucalyptus delegatensis*
This is one of the tallest of all eucalyptus, regularly attaining heights in excess of 60m (197ft) in the mountains of Tasmania. In cultivation, in the USA, it is more likely to reach heights of around 30m (100ft). It has a straight, clean trunk and sparse airy crown. The juvenile bark is smooth, bluish-grey and shed in narrow, vertical ribbons; in maturity it becomes rough and fibrous. The adult leaves are lanceolate, dull sage-green and up to 15cm (6in) long.

Silver Dollar Tree

Eucalyptus polyanthemos

This tender gum is native to New South Wales and Victoria, Australia. It was introduced into the USA in the late 19th century. It is the only eucalyptus to be seen growing in the eastern states outside southern Florida. It is cultivated in parks and gardens from Atlanta to west of New Orleans, inland Georgia and Alabama, as well as in California. Although relatively hardy, it is often cut to the ground by frost and regrows as a shrubby bush rather than a tree.

Identification: The bark is orange red and fibrous, becoming shaggy in maturity. Both the juvenile and adult leaves are almost round and a bright glaucous, silvery blue-white colour, hence the name silver dollar. The juvenile leaves are borne opposite on the shoots, and the adult leaves are alternate. From a distance this tree is very distinctive with its light silvery colouring. The flowers are creamy white, small and borne in clusters in early spring.

Distribution: Australia. USA zones 8–10.
Height: 30m (100ft)
Shape: Broadly columnar
Evergreen
Pollinated: Insect
Leaf shape: Orbicular

Above: Small clusters of creamy, white fragrant flowers are borne in early spring.

DOGWOODS AND HANDKERCHIEF TREE

The flowering dogwoods are some of the most beautiful trees in North America. They have been widely cultivated as ornamental specimens in parks and gardens from the eastern seaboard to the west coast. Their small insignificant flowers are surrounded by coloured bracts which act as protection for the flowers.

Flowering Dogwood

Cornus florida

This beautiful small tree is common in North America. It has a natural range that extends from Portland, Oregon, east to Maine and south to Texas. It has distinctive bark that becomes deeply fissured into small, square, red-brown blocks. It is slow-growing and eventually makes a bushy, upswept tree with a low crown. The cultivar 'Cherokee Chief', which has deep pink flower bracts, is common in cultivation.

Distribution: North America.
Height: 12m (40ft)
Shape: Broadly spreading
Deciduous
Pollinated: Insect
Leaf shape: Ovate

Identification: Flowering dogwood has untoothed and taper-pointed leaves that are ovate to elliptic, up to 10cm (4in) long and 5cm (2in) across. They are dark green with a slight sheen above, paler with some white soft pubescence beneath. In autumn they turn through pink to a stunning rich, burgundy-red. The flowers have a distinct notch at the tip. They are followed by glossy, bright red berries.

Left: The flowers are tiny, green and produced in a dense cluster that is surrounded by four 5cm- (2in-) long, white bracts.

Pacific Dogwood

Cornus nuttallii

Distribution: British Columbia south to California.
Height: 25m (80ft)
Shape: Broadly conical
Deciduous
Pollinated: Insect
Leaf shape: Elliptic

The Pacific dogwood grows naturally in lowland forests beneath larger trees, such as the Douglas fir, from Vancouver Island along the Coast Range to south California and the western flanks of the Cascade Sierra Nevada. It has been widely cultivated as an ornamental tree outside this region in parks and gardens. In late spring it produces some of the biggest bracts of any dogwood. In cultivation it rarely attains its full potential height, more often growing as a multi-stemmed, large shrub, or small tree.

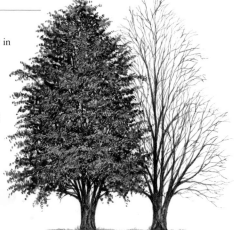

Identification: The bark is smooth, grey, becoming cracked into irregular plates in maturity. The untoothed, pointed leaves are elliptic, sometimes obovate, up to 15cm (6in) long and 7.5cm (3in) across, dark green above, paler beneath, with some pubescence. In autumn they turn bright red. After flowering, small oval-shaped, shiny red berries appear in clusters.

Far left: The flowers are small, green and borne in dense, hemispherical clusters. Four to seven large creamy white (sometimes blush-pink) bracts, up to 7.5cm (3in) long, surround each cluster.

OTHER SPECIES OF NOTE

Alternate-leaved Dogwood

Cornus alternifolia

As the name suggests, this species of dogwood is unusual in having leaves that are borne alternately on the shoot; most dogwoods have opposite leaves. This large shrub, or small multi-stemmed tree, is native to eastern North America from Newfoundland to Florida. It is sometimes known as the pagoda dogwood because of the tiered effect created by its horizontal branches.

Cornus 'Eddie's White Wonder'

This is an extremely popular ornamental hybrid between the two main American dogwoods: flowering dogwood, *Cornus florida*, and the Pacific dogwood, *C. nuttallii*. It has large white bracts, which appear consistently year upon year, and leaves that turn a brilliant orange-red colour every autumn. It was first developed in America in the 1960s.

Japanese Strawberry Tree *Cornus kousa*

This beautiful small tree, native to Japan and Korea, was introduced into North America in the 1870s and has since become widely cultivated in parks and gardens across the USA. It differs from the American dogwoods in having showy, pointed creamy white, or pink-blushed, bracts, and red, edible strawberry-like fruits, which hang from the branches in late summer to early autumn. The variety *chinensis* is a taller, more open form with larger leaves. It was introduced into America in 1907. *See also page 410.*

Handkerchief Tree

Dove tree, Ghost tree *Davidia involucrata*

This beautiful tree was introduced into the West from China in 1904, by the plant collector Ernest Wilson, who had been commissioned by Veitch's nursery to collect propagation material from "this most wondrous of species". All of the tree's common names refer to the white hanging leaf bracts that appear in late spring.

Identification: The bark is orange-brown with vertical fissures, creating flaking, irregular plates. The leaves, up to 15cm (6in) long and 10cm (4in) wide, are sharply toothed with a drawn-out, pointed tip. They are glossy bright green above and paler with some hairs beneath. In times of drought they roll into a cigar shape in an effort to reduce water loss by transpiration. The flowers appear in late spring. They are small, numerous, clustered into a ball and have conspicuous lilac anthers. The fruit is a green-purple husk containing a single, hard nut, inside which are up to five seeds.

Distribution: Western China. USA zones 6–8.
Height: 25m (82ft)
Shape: Broadly conical
Deciduous
Pollinated: Insect
 Leaf shape: Cordate

Above: Surrounding the flowers are two large white bracts of unequal size, up to 20cm (8in) long, which flutter in the breeze.

Golden Raintree

Koelreuteria paniculata

This Asian tree, sometimes called "pride of India" or "China tree", is particularly valued for its golden-yellow flowers, which appear in the height of summer. It has long been planted as an ornamental species in parks, gardens and streets throughout the USA. After flowering, three-sided papery, pink, bladder-shaped capsules develop, which contain three hard black seeds.

Identification: The bark is pale brown, smooth, becoming shallowly fissured in maturity. The large, attractive leaves are pinnate, sometimes bipinnate, up to 45cm (18in) long, and divided into 10cm- (4in-) long, toothed, dark green leaflets, which turn butter-yellow in autumn. This tree has golden-yellow flowers, 1cm (½in) across, which are carried in conical-shaped panicles up to 45cm (18in) long, at the tips of the growing shoots. After flowering, bladder-like seed capsules develop.

Distribution: China and Korea. USA zones 5–9.
Height: 12m (40ft)
Shape: Broadly spreading
Deciduous
Pollinated: Insect
Leaf shape: Pinnate

Above: The flowers are greenish-pink, gradually fading to pale brown. In China, the seeds they contain were made into decorative necklaces.

HOLLIES AND BOX

There are more than 400 species of temperate and tropical, evergreen and deciduous, trees and shrubs in the Aquifoliaceae family; the majority belong to the holly, or Ilex, genus. Hollies are dioecious (either male or female). The leaves occur alternately on the shoot and the fruit is a berry. Holly has long been associated with the Christmas season.

Common Holly

Ilex aquifolium

Holly is one of the most useful and ornamental trees of the temperate world. It is extremely hardy, and its dense foliage provides better shelter in exposed coastal and mountainous localities than just about any other tree. Holly has long been considered an integral part of Christmas celebrations and its bright berries cheer up the dullest of winter days. Holly timber is dense and hard and has been used for making just about everything, from piano keys to billiard cues. The common holly has given rise to numerous attractive garden cultivars.

Identification: The bark is silver-grey and smooth even in maturity. The leaves are elliptic to ovate, up to 10cm (4in) long, glossy dark green and waxy above, and pale green beneath. They are extremely variable: some leaves have strong spines around the margin; others are spineless. Both the male and female flowers are small and white with a slight fragrance; they appear on separate trees clustered into the leaf axils in late spring and early summer. The fruit is a round, shiny, red berry up to 1cm (½in) across, borne in clusters along the shoot in winter.

Right: The dense foliage of holly makes it a useful hedging plant.

Distribution: Whole of Europe, western Asia and North Africa. It survives in USA hardiness zones 6–8.
Height: 20m (66ft)
Shape: Broadly columnar
Evergreen
Pollinated: Insect
Leaf shape: Elliptic to ovate

Right: Holly flowers are scented and appear from spring into summer.

American Holly

Ilex opaca

This native American tree grows wild in eastern USA, from Long Island south to Florida, and is common as a planted roadside tree in Tennessee, Louisiana, Arkansas and eastern Texas. In the wild it is most prevalent on coastal sandy soils. It is similar to the common holly, *Ilex aquifolium*, except the leaf is less glossy above and it has a more pronounced yellow colour beneath, and there is less variability in the number of spines on the leaf margin. It produces brilliant red berries in winter.

Left: There are several cultivars and varieties of Ilex opaca *in North America including the form xanthocarpa, which has bright yellow fruits.*

Identification: The bark is grey and smooth, becoming finely lined in maturity, with dark yellow-green fissures. The leaves are elliptic, up to 10cm (4in) long and 5cm (2in) across. They are matt dark green above, yellow-green beneath, with spines at the tip and around the leaf margin. Both the male and female flowers are small, dull white and borne in leaf axils on separate trees in late spring. The fruit is a red, shiny spherical berry up to 1cm (½in) across.

Distribution: Eastern North America.
Height: 20m (66ft)
Shape: Broadly conical
Evergreen
Pollinated: Insect
Leaf shape: Elliptic

Japanese Holly *Ilex crenata*
Native to both Japan and Korea, this
attractive evergreen plant is more a tall
shrub than a tree, seldom attaining
heights in excess of 4m (13ft). It has
stiff, deep green, glossy, small leaves,
which are 1cm (½in) long and more
akin to those of common box than
holly. These are densely borne on
reddish-brown shoots, which also
carry globular, glossy black berries in
winter. It survives in the warmer
areas of zone 5.

Chinese Holly *Ilex cornuta*
Also known as horned holly because of
its horn-like spines, this small evergreen
tree is native to China and Korea, and
rare in cultivation. It has slightly larger
red berries than common holly and a
rectangular-shaped leaf with a large spine
at each corner, plus smaller intermediate
spines. It is slow-growing with a neat
compact habit. *See also page 412.*

Highclere Holly *Ilex x altaclarensis*
The term Highclere holly has come to
represent a whole group of ornamental
holly cultivars developed from the original
Ilex x altaclarensis hybrid between the
common holly, *I. aquifolium*, and the
Madeira holly, *I. perado*. The original
hybrid was developed at Highclere
Castle, England, in 1838. Most
of the cultivars have broad, rounded,
glossy leaves. One of the most
popular cultivars is 'Golden King'. *See
also page 413.*

Yaupon

Ilex vomitoria

This small tree, or large shrub, grows naturally on
the Coastal Plain from Virginia to Texas. It gets its
botanical name *vomitoria* from the fact that at one
time Native Americans would make an infusion of
the leaves, which they then drank in large
quantities causing severe vomiting. They continued
to drink the infusion for two or three days until
they had sufficiently cleansed themselves. This
species is tender and although widely
planted in southern United States
it is seldom seen growing
successfully in northern
states. It has become
naturalized in Bermuda.

Identification: Yaupon has
smooth pale grey bark and
shoots that arise from
stout, horizontal
branches. It is a
densely branched small
tree with a central trunk
rarely more than 45cm
(18in) in diameter. The
leaves, which persist for
two years, are glossy dark
green above and pale yellow-
green beneath, narrowly oval or ovate,
tapered at the base and blunt at the tip
with irregular, small spines. Both male and
female flowers are small, white and borne in
clusters in the leaf axils on separate trees in
spring. The fruit is a bright orange-red berry.

Distribution: South-eastern
USA.
Height: 6m (20ft)
Shape: Broadly spreading
Evergreen
Pollinated: Insect
Leaf shape: Oval

*Above: The leaves
are up to 10cm (4in) long
and 5cm (2in) broad.*

*Right: The
flowers are
borne in the
leaf axils.*

Common Box

Buxus sempervirens

This small tree, or spreading shrub,
has dense foliage and has been
grown for centuries in gardens
for hedging, screening and
topiary. It is a favourite for
use in defining knot gardens
and parterres, and clips well.
It withstands dense shade and
will happily grow beneath the
branches of other trees. It has
hard, cream-coloured wood,
which has been extensively used for
wood engraving and turnery.

Identification: The bark is fawn or
buff-coloured, smooth at first, then
fissuring into tiny plates. The
leaves are ovate to oblong,
2.5cm (1in), rounded at the tip
with a distinctive notch, glossy
dark green above, pale green
below and borne on angular
shoots. Both male and female
flowers are produced in
mid-spring; they are small,
pale green with yellow
anthers and carried
separately in the same
clusters on the same trees.

Distribution: Europe, North
Africa and western Asia. It
survives in USA hardiness
zones 5–10.
Height: 6m (20ft)
Shape: Broadly conical to
spreading
Evergreen
Pollinated: Insect
Leaf shape:
Ovate

*Far left: The fruit is a small woody
capsule holding up to six seeds.*

*Right: Male and female flowers are produced
separately in the leaf axils.*

BUCKEYES AND HORSE CHESTNUTS

The horse chestnut genus, Aesculus, contains some of the most popular and easily recognizable ornamental trees in the world. There are just 15 species, all native to northern temperate regions, where they are widely grown in parks, gardens and arboreta for their stately habit, and attractive flowers and fruit. All horse chestnuts have compound, palmate leaves and large flowers borne in upright panicles.

Californian Buckeye

Aesculus californica

There are six different species of American buckeyes, or horse chestnuts, as they may be known, five of them are native to eastern USA, and this one is native to California. It is found in the low, dry foothills from Shasta to the Coast Ranges and south along the western slopes of the Sierra Nevada. It is low-growing, with branches emerging from the trunk 30cm (12in) from the ground. The flowers have the strongest fragrance of any buckeye.

Identification: The juvenile Californian buckeye has pale grey, smooth bark, which becomes scaly, thick and a pale pink-grey colour in maturity. The winter leaf buds are large, red-brown and very resinous. The leaves are palmately compound with five to seven oblong, toothed leaflets, up to 15cm (6in) long and 7.5cm (3in) broad. They are yellow-green above and sage-green beneath. The small flowers are white, or pale pink, and are borne in dense upright columnar panicles, up to 20cm (8in) long. These are followed by glossy brown pear-shaped seeds, individually protected in a pink-green casing.

Distribution: California.
Height: 10m (33ft)
Shape: Broadly spreading
Deciduous
Pollinated: Insect
Leaf shape: Compound palmate

Right: Autumn leaf colour is not significant.

Left: The flowers appear in early summer.

Yellow Buckeye

Sweet buckeye *Aesculus flava*

Sometimes referred to as *Aesculus octandra*, or sweet buckeye, this handsome, round-headed tree was introduced from North America into Europe as early as 1764. *Flava* means yellow and refers to the yellow flowers that appear in early summer. This is one of the best horse chestnuts for autumn colour because the leaves turn a stunning orange-red in early autumn.

Identification: The bark is brown-grey, flaking in maturity into large irregular-shaped scales. Branches tend to be horizontal or even drooping with a characteristic sweep upwards towards the tip. The leaves are compound and palmate, with five sharply toothed, dark-green leaflets, each up to 15cm (6in) long, all joining a pea-green leaf stalk at a common point. The flowers are yellow with a pink blotch and borne on upright panicles up to 15cm (6in) long in late spring and early summer. The fruit, two brown nuts, or "conkers", are encased in a smooth, round husk, up to 5cm (2in) across.

Distribution: USA: from Pennsylvania to Tennessee and Georgia, and west into Ohio and Illinois.
Height: 30m (100ft)
Shape: Broadly conical
Deciduous
Pollinated: Insect
Leaf shape: Compound palmate

Left: The yellow buckeye is named after its flowers.

Right: The fruit is smooth.

Red Buckeye

Aesculus pavia

Red buckeye is native to the Coastal Plain from North Carolina to Florida and east to the Mississippi River Valley, where it grows in moist woods and thickets. It is a small tree, sometimes little more than a shrub, with a slightly weeping, pendulous habit to the outer branches. It is one of the parents of the hybrid red horse chestnut, *Aesculus* x *carnea*, to which it gives the red colour of its flowers. Red buckeye has been in cultivation in parks and gardens since the 18th century.

Identification: The bark is dark grey and smooth, becoming cracked in maturity. The leaves are palmately compound, with five elliptic, sharply toothed and pointed, shiny dark green leaflets, up to 15cm (6in) long. The flowers have, without doubt, the best red colour of any buckeye, and far better than that of its hybrid offspring. They are slender, bright red, borne in upright panicles up to 20cm (8in) long in early summer. These are followed by small pear-like fruits, which open to reveal one or two glossy mahogany-brown seeds.

Distribution: South-east USA.
Height: 5m (17ft)
Shape: Broadly spreading
Deciduous
Pollinated: Insect
Leaf shape: Compound palmate

Left: The flowers are at their best in June and July.

Right: The fruits resemble small unripe pears.

Ohio Buckeye

Aesculus glabra

This tree has the largest natural distribution of any North American buckeye. Its range extends from Pennsylvania to Tennessee in the Allegheny valley bottoms, and westwards into Texas. It is also widely planted as an ornamental tree in parks and gardens throughout this range because of its beautiful yellow flowers, which appear early every summer.

Identification: Ohio buckeye has smooth grey bark at first, becoming very rough and flaky in maturity. The leaves are palmately compound with scarcely any leaf stalk. There are five elliptic leaflets, up to 20cm (8in) long, glossy green above, paler beneath, turning a good orange-yellow in autumn. The flowers are pale lemon-yellow, 2.5cm (1in) long, and densely borne in upright conical panicles up to 15cm (6in) long. Most years the flowers are borne in profusion right across the whole canopy, producing a magnificent sight in early summer.

Distribution: South-east and central USA.
Height: 10m (33ft)
Shape: Broadly spreading
Deciduous
Pollinated: Insect
Leaf shape: Compound palmate

Above: The fruit has a prickly poisonous casing.

MAPLES

There are more than 100 species of maples, Acer, in the world and countless cultivars, particularly of the Japanese maples. They are mainly deciduous and predominantly found throughout northern temperate regions, with a few extending into subtropical Asia. They range in size from mighty American giants to slow-growing Japanese bonsai. Many are cultivated for their attractive foliage and graceful habit.

Ash-leaved Maple

Box elder *Acer negundo*

This variable small to medium-size maple is found growing wild across North America, particularly alongside rivers and in moist soils. The leaves do not resemble those on the Canadian flag, but are pinnate with up to seven leaflets, which individually resemble the leaves of elder, *Sambucus*. The name "box" is derived from the timber, which is white and dense, like boxwood.

Identification: The bark is brown to silver-grey, thin and smooth. The leaves are pinnate, with each leaflet approximately 10cm (4in) long and sometimes lobed. Leaflets are arranged opposite in pairs, with a terminal leaflet that is usually slightly bigger than the rest. They are rich green above and lighter green with some hair beneath. Both male and female flowers are small, yellow-green and borne on separate trees in spring, just as the leaves are emerging. The male flowers are tassel-like with long drooping stamens; the females soon develop the familiar seed wings. The fruit is the classic, downward-pointing, two-winged seed.

Distribution: North America.
Height: 20m (66ft)
Shape: Broadly columnar
Deciduous
Pollinated: Insect
Leaf shape: Pinnate

Left: Flowers hang, tassel-like, from the outer twigs. The seeds each have two wings to catch the wind and spin as they fall from the tree. The leaves are different from those of most maples.

Red Maple

Acer rubrum

One of the most striking of all American maples, from its bright red showy flowers in spring, until its stunning autumn colour, this is a tree not to be missed. It has a natural range that extends from eastern Newfoundland to Ontario in the north, south to Florida and westwards into Texas. Red maple grows particularly well in wet lowland areas. It is a common tree in parks, gardens and cities right across its natural range.

Identification: The bark is dark grey and smooth, even in maturity. The leaves are palmate, up to 10cm (4in) long, and broad, with three or five coarsely serrated lobes. The upper surface is dark matt green; the underside is sage-green to almost white with yellow pubescence around the leaf veins. Small red flowers appear on bare branches in early spring. Both male and female flowers are bright red and they appear on slender red stalks in dense clusters in early spring. These are followed by red two-winged seeds, each about 2.5cm (1in) long.

Distribution: Eastern and central North America.
Height: 30m (100ft)
Shape: Broadly columnar
Deciduous
Pollinated: Insect
Leaf shape: Palmate

Right: The winged seeds.

Left: The leaves turn scarlet in autumn.

Silver Maple

Acer saccharinum

This is one of the fastest-growing North American maples, and is widely planted as an ornamental specimen for parks and gardens. It is altogether more refined than sycamore, having a light, open crown with bicoloured leaves, which catch the light as they flutter in the breeze. It does have rather brittle wood, which means that it has a tendency to drop its branches – sometimes with no warning.

Identification: The bark is grey and smooth when young, becoming flaky with epicormic growth in maturity. The leaves are palmate, up to 15cm (6in) long and wide, and have five sharply toothed lobes, each ending in a sharp point. They are light green above and glaucous with some hair beneath. The leaves are borne on lax stalks up to 15cm (6in) long, allowing them to flutter in even the lightest breeze. Both male and female flowers are small and greenish-yellow. They are clustered together on the young shoots as the leaves begin to emerge. Each winged seed is up to 2.5cm (1in) long.

Distribution: Eastern North America from Ontario to Florida.
Height: 30m (100ft)
Shape: Broadly columnar
Deciduous
Pollinated: Insect
Leaf shape: Palmate

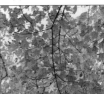

Left: In mid-autumn the leaves turn yellow before dropping.

OTHER SPECIES OF NOTE

Black Maple *Acer nigrum*
This maple is considered by some to be a sub-species of the sugar maple, *A. saccharum*. It is certainly closely related, but has larger, darker leaves and a more open pattern of growth. In autumn, the leaves become a rich yellow. It has a similar natural range to that of sugar maple, but is not as common in cultivation.

Canyon Maple *Acer grandidentatum*
The canyon maple is also considered to be a subspecies of sugar maple. It may be referred to as bigtooth maple because of its large lobed leaves. It is native to damp canyons in the southern parts of the Rocky Mountains, where it grows at altitudes of up to 2,500m (8,000ft). It is a much smaller tree than the sugar maple, seldom attaining heights in excess of 33ft (10m).

Norway Maple *Acer platanoides*
Native to northern and central Europe, Norway maple was introduced into North America 100 years ago. Since then, it has become a common tree in cultivation across much of northern North America, particularly in cities and towns. At first glance it is similar to sugar maple, but it has a smoother bark in maturity and more prominent yellow flowers in spring. *See also page 419.*

Paperbark Maple *Acer griseum*
This beautiful small tree was discovered in China, in 1901. It has striking, cinnamon-coloured, wafer-thin, peeling bark, which flakes away to reveal fresh orange bark beneath. It has distinctive trifoliate leaves, which turn burgundy-red and orange in autumn. *See also page 419.*

Sugar Maple

Acer saccharum

The sugar maple has the most striking scarlet-orange, autumn leaf-colours. It has a natural range from Quebec and Nova Scotia, south to North Carolina and west to Missouri, but is commonly cultivated throughout eastern and central North America. This tree is the source of maple syrup, which is produced from its boiled sap. Its timber is hard and resistant to wear and has been used for dance floors.

Identification: The bark is brown-grey, smooth at first, becoming shallowly fissured and flaking in maturity. Each leaf is mid- to dark green above and paler beneath, with some pubescence in the vein axils. The flowers are small, yellowish-green and borne in drooping open clusters in early spring just as the leaves emerge from bud.

Below: The fruit is a two-winged seed up to 2.5cm (1in) long.

Distribution: Eastern North America.
Height: 35m (100ft)
Shape: Broadly columnar
Deciduous
Pollinated: Insect
Leaf shape: Palmate

Below: The palmate leaves have five prominent tapered lobes that run to long points.

Right: Each leaf may be up to 15cm (6in) long and broad.

Smooth Japanese Maple

Acer palmatum

Smooth Japanese maple was discovered in 1783 and introduced to the West in 1820. Surprisingly though, it was almost another 80 years before it became popular and began to be widely planted. The famous acer glade at Westonbirt Arboretum in England was not planted until 1875. Today there are hundreds of cultivars of smooth Japanese maple. In the wild the species grows within, or on the edge of, mixed broad-leaved woodland, providing dappled shade and shelter.

Distribution: China, Taiwan, Japan and Korea. USA zones 5–8.
Height: 15m (50ft)
Shape: Broadly spreading
Deciduous
Pollinated: Insect
Leaf shape: Palmate

Identification: The bark is grey-brown and smooth, even in maturity. The overall shape of the tree is like a large natural bonsai, with horizontal, spreading, meandering branches forking from the main stem quite close to the ground. The leaves are palmate with between five and seven deep, pointed lobes, which have forward-facing serrations around the margin. They are up to 10cm (4in) across. The flowers are burgundy-red with yellow stamens. They are borne in upright or drooping clusters as the leaves emerge in spring. The fruit is green to red winged seeds carried in pairs; each wing is up to 1cm (½in) long and clustered together on the branch with up to 20 other seeds.

Below left: In autumn, the leaves turn red and gold before dropping.

Right: New leaves emerge a bright green colour.

Oregon Maple

Bigleaf maple *Acer macrophyllum*

The big leaves are the main characteristic of this handsome North American species, which inhabits riverbanks, moist woods and canyons. In fact everything about this tree is big: its trunk, flowers and fruit are also among the largest for the genus. The timber of Oregon maple is highly valued in America, where it is used to make furniture.

Distribution: Western North America from British Columbia to California.
Height: 25m (82ft)
Shape: Broadly columnar
Deciduous
Pollinated: Insect
Leaf shape: Palmate

Identification: The bark is grey-brown and smooth, becoming vertically fissured in maturity. The leaves are palmate with large, coarsely toothed lobes cutting deep into the leaf centre. They are up to 25cm (10in) long and 30cm (12in) across, grass-green, and carried on long, buff-coloured leaf stalks. The flowers are green-yellow, fragrant and hang in conspicuous clusters up to 20cm (8in) long as the leaves unfurl in spring. The fruit has paired wings, each up to 5cm (2in) long, covered in fawn bristles and containing one seed at its base.

Below: The flowers appear in spring as the new leaves emerge.

Below left: The winged seeds are held on the tree in small bunches.

Fullmoon Maple *Acer japonicum*
Native to Japan, this tree is cultivated in USA zones 5–7. It has produced some of the finest and most popular ornamental cultivars, including the vine-leaved 'Vitifolium', 'Aconitifolium' and the golden-leaved 'Aureum', which is now considered a species in its own right with the name *A. shirasawanum*. See also page 420.

Cappadocian Maple *Acer cappadocicum*
Native to the Caucasus Mountains, this round-headed, large tree has palmate leaves with five to seven taper-pointed, untoothed lobes. The leaves are borne on long stalks, which, when cut, exude a milky white sap. In autumn the leaves turn a butter-yellow colour before dropping. See also page 419.

Nikko Maple *Acer maximowiczianum*
A delightful, round-headed, deciduous medium-size Japanese tree with trifoliate leaves, the under-sides of which are covered with soft blue-white hairs. It is a fine maple for autumn colour. It thrives in USA zones 4–8. Leaflets gradually turn from green through yellow and orange to red.

Rocky Mountain Maple *Acer glabrum*
Otherwise known as rock maple, this small, bushy tree is native to western North America, from Montana to New Mexico, where it grows on riversides and in moist woodlands. It has variable leaves, with three or five lobes. It has dull red shoots that are prominent in winter.

Moosewood

Striped maple *Acer pensylvanicum*

In North America moose eat the bark of this tree; however, striped maple is far more descriptive because of the way the grey-brown bark is beautifully striped with vertical, wavy white lines. This species thrives in moist woodlands. There is a popular cultivated garden form of moosewood called 'Erythrocladum', which has bright crimson shoots and winter buds.

Distribution: Eastern North America.
Height: 10m (33ft)
Shape: Broadly columnar
Deciduous
Pollinated: Insect
Leaf shape: Oblong

Identification: The striped bark develops at a young age; immature shoots are green, ripening to reddish-brown before developing vertical white lines (within three years). The leaves are up to 15cm (6in) long, oblong with three triangular, taper-pointed, toothed lobes cutting into the top half of the leaf. They are deep green and crinkly with pronounced veining above and some rust-coloured pubescence beneath. The inconspicuous green flowers are borne in weeping clusters in spring. The fruit is a small two-winged seed; each wing is 2.5cm (1in) long.

Left: The distinctive striped bark.

Right: The winged seeds.

Norway Maple

Acer platanoides

This fast-growing, handsome, hardy maple has been cultivated as an ornamental species for centuries. It has a large, spreading crown with upswept branches and is as much at home in parkland settings as in woodland. Recently, smaller cultivars have been developed, which are being planted in great numbers alongside roads.

Identification: The bark is grey and smooth when young, becoming vertically ridged and fissured in maturity. The leaves are rather like the leaf on the Canadian flag: palmately lobed, with five lobes, each ending in several sharp teeth and a slender point. Each leaf is up to 15cm (6in) in length and width, bright green and borne on a long, slender, pink-yellow leaf stalk. The flowers are bright yellow, sometimes red, and borne in conspicuous drooping clusters in spring as the leaves emerge.

Distribution: South-west Asia and Europe, north to Norway. USA zones 3–7.
Height: 30m (100ft)
Shape: Broadly columnar
Deciduous
Pollinated: Insect
Leaf shape: Palmate

Left: The fruit is a pair of green-yellow winged seeds borne in clusters. Each wing is up to 5cm (2in) long.

Right: Fresh foliage is a light green colour.

Right: Flowers may be either yellow or red.

ASHES AND CATALPAS

There are about 65 species within the ash genus, Fraxinus. All have pinnate leaves and are found within temperate regions of the world, primarily North America, Europe and Asia. They are hardy, fast-growing deciduous trees that tolerate exposure, poor soils and atmospheric pollution. The catalpas make up a genus of eleven species of beautiful flowering trees, mainly native to North America and China.

White Ash

Fraxinus americana

The white ash is a common North American tree that has a natural range extending from Nova Scotia east to Wisconsin, and south to Texas and Florida. It was first introduced into cultivation in 1724 and is now widely planted in parks and cities throughout this region. White ash produces clean, straight, strong flexible timber, which is used to make baseball bats, polo mallets, hockey sticks and rowing oars.

Identification: The bark is grey, with prominent narrow fissures that become deep in maturity. The winter leaf buds are rusty brown and borne on green shoots. The leaves are pinnate, to 35cm (14in) long. Each has up to nine short-stalked, ovate to lanceolate, sparsely toothed, taper-pointed leaflets, each 12cm (4½in) long, which are dark green above and pale green to white beneath. Male and female flowers are purple, small and appear in spring on separate trees before the new leaves emerge.

Distribution: Eastern North America.
Height: 28m (94ft)
Shape: Broadly columnar
Deciduous
Pollinated: Insect
Leaf shape: Pinnate

Right: White ash flower.

Right: The fruit is a winged seed, 5cm (2in) long, borne in dense pendulous clusters.

Black Ash

Brown ash *Fraxinus nigra*

Black ash, or brown ash, as it is sometimes known, grows further north than any other American ash. It occurs naturally from Manitoba to Newfoundland and south to West Virginia. It is also planted as a street tree in northern cities. It gets its name from its timber, which has dark brown to black heartwood, surrounded by a ring of almost white sapwood. Black ash thrives in wet, swampy areas, and on the banks of streams and lakes.

Identification: The bark is grey, slightly tinged with red, becoming thick with corky scales in maturity. Winter buds are dark brown to black and slightly velvety to the touch. The pinnate leaves are up to 40cm (16in) long, with up to eleven 10cm- (4in-) long, oblong to lanceolate, long-pointed, toothed leaflets, which are dark green above and paler beneath, with tufts of pubescence along the midrib. Dark purple male and female flowers appear on separate trees in early spring, before the leaves appear. These are followed by pendulous clusters of green, single-winged seeds, which ripen to pale brown in autumn and remain on the tree well into winter.

Distribution: Southern Canada and northern USA.
Height: 28m (94ft)
Shape: Broadly columnar
Deciduous
Pollinated: Insect
Leaf shape: Pinnate

Left: The green seeds ripen to pale brown in autumn.

Below: The pinnate leaves have up to five pairs of opposite leaflets and one terminal leaflet.

Green Ash

Fraxinus pennsylvanica

This is the most widespread of all American ashes. Its natural range extends from Nova Scotia to Alberta, and south to the Gulf Coast, Texas. It prefers rich, moist soils, but has been planted as a street tree in towns, both within and to the west of its natural range. It is a fast-growing tree, quick to establish on reclaimed land and widely used for wind protection.

Identification: The bark is grey-brown with narrow, interlacing ridges. The winter leaf buds are chocolate-brown and slightly pubescent. It has pinnate leaves, to 30cm (12in) long, with up to nine ovate to lanceolate, taper-pointed leaflets, 10cm (4in) long, sharply toothed around the margin, but sometimes untoothed. The flowers appear in early spring before the leaves. They are small, usually purple and carried in clusters. They are followed by single-winged seeds, up to 5cm (2in) long, which are borne in pendulous lusters.

Far right: Male and female flowers are borne on separate trees.

Distribution: Central and eastern North America.
Height: 25m (80ft)
Shape: Broadly columnar
Deciduous
Pollinated: Insect
Leaf shape: Pinnate

Right: The leaves are glossy dark green above, and pale, almost sage-green beneath.

OTHER SPECIES OF NOTE

Blue Ash *Fraxinus quadrangulata*
This small tree gets its name from its square, four-angled young shoots, which are slightly winged. Blue ash has a natural range from Ohio west to Missouri, and south to Georgia. The blue in the name refers to the inner bark, which early settlers used to make blue dye.

Oregon Ash *Fraxinus latifolia*
This ash is native to the west coast from Washington State south to central California along the flanks of the Sierra Nevada. It has been widely planted as a shade-giving tree in cities in the south-west. It produces timber and has large leaves, up to 30cm (12in) long.

European Ash, Common Ash
Fraxinus excelsior
This large, fast-growing tree is widespread throughout Europe from the western Mediterranean eastward into Russia. It has been grown in North America for over 100 years. It is similar in form to white ash, *Fraxinus americana*. *See also page 426.*

Narrow-leaved Ash *Fraxinus angustifolia*
This large, elegant, fast-growing tree, native to southern Europe and North Africa, is better

known in cultivated form rather than as a species. There are several cultivars, including 'Pendula' and 'Raywood', which are widely planted. *See also page 426.*

Velvet Ash

Fraxinus velutina

This small, pretty tree, which is sometimes known as the Arizona ash, grows wild from Texas west to California and south into Mexico. It gets its common name from the dense covering of grey velvety down that regularly covers the leaves, stalks and shoots. Velvet ash is planted as a shade-giving street tree, particularly in California.

Identification: The bark is thick, grey, sometimes tinged with red, and deeply fissured when mature into broad, flat, broken ridges. Velvet ash has dark brown winter buds. The leaves are 10cm (4in) long, with up to five ovate leaflets, although more commonly three. Each leaflet is up to 5cm (2in) long and normally covered with soft, dense grey-white hairs. They are dark green above and paler beneath. The flowers are deep purple coloured and appear on the tree in March and April before the leaves appear. Male and female flowers are borne on separate trees.

Right: Purple flowers appear in early spring.

Below: The seeds are narrow, oblong and 2.5cm (1in) long.

Right: The leaflets run to a long even point.

Distribution: South-west USA.
Height: 12m (40ft)
Shape: Broadly columnar
Deciduous
Pollinated: Insect
Leaf shape: Pinnate

Western Catalpa

Northern catalpa *Catalpa speciosa*

Sometimes known as the northern catalpa, this large, vigorous tree is native to the lands around the Mississippi and Ohio rivers in Illinois, Indiana, Missouri, Arkansas and Kentucky. It is also widely cultivated in parks and gardens elsewhere including on the west coast in British Columbia, Washington State and Oregon. It is a much taller and tougher tree than its southern cousin *Catalpa bignonioides*. This vigorous tree is not for small gardens. In North America the wood is prized for its natural durability and ability not to degrade or rot in wet conditions. It is quite often used to make untreated fence posts, which are then sunk into moist soil.

Identification: The bark is dark grey and coarsely ridged. The leaves are broadly ovate, up to 30cm (12in) long and 20cm (8in) wide, tapering at the tip to a long point. They are glossy dark green above, slightly lighter beneath, quite thin and lax. The flowers are bell-shaped, 5cm (2in) long, white, spotted with yellow and purple, and borne in upright open panicles in summer. These are followed by pendulous slender, bean-like pods, up to 45cm (18in) long, which persist on the tree into winter.

Below: When young the leaves are covered with slight pubescence.

Right: The seeds are contained within long, pendulous bean-pods.

Right: This large tree is perfect for parks and arboreta.

Distribution: South-eastern USA.
Height: 40m (130ft)
Shape: Broadly columnar
Deciduous
Pollinated: Insect
Leaf shape: Ovate

Crepe Myrtle

Lagerstroemia indica

Although native to China and Korea, this beautiful, upright, bushy little tree is widely planted as an ornamental in parks and gardens throughout the southern states of the USA. Elsewhere it is rather tender and requires a sheltered, sunny position. The main attraction of crepe myrtle is its lilac, deep pink flowers, which appear from late summer well into autumn.

Identification: Crepe myrtle has pretty bark, which is smoothly ribbed and mottled grey, pink and cinnamon. The leaves are opposite, alternate or in whorls of three; they are privet-like, obovate, untoothed around the leaf margin and up to 5cm (2in) long and 2.5cm (1in) wide. The flowers are borne in terminal panicles, up to 15cm (6in) long, with crinkly deep pink petals, which contract at the base into a slender claw. A distinctive feature of this tree is its multi-stemmed habit, with several stems rising from the base through 360 degrees.

Distribution: China and Korea.
Height: 6m (20ft)
Shape: Broadly spreading
Deciduous
Pollinated: Insect
Leaf shape: Obovate

Right: The deep pink flowers of the crepe myrtle are borne in late summer to mid-autumn.

Left: The leaves are thick, tough and reminiscent of privet.

Foxglove Tree

Paulownia tomentosa

This beautiful flowering tree is native to the mountains of central China. It takes its genus name from the daughter of Czar Paul I of Russia, Anna Paulownia. The spectacular pale purple, foxglove-like flowers appear on spikes in late spring. The timber has a certain resinous quality and was used in China and Japan to make a stringed instrument similar to a lute. Quite often *Paulownia* is coppiced for its foliage, which on juvenile shoots can be up to 45cm (18in) across.

Identification: The bark is rather like beech, being grey and smooth, even in maturity. The leaves are ovate, up to 45cm (18in) wide and long, heart-shaped at the base, with two large, but normally shallow, lobes on each side. They are dark green, with hair on both surfaces and shoots. The shoots are soft and pithy. Each trumpet-shaped, pale purple flower, blotched inside with dark purple and yellow, is 5cm (2in) long. Flowers are on upright panicles up to 45cm (18in) tall.

Distribution: Central, eastern China. USA zones 5–9.
Height: 20m (66ft)
Shape: Broadly columnar
Deciduous
Pollinated: Insect
Leaf shape: Ovate

Left: The fruit is a green, pointed, egg-shaped, woody capsule containing several winged seeds. The purple flowers resemble foxgloves.

OTHER SPECIES OF NOTE

Yellow Catalpa *Catalpa ovata*
This rare, small, spreading tree is native to China. It has ovate leaves, which are more distinctly lobed than either of its two North American cousins. It has white flowers, which are suffused with yellow. The flowers open in late summer and are followed by dark brown seed pods, each up to 30cm (12in) long, in autumn. The flowers are borne in upright panicles in late summer

Russian Olive *Elaeagnus angustifolia*
Otherwise known as 'Oleaster', this attractive, spiny small tree, or large shrub, is native to western Asia. It produces fragrant yellow flowers in early summer and has silver-grey, willow-like leaves. Russian olive is very resistant to heat, drought and cold, and is widely planted in the midwest and south-west USA along roads, in shelter belts and on industrial sites.

Indian Bean Tree

Catalpa bignonioides

The Indian part of the name refers to the Native Americans, who used to dry and paint catalpa seeds and wear them as decoration. This is one of the last trees in its region to flower, and is normally at its best in midsummer. It tolerates atmospheric pollution well, and has become widely planted in towns and cities, despite its broad, spreading crown.

Identification: Catalpa has grey-brown bark, becoming loose and flaking in patches in maturity. The leaves are broadly ovate, up to 25cm (10in) long and 15cm (6in) wide, rarely lobed, and heart-shaped at the base. On emerging from the bud they are bronze, gradually turning grass-green with some hair beneath. Each leaf is borne on a long, lax leaf stalk. The branches are quite brittle and prone to breakage in summer.

Distribution: South-east USA.
Height: 20m (66ft)
Shape: Broadly spreading
Deciduous
Pollinated: Insect
Leaf shape: Ovate

Right: The seed pods are 40cm (16in) long.

Below: Each trumpet-shaped flower is up to 5cm (2in) long.

PALMS AND YUCCAS

There are almost 150 genera within the Arecaceae (Palm) family. The majority of these are indigenous to tropical or subtropical regions of the world. However, one or two are native to the United States and others are cultivated for their fruit or for ornamental purposes in many temperate parts of the world.

Canary Island Date Palm

Phoenix canariensis

This is the most majestic and stately of all palms that thrive outside the tropics. Although native only to the Canary Islands, it is widely planted as an ornamental species in warm temperate regions throughout the world. In the USA it is commonly planted on sea fronts, and along avenues from Florida west to California. Many of the best specimens in Florida were blown over by Hurricane Andrew in 1992.

Right: The leaves are up to 5m (16ft) long evergreen fronds.

Identification: The Canary Island date palm has a long, straight, golden-brown fibrous stem with reptilian-like scales, formed by the shedding of previous fronds. It may be up to 1.5m (5ft) in diameter at the base, which tends to splay out just above ground level. The leaves are pectinate (comb-like) fronds, which gracefully arch skywards before drooping towards the tip. Golden-yellow flower spikes, up to 2m (6.5ft) long, are borne in the spring, followed in warm climates on female trees by bunches of purple-brown fruits.

Distribution: Canary Islands.
Height: 12m (40ft)
Shape: Broadly spreading
Evergreen
Pollinated: Insect
Leaf shape: Pectinate

California Washingtonia

Washingtonia filifera

The California washingtonia is native to Palm Springs and south to the Mexican border. It has, however, been planted as an ornamental species further north in California and, to a lesser degree, in Florida. A distinctive characteristic of this tree is the way it carries its old, dead, fan-shape leaves around the stem, below the live crown of evergreen leaves. The species is named, appropriately enough, in honour of the former president and has nothing to do with the state.

Identification: This attractive palm has a light brown, stout, columnar stem, sometimes broadening towards the base. The leaves are fan-shaped, and divided nearly to the middle into up to 70 slender, pointed lobes and carried on 1.5m (5ft) long, spine-edged stems. Panicles of yellow flowers up to 3m (10ft) long are borne in summer, persisting dead on the tree long into autumn. The fruit is an erect, short-stalked black berry with thin dry flesh.

Left: The fruit of California washingtonia is an ovoid brown-black berry.

Right: Attached to each fan-shape frond are thin straw-like threads.

Distribution: California.
Height: 23m (75ft)
Shape: Broadly columnar
Evergreen
Pollinated: Insect
Leaf shape: Flabellate (fan-shaped)

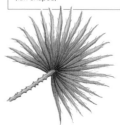

Cabbage Palmetto

Sabal palmetto

The cabbage palmetto grows naturally throughout peninsular Florida, the Florida Keys, coastal Georgia and South Carolina. Elsewhere in southern USA it has been widely planted in parks, gardens, and streets near the coast. It is also cultivated in Hawaii. The seeds of the cabbage palmetto are buoyant and salt resistant. Near coastal areas, water is an important means of seed dispersal. In some areas seeding is so successful that "pure forests" of the plant may cover 10ha (25 acres).

Identification: An erect, unbranched tree with a uniform stem diameter of 30–60cm (12–24in). The grey trunk is covered with interlacing leaf stubs, known as boots, which persist before breaking off to give the stem a smooth appearance. The leaves are fan-shaped, palmately divided and spineless, with a prominent arching midrib. Cream to yellowish-white flowers, borne in drooping clusters up to 2m (6ft) long, are produced between April and August.

Left: The leaves may be up to 3m (10ft) long.

Distribution: South-eastern USA.
Height: 25m (82ft)
Shape: Broadly columnar
Evergreen
Pollinated: Insect
Leaf shape: Flabellate (fan-shaped)

Right: The black, fleshy fruits contain a single seed.

OTHER SPECIES OF NOTE
Blue Hesper Palm *Brahea armata*
This beautiful tree has the bluest leaves of any palm. It is native to Baja California, Mexico, where it inhabits dry canyons. It reaches heights of 12m (40ft), but is slow-growing and takes a long time to reach this height. The flowers are creamy white and are borne in profusion in distinct, long, weeping inflorescences.

Jelly Palm *Butia capitata*
Also known as the pindo palm, this beautiful small palm is native to Brazil, but has been widely cultivated in southern coastal areas of the USA. It has grey-green to silver arching fronds, and fragrant yellow flowers, tinged with purple. These are followed by yellow fruits, which can be used to make jelly or wine.

Mexico Fan Palm *Washingtonia robusta*
The Mexican fan palm grows taller than its Californian cousin and has a thinner trunk. Although not native to the USA, it is widely cultivated as a single-trunked street palm in the south-west. It has dense grey-green fan-shaped foliage and leaf stalks that are tinted red.

Chilean Wine Palm *Jubaea chilensis*
Otherwise known as honey palm, or syrup palm, this spectacular tree, with its straight, symmetrical, elephant-grey trunk, has become a rarity in its native Chile largely because of over-felling for its sugary sap content, which is used to make wine. Chilean wine palms are widely planted as an ornamental species in warm coastal areas of the USA. Each grey-green pinnate leaf may be up to 4m (13ft) long.

Joshua Tree

Yucca brevifolia

The Joshua tree is one of the most characteristic trees of the Mohave Desert. It has a natural range from southern California, Mexico and western Arizona, eastward into southern Nevada and south-western Utah. It is named after Mormon Brigham Young, who led a group of Mormons to Utah. As they crossed the Salt Lake Desert, Young is said to have pointed at a yucca tree's outstretched arm-like branches and said, "There is Joshua welcoming us to the Promised Land."

Identification: The bark is soft and cork-like, rough and fissured, reddish-brown to grey with trunks up to 1.2m (4ft) in diameter, quite often single-stemmed but sometimes two- or three-stemmed. Erratic branching may begin as low as 1m (3ft) from the ground. The branches are erect, ascending or spreading and in maturity form a dense, compact, rounded top. The flower is contained within a big ovoid bud that unfolds to a stout 25cm- (10in-) long, greenish-white flower.

Distribution: South-west USA.
Height: 15m (49ft)
Shape: Broadly spreading
Evergreen
Pollinated: Insect
Leaf shape: Pectinate

Above: The leaves are short, sharply pointed and closely set spines.

Right: The flower has a scent of mushrooms.

TREES OF TROPICAL AMERICA

Tropical America roughly equates to an area from Southern California,
Florida and the Gulf of Mexico to the West Indies and Amazonian
jungles of Brazil and further south into Argentina. It is a vast region of
large, low-lying landmasses, wind-blown islands and arid mountain
ranges. The trees that inhabit these areas vary enormously. The majority
of the trees are evergreen, but if they are deciduous, it is often only
fleetingly, or to advertize glamorous flowers. Numerous tropical flowers
are large and intoxicatingly beautiful. Within the following pages you
will find exotic flowering trees such as the Jacaranda and the Yellow
Trumpet Flower tree and coastal trees such as the Red Mangrove and
White Buttonwood Tree. In addition to native tree species there are also
cultivated ornamental species included here that originate from other
parts of the world but which grow quite happily in tropical America.

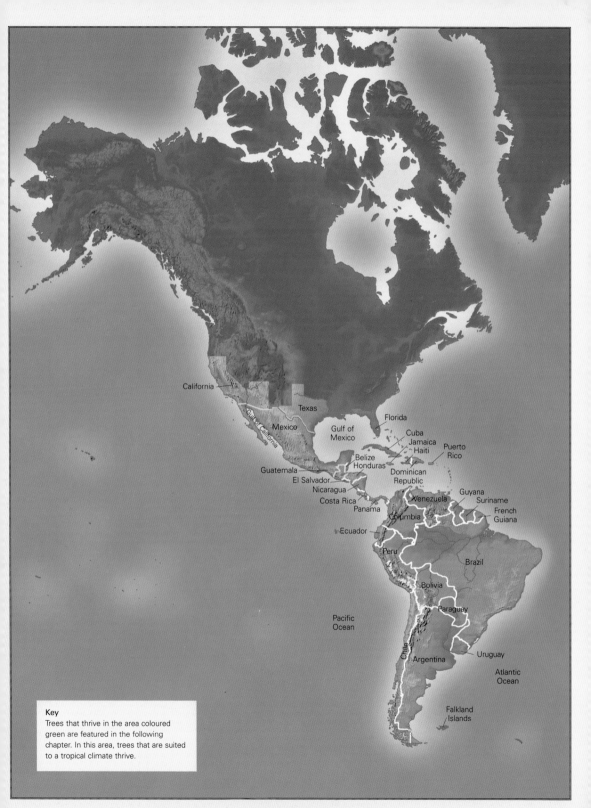

California

Texas

Mexico

Gulf of California

Florida

Gulf of
Mexico

Cuba
Jamaica
Haiti

Puerto
Rico

Belize
Honduras

Dominican
Republic

Guatemala

El Salvador

Nicaragua

Costa Rica

Panama

Venezuela

Guyana
Suriname
French
Guiana

Columbia

Ecuador

Peru

Brazil

Bolivia

Paraguay

Pacific
Ocean

Chile

Argentina

Uruguay

Atlantic
Ocean

Falkland
Islands

Key
Trees that thrive in the area coloured
green are featured in the following
chapter. In this area, trees that are suited
to a tropical climate thrive.

CONIFERS

*Conifers belong to a botanical grouping of plants known as gymnosperms, where the
naked seeds are held within a cone. The majority are evergreen trees with leaves
reduced to needles or scales. Many of them live to a great age. There are about
840 species of gymnosperms, in 86 genera.*

Caobilla

Podocarp, Wild pine *Podocarpus coriaceus*

This evergreen tree, belonging to the Taxaceae family, grows in mountain
forests on certain islands in the Caribbean, notably on Puerto Rico. In
Trinidad it is known as wild pine. The wood is soft and easily carved,
and has been used for making furniture, partly as a result of which
mature trees are now scarce. Mature specimens may reach 9m
(30ft) with a narrow or spreading crown.

Identification: An evergreen tree with scaly bark that peels off in strips. The
inner bark is pink, and the heartwood yellow or brown. The young twigs are
green when young, becoming brown with age, and bear alternate, almost
stalkless, leaves, which are yellow-green on the underside. The leaves
are crowded on the twigs and are long and narrow, with a leathery
surface. Male and female trees are separate. The male
cones are yellow-green, turning brown, occur singly at the
base of the leaves, and are unstalked. The naked seeds are
small and grey, becoming pointed and with a bright red
base as they ripen.

Left: Seeds develop
on a fleshy red or
purple base.

Distribution: Puerto Rico,
St Kitts, Montserrat,
Guadeloupe, Dominica,
Martinique, St Lucia, Trinidad
and Tobago.
Height: 9m (30ft)
Shape: Variable
Evergreen
Pollinated: Wind
Leaf shape: Linear, unstalked

*Left: The stalkless leaves are
alternately arranged on the twig.*

Mexican Swamp Cypress

Taxodium mucronatum

Distribution: Mexico and
Guatemala.
Height: 30m (100ft)
Shape: Tapering
Deciduous
Pollinated: Wind
Leaf shape: Linear

This species, closely related to the bald or swamp
cypress (*T. distichum*), is common in parts of Mexico
and also occurs in a few places in Guatemala. It
grows besides streams or in shallow water, at
altitudes of up to 1,400m (4,592ft). The wood is
light to dark brown or yellowish and polishes
well, but is weak and soft. Even so, it is used
in Mexico for construction as it is resistant to
decay and insect attack. It is a decorative tree,
particularly attractive at the turn of the year
when the leaves become yellow and red.

Identification: It is a large tree with a tall, straight trunk,
enlarged at the base, and covered with light brown or
brownish-red bark. The leaves, 5–10mm (¼–½in) long, are
arranged in two ranks on the branches, and are thin and
soft in texture. The male flowers appear in slender,
drooping panicles, and the female ones are
solitary, or in pairs, near the branch ends.

Far left: The cones are about 2.5cm (1in) in diameter.

Left: The flowers appear in panicles

Norfolk Island Pine
Araucaria heterophylla
From Norfolk Island but not a pine, this beautiful, fast-growing conifer reaches 60m (200ft) and grows successfully throughout the tropics. Hawain planta-tions provide timber for masts. It is a symmetrical, upright, formal-looking tree and is conical with a regular branching pattern. The soft, curved leaves are bright green and glossy. This tree will thrive in deep sand and is wind tolerant. As a result, it is often planted in coastal locations. It is tolerant of low light levels and is sold as a houseplant in temperate climates.

Mexican White Pine *Pinus ayacahuite*
A native of the moist mountain regions of Mexico, Guatemala, El Salvador and Honduras, this species can grow to a height of 45m (147ft) in the wild, but is usually shorter in cultivation. Its bark is greyish-white and smooth on young trees, later becoming light brown or copper, and broken up into rectangular plates. The leaves are in bundles of five, pale green to silvery, and the resinous cones are narrow and up to 45cm (18in) long. This is one of Central America's most attractive pines, with foliage that glistens in the sunlight.

Ocote Pine *Pinus oocarpa*
This pine grows wild in the mountains from Mexico south to Nicaragua. It is probably the most abundant pine in Guatemala, where it is an important source of timber. Its bark is thick, rough and grey, and deeply fissured into broad plates. It has a dense, rounded crown, particularly in older trees. The stiff needles are in bundles of three to five, are olive- or grass-green, and up to 30cm (12in) long. The cones are broadly ovoid and up to 10cm (4in) long. The wood is pale and yellowish, and is used for building work and also for furniture.

Smooth-barked Mexican Pine
Pinus pseudostrobus
A pine of moist forests, this species is widely distributed in mountain regions from Mexico to Nicaragua (the southern limit for mountain pines in Central America). It forms a medium to large tree with whorls of branches spreading horizontally, and has a dense, rounded crown. Its bark is smooth and grey, darkening to brownish-grey or blackish. Its leaves are in fives, light to dark green, flexible, drooping, and are up to 35cm (14in) long.

Caribbean Pine

Cuban pine *Pinus caribaea*

Also commonly called the Cuban pine, this conifer is grown commercially for its timber, which is resinous, and for the making of turpentine. The mature, open, broad crown is rounded and consists of heavy, spreading branches.

Identification: The bark varies from grey to brown and naturally sheers off in large, flat plates. The winter buds at the branch tips are cylindrical, producing the leaves, which have adapted into thin needles. Each leaf is 30cm (12in) long, deep green and glossy. Leaves occur in bundles of three to five. The male cones consist of many catkins bunched together, producing large amounts of pollen. The female cones may be oval or conical and are 10–13cm (4–5in) long by 5–6cm (2–2¼in) wide. They are covered in glossy, reddish-brown scales with a prickle at the end of each, and contain black, triangular seeds.

Distribution: Central America, south-east United States, Honduras and Cuba.
Height: 30m (100ft)
Shape: Domed
Evergreen
Pollinated: Wind
Leaf shape: Needle

Right: The foliage and cones easily identify this tropical pine.

Mexican Cypress

Cupressus lusitanica

This native of Mexico and Central America has been introduced to many other places such as Florida, Puerto Rico, and from Colombia to Chile. It is an attractive, aromatic tree useful as an ornamental and also in forestry, and has a dense, narrow crown with dark green foliage. It takes cutting and pruning well, and is therefore useful as a hedge tree. A number of varieties exist, with various shapes, including a long, narrow form and one with weeping or drooping branches.

Identification:
Naturally grown specimens have a tall, straight trunk with reddish-brown, somewhat scaly bark. The twigs are slender, and covered with tightly pressed, scale-like, pointed leaves. The male cones develop at the ends of short branches, and are greenish-yellow and cylindrical. The female cones are brown when fully ripe, and open to release the winged seeds.

Distribution: Mexico, Guatemala, El Salvador, Honduras.
Height: 13.5m (45ft)
Shape: Slender
Evergreen
Pollinated: Wind
Leaf shape: Scale-like

Above: Female cones have six to eight scales.

Below: The foliage is delicate, with closely pressed, scale-like leaves.

ANNONAS

Annona is a large genus of more than 100 species within the family Annonaceae. The species are all similar: they are tropical and subtropical trees, usually evergreen, with large, simple, oblong, smooth-margined and aromatic leaves. The fruit-scented flowers are fleshy, emerging directly from old wood. The fruit is made of many fused segments and is normally edible.

Custard Apple

Annona squamosa

The custard apple is grown for its delicious fruit, sometimes described as tasting like strawberries and cream. The fruit is eaten fresh or processed into confectionery and drinks. The tree has an open crown of zigzagging branches and needs high humidity, and is only seen in very humid tropical areas.

Distribution: North of South America and West Indies.
Height: 6m (20ft)
Shape: Spreading
Semi-deciduous
Pollinated: Beetle
Leaf shape: Lanceolate to oblong

Identification: The leaves, which are fragrant when crushed, vary in shape and may be 9–15cm (3½–6in) long. They are dull, pale green and smooth with minute dots on both surfaces, and may drop in dry spells. The pleasantly scented flowers occur all year round. They have three fleshy petals 5cm (2in) long, are greenish-yellow and found singly or in small clusters. The fruit occurs with the flowers. They are greenish-yellow but with a bluish-green surface bloom. Each fruit is 5–13cm (2–5in) long, round- or heart-shaped and made up of prominent lumps, which, when ripe, may be pulled apart. The white flesh has a smooth texture and is sweet.

Right: The fruit has custard-like flesh, and the leaves are scented.

Soursop

Annona muricata

The soursop is the easiest *Annona* to grow in the tropics and carries the largest fruit, weighing up to 1kg (2lb). The prolifically produced fruit appears throughout the year. It is not sour as the name suggests, but has unpleasant smelling skin and is often rather fibrous. It is rarely eaten fresh, but instead is processed into refreshing drinks and ices.

Identification: Sometimes seen as a multi-stemmed tree, the branches are sharply ascending and begin low on the trunk; young growth is covered in silky brown hairs. The leaves are 15cm (6in) long, slightly curved, variable in shape, bright, glossy dark green above and rusty below, with an unpleasant aroma if crushed. The rather peculiar flowers appear year round from the trunk and branches. They have three very thick, cardboard-like petals, are 5cm (2in) long, pale greenish-yellow and fragrant. The fruit is yellow when ripe, often oval, yet distorted in shape, being 30cm (12in) long and covered in short, fleshy spines. The skin of the fruit is thin. The flesh is firm, white, juicy, pleasantly fragrant and embedded with black seeds.

Distribution: West Indies and north of South America.
Height: 7m (23ft)
Shape: Columnar
Evergreen
Pollinated: Beetle
Leaf shape: Ovate, obovate, elliptic to lanceolate

Right: The simple, glossy soursop foliage smells unpleasant.

Left: The flowers of the soursop are stiff and the fruit prickly.

Cherimoya

Annona cherimola

Distribution: Peru and Ecuador.
Height: 8m (26ft)
Shape: Spreading
Briefly deciduous
Pollinated: Beetle
Leaf shape: Ovate, elliptic or lanceolate

Found in mountain valleys in its native Andes, the cherimoya is suited to cooler, drier conditions than many others in this genus. It forms an attractive, low-branched, spreading tree with nicely scented leaves. The cherimoya is grown in various parts of the world for its tasty, slightly acidic fruit.

Right: The fruit grows slowly, ripening in mid- to late spring.

Identification: The leaves, which drop briefly in the spring, are rather variable in shape. They are a dull, deep green with velvety undersides, 25cm (10in) long and strongly scented. The fragrant, hanging flowers are produced in the middle of summer. They consist of three thick, fleshy petals, are 2.5cm (1in) long and vary from greenish-yellow to reddish-brown on the outside, and pale yellow or off-white with a purple central blotch on the inside. The ripe fruit is yellow, 15 x 10cm (6 x 4in) and covered in large overlapping scales, each with a small black spot on it. The flesh is white and pulpy.

OTHER SPECIES OF NOTE

Ilama *Annona diversifolia*
This spreading tree from lowland areas of western Mexico and Central America reaches 7m (23ft) in height. It has tasty fruit, but may not produce it in great quantity. Although grown only on a local scale, many varieties are raised. Some have fruit with rich red flesh, with others it is white, pink or purple. The 2.5cm (1in) flowers are maroon with furry petals and are held on long stalks. The aromatic leaves are glossy green above, dull below and 15cm (6in) long. The fruit is variable in shape and texture, and may be light green, deep pink or even purple.

Pond Apple *Annona glabra*
Occurring in swampy and mangrove areas of southern Florida, northern South America, Peru and West Africa, the pond apple tree grows to 12m (40ft) tall. Its evergreen leaves are glossy above, paler and hairy below, and vary in shape and size. The large, thick flowers grow in pairs in summer. They are maroon inside and yellow with red spots on the outside. The round, ovoid or cone-shaped fruit is greenish-yellow, 7.5cm (3in) long and inedible.

Poshte *Annona scleroderma*
Reputed to be one of the tastiest of all annonas, the poshte is unfortunately rarely seen outside its native Mexico, Belize, Guatemala and Honduras. It is grown in Guatemala on a local scale, but being a 20m- (66ft-) tall evergreen tree, it is difficult to harvest and causes excessive shade over other crops. The leathery, lanceolate, shiny leaves are 25cm (10in) long and 7.5cm (3in) wide. The tough-skinned fruit may be green, green with brown spots or reddish. The flesh is smooth and either creamy or grey.

Bullock's Heart

Annona reticulata

The fruit takes time to develop, and is less pleasantly flavoured than other annonas. Nonetheless, the bullock's heart is grown locally for its fruit in the tropics. Depending on location, it may drop its leaves for part of the year or stay evergreen.

Identification: The 20cm (8in) long leaves are dark green, smooth, pointed, and dotted on the surface. If crushed they release an unpleasant odour. The fragrant flowers hang in clusters from the leaf axils on new wood. They are yellow or yellowish-green with a purplish blotch or tint inside, 2.5cm (1in) long and have narrow, fleshy petals. The fruit may be heart-shaped, oval or conical, weighing up to 1kg (2lb), but often less, and 7.5–16cm (3–6½in) across. It is greenish-yellow, becoming attractively reddish-brown or rosy on the side that is facing the sun. The surface is smooth and lined. The flesh of the fruit is creamy white and pulpy.

Distribution: West Indies and northern South America.
Height: 10m (33ft)
Shape: Spreading
Semi-evergreen
Pollinated: Beetle
Leaf shape: Oblong-lanceolate

Above: Bullock's heart's flowers appear near the growing tips.

Above: The fruit may contain hard or grainy sections within the flesh.

LAUREL FAMILY

The Lauraceae family is made up mostly of aromatic, evergreen, tropical and subtropical trees and shrubs. The leaves are often irregularly spaced and clustered at the branch tips. They are generally elliptical and glossy with smooth margins – typical rainforest leaves. The six-lobed flowers are small, greenish or yellow and appear singly along stalks in clusters. The fruit is a one-seeded berry or drupe.

Avocado Pear

Persea americana

Avocados naturally grow in wet lowlands, but have been planted extensively throughout the tropics. They are grown for their tasty and highly nutritious, savoury fruit, which is rich in minerals, oils and sugars. This fast-growing tree initially forms a round head but may become spreading in maturity. As the plants need to cross-pollinate to produce fruit, two or more are usually grown together.

Identification: The trunk is short with dark fissured bark. The leaves are leathery, elliptical, heavily veined, and up to 45cm (18in) long. They are dark green and glossy above, and coated with a bloom below. The green, branched racemes of fragrant flowers arise in the axils from autumn to spring. Each flower measures 1cm (½in). The fruit may weigh up to 1kg (2lb) but is usually smaller, measuring about 10–15cm (4–6in) long. It is pear-shaped and purple to greenish-brown with leathery skin.

Left: The fruit has a buttery texture and is often eaten with spices and sugar.

Distribution: Mexico and West Indies.
Height: 18m (60ft)
Shape: Domed
Evergreen
Pollinated: Insect
Leaf shape: Elliptic

Right: The leaves carry a pale bloom on their undersides.

Slugwood

Guajón, Aguacatillo, Laurier madame *Beilschmiedia pendula*

Distribution: Caribbean: Cuba, Jamaica, Dominican Republic, Puerto Rico, St Thomas, Lesser Antilles (St Kitts to St Vincent).
Height: 23m (75ft)
Shape: Variable
Evergreen
Pollinated: Insect
Leaf Shape: Broad, elliptic

This Caribbean tree is known by several different names, including guajón, aguacatillo and laurier madame. Slugwood is its usual name in Jamaica. The fruit consists of fleshy berries, ripening from green to black, and is rather olive-like, with a single large seed, borne from spring to autumn. It is not eaten by people, but is apparently consumed by pigs and other livestock in Cuba. This is a timber tree, used for carpentry, furniture, flooring and shipbuilding; the wood is quite hard, strong and heavy, and good for shaping, planing and sanding.

Identification: Medium-size evergreen tree with dark brown, smooth, slightly fissured bark. The broad leaves (green above, paler beneath) are mostly almost hairless, alternate and untoothed, with a short stalk. The foliage, bark and twigs have a spicy aroma. The flowers develop in clusters and are yellow-green when open, on slightly hairy branches. The fruit consist of fleshy, single-seeded green berries, which turn black when ripe, and resemble olives or small avocados.

Right: A twig, showing development from flower to young and mature fruit.

Sweetwood

Misanteco, Gulf licaria, Laurel blanco *Licaria triandra*

This a rare native tree in southern Florida, where it is called Gulf licaria. It is also found locally in Cuba, Jamaica, Haiti, the Dominican Republic, Puerto Rico and Martinique. Sweetwood is its name in Jamaica, while in Cuba it is known as laurel blanco. Like several members of the laurel family, its foliage, bark and twigs are spicy. In Puerto Rico it favours moist forests on limestone, in the north of the island.

Identification: This small, evergreen tree develops a broad, rounded crown, and has potential for planting as a shade tree. The bark is dark brown and scaly. Its strong timber is used for posts and general construction. It has slender twigs that are rather reddish when young, and these have fine hairs and raised lenticels. The alternate, stalked leaves have broad blades and are shiny dark green, mostly with a long, tapering point. The flowers are small and white, in branched clusters, and develop into green fruit, ripening to dark blue.

Distribution: Southern Florida, Greater Antilles, Martinique.
Height: 9m (30ft)
Shape: Rounded
Evergreen
Pollinated: Insect
Leaf shape: Broad, elliptic, pointed

Left: The white flowers develop in clusters.

Far left: Each fruit sits in a thick red cup, rather like an acorn.

OTHER SPECIES OF NOTE

Persea cultivars
Avocado cultivars are selected for many fruiting characteristics, including non-stringy flesh, small seeds, good storage (which is important) and firm attachment to the tree. The trees must produce steady yields, remain small, and have a spreading habit. Each cultivar has different characteristics. Fruit can vary from 5cm (2in) to 60cm (2ft) long, and the skin can be light green, dark green, brownish, purple or red. The flesh may be fibreless, thick and creamy, or watery, insipid and fibrous. The most popular are the Mexican and Guatemalan crosses: 'Fuerte' matures in winter and spring with smooth, green skin, but fruits in alternate years; 'Hass' has a purple to black warty skin, and is produced in spring and summer.

Laurel Espada *Ocotea floribunda*
This is a medium-size evergreen tree, growing to 18m (60ft), with smooth, light brown bark and long, spreading branches. Like many members of the family, its twigs, bark and leaves are, in fact, quite spicy. The greenish-white flowers are borne in branched clusters, and the fruit is small and black. Flowering is normally from October through to December, and the fruit appears from February through to July. It grows in forests from Cuba, Jamaica and Puerto Rico through the Lesser Antilles to Trinidad. In Jamaica it is known as black sweetwood. This genus contains about 350 species.

Jamaica Nectandra

Laurel avispillo, Sweetwood, Black torch

Nectandra coriacea

This small tree is often planted for shade in southern Florida and in Cuba, and its clusters of fragrant flowers scent the air and provide a source of food for insects, including bees. It is rather a small tree, with attractive, shiny, dark green, leathery leaves, and smooth grey bark. In the wild it grows in the moist limestone forests of Puerto Rico, and is also found from the Florida Keys and right through the West Indies from the Bahamas and Cuba to Tobago, as well as on the Yucatán Peninsula (Mexico), Guatemala and Honduras. In Jamaica it is called sweetwood, and black torch or sweet torchwood in the Bahamas.

Distribution: Mexico and West Indies.
Height: 8m (25ft)
Shape: Narrow
Evergreen
Pollinated: Insect
Leaf Shape: Elliptic

Identification: A small tree with a trunk about 30cm (1ft) in diameter. The twigs are slender, green and slightly hairy, and the alternate leaves are shiny, with obvious veins on both surfaces. The small, white flowers appear in clusters.

Right: The white panicles develop into dark blue or blackish fleshy fruits (above), each containing a red-brown seed.

BUCKWHEAT AND POKEWEED FAMILIES

The buckwheat family, Polygonaceae, contains mostly temperate plants from the Northern Hemisphere. Their small flowers are usually held in spikes and produce one-seeded fruit. The majority of plants in the pokeweed family, Phytolaccaceae, are tropical, from South America and Africa. Many have succulent leaves, some are spiny and many have poisonous sap.

Sea Grape

Coccoloba uvifera

Distribution: Coastal tropical America and West Indies.
Height: 9m (30ft)
Shape: Variable, domed
Evergreen
Pollinated: Insect
Leaf shape: Kidney (reniform)

The beautiful sea grape is completely salt tolerant and will grow right on the beach. It has been planted in coastal locations throughout the tropical and warmest temperate regions of its range. Tree shape and size vary immensely, and are dependent on climatic factors. The sea grape can be dense and domed, or multi-stemmed, sprawling and untidy. Whatever its shape, this tree's distinctive leaves make it easy to recognize.

Identification: The thick trunk has grey, fissured bark. The leaves are very tough, leathery and stiff. Olive-green and veined in red, pink or white, they are 20cm (8in) across. The leaves turn a rich orange or maroon before dropping. The scented, greenish-white flowers are produced year round, but are particularly abundant in the spring and summer. They are held in dense, erect clusters, 25cm (10in) long. The purple fruit occurs in long, hanging bunches like grapes – each fruit is 2cm (¾in) wide. The fruit has an acidic flavour and is used to make jellies.

Right: Male and female flowers are separate. Female flowers produce the grape-like bunches of edible fruit.

Bella Sombre

Phytolacca dioica

Bella sombre is Spanish for "beautiful shade", and this tree is often planted for shade in villages. The wonderfully sculptured, buttressed and spreading surface roots create natural seating up to 2m (6½ft) high, and spread across an area up to 18m (60ft) in diameter. The bella sombre tree is often multi-stemmed, and stores large amounts of water in its massive trunks. It is a fast-growing species native to grassy plains, and is fire and wind resistant. The tree is very highly revered in Argentina, and often lives to a very great age.

Distribution: South Brazil, Uruguay, Paraguay and north Argentina.
Height: 20m (66ft)
Shape: Domed
Semi-evergreen
Leaf shape: Elliptic

Identification: The bark of the sturdy trunks and surface roots is white. The soft, thick leaves are smooth and 10cm (4in) long with a prominent midrib that is red when the leaves are young. Before falling, the leaves turn yellow and then purple. The small, white flowers are held in pendulous clusters 10cm (4in) long. The fruit is a small berry, ripening through yellow and red to black. When ripe, it is fleshy with reddish-purple juice.

Right: Trees may drop their leaves in autumn or during cold or dry spells. Each tree is male or female, with only the female trees producing berries.

NETTLE AND CASUARINA FAMILIES

*The nettle family, Urticaceae, is mainly tropical and includes only a few trees, many of which
have stinging hairs. Their small flowers are usually green, and when the pollen is ripe, it is released
when the anthers suddenly uncoil. The casuarina family, Casuarinaceae, contains four genera,
and the best is featured below.*

Flameberry

Urera caracasana

This unusual tree is armed with
stinging hairs on its leaves;
presumably it evolved as an anti-
grazing device, and indeed it is
often known as "stinging nettle".
The dangerous hairs are mainly
on the undersides of the leaves,
on the midrib, and lie flat,
injecting their poison (formic
acid) only if brushed in one
direction. A small tree, it has
stout, rather fleshy twigs and large
leaves. Partly because of its
deterrent properties, it is sometimes
planted as a hedge, or living fence. In the
wild, it tends to grow scattered in the
understorey of mountain forests.

Identification: The large leaves
have long stalks and shallowly
toothed margins. There are also
stinging hairs on the stalks and
on the branches of the flower
clusters. The latter have a good
supply of very small, greenish
or pink flowers. The fruit is juicy
and orange-red.

*Right: The toothed leaves
are large and nettle-like.*

*Left: The fleshy
fruits grow
in clusters.*

Distribution: Broad range in
tropical America, in the
Caribbean islands,
and from Mexico to
Peru, Brazil, Paraguay
and Argentina.
Height: 9m (30ft)
Shape: Variable
Evergreen
Pollinated: Insect
Leaf shape:
Cordate

Australian Pine

Casuarina equisetifolia

This elegant, wispy tree looks like a pine, hence its common name.
However, it is not a true pine. Fast-growing, this species has the ability
to fix nitrogen into the soil by its roots, and is tolerant of wind and
some salinity. It is used for windbreaks, soil stabilization and dune
reclamation in coastal regions. It is also grown for its timber,
which is used for making boats, furniture and houses. This species
may live for several hundred years. Though not native in the
region, this species is established in Hawaii, Puerto Rico, the
Bahamas, Caribbean islands and coastal Florida.

Identification: The short trunk has thick, brown, peeling bark, while the
long, weeping branches are silvery grey. From the branches arise 10–20cm-
(4–8in-) long, extremely narrow, downy branchlets. These branchlets
resemble long pine needles and are coated in minuscule triangular leaves.
The flowers appear in May and June. Male flowers are red, tufted, catkin-
like and measure 4cm x 5mm (1½ x ¼in). Smaller female flowers are
greyish-brown and globular. The cone-like greenish-grey fruit takes five
months to develop.

*Right and far right: The tiny scale leaves
are adapted to coastal conditions.*

*Left: The compound, cone-like fruit is
highly misleading as an identifying
feature, as this tree is not a conifer.*

Distribution: Coastal
regions of north-east
Australia, South-east Asia
and Polynesia.
Height: 35m (115ft)
Shape: Columnar
Evergreen
Pollinated: Wind
Leaf shape: Reduced to
tiny scales

PAPAYA AND RELATIVES

The papaya family (Caricaceae), the Flacourtiaceae, the Moringaceae and the Elaeocarpaceae are all related within the subclass Dilleniidae. The Caricaceae has about 30 species, which have large fruits with a fleshy coat. The Flacourtiaceae has many tropical species, but the Moringaceae has only a single genus with a dozen species, while the Elaeocarpaceae has 540 species – mainly tropical trees and shrubs.

Wild-coffee

Guassatunga *Casearia sylvestris* (Flacourtiaceae)

This is a widespread tree typical of open sites such as roadsides, coastal forests and in the forest understorey. Although often only a small tree or large shrub, it does sometimes grow taller, up to 20m (65ft). The fragrant flowers are particularly attractive to honeybees.

Identification: The alternate leaves are long with wavy margins and are rather shallowly toothed. The clusters of tiny yellowish- or greenish-white flowers appear at the base of each leaf close to the point of insertion on the twig. From these the red fleshy seed capsules develop, each with usually three brown seeds. The bark is grey and smooth. The seeds are a source of oil, used for treating leprosy, while the leaves are used traditionally for fever and snakebite.

Above: The fruits are fleshy.

Right: The flower clusters grow from the base of the leaves.

Distribution: Cuba, Jamaica, through Antilles to Trinidad and Tobago, Mexico, Peru, Brazil, Argentina and Uruguay.
Height: 4.5m (15ft)
Shape: Spreading
Evergreen
Pollinated: Insect
Leaf shape: Lance-shaped to elliptic

Horseradish Tree

Drumstick tree *Moringa oleifera* (Moringaceae)

This ornamental tree is planted widely in tropical regions, often in gardens, or along roadsides or in hedgerows. It withstands pruning well, and grows back vigorously. It also produces large numbers of clustered, fragrant white flowers, and in Florida gardens, for example, flowers throughout the year. The thick roots, which have a taste not unlike horseradish, are used as a condiment in some places, and extracts of the bark and resin have medicinal properties. The large seeds from the bean-like pods yield oil used as a lubricant, and also in perfume. Honeybees find the flowers attractive.

Left: The young leaves and flowers are edible, and are sometimes cooked as a vegetable.

Right: The seed pod splits open when ripe.

Distribution: South-east Asia, East Indies, India, but now widespread in tropics.
Height: 9m (30ft)
Shape: Spreading
Deciduous
Pollinated: Insect
Leaf shape: Compound, pinnate

Identification: A small tree with rather fragile branches, feathery foliage and clusters of prominent white, perfumed flowers. The seeds develop in pods, up to 35cm (14in) long, which hang down from the twigs. These split to release several winged seeds.

Motillo

Sloanea berteriana (Elaeocarpaceae)

This is a large tree found in the wild in tropical mountain forests of certain Caribbean islands, where it is patchily dominant and may appear above the main forest canopy. The trunk grows straight and tall and develops obvious buttresses or flanges at the base – a common growth habit of rainforest trees, which gives support and stability in shallow, damp soils. The wood is very hard and finds a use as durable timber, although it is said to be attacked by termites.

Identification: The bark is smooth and dark grey with reddish warty lumps, and the alternate dark green leaves are large, elliptic and tapering. The flowers, which are pale yellow, are arranged in clusters (racemes). The fruit is a capsule that splits into four to release the seeds when ripe.

Distribution: Caribbean: Hispaniola, Puerto Rico, Lesser Antilles.
Height: 30m (100ft)
Shape: Straight
Evergreen
Pollinated: Insect
Leaf shape: Elliptic

Top left: Pale yellow motillo flowers appear in clusters.

Left: The large elliptic leaf tapers towards the tip

Papaya

Carica papaya

The popular papaya fruit is tasty, juicy and has a distinctive flavour. It is grown throughout the tropics, and the fruit is exported to temperate regions. It is very fast growing, easy to cultivate and crops heavily, even from a young age. This herbaceous "tree" has a single stem or may branch a little into a flat crown when older, and the leaves only ever remain on the growing tips. The stem always remains soft, becoming woody only at the base even when mature. The enzyme papain is contained within the leaves and fruit and is used for tenderizing meat.

Above: Deep indentations in the trunk remain where the leaf stems were once attached.

Distribution: South America.
Height: 6m (20ft)
Shape: Columnar or spreading
Evergreen
Pollinated: Insect
Leaf shape: Round (orbicular) but heavily lobed

Identification: The stem remains light with old leaf scars evident. Leaves are 60cm (24in) long, dark green and heavily incised into five to seven lobes, each further incised. Leaf stems are 60cm (24in) long. The fleshy flowers appear year round, borne on the stem, and are creamy or greenish-white, and 6cm (2in) across. Trees may be either sex or both. The fruit is orange-yellow when ripe, pear-shaped or round, smooth and up to 30cm (12in) long but usually 20cm (8in) long.

Left: Papaya leaves may help to aid digestion when taken medicinally.

Above: The papaya is a popular, yet short-lived, cropping tree.

Left: Papaya fruits are common in the tropics. They hang close to the stem among the leaf stems.

Elephant Apple

Dillenia indica (Dilleniaceae)

This spectacular tree is common in cultivation. It is grown for the combination of stunning, unusual foliage, beautiful, scented flowers and large, edible fruit. The fruit consists of heavily swollen overlapping sepals, rolled into a ball containing a sticky green mass of seeds. It is musk-scented, tasting like an unripe apple, and is used to make cooling drinks and jellies. The fruit are apparently popular with elephants! The tree has an open broad crown above a short, dark trunk, with leaves concentrated towards the branch tips.

Identification: The trunk has rich orange-brown bark and few branches. The leaves are heavily corrugated, up to 75cm (30in) long, toothed, leathery and smooth on the upper surface but rough below. The flowers appear in late spring and early summer, and are fragrant, 20cm (8in) across, creamy yellow to pure white with a mass of central golden stamens. The fruit reach 15cm (6in) across and are green.

Distribution: East India and South-east Asia. USA hardiness zone 9.
Height: 18m (60ft)
Shape: Domed
Semi-evergreen
Pollinated: Insect and beetle
Leaf shape: Elliptic-oblong

Left: The enormous solitary flowers face downwards; they are the largest of all Malaysian flowers and last only a day. The leaves are altogether rather unusual for a tropical tree.

Far left: The ripe fruit is huge and edible and hangs down from the tree. Unripe fruit is made into chutneys.

Left: The leaves are toothed and leathery.

Jamaica-cherry

Muntingia calabura (Tiliaceae)

Distribution: Cuba, Jamaica, Hispaniola, Trinidad and Tobago; also from southern Mexico to Venezuela, Peru, Bolivia and Brazil. Introduced to southern Florida and Hawaii.
Height: 7.5m (25ft)
Shape: Variable
Evergreen
Pollinated: Insect
Leaf shape: Lanceolate

A small, rapidly growing tree native through much of Central and South America, this species has a fibrous inner bark, the silky fibres of which have been used traditionally for making baskets and rope. It is also used as a shade tree and is commonly planted for this purpose. Its rapid growth and ability to spread have turned it into something of a weed in certain areas. It flowers and fruits throughout the year, and the flowers have been used medicinally, while the berries are edible and juicy, with a slightly sweet flavour.

Identification: This small evergreen tree has smooth brown bark with stringy, pale, inner bark, and grey twigs, which turn brown with age. The leaves are alternate and toothed, green and softly hairy. The flowers are quite large, with five rounded white petals. The fruit is a yellowish or reddish berry containing tiny brown seeds.

Below left: The cherry-like fruit is rounded.

Right: The flowers arise from the leaf bases.

Sandpaper Tree

Chaparro *Curatella americana* (Dilleniaceae)

This shrub or small tree is distributed throughout the subarid regions of Central America, Cuba and South America. It is known by a number of different names, including chaparro and lengua de vaca (meaning cow's tongue), a reference to the abrasive nature of the leaves, which contain a considerable amount of silica and are commonly used as a substitute for sandpaper to polish articles of wood and metal, and to clean kitchen utensils. In Brazil, a decoction of the leaves is used to treat wounds. The wood is hard and heavy, difficult to cut and plane, but very durable. It is used for a variety of purposes, including fuel, charcoal, fence posts, frames and even cabinet-making. In some regions the bark, which is rich in tannin, is used for curing skins.

Identification: The white or pinkish flowers, arranged in clusters, are unpleasantly scented. These are followed by hairy fruits containing black seeds that have been used for flavouring chocolate.

Distribution: Western Mexico to Panama, Cuba and tropical South America.
Height: 6m (20ft)
Shape: Spreading
Semi-evergreen
Pollinated: Insect
Leaf shape: Oval or elliptic

Left: The hairy fruit contains two seeds.

Left: The white flowers grow in clusters and have an unpleasant smell.

Florida Trema

Jamaican nettle-tree, guacimilla *Trema micrantha* (Ulmaceae)

A small, evergreen, fast-growing tree, with a spreading crown and drooping branches and leaves. It grows naturally in open forests and clearings, but has been widely naturalized and indeed become invasive in some areas. The timber is rather soft and light and is used mainly for posts, tea-chests and matches, and also as a fuel, and the pale brown bark yields a strong fibre. The tree has also been used to provide shade in coffee plantations.

Identification: The trunk, which grows to a diameter of 30cm (12in), is covered with light brown, smooth or slightly fissured bark. The open crown has horizontal or slightly drooping branches. The leaves are alternate, toothed and hairy, and the fresh foliage is poisonous to wild animals and livestock. The flowers, which are small and green, grow in clusters near the leaf bases and usually consist of both male and female flowers. The female flowers develop into tiny rounded, fleshy fruit, each with a single black seed. Seed dispersal is mainly via birds, which eat the fruits, then pass the seeds in their droppings. Flowering and fruiting occurs throughout the year.

Distribution: Central and southern Florida, Cuba and West Indies to Trinidad and Tobago, Mexico, Argentina and Brazil.
Height: 12m (40ft)
Shape: Spreading
Evergreen
Pollinated: Wind
Leaf shape: Lanceolate, long-pointed at apex

Left and right: The alternate leaves show distinct toothed margins, and the flowers develop in small clusters, arising from the leaf stalk bases.

ELM FAMILY

*The elm family (Ulmaceae) has about 175 species of trees and shrubs, mainly in the
Northern Hemisphere, from tropical to temperate regions. Their flowers are small and
wind pollinated, and many species are important as timber trees. The leaves are simple,
and often arranged spirally on the twigs.*

Mexican Elm

Ulmus mexicana

Elms are found wild only in the Northern Hemisphere,
and this species is native throughout Central America. It
is a large tree of wet forest regions, with a crown as
much as 20m (66ft) high and almost as broad. The
trunk, which can be over 1m (3ft) in diameter, is
covered with scaly, grey bark. The branches grow
upwards at an angle, and bear leaves in two rows
along the branchlets. The wood is heavy, hard and
strong, and varies from light to dark
brown. The bark is
astringent, and in some
areas is used as a
treatment for coughs.

Distribution: Mexico to
Panama.
Height: 40m (130ft)
Shape: Crown broadly
spreading
Deciduous
Pollinated: Wind
Leaf shape: Lanceolate or
narrowly ovate to
ovate-oblong

Identification: The leaves are small, only
4–13cm (1½–5in) long and 2–5cm (1–2in)
wide. The inflorescences emerge from buds
in the axils of fallen leaves, and are
composed of yellow flowers in whorls of
three or four. Each dry fruit has one seed.

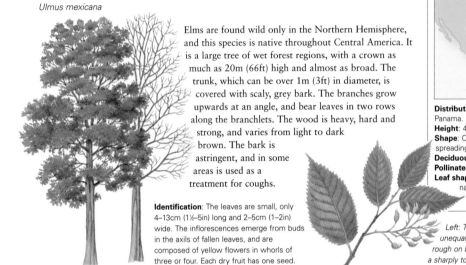

*Left: The leaves are very
unequal at the base, often
rough on both surfaces and with
a sharply toothed margin.*

Almez

Celtis trinervia

This small or medium-size deciduous tree is found in
some of the islands of the Caribbean and also in
southern Mexico and Guatemala. On Puerto Rico it
is rare, and grows mainly in thickets and forests
near the coast, especially in the south-west, in
moist limestone valleys, from sea level up to
about 90m (300ft). It flowers and fruits rather
irregularly throughout the year. The wood is very
hard and yellowish in colour.

Distribution: Greater
Antilles, Virgin Islands,
Mexico, Guatemala.
Height: 15m (50ft)
Shape: Variable
Deciduous
Pollinated: Insect
Leaf shape: Narrowly
ovate

Identification: The leaves are alternate in
two rows, and each leaf has three main
veins (hence the specific name), and toothed
margins towards the pointed tip. The flowers
are very small, yellow-green and clustered near
the leaf bases. The fruit is single, black and fleshy.
The light brown or grey, smooth bark has fine
fissures, and the twigs are slightly hairy when young.

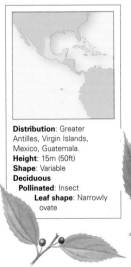

*Far left: The three main veins in the
leaves are characteristic.*

Left: This tree has long-stalked leaves.

HIBISCUS FAMILY

Most members of the Malvaceae family are herbaceous shrubs, many from temperate areas. The trees are fast growing and have soft wood. Mallow flowers have five petals, are usually asymmetrical and are often showy; many of the family are grown as garden ornamentals. The fruit is usually a capsule, more rarely a berry.

Sea Hibiscus

Seaside majoe *Hibiscus tiliaceus*

Distribution: Brazil, Peru, Mexico, Caribbean region, Florida. Throughout the tropics; probably native to the Old World.
Height: 6m (20ft)
Shape: Broad-crowned
Evergreen
Pollinated: Insect
Leaf Shape: Rounded, cordate

A beautiful small tree often found growing in coastal, swampy soils, it is also commonly grown as a garden ornamental. It often has a mangrove-like habit in saline swamps, rooting freely in the mud. The flowers are large and showy, yellow at first, turning orange and then reddish as they age. The tree grows vigorously and resprouts well after cutting, even from fence posts. It has a number of uses: the stringy bark for rope, matting and coarse cloth; various parts in medicine; and the flowers attract bees and are a source of honey.

Identification: The leaves, which are alternate, have long stalks, and prominent veins, and are a shiny yellow-green above, densely hairy beneath. The young twigs and the seed capsules are also hairy. The bark is grey and smooth, and fibrous internally.

Right: The five-petalled flowers produce pointed fruit capsules, which split to release dark brown or blackish seeds.

Portia Tree

Thespesia populnea

This tree is often confused with the mahoe, and there are numerous similarities between them. The portia tree is very salt tolerant, growing on seashores and in sandy places, and has a dense, spreading crown. The trunk, although sometimes contorted, has good, hard timber with chocolate-brown heartwood, which is used for furniture.

Identification: The trunk is short and dark, and the leaves dull, deep green with prominent lighter veining. Leathery and dotted with glands above, the leaves are 6–12cm (2½–4½in) long and have a nectar zone at the base. The solitary, yellow flowers are produced throughout the year. They are tightly trumpet-shaped with overlapping petals 5cm (2in) long. The fruit is a leathery, dark grey or brown, cup-shaped capsule, 2.5–5cm (1–2in) wide with woolly seeds.

Above: A portia can be mistaken for a mahoe but has rugged bark and yellow flower stigmas.

Distribution: Coastal throughout all tropics.
Height: 20m (66ft)
Shape: Rounded, spreading
Evergreen
Pollinated: Insect
Leaf shape: Cordate to ovate

Above and left: The flowers open in the evening attracting night-flying moths. From daybreak they fade to orange, pink or maroon to attract day-flying insects. They stay on the tree for a few days.

KAPOK FAMILY

The kapok family of tropical trees is especially well represented in South America, and includes some outstanding species. Many have thick or swollen trunks for water storage and spectacular flat-topped, spreading crowns. Their leaves are often lobed and clustered towards the tips of the thick branches. Bombacaceae flowers, with five petals and many stamens, are usually large and showy.

Pochote

Ceiba aesculifolia

This tree is closely related to kapok, and indeed it has been planted in some regions, such as in Guatemala, for its cotton-like fibres, which are used for similar purposes to those of kapok. It is also sometimes planted as an ornamental and to provide shade.

Identification: Pochotes are medium or large deciduous trees, with conical spines on the otherwise rather smooth trunk and twigs. The alternate leaves have five to eight toothed leaflets, and long, slender stalks. The leaflets are pale green beneath, and pointed towards both the tip and the base, and have short, hairy stalks. The flowers are large, with yellowish, hairy, spreading petals up to 15cm (6in) in length, and long, protruding stamens. The fruit consists of large oblong capsules.

Right: Inside the brown fruit, the seeds are protected by masses of brownish-white, cotton-like hairs.

Distribution: Southern Mexico, Guatemala, Honduras, El Salvador; introduced more widely.
Height: 50m (165ft)
Shape: Spreading
Deciduous
Pollinated: Bat
Leaf shape: Palmate

Left: The large bronze flowers open in late evening.

Kapok

Ceiba pentandra

This tree was sacred to the ancient Maya of Central America, and today is often seen in market places. It probably originated in South America but has become so widespread that it is difficult to be certain. The kapok has a distinctive outline: its huge, thick trunk is heavily buttressed and often covered with thick spines. The thick, heavy branches are held at right angles to the trunk, and the tree eventually becomes as wide as it is tall. Kapok fruit yields fine silky filaments, which are used to stuff pillows and life jackets.

Identification: The bark is grey. The leaves are 30cm (12in) wide and divided into between five and seven mid-green leaflets, each lanceolate and 15cm (6in) long. The fragrant flowers appear in spring, when the tree is leafless (if deciduous). The flowers are 15cm (6in) across, woolly and white, creamy pink or yellow. The fruit pod is 15cm (6in) long, narrowly elliptical, leathery and dark.

Distribution: Throughout the tropics (America, Africa and Asia).
Height: 60m (200ft)
Shape: Conical
Semi-evergreen
Pollinated: Bat
Leaf shape: Round (orbicular) and divided

Right: Mature trees yield up to 900 fruits. They are harvested and laid out in the sun until they open.

Water Chestnut

Pachira aquatica

The seeds of this tree are eaten raw or roasted. Although they are called water chestnuts, they are completely unrelated to the water chestnuts used in Chinese cooking. This species occurs on damp ground and along watercourses. It has a very dense canopy and a heavy, buttressed trunk.

Identification: The bark is grey. The leaves are divided into between five and nine leaflets. They are smooth, 10–30cm (4–12in) long and bright green with lighter midribs and veins. The flower buds are obvious, solitary, thick, brown, velvety spikes poking out from the leaf axils. The flowers have five narrow petals up to 35cm (14in) long, pale buff on the top and brown underneath. They encircle hundreds of 15–20cm- (6–8in-) long stamens, which may be red, purple, pink or white. The fruit pod is up to 38cm (15in) long and 13cm (5in) across, velvety, reddish-brown and contains the seeds in pulp.

Distribution: Tropical America and West Indies.
Height: 18m (60ft)
Shape: Spreading
Evergreen
Pollinated: Bat
Leaf shape: Round (orbicular) and divided

Left: The flowers are fragrant and showy but open at night, each lasting for only 24 hours.

OTHER SPECIES OF NOTE

Wild Chestnut *Pachira insignis*
The edible seeds in the pod of this tree are the "chestnut". This buttressed tree from the West Indies and Mexico grows to 18m (60ft). It has large leaves divided into five to seven egg-shaped to oblong, glossy leaflets. The spidery-looking flowers are fleeting. They have five fleshy, pale pink, crimson or brownish petals, which are long and narrow, and elegantly curl back in on themselves. Held within the petals are many pale, delicate stamens. The fruit pods are 20–25cm (8–10in) long. It is sometimes planted as an ornamental or shade tree, and is also a honey plant. The seeds, which are eaten raw or toasted, taste like the sweet chestnut.

White Floss Silk Tree *Chorisia insignis*
This fast-growing tree from Peru and northeastern Argentina has an open, sprawling crown and grows to 12m (40ft) tall. The smooth trunk has green to grey bark, with a few thick spines, and is swollen. It may measure up to 1.8m (6ft) in diameter. The deep green, deciduous leaves comprise five to seven broad overlapping leaflets, each 15cm (6in) long. In autumn the 15cm (6in) wide, trumpet-shaped flowers appear in clusters at the branch tips. The flowers have five waxy petals and are pale yellow when they open but change to orange or purple and then white. They may have brown markings but are highly variable. The old pale flowers hang on the tree after they have died. The woody fruit contains seeds in kapok floss.
The closely related floss silk tree, *C. speciosa*, is considered to be one of the most beautiful of flowering trees. Its pink flowers are large and showy and appear before the leaves.

Red Silk Cotton Tree

Bombax ceiba

Now found throughout the tropics, this tree is popular for its dramatic flowering display, and in India the thick flower petals are added to curries. The seed pod contains kapok but of an inferior quality to that of the real kapok tree. The tree is fast growing and has soft wood. The trunk is heavily buttressed and may have thick spines when young, as may the branches, which form in whorled tiers.

Identification: The bark is grey. The glossy leaves are divided into between three and ten leaflets, each 25cm (10in) long, dark green above and paler below. The flowers appear along the branches in late winter while the tree is briefly leafless. They are 28cm (11in) across and have five succulent, curved petals, which are bright shining scarlet, pale red or vermilion, and surround many bright red stamens. The fruit develops in late spring. It is a brown pod, 15cm (6in) long, and contains kapok.

Distribution: Tropical South America.
Height: 36m (120ft)
Shape: Spreading
Deciduous
Pollinated: Bird
Leaf shape: Round (orbicular) and divided

Above: As the flowers drop to the ground they form an ephemeral red carpet.

Above: The leaves are massive.

Balsa Wood

Ochroma lagopus

Distribution: Central and north South America.
Height: 21m (70ft)
Evergreen
Pollinated: Bat
Leaf shape: Cordate

Balsa is renowned for its incredibly light wood, which is used for floats, rafts, aircraft construction and insulation, among other things. Balsa wood is the lightest wood known, weighing just 9kg per cubic metre (7lb per cubic foot). The tree is incredibly fast growing and is common in its native haunts, colonizing secondary rainforest in dense patches.

Identification: The straight trunk has smooth, brown bark. The leaves are easily recognized, as they are immense – 60cm (24in) long with leaf stems equally long. Rough textured and weakly divided into angular lobes, the leaves occur in groups of five to seven. Each leaf is pale green with toothed margins, and downy below. The solitary flowers are funnel-shaped, pale brown or yellow. The semi-woody fruit is produced in spring, and is rather curious: brown, velvety and 18cm (7in) long, it is ridged longitudinally and stands erect on the branches. When the fruit splits open it reveals floss, making it look like a soft, brown brush.

Above: The fast-growing, short-lived balsa can prove a weed in some localities. In Spanish, the name translates as raft or dinghy.

Left: Each giant flower lasts only one night, and may produce up to 20ml (4 tsp) of nectar to attract bats during that time.

Left: The huge leaves are unusual within the forest canopy. The largest leaves are seen on young trees.

Garrocho

Swizzlestick tree *Quararibea turbinata*

The natural habitat of this small tree is a deep shady site in a moist forest, where it typically forms part of the understorey. It has a straight trunk with grey-brown bark, and branches arranged characteristically in distinct whorls of four or five. The inner bark is yellow. The leaves taper to a point, and produce a strong smell, especially when dry. Flowering is mainly from February to May. The wood makes sturdy sticks, and the rings of branches make very good coat hangers or hat-racks.

Identification: The leaf-bases have a pair of grey, scale-like stipules, which fall off as the leaves age, leaving behind distinct scars. The flowers grow close to the twigs, and each has five pale whitish petals. The fruit is round, fleshy and orange, supported at the base by the calyx, and each containing one or two large seeds.

Distribution: Mainly Caribbean – from Haiti and the Dominican Republic to Puerto Rico and Lesser Antilles; Surinam.
Height: 6m (20ft)
Shape: Rather straight, with whorled branches
Evergreen
Pollinated: Insect
Leaf shape: Short-stalked, elliptic

Right: Note the tapering leaf and the flowers inserted close to the twig.

Left: Swizzlesticks are traditionally made from the twigs and used for stirring drinks.

Floss Silk Tree

Chorisia speciosa

The floss silk tree is grown for its beautiful and delicate cup-shaped flowers, which are quite different from those of other members of this family. It is thought that no two floss silk trees have identical flowers. This species grows quickly and has soft wood. The trunk is swollen at the base and has thick thorns; the number and density of thorns varies between trees. The branches are angular and sprawling.

Identification: The bark is green when young and turns grey as the tree ages. The leaves are divided into between five and seven leaflets, each long and narrow with a toothed margin and a long leaf stalk. The flowers appear in the leaf axils through autumn and winter. They are 8cm (3in) across and may be red, pink, white or yellowish with gold or white throats, and purple or brown dots and striations. The large, capsular fruit is pear-shaped and contains cotton-like silky white kapok.

Distribution: Brazil.
Height: 15m (50ft)
Shape: Spreading
Deciduous
Leaf shape: Round (orbicular) and divided

Left: The trunk swells as it matures, and may lose its lower spines with age.

Right: The mid-green leaves drop in autumn and winter.

Above: Speciosa means "showy," describing the beautiful flowers.

Shaving Brush Tree

Pseudobombax ellipticum

This fast-growing tree is grown for its beautiful winter flowers, which open at night, and its colourful reddish-bronze young leaves, which contrast well with the pale green branches in spring. This species may have one or many short stout trunks.

Identification: The bark is pale grey with vertical green stripes. The leaves often droop when mature and are divided into five to seven leaflets. Each leaflet is dark green with a lighter midrib and veins, 15–30cm (6–12in) long, elliptic to egg-shaped with the stalk at the narrow end and fine hairs on both sides. The leaves drop in the winter, and flower buds that resemble large acorns develop through the winter; in spring they enlarge rapidly into brown velvety spikes 10cm (4in) long. The spikes open to reveal masses of thick 15–20cm (6–8in) long white or deep pink stamens. The fruit pods are woody, pear shaped to round containing kapok floss and seeds.

Distribution: Guatemala, southern Mexico and the West Indies.
Height: 9m (30ft)
Shape: Spreading
Deciduous
Pollinated: Bat
Leaf shape: Round (orbicular) and divided

Right: The flowers and foliage are often mistaken for those of the water chestnut tree.

COCOA FAMILY

The Sterculiaceae family is found mainly in the tropics and includes trees, shrubs, climbers and herbs, with about 1,500 species. The flowers have three to five sepals and may have either five or no petals. The fruit may be fleshy, leathery or woody, and the seed may or may not have an outer covering. This family includes some important crop and timber trees.

Cacao

Theobroma cacao

Cacao originated and was first harvested in Central America. Today it is also cultivated in the West Indies, tropical Africa, Java and Sri Lanka for its beans, which are the source of cocoa, the key ingredient in chocolate. Cocoa bean pods are harvested and opened to collect the beans, which are fermented for a few days and then dried in the sun to cure them. These cured beans are roasted, ground and heated to extract the cocoa butter and cocoa solids.

Distribution: Central America.
Height: 9m (30ft)
Shape: Domed
Evergreen
Pollinated: Insect
Leaf shape: Oblong-elliptic

Identification: The deep green, leathery leaves are smooth, often with dry, crispy edges or tips, and are 25cm (10in) long. Flowers emerge directly from the trunk and older branches all year round and are abundant in spring. Creamy yellowish or pinkish, they are 1cm (½in) wide and have five petals. The fruit is an ovoid, longitudinally ribbed pod 20cm (8in) long. It may be brown, maroon or orange.

Right: The fruit contains 50–100 beans. The 2cm- (¾in-) long beans are set in a slimy white pulp, which has a lemony flavour. The fresh beans may be deep royal purple inside.

Left: Pods vary in colour, size, shape and texture. They may have smooth or warty skin.

Right: Leaves are pale maroon and drooping when young; this is thought to deter pests.

West Indian Elm

Guazuma ulmifolia

A small to medium-size tree characteristic of stream banks and clearings. It grows rapidly in both dry and moist areas. The light pink-brown wood is used to make fence posts, furniture, boxes and barrels, tool handles and violins. The flowers attract honeybees.

Right: After the flowers have withered, hard, warty, rounded fruits develop.

Distribution: West Indies, Central and South America.
Height: 15m (50ft)
Shape: Rounded crown
Evergreen: Except in areas with a very dry season
Pollinated: Insect
Leaf shape: Ovate-lanceolate

Identification: The trunk, up to 60cm (2ft) in diameter, has grey or grey-brown bark. The branches are horizontal and end in long, slender twigs. The thin leaves are up to 13cm (5in) long, with long-pointed tips and finely toothed margins. At night, the leaves hang down vertically. The small, slightly scented flowers have yellow petals and are in clusters at the base of the leaves.

Panama Tree

Sterculia apetala

This species is the national tree of Panama, which is found in tropical and subtropical forests and alongside rivers, where it thrives. It is grown in gardens and as a street tree, and has become naturalized in the West Indies. The Panama tree is fast growing and has many uses in addition to its fine stature as an ornamental, shade-bearing tree. It is a useful species for reforestation and erosion control.

Distribution: Central America, northern South America and the West Indies.
Height: 40m (130ft)
Shape: Rounded
Deciduous
Pollinated: Insect
Leaf shape: Compound palmate

Identification: The trunk can be up to 2m (6ft) in diameter and has grey, smooth bark. The five-lobed leaves cluster towards the branch ends; the lobes are 15–50cm (6–20in) long. The flowers are 2.5–3.5cm (1–1½in) wide, in branched structures. The woody fruit is yellow to grey and 30cm (12in) long, and opens to reveal the 2.5 x 1cm (1 x ½in) black seeds.

Far left: The edible seeds are rich in starch and fats.

Cola Nut

Cola acuminata

"Cola" is a world-renowned drink, yet few people know that it is also a tree. The "nuts" (really seeds) of this tree are two per cent caffeine, and were originally used in the cola drink. The tree is cultivated in Sri Lanka, the West Indies, Malaysia and west Africa. In the tropics its seeds are chewed for medicinal purposes, for their stimulating effects and to enable people to undertake feats of endurance. They are no longer used in the drink to which they gave their name and are now little used in the West. The tree grows in humid lowlands.

Identification: The leaves are leathery, dark green and 10–15cm (4–6in) long. The flowers are found in clusters of 15 throughout the year, or, on some trees, only in winter. The flowers are 1cm (½in) across and have no petals. However, they do have five pale yellow sepals, each with central purple markings. The green, warty fruit is a 13–18cm- (5–7in-) long pod.

Distribution: Tropical west Africa. USA zones 11–12.
Height: 12m (40ft)
Shape: Spreading
Evergreen
Pollinated: Insect
Leaf shape: Oblong-ovate

Below: The ugly cola fruit contains the "cola nuts". White nuts are popular for chewing, and command the best price.

Right: The long-lived cola tree may yield fruit for 100 years.

ANNATTO FAMILY

*This small family consists of a handful of shrubs and small trees. Members of the Bixaceae have large
leaves that are often lobed. They have resin cells within them and small appendages (stipules) at the base
of the long delicate leaf stem. The flowers have four or five petals, many yellow stamens and are held in
branched clusters. The fruit is a many-seeded capsule, which splits into sections when ripe.*

Annatto

Bixa orellana

Tribal peoples use bright red dye from the annatto's greasy
seeds cosmetically, and plantations have been set up to
supply the export market to Europe and North America,
where the pigment is used for
lipstick and colouring foods,
such as cheese. This densely
crowned tree or shrub with
multiple branching has
pretty flowers, and is
popular in tropical
gardens, where it is grown
as an ornamental or
hedging plant.

Identification: The alternate,
glossy leaves are light green with
prominent veins, measure
20 x 15cm (8 x 6in) and have a
reddish tone when young. The
bark is light brown. The flowers
occur in clusters at the ends of
twigs or small branches. Each
flower is pink or white with purple
tones, 5cm (2in) across and has
masses of fluffy, central stamens.
The fruit is a flattened ovate
capsule, 5cm (2in) long. Coated in
dense, soft spines, it may be
white, red, pink or brown. The
seeds inside are deep red.

Distribution: Tropical
America and West Indies.
Height: 7m (23ft)
Shape: Domed
Evergreen
Pollinated: Insect
Leaf shape: Broadly ovate

*Left: Attractive,
dense foliage
makes Bixa ideal
for hedging in
tropical gardens.*

*Right: The lovely flowers appear
for most of the year. Although
they are short-lived, they appear
in continual succession, soon
followed by attractive seed pods.*

Buttercup Tree

Wild cotton tree *Cochlospermum vitifolium*

This fast-growing tree with soft, brittle branches is grown for its intense yellow flowers,
which are borne on bare branches. It is sometimes grown as a hedge, and there are varieties
with double flowers. The buttercup tree is also commonly called the wild cotton tree due to
the white floss that covers the seeds. This floss is used like kapok to stuff cushions and soft
toys. The buttercup tree has a rather open,
sparsely branched canopy. Some botanists
consider it to be the sole genus in its own
family, Cochlospermaceae.

Identification: The 30cm- (12in-)
wide, vine-like leaves are
deeply divided into
between five and seven
lobes, each toothed along
the edges. Held in erect,
branched clusters, the flowers
occur for three months in late
winter and spring while the
tree is leafless. The brown, elliptic fruits
are 7.5cm- (3in-) long capsules with a
velvety texture. Split into five sections,
they contain kidney-shaped, dark brown seeds
covered in floss.

Distribution: Tropical
America.
Height: 12m (40ft)
Shape: Spreading
Deciduous
Leaf shape: Round (orbicular)
and lobed

*Left: The flowers are 12cm (4½in)
across, golden-yellow, and have
masses of central stamens.*

CECROPIA FAMILY

These plants have prominent stilt roots and sheaths or caps protecting their growing tip. They often have palmate, lobed leaves and produce brown latex in the shoot tips. The cecropia family (Cecropiaceae) is very closely related to the fig family, Moraceae, and also to the nettle family, Urticaceae. This family contains 180 species of trees, shrubs and lianes, in six genera.

Guarumo

Cecropia insignis

This fast-growing, softwood species inhabits wet lowland rainforest, and is a pioneer species, colonizing open or recently disturbed places with plenty of light. The guarumo grows into a large, open-crowned tree with branches radiating in tiers. Its trunk and thick branches are hollow, providing a home for aggressive ants, which defend it from leaf-cutting ant species. The large, umbrella-like leaves of this species are very eye-catching.

Identification: The trunk is pale in colour and produces milky sap: the twigs are reddish-brown. Each of the dramatic leaves is round, up to 1m (3ft) across and heavily lobed, usually with seven separate lobes. Lobes are oblong to egg-shaped, with the narrow end nearest the leaf stalk. The tiny flowers are densely clustered on spikes: the male and female flower spikes are similar, 6–12cm (2½–4½in) long x 1cm (½in) wide, initially enveloped in a pink to brownish-red spathe (a modified leaf), pale green and generally erect. The tiny green fruit is a dry nut with one seed, held on a spike up to 21 x 1cm (8½ x ½in).

Above: The leaves are rough on the upper surface.

Distribution: Costa Rica.
Height: 25m (80ft)
Shape: Irregularly domed
Deciduous
Pollinated: Insect
Leaf shape: Orbicular, deeply lobed

Right: Each spike carries numerous tiny seeds, which are popular with birds.

OTHER SPECIES OF NOTE
Amazon Grape *Pourouma cecropiifolia*
This tree is grown for its huge leaves, and for the fruit that it produces prolifically over three months, from the age of three years. It has a light tan trunk, stilt roots and short, very wrinkly branches, often containing brown latex. It grows on damp ground, exploiting the light from gaps in the forest canopy. The beautiful circular leaves consist of 10–13 lobes. When young, they are burgundy and droop, but they flatten out as they mature. The yellowish-green fruit is ovoid, 2.5cm (1in) long and covered in dense, velvety hair. Each contains a large seed and sweet, juicy pulp with a gummy, sticky texture. The pulp is used to make sweet wine, jam and jellies.

Trumpet-tree

Guarumo *Cecropia peltata*

This medium to large tree has a spreading crown formed from upwardly curving branches. Usually evergreen, in areas with a pronounced dry season it is deciduous. The branches and twigs are often hollow and frequently inhabited by colonies of ants.

Identification: Notable for its large lobed leaves, up to 75cm (2½ft) in diameter. The bark is smooth and grey, and the young branches are green and hairy. Individual trees are either female or male (the tree is dioecious), and the clusters of tiny flowers and fruits develop at the leaf bases.

Distribution: Venezuela, Colombia, Guyana, Surinam, French Guiana, Mexico, Costa Rica, West Indies from Jamaica and Cuba to Trinidad and Tobago.
Height: 21m (70ft)
Shape: Spreading
Evergreen or dry-deciduous
Pollinated: Insect
Leaf shape: Large, peltate, lobed

Above left: The fruits are liked by bats, which are a major agent of seed dispersal.

MULBERRY FAMILY

The diverse family Moraceae includes mostly tropical trees, shrubs, herbs, climbers and stranglers. All members have milky sap and distinctive conical caps that cover the growing tips of twigs. The leaves are simple and often large. Flowers are of one sex, generally small and clustered in spikes, discs or hollow receptacles. The fruit is fleshy with a single, hard stone, and often many are grouped into one body.

Panama Rubber

Castilla elastica

A large tree with a trunk up to 1m (3ft) in diameter supported by buttresses, which form at the base of mature specimens. The bark is light brown with fine fissures, and when cut it oozes latex, which coagulates on exposure to the air. In the past it was an important source of rubber, both from wild trees and from plantations. Nowadays most rubber comes from the para rubber tree (*Hevea brasiliensis*), an unrelated species, although some latex is still collected from wild trees. The tree is fast growing and is occasionally planted beside roads for shade. The wood is fairly soft and not durable, but can be used for fuel.

Identification: The long, slightly drooping hairy twigs have hairy leaves in two rows. The leaves are up to 45cm (18in) long and 20cm (8in) wide, heart-shaped at the base and with a short, blunt point at the tip, and minute tufts of hairs along the edges. Male and female flowers are in separate clusters on the same tree, and are yellow-green. The clusters of female flowers develop into multiple fruits, which are disc-shaped and 5cm (2in) across.

Right: The ripe fruit is red and juicy, with a sour taste. Each contains one white oblong seed.

Distribution: Mexico to northern South America.
Height: 21m (70ft)
Shape: Crown spreading
Evergreen
Pollinated: Insect
Leaf shape: Oblong-obovate

Breadfruit

Artocarpus altilis

It was the lavish attention received by breadfruit saplings that caused the infamous mutiny on the *Bounty*. The trees now thrive in the West Indies and are grown throughout the humid tropics for their valuable and plentiful fruit. The fruit is rich in carbohydrate, and tastes and is cooked like potato. The cooked seed is also eaten and tastes like chestnut.

Left: Breadfruit leaves are huge and glossy green.

Identification: These fast-growing trees have smooth bark, ascending branches and a dense bushy crown. The leaves are very dramatic looking. They are 60–90cm (24–36in) long, ovate and deeply cut into six to nine lobes. Deep glossy green above, they have a rougher texture and are paler below. The minute green flowers are found on a round organ, which looks like a developing young fruit. The compound fruit is round or ovoid, 10–20cm (4–8in) long, weighs up to 4–5kg (10lb) and is green with a bumpy surface. Breadfruit does not usually have seeds – those that do produce seeded fruit are called breadnuts.

Distribution: Malaysia, Indonesia, Pacific Islands.
Height: 20m (66ft)
Shape: Columnar to domed
Evergreen
Pollinated: Wind and insect
Leaf shape: Ovate

Above: The compound fruit oozes white sticky latex when cut, but is a popular, tropical staple food.

Jackfruit

Artocarpus heterophyllus

Jackfruit trees are grown for their gigantic compound fruit, which measures up to 90cm (36in) long x 50cm (20in) across and weighs up to 18kg (40lb). The fruit varies enormously between trees. It is full of starches – 23 per cent of the sticky, pink to golden-yellow, waxy flesh is carbohydrate. Jackfruit flesh has a strong, unpleasant smell but a sweet taste. The seeds within the flesh are also eaten. These fast-growing trees are cultivated throughout the wet tropics.

Identification: The reddish-brown, straight trunk carries a dense crown. Juvenile leaves are often lobed, whereas mature leaves are oblong to egg shape with the leaf stalk at the narrow end, dark green, leathery, 10–20cm (4–8in) long and downy beneath. The flowers are minute, greenish and emerge directly from the trunk and older branches. The fruit contains numerous 3cm- (1¼in-) long seeds with a gelatinous covering.

Distribution: India to Malaysia.
Height: 20m (66ft)
Shape: Domed, columnar
Evergreen
Pollinated: Wind and insect
Leaf shape: Obovate

Left: The yellowish-green fruit has short fleshy spines, and hangs from the trunk.

Right: The leaves are arranged alternately.

OTHER SPECIES OF NOTE

False Breadnut *Pseudolmedia spuria*
This tree, which is something of a rarity on Puerto Rico, is also found in Cuba, Hispaniola and Jamaica, as well as in southern Mexico, Honduras and Guatemala. It has long, pointed, rather narrow leaves, and minute, stalkless flowers at the leaf bases. The tree grows to 15m (50ft), and has a rough, scaly bark, and milky latex. The edible fruit, which is red and rather cherry-like, is enclosed in a fleshy calyx, and contains a single seed. Indeed the tree is known as cherry in some regions, although it is related not to the true cherry, but to mulberry and figs.

Ramón *Trophis racemosa*
Although found in the Caribbean (Greater Antilles), Mexico, and Honduras to Venezuela, Colombia, Ecuador and Peru, this is rather a rare tree in cultivation. It has alternate, narrow, elliptic leaves, and like many other members of the family the sap is milky. It is a medium-size, evergreen tree growing to about 21m (70ft), with smooth, grey bark becoming scaly with age. The male flowers are catkin-like clusters, while the female flowers are in shorter clusters on separate trees. The tree flowers rather irregularly at any season, and produces small, edible fruit with rather little flesh.

Fustic

Mora *Chlorophora tinctoria*

This relative of the osage-orange of the southern United States is widespread in tropical America. It was once an important source of yellowish (khaki) dye, which was exported to Europe and other places. The tree is spreading and often spiny, and its timber is used for many things, including boats, sleepers, flooring, furniture and veneers. The bark is also used in tanning, and the resinous latex for waterproofing boats, and in medicine.

Distribution: Caribbean islands; Mexico to southern Brazil, Peru, Bolivia and Argentina.
Height: 15m (50ft)
Shape: Spreading
Deciduous
Pollinated: Insect
Leaf shape: Elliptic

Below: The leaves are pointed and alternately arranged on the twigs.

Identification: The bark is smooth, light grey or yellowish, with raised lenticels; the inner bark is orange with creamy latex. The yellow-green alternate leaves are arranged in double rows on the twigs, and are pointed and often slightly hairy, with toothed margins. The male and female flowers are on separate trees (the tree is dioecious). Male flower clusters droop from the leaf bases, while the female flowers are crowded into globular clusters. The latter develop into multiple fruits, which are juicy, sweet and edible.

FIGS

This large genus of plants, also in the mulberry family, has around 750 species growing predominantly in the tropics and subtropics. Figs are enormously varied, and range from small-leafed climbers to huge trees and epiphytes (plants that grow on others). The infamous "strangling" figs begin their lives as small epiphytes. Fig flowers are tiny and enclosed within a fleshy receptacle. This receptacle is the fig itself.

Shortleaf Fig

Ficus laevigata

Distribution: Southern Florida and West Indies.
Height: 18m (60ft)
Shape: Crown spreading
Evergreen
Pollinated: Insect
Leaf shape: Elliptic-oblong

A small to medium-size tree, which, like some other related species, probably starts as a young plant high in the fork of another tree where a bird has dropped a seed. The young tree puts out aerial roots, which grow to the ground, usually uniting to form a trunk. The tree then grows rapidly, often overwhelming the host plant. This species has smooth, whitish bark, which becomes slightly fissured with age. When cut, white latex oozes out. Although the wood is tough it is not durable, and is subject to attack by termites. Nevertheless it is suitable for boxes and crates, interior construction, light carpentry and even for making guitars. Since cuttings root readily, it is also excellent for making live fence posts.

Right: The long leaves are shiny.

Above: The small fig fruits are attractive to birds.

Identification: The green-grey twigs have alternate leaves, varying in shape and size. They can grow to 15cm (6in) long and 7.5cm (3in) broad, with a short point at the tip, and are rounded or slightly heart-shaped at the base. The upper side is slightly shiny with numerous tiny dots, raised on dry leaves. The multiple fruit is 1cm (½in) in diameter and tasteless.

Amate

Ficus obtusifolia

This fig species grows into a medium-size evergreen tree with a smooth trunk and light brown bark, and the familiar milky white latex. A typical habitat for the wild tree is coastal forest, from sea level to about 120m (400ft).

Identification: The alternate leaves are large, ovate or obovate, with the blades up to about 23cm (9in) long and 13cm (5in) wide, rounded or blunt at the apex. The fruits are like small figs, and usually develop in pairs near the leaf bases. This is the typical multiple fruit (syconium), which contains many tiny male and female flowers, with a small round opening at the tip.

Distribution: Virgin Islands (only on St Croix), Lesser Antilles; also mainland tropical America from central Mexico and Honduras to Colombia, Venezuela and northern Peru.
Height: 13.5m (45ft)
Shape: Variable
Evergreen
Pollinated: Insect
Leaf shape: Ovate, elliptic or obovate

Left: The small fig fruits grow close to the base of the rounded leaves.

Bo Tree

Ficus religiosa

It is said that the Buddha was sitting beneath a bo tree when he attained enlightenment. This type of fig is incredibly long lived, with specimens thought to be more than 2,000 years old. It is sacred to Buddhists and Hindus, and is regularly seen growing in the grounds of temples. A strangling climber, it may start its life on house roofs or gutters. Despite the problems this can cause, it is rarely removed because of its sacred status.

Identification: The great trunk has slight buttressing and dark brown bark. Most mature specimens have only a few aerial roots and some surface roots. The open crown, which is as wide as the tree is tall, consists of heart-shaped leaves with long, elegant tails. Each leaf is 20cm (8in) long x 15cm (6in) wide and blue-green with a pale midrib. The leaves have long stalks on which they move in the slightest breeze, and drop briefly in late winter. The tiny dark purple or brown figs grow in pairs in leaf axils along the branches.

Distribution: India, Burma, Thailand and Southeast Asia. Bo trees grow in tropical areas of the USA.
Height: 30m (100ft)
Shape: Spreading
Deciduous
Pollinated: Wasp
Leaf shape: Cordate

Right: The elegant, wispy-tailed leaves of the bo tree are used in arts and crafts in the West.

Indian Rubber Tree

Ficus elastica

A mature specimen is an impressive sight. Curtains of aerial roots form a veritable forest of high-buttressed trunks, while the surface roots swarm over the soil. The tree lives wild in tropical and subtropical forests, but is grown throughout Asia for shade and ornament. In temperate countries, this species is known as the rubber plant and is grown in pots indoors. The milky latex tapped from the trunk was the traditional rubber of commerce until *Hevea* rubber was discovered.

Identification: Each leaf measures more than 30cm (12in) long and 15cm (6in) wide and has a single, prominent midrib. Young leaves are tinged pink, and a long pink or red sheath protects the growing tip. The leaves form a dense crown at the end of clear branches. The oval, 2cm- (¾in-) long, greenish-yellow figs are crowded in pairs in the leaf axils towards the ends of twigs on trees over 20 years old. Figs are produced all year round.

Below: The spirally arranged foliage is simple, dark green, very smooth, thick and leathery.

Distribution: East Himalayas, northeast India, Burma, north Malay Peninsula, Java, Sumatra. Tropical areas of the USA.
Height: 60m (200ft)
Shape: Spreading
Evergreen
Pollinated: Wasp
Leaf shape: Oblong to elliptic, tip pointed

RUBBER FAMILY

A large family of more than 300 genera, the Euphorbiaceae includes herbs, climbers, shrubs and trees, many with white poisonous sap. The leaves are highly variable, and the small flowers are often without petals. The flowers are either male or female and occur on individual stalks in bunched clusters called cymes, or on branched structures known as panicles.

Rubber

Hevea brasiliensis

This erect, fast-growing tree is the source of natural rubber. When the tree reaches five or six years old it is "tapped" by cutting a long, slanting channel into the bark at about 1m (3ft) from the ground. A white, milky latex flows from the channel and is collected in cups. The latex is then strained, standardized to a set density and coagulated by the addition of acetic acid. The resultant white spongy material, rubber, may be processed in a number of ways and is smoked for preservation.

Identification: The bark is patchy, pale brown or grey and smooth. The spirally arranged leaves have long stalks and smooth, elliptic, dark green leaflets, each 20cm (8in) long. During a dry period, they turn orange and fall off, to be followed by the appearance of the flowers. Small, greenish-white and scented, they are held on panicles, which grow from the axils. The fruit is a smooth, greenish-brown, 3cm- (1¼in-) long, three-sectioned capsule.

Distribution: Amazonian (Brazil) and Orinoco (Venezuela) river basins.
Height: 40m (130ft)
Shape: Variable
Semi-evergreen
Pollinated: Insect
Leaf shape: Trifoliolate

Left: The trees are tapped with diagonal cuts in the bark.

Right: The three-sectioned fruit explodes when ripe.

Sandbox Tree

Hura crepitans

Distribution: West Indies, Mexico, Central America and northern South America.
Height: 60m (200ft)
Shape: Spreading rounded
Deciduous
Pollinated: Insect
Leaf shape: Cordate

Right: The flowers are small and dark red.

Far right: The fruit is pumpkin-like.

Every part of this tree is highly poisonous, and the sap may cause blindness if it contacts the eye. The fruit resembles a miniature brown pumpkin, and when ripe it bursts open explosively, discharging its seeds over quite some distance. In the past, these fruits were harvested then filled with sand and used as quill stands. Now they are occasionally filled with molten lead and sold as paperweights.

Identification: The straight trunk has buttresses and carries a dense crown of brittle branches covered in thick, dangerous spines. Held on long leaf stems, the thick, glossy leaves are dark green, up to 30cm (12in) long, with light veining on the upper surface. The female flowers are carried on a thick, pendulous spike 15cm- (6in-) long, and the male ones on a structure resembling an ear of corn. The 7.5cm- (3in-) wide fruit has a grooved surface and is made up of 15–20 sections, each containing a flat, pale brown seed.

Candleberry Tree

Aleurites moluccana

This fast-growing native of hillside forests has been cultivated for hundreds of years, and is now naturalized throughout the tropics. Annually each tree produces up to 46kg (100lb) of poisonous nuts, which are 50 per cent oil and burnt for light, hence the tree's common name. The nutshells are used as beads and yield a dye, while the timber is a popular choice for canoe- and house-building.

Identification: The thick, straight trunk has relatively smooth grey bark. Leaves are clustered toward the branch tips, have oil glands and are slightly scented if crushed. Each leaf is 10–20cm (4–8in) long, divided into three or five lobes and has pale rusty down on the underside. Young leaves and shoots are coated in fine, white down. Tiny, white, bell-shaped flowers are produced throughout the year in long, terminal panicles. The rough-skinned, hard, pale green fruit is a 5cm- (2in-) wide ball.

Distribution: Moluccas and South Pacific Islands. Tropical USA.
Height: 18m (60ft)
Shape: Domed
Evergreen
Pollinated: Insect
Leaf shape: Broadly ovate

Left: The fruit contains one seed and is poisonous when raw, but can be eaten cooked.

Left and right: The juvenile and mature leaves differ in shape.

OTHER SPECIES OF NOTE

Coral Plant *Jatropha multifida*
This little tree from South America reaches 6m (20ft) tall, and has amazing leaves and colourful flowers. The leaves are round and up to 30cm (12in) across, but heavily divided into up to 12 leaflets, each of which has many incisions towards its tip. The leaves and seeds are poisonous but used locally for medicine. The small, red flowers appear throughout the year in flat-topped clusters above the tree. Each cluster stands on a long, upright stem.

Manchineel, Poison-guava
Hippomane mancinella
This tree is deadly poisonous, and all the more dangerous because it bears attractive, apple-like juicy fruit which is sweet-scented and palatable. Eating it causes nausea, diarrhoea, muscular weakness, and sometimes death. The plant is also poisonous to livestock. Nevertheless, it is an attractive evergreen tree, to 12m (40ft), with a spreading crown. It is widely distributed on tropical shores, the fruit drifting in ocean currents, and this partly explains why it was notorious for poisoning marooned sailors. The milky sap is irritating to the skin and dangerous if it contacts the eyes, causing blistering and blindness. Legends abound: sleeping beneath it was reputed to be dangerous. Some indigenous people tipped poison arrows with its sap. It may be found in southern Florida, from the Bahamas to Trinidad and Tobago, and also on Pacific and Atlantic coasts of Mexico, Venezuela, Colombia, and Ecuador, as well as the Galapagos Islands.

Peregrina

Jatropha integerrima

This tree is grown for its continuous display of vibrant, intense cerise or scarlet flowers. In the wild it often grows as a multi-stemmed tree, and it may be pruned or trained in gardens to retain its young, shrub-like habit or force it to grow as a single-stemmed specimen. In temperate countries it is sold as a houseplant.

Identification: The bark is dark brown and fissured. The glossy leaves alternate on each side of the stem, are deep green with paler veining and have a pair of glands near the base. They are 4–15cm (1½–6in) long, vary from elliptic to egg-shaped, have smooth margins and may be partially and irregularly lobed with a long, slender point. The flowers are in long cymes protruding from the axils or the ends of branches. Each is either male or female, 2.5–5cm (1–2in) wide and has five petals; the male flowers have yellow anthers. The fruit is nearly round in shape, 1–1.5cm (½–⅔in) wide and split into three sections when ripe.

Right: The flower cymes bear many more male than female flowers.

Distribution: Cuba, West Indies and Peru.
Height: 6m (20ft)
Shape: Columnar
Evergreen
Pollinated: Insect
Leaf shape: Irregular

BRAZIL NUT FAMILY

Lecythidaceae includes shrubs and trees – many of the latter being large, rainforest, emergent species. The plants have a characteristic odour, tough fibres in their stems and leaves with toothed margins. The family is closely related to the myrtle family, and this is reflected in the flowers, which have numerous stamens, and are often large and showy. The fruits are large berries or capsules, and the seed is nut-like.

Cannonball Tree

Couroupita guianensis

A mature cannonball tree with fruit and flowers is an impressive sight. The large, waxy flowers hang the full length of the trunk and are interspersed with tough, sinuous cords holding large, cannonball-like, reddish-brown fruit.

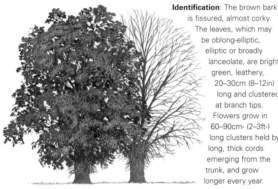

Identification: The brown bark is fissured, almost corky. The leaves, which may be oblong-elliptic, elliptic or broadly lanceolate, are bright green, leathery, 20–30cm (8–12in) long and clustered at branch tips. Flowers grow in 60–90cm- (2–3ft-) long clusters held by long, thick cords emerging from the trunk, and grow longer every year.

Distribution: Northern South America including the Amazon basin.
Height: 30m (100ft)
Shape: Columnar
Deciduous
Pollinated: Bat
Leaf shape: Variable

Above and right: The spherical fruit is 25cm (10in) wide. When ripe, it falls to the ground, exploding and releasing its foul-smelling red pulp.

Right: Flowers are 7.5–12cm (3–4½ in) wide, and strangely scented.

Brazil Nut Tree

Bertholletia excelsa

This emergent rainforest tree has a small crown topping a trunk that is clear of branches for much of its height. The fruit holds 10–15 Brazil nuts, and is a favourite food of cat-size rodents called "agoutis". Agoutis, which live on the ground, open the fallen fruit to feed on the nuts. Like squirrels, they have the habit of burying some for later; a few are never dug up again, and they take root and grow. These trees do not fare well in plantations, and nuts are still collected from the wild.

Below: The hard fruit takes about 15 months to develop. A large tree may yield 300 fruits in one season.

Distribution: Amazon basin.
Height: 30m (100ft)
Shape: Oval
Evergreen
Pollinated: Bee
Leaf shape: Oblong

Identification: The alternate leaves are dark green, leathery and large. Before dropping, they turn brownish-red. The flowers appear on thick branches above the foliage in long, branched clusters. Each individual flower is yellow and 2.5cm (1in) wide. The fruit is attached to a long woody stem. It is round, brown, hard and 10cm (4in) across. The fruit contains the hard-shelled, angular seed that is the edible Brazil nut.

Far left: Brazil nut trees require cross-pollination (with another tree) to produce fruit.

Left and right: The leaves have wavy edges.

Barringtonia

Barringtonia asiatica

This handsome tree is native to tropical Asia, but is planted as an ornamental and shade tree in the New World. It is quite often seen in parks and botanical gardens. In its native habitat it forms stands close to the shore, and its cork fruit can float and spread via the sea, like the coconut. The large, fragrant flowers open in the evening and are mainly pollinated by bats. In its native region, the trunks are used to make canoes, the buoyant fruits are fashioned into fishing floats, while the bark, fruit and seed are used as fish poison and traditional medicine.

Distribution: Native to south Pacific region, but planted in southern Florida, Hawaii, Puerto Rico, Jamaica, Dominica and Trinidad.
Height: 9m (30ft)
Shape: Spreading
Evergreen
Pollinated: Bat
Leaf shape: Large, obovate

Identification: The large leaves are shiny and dark green, and tend to be crowded towards the ends of the branches. The flowers are very large with whitish petals about 7.5cm (3in) long. The hard, heavy fruit has a thick, corky, fibre-rich husk. Inside is the large rounded fruit, about 5cm (2in) in diameter.

Far left: The flower has protruding stamens.

Left: The husk germinates within the fruit.

OTHER SPECIES OF NOTE

Stinkwood *Gustavia augusta*
This evergreen timber tree or shrub from Guyana and the Amazon grows up to 22m (73ft). The leaves vary from egg- to teardrop-shaped, with the stalk at the narrow end. They grow in tufts from the branch tips. They measure 48cm (19in) long x 13cm (5in) wide, and are pink when young. The scented flowers have six to nine white petals tinted pink below, and appear in clusters, each up to 20cm (8in) across. The fruit is spherical and 7.5cm (3in) in diameter.

Paradise Nut *Lecythis zabucajo*
This tree is closely related to the Brazil nut, but is much less well known outside its native range. The nut has a delicate flavour and is said to be superior to Brazil nuts. However, they are more difficult to collect than Brazil nuts as the seed drops from the shells, and they are therefore more expensive. Once the nuts have fallen, they must be gathered quickly before they rot. Often, the nuts are extracted from the fruit while still on the tree, by birds or monkeys. The tree provides good timber and has become quite rare.

Cream nut

Lecythis pisonis

This tree is grown ornamentally for the stunning effect created when the purple flowers and new young pink leaves unfurl, turning the entire crown pink and mauve. It is also highly regarded for its tasty nuts, which can be hard to find because monkeys and other animals are fond of eating them too.

Identification: The trunk carries ascending branches and a dense crown. It has grey bark with deep vertical fissures. The smooth, leathery leaves have specks on them, and have toothed margins and a prominent midrib. The flowers form in clusters at the ends of the twigs and branches. The hard fruit is cinnamon coloured, 20cm (8in) long, and contains the delicious, red to brown, elliptical seeds, each of which is 5cm (2in) long.

Distribution: Eastern tropical America.
Height: 30m (100ft)
Shape: Domed
Deciduous
Pollinated: Insect
Leaf shape: Oblong-elliptic

Right: The rough-skinned fruit has a closely fitting lid and contains delicious seeds.

Below: The large, purple to white flower has a dense central disc of stamens surrounded by six petals.

CHICLE TREE FAMILY

These tropical and subtropical trees and shrubs of the Sapotaceae family are an ecologically important part of the South American rainforest. They all have milky sap and leaves with smooth margins. The small flowers are whitish, greenish or tan and have four to eight petals fused into a tube at the base. The often edible fruit is fleshy, and the seeds are big, shiny and dark brown with a lighter coloured scar.

Chicle Tree

Manilkara zapota

The sweet fruit of this tree is very popular in tropical America, where it is eaten raw and made into syrups and preserves. The trunk produces a gum, which may be tapped every two or three years. Called "chicle", this was the original base for chewing gum, but it is now rarely used. Chicle trees are grown in plantations in tropical America and the Far East. The thick branches, closely set in tiers, have incredibly dense foliage.

Distribution: Mexico, Belize, Guatemala, northern Colombia.
Height: 35m (115ft)
Shape: Domed
Evergreen
Pollinated: Insect
Leaf shape: Elliptic

Identification: The bark is grey to brown and made up of small, interlocking plates. The 13–15cm- (5–6in-) long, leathery leaves are glossy dark green with a prominent midrib and are clustered towards the branch tip. The flowers are small, greenish- or creamy white, tubular and found in the leaf axils, while the 8cm- (3in-) wide fruit is spherical to egg-shaped and has rough, matt brown skin. The flesh varies in colour from cream to yellowish- or even reddish-brown.

Left: The leaves are glossy and attractive.

Right: The fruit is produced all year and has a grainy, pear-like texture.

Sapote

Mamey *Pouteria sapota*

This medium-size or large tree is one of the best known native fruit trees in the region, and it is sometimes cultivated. It bears large, edible fruit, which is brown and egg-shape, about 15cm (6in) long, and with a sweet, pinkish flesh and milky sap. These are either eaten raw, or made into various preserves and jellies, or used to flavour ice cream. The seed is also ground as a flavouring, though some reports claim it is poisonous. The seeds yield oil, which the Aztecs used to apply to their hair. The flowers are attractive to honeybees. The wood is moderately hard and strong, and is sometimes used in carpentry.

Identification: The bark is red-brown and rather shaggy, and the stout twigs have rust-red hairs towards their tips. The leathery leaves are alternate but clustered towards the ends of the twigs, and their blades are up to 36cm (14in) long, tapering towards the base. The flowers grow close to the twigs and have pale yellow corollas.

Below: The fan-like clusters of leaves are at the end of a twig.

Distribution: Southern Mexico, Central America to Nicaragua. Planted from southern Florida and Bermuda, throughout the West Indies.
Height: 18m (60ft), occasionally 30m (100ft)
Shape: Rounded crown
Evergreen or deciduous
Pollinated: Insect
Leaf shape: Lanceolate

Right: The egg-shape fruit is large and edible.

Star Apple

Chrysophyllum cainito

This slow-growing tree occurs in wet lowlands and foothills. The fruit, which is found only on mature trees, is eaten when soft to the touch and has a cool, refreshing, sweet flavour. The name "star" refers to the shape of the fruit – in cross-section the seed chambers radiate from the centre like a star. The tree has a short trunk and may be as broad as it is tall. Its thick, pendant branches have weeping tips and carry a dense mass of foliage.

Left: The delicious fruit has white or purple flesh and dark brown to black seeds.

Identification: The bark is grey-brown and becomes deeply fissured as the tree ages. The 10–15cm- (4–6in-) long leaves are deep shiny green above and lustrous with copper-coloured velvet below. The young branches also have a copper-coloured down. Small, white, purplish or yellow flowers appear in summer and are barely visible, due to the thick foliage. The smooth-skinned, round fruit ripens in spring and is up to 10cm (4in) across. The fruit ripens to either a dark purplish-red or to white, depending on the variety.

Right: The fruit's skin must not be eaten, because it contains bitter latex.

Distribution: Central America and West Indies.
Height: 30m (100ft)
Shape: Domed to columnar
Evergreen
Pollinated: Insect
Leaf shape: Oblong-elliptic

OTHER SPECIES OF NOTE

Balata *Manilkara bidentata*
This evergreen tree from the West Indies, Panama and South America produces gum balata, a latex similar to, and sometimes used as a substitute for, gutta percha. It also has hard, dense, durable wood. It has a short trunk and a massive oblong crown, and may reach 30m (100ft) tall. The narrowly oblong leaves are 25cm (10in) long, leathery, shiny and deep green above and greyish and velvety below. They have prominent yellow midribs. The small flowers are white and form in clusters in the leaf axils. The yellow spherical fruit is 2cm (¾in) across.

False Mastic *Sideroxylon foetidissimum*
This evergreen tree is native in Florida, throughout the West Indies, and is also found in south-east Mexico and Honduras. It grows to 15m (49ft) high, although 24m (78ft) has been recorded. It has a straight trunk, up to 30cm (12in) in diameter, and a dense, irregular crown. On young trees the bark is smooth, with only small fissures and horizontal cracks, but on older, larger trees it becomes deeply furrowed, splitting into plates. The alternate leaves are elliptic-oblong, slightly shiny, and yellowish-green. The numerous flowers are yellow, about 1cm (½in) across, usually in small clusters along the stems, and have a curiously pungent, cheesy smell. The fruits are yellowish, 2cm (¾in) long, and contain one large brown seed. The wood is hard, heavy and strong, excellent for making boats, planks, furniture and fences. The tree is suitable as an ornamental because of its abundant flowers, and it is also said to be a useful honey plant.

Damson Plum

Satin Leaf *Chrysophyllum oliviforme*

This slow-growing, long-lived tree has particularly attractive foliage. The leaves have shimmering velvety red or copper undersides, leading to its other name, "satin leaf". It is grown in towns to form an avenue or as a shade tree, and has edible fruit, which varies in flavour from plain and insipid to quite tasty.

Identification: The trunk is reddish-brown, scaly, sometimes thorny and carries weeping branches. The glossy, 10–20cm- (4–8in-) long leaves are dark green above and a rich tone below, while the 5mm- (¼in-) long, five-petaled flowers are white, cream, grey or greyish-green. The latter appear in clusters in the leaf axils throughout the year, and are particularly abundant in late summer and early autumn. Like the flowers, the fleshy fruit is well hidden among the leaves. When ripe, the fruit is dark purple, shiny, up to 4cm (1½in) in length and contains one seed.

Above: Although naturalized in Hawaii, the damson plum has become endangered in its native Florida.

Left: The name Chrysophyllum, meaning "gold leaf," alludes to the coppery underside of the leaf.

Distribution: West Indies and southernmost Florida.
Height: 12m (40ft)
Shape: Oval
Evergreen
Pollinated: Insect
Leaf shape: Ovate-oblong

CLUSIA FAMILY

The trees in the Guttiferae family have oil glands and ducts on their leaves, which give a clear spot effect. Many also yield resins. Most are tropical trees or shrubs, and some are semi-epiphytic, using other plants to support them. They often produce latex, which may be white, yellow or even orange, and many have stilt roots. This family includes several useful timber trees, and some species grown for their fruit.

Autograph Tree

Clusia rosea

This tree earns its name from its leaves, which are so thick that one can carve words into them – historically, they have even been used as playing cards. The tree may start life on rocks or as an epiphyte, becoming a strangler with aerial roots forming many trunks. It grows quickly into a sprawling, irregular tree with horizontal branches and a dense crown. Being adapted to salt spray, high winds and sandy, saline soil, and with surface wandering roots, it occurs naturally and is planted in coastal locations.

Identification: The tree has yellow sap and thick, bright green leaves 7.5–20cm (3–8in) long. The lightly scented flowers have thick, waxy petals. They appear intermittently throughout the year, but are particularly abundant in late summer. Solitary and white, ageing to pink, they have many bright yellow stamens and are 5–9cm (2–3½in) across. The fruit is round, pale green, 5–9cm (2–3½in) across, and bursts open to reveal red seeds embedded in black, poisonous resin.

Distribution: Caribbean, Florida Keys, and south-east Mexico.
Height: 15m (50ft)
Shape: Spreading
Evergreen
Pollinated: Insect
Leaf shape: Obovate

Left: The lovely scented flowers are short-lived, becoming brown after only a few days.

Right: The thick, tough, waxy leaves are designed to withstand harsh coastal conditions.

Cupeillo

Clusia krugiana

Distribution: Puerto Rico and Dominican Republic.
Height: 12m (40ft)
Shape: Crown spreading
Evergreen
Pollinated: Insect
Leaf shape: Obovate

This small or medium-size tree has a trunk up to 30cm (12in) in diameter bearing a crown of thick branches, sometimes supported by a few prop roots. If its smooth, grey bark is damaged, the yellow or orange latex seeps out, coagulating on exposure to the air. Flowering and fruiting is thought to continue through the year. The light brown wood is hard and heavy, but has little value as timber, and is used mainly for fuel.

Right: Several light brown seeds are embedded in the orange pulp.

Right: The yellow flowers are attractive.

Identification: The stout, brownish twigs, ringed at the nodes, bear very thick, leathery, dark green leaves, up to 13cm (5in) in length, 10cm (4in) in width, with scarcely visible veins. The small, yellow flowers are arranged in branched clusters at the ends of the stems, male and female flowers on separate trees. The female flowers develop into round, green fruit, which retains the enclosing calyx at the base, and also the five blackish stigmas at the apex.

Palo de Cruz

Rheedia portoricensis

This small tree is found growing wild only in the forests and thickets of the coastal regions of Puerto Rico and on the neighbouring island of Vieques. Its trunk, only about 10cm (4in) in diameter, has smooth or slightly fissured brown bark and bears a crown of horizontal or slightly drooping branches with dark green foliage. A pale yellow latex is found in the inner bark, twigs, leaves and fruit. Characteristic of this species are the green or grey twigs that occur in pairs opposite each other, at right angles to the main axis. This regular, cross-like branching has given rise to the local Spanish name for the tree. The light brown wood is very hard and heavy, but as the trees are small it is mainly used for posts. It is regarded as a handsome tree, and may therefore have some potential ornamental value.

Identification: The small, spine-tipped leaves are arranged opposite each other along the stems. They are stiff, thick and shiny, and grow up to about 7.5cm (3in) long and 5cm (2in) broad, dark green on the upper surface and light green beneath. The small flowers, less than 1cm (½in) across, are pale yellow with a tinge of pink. They grow singly or in small groups at the base of the leaves.

Distribution: Puerto Rico, Vieques.
Height: 6m (20ft)
Shape: Crown narrow
Evergreen
Pollinated: Insect
Leaf shape: Elliptic-obovate

Left: The yellow elliptical fruit, is about 4cm (1¾in) long.

Barillo

Symphonia globulifera

A large tree, common at sea level in wet or swampy forests along the Atlantic coast of Central America, barillo resembles the American elm (*Ulmus americana*) in general appearance. The stout trunk, occasionally more than 1m (3ft) in diameter, is sometimes supported by stilt roots. The rough, dark bark contains yellowish resin, from which this tree derives its Spanish name of *leche amarillo*. On exposure to the air, this resin becomes black and pitch-like, and in some regions is used for waterproofing boats. The hard, heavy timber is used for building purposes, carpentry, crates and boxes, railway sleepers and fuel. Small quantities have been exported to North America and Europe, mainly for use as veneers.

Identification: The branches of this tree spread out horizontally, or droop slightly, and bear short-stalked, leathery leaves. The flowers, with round, red petals, are followed by small, ovoid, dark green, berry-like fruit that become brownish or yellowish with age.

Distribution: Atlantic coast of Central America, from Guatemala to Panama; West Indies; coastal South America; tropical Africa.
Height: 30m (100ft)
Shape: Crown rounded
Evergreen
Pollinated: Bird
Leaf shape: Lanceolate

Above: Each leathery fruit contains one to three seeds.

MIMOSA SUBFAMILY

The Mimosoideae are a subclass of the large pea family, the Leguminosae. There are almost 3,000 species, including trees, shrubs and some herbs; most have finely divided leaves, and the acacias are probably the most familiar members. The flowers tend to be small and are often in eye-catching clusters. There are 1,200 species of Acacia, 900 of which occur in Australia.

Guaba

Inga vera

Distribution: Jamaica, Cuba, Haiti, Dominican Republic, Puerto Rico and possibly Mexico.
Height: 18m (60ft)
Shape: Spreading
Evergreen
Pollinated: Insects, birds, and bats
Leaf shape: Alternate, pinnate

The range of this medium-size, spreading tree has been considerably extended due to its use as a shade tree in coffee plantations, and this has blurred its natural distribution somewhat. The genus is a large one, with 350 species. The flowers open at different times and are pollinated by insects and birds, and possibly also by bats at night. The timber is used for posts and furniture.

Identification: The pinnate leaves have three to five pairs of large, drooping, hairy leaflets. The trunk may reach 1m (3ft) in diameter, and the bark is grey-brown and smooth at first, becoming fissured with age. The fruit is a brown, hairy, slightly curved pod.

Left: The whitish flowers have long, protruding stamens, giving them a feathery appearance. Each flower opens only for a short period of just a few hours.

Ice Cream Bean

Inga edulis

This fast-growing tree is used in its native home to provide shade in coffee plantations. It is also grown for its seed pods, which contain sweet, white pulp that tastes like vanilla ice cream.

Identification: The trunk has smooth, grey bark and may be multi-stemmed. The spreading branches are heavily clothed with leaves, providing dense shade. The branches are somewhat brittle and occasionally break under their own weight. The leaves are 60cm (24in) long, and have three or four pairs of dark green leaflets with lighter veining. Each leaflet is 10cm (4in) long, rough textured and elliptical. The stem between each pair of leaflets is winged. The flowers appear sporadically throughout the year, but are most common in the spring and summer. They have small, brown petals and long, white stamens, and are clustered together like tight powder-puffs. The greenish-brown pods are 30–60cm (12–24in) long, oblong in cross section and velvety.

Distribution: West Indies, Central America and northern South America.
Height: 12m (40ft)
Shape: Spreading
Evergreen
Pollinated: Hummingbird and bee
Leaf shape: Pinnate

Above right: Seeds are encased in soft pulp.

Left: Winged leaf stems are typical for the Inga genus.

Right: The ice cream bean forms a dense mass of foliage.

Sweet Acacia

Aroma *Acacia farnesiana*

This tree spreads rapidly and is naturalized in Florida and Louisiana, as well as being occasionally planted in gardens. It is the source of perfume, which is distilled from its flowers – these being known in the trade as "cassie flowers" – and is also grown for this purpose in southern Europe, where it is sometimes called "mimosa". Not surprisingly, the flowers attract bees, and this is a good honey plant. The foliage and twigs of this multi-use species are eagerly browsed by livestock, and the pods and bark are used in the tanning industry. Bunches of dried flowers retain a pleasant perfume, and are sometimes used to scent and freshen linen.

Identification: A small tree with dark brown, rather smooth bark, and paired spines at the base of its feathery leaves. The flowers are arranged in tight, bright yellow balls on hairy stalks, and are pleasantly perfumed. The fruits are typical legume bean-like pods, each with several brown seeds, and they remain on the tree long after ripening.

Distribution: California, Texas, Arizona, Mexico, West Indies, through Central and South America to Chile and Argentina.
Height: 3m (10ft)
Shape: Spreading
Deciduous
Pollinated: Insect
Leaf shape: Feathery (twice-pinnate)

Left: The globular flowerheads are sweet-scented and golden-yellow.

Mesquite

Algarobbo *Prosopis juliflora*

This spiny tree has a wide distribution – from California right through to Central and South America – and it is also widely naturalized in the tropics elsewhere. It is a multi-use species, yielding durable, rot-resistant timber, fuelwood and high-quality charcoal. Its bark is used for tanning leather, and its flowers attact honeybees. Native Mexican and American people traditionally used the pods to grind into a kind of flour, for use in cooking. Mesquite pods are nutritious, and are also eaten by animals, including cattle.

Identification: A small tree with a rather crooked trunk, angled branches and twigs, and paired spines at the nodes. The leaves are composed of up to 25 pairs of narrow leaflets, and the small flowers dangle in tight clusters. The fruit is a bean-like pod up to about 23cm (9in) long, containing brown seed in a sweet, edible pulp.

Distribution: South-west USA, through Mexico and the Caribbean islands to Colombia and Venezuela; naturalized in Hawaii and elsewhere.
Height: 9m (30ft)
Shape: Broad-crowned, spreading, flat-topped
Deciduous
Pollinated: Insect
Leaf shape: Feathery (twice-pinnate)

Left: The catkin-like cylindrical flower clusters attract insects including honeybees.

Manila Tamarind

Pithecellobium dulce

This plant has thorns on all its branches and, when kept pruned as a shrub, makes a good spiny hedge. The Manila tamarind has several other uses: yellow dye is made from its bark, a drink is made from the fruit pulp, and its pods are collected for animal fodder. It is suited to dry conditions, and has a light and airy canopy with ascending branches.

Identification: The pale grey bark has longitudinal ridges. The leaves have one pair of side stalks, each with only a single pair of leaflets. Each leaflet is 2.5–5cm (1–2in) long, blunt-ended and matt greyish-green when mature. The young leaflets are dull maroon. The overall effect of the leaves makes the tree look congested. The tiny, greenish flowers are packed into round heads 2cm (¾in) wide, which are held on branched clusters springing from the leaf axils. The pods are 12–15cm (4½–6in) long, 1cm (½in) wide, lobed and spirally twisted.

Distribution: Mexico and Venezuela.
Height: 15m (50ft)
Shape: Domed
Evergreen
Pollinated: Insect
Leaf shape: Bipinnate

Right: As the pods mature, they twist up. They contain three to nine shiny black seeds in pink and white edible pulp.

Yellow Rain Tree

Albizia saman

The grass underneath this tree is often green when the surrounding grass has dried out and died. This was once attributed to the tree making rain overnight, hence its name. In reality, the leaves close at night and during showers, allowing rain to fall on to the grass below when that beneath other trees receives far less or none. The yellow rain tree is widely planted in the tropics for shade – its crown, which has a symmetrical form with ascending branches, attains a spread of 60m (200ft). The pods contain a sugary pulp, which is favoured by cattle and used for fodder.

Identification: The bark is grey and lightly fissured. The leaves are 30cm (12in) long with three to six pairs of side stalks, each carrying six to eight pairs of leaflets. Each leaflet is 2.5–5cm (1–2in) long, mid-green above, pale green below and oblong to diamond-shaped. The delicate flowers occur throughout the year and are particularly common from spring to summer. They have small petals but long stamens, which together give the look of an airy, pink-tipped powder-puff. The pods are 15–25cm (6–10in) long, flat, black and contain brown seeds.

Distribution: West Indies, Central America.
Height: 35m (15ft)
Shape: Spreading, domed
Semi-deciduous
Pollinated: Insect
Leaf shape: Bipinnate

Right: The leaves close up an hour or more before sunset, and open an hour or so after sunrise. It is thought that this allows moisture through the canopy, and enables numerous epiphytes to live on the tree's trunk and branches.

Powder-puff

Calliandra haematocephala

This plant is grown for its amazing flowers – large, soft powder-puffs of intense scarlet or the darkest pink. It may be grown as a large shrub or pruned to give it a more tree-like shape. The branches droop and sprawl somewhat, but are amply covered with thick foliage. The flowers first appear when the plant is quite small.

Identification: The leaves are composed of two pinnae, each 25cm (10in) long and consisting of five to ten pairs of leaflets. Each leaflet is oblong to sickle-shaped, deep green when mature and 4cm (1½in) long. When young, the foliage weeps and is a soft coppery pink. The 10cm- (4in-) wide flower clusters contain hundreds of individual flowers with their petals obscured by the numerous, 6cm- (2½in-) long, red stamens. The flowers appear mostly in the autumn and winter months.

Distribution: Bolivia.
Height: 9m (30ft)
Shape: Spreading
Evergreen
Pollinated: Hummingbird and insect
Leaf shape: Bipinnate

Left: The tight flower buds are reminiscent of small-berried fruit, and burst open to reveal the long stamens.

Right: The flowers are short-lived, lasting only a day or two.

OTHER SPECIES OF NOTE
Koa *Acacia koa*
Native to Hawaii, this tree is found on slopes throughout the island in all except the driest locations. On Hawaii, it is a popular choice for reforestation. The wood is red and was once used for war canoes. The koa grows quickly and reaches 30m (100ft) tall with an open, spreading crown of thick, contorted, horizontal branches. In ideal conditions, the trunk may reach 3m (10ft) in diameter. The koa is tolerant of salty air and soil, and on coasts forms a smaller, more contorted tree.
The leaf stems are expanded into evergreen phyllodes, sickle-shaped and 15cm (6in) long. The spring flowers are pale yellow and form spherical clusters.

Ear Pod Tree

Enterolobium cyclocarpum

This upright tree is grown for the novelty value of its pods, which look uncannily like human ears. These pods may be eaten when young and are often collected for animal fodder. The bright red seeds are used for jewellery and the timber is of high quality. The ear pod tree can grow as wide as it is tall and has thick, ascending branches.

Identification: The bark is light grey and smooth, while the leaves are bright green and feathery, consisting of four to eight pairs of pinnae, each with 12–24 pairs of leaflets. The leaflets are 1.5cm (⅝in) long and oblong to sickle-shaped. The tree blossoms in spring, producing sprays of tiny white flowers clustered into balls. Each flower has greenish-white, 5mm- (¼in-) long petals and longer, white stamens. The seed pods often appear in the dry season, when the tree is leafless. They are deep russet brown, shiny and 8–16cm (3–6¼in) long.

Distribution: Venezuela.
Height: 30m (100ft)
Shape: Spreading
Deciduous
Pollinated: Insect
Leaf shape: Bipinnate

Left: The pods are produced in large numbers and contain a dry, sugary pulp – a valuable fodder at the end of the dry season.

Right: The leaves are fine and feathery.

CAESALPINIA SUBFAMILY

The legumes include well over 600 genera spread across the globe, and they are particularly common in the tropics. The family includes annuals, herbaceous plants, shrubs, trees and climbers. The trees play an important role in the forests of South America and Africa. The Caesalpinia subfamily is distinguished by flowers with five petals, and one odd-sized petal is enclosed by the others.

West Indian Locust

Hymenaea courbaril

An attractive forest tree, with a trunk at least 1.2m (4ft) in diameter, sometimes supported by buttresses, and covered by a thick layer of smooth, grey bark. This is an important timber tree, being used for furniture, wheels and cogs, railway sleepers, veneers and cabinet work, etc. The tree is ommercially important as the source of South American copal, used in varnishes. A good shade tree, but not for planting near houses because of the unpleasant odour of the fruits.

Left: Each leaf has two shiny green leaflets, each up to 10 x 4cm (4 x 1½in) and narrowing near the base.

Identification: The stout branches forming the crown terminate in sturdy brown twigs bearing compound leaves. The flattened flower clusters stand upright at the ends of the branches, and consist of numerous whitish flowers. The pods contain pockets of gum, and large, dark red seeds embedded in thick, pale yellow pulp. The pulp is edible.

Distribution: West Indies; Central and South America.
Height: 20m (65ft)
Shape: Crown rounded and spreading
Evergreen
Pollinated: Insect and bat
Leaf shape: Oblong, but unequal-sided

Left: The flowers develop into rough, dark brown pods, up to 10 x 5cm (4 x 2in).

Flame of the Forest

Flamboyant tree *Delonix regia*

Also called the flamboyant tree, the flame of the forest flowers in late spring and early summer when it becomes one mass of intense vermilion blossoms, completely obliterating from sight any foliage across its incredibly wide, flat-topped crown. The tree is also eye-catching in fruit, when hundreds of long pods hang from its horizontal branches. Even when it is in leaf the tree has a pleasant, airy appearance. It has been planted in considerable numbers throughout the tropics including the USA, but with its spreading, shallow roots and eventual buttresses, it has not proved popular as a street tree.

Right: This fast-growing tree may grow to 7.5m (25ft) in four years.

Identification: The smooth bark is light brown or grey, and the trunk carries thick branches, which are never straight. The leaves are delicate, 60cm (24in) long, bright green above and lighter below. The flowers have four red petals, and one larger white petal with yellow and red streaks. The dark brown, flattened seed pods are up to 60cm (24in) long.

Distribution: Madagascar.
Height: 20m (66ft)
Shape: Spreading
Deciduous
Pollinated: Bird
Leaf shape: Bipinnate

Above: Profuse, beautiful flowers give rise to masses of hard, woody pods, which remain on the tree even when splitting open.

Rose of Venezuela

Brownea grandiceps

This slow-growing, handsome tree is notable for its display of impressive flowers and fine foliage. Despite being the largest flowering member of its genus, it is not heavily planted in the tropics. The leaves display an interesting piece of behaviour – they cover the flowers by day to protect them from the sun, then move aside to reveal them at night. The rose of Venezuela grows naturally in mountain forests.

Distribution: Northern Venezuela.
Height: 18m (60ft)
Shape: Domed
Evergreen
Leaf shape: Pinnate

Identification: The dense crown has leaves up to 90cm (36in) long divided into five to eleven pairs of long, narrow leaflets. Young leaves are translucent pink or bronze and hang; when mature, they are bright green, leathery and flat. The delicate flowers are bright red and tubular with long, protruding anthers. They occur in clusters of about 50, in large hanging balls towards the branch tips. Each cluster is 25cm (10in) wide. The wide, flattened seed pods are 25cm (10in) long.

Left: Flowers appear year round and are particularly abundant in spring and early summer.

Pink Shower Tree *Cassia grandis*
The thick canopy of coral pink flowers this tree produces falls quickly in early spring to form a pink carpet below. This species comes from Central America. It has a spreading crown and grows to 18m (60ft) tall. The leaves are pinnate, 30cm (12in) long and mid-green. The black, cylindrical pods may be up to 38cm (15in) long, and contain flat, yellow seeds.

Jerusalem Thorn *Parkinsonia aculeata*
This spiny shrub or small tree is native to the southern United States and Mexico, but has been extensively planted elsewhere as a hedge plant or ornamental. Nowadays it is found from California to Florida, southwards to Central and South America and the West Indies, and even in the Old World tropics.

It grows to about 6m (20ft), often branching near the ground, and has an open crown of spreading branches. The smooth, thin bark is at first yellowish or bluish-green, but becomes brown and fissured on larger, older trunks. The slender, slightly zigzag green stems bear specialized leaves, consisting of a 2cm- (¾in-) long spine and two or four dangling axes, up to 30cm (12in) long, each edged by 20–30 pairs of tiny, oblong, deciduous leaflets. At the base of each leaf is a pair of short spines. The colourful, fragrant flowers have five bright yellow petals, the upper one often tinged red, 10 stamens with green filaments and orange-brown anthers, and a reddish ovary and style. The leathery, brown, pointed pods, up to 7.5cm (3in) long, are pinched between the seeds. The wood is too brittle to be used for construction, and is useful only for fuel. Leaves and pods are eaten by livestock, and an infusion of the leaves has been used in domestic medicines.

Dividivi

Caesalpinia coriaria

This small deciduous tree is native mainly in the Caribbean but has been widely planted elsewhere, partly as a source of tannin from its pods. The bark is also rich in tannin. The tree has feathery foliage and an irregular, spreading crown, often flattened at the top, and the flowers are fragrant, attracting bees.

Identification: The light green leaves have finely hairy axes, and each branch (secondary axis) carries up to 24 tiny leaflets, giving an almost fern-like appearance. The flowers have yellow or whitish petals, and are arranged in clusters. The fruit is a thick, hard pod, at first light brown, but turning reddish and twisting into a circular or S-shape. The wood is very heavy and hard, and takes a polish well.

Distribution: Greater and Lesser Antilles; Mexico to Colombia and Venezuela. Bahamas and Trinidad (introduced).
Height: 7.5m (25ft)
Shape: Variable
Deciduous
Pollinated: Insect
Leaf shape: Bipinnate

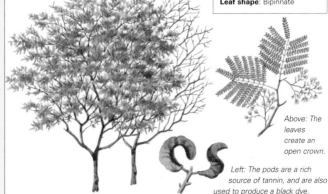

Above: The leaves create an open crown.

Left: The pods are a rich source of tannin, and are also used to produce a black dye.

BEAN SUBFAMILY

There are more than 12,000 species in this legume subfamily (Faboideae). It contains mainly herbs (such as clovers and vetches), but also some shrubs (such as Broom) and some trees, including Laburnum. The flower structure is the typical pea flower, with a large standard petal, lateral wing petals, and a keel formed by two fused petals, adapted to pollination by insects and sometimes by birds.

Common Coral Tree

Erythrina crista-galli

This fast-growing plant has soft wood, and is grown as a multi-stemmed tree in tropical regions and as a herbaceous plant in warm temperate areas, where it is cut to the ground by the cold each winter. The stems are covered in thick, 7mm- (⅜in-) long, curved thorns, and even the leaf stems carry spines. The large, long-lasting flower panicles are produced throughout the year, and are the showiest in the genus.

Left: As it matures, the tree gains rough fissured bark and contorted branches.

Above and below left: These stunning flowers are adapted to pollination by birds through their red colour, tubular shape, copious amount of nectar and sturdiness.

Distribution: Brazil.
Height: 9m (30ft)
Shape: Spreading, irregular crown
Evergreen
Pollinated: Bird
Leaf shape: Trifoliate

Identification: The trunk has ridged bark and grows into a gnarled form. The leaves are deep green, smooth and leathery with elliptic leaflets each measuring 7.5cm (3in) long. The flowers are scarlet to deep pink, and 5–7.5cm (2–3in) long. They form an inflorescence containing up to 100 flowers, which often hangs down. The flowers appear in cycles of six weeks. The smooth pods are up to 30cm (12in) long and contain grey seeds.

Cabbage-bark

Dog-almond *Andira inermis*

This is a striking, beautiful tree, especially when it is in full bloom, when it boasts clusters of purple or pink, pea-shaped flowers, which attract insects, notably honeybees. It is sometimes planted as a shade tree or ornamental in parks and gardens. Its strange name derives from the distinctive smell of the cut bark – not unlike cabbage. The bark is poisonous, as are the seeds, but it is also reputed to have medicinal properties, killing parasitic worms. The heartwood is attractively patterned and is consequently suitable for furniture.

Far right: The fruit is rounded, fleshy and olive-like.

Right: The leaves are arranged opposite on the twig.

Identification: This much-branched tree has scaly bark and rather sturdy twigs, which are covered in fine hairs when young. The pinnate leaves have shiny, pointed green or yellow-green leaflets. The flowers are pink or dark red, and develop in branching clusters, while the fruit has a rounded, fleshy outside and is hard on the inside.

Distribution: Mexico, Peru, Bolivia, Brazil, southern Florida (introduced), west tropical Africa.
Height: 15m (50ft)
Shape: Rounded
Deciduous
Pollinated: Insect
Leaf shape: Pinnate

Left: The pea-like flowers are stunningly pretty.

Pea-tree

Quick-stick, Mother-of-cocoa *Gliricidia sepium*

This small tree has pretty pea-like flowers arranged in clusters mainly close to the wood of older branches, and opening between December and May. The timber is strong and heavy, and has been used as railway sleepers, and to make sturdy posts. One name is "mother-of-cocoa", referring to its use as a shade tree in cocoa plantations, where it also enriches the soil. Many parts of this tree are poisonous, and have been used to kill rodents, although the flowers attract honeybees.

Identification: The pinnate leaves have numerous elliptic leaflets with hairy stalks and green or greyish blades. Each flower has a spreading, butterfly-shaped corolla with pink or purplish-white petals, and resembles that of a sweet-pea. The fruit pods are yellow-green at first, ripening to brownish-black, and contain blackish seeds.

Distribution: Mexico, Colombia, Venezuela; introduced in Caribbean islands from Cuba to Trinidad, and also in southern Florida, Brazil, and in Africa and south Asia.
Height: 7.5m (25ft)
Shape: Variable
Deciduous
Pollinated: Insect
Leaf shape: Pinnate

Left: This tree is well-named as the individual flowers are like those of the sweet-pea.

OTHER SPECIES OF NOTE

Swamp Immortelle *Erythrina fusca*
This tree is found across a very wide natural range, which includes the tropics of America, Africa and Asia. It is a deciduous tree with a rounded crown that may grow to 24m (80ft) tall and have a spread almost equally large. The swamp immortelle is grown for its scarlet flowers, which are densely crowded into 25cm- (10in-) long sprays. The flowers appear in spring and summer, and have a brick-red upper petal and brownish-maroon to cream wings and keel. The tree grows with a crooked, buttressed trunk, which loses its thick curved spines when mature. The leaves have three deep green, smooth and leathery elliptic leaflets, each 7.5cm (3in) long. The narrow pods are 30cm (12in) long.

Mountain Immortelle *Erythrina poeppigiana*
From eastern Peru and Brazil, this tree has been widely introduced into the Caribbean and Costa Rica. Growing up to 24m (80ft) tall, it is sometimes used as a shade tree in cocoa plantations. In spring, and occasionally in late summer, it can be seen from a long way off due to the abundant scarlet to deep pink flowers covering its dome-shaped crown. The flowers are pollinated by small birds. The mountain immortelle has thorny bark covering a soft-wooded trunk, which usually exceeds 1m (3ft) in diameter. The leaves have three leaflets: the lower two are 10cm (4in) across, and the terminal leaflet is 15cm (6in) wide. The pods are 12cm (4½in) long and contain two seeds.

Pride of Bolivia

Tipuana tipu

The pride of Bolivia is a fast-growing tree that forms a thick, straight trunk with buttresses. This tree is common in Bolivia, and one valley there has so many of them that it is known simply as Tipuana. Once it has passed through a young, ungainly stage, the pride of Bolivia normally grows into a wide, spreading tree with horizontal, zigzagging branches. It has been planted around South America, in North America and in the south of France for its spring and summer flowers, attractive shape and abundant shade.

Identification: The dark brown trunk is usually short in cultivated trees. The leaves are 30cm (12in) long and composed of 13–21 leaflets, each dark to yellowish-green and oblong. The butterfly-like flowers vary from pale yellow to orangey yellow. They are in terminal clusters. The fruit appears in autumn and is a winged key, 5–10cm (2–4in) long and brown.

Below: This drought-tolerant species produces its flowers in spring and summer.

Distribution: South America.
Height: 30m (100ft)
Shape: Spreading
Semi-evergreen
Pollinated: Insect
Leaf shape: Pinnate

Fish-poison Tree

Piscidia carthagenensis

A medium-size tree common on coasts and coastal hills, often in seasonally dry regions. It is also planted in gardens and parks. In some regions, including the West Indies, the root bark, young branches and crushed leaves were thrown into the water to assist in fishing. The effect on the fish is to render them temporarily helpless (hence the tree's common name). They float to the surface. where they are easily caught, but they apparently recover and swim off if left alone. The wood is hard and heavy.

Identification: The pinnate leaves typically have seven or nine elliptic, grey-green, fine-haired leaflets. The flowers are pea-like, pink and arranged in clusters (panicles), often appearing before the leaves. The fruit is a rather unusual pod, with four broad, papery wings along the sides. Inside the fruit are several bean-like, brown seeds.

Distribution: Islands of the Caribbean; coasts of Venezuela, Colombia, Ecuador, north-west Peru, Panama along Pacific coast to southern and western Mexico.
Height: 11m (35ft)
Shape: Variable
Deciduous:
Pollinated: Insect
Leaf shape: Pinnate

Above: The attractive pink flowers are arranged in clusters on the tree.

Left: The fruit is highly unusual in shape, with distinct flanges.

Right: Like many members of the subfamily, the fish-poison tree has pinnate leaves.

Geno-geno

Lonchocarpus domingensis

This deciduous tree is native to southern and western Puerto Rico and some other Caribbean islands. In Tobago it can be found in semi-deciduous forests at the northern tip of the island. Here the canopy is about 15m (49ft), and it is co-dominant with other trees such as *Bursera simaruba*. The pale or yellowish wood is fairly strong and is used mainly for posts. It flowers mainly in the spring, and the fruit ripens in summer. The bark has been used for rope. It is planted occasionally as a shade tree or ornamental, and is also attractive to honeybees.

Identification: The leaves have seven to eleven untoothed leaflets, usually pointed. The flowers are pea-shaped, pale rose or violet and appear in clusters (racemes or panicles). The fruit is a pod covered in fine brown hairs, and contains several flat, dark brown seeds. The bark is brown, with pale dots.

Below: The leaves have a medicinal use.

Distribution: Cuba, Hispaniola, Puerto Rico, Guadaloupe, Martinique, Tobago.
Height: 21m (70ft)
Shape: Spreading
Deciduous
Pollinated: Insect
Leaf shape: Pinnate

Right: The flattened pods contain dark brown seeds.

MACADAMIA FAMILY

The Proteaceae are found in warm regions of the Southern Hemisphere, and are well represented in Australia and South Africa. Many species produce showy, long-lasting flowers used in the cut-flower industry. The leaves are often thick and waxy or hairy – adaptations for water retention. There are 1,600 species belonging to 77 genera in this family.

Silk Oak

Silky oak *Grevillea robusta*

This pretty, medium-size tree is native to Australia, but is widely planted in other tropical and subtropical regions, including the West Indies and Central and South America. It has divided, almost fern-like leaves, and showy flowers, which produce copious nectar – attracting birds as well as insects. Often planted for shade, for example along roads, it also propagates readily and grows rapidly. It is also drought resistant and cold hardy, but can become ragged with age, and the branches tend to break rather easily. The timber is used for furniture, and has prominent rays.

Identification: The bark is smooth, grey, becoming furrowed with age. The leaves are rather delicate and fern-like, and the yellowish flowers are crowded together in unbranched clusters. The fruit is pod-like, broad and flattened and split open on one side to release the winged seeds.

Left: Silk oak flowers appear orange-yellow in mid-spring.

Distribution: Australia; introduced and naturalized in the West Indies, and from Mexico to Brazil, Argentina and Peru; also in southern Florida, southern California and southern Arizona.
Height: 21m (70ft)
Shape: Variable
Evergreen
Pollinated: Insect and bird
Leaf shape: Pinnate

OTHER SPECIES OF NOTE
Queensland Nut
Macadamia ternifolia
This is a medium-size tree, related to *M. integrifolia*, and likewise produces edible seeds. A native of Queensland and New South Wales in Australia, it is also grown in the Caribbean area, notably in Puerto Rico, mainly as an ornamental tree. It has whorled, narrow, oblong leaves, and short-stalked whitish flowers in drooping clusters. The rounded fruit is about 2.5cm (1in) in diameter and splits into two when ripe to release the single, hard, thick-shelled, edible nut.

Macadamia Nut

Macadamia integrifolia

The delicious nuts for which this species is famous are found inside the fruit. Macadamia nut trees are grown throughout the tropics, particularly in Australia and Hawaii, where they were introduced in 1890. The trees grow naturally in eastern Australia's rainforests, but most grown commercially are selected, grafted varieties. The wild tree is handsome with a dense, wide crown.

Identification: The leaves are leathery, glossy, dark green and up to 30cm (12in) long. They appear in whorls, have wavy-toothed margins and yellowish midribs. The tiny flowers form dangling tassels, 10–30cm (4–12in) long in winter and spring. Each flower is white, cream or pale pink. The fruit is usually ready in late summer, when it hangs in long clusters. Each fruit is spherical, 2.5cm (1in) across and green, with a broad scar revealing the inner husk. The shell and husk are hard to break and poisonous.

Distribution: Queensland and northern New South Wales, Australia. Hawaii.
Height: 21m (70ft)
Shape: Domed
Evergreen
Pollinated: Insect
Leaf shape: Oblanceolate

Above: The fruit takes up to nine months to mature.

GUAVA FAMILY

Many Myrtaceae are evergreen trees and shrubs, having leaves with a distinctive, spicy scent. They usually have smooth margins, and grow opposite one another on the stem. The bark is often papery, peeling or splotched with pale and reddish patches. The flowers are arranged in various ways but often have many stamens, giving them a powder-puff look.

Weeping Paperbark

Melaleuca quinquenervia

This tree occurs naturally in swampy ground, but is very adaptable to even dry soils and has been planted throughout the tropics. In the Everglades of Florida, the tree has become naturalized and is proving a threat to the local, indigenous species. In Hong Kong, the weeping paperbark has a different reputation. There it is widely planted by the government to stabilize swampy farming ground, and considered invaluable in land reclamation.

Identification: The thick, shaggy, peeling bark is pale cinnamon-brown to white. The tree emits volatile oils that deter insects. The smooth, shiny, hard leaves are a bluish grey-green, flat, 4–10cm (1½–4in) long and have parallel veins. The leaves are distilled to produce an essential oil with many uses.

Right: The white flowers form bottlebrush-like inflorescences 10cm (4in) long. The flowers release large amounts of pollen, causing problems for hay fever sufferers.

Distribution: Eastern coastal Australia, New Guinea and New Caledonia. Florida.
Height: 18m (60ft)
Shape: Columnar to spreading
Evergreen
Pollinated: Bird
Leaf shape: Elliptic-lanceolate

Allspice

Pimenta dioica

The fruit, sold as allspice, is often mistakenly thought to be a mixture of different spices. This error is understandable because, quite apart from the fruit's name, allspice has a scent similar to a combination of clove, nutmeg and cinnamon. Allspice trees are widely grown in Jamaica, from where the spice is exported. The fruit is collected before it is completely ripe and dried in the sun for up to ten days. After drying, the fruit looks similar to pepper, so the genus is named *Pimenta*, from the Spanish for "pepper". The berries are an essential part of Caribbean cuisine and have medicinal properties.

Identification: This dense-crowned tree is aromatic in every part. The trunk is short and has pale grey peeling bark. The leaves are glossy, mid-green with prominent veining below, and are 15–20cm (6–8in) long. The flowers appear in spring and early summer in short panicles, which are in axils near the branch tips. Each flower is white or pale green, scented and tiny. The valuable fruit, 5mm (¼in) across, is produced in summer, and is picked when green and is black when ripe.

Distribution: Caribbean, southern Mexico and Central America.
Height: 12m (40ft)
Shape: Oblong
Evergreen
Pollinated: Insect
Leaf shape: Oblong-elliptical

Left: The allspice tree's stems, bark, leaves and flowers are all scented, filling the air around with a thick aroma. The tree also yields an oil used in perfumes and liqueurs.

Guava

Psidium guajava

This fruit tree is grown extensively throughout the tropics and into temperate areas, where it has proved itself capable of surviving slight frosts. It is popular because it is such an accommodating, undemanding tree and readily produces tasty fruit. Although it has a slightly unpleasant, grainy texture, the fruit is eaten raw and is highly nutritious, containing large amounts of vitamin C.

Above: Guava fruit is made into drinks, conserves and confectionery.

Distribution: West Indies to Peru.
Height: 10m (33ft)
Shape: Domed
Evergreen
Pollinated: Insect
Leaf shape: Oblong-elliptic

Identification: The distinctive, brown bark flakes off leaving mottled, green patches on the trunk and branches. The leathery leaves form a dense crown. They are up to 15cm (6in) long, downy below, yellowish-grey-green and heavily veined. The white flowers have hundreds of stamens and appear mostly in spring and early summer. They are slightly scented, about 2.5cm (1in) wide and occur in the axils. The fruit is a yellowish-green or pinkish tone when ripe.

Left: The round, lumpy fruit is heavily scented and measures 7cm (2¾ in) across.

OTHER SPECIES OF NOTE

Jamaica Pepper *Pimenta officinalis*
The fruit of this Jamaican tree has a peppery flavour and a range of uses, including cooking, aromatherapy and potpourri. The species is similar to allspice, although Jamaica pepper does not grow quite as tall, and has flattened branches that are more oblong in cross-section. An essential oil called "pimento" is extracted from the leaves of Jamaica pepper and is used in the manufacture of perfume.

Bay Rum Tree *Pimenta racemosa*
This West Indian tree grows to 12m (40ft) and is aromatic in every part. The leaves and twigs contain a pale yellow oil called myrcia, or bay oil, which is extracted by distillation. The oil is used in cosmetics, medicine and flavouring. The leaves are sometimes distilled in rum, which is then called "bay rum". The bark is pale and peels, while the leaves are thick, bright green and oblong. The tree has white flowers tinged red. The pea-size black fruit is eaten by birds and can be used in cooking. It is an invasive weed in Hawaii.

Birchberry *Myrcia splendens*
This small evergreen grows to 9m (30ft). It grows throughout the West Indies, and in Colombia, Peru, Bolivia, Brazil and Surinam, usually in mixed forests and clearings. It has long, pointed, shiny, short-stalked leaves and terminal clusters of white, fragrant flowers with prominent stamens. The fruit is fleshy, green at first, ripening to dark blue or blackish, and each contains a single large seed. The fruit is said to be edible, and the wood is used for making posts.

Strawberry Guava

Psidium littorale

A narrow, leggy, upright shrub or small tree, the strawberry guava has a dense crown and produces small fruit in large quantity. The fruit is juicy and has a similar taste and texture to strawberries, although it is a little more acidic and grainy. The strawberry guava is a slow-growing tree cultivated in tropical and warm temperate regions. In the latter it may be severely cut back by the winter cold, whereas in the former it may become naturalized and a serious problem.

Distribution: Eastern Brazil.
Height: 6m (20ft)
Shape: Columnar
Evergreen
Pollinated: Insect
Leaf shape: Oblong-obovate

Identification: The tree has smooth, reddish or deep brown bark that flakes to reveal a mottling of greyish green below. The short-stalked leaves are smooth, glossy, thick and tough. Bright green, they have lighter midribs, are downy below and measure 7.5–10cm (3–4in) long. The single white or yellow flowers are 2.5cm (1in) across and scented. The round fruit is smooth-skinned, 2.5–5cm (1–2in) across, red or yellow when mature and has white flesh containing many seeds.

Right: The fruit may be eaten raw, but is usually used to make jams and jellies.

CREPE MYRTLE FAMILY

The Lythraceae family includes herbaceous plants, trees and shrubs but only a few are well known, and only a handful are used in horticulture. The trees have simple, smooth-edged leaves positioned opposite one another on the stem. The star-shaped flowers have petals that are crumpled up when in bud and appear in panicles, racemes or cymes. The fruit is a capsule or berry containing many seeds.

Queen's Crepe Myrtle

Pride of India *Lagerstroemia speciosa*

This tree is grown as an ornamental plant for its large panicles of showy, pink flowers – the name *speciosa* actually means "showy", It grows wild in humid forests and along forested waterways. The queen's crepe myrtle has a dense crown that loses its leaves in the cooler winter months. The tree flowers in summer.

Identification: The unusual bark is pale grey and often flakes off in large chunks, leaving concave indentations and resulting in the trunk having a yellowish mottling. The leaves have prominent veining and may have scalloped margins. They are 18cm (7in) long and 7cm (2¾in) (wide, dark green and rough. The flowers form in erect panicles up to 60cm (24in) tall on the top of the tree. Each individual flower is 8cm (3in) across and has six crinkled, pink petals, which fade to purple as they mature. The small fruit sits in a star-shaped structure formed by the sepals, and the ovoid woody capsule has six sections. Each section of the fruit contains a winged seed.

Distribution: India, Sri Lanka, Burma, southern China and south-east Asia. USA hardiness zones 10–11.
Height: 24m (80ft)
Shape: Spreading and round
Deciduous
Pollinated: Insect
Leaf shape: Elliptic

Above left: Leaves turn bright red before dropping.

Left: Cultivated forms have flowers in different hues.

Tulip-wood

Physocalymma scaberrima

This tree is the only species in its genus, and it is native to the tropical regions of northern South America. The timber is used mainly for making furniture. It is fairly straight-grained, moderately hard and easy to work, and becomes smooth and lustrous when polished. It is also durable, though may be subject to insect attack. Characteristic of the species are the oil or resin canals that are present both in the bark and in the wood. The oil is used in perfumery.

Identification: It is tall, but has rather a slender, columnar trunk. There are no branches until about 5m (16½ft) from the base, and then they continue, wide-spreading, to the top of the tree. The bark is pinkish-brown and scaly, the sapwood is pinkish-brown or yellowish and the heartwood purplish-red or dark brown. The leaves are rough, leathery, shiny and up to 10cm (4in) in length. The showy flowers, with a dark purple calyx and a bright pink corolla, are arranged in clusters.

Far right: The beautiful flowers of this tree produce sweet nectar, which attracts forest birds.

Right: The buds appear at the end of the twigs.

Distribution: Northern South America.
Height: 25m (80ft)
Shape: Crown spreading
Evergreen
Pollinated: Bird
Leaf shape: Obovate

RED MANGROVE FAMILY

Many of the trees and shrubs in the Rhizophoraceae family are mangroves, living in brackish and salty water along tropical coasts. Several allow their seeds to germinate while still attached to the branches, giving them a better chance of getting established in between the tides. Leaf shape and size varies considerably, but flowers are star-shaped, and either solitary or produced in groups in the axils.

Red Mangrove

Rhizophora mangle

Distribution: Coastal tropical America and West Africa.
Height: 30m (100ft)
Shape: Domed or irregular
Evergreen
Pollinated: Wind or self
Leaf shape: Elliptic

Right: The thick, waxy leaves are well adapted to harsh coastal conditions.

The red mangrove is an incredibly important species ecologically. Able to withstand saline conditions, it grows right down to the low tide mark, forming dense, often storm-proof thickets along coastlines and providing shelter for young fish and nesting sites for birds. The red mangrove is able to survive where it does by excreting excess salt, and by having pores on its roots that allow gaseous exchange when exposed to the air. This species is incredibly slow-growing and forms distinctive, branching stilt roots. As time passes, the main trunk dies until eventually the aerial roots alone support the plant.

Identification: The bark is pinkish-red when young and grey when mature. The leaves sit opposite one another on the branch, and are deep green with a prominent paler midrib. Thick, succulent and glossy, they may be up to 20cm (8in) long. The flowers appear throughout the year in groups in the axils. They are cream, 2cm (¾in) wide and have four thick petals. The fruit is 2.5cm (1in) long, brown and contains a single seed. The seedling may grow to 30cm (12in) before dropping from the tree.

Goatwood

Cassipourea guianensis

While most mangrove species inhabit coastal saltmarshes and swamps, goatwood prefers damp forests, from sea level up to about 915m (3,000ft). It is widespread, but not always common on many of the Caribbean islands, or in parts of Central America and northern South America. This shrub or small tree has dark grey bark and horizontal branches. Its wood is fairly hard and is used for poles, posts and carpentry.

Identification: The hairless leaves are opposite, spreading in two rows, with thin blades, shiny green above and yellow-green beneath. The flowers develop at the leaf bases, and are small and bell-shaped, with white petals. Flowering is throughout the year, and irregular. The fruit is berry-like with three to four cells and the seed has a yellow covering.

*Below:
The fruit in the axils.*

Distribution: Greater and Lesser Antilles, Trinidad; Mexico, through Central America (not El Salvador), to Guyana, Brazil, Peru and Ecuador.
Height: 6m (20ft)
Shape: Variable
Evergreen
Pollinated: Wind and insect
Leaf shape: Elliptic to ovate

Left: The small flowers of goatwood are inconspicuous, at the bases of the leaf stalks.

SOAPBERRY FAMILY

The Sapindaceae family contains a large number of very diverse but mostly tropical trees, shrubs and climbers. The leaves may be simple, pinnate, bipinnate or even tripinnate. The small flowers, normally with three to five petals, form in branched clusters or in bunches with each flower on an individual stem. The fruit is also highly variable but is always composed of three sections.

Ackee

Blighia sapida

The tasty fruit of the ackee is a popular ingredient in West Indian cooking, but extreme care must be exercised when preparing it. The thick, creamy flesh can be fried or boiled as a vegetable, but it contains highly poisonous seeds, which must be removed before cooking.

Identification: The tree is fast-growing and forms a handsome, dense crown. The trunk is short and thick with grey bark. The leaves consist of three to ten egg-shaped to oblong leaflets, each of which is glossy, mid-green above and paler below, 15–30cm (6–12in) long with prominent veining. The scented flowers are hairy, white and hang from the tree. The smooth-skinned fruit is spherical to pear-shaped, and triangular with rounded corners in cross-section. When ripe, it turns rosy pink, apricot or red and measures 7.5–10cm (3–4in) long. The fruit divides into three sections, each containing a shiny black seed surrounded by white flesh.

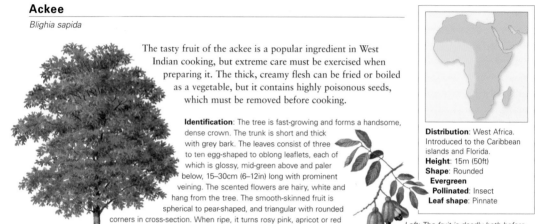

Distribution: West Africa. Introduced to the Caribbean islands and Florida.
Height: 15m (50ft)
Shape: Rounded
Evergreen
Pollinated: Insect
Leaf shape: Pinnate

Left: The fruit is deadly both before ripening and soon after bursting open.

Guayo

Talisia oliviformis

A tree of medium height that grows wild in wooded ravines or thickets at low altitudes, and is often planted near dwellings. It is one of 40 species of *Talisia*, all of which are confined to the tropical regions of America. It is best known and cultivated for its fruit, which is rounded and about 2.5cm (1in) across, with a firm texture and sage-green rind. It becomes yellowish on maturity and encloses a considerable amount of orange-red pulp, which has an agreeably acid flavour.

Identification: The leaves are composed of four leaflets, arranged in opposite pairs, thin and leathery, and 5–12cm (2–4½in) in length. The inflorescences spring from the axils of the leaves, and are often clustered at the ends of the branches. They are usually small, shorter than the leaves, and densely hairy. The tiny flowers, only 3–4mm (⅛in) long, have white petals fringed with hairs.

Distribution: Mexico, Guatemala, Honduras, Colombia and Venezuela.
Height: 18m (60ft)
Shape: Crown spreading
Evergreen
Pollinated: Insect
Leaf shape: Elliptic to lanceolate-oblong

Left: The fruit is eaten fresh and made into juice and jam, and the seeds are eaten roasted.

Guara

Candlewood-tree *Cupania americana*

In the wild this medium-size tree grows typically on moist sites near the coast, or in forests along rivers. Because of its broadly spreading crown and large leaves it is also sometimes planted as a shade tree. The light brown wood is subject to attack by termites. It is, however, used for posts, poles, general construction and in shipbuilding. The leaves and also the seeds are said to possess medicinal properties, and the flowers attract insects, including honeybees.

Identification: In young trees the grey bark is fairly smooth, but with age this becomes rough and broken into plates. The stout, hairy twigs bear alternate leaves. They are pinnate, with up to eight large leaflets, which are rounded and with a notch at the tip, with wavy, toothed margins. On the underside they are covered in dense, soft hairs, and above are shiny, with hairy veins. The small, white flowers are arranged in branched clusters, and develop into round, reddish-brown seed capsules, opening in three parts to reveal the shiny black seeds.

Right: The leaves are a characteristic shape, with large, rounded leaflets, notched at the tip.

Distribution: Greater and Lesser Antilles, Barbados, Trinidad and Tobago, Venezuela and Colombia.
Height: 15m (50ft)
Shape: Rounded crown
Evergreen
Pollinated: Insect
Leaf shape:
Pinnate

Soapberry

Sapindus saponaria

Distribution: California and Florida, throughout Central America and the West Indies, to Peru, Brazil, and south to Paraguay and Argentina.
Height: 18m (60ft)
Shape: Crown broad
Evergreen
Pollinated: Insect
Leaf shape:
Pinnate, with elliptic-lanceolate leaflets

A small to medium-size tree, that grows wild or is cultivated in many regions, including tropical areas in the Old World. The yellow or light brown wood is hard and heavy, and is used for posts and in carpentry. The common name refers to the fruit being used as a substitute for soap. Since the fleshy part is up to 30 per cent saponin, it produces abundant suds when placed in water. A medicinal oil can be extracted from the seed, and the roots and leaves are used in home medicines. It is also useful as a honey plant and as a shade tree.

Centre left:
The seeds can be used whole as necklace beads and, when crushed, as a fish poison or insecticide.

Left: The tiny flowers have a feathery appearance.

Identification: The trunk grows to more than 30cm (12in) in diameter, and is covered with light grey or brown bark, fairly smooth though warty at first, becoming finely fissured and scaly with age. The stout twigs have pores that appear as raised, reddish-brown dots. They bear alternate leaves 20–40cm (8–16in) long, composed of three to six pairs of stalkless leaflets, 15cm (6in) long and 7cm (2¾in) broad, with sometimes a single terminal one, and a characteristic winged stalk. The male flowers are produced in vast quantities, raining down and littering the ground beneath. The shiny brown globular fruits contain a yellow, sticky, poisonous flesh.

CASHEW FAMILY

The Anacardiaceae family includes a number of economically important tropical trees. It also contains shrubs and some temperate plants. Many members of the family have resinous bark and poisonous leaves with a strong odour. Leaves are pinnate or simple and arranged alternately or in whorls. Flowers are five-petalled stars, held in branched clusters, while the fruit has firm flesh surrounding a single seed.

Mango

Mangifera indica

The mango is thought to have been cultivated for more than 4,000 years. Mangoes are most widely grown in India, where legends surround the tree, and numerous varieties have been developed. The genus name comes from a mixture of Hindi and Latin: "mango" is the original Hindi name for the tree and *fera* is the Latin verb "to bear". The fruit of the mango tree is juicy.

Distribution: India to Malaysia. Introduced into Florida and Brazil.
Height: 30m (98ft)
Shape: Domed
Evergreen
Pollinated: Insect
Leaf shape: Lanceolate

Right: The fruit varies greatly in shape, size and colour.

Identification: The trunk is buttressed when mature and carries a dense crown. The drooping leaves are red when young, and deep green and glossy when mature. The flowers appear at the ends of twigs in late winter in loose, branched clusters. Each cluster contains thousands of tiny blossoms, which may be pink, yellow, green, brown or white.

Right: The leaves reach up to 30cm (12in) long.

Cashew Nut

Anacardium occidentale

The tasty, kidney-shaped cashew nut is produced individually inside a fleshy husk. The husk contains an extremely acrid, resinous sap, which can burn human skin. Once the husk is removed, the nuts are roasted, explaining their relatively high price. The stem from which the nut hangs swells into a 10cm- (4in-) long, fleshy, pear-shaped organ, which is red when ripe. Called the "cashew apple", this can also be eaten. The cashew nut tree is fast growing and untidy-looking, and can bear fruit from a young age. The cashew tree favours areas with long, hot dry seasons.

Identification: The bark is light grey to brown. The smooth, leathery leaves are 15cm (6in) long, mid-green and blunt-ended or notched at the tip. The tiny yellow flowers occur early in the wet season in erect, branched clusters at the ends of twigs and branches. They are fragrant at night, and fade to pink when mature. The fruit, which contains a single nut, is grey or brown and 4cm (1½in) long.

Distribution: West Indies and tropical America.
Height: 10m (33ft)
Shape: Spreading, irregular
Evergreen
Pollinated: Insect
Leaf shape: Oval-obovate

Right: The cashew apple grows above the nut. It is eaten raw and is used in a fermented drink.

Brazilian Peppercorn Tree

Christmas berry tree *Schinus terebinthifolius*

All parts of this tree have a spicy scent, and may cause irritation if they come into contact with the skin. The small, pink to red fruit is the pink peppercorn, which is often mixed with green and black peppercorns for taste and decorative effect. The fruit appears at Christmas time, giving the species its other common name, the Christmas berry tree. The tree is fast growing and forms a dense crown of brittle branches, which may naturally ooze sap. It grows readily from seed and has become naturalized in many parts of the world, including Hawaii and Florida, where it is now an invasive weed.

Identification: The leaves are 10–18cm (4–7in) long, dark green and divided into seven blunt-ended, elliptical leaflets (three pairs and one terminal). Each leaflet is 2.5–5cm (1–2in) long and has pale veins. The tiny white or greenish-white flowers form in dense, erect, branched clusters 5–15cm (2–6in) long. The fruit is spherical and 5mm (¼in) across.

Distribution: Tropical Central and South America.
Height: 9m (30ft)
Shape: Rounded
Evergreen
Pollinated: Insect
Leaf shape: Pinnate

Left: The pink "peppercorn" fruit is produced in abundance. It does not have a peppery flavour, rather a sweet, subtle taste, but looks very similar to peppercorns.

OTHER SPECIES OF NOTE
Pepper Tree *Schinus molle*
Native to the deserts of Peru's Andean region, this tree thrives in sandy, dry places in tropical and temperate regions, and may become a pest. It grows quickly to 15m (50ft) tall and has a rounded crown, graceful weeping branches and fine blue-green, pinnate foliage. The small, pink fruit may be substituted for peppercorns.

Hog Plum *Spondias mombin*
This handsome tree occurs wild in rainforest areas of the West Indies, Central America and northern South America. The orange to yellow fruit forms in clusters and tastes acidic, often with an unpleasant flavour similar to the smell of paint thinner. The tree has thick, fissured, pale cinnamon bark on a heavy trunk and a spreading crown of light green, pinnate foliage.

Yellow Mombin *Spondias dulcis*
This tree reaches just 9m (30ft) tall and may grow as a large, sprawling shrub. It comes from tropical America and the West Indies and has 10–25cm- (4–10in-) long, light green, pinnate leaves. The branched clusters of tiny pink or purple flowers appear in spring and produce small, yellow, orange, red or purple fruit with an acidic, plum-like flavour. See also page 476.

Purple Mombin

Purple-plum *Spondias purpurea*

This is a small tree, with edible fruit that resembles small plums in both appearance and flavor. It is widely distributed in tropical America, and commonly planted in southern Florida, and also throughout most of the Caribbean. The fruit can be eaten raw, or cooked, or incorporated into wine or other alcoholic drinks. In some parts of Central America, including Mexico, this is one of the major fruits. It is a handsome tree, with spreading branches and clusters of pink or red flowers.

Distribution: Mexico, Peru, Brazil; naturalized through the West Indies; introduced to Florida and parts of the Old World tropics.
Height: 9m (30ft)
Shape: Spreading
Deciduous
Pollinated: Insect
Leaf shape: Pinnate

Below: The small, plum-like fruit is edible, but has a rather sour taste.

Identification: The bark is grey or brown and smooth, turning rougher on older wood, and the branches are large, but somewhat brittle. The alternate leaves are pinnate and have up to 25 thin, yellowish-green leaflets. Flowers develop in clusters (panicles), and are small, five-lobed and red or pink.

MAHOGANY FAMILY

This family includes many important timber trees, some with sweetly scented wood. It also contains trees and shrubs with edible fruit or valuable seeds. The Meliaceae are tropical or subtropical trees and shrubs with pinnate or bipinnate leaves. The flowers have four or five petals and appear in branched clusters. The leathery-skinned fruit often contains seeds with wings.

Mahogany

Swietenia mahagoni

Distribution: Central America and West Indies.
Height: 20m (66ft)
Shape: Rounded
Evergreen
Pollinated: Insect
Leaf shape: Pinnate

This very slow-growing, long-lived tree is famous for its hard, red, glowing timber, which polishes to a high shine. It has been a favourite choice of cabinet-makers ever since it was first discovered in the 17th century, and is now threatened in the wild due to over-collection. In some places it is grown as a shade or avenue tree, as it spreads out when fully mature. It is cultivated throughout the tropics and flourishes in drier climates, such as that of India.

Identification: The buttressed trunk has dark, reddish-brown, scaly bark and carries a crown that becomes open when the tree reaches maturity. The leaves have five to seven pairs of 7cm- (2¾in-) long, ovate to sickle-shaped, dark green leaflets. The insignificant flowers are greenish-yellow or white, scented and form in branched clusters from the leaf axils in spring and summer.

Right: The fruit is an oval, woody capsule, 10cm (4in) across, and contains 45–55 winged seeds.

Chinaberry

Bead tree *Melia azedarach*

In India this tree is venerated and grown for its pretty, honey-scented flowers, which are used as temple offerings. It is often called the "bead tree", as its poisonous seeds have a hole through them, making them ideal for threading. It was once grown in Italy specifically for the making of rosaries. The chinaberry is a short-lived tree that grows quickly and easily in dry tropical and subtropical areas. In some places it is considered a weed.

Identification: The trunk has smooth, thin, dark purplish or greyish-brown bark and carries brittle branches crowded with 50cm- (20in-) long leaves. The leaves have three to five pairs of pinnae, each with three to five pairs of leaflets. The leaflets are mid- to light green, ovate and have toothed margins. The flowers appear in large, branched clusters, which sprout from the leaf axils in spring. Each flower is pale pink with a dark purple tube at the centre and up to 2cm (¾in) wide. The fruit appears in autumn; it is oval, pale yellow and 2.5cm (1in) long.

Distribution: From Iraq to Japan to Australia. Naturalized in the south-eastern USA.
Height: 12m (40ft)
Shape: Spreading
Deciduous
Pollinated: Bee
Leaf shape: Bipinnate or tripinnate

Right: Toothed leaves.

Left: The chinaberry may produce its fragrant flowers all year round, and from a very young age.

American Muskwood

Trompillo *Guarea trichilioides*

One of the commonest trees in moist forests of Puerto Rico, where it is also found in coffee plantations. It has been introduced to southern Florida, where it serves as a useful shade tree. It regenerates quickly and also withstands the shade of taller trees. The timber has a pretty grain and takes polish well, and is used for furniture, as well as for general building.

Right: The seed capsules (above right) grow close to the flower clusters.

Identification: A large tree with a dense crown, and large leaves with up to 20 dark green, rather glossy leaflets. The bark is brown or reddish and rough, with longitudinal fissures. The lateral flower clusters (panicles) consist of many, small, fragrant greenish-white flowers, maturing into red-brown, followed by rounded seed capsules, which dangle rather like bunches of grapes.

Distribution: Cuba, Hispaniola, Trinidad, Costa Rica, Panama, Brazil and Argentina. Introduced to Florida.
Height: 23m (75ft)
Shape: Spreading
Evergreen
Pollinated: Insect
Leaf shape: Pinnate

OTHER SPECIES OF NOTE

Honduran Mahogany
Swietenia macrophylla
Once an important timber tree in Central and South America, the Honduran mahogany is incredibly valuable. It grows in lowland rainforests but huge areas have now been depleted due to over-collection. Unfortunately, this species is difficult to establish in plantations, due to pests. It grows with a straight, buttressed trunk to 45m (150ft) tall and has rough, brown bark. The pinnate leaves are 38cm (15in) long and have up to six pairs of leaflets. The flowers are insignificant, but the woody, brown fruit is 15cm (6in) across and hangs on 30cm (12in) stems.

Broomstick *Trichilia hirta*
This is a small deciduous tree with a dense rounded crown, and alternate, pinnate leaves. It grows on the islands of the Caribbean and in Mexico, Ecuador, Peru, Brazil and Venezuela, and like many tropical species has also been introduced to Florida, where it provides both shade and honey. In Venezuela the wood was used for making paddles and oars. It grows to about 15m (50ft), and the trunk has rough, furrowed bark. The alternate, pinnate leaves are shiny and green, and slightly hairy beneath. The fragrant flowers are small and greenish-white, in narrow clusters (panicles) towards the ends of the twigs, and the fruits are rounded and greenish-brown.

Cigar Box Cedar

Jamaican cedar *Cedrela mexicana*

This tree produces a mahogany-like timber, which is used for cabinets and cigar boxes. The wood is light reddish-brown, aromatic and termite-resistant. The cigar box cedar is sometimes called the Jamaican or Honduran cedar, and has been over-exploited in its native forests. The genus name *Cedrela* was given because of the similarity of the wood's scent to that of true cedars, *Cedrus*. The cigar box tree is fast growing, has brittle branches and forms an untidy, thin, open crown.

Identification: The trunk has pale brown bark and reaches 90cm (36in) wide. The leaves are up to 60cm (24in) long and divided into between six and eight pairs of leaflets. Each leaflet is oblong to elliptic, smooth, pale green and up to 12cm (4½in) long. The small, white flowers appear at the ends of twigs and branches in pyramidal branched clusters 30cm (12in) long. The fruit is hard, brown, oblong, 4.5cm- (1¾in-) long pods, which split open to release winged seeds.

Distribution: West Indies and Central and South America.
Height: 35m (115ft)
Shape: Narrow
Evergreen
Pollinated: Insect
Leaf shape: Pinnate

Above: The woody fruit takes nine to ten months to develop. When ripe it splits into five sections revealing a woody, central core and numerous winged seeds.

CITRUS FAMILY

Many of these plants are strongly scented, often with a citrus-like aroma, and yield valuable oils. The oils are found in translucent glands, often visible in the flowers, fruit, leaves and bark. The Rutaceae family is composed mostly of trees and shrubs, a number of which have thorns, but throughout the family botanical features are highly variable.

Satinwood

Yellowheart *Zanthoxylum flavum*

A medium-size tree found mainly in the Caribbean region, and highly valued for its decorative wood, which has a satiny sheen, and is used for making fine furniture, veneers and panelling. Exploitation for its timber has sadly diminished stocks to the point where native stands are increasingly rare. It is, however, also planted for shade, and as a honey source.

Below: The leaves are arranged opposite on the twig. The flowers and fruit grow in clusters.

Identification: The bark of this tree is thin and grey and rather smooth, and the inner bark has a distinct citrus taste. The young twigs are hairy, and the branched flower clusters (panicles) are made up of small, yellowish, five-lobed, fragrant flowers. Male and female flowers are borne on separate trees (the tree is dioecious). The fruit is a small, stalked pod containing a single shiny black seed.

Distribution: Bermuda, Bahamas, Cuba, Hispaniola, Puerto Rico, Lesser Antilles, Jamaica. Also reported from Florida Keys, where it is very rare and restricted to just a handful of locations.
Height: 15m (50ft)
Shape: Spreading
Evergreen
Pollinated: Insect
Leaf shape: Pinnate

Lime

Citrus aurantifolia

Distribution: East Indies (native); introduced in Mexico, West Indies, Florida and parts of South America.
Height: 6m (20ft)
Shape: Variable
Evergreen
Pollinated: Insect
Leaf shape: Elliptic

This familiar citrus tree is best known for its small, green fruit, which is widely used in flavouring, and for making drinks, and in cooking, and also for dyeing and in medicine. Oil from the rind and seeds is also used for making soap. Lime fruit is sharp, but sweeter than lemon. Although it is native to the East Indies, it was introduced to the New World (especially the Caribbean) more than 400 years ago, and this is now the main area of production, along with southern Florida. The fruit is picked and shipped young, and travels well. The flowers are attractive to honeybees.

Identification: A small spiny, aromatic tree or shrub with shiny, leathery green leaves and small (compared with other citrus fruits) green fruits, turning yellowish when fully ripe. The whitish flowers are softly fragrant, and each has four or five petals.

Left: The lime fruit is similar to a lemon, but smaller and with a greener colouring.

LIGNUM VITAE AND INCENSE-TREE FAMILIES

The lignum vitae family (Zygophyllaceae) contains about 285 species of mostly tropical trees, shrubs and herbs, many found in arid areas. Their stems are often swollen at the nodes. The 540 species of the incense-tree family (Burseraceae) are tropical trees or shrubs, mostly from the Americas, or found in northeast Africa. Their bark is usually rich in resins.

Lignum Vitae

Guaiacum officinale

The wood of this pretty, extremely slow-growing tree has outstanding characteristics. It is possibly the heaviest wood in the world, weighing 1,307kg per cu m (67lb per cu ft). It even sinks in water. It is the hardest wood used commercially and has a high content of oily resin. The latter gives a good level of lubrication, lending the wood resistance to rot, termites, fungus, borers and harsh chemicals. It is particularly favoured for use on boats, where bearings of this wood will outlive metal. The name *lignum vitae* translates as "wood of life"; in 16th-century Europe the tree was thought to have great healing properties. Due to over-harvesting these trees are now facing a very high risk of extinction in the wild.

Identification: The short trunk has dark grey bark and may ooze greenish resin. The crown is dense. The 10cm- (4in-) long leaves are composed of four to six obovate, blunt- ended, 2.5cm- (1in-) long leathery leaflets. The beautiful, fragrant, felty flowers appear twice a year, and are 2.5cm (1in) across with four or five petals. The fruit is often seen with the flowers, and is yellow or orange, heart-shaped with a moist leathery skin and 2.5cm (1in) across.

Distribution: West Indies, Panama, Colombia and Venezuela.
Height: 9m (30ft)
Shape: Spreading
Evergreen
Pollinated: Insect
Leaf shape: Pinnate

Far left: The deep blue flowers fade to silvery blue.

Left: The colourful fruit holds up to five hard, oblong seeds.

Incense Tree

Gumbo-limbo *Bursera simaruba*

A fine, spreading tree with aromatic foliage and a smooth, coppery bark, which characteristically peels off in flakes, revealing the newer bark beneath, which is greenish-brown. The bark exudes a grey resin, which smells of paint thinner. This resin is used in making glue, varnish, and incense. It has also been used as a traditional medicine. An attractive tree, it is often planted along roads or as an ornamental, notably in Florida. The timber is used for light carpentry, plywood and matches.

Identification: A thick-trunked tree with sturdy, spreading branches. The small, whitish or yellow-green flowers are five-lobed and arranged in terminal or lateral clusters (panicles). The angled, pointed fruit splits into three when ripe, to release the pale seeds.

Distribution: Southern Florida, West Indies from Bahamas and Cuba to Trinidad and Tobago; Mexico to Colombia, Venezuela, Guyana.
Height: 12m (40ft)
Shape: Spreading
Deciduous
Pollinated: Insect
Leaf shape: Pinnate

Left: The small flowers develop into pointed fruits.

Right: The leaves, which also smell when crushed, are pinnate, and about 20cm (8in) long.

BUTTONWOOD FAMILY

The Combretaceae family includes trees, climbers and shrubs. Its members vary significantly and have few consistent features. Many of the trees have large yet narrow buttresses and yellow inner bark, and the flowers usually have greatly reduced petals and protruding anthers. The fruit, which is dry, is dispersed by water or wind, and has wing-like structures protruding from it.

White Buttonwood

White-mangrove *Laguncularia racemosa*

Distribution: Coasts of tropical America, from Mexico to Ecuador, Peru, and Brazil, southern Florida, Bermuda, and most of West Indies; also in west Africa.
Height: 12m (40ft)
Shape: Variable
Evergreen
Pollinated: Insect
Leaf shape: Elliptic

Like other mangroves, this tree grows mainly in salt or brackish water on muddy and silty shorelines. It is fast growing, often reaching maturity and flowering in less than two years. It also sprouts vigorously after cutting, and trees may therefore develop rather tangled shapes. The strong, heavy timber is used for making tool handles, posts, and in general construction. The fleshy, rapidly germinating fruit floats when it falls into water, and this is its main means of dispersal.

Left: Like those of many species growing in salty conditions, the leaves are tough and leathery.

Identification: The bark of this mangrove is grey-brown and rough, with a paler, bitter inner bark. The leaves are opposite, leathery and rounded, being yellow-green, with reddish stalks. The pale, bell-shaped flowers develop in clusters (panicles), and are fragrant. The rather fleshy fruit is green, turning brown when ripe, and each one has a single large seed.

Tropical Almond

Terminalia catappa

The nuts of this tree are incredibly hard and popular with humans and animals. The tree is highly tolerant of salt, and is often grown along beaches to provide shade and help stabilize the soil. Its reddish timber is used for boat construction. The tropical almond is a good-looking tree with horizontal tiers of foliage that spread out to make it wider than it is tall. It thrives in tropical cities throughout the USA.

Identification: The trunk is short and dark, and the smooth, glossy leaves cluster towards the branch tips. The leaves are deep green turning bright orange, red or purple before dropping at any time of year. The flowers occur mostly in summer on 23cm- (9in-) long spikes, produced near the branch tips. The fruit is greenish-yellow or red, almond shaped and 5cm (2in) long.

Above: The inconspicuous but fragrant flowers are greenish-white to cream.

Left and right: Leaves are leathery and 30cm (12in) long.

Distribution: Tropical coastal Asia.
Height: 24m (80ft)
Shape: Spreading
Deciduous
Pollinated: Insect
Leaf shape: Obovate

IVY FAMILY

The ivy family, Araliaceae, spans temperate and tropical regions and encompasses trees, shrubs, climbers
and herbs. Some are prickly, and in tropical countries may be epiphytic or semi-epiphytic. They are
grown for their foliage yet often have an unpleasant scent. Their alternate leaves vary immensely, whereas
flowers are more distinctive, small and usually in umbels. The fruit is often a small, black berry.

Matchwood

Morototo *Didymopanax (Schefflera) morototoni*

A distinctive, rather umbrella-
shaped tall tree of wet tropical
forests, it has a smooth, grey,
unbranched trunk topped by
a crown of radiating branches
bearing large, palmately
compound leaves. Although the wood is
used for building, it is susceptible to termite attack,
and is therefore more suitable for crates, plywood
or matchsticks.

Identification: The bark bears faint horizontal markings, and
the inner bark has a distinctive spicy flavour. Each leaf has
a long, strong stalk and has usually 10 or 11 oblong leaflets,
each about 30cm (12in) in length. The leaves are alternate
and grow close together. The flowers, which have white,
somewhat pointed, petals, grow in broad, umbel-like
panicles. The fruit is a flattened berry, containing a pair
of brown, flat seeds.

Below: Birds feed
on the fruits
and help to
disperse the
seeds.

Distribution: Widespread
from southern Florida
(planted) through West Indies
to Mexico, Guyana, Bolivia,
Brazil and Argentina.
Height: 18m (60ft)
Shape: Spreading
Evergreen
Pollinated: Insect
Leaf Shape: Linear

Above: The white
flowers of this tree
grow in spreading
clusters.

Left: The leaves are large
and long-stalked, with
spreading leaflets.

Pollo

Angelica tree *Dendropanax arboreus*

Distribution: Widespread
from southern Florida
(planted) through West Indies
to Mexico, Colombia,
Venezuela, Peru and Bolivia.
Height: 12m (40ft)
Shape: Spreading
Evergreen
Pollinated: Insect
Leaf Shape: Ovate

This widespread, medium-size tree is
typically found in lower
mountain tropical forests,
but is also planted,
sometimes to give shade
to crops of coffee. In
some areas the leaves and
roots have been used in
traditional medicine.
Extracts have been
found to be cytotoxic, and
this species is being tested for
anti-cancer compounds. The
flowers are attractive
to honeybees and
other insects.

Identification: The bark
is grey, and often warty,
and the green twigs
turn grey with age. The
leaves are alternate,
and have long,
green stalks with
blades up to
20cm (8in) long
and 9cm (3½in) in
width. The flowers
are tiny, with yellow
petals, in tight clusters
(a raceme of umbels). The
fruit, a rounded, fleshy berry,
is pale green at first,
gradually ripening
to black.

Right: The flowers are
small and in dense
clusters.

Left: The seeds are mainly
dispersed by birds.

FRANGIPANI FAMILY

This family is renowned for its toxic properties. Plants contain a large quantity of poisonous, milky latex, which, in some species, is of value to humans. The family is also valuable for its contribution to ornamental horticulture. Most of the Apocynaceae are tropical, and many are shrubs. The simple leaves are usually opposite, the five-petalled flowers are funnel-shaped and the fruit is usually dry and in pairs.

Frangipani

Plumeria rubra

The legendary frangipani is regarded as one of the world's most beautifully scented flowers. It is thought a botanist named Frangipani first distilled the perfume in the sixteenth century, hence the common name. The trees are found growing in temple grounds of Buddhists, Hindus and even Muslims, and the flowers are used as offerings. In Hawaii garlands made of these flowers are used on special occasions, and to greet visitors. Although the flowers may be white, red, yellow or pink, the form *P. rubra* f. *acutifolia,* with white flowers with golden centres, is most widely planted.

Identification: The fleshy round stems are rubbery and green when young, woody and pale grey when mature. Branching is sparse and candelabra-like. The thick, 30cm-12in-) long leaves with paler midribs cluster at the branch tips. The 8cm- (3in-) wide twisted flowers form in terminal clusters. The fruit grows in pairs of 15cm- (6in-) long leathery pods.

Distribution: Southern Mexico to Panama.
Height: 8m (26ft)
Shape: Domed
Semi-evergreen
Pollinated: Insect and self
Leaf shape: Elliptic-obovate

Above left: The leaves are long and tapering.

Left: Each funnel-shaped flower has five waxy petals and an intoxicating perfume.

West Indian Jasmine

Milk tree *Plumeria alba*

This small tree gets one of its common names from the abundant milky juice that exudes when it is cut. It is found wild only on some of the islands of the West Indies, and does not appear to be much cultivated, despite its attractive appearance. The white, or cream species that is often grown, is in fact a colour variant of *P. rubra*. The light brown wood is hard, heavy and tough. It is usually used only as fuel, but where the trunk is of sufficient size it can be useful for carpentry.

Identification: The trunk rarely exceeds 10cm (4in) in diameter, and with only a few branches it often resembles a shrub. The stout, yet soft, rather brittle branches end in a cluster of think, leathery leaves, up to 38cm (15in) long but only about 5cm (2in) wide. They are shiny green above, white and densely hairy beneath, with downturned margins. The flower stalks, up to 20cm (8in) long, bear a flattened cluster of very fragrant, waxy, white flowers. The fruit is about 15cm (6in) long and 1cm (½in) wide, and contain numerous flat, winged seeds.

Distribution: Puerto Rico; Lesser Antilles.
Height: 5m (16½ft)
Shape: Variable
Evergreen
Pollinated: Insect
Leaf shape: Narrow, tapering

Left and right: The flowers can be 5cm (2in) long and broad, and if successfully pollinated they develop into a pair of brown pod-like follicles.

White Frangipani

Plumeria obtusa

One of the most popular frangipanis is this 8m- (26ft-) tall evergreen tree from Mexico and the Caribbean islands. It is endowed with intensely fragrant, pure white blossoms. The fragrant, waxy, flower clusters appear on long stalks between the terminal bunches of leaves. As with other frangipanis, the flowers develop all year round in constantly wet areas, or in the wet season only in monsoon areas. The attractive leaves are dark green, glossy, obovate and 15–30cm (6–12in) long. Dwarfing varieties have been developed to be more shrub-like. Although not seen as often in cultivation as *P. rubra*, it is an attractive shrub or tree.

Identification: The trunk grows to a diameter of about 25cm (10in), and has grey, smooth or slightly furrowed bark. The green twigs, which turn grey as they age, produce abundant milky white latex, which is sometimes irritating to the skin.

Distribution: Mexico (Yucatán), Honduras, Bahamas, Cuba, Hispaniola, Puerto Rico, Jamaica.
Height: 4.5–12m (15–40ft)
Shape: Variable
Evergreen
Pollinated: Insect
Leaf shape: Obovate, notched at tip

Left: Each flower produces two long pods, which split open to release many flat, winged seeds.

OTHER SPECIES OF NOTE
Palo Rosa *Aspidosperma polyneuron*
This magnificent tree, native to central Brazil, Paraguay and north-east Argentina, grows to 42m (140ft) tall, with a straight trunk for the first 20–30m (66–100ft), and a diameter of 1.5m (5ft). Its thick bark is ash-grey or slightly reddish, with deep, more or less parallel fissures. This is topped by a crown of twisted branches, which divide repeatedly down to the smallest branchlets. The evergreen leaves are simple, rather leathery and very variable in shape. The small whitish or yellowish flowers are followed by woody fruit containing numerous winged seeds. The wood is hard, fairly heavy, strong and resistant, and is used for furniture and building.

Quebracho Blanco *Aspidosperma quebracho-blanco*
This tree can grow to about 25m (85ft), and like the previous species it has a straight lower trunk, but in this case branching occurs from about half way up, ending in an irregular conical crown. The leaves are evergreen, lanceolate and spine-tipped. The scented yellowish-white flowers develop in clusters from September to January, and produce grey-green woody capsules, 7–12cm (2¾–4½in) in length, containing numerous roundish seeds. The wood is heavy and hard, and the bark contains tannin and other medicinal substances.

Yellow Oleander

Thevetia peruviana

The sap and fruit are extremely poisonous, and yet the deadly poisonous seeds contain beneficial chemicals that are extracted for use in heart medicines. Curiously the seeds are also thought to be lucky, and are carried as charms or worn as pendants. In addition to the typical yellow flowers, forms exist with white, orange or apricot flowers. In some plants they are pleasantly scented, while others have no scent. Often used as a fast-growing hedge or screen, the foliage gives an unusual, soft appearance.

Distribution: South-east Mexico, Belize and the West Indies.
Height: 9m (30ft)
Shape: Domed
Evergreen
Pollinated: Insect
Leaf shape: Lanceolate

Above and right: The foliage is evergreen, and the flowers appear all year round.

Identification: The brown trunk is often multi-stemmed and rarely upright. The bright green, glossy leaves cluster at the tips of the branches forming a dense crown. Each leaf is 10–15cm (4–6in) long. The terminal clusters of a few flowers appear throughout the year. Each flower is tubular-shaped and 8cm (3in) long. The fruit is a rounded, four-sided, 4cm- (1½in-) wide, hard, fleshy pod. When ripe it is black.

POTATO FAMILY

The important potato family, Solanaceae, is very large and contains nearly 3,000 species; it is found worldwide, but especially in South America. It contains trees, shrubs, lianes and herbs, including the familiar potato and tomato. Although parts of certain species may be edible, it's worth stressing that many contain poisons.

Lady-of-the-Night

Brunfelsia americana

This shrub or small tree is very popular with gardeners, chiefly because of its masses of attractive cream flowers, which are some of the most fragrant of the family. The scent develops in the evening, and lasts all through the night, attracting moths. It thrives and flowers best in humid conditions, and the perfume is reported to be detectable from 30m (100ft) away. Flowering is in cycles, with hundreds opening together. Growth is straight, with moderate branching and pruning is unnecessary, making this an ideal garden shrub or tree. In the wild it is found in moist, coastal forests, from sea level to about 600m (2,000ft).

Identification: The alternate leaves are borne on short side twigs, and are shiny above. The flowers are solitary, the large corolla emerging from the bell-shaped calyx as a narrow tube 5cm (2in) in length, with five rounded, spreading lobes about 4cm (1½in) across. The fruit (reputedly poisonous) is round, yellow, and contains brown seeds.

Right: The enormous flowers are a spectacular feature of this tree.

Distribution: Hispaniola, Puerto Rico, Virgin Islands, Lesser Antilles; planted in southern Florida, Colombia and Venezuela.
Height: 4.5m (15ft)
Shape: Variable
Evergreen
Pollinated: Insect
Leaf shape: Elliptic to obovate

Tree Potato

Solanum wrightii

This incredibly fast-growing tree has been recorded at 9m (30ft) high with an equal spread in only two years. Inevitably this cannot last, and trees are said to lose their condition after only four years. The flowers open as deep purple and fade to white over a couple of days. As they are in clusters and appear throughout the year, the tree almost always has a colourful collection of purple, mauve and white flowers. In some gardens it is kept pruned as a shrub; this treatment inhibits flowering but extends the life, and encourages the hairy, ornamental leaves to become huge.

Identification: The soft-wooded, pale grey trunk is often multi-stemmed. The bright green leaves vary enormously in size depending on the way the plant is grown: as shrubs they can reach 45cm (18in) in length, but as trees they are more normally 25cm (10in) long. Each is deeply incised into angular lobes and covered in coarse hairs. The midrib and main veins carry thorns. The round fruit is 5cm (2in) across, and orange-yellow to brown when ripe. It contains four cavities filled with pulp and flat seeds.

Distribution: Bolivia and adjoining area of tropical Brazil.
Height: 12m (40ft)
Shape: Domed
Evergreen
Pollinated: Insect
Leaf shape: Ovate

Left: The flowers are crumpled up in bud. When open they are 8cm (3in) across and have a cluster of central golden stamens. They have five petals and form in small clusters.

BORAGE FAMILY

The majority of the Boraginaceae family are herbs with just a few trees, shrubs and climbers included. Many of the woody species are tropical. They have simple, hairy leaves, usually alternately arranged and smooth edged. Stems are often covered in stiff hairs, too. The five-petalled flowers are occasionally solitary, but more often in cymes. The fruit has one to four seeds and is usually dry and hard.

Salmwood

Cordia alliadora

This attractive, fast-growing yet long-lived pioneer species is often found on disturbed land within humid and dry regions. It is grown throughout its native range for its quality timber, used in numerous products including veneers, furniture, and boat and housing construction. The flowers are a major source of nectar for eekeeping, producing a thick, pale honey. The crushed leaves have a distinctive onion-like odour. Some trees have hollow, swollen nodes, which are inhabited by ants.

Identification: The thin trunk, which may have small buttresses, has smooth, pale grey or brown bark, and carries a thin, open crown. The dark green leaves reach 18cm (7in) and are covered in hairs below. Flowers appear mostly in summer, and a large tree may produce as many as 10 million in one season. They are 1cm (½in) long and in 10–30cm-(4–12in-) long inflorescences. The dry, brown fruit is up to 1cm (½in) long with a parachute formed from the expanded petals.

Distribution: Northern Mexico through to northern Argentina and Paraguay and the islands of Cuba to Trinidad.
Height: 40m (130ft)
Shape: Oblong
Evergreen
Pollinated: Insect
Leaf shape: Elliptic

Left: Trees can flower from as young as two years, although viable seed is produced only from five-year-old trees. In mature specimens, up to one million seeds can be produced annually.

Geiger Tree

Cordia sebestena

The attraction of this tree lies in its virtually continual succession of bright vermilion flowers, and its tolerance of dry conditions and salt-laden air. It is a popular ornamental tree in gardens and streets throughout its native range. It is sometimes also grown as a shrub. In addition, the tree has a number of medicinal uses, particularly in relation to breathing difficulties. The sweet, edible fruit is used in some areas as a remedy for coughs, while the bark, flowers or fruit may be used to make a sugary syrup.

Identification: The trunk is rarely straight and may be multi-stemmed. Interestingly, the stiff leaves are hairy and rough on the upper surface and smooth below. They are also dark green above and paler below, 15cm (6in) long and may have a slightly toothed margin. The veins are paler than the leaf and depressed on the upper surface. Each flower is funnel-shaped, 4cm (1½in) long and a similar width. The petals are crinkled like crepe, and there are central yellow stamens. The flowers are in terminal clusters and are particularly abundant in the summer. The white fruit is oval and 1cm (½in) long.

Distribution: West Indies and Venezuela.
Height: 8m (26ft)
Shape: Oblong to spreading (variable)
Evergreen
Pollinated: Insect
Leaf shape: Ovate

Left: The clusters of flowers include bisexual and male ones; the male flowers are smaller but occur in a greater numbers.

TEAK FAMILY

This large family contains well-known and useful plants. It is found mostly in the Southern Hemisphere and includes herbs, climbers, shrubs and trees, some of which are aromatic. Verbenaceae often have square-shaped twigs, and flowers with a long tube divided into five petals. The fruit is a hard capsule or fleshy with a hard stone, divided into four sections, each with one seed.

Teak

Tectona grandis

The wonderful hard timber of the teak tree was first taken to Europe in the early 1800s and has been introduced in the USA. It has remained a popular choice for quality furniture production ever since. As a result, the monsoon forests of which it is a native have been stripped of their specimens. Originally elephants would have been used to shift the timber before it was floated downriver out of the forest. Now, the fast-growing teak is planted in large plantations across its indigenous area.

Identification: The straight trunk carries many tiered branches and has pale grey, soft, fissured, peeling bark. The leaves are of colossal size, up to 80cm (32in) long and 40cm (16in) wide, with undulating margins and prominent veining. They are rough and leathery, mid-green above and covered in soft white hairs below. The tiny cream flowers are found in large panicles 45cm (18in) long in early summer. The fleshy fruit is round, 2cm (¾in) across and purplish-red or brown.

Right: The old bark peels off in small, thin, oblong pieces, revealing the yellow inner bark.

Left: The flowers appear after the tree has put on its new leaves in the wet season.

Distribution: Tropical India to Vietnam. Tropical America.
Height: 35m (115ft)
Shape: Oblong
Deciduous
Pollinated: Insect
Leaf shape: Widely elliptical

Florida Fiddlewood

Citharexylum fruticosum

This small, slender tree or shrub is often planted in gardens, hedgerows or alongside roads as an ornamental, and its fragrant flowers are attractive to honeybees. It is moderately salt-tolerant and is therefore often planted near the shore, where it grows well on sandy soils. Fiddlewood has heavy, close-grained timber, mainly used for rough building and fences, although, as may be guessed from its name, it has been used for musical instruments, including violins.

Right: The showy white flowers appear in the summer months, and provide a striking contrast with the leaves.

Identification: The young twigs have a characteristic four-angled shape. The leaves are opposite, and yellow-green with yellow or orange stalks. The flowers are borne in clusters (racemes), and the individual flowers are small, with a five-lobed white corolla. The fleshy fruit dangles down in tight clusters and is attractive to birds and other wildlife. Flowering and fruiting is throughout the year.

Distribution: Central Florida, south to West Indies; Venezuela to Surinam.
Height: 12m (40ft)
Shape: Variable, slender
Evergreen
Pollinated: Insect
Leaf shape: Elliptic

QUININE FAMILY

This is an important and virtually wholly tropical family of trees, shrubs, climbers and herbaceous plants. A number of the genus Rubiaceae have economic and/or ornamental value. The family is easy to recognize. Leaves always have smooth margins, and are most often arranged as opposites. Flowers are usually tubular with four or five flared petals, and the fruit is usually divided into two sections.

Quinine Tree

Cinchona officinalis

Distribution: Ecuador and Peru.
Height: 10m (33ft)
Shape: Oblong to rounded
Evergreen
Pollinated: Insect and hummingbird
Leaf shape: Ovate-lanceolate

One of the most important medicinal discoveries of all time was the quinine tree. The bark of *Cinchona* plants has provided the antimalarial drug "quinine" since at least 1638, when it cured the Countess of Cinchon in Peru. Commercial plantations were not developed though until the 1800s in India and Asia. After World War II synthetic antimalarial drugs were developed, but due to a build-up of resistance, quinine continues, to some extent, to be used. The trees naturally grow in humid lowland forests.

Identification: There is great variation within each *Cinchona* species, and hybrids are readily produced. The leaves of *C. officinalis* are generally smooth, shiny, mid-green and 7.5–15cm (3–6in) long. The tubular flowers vary from red to pale pink. They are covered in fine, silky hair, are often heavily fragrant, and found in terminal and axillary panicles. The ovoid fruit is 1.5cm (⅝in) long, and splits into two to release numerous winged seeds.

Right: The cinchona bark is usually harvested by either coppicing the trees every six years, or by carefully shaving the bark off two sides of the trunk at any one time, without damaging the cambium.

Genipap

Jagua *Genipa americana*

This widespread tree is frequently planted for shade and ornament, but also for the edible fruit and useful timber. It is also attractive to honeybees. The juice of the young fruit has been used as a dye, notably by Native Americans. The juice has been investigated for its antibiotic properties. The wood has a range of uses: tools, boxes, furniture, veneers, chests, barrels and shipbuilding. The foliage is eaten by cattle, and the bark, rich in tannin, is used for curing leather.

Identification: A medium-size tree with an upright trunk, and large, dark green, opposite leaves. The flowers are large, five-lobed and pale yellow, in short, terminal clusters. The yellow-brown fruit has sour, edible flesh, sweetening slightly when over-ripe, and contains several flat seeds.

Distribution: Cuba, Hispaniola, Puerto Rico, Lesser Antilles, Trinidad and Tobago; Mexico south to Ecuador, Peru, Bolivia, Brazil, and Argentina.
Height: 18m (60ft)
Shape: Spreading
Deciduous
Pollinated: Insect
Leaf Shape: Elliptic

Far left: The ripe fruit makes tasty preserves, sour refreshing drinks, as well as various alcoholic drinks, when fermented.

JACARANDA FAMILY

Bignoniaceae is one of the more readily recognized families. Its members are native to the tropics and subtropics and include trees, shrubs, a few herbs and many climbing plants. Their funnel-shaped flowers are usually found in clusters and are some of the most flamboyant. Their compound leaves are opposite. The fruit is normally long, splitting into two to release numerous flat, winged seeds.

Candle Tree

Parmentiera cerifera

This tree is grown for the oddity of its fruit, which hangs in great abundance from the trunk and branches of mature trees. The fruit has a distinctive apple-like scent and bears a strong resemblance to old-fashioned, hand-dipped candles, which is how the common name came about. In its native habitat the fruit is eaten and in many areas it is used as cattle fodder.

Identification: The tree often has many trunks and may grow as a large shrub. The leaves drop only briefly and consist of three ovate leaflets, each less than 2cm (¾in) long, and have a winged leaf stem. The waxy flowers appear individually or in groups directly from the trunk and larger branches throughout the year. They are bell-shaped, pale greenish- to creamy yellow, up to 7cm (2¾in) long and open in the evening. The smooth, fleshy, cylindrical fruit is pale yellow, measures up to 60cm (24in) long and appears mostly in the drier months.

Distribution: Panama.
Height: 8m (26ft)
Shape: Rounded
Deciduous
Pollinated: Bat
Leaf shape: Trifoliate

Left: The candle-shape fruit has very waxy skin. Unusually for this family it does not split open.

Far left: The leaves turn yellow when they fall from the trees.

Left: These unusual-looking trees are said to have medicinal properties. They have spread from their cultivated areas and become naturalized in Australia.

Calabash Tree

Crescentia cujete

Calabashes are gourds, and were originally used as water carriers, but are now more likely to be seen as musical instruments, cups, ornaments or bags. Calabash maracas still feature in Afro-Caribbean music. The fruit is hollowed out, highly polished and often carved on the outside. To make an hourglass or other shapes, the fruit is tied with string while immature.

Right: Calabashes are green while immature, ripening through yellow to brown.

Identification: The short trunk has fissured, light grey bark and carries a dense to open crown of heavily foliaged, rarely branched, long, spreading, semi-pendulous branches. The leaves are in clusters of three to five, and they jut out along the length of the branches in an inelegant fashion. Each leaf is dark green, glossy and 10–15cm (4–6in) long. The unpleasantly scented flowers form directly from the trunk and larger branches; they are off-white with purple markings and 5cm (2in) long. The fruit is ovoid or round, brown when ripe and up to 30cm (12in) long.

Distribution: Throughout Central America, northern South America, West Indies and southern Mexico.
Height: 13m (43ft)
Shape: Spreading
Evergreen
Pollinated: Bat
Leaf shape: Obovate

Jacaranda

Jacaranda mimosifolia

Distribution: Paraguay, southern Brazil and northern Argentina.
Height: 15m (50ft)
Shape: Domed
Deciduous
Pollinated: Insect
Leaf shape: Bipinnate

While leafless, the clear mauve flowers of the jacaranda cover the crown, creating a unique and unforgettable sight. The flowers fall to form a blue carpet below. In addition, this fast-growing tree has delicate ferny foliage justifying its use as a pot plant and in gardens of humid tropical areas, where it flowers less reliably. This is one of the rare trees commonly called by its botanical name.

Identification: The trunk has grey bark. The airy, well-shaped crown is as wide as the tree is tall. The leaves measure 20–45cm (8–18in) in length and consist of 8–20 pairs of pinnae, each carrying 10–28 pairs of leaflets. Each downy leaflet is bright green, ovate to elliptic and 1cm (½in) long. The dense terminal panicles of 5cm- (2in-) long trumpet-like flowers appear in spring and summer. The fruit is a 5cm- (2in-) wide, flattened, round to oblong, rich brown, leathery pod containing winged seeds.

Above and right: The jacaranda is a beautiful tree. The fine, fern-like foliage casts delicate shade below.

OTHER SPECIES OF NOTE
Jicara *Crescentia alata*
From southern Mexico through to Costa Rica grows this 9m (30ft) evergreen tree. It has long, thin, stem-like branches and a short trunk. The trees were thought to have Christian significance, as the leaves form the shape of a cross. Each trifoliate leaf is composed of a winged leaf stem, and three leaflets arranged at right angles to one another. The entire leaf is 12cm (4½in) long and dark green. The flowers form in pairs on the trunk and larger branches; they are 6cm (2½in) long, greenish-yellow to brown with purple markings. The round gourd-like fruit reaches 13cm (5in) across.

Cow Okra *Parmentiera aculeata*
A small tree, up to 10m (33ft), from secondary forest, in Central America and Mexico. It is grown for the edible fruit, medicinal properties of the roots, shade and ornament. In Australia it has become a weed, posing a threat to the native flora. It may grow with a shrubby, multi-stemmed habit, and has ascending branches and grey, fissured bark. The trifoliate leaves have thorns at the base and are dark green with paler veins. Leaflets vary in size up to 15cm (6in) long. The flowers emerge directly from the trunk(s) and older branches throughout the year. They are funnel-shaped, greenish-cream with purple markings and 5cm (2in) long.

Yellow Trumpet Flower

Tecoma stans

This fast-growing plant forms a large shrub or small tree. It can be grown as a hedge or screen and is popular in gardens, as it is reliable and flowers over a long period, specially in the spring and autumn. If pruned after flowering, the tree is encouraged to produce more flowers. It grows well in arid and semi-arid zones, but may cause problems for some people, as the flowers produce a large quantity of pollen.

Identification: This tree is often multi-stemmed, and the trunks have smooth, light grey to brown bark. The opposite leaves are 20–25cm (8–10in) long and consist of five to eleven leaflets. Each leaflet is 6–8cm (2½–3in) long, lanceolate, light green, smooth, thin and heavily toothed. The 4cm- (1½in-) long flowers are clustered in rounded terminal panicles. The fruit is an 20cm- (8in-) long, leathery, rich brown, thin bean-like pod. It contains the two-winged seeds.

Distribution: West Indies, Mexico, Central America and northern South America including Peru.
Height: 9m (30ft)
Shape: Spreading
Evergreen
Pollinated: Insect
Leaf shape: Pinnate

Above and left: The flowers are an attractive trumpet shape and a beautiful golden-yellow.

Right: Leaves are somewhat variable.

Golden Trumpet-tree

Tabebuia chrysantha

Distribution: Mexico to Venezuela.
Height: 30m (100ft)
Shape: Rounded, spreading
Deciduous
Pollinated: Insect
Leaf shape: Compound palmate

Right: Breathtaking in flower, this tree produces a profusion of golden trumpets. In the wild, it grows in forested, riverine and coastal localities and is a feature of secondary forests.

This genus has earned a reputation as being one of the most worthwhile trees for planting in the Americas. There are numerous species to choose from, providing a vast choice of colour, and the majority have outstanding displays of flowers over a long period, particularly in the winter months. Many are tolerant of coastal conditions, flooding or dry conditions, and are rarely attacked by pests and diseases. This species has deep yellow flowers in large clusters while it is leafless. Its timber yields a mulberry-colour dye, and it is also valued for making furniture, flooring and bowls.

Identification: The tree often has an irregular trunk, and the narrow branches have a zigzagging habit, creating an open haphazard crown. The leaves fall in late winter or spring; they are up to 25cm (10in) across and divided into five hairy, ovate leaflets up to 18cm (7in) long. The trumpet-shape flowers have pink streaks inside, are lightly scented, 8cm (3in) long and appear towards the branch tips from late winter through to summer. The fruit pods are slightly hairy.

White Cedar

Tabebuia heterophylla

Distribution: Caribbean islands, and naturalized in southern Florida.
Height: 18m (60ft)
Shape: Rather narrow-crowned
Mainly deciduous
Pollinated: Insect
Leaf Shape: Palmate

This is both a valuable timber tree, and also one of the most beautiful and ornamental of tropical trees. Widespread in forests, it is also popular in parks and gardens, where it is notable for its abundant, large pink flowers, which sometimes cover the tree, even before the leaves are fully out, and which carpet the ground beneath when they fall. In areas with a pronounced dry season, leafless trees may burst into full blossom, standing out like beacons in the forest. The timber is fairly hard and strong, and takes a high polish, and is used for furniture and veneers. Several species are known by the name "Pau d'arco". Their inner bark has been used to treat a variety of diseases, from cancer to fungal infections, and a popular herbal remedy is said to stimulate the immune system.

Identification: The bark is rough, furrowed, and grey-brown. The leaves are opposite, grow to about 30cm (12in) long, and usually have five leaflets. Each flower is tubular and five-lobed, and about 9cm (3½in) long. The fruit is a long, dangling pod containing many light brown seeds.

Right: The large, showy flowers make this one of the most beautiful of flowering ornamental trees.

Above: Tabebuia species are coming under pressure from collection of their bark for use in herbal remedies.

Pink Trumpet Tree

Tabebuia rosea

This tree is grown for its stunning floral display and handsome foliage, and as a shade tree for coffee and cocoa throughout the tropics. In areas without a pronounced dry season, flowering is reduced, and the tree may be virtually evergreen. It is also grown for timber in forestry plantations, and the heavy, durable wood is used in construction and furniture-making.

Identification: The massive straight trunk has rough, furrowed grey bark, is often buttressed and carries well-spaced branches. Dark green leaves are up to 30cm (12in) across and form from three to five elliptic leaflets of varying size, the largest measuring 15cm (6in) in length. Numerous terminal and axillary inflorescences carry clusters of trumpet-shaped, pale to dark pink to mauve flowers with crinkled petals in spring, and sporadically through the year. The fruit splits to reveal winged seeds attached to a central core.

Distribution: Mexico to Venezuela to Ecuador.
Height: 27m (90ft)
Shape: Oval to cylindrical
Deciduous
Pollinated: Insect
Leaf shape: Compound palmate

Left: Often grown for its timber, this multi-use tree is stunning when in full flower.

Far left: The fruit is a dark brown, straight, round pod.

African Tulip Tree

Spathodea campanulata

This outstanding tree is easy to spot and recognize. It is grown throughout the tropics, including the USA, for its spectacular display of intense orange-red flowers radiating against the dark foliage. A pure yellow form is occasionally seen, too. In some places these fast-growing trees are used to mark land-ownership boundaries. Their soft wood is brittle, often resulting in damage in windy conditions.

Identification: The pale trunk carries only a few thick branches but a dense crown. The 60cm (24in), dark green leaves are composed of 9–21 ovate leaflets, each about 10cm (4in) long. The terminal flowers appear throughout the year, but are more pronounced in the wet season. Domes of tightly packed buds open in succession over many weeks. Each tulip-shaped flower is 10–15cm (4–6in) long, yellow inside, and red outside with a frilly golden edge to the petals and an unusual scent. The smooth, woody pods are 20cm (8in) long, 5cm (2in) wide, and split open to release hundreds of winged seeds.

Distribution: Uganda.
Height: 25m (82ft)
Shape: Oblong
Evergreen
Pollinated: Bat
Leaf shape: Pinnate

Left and right: The finger-like flower buds are full of water and when squeezed will squirt water.

PALMS

The palms, Palmae, are monocotyledons. There are 200 genera and 2,650 species, the majority of which come from tropical and subtropical regions, where they are a common feature in wild and cultivated areas. Most palms have hard, woody upright stem(s) giving a tree-like appearance. The stem does not branch, is pithy and topped with a crown of readily recognizable fronds.

Broom-palm

Brittle Thatch-palm *Thrinax morrisii*

This small palm grows naturally on limestone hills and cliffs, and also coastal sands, from sea level to about 300m (1,000ft). It is quite decorative and is sometimes planted for ornament. It is slow growing, with a single, slender, grey trunk, topped by a crown of about 20 large fan-like brittle leaves.

Left: As suggested by the common names, this tree's stiff leaves are sometimes used for thatching and making brooms.

Identification: The leaves are alternate and spreading, with blades up to 1.2m (4ft) long. The uppermost leaves are erect, and are surrounded by outer drooping leaves. The leathery leaf segments are mostly forked at the tip. The cluster of flowers develops among the leaves and is 60–180cm (2–6ft) long. The flowers are slightly fragrant. The fruit has a whitish, rather bitter flesh, and a single shiny brown seed.

Distribution: Southern Florida, Bahamas, Cuba, Hispaniola, Puerto Rico, Virgin Islands; also Mexico (Yucatán) and Honduras.
Height: 4.5m (15ft)
Shape: Single-stemmed palm
Evergreen
Pollinated: Wind, insect
Leaf shape: Palmate, fan-shaped

Royal Palm

Roystonea regia

When one sees a dramatic, awe-inspiring avenue of palms in the tropics, it is likely to be *Roystonea*. Their fast, strong-growing nature, straight upright trunk and dense crown of feathery fronds makes them extremely useful for formal planting. Within the landscape gardening industry they are highly regarded and very widely planted, in both tropical and subtropical regions. The growing tip, which is called the palm heart or cabbage, is often eaten as a vegetable, but this involves killing the palm.

Identification: The thick, smooth, pale grey or white trunk has distinctive rings and becomes swollen in the centre with age. The huge, arching fronds reaching up to 6m (20ft) in length are composed of numerous deep green, narrow pendulous leaflets, each up to long. The small, white flowers are found densely packed on 1m (3ft) branched plumes. The fruit is oval and 1.5cm (⅝in) long.

Below: The Royal palm requires a reliable supply of water to grow well. In the wild it can be found in swampy locations.

Distribution: Cuba.
Height: 30m (98ft)
Shape: Single-stemmed palm
Evergreen
Pollinated: Insect and/or wind
Leaf shape: Pinnate

Right: Ripe fruit is reddish-purple.

Below: The elegant leaves arise from a deep green shaft.

Assai

Euterpe edulis

Large stands of this fast-growing graceful palm dominate damp areas of rainforest in the Amazon basin. The fruit is edible and can be used to make a nutritious drink, assai, by soaking in water. The palm hearts are also popular, although their harvest kills the palm. The heart is harvested from the young growing tip when the palm is three-and-a-half years old. The hearts are canned and exported from South America. Other species of *Euterpe* are multi-stemmed and need not be killed during the harvest of the heart.

Left: Assai is a fast-growing, tolerant palm.

Identification: The smooth trunk is slender, reaching about 15cm (6in) in diameter. It is grey with long, green, clasping leaf bases at the top. The deep green fronds are up to 3m (10ft) long and elegantly arching. Fronds consist of narrow, weeping leaflets up to 90cm (36in) long. The small white flowers on erect panicles produce large quantities of purple or black fruit, 5mm (¼in) across.

Distribution: Amazon basin, Brazil.
Height: 30m (98ft)
Shape: Single-stemmed palm
Evergreen
Pollinated: Insect
Leaf shape: Pinnate

Right: The fruit is popular with forest birds and mammals.

Left: Assai foliage is particularly elegant.

Ruffle Palm *Aiphanes caryotifolia*
From northern South America, this palm's widespread habitat includes deciduous and rain forests. It is common in disturbed areas, and is cultivated locally for the edible red fruit and seeds. It grows to 9m (30ft), with a single stem clothed in long black spines. The softly arching fronds have roughly triangular leaflets with jagged edges.

Carnauba Wax Palm
Copernicia prunifera
From low-lying areas of northeast Brazil comes this slow-growing, 12m (40ft), slender palm. The distinctive stem is clothed on the lower half only with old leaf bases. The tough carnauba wax found on the lower leaf surfaces is collected, and used in polish and foodstuffs.

Jelly Palm *Butia capitata*
This tough palm from the open drier areas of southern Brazil, Paraguay, Uruguay and northern Argentina grows in tropical to cool temperate environments. It grows to 6m (20ft) with a thick trunk up to 1m (3ft) diameter. The 2.5cm (1in) wide yellow fruit is found in huge clusters, and is harvested to make jellies and wine.

Coconut

Cocos nucifera

Tropical beaches would be incomplete without coconut palms, which are now thoroughly naturalized on tropical shores throughout the world. Coconut trees are also widely planted for their fruit, and as an ornamental. They can grow in sand and are incredibly tolerant of windy, salty conditions. Every part of this palm can be used: the leaves for thatch, the growing tip for palm cabbage, the trunk for construction, the flower for toddy, the fruit for food, drink and oil, and the fruit husk for matting and fuel. It is grown inland and in coastal areas.

Identification: Slender, often curved trunks are swollen at the base, where new roots emerge. The lightly arching fronds grow to 6m (20ft) with long, hanging, deep green leaflets. The 1m- (3ft-) long branched inflorescence carries small, cream flowers. The fruit is a hard, triangular sphere, 12in (30cm) long and green or yellow.

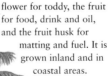

Left: The tough leaves can withstand strong coastal winds. Older leaves turn yellow before dropping off.

Distribution: Native to the tropical east, now widely naturalized and planted.
Height: 18m (60ft)
Shape: Single-stemmed palm
Evergreen
Pollinated: Insect and wind
Leaf shape: Pinnate

Below: A coconut fruit may float at sea for many months and still be able to germinate.

TREES OF BRITAIN AND EUROPE

The range of climatic variation found within Europe makes it one of the most diverse continents. There are sun-baked lands surrounding the Mediterranean, exposed snow-covered mountains in Scandinavia, plentiful rainfall and mild temperatures in the United Kingdom and dry tundra permafrost in north-eastern Russia. These diverse and sometimes extreme conditions enable a rich and varied population of tree species to grow. Ironically, the majority of these trees are not native to Europe, as the effects of the last Ice Age, which ended 12,000 years ago, meant that many European species perished. Since then, through the travels of European plant hunters, Europe has become home to a vast collection of species obtained from temperate regions elsewhere. Trees from South and North America, South Africa, Australasia and Asia are all now to be found thriving in Europe.

The following pages provide a comprehensive profile of the trees that thrive in Britain and Europe. The associated descriptions will clarify how each tree can be identified at all times of the year, even in winter. Other information contained in fact boxes provides general points of interest about each tree and covers such things as map and country of origin, average size, shape and how each tree is pollinated.

PRIMITIVE CONIFERS

At the end of the Carboniferous period, 286 million years ago, the first conifers, or gymnosperms, began to evolve. These trees protected their seeds in cones and had a much more efficient reproductive system than earlier evolving trees. The following are direct descendants of the first gymnosperms.

Chinese Plum Yew

Cephalotaxus fortunei

This small, handsome evergreen tree, not dissimilar to yew, comprises a series of erect stems each clothed in distinctive whorls of branches. Chinese plum yew was introduced into Europe by the Scots Victorian plant hunter Robert Fortune in 1849, hence the botanical name *fortunei*. It grows naturally as a woodland species and, as such, prefers to be planted in dappled shade rather than full sun.

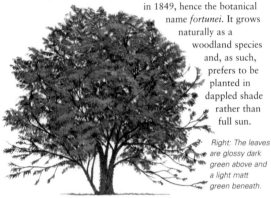

Right: The leaves are glossy dark green above and a light matt green beneath.

Identification: The bark of the Chinese plum yew is red-brown and flaking, rather like the English yew, *Taxus baccata*. The soft needle-like leaves are up to 7.5cm/3in long. Both male and female flowers are small and pale yellow, produced on separate trees in spring. The male flowers are borne in the leaf axils, the females at the shoot tips. On female trees these are followed by purple-brown oval fruits.

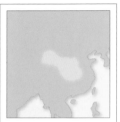

Distribution: Central China.
Height: 15m/50ft
Shape: Broadly spreading
Evergreen
Pollinated: Wind
Leaf shape: Linear

Right: The needles each have two white bands of stomata.

Right: Each fruit is 2.5cm/1in long and contains a single seed.

Monkey Puzzle

Chile pine *Araucaria araucana*

This is a uniquely bizarre tree for its triangular, very sharp, pointed leaves and distinctive whorls of long branches. It was introduced into European cultivation in the late 18th century. It is widely admired for its architectural habit, but often looks misplaced. Even in its native Andean forest it is an impressive oddity. Female monkey puzzle trees produce cones 15cm/6in in length, which take more than two years to ripen and fall. The seed is edible.

Identification: When young, the tree has a slightly rounded conical outline, with foliage to ground level. As it matures, the crown broadens and the lower branches fall away. This reveals an impressive trunk with horizontal folds of grey bark, similar in appearance to elephant hide.

Above: The mature tree's distinctive bark.

Right: The male cones are borne in clusters at the tips of shoots.

Distribution: Forms groves in the Andean forests of Chile and south-western Argentina.
Height: 50m/164ft
Shape: Broadly conical, becoming domed in maturity
Evergreen
Pollinated: Wind
Leaf shape: Linear to triangular

Left: The ovoid female cone contains up to 200 seeds.

Maidenhair Tree

Ginkgo biloba

Distribution: Originating in China, thought to be from the provinces of Anhui and Jiangsu. It is widely cultivated throughout the Northern Hemisphere, including Japan and Europe.
Height: 40m/130ft
Shape: Broadly conical
Deciduous
Pollinated: Wind
Leaf shape: Fan

Fossil records show that *Gingko biloba* existed over 200 million years ago. It was introduced into general cultivation in 1754. It produces male and female flowers on separate trees. When ripe, the fruit has a rancid odour; the seed beneath this pungent flesh is edible if roasted. *Ginkgo* has an attractive outline.

Identification: This deciduous tree is unique in producing fan-shaped leaves, which resemble those of the maidenhair fern, *Adiantum*, hence its common name. The foliage is produced on characteristic short shoots, most apparent in winter. The bark is pale grey.

Above left: The foliage turns golden yellow in autumn.

Left and above right: The fruit is orange-brown when ripe and has a single edible kernel.

OTHER SPECIES OF NOTE

Manio *Podocarpus salignus*
Native to Chile, this tree is commonly referred to as the willowleaf podocarp as its leaves are linear and sickle-shaped, resembling those of a willow. It has gently pendulous branches and graceful foliage, and can grow to 20m/65ft, though most specimens in Europe are far smaller.

Californian Nutmeg *Torreya californica*
At first glance the Californian nutmeg looks similar to the plum yews, *Cephalotaxus*. However it is easily distinguished by its sharply pointed, needle-like evergreen leaves. It originates from California, where it can grow to heights in excess of 30m/100ft. It has been widely planted in gardens across northern Europe. *See also page 101.*

Plum Yew *Cephalotaxus harringtonia*
The origin of this tree is unknown but it has been in cultivation in Japan for centuries. It was introduced to Europe in 1829 and is sometimes referred to as the cow's tail pine. It is an attractive small evergreen, seldom attaining heights in excess of 10m/33ft. It has foliage that at first glance is similar to that of yew, but the fruit is purple-brown and nutmeg-shaped, and resembles a small domestic plum.

Prince Albert's Yew

Saxegothaea conspicua

The genus *Saxegothaea* is monotypic, meaning that this tree is the only species in it. It is an evergreen tree that forms part of the temperate rainforests of southern Chile and adjacent Argentina. It is found growing in association with other forest species, such as *Nothofagus dombeyi*, *Drimys winteri* and *Podocarpus nubigena*, which are all prized for timber. It is cultivated throughout the warmer regions of the Northern Hemisphere, including Europe, as an ornamental tree. Both its generic and its common names commemorate Albert of Saxe-Coburg-Gotha, the consort of the British Queen Victoria.

Above: Needles of the Prince Albert's yew are slightly curved with a sharp tip and are up to 3cm/1¼in long.

Distribution: In lowland areas along the base of the west Andean slopes, from southern Chile into south-west Argentina.
Height: 15m/50ft
Shape: Broadly conical
Evergreen
Pollinated: Wind
Leaf shape: Linear

Identification: The tree grows to a height of 15m/50ft or more, developing a slender, conical crown in its native environment and a more bushy habit in cultivation. The foliage is similar in appearance to that of yews in the genus *Taxus*. The fruits are thick, round and composed of fleshy scales.

Right: The leaf on the right shows the topside view and that on the left shows the underside colouring.

YEWS

The genus Taxus *is present in Europe, North America and Asia. All the species are mainly confined to the middle latitudes, though some grow in tropical highlands. Most are grown as ornamental trees and there are many cultivars. Yews are poisonous, and most species yield the alkaloid taxol, which is used in the treatment of cancer.*

Japanese Yew

Taxus cuspidata

The Japanese yew grows predominantly in Japan but also occurs naturally in parts of China and eastern Russia. It is a slow-growing, very hardy species with a rather sprawling habit. It was introduced into Europe in 1855 by the Scottish plant hunter Robert Fortune. Today, there are more than 90 named forms of the Japanese yew and 130 hybrids – many crossed with the English yew, *T. baccata* – in common cultivation.

Identification: The bark is reddish brown, flaking in maturity. The leaves are 2.5cm/1in long, dark green above and yellow-green beneath with obvious yellow stomatic banding. They are arranged in two ranks and stand erect from the twig – often forming a narrow V-shaped trough. The fruit is similar to that of the English yew but is normally carried in greater profusion.

Distribution: Japan and north-east Asia.
Height: 15m/50ft
Shape: Broadly spreading
Evergreen
Pollinated: Wind
Leaf shape: Linear

Left: The crown is broadly spreading with wide open branching, which gives a sprawling habit.

Above: The needle-like leaves are arranged in two erect ranks at each side of the twig forming a V-shaped trough.

English Yew

Common yew *Taxus baccata*

The English yew develops a very dense, evergreen canopy, which gives this tree a sombre feel that is heightened by its long association with burial grounds and churchyards. Yew wood is extremely durable and is valued in the production of furniture and highly decorative veneers used in cabinet-making. It was once commonly used for making bowstaves. A number of cultivars have been created, and one of the most striking is 'Standishii', which has an upright habit and golden-yellow foliage.

Identification: The tree develops a broad and loosely conical outline. Its leaves are glossy above with a central groove and the bark is rich brown with a purple hue. The male cones shed pollen with cloud-like abundance in spring. The fruit is fleshy, turning red at maturity, around an olive-green seed.

Below: Yew berries are eaten by birds but the poisonous seeds inside are not digested.

Distribution: Europe, including Britain, eastwards to northern Iran and the Atlas mountains of North Africa.
Height: 20m/65ft
Shape: Broadly conical
Evergreen
Pollinated: Wind
Leaf shape: Linear

Right: Yew leaves are needle-like in appearance.

Himalayan Yew

Taxus wallichiana

The Himalayan yew grows naturally throughout the Northern Hemisphere including Europe and North America. It is prolific in India and the Himalayas. *T. wallichiana* is found growing wild from Afghanistan eastwards through the Himalayan region and north-eastern India into south-western China. The tree is particularly rare in cultivation, with few specimens having been planted outside botanical gardens and arboreta.

Identification: The bark is red-brown with purple patches, flaking in maturity. The leaves differ from those of the English yew in being narrower and longer, to 5cm/2in. Both male and female flowers are small and yellow-green, and are borne on separate trees in early spring. The male flowers produce copious amounts of yellow pollen. The ripe fruit, which is bright red and fleshy, contains a single seed.

Distribution: Asia.
Height: 20m/65ft
Shape: Broadly conical
Evergreen
Pollinated: Wind
Leaf shape: Linear

Right: The leaves have a distinctive sickle-like curve and end in a sharp point.

OTHER SPECIES OF NOTE

Pacific Yew *Taxus brevifolia*
This small evergreen tree is native to western North America, from British Columbia to California, where it inhabits canyons and gullies. The branches are slender and slightly pendulous and the winter buds are covered with golden scales. It has needle-like dark green leaves, 2.5cm/1in long. The anti-cancer drug taxol was originally isolated from the bark of this species in the 1960s. *See also page 103.*

Canadian Yew
Taxus canadensis
One of the hardiest of all yew species, this small evergreen tree is native to eastern North America from Newfoundland to Virginia. Unlike most yews the Canadian yew has both male and female flowers on the same tree. The leaves are more pointed than those of the English yew; otherwise it is very similar in appearance to its European cousin.

Hybrid Yew *Taxus x media*
This is a hybrid cross between the Japanese yew, *T. cuspidata*, and the English yew, *T. baccata*. It was bred by T. D. Hatfield at the Hunnewell Pinetum, Wellesley, Massachusetts, around 1900. It is a vigorous, medium-size tree with a spreading habit. Scores of cultivars have been developed from the hybrid, including 'Brownii', which is quite often used for hedging.

Irish Yew

Taxus baccata 'Fastigiata'

Two female saplings of this distinctive erect form of common yew were originally found growing wild on the mountains above Florence Court in County Fermanagh, Northern Ireland, by a farmer called George Willis, in 1740. Since then, the cuttings taken from these two trees have resulted in thousands of Irish yews growing in churchyards, gardens and arboreta in western Europe.

Identification: The Irish yew is easily recognized by its sombre dark green foliage and upright pillar-like habit, which has made it a favourite for planting in classical or formal gardens throughout Europe. Although it can reach a height of nearly 20m/65ft it more commonly grows to 7–10m/22–33ft with a spread of up to 5m/16ft. Branches on old trees quite often break away from the vertical form, particularly when weighed down during and after heavy falls of wet snow. There is also a golden form of the Irish yew, *T. baccata* 'Fastigiata Aurea', which has bright yellow-green foliage.

Distribution: County Fermanagh, Northern Ireland.
Height: 19m/60ft
Shape: Narrowly columnar
Evergreen
Pollinated: Wind
Leaf shape: Linear

Left and below: The needle-like leaves of Irish yew are slightly darker green than the English yew and are arranged radially on the twig.

FALSE CEDARS AND CYPRESS

Trees belonging to the genus Chamaecyparis, or false cypress, have a number of obvious characteristics in common. All are evergreen, and their leaves are arranged in flattened sprays and have a pungent aroma when crushed. The habitats from which these species originate are generally wet and they all produce very durable timber.

Leyland Cypress

x *Cupressocyparis leylandii*

This fast-growing conifer is a hybrid between two American species: Monterey cypress, *Cupressus macrocarpa*, and Alaska cedar, *Chamaecyparis nootkatensis*. The hybrid cross has never occurred naturally in the USA, because the natural ranges of the two parents do not overlap. Instead it originated in 1888 at Leighton Hall, Powys, Wales, where the two parents were planted close to each other in a garden. Since then, Leyland cypress has become very popular for hedging and screening because it is extremely fast-growing, quite often exceeding 2m/6ft in one year. However, it is suitable for planting as hedging close to buildings only if it is regularly trimmed.

Below: The shoot tip and fruit.

Identification: The bark is red-brown, developing shallow fissures as it matures. The leaves are small and scale-like with pointed tips, dark green above, lighter green beneath and borne in flattened sprays. Male and female flowers are found on the same tree. The male flowers are yellow, the female green; both appear in early spring at the tips of the shoots. The fruit is a globular woody brown cone approximately 2cm/¾in diameter.

Distribution: Of garden origin as a hybrid in the United Kingdom. Widely planted throughout Britain and Europe.
Height: 30m/100ft
Shape: Narrowly columnar
Evergreen
Pollinated: Wind
Leaf shape: Scale-like

Japanese Red Cedar

Cryptomeria japonica

Distribution: Found in Japan in Honshu, Shikuka and Kyushu. It is also found in Zhejiang and Fujian provinces in China.
Height: 30m/100ft
Shape: Broadly conical
Evergreen
Pollinated: Wind
Leaf shape: Linear

This stately, fast-growing conifer produces a large, straight trunk that tapers quickly from a broad base above the roots. Its reddish-brown bark is soft and fibrous and peels off to hang in long strips from the trunk. It was introduced into Europe in 1842 and is extensively grown in parks, gardens and arboreta across western Europe. Its timber is strong and pinkish-brown.

Identification: The crown of the tree is narrow when young, broadening with age. Often the heavy branches sweep downwards before rising again at the tips. The very aromatic foliage is a system of bright green branchlets covered with hard, forward-facing needles 1.5cm/⅝in long. The ovoid male flowers are yellowish-brown, clustered along the final 1cm/⅜in of each branchlet. They are bright yellow when ripe, and shed pollen in early spring. The female flowers are green rosettes, found on the same tree as the male flowers. The cones are globular, 2cm/¾in across, and held on upright, stiff stalks.

Above: Branches occasionally touch the ground, causing layering.

Right: At the base of each needle is a long protruding keel, which runs down the branchlet.

Incense Cedar

Calocedrus decurrens

The incense cedar is grown widely in western Europe. The natural habit of the tree is unusual in that it develops a columnar, almost fastigiate, form. Shiny, mid-green leaves develop in flattened sprays produced on branches that are almost horizontal to the main stem. It has a very attractive, flaky bark, grey to reddish-brown. There are only two other species of tree in this genus, C. *macrolepis* from China and C. *formosana* from Taiwan.

Identification: The foliage of the incense cedar is dense, dark green and usually present to the base of the tree, with only a short exposed bole. The male and female flowers are produced on the same tree. Often, abundant quantities of oblong cones are produced and become pendulous with their own weight.

Above: The red-brown bark of the incense cedar is similar to that of the giant redwood.

Far left: The yellow-brown cones have six overlapping scales.

Distribution: Western North America, from mid-Oregon southwards to Baja California in northern Mexico.
Height: 40m/130ft
Shape: Narrowly columnar
Evergreen
Pollinated: Wind
Leaf shape: Linear scale-like

OTHER SPECIES OF NOTE
Hinoki Cypress *Chamaecyparis obtusa*
This cypress is native to Japan, where it is cultivated as an ornamental tree. It was first grown in Europe in the 1860s. It produces a valuable timber. The crown develops a fairly broad conical shape. The bark is soft, stringy and greyer than that of other *Chamaecyparis* species. Bright stomatal banding under the leaves gives an almost variegated appearance.

Sawara Cypress *Chamaecyparis pisifera*
This is a medium-size, highly ornamental Japanese evergreen tree, which has a conical shape and an open branching habit. It has attractive reddish-brown bark and light green foliage, which is produced in flattened sprays and, when crushed, emits a pungent, resinous scent. Small cones the size of peas are produced in dense clusters. It was introduced into Europe in 1861.

Patagonian Cypress
Fitzroya cupressoides
This beautiful large tree, with a cypress-like habit, is native to Chile and Argentina and was introduced into Europe in 1849. It produces pendulous sprays of blue-green foliage that are distinctly marked beneath each needle with two white stomatal bands. It is common in cultivation but seldom attains such large proportions as in the wild, where it may grow up to 50m/165ft. *See also page 108.*

Lawson Cypress

Port Orford cedar, Oregon cedar
Chamaecyparis lawsoniana

The Lawson cypress develops into a conical tree up to 40m/130ft tall, with reddish-brown fibrous bark and scented foliage that has distinctive stomatal markings on the underside of the leaves. In the Pacific north-western USA, where this species originates, it remains a very important source of timber, with many uses from boat-building to cabinet-making. Many cultivars have been produced, which vary widely in form, foliage and colour.

Identification: The young tree has smooth, brown-green, shiny bark, and a pendulous dominant shoot, not seen in the mature tree. It produces globular cones on the foliage tips, which are at first fleshy with a bluish purple bloom and become woody and wrinkled.

Below: The cones are globular, 7mm/¼in in diameter and purple-brown. They remain on the tree long after the seed has been shed.

Distribution: North-western USA, from south-west Oregon to north-west California. Introduced into Europe in 1854 and widely planted in gardens across the continent.
Height: 40m/130ft
Shape: Narrowly conical
Evergreen
Pollinated: Wind
Leaf shape: Linear scale-like

Below: The top side of the foliage is dark green to blue and when crushed smells of parsley.

FALSE CYPRESSES AND THEIR CULTIVARS

The trees included below are commonly known as false cypresses. They have characteristics of the true cypresses, but belong to different genera. Like the true cypresses, they are grouped within the Cupressaceae family. However, true cypresses belong to the genus Cupressus.

Ellwood's Cypress

Chamaecyparis lawsoniana 'Ellwoodii'

This slow-growing, columnar cultivar of Lawson cypress was raised at Swanmore Park, Bishops Waltham, Hampshire, England, in the late 1920s. It takes its name from Mr Ellwood, the head gardener at Swanmore Park at the time. Originally thought of as a dwarf tree ideal for planting in rock gardens, it soon became clear that it had the potential to outgrow all but the largest rockeries.

Identification: Ellwood's cypress makes a distinctive, tightly packed, almost impenetrable column of strongly ascending branches. It has short, rather feathery, spray-like evergreen foliage, which is predominantly grey-green but turns a steely blue-green in winter. A feature of this tree is that the juvenile foliage is always present, giving a rather soft appearance. In maturity the top of the column becomes irregular, with multiple pinnacles of foliage.

Distribution: Of UK garden origin.
Height: 10m/33ft
Shape: Narrowly columnar
Evergreen
Pollinated: Wind
Leaf shape: Linear scale-like

Above: Each small, irregularly shaped spherical cone contains hundreds of tiny seeds.

Left: A common and distinctive feature of this tree is the way it produces juvenile foliage throughout its life, which gives the whole tree a soft appearance even in maturity. The foliage is short, rather feathery and a metallic blue-green colour in winter.

Lawson Cypress 'Erecta Viridis'

Chamaecyparis lawsoniana 'Erecta Viridis'

This is one of the oldest of all Lawson cypress cultivars and still one of the most popular. It was raised at the Knaphill nursery of Anthony Waterer in Surrey, England, in the 1850s, and is believed to have arisen from only the second batch of seed of Lawson cypress ever imported into Europe from California. Originally called simply 'Erecta', its name was changed to 'Erecta Viridis' in 1867. Although relatively slow-growing, it is potentially a large tree and there are several old specimens around the British Isles that are 28m/80ft tall. It can be used as a hedging tree or as an isolated specimen to be grown in a lawn. It has a compact shape and dense foliage and grows well on free-draining soil.

Identification: 'Erecta Viridis' has perhaps the brightest green foliage of any Lawson cypress and maintains this vibrancy throughout the winter. It has a fastigiate shape, with ascending branches that sweep dramatically skywards at the tips. There will quite often be between two and six main stems growing from the base, which help to develop a rather billowing multiple top. In maturity its tight columnar form becomes more open and lax, as old branches fall outwards away from the main stem(s).

Distribution: Of UK garden origin.
Height: 28m/80ft
Shape: Columnar
Evergreen
Pollinated: Wind
Leaf shape: Linear scale-like

Right: The foliage is bright, rich green and borne in large flattened sprays.

Taiwan Cypress

Formosan cypress *Chamaecyparis formosensis*

In its native habitat this is an impressive tree, growing to 60m/200ft, with a trunk of 20m/65ft or more in girth. Introduced into cultivation in the early part of the 20th century, it has yet to be recorded at the great size of its wild form. As with many of the false cypresses, its timber is noted for being durable and resistant to moisture. Since its introduction into Europe in 1910, it has been widely planted in arboreta and botanic gardens across the continent.

Identification: The tree has a reddish bark with regular, shallow fissuring. The leaves are flat and produced in broad sprays; the individual leaves are scale-like. The small oblong cones have brown wrinkled scales that are flat or slightly protuberant, and are carried above the foliage.

Distribution: Mountainous regions of central and northern Taiwan.
Height: 60m/200ft
Shape: Broadly conical
Evergreen
Pollinated: Wind
Leaf shape: Linear scale-like

Left: The lower branches are level and sweep up towards the tip.

Left: The scale-like needles are light yellow-green and when crushed have the aroma of seaweed.

Fletcher's Cypress

Chamaecyparis lawsoniana 'Fletcheri'

This common, attractive cultivar is named after the Fletcher brothers, who ran a tree nursery at Chertsey in Surrey, England, in the early part of the 20th century. It was developed from a "sport" on a Lawson cypress, which was found growing near the nursery in 1911. The sport showed the interesting characteristic of having permanently semi-juvenile foliage. The Fletchers tested it in the nursery for reversion, and then named and distributed it in 1923. Today, one of the finest specimens is to be seen at Bedgebury Pinetum in Kent, England. It is a slow-growing tree that is often erroneously planted in rock gardens, where it soon becomes far too large.

Identification: Fletcher's cypress is normally a broad columnar multi-stemmed tree 10–15m/33–50ft tall, with regular ascending sprays of foliage on the outer side of vertical shoots. The feathery foliage is blue-grey-green, becoming bronze in winter. The shoots are dark pink-purple, turning purple-brown as they mature. In maturity the basal branches commonly brown and die.

Distribution: Of UK garden origin.
Height: 15m/50ft
Shape: Broadly columnar
Evergreen
Pollinated: Wind
Leaf shape: Linear scale-like

Above: Small irregularly shaped cones ripen in winter.

Below: The foliage is bronze tipped in winter.

TRUE CEDARS AND FALSE FIRS

Although there are only four true cedars, they are without doubt the real stars of the coniferous world. Nothing can touch them for sheer majesty and dignity. Three originate from around the Mediterranean and the fourth grows a little further east in the Himalayas. The false firs, on the other hand, are all to be found in either North America or Asia.

Deodar

Cedrus deodara

In the days of the British Empire, huge deodars 75m/245ft tall were found, some of them over 900 years old. Sadly, most of these have been felled for their timber. The deodar has light brown, very durable timber, which is highly prized. It is widely planted all over Europe as an ornamental tree, rather than for its timber.

Below: The barrel-shaped cones are 12cm/4¾in long, ripening to dull brown.

Identification: In young trees the bark is smooth and dark grey, but on older trees it becomes cracked and covered with pink-grey fissures. The juvenile foliage is blue-grey, becoming dark green with age. The deodar is narrowly conical when young, and broadens as it matures. It is easily distinguished from other cedars by the drooping ends to its branches. The needles, which are 4cm/1½in long, are arranged in whorls around the shoot. The male flowers are very prominent and erect, purple ripening to yellow, up to 8cm/3in long; they shed copious amounts of pollen in late autumn.

Distribution: Western Himalayas, Kuram Valley to Kumaon and on to Afghanistan.
Height: 50m/165ft
Shape: Broadly conical
Evergreen
Pollinated: Wind
Leaf shape: Linear

Right: The needles of the deodar are sparse.

Cedar of Lebanon

Cedrus libani

This large, stately tree is probably the best known of all the cedars. It has been revered for thousands of years, and in biblical times it was a symbol of fertility. King Solomon is believed to have built his temple using its timber. On Mount Lebanon it grows at altitudes up to 2,140m/7,020ft. Although numbers are decreasing in the wild, it is widely planted as an ornamental tree in parks, gardens and arboreta in Britain and Europe.

Identification: The young tree is narrow and conical; after about 40 years it broadens rapidly, with level branches so long they seem to defy gravity. The bark is a dull brown with even, shallow fissures. The 3cm/1¼in needles are grey-blue to dark green (depending on the provenance of the individual tree), growing in dense whorls on side shoots and singly on fast-growing main shoots. The erect, barrel-shaped cones are grey-green, maturing to purplish brown.

Distribution: Mount Lebanon, Syria and the Taurus Mountains in south-east Turkey.
Height: 40m/130ft
Shape: Spreading
Evergreen
Pollinated: Wind
Leaf shape: Linear

Right: The cones are 12cm/4¾in long.

Left: Broad spreading habit.

Atlas Cedar

Cedrus atlantica

The natural range of this beautiful tree is in the Atlas Mountains, where it grows along the snowline at 1,500–2,200m/4,900–7,200ft above sea-level. It is sometimes considered to be a geographical sub-species of the cedar of Lebanon, *C. libani*, but is distinguished by its ascending branches. In its natural range the foliage varies from dark green to grey-blue. In cultivation it is the glaucous form, *C. atlantica* 'Glauca', that is most commonly planted. It grows in parks and gardens in western Europe.

Identification: The bark is slate grey, smooth at first becoming fissured into scaly plates in maturity. The needle-like leaves, up to 2.5cm/1in long, are borne in dense whorls on short side shoots and singly on the longer leading shoots. Both the male and female flowers are erect catkins; males are yellow, females green. The male flowers, up to 5cm/2in long, are conspicuous in autumn. Once the pollen has been released they fall to the ground. The fruits are barrel-shaped upright cones, to 7.5cm/3in long, borne in rows along the branches.

Distribution: Algeria and Morocco.
Height: 40m/130ft
Shape: Broadly conical
Evergreen
Pollinated: Wind
Leaf shape: Linear

Left: Needles.

Left: After two to three years the cones ripen and release numerous winged seeds.

Douglas Fir

Pseudotsuga menziesii

Distribution: North-west Pacific seaboard, from Mexico through USA to Canada, including Vancouver Island.
Height: 75m/245ft
Shape: Narrowly conical
Evergreen
Pollinated: Wind
Leaf shape: Linear

Below: The cones have bracts that project from each scale.

Douglas fir is one of the most commercially important timber-producing trees in the world. It has been planted throughout North America, Europe, Australia and New Zealand. It is a huge tree, attaining heights in excess of 75m/245ft. Quite often there is no branching for the first 33m/110ft. The bark is corky and deeply fissured in maturity; young trees have smooth, shiny grey-brown bark that is pock-marked with resin blisters.

Identification: When young this majestic tree is slender and regularly conical, with whorls of light ascending branches. In old age it becomes flat-topped, with heavy branches high up in the crown. The needles are up to 3cm/1¼in long and rounded at the tip. They are rich green, with distinctive white banding beneath, and arranged spirally on the shoot. When crushed the foliage emits a sweet citrus aroma. The male flowers are yellow and grow on the underside of the shoot. The female flowers are green, flushed pink to purple at the tip, and grow in separate clusters on the same tree. The fruit is a hanging cone, up to 10cm/4in long, green ripening to orange-brown, with distinctive three-pronged bracts.

OTHER SPECIES OF NOTE

Big-cone Fir
Pseudotsuga macrocarpa
Native to south-west California, this rare tree has dull grey

bark with wide, vertical orange fissures. Its crown is broadly conical with level branches. The needles are up to 5cm/2in long, stiff, pointed and widely spaced all around the shoot. The cylindrical cones grow up to 18cm/7in long. It was first grown in Britain in 1910. *See also page 121.*

Japanese Fir
Pseudotsuga japonica
This tree, which is found in south-east Japan, is rare in the wild and uncommon in cultivation. It has a flattened crown. The leaves are soft, light green, 2.5cm/1in long, blunt and notched at the tip. No fragrance is emitted when the foliage is crushed. The cone is the smallest of the genus at 5cm/2in long; its scales are few and smooth, with a spreading bract that is bent slightly outwards.

TRUE CYPRESSES

These trees are closely related to the genus Chamaecyparis, *in that their leaves are scale-like and produced in sprays. Unlike the false cypresses, their foliage is not flattened. Their cones are composed of fewer scales – between six and eight – and are twice the diameter, but contain less seed. True cypresses are distributed throughout regions of North America, Europe and Asia.*

Himalayan Cypress

Bhutan cypress *Cupressus torulosa*

Despite growing at elevations in excess of 3,300m/10,800ft in the Himalayas, this slow-growing species is not particularly hardy in cultivation in northern Europe. Consequently it is relatively uncommon and is mostly confined to arboreta, tree collections of botanic gardens and gardens that benefit from the warmth of the Atlantic Gulf Stream. Even here, patches of browning foliage in the canopy are commonplace. Where it does grow well it makes an attractive tree with weeping foliage. It was introduced into Europe in 1824.

Distribution: Western Himalayas to south-west China; also central and north Vietnam.
Height: To 20m/65ft
Shape: Columnar with conical top
Evergreen
Pollinated: Wind
Leaf shape: Linear scale-like

Identification: The overall form of this tree is columnar, becoming conical towards the top, with slender branches that begin level, but then curve downwards towards the tips, where bright yellowish-green foliage hangs in dense irregular bunches. When crushed, the foliage smells of newly cut grass. The brown or greyish bark on mature trees peels off in long strips, revealing fresh red-brown bark beneath.

Right: Clusters of small, 1cm/½in-long cones are conspicuous in autumn, when they ripen from blue-green to a dark red-brown.

Cedar of Goa

Mexican cypress, Portugal cedar *Cupressus lusitanica*

The origins of this tree are rather confusing. It is thought to have been cultivated in England since the late 17th century, having been introduced from Portugal, where it was once believed to be a native species. Its botanical name is derived from Lusitania, the Roman province established in the region occupied by Portugal. However, the tree has never been found growing wild there, or for that matter in the former Portuguese settlement of Goa in western India, despite its common name. It is now believed to have been introduced into Portugal from Mexico in the 16th century by Portuguese missionaries. More recently, it has been planted in parts of Africa as a forest tree. Its timber has been used for general construction, for posts and poles, although its durability is questionable.

Identification: On old trees, the rich, dark brown bark peels away in vertical fibrous strips. The leaves are small, scale-like, grey-green in colour and borne on pink to dark red shoots in short, broad sprays. In early spring the tips of each shoot are covered in numerous small male flowers of yellow to creamy-brown. These are followed by ovoid cones, 1.5cm/¾in across, which are glaucous green in the first year, ripening to dark, shiny purple-brown in the second year. Each cone scale has a hooked spine in the centre.

Distribution: Mexico and Guatemala.
Height: 30m/100ft
Shape: Narrowly conical
Evergreen
Pollinated: Wind
Leaf shape: Linear scale-like

Left: The grey-green leaves are scale-like and borne on pink shoots in short, broad sprays.

Monterey Cypress

Cupressus macrocarpa

With an incredible ability to withstand exposure to salt-laden winds, this tree has become as common a sight in the exposed coastal habitats of Europe as in its native California. It can attain a height of 40m/130ft, but is often stunted by extreme conditions. In maturity it becomes flat-topped, with spreading horizontal branches. In cultivation it is best known for being the female parent of the leyland cypress, × *Cupressocyparis leylandii*. The strong, durable timber is often used for structural work.

Right: Cupressus macrocarpa 'Donald Gold' is a variety of Monterey cypress.

Identification: Mature trees display a great variability in habit, from a dense crown of ascending branches to a more horizontal cedar-like form. Leaves are arranged in loose, circular sprays around the shoots. When crushed, the foliage releases an aromatic odour.

Distribution: USA: two sites near Monterey, California, at Cypress Point and Point Lobos.
Height: 40m/130ft
Shape: Columnar to spreading
Evergreen
Pollinated: Wind
Leaf shape: Linear scale-like

Left: Cones are up to 4cm/1½in across.

OTHER SPECIES OF NOTE

Chinese Weeping Cypress *Cupressus funebris*
Native to China, this species grows along the Yangtze Valley. It is planted an an ornamental tree in Europe. It is similar to the false cypresses in having foliage produced in flattened sprays. The habit is attractive and often pendulous. Immature plants have a fine, soft foliage that is retained for a number of years.

Smooth Arizona Cypress *Cupressus arizonica* var. *glabra*
This hardy, small to medium-size cypress grows in European arboreta, where it inhabits dry, rocky mountain slopes and has attractive, peeling red bark, which turns purple with age. It has a dense, conical habit with ascending branches that end in red shoots. The foliage is blue-grey speckled with spots of white resin. A form of this tree known as 'Pyramidalis', which has strikingly blue foliage, is common in cultivation.

Kashmir Cypress *Cupressus cashmeriana*
Curiously, this tree has never been found growing in the wild but it was introduced into Europe from Asia in 1862. It is a graceful and beautiful tree with ascending branches, which are adorned with pendulous sprays of silver-blue foliage. In colder regions of northern Europe this tree will not survive outside, but it makes a splendid specimen for a large conservatory.

Italian Cypress

Cupressus sempervirens

This is a fascinating tree because of its ability to retain a tight columnar form throughout its life. There is no other conifer, except the monkey puzzle, that has such a strong sense of architecture. It is the space between the plantings of these trees that characterizes the hills and roadside verges of Tuscany, in Italy, and the western Mediterranean. The foliage is a dull grey-green and, unusually for cypress, has no noticeable scent when crushed.

Identification: The Italian cypress can attain a height of 18m/60ft or more in its natural habitat. The bark is predominantly grey with some brown colouring. The cones are larger than in most trees in this genus, growing to 3.5cm/1½in, similar to those of the Monterey cypress. They are retained on the tree for many years.

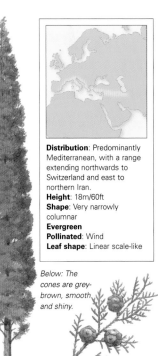

Distribution: Predominantly Mediterranean, with a range extending northwards to Switzerland and east to northern Iran.
Height: 18m/60ft
Shape: Very narrowly columnar
Evergreen
Pollinated: Wind
Leaf shape: Linear scale-like

Below: The cones are grey-brown, smooth and shiny.

JUNIPERS

The junipers are similar to the true cypresses, Cupressus, in having two types of leaves on the same plant, both juvenile and scale-like. Unlike cypresses, their fruit is a fleshy cone in which the scales have fused together to give a berry-like appearance. There are at least 50 species, mostly occurring in the Northern Hemisphere, and in many dry regions junipers are the dominant forest cover.

Syrian Juniper

Juniperus drupacea

With the longest needles and largest fruit of the junipers, the Syrian juniper has a distinctive, fine outline, developing into a tall columnar tree. It thrives in Greece and Turkey in mountains and coastal forests. It usually reaches a height of about 15m/50ft, though the tallest recorded specimen, in Turkey, is about 40m/130ft. The Syrian juniper has a similar distribution to that of *J. excelsa*, the Grecian juniper. Between the two in distribution and extending further north is *J. foetidissima*, the stinking juniper.

Identification: The crown of this juniper is columnar to conical in shape. The trunk has orange-brown bark, which is shed in fine vertical strips. The leaves have two white bands of stomata on the inner surface and are shiny mid-green on the outer surface. They are arranged in groups of three.

Above: The needles are very stiff, and can be up to 2.5cm/1in long. They are sharply pointed and are arranged in whorls of three. The cone is 2.5cm/1in across; blue-green at first, it changes colour to a blackish purple as it matures.

Distribution: Range extends through southern Europe and northern Africa. Found on rocky slopes in forest or scrub, throughout Syria into Turkey and in parts of Greece.
Height: 15m/50ft
Shape: Columnar
Evergreen
Pollinated: Wind
Leaf shape: Linear scale-like

Common Juniper

Juniperus communis

The common juniper is believed to be the most widespread tree in the world, growing naturally from Alaska, Greenland, Iceland and Siberia south through most of Europe, temperate Asia and North America. It is a hardy tree that tolerates intense cold, exposed coastal locations and high mountain ranges. As a tree it seldom attains heights in excess of 5m/16ft, and it often grows as a multi-stemmed shrub.

Below: The needle-like leaves are grey-green, sharply pointed, carried in whorls of three with each needle up to 1cm/½in long. The juniper berries are easy to identify on the twigs.

Identification: Depending on the degree of exposure of its location, the overall shape of common juniper may be thin and tree-like or wide-spreading and shrub-like. It has thin, dark red-brown bark that peels in vertical papery strips. The leaves are needle-like, sharply pointed and up to 1cm/½in long. They are grey-green and carried in whorls of three along the shoots. The yellow male and green female flowers are borne on separate trees in clusters within the leaf axils. The fruit is a green berry-like cone that takes between two and three years to ripen. When ripe it turns a glaucous purple-black.

Right: The cones, which are commonly known as juniper berries, are used to give gin its characteristic flavour.

Distribution: Europe, Asia and North America.
Height: 6m/20ft
Shape: Narrowly conical
Evergreen
Pollinated: Wind
Leaf shape: Needle-like

Chinese Juniper

Juniperus chinensis

This is the conifer most commonly used for bonsai. It was introduced to Europe in 1804. Male and female flowers are borne on different trees. It has been in cultivation for centuries and has many cultivars, including 'Keteleeri', which makes a dense, regular and narrowly conical tree; the old and widely planted 'Pfitzeriana', known as the Pfitzer juniper; and 'Hetzii', a very vigorous hybrid, which has an upright and a spreading form.

Above: The mature foliage has dark green scale-like needles with paler banding.

Right: When ripe, the cones are dark purple with a pale grey bloom.

Identification: The Chinese juniper has an erect, narrow and conical growing habit. The bark is grey to reddish-brown, peeling off in strips. The leaves are dark green on the outer surface and have a broad green stripe on the inside, separated by two white stomatal bands. The cones are rather lumpy in appearance and measure approximately 6mm/¼in across.

Distribution: Widely distributed through north and east China. Also present in Inner Mongolia and around Japan, restricted to the coastal areas of Honshu, Kyushu and Shikoku.
Height: 25m/80ft
Shape: Narrowly conical
Evergreen
Pollinated: Wind
Leaf shape: Linear scale-like

Right: Young needles are wedge-shaped.

OTHER SPECIES OF NOTE

Temple Juniper
Juniperus rigida
Native to Japan, Korea and northern China, this slow-growing, small to medium-size tree is planted in the grounds of Japanese temples. It was introduced into Europe in 1861 but is relatively uncommon in cultivation. It has dull grey, peeling bark and glossy, bright green needles set in sparse whorls of three.

Eastern Red Cedar
Juniperus virginiana
Also known as pencil cedar, this North American species has a dense pyramidal to columnar habit and dense foliage that is sage-green above and grey-green beneath. It has red-brown bark that exfoliates in long strips. The fruit is berry-like, light green in spring and dark blue when mature in autumn. The wood has moth-repellent properties and is common in Europe. *See also page 110.*

Flaky Juniper *Juniperus squamata*
Also known as the Himalayan juniper, this small bushy tree, with a natural range from Afghanistan to China, is uncommon in Europe. It has nodding tips to the shoots, dense foliage with awl-shaped, sharply pointed leaves in whorls of three, the upper surface of which are green-white, and purple-black fruits containing one seed. It was introduced into Europe in 1824.

Drooping Juniper

Juniperus recurva

Drooping juniper is so-called because of its weeping foliage, which descends from upswept branch ends. This interesting, slow-growing tree was introduced into Europe by the Veitch Nursery of Chelsea, England, in 1861. Its natural range in the Himalayas overlaps with that of the flaky juniper, *J. squamata*. Although drooping juniper is relatively uncommon in cultivation, the variety *coxii* is widely cultivated, and differs from the species in having orange peeling bark and a much more open habit.

Identification: The bark is dark red-brown and peels in maturity into long vertical strips. The leaves are needle-like, forward pointing, 5–8mm/¼–⅜in long, grey-green with two distinct bands of blue-white stomata. They are borne on red-brown shoots, which, when shaken, emit a dry rustling sound. Both male and female flowers are green and are borne in small clusters at the tips of the shoots on the same tree. The small oval fruit is purplish-brown to black, resembling a black berry.

Distribution: From eastern Himalayas to Japan.
Height: 15m/50ft
Shape: Narrowly conical
Evergreen
Pollinated: Wind
Leaf shape: Linear scale-like

Right: Small needle leaves point forward along the shoot.

Below: The foliage weeps or droops at the branch ends.

Canary Island Juniper

Canary cedar *Juniperus cedrus*

The Canary Island juniper is native to the islands of La Palma, La Gomera, Tenerife, Gran Canaria and Madeira. It occurs in the high mountain regions of these islands alongside the Canary pine, *Pinus canariensis*. On Tenerife it can be found growing from old lava flows at 2,000m/6,560ft above sea level on Mount Teide. Its timber is highly prized, but in recent years the natural distribution of this tree has been dramatically reduced through deforestation and forest fires.

Distribution: Canary Islands and Madeira.
Height: 15m/50ft
Shape: Broadly conical
Evergreen
Pollinated: Wind
Leaf shape: Linear scale-like

Identification: This wide and somewhat pendulous-branched, rather bushy tree has a low open crown and dark grey-green foliage arranged oppositely, or in whorls, upon silver-white pendulous shoots. The bark of the trunk and main branches is red-brown and the fruits are globular in shape, up to 1.5cm/½in in diameter, bright green at first, becoming dark red on ripening. This is a dioecious species, having both male and female individuals.

Right top: The fruits of this juniper are rounded, bright green at first but ripening to a distinctive dark red colour.

Left and right: The foliage is a dark grey-green colour and borne upon silver-white pendulous shoots.

Greek Juniper

Juniperus excelsa

This hardy, shapely tree is native to mountainous regions from Greece and the southern Balkans to Pakistan. It occasionally occurs as pure forest and in Greece there are several ancient specimens that are over 500 years old. Greek juniper is normally a monoecious species, with both male and female flowers occurring on the same tree, although occasionally single sex species do occur. It was first introduced to cultivation in western Europe in 1806. A common garden cultivar of this species is the columnar 'Stricta', which retains its juvenile foliage.

Below: The flattened foliage sprays carry small purple-brown fruits.

Identification: Greek juniper has light brown bark, which in maturity, peels off in vertical strips, and long, slender, thread-like branches densely covered with sharply pointed grey-green foliage. The juvenile leaves are needle-like, 5mm/¼in long and borne in twos or threes on the shoots. The adult leaves are flattened and scale-like. The globular fruits, which ripen in the second year, are 1cm/½in in diameter, dark purple-brown covered with a blue-white bloom.

Distribution: South-east Europe to south-west Asia.
Height: 21m/70ft
Shape: Broadly conical
Evergreen
Pollinated: Wind
Leaf shape: Linear scale-like

Right: The mature leaves are scale-like.

Juniperus x media

This is a dwarf variable hybrid species between the Chinese juniper, *J. chinensis*, and the Common savin, *J. sabina*. It is the origin of around 85 named cultivars now common in cultivation in gardens throughout Europe. These include 'Pfitzeriana', 'Plumosa', 'Blue and Gold', and 'Mordigan Gold', which has bright golden summer foliage.

Phoenician Juniper *Juniperus phoenicea*

This small tree is native to southern Europe, North Africa and possibly the Canary Islands. It was introduced to Britain and northern Europe as early as 1683. It has a broadly conical habit and bright green foliage, which when crushed has an aroma reminiscent of paint.

Creeping Juniper *Juniperus procumbens*

As the name suggests, this is a low-growing dwarf juniper, which is much used for ground cover or as a rockery plant. In Japan it grows wild on the coast of Kyushu. It is a sturdy, dense little tree with stiff branches thickly covered with blue-green, sharply-pointed leaves.

Common Savin *Juniperus sabina*

This handsome dwarf juniper, widely distributed in the wild from the Pyrenees to the Caucasus, has been cultivated since ancient times in the Mediterranean region, and was introduced into England in 1548. It has resulted in many popular cultivars, including 'Blue Danube', 'Erecta' and 'Arcadia'. When crushed, the foliage of the true species emits a pungent, unpleasant odour.

Prickly Cypress

Formosan juniper *Juniperus formosana*

Native to southern China, where it is widespread, and Taiwan, this beautiful small, graceful tree is somewhat tender and will not flourish in colder regions of Europe. There is a splendid specimen at Bedgebury Pinetum, Kent, England. It was introduced into Europe around 1844, although it was originally confused with *J. taxifolia* and was not correctly named until 1908. It has similar characteristics to those of the sharp cedar, *J. oxycedrus*, which is native to the Mediterranean, Iran and the Caucasus Mountains.

Identification: This beautiful tree has fibrous brown bark, which peels in thin, narrow strips. It has a loose, elegant habit, open crown and sparsely set, very large, spiny forward-pointing leaves held on pendulous branchlets. The leaves are up to 1cm/½in long, awl-shaped, borne in whorls of three, blue-green in colour, with two bands of white stomata separated by the central midrib.

Distribution: South China and Taiwan.
Height: 12m/40ft
Shape: Broadly columnar
Evergreen
Pollinated: Wind
Leaf shape: Linear scale-like

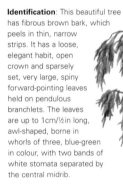

Above: The globular fruits are olive-green in the first year, maturing to orange-red, or reddish-brown, in year two.

Shore Juniper

Juniperus conferta

This is a prostrate shrub rather than a tree, but it is widely used as low ground cover in areas close to the sea. It is native to coastal areas of Japan and Sakhalin, particularly in the sand dunes of Hakodate Bay in Hokkaido. It was identified by the Russian botanist Maximowicz in 1861 and introduced into Europe by the English plant hunter Ernest Wilson in 1914. It is closely related to the creeping juniper, *J. procumbens*.

Identification: This is a prostrate evergreen with short, angular, ascending branches and young shoots that are densely clothed with sharply pointed, glossy, pale green linear leaves, up to 5mm/¼in long, which have a distinctive band of white stomata on the upper surface. The globular fruits are 12mm/½in in diameter, purple-black and covered in a glaucous bloom. Inside each fruit there are three triangular seeds.

Distribution: Japan.
Height: 2m/6ft
Shape: Prostrate
Evergreen
Pollinated: Wind
Leaf shape: Linear scale-like

Left: Shore juniper has short, pale green linear leaves which are sharply pointed. The tips turn yellow.

THUJAS AND HIBA

The Arborvitae or Thuja species are similar to Chamaecyparis species, such as Lawson cypress, except that they have larger and broader scale-like leaves, which emit a more pleasant aromatic fragrance when crushed and have cones with overlapping scales. Both Thuja and Thujopsis are perfectly hardy in Europe and will thrive in almost any soil, providing it is well-drained.

Japanese Arborvitae

Thuja standishii

The name Arborvitae means 'tree of life' or 'tree of everlasting life' and refers to the evergreen foliage of this species. In fact, as with all evergreen trees, the foliage does die and is replaced, but gradually over a period of years rather than all at once each autumn. This tree is easily recognized by its lax yellow-green foliage and open crown, together with the citronella-like fragrance emitted by the foliage when crushed. In Japan it is one of the 'five sacred trees' from which Shinto shrines are built. It was introduced to Europe by the Scottish plant collector Robert Fortune in 1860.

Identification: The bark is deep red, smooth at first, peeling away into long strips and plates in maturity, from both the trunk and larger branches. Each spreading branch sweeps skywards towards the tip and is densely clothed in lax, nodding sprays of yellow-green foliage. The male flowers are dark red and the female flowers are green; both appear at the tips of the shoots on the same trees in spring. The fruit is a very small cone, 1cm/½in long, covered with approximately ten scales, green at first, ripening to red-brown.

Distribution: Central Japan.
Height: 25m/80ft
Shape: Broadly conical
Evergreen
Pollinated: Wind
Leaf shape: Scale-like

Right: The leaves are yellowish-green and carried in elegant drooping sprays.

Left: Male and female flowers are borne at the tips of the shoots in spring.

Korean Arborvitae

Thuja koraiensis

This beautiful small tree from north-east China and Korea, where it inhabits woodland in mountainous areas, was introduced into Europe by the English plant collector Ernest Wilson in 1917. It is a striking tree that deserves to be more widely planted, being largely confined at present to botanic gardens and arboreta. It has broad, flat foliage which, when crushed, emits a scent of almonds and marzipan.

Right: Male and female flowers are green with black markings and borne at the shoot tips.

Right: The scale-like leaves are flat, broad and silver-white beneath.

Identification: The bark is pinkish-brown, peeling away in thin scales. The scale-like leaves are flat, broad, grass green above and a remarkable silver-white colour beneath, bordered by pale green. Each spray of leaves is borne in a flattened plane on coppery-orange, stout shoots. Both male and female flowers are green tipped with black and appear at the ends of the shoots in spring. The fruit is an oblong, upright cone, 1cm/½in long, green-yellow maturing to orange-brown.

Distribution: North and central Korea.
Height: 10m/33ft
Shape: Narrowly conical
Evergreen
Pollinated: Wind
Leaf shape: Scale-like

Western Red Cedar

Giant arborvitae *Thuja plicata*

This evergreen tree originates in the north-western Pacific coastline of America, where it is a major component of the moist, lowland coniferous forests. Individual living trees over 1,000 years old have been recorded, and its timber has been utilized for centuries. Native Americans burnt out the trunks to make canoes, and it is an economically important timber, being straight-grained, soft and easily worked. It has been widely used to make roofing shingles and is grown for timber in Europe and New Zealand. Its many cultivars include a variegated form called 'Zebrina'.

Identification: This very tall, narrow, conical evergreen tree grows up to 50m/165ft. Individual specimens with low branching may layer to form a secondary ring of vigorous, upright trunks. The foliage is dark green and glossy above, with a sweetly aromatic scent when crushed. The bark is reddish-brown, forming plates in maturity.

Left: The shoots are coppery-brown with sprays of deep glossy green, scale-like needles that are flattened in one plane.

Distribution: USA: originating from the Pacific coastline of North America, it grows from southern Alaska, through British Columbia, southwards to Washington and Oregon to the giant coastal redwood forests of California.
Height: 50m/165ft
Shape: Narrowly conical
Evergreen
Pollinated: Wind
Leaf shape: Linear scale-like

OTHER SPECIES OF NOTE

Chinese Thuja *Thuja orientalis*
A species from Korea, northern and southern China, this differs from other *Thuja* in having foliage that is arranged in vertical sprays, giving it a distinct character as a specimen tree. Cultivars include 'Aurea Nana', a golden, slow-growing form, and 'Elegantissima'. *See also page 109.*

White Cedar *Thuja occidentalis*
This narrowly conical, medium-size tree, to 20m/65ft, is native to eastern Canada and south-eastern USA, where it grows at high altitudes in forests on rocky outcrops. It has twisted sprays of mid-green foliage, which when crushed emit a scent of green apples. It is thought to be the first North American tree to have been introduced into Europe. *See also page 108.*

King William Pine
Athrotaxis selaginioides
From a distance this tree looks like the Japanese cedar, *Cryptomeria japonica*, as it has similar foliage. Close up, the bark is like that of the American giant redwood, *Sequoiadendron giganteum*. However, the King William pine is in fact a Southern Hemisphere tree, originating from the temperate rainforests of Tasmania, where it grows alongside eucalyptus at altitudes in excess of 1,000m/3,300ft above sea level. It was introduced into Europe in 1857.

Hiba

Thujopsis dolabrata

Distribution: Japan: From the southern islands of central Honshu, northwards to Shikoku and Kyhshu. A distinctive form, *T. dolabrata* var. *hondae* 'Makino', is unique to northern Honshu and southern Hokkaido.
Height: 20m/65ft
Shape: Broadly conical
Evergreen
Pollinated: Wind
Leaf shape: Linear scale-like

This monotypic genus consists of a single species of evergreen tree, which is distinguished from *Thuja* in having broad leaves with distinctive white undersides. It was introduced to Britain in 1853. In cultivation it is slow in growth and for the first ten years often develops no further in form than that of a dense, evergreen shrub. As a mature tree, the habit of *Thujopsis* can vary from tall, upright and columnar to low-branching, multi-stemmed and broadly conical.

Identification: The foliage is yellow-green, glossy and hard. The white undersides of the needles are bordered by a dark green margin. The ovoid cones are 1.25cm/½in long, green becoming brown. The bark is red-brown to grey, peeling off in fine strips in maturity .

Right: The scale-like, 6mm/¼in long needles form flattened sprays.

REDWOODS AND HEMLOCKS

The conifers in this group are all members of the Taxodiaceae and Pinaceae *families and are found in the Northern Hemisphere. The group includes some of the biggest, tallest and oldest trees in the world. The coast and giant redwood are evergreens originating in California, while the dawn redwood and swamp cypress are deciduous conifers. All have distinctive fibrous, reddish-brown bark.*

Coast Redwood

Sequoia sempervirens

The *Sequoia* takes its name from a native American Cherokee called Sequoiah. It was introduced into Europe in 1840 and is widely grown in parks and arboreta in northern and western Europe. The trunk is quite often branchless for two-thirds of its height. It grows to 100m/330ft tall.

Left: The cones are 2–3cm/ ¾–1¼in long.

Identification: Young trees have a cone-like form with widely spaced, level, slender branches, up-curved at the tips. Old trees become columnar with flat tops and branches that sweep down. The leading shoots have small, pinkish-green needles arranged spirally. The needles on the main and side shoots are arranged in two flat rows, 1–2cm/½–¾in long, dark green above and speckled with two bands of white stomata on the underside. The male flowers are yellowish-brown; the female flowers are green, in separate clusters on the same tree.

Distribution: USA: found in a narrow coastal band running for approximately 800km/500 miles from Monterey, California, to the Oregon border.
Height: 100m/330ft
Shape: Narrowly conical
Evergreen
Pollinated: Wind
Leaf shape: Linear

Left: The fissured, reddish-brown, thick, spongy bark is fire resistant, protecting the tree from forest fire.

Giant Redwood

Sequoiadendron giganteum

The largest living organism in the world is a giant redwood called "General Sherman". Some giant redwoods are up to 3,500 years old. They thrive in any soil, site or exposure with a moderate supply of moisture but do not grow well in heavy shade. The bark is red-brown, soft, thick and fibrous. It was introduced to Europe in 1853.

Left: Needles and two-year-old brown cones.

Distribution: USA: restricted to 72 groves on the western slopes of the Sierra Nevada, California.
Height: 80m/260ft
Shape: Narrowly conical
Evergreen
Pollinated: Wind
Leaf shape: Linear

Right: The trunk of a redwood may grow to more than 3m/10ft in diameter.

Identification: The crown of the tree is conical at first, becoming broad in old age. The leaves grow to 8mm/⅛in, and are sharp-pointed with spreading tips. They are matt grey-green at first, covered with stomata, and turn a dark, shiny green after three years. When crushed, the foliage emits a fragrance of aniseed. The male flowers are yellowish-white, held at the ends of minor shoots, and shed pollen in early spring. The female flowers are green, and develop into bunches of green ovoid cones, which ripen to brown in their second year.

Southern Japanese Hemlock
Tsuga sieboldii
In Europe this is a small to medium-size tree, but in its natural habitat in southern Japan it can reach heights in excess of 30m/100ft. It was introduced into Europe in 1853 by the German physician and plant collector Philipp Franz von Siebold. The foliage is similar to that of the American hemlocks, but it normally has multiple stems from ground level and dark grey bark with rectangular pink fissures.

Himalayan Hemlock
Tsuga dumosa
The Himalayan hemlock is found growing wild from north-west India to northern Burma and on into China, where it attains heights in excess of 50m/165ft. However, in cultivation elsewhere, including Europe, it seldom reaches 20m/65ft. Its bark is pink-brown and scaly, rather like that of the larch. The needles are relatively long for a hemlock, 3cm/1¼in, hard and rigid, green-blue above with two silver stomatal bands beneath.

Western Hemlock

Tsuga heterophylla

This tall, elegant tree has weeping branches and soft, pendulous foliage. However, this softness is deceptive: western hemlock is as hardy as any other conifer. It has been widely planted for timber in forests throughout western Europe since its introduction in 1851. It is extremely shade-tolerant, out-growing its competitors in the thickest forest.

Identification: The tree has a narrow conical shape, with ascending branches that arch gently down towards the tip. The leading shoot is always lax. The bark is reddish-purple in young trees, becoming dark purple-brown with age. The needles are 2cm/¾in long, deep dark green above with two broad blue-white stomatal bands beneath. New growth is bright lime green in spring, contrasting dramatically with the sombre mature foliage. Both male and female flowers are red. Much pollen is shed in late spring. The cones are pendulous, egg-shaped, 2.5cm/1in long, with few scales, pale green ripening to deep brown.

Distribution: West coast of North America.
Height: 60m/200ft
Shape: Narrowly conical
Evergreen
Pollinated: Wind
Leaf shape: Linear

Left and below: Small egg-shaped cones appear in late summer at the tips of branches.

Mountain Hemlock

Tsuga mertensiana

Native to the west coast of North America from Alaska to California, this handsome tree has a columnar crown of grey pendulous foliage. The mountain hemlock is sometimes mistaken for *Cedrus atlantica* 'Glauca', as it has thick blue-grey needles, which radiate all around the shoot. It thrives in Europe.

Identification: The bark is dark orange-brown, becoming vertically fissured into rectangular flakes in maturity. The branches are slightly drooping, with weeping branchlets hanging from them. The shoot is a shiny pale brown. The needles are similar to a cedar's, 2cm/¾in long, dark grey-green to blue-grey, and are borne radially all over the shoot. The cone is spruce-like, 7cm/2¾in long, cylindrical and buff-pink maturing to brown. The male flowers are violet-purple, borne on slender drooping stems. The female flowers are erect and have dark purple and yellow-green bracts. Although closely related to the western hemlock, it is seldom planted in European forests for timber production because it is a slower growing species and the timber is often extremely knotty and difficult to work. It was introduced into Europe in 1851.

Above: The needles are blue-green and cedar-like. The cone resembles that of spruce.

Distribution: West coast of North America, from Alaska to California.
Height: 30m/100ft
Shape: Columnar
Evergreen
Pollinated: Wind
Leaf shape: Linear

Left: The needles have a definite bluish tinge and radiate out from the twigs. Viewed end-on, the shoots appear star-like.

SWAMP CYPRESS AND CHINESE FIR

Swamp cypress and dawn redwood are widely planted as ornamental trees in parks and gardens throughout Europe – their main attraction being their soft foliage, which turns bright yellow or orange before falling in autumn. The remaining trees in this section are less common but can be found in botanic gardens and arboreta.

Japanese Umbrella Pine

Sciadopitys verticillata

The Japanese umbrella pine grows at elevations of 180–1,520m/590–5,000ft on rocky slopes and ridges. It has been widely planted in other parts of the world, including Europe, as an ornamental species, because of its unusual leaf formation and attractive, regular shape. In Japan its timber, which is pure white, springy and very durable, is used for making bathtubs, casks and boats.

Identification: This distinctive tree has widely spaced whorls of shiny green needles, which are deeply grooved and grow up to 12cm/4¾in long. Each whorl sits about 3.5cm/1½in apart from its neighbour on a buff-brown shoot. The male flowers are globular, yellow and green and bunched in clusters of 12. The green female flowers appear on the same tree, held at the end of each shoot.

Distribution: Japan: the mountains of central and southern Honshu.
Height: 33m/110ft
Shape: Conical
Evergreen
Pollinated: Wind
Leaf shape: Linear

Below: The fruit is an egg-shaped cone up to 7.5cm/3in across.

Right and left: The arrangement of the needles within each whorl resembles the ribs of an umbrella – hence the common name.

Chinese Fir

Cunninghamia lanceolata

The Chinese fir is a handsome tree with a domed crown of short, drooping branches. At first glance there is a similarity with the monkey puzzle. It has prickly, lance-shape needles, which are glossy dark green. It grows in stands on Chinese mountainsides up to an elevation of 1,520m/5,000ft, enduring hot summers and high humidity. It thrives in Europe.

Right: A male flower.

Right: Female flowers.

Identification: The bark is chestnut brown, with parallel, vertical shallow fissures running down the trunk. It has a columnar or conical shape with a domed top. The branches are widespread, giving a sparse appearance often concealed by the drooping foliage. The needles grow to 6cm/2½in long, spirally set on the shoots, but twisting to lie in just two planes on each side of the shoot. They are deep, glossy green on top, with two striking white bands beneath. The male flowers are yellow-brown, borne in clusters at the shoot tips, while the female flowers are yellow-green and held singly on terminal branchlets. The fruit is a rounded cone, 4cm/1½in across, bright green maturing to brown.

Distribution: Central and southern China south of a west-east line from Sichuan, Hubei and Honan to Guangxi, Guangdong, Fujian and Hong Kong.
Height: 25m/80ft
Shape: Broadly columnar
Evergreen
Pollinated: Wind
Leaf shape: Lanceolate

Left: The distinctive, glossy, dark green foliage of the Chinese fir makes it an excellent ornamental species.

Swamp Cypress

Bald cypress *Taxodium distichum*

Also known as the bald cypress because of its deciduous habit, this tree grows naturally in wet conditions and can tolerate having its roots submerged for several months. In these conditions it will produce aerial roots known as "knees" or "pneumatophores", which provide oxygen to the roots. It is an excellent tree for colour; the leaves turn from old gold to brick red in early to mid-autumn.

Right: Autumn needles.

Left: Cones are borne on the same trees as male flowers.

Identification: The crown is typically conical, although some trees develop a rather domed appearance in maturity, with heavy, low, upswept branches. The bark is a dull reddish-brown and is frequently fluted. The shoots are pale green, up to 10cm/4in long, with soft, flattened leaves 2cm/¾in long, arranged alternately along the shoot; they emerge late in the season. The male flowers, to 5–6cm/2–2½in, are prominent throughout the winter as three or four catkins held at the end of each shoot. These lengthen to 10–30cm/4–12in when pollen is shed in early spring. The female cones are on a short stalk, globular and light green until ripe.

Right: The deciduous, needle-like foliage turns red in autumn.

Distribution: South-eastern USA: Delaware to Texas and Missouri.
Height: 40m/130ft
Shape: Broadly conical
Deciduous
Pollinated: Wind
Leaf shape: Linear

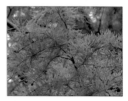

OTHER SPECIES OF NOTE
Pond Cypress *Taxodium ascendens*
This broadly conical tree from the south-eastern USA reaches a height of 40m/130ft. It tolerates wet soil but also grows in drier situations. It has linear leaves 1cm/⅜in long, which are closely pressed around the upright, deciduous shoots. The bark is red-brown, thick and heavily fluted. The male flowers are yellow-green, and held in catkins up to 20cm/8in long. The female flowers are green and appear in clusters at the base of the male catkins. The fruit is a green globular cone, 3cm/1¼in across.

Chinese Swamp Cypress
Glyptostrobus pensilis
This small tree seldom reaches heights in excess of 10m/33ft. It originates from south-east China, where it grows in swamps and along riverbanks. However, it is now very rare in the wild. It has linear, scale-like leaves, 1.5cm/⅝in long, which are arranged spirally on deciduous side shoots. The bark is grey-brown and the flowers are insignificant. The fruit is an egg-shaped green cone up to 2.5cm/1in long. This fairly tender tree does not thrive in northern Europe.

Dawn Redwood

Metasequoia glyptostroboides

Until this beautiful tree was discovered growing in east Sichuan by the Chinese botanist T. Kan in 1941, it had been seen only as a fossil and was deemed extinct. It was introduced to the West in 1948. Since then it has become a popular species for ornamental planting. It has bright orange-brown stringy bark and the trunk is quite often fluted.

Identification: The crown is conical in most trees, although some are broad with upswept branches. When grown in the open the crown is dense, but in shade it becomes sparse. The leaves are down-curved at the tips, 2cm/¾in long, bright green above with a pale band each side of the midrib beneath. The male flowers are ovoid, set on panicles up to 25cm/10in long. The female cones are green ripening to brown, 2cm/¾in across with stalks 2cm/¾in long.

Distribution China: the Shui-sha valley, in the north-west part of Hubei and into Sichuan.
Height: 40m/130ft
Shape: Narrowly conical
Deciduous
Pollinated: Wind
Leaf shape: Linear

Below: The leaves are positioned opposite each other on the shoot, which is bright green.

TRUE FIRS

The diversity among European and Asian firs is quite remarkable. They include some of the tallest firs in the world and some of the smallest. They can be found growing wild from China to Spain. Several have been adopted as ornamental species and planted just about everywhere, from large arboreta to small town gardens. All are handsome trees, producing lush foliage, good symmetry and attractive cones.

European Silver Fir

Abies alba

Distribution: Pyrenees, France, Corsica, the Alps and the Black Forest south to the Balkans.
Height: 50m/165ft
Shape: Narrowly conical
Evergreen
Pollinated: Wind
Leaf shape: Linear

This species is long-lived for a conifer – some specimens are known to be over 300 years old. Although widely planted for timber, it is very susceptible to aphid damage, which can be fatal in close-grown plantation conditions. It is widely used as a Christmas tree in many parts of Europe. Prolific natural regeneration from seed is a characteristic of the species.

Identification: Young trees are symmetrical, with slightly ascending branches. In maturity the stubs of dead branches cover the trunk and the leading stem becomes heavily forked. In young trees the bark is smooth and dull grey. Older trees have a paler bark with shallow pink-brown fissures. The needles are 1–2cm/½–¾in long, shiny green above with noticeable linear grooves and white stomatal banding below. They have rounded tips and are flattened each side of the shoot. The cones are clustered on just a few branches at the top of the tree. They are red-brown, cylindrical, up to 15cm/6in long and disintegrate on the tree. In spring, new growth is an attractive bright lime-green but is quite often burnt by the sun melting late frost.

Right: The long cones stand upright from the finger-like shoots.

Korean Fir

Abies koreana

This is an alpine species and the smallest of all firs. It originates from the volcanic island of Quelpeart, where it grows in vast forests on mountain slopes up to 1,000m/3,300ft. It has become a favourite for planting in gardens in Europe because of its manageable size and profusion of purple-blue cones on even the youngest trees.

Identification: The Korean fir forms a broad, tall shrub or small tree. It has dark olive-green to black bark, which is pock-marked with light freckle-like lenticels. The shoots are pale fawn and slightly hairy, and are covered in a profusion of short, stubby, dark green needles, 1–1.5cm/½–⅜in long, which curve upwards from the shoot, almost obscuring it from view. On the underside of the needles are two bright white stomatal bands. The male flowers are red-brown, normally covered in resin and clustered all around the side shoots. The female flowers are dark red to purple, ripening to attractive, dark blue-purple cones up to 7cm/2¾in long. These are normally covered with a sticky white resin.

Above: The leaf buds.

Distribution: South Korea.
Height: 15m/50ft
Shape: Broadly conical
Evergreen
Pollinated: Wind
Leaf shape: Linear

Below: The male flowers.

Right: The cones stand upright from the shoots.

Noble Fir *Abies procera*
This tree has a stately, noble appearance with a long, straight stem, and large cones that stand proudly above the surrounding foliage. It has smooth, silver-grey bark with occasional blisters, and blue-green needles 3.5cm/1½in long. When crushed they emit a pungent smell. It grows in western Europe. *See also page 116.*

Veitch's Silver Fir *Abies veitchii*
This beautiful, fast-growing Japanese tree was introduced into Europe in 1879. It has densely arranged, upcurved needles, 2.5cm/1in long, which are dark green above and silver beneath. The fruits are barrel-shaped, upright, purple-blue cones that stand proud on the topmost branches.

Greek Fir *Abies cephalonica*
Native to the island of Cephalonia and the mountains of southern Greece, where it reaches 30m/100ft tall, this handsome fir has rigid, sharply pointed, glossy dark green needles up to 2.5cm/1in long. The underside of each needle has two silver-grey bands of stomata. It is one of the earliest firs to start producing new growth in spring and as a result it is sometimes damaged by frost when planted in northern Europe.

Grand Fir *Abies grandis*
This tree has graceful, downward-sweeping branches with upturned tips, the lower boughs reaching the ground. The needles, up to 5cm/2in long, are glossy green on top, silvery below. *See also page 117.*

Delavay Fir

Abies delavayi

This handsome medium-size tree is believed to have been introduced into Europe in 1918. However, there is some suggestion that the original trees may have been the Faber fir, *Abies fabri*. The Delavay fir is named after the French missionary Jean Marie Delavay, who discovered the tree in Yunnan in 1884. It is common in cultivation in botanic gardens and arboreta. Some of the largest specimens in Britain are found in west coast Scottish collections such as Benmore in Argyll.

Identification: The crown is symmetrical but rather sparse and spiky, with strong ascending branches bearing short red-brown shoots. The bark is smooth, pale grey, becoming fissured with age. The needles, up to 4cm/1½in long, are borne all around the shoots. They are deep blue-green above with two bright silver stomata bands beneath. The fruit is a distinctive barrel-shaped upright cone, up to 10cm/4in long, purple-blue maturing to dark brown, with small bract-like curved spines emerging from each cone scale.

Distribution: Yunnan, China and Burma, extending into northern India.
Height: 20m/65ft
Shape: Broadly conical
Evergreen
Pollinated: Wind
Leaf shape: Linear

Above: The needles are blue-green above with two silver-white stomata bands beneath. The cone is barrel-shaped.

Caucasian Fir

Nordmann fir, Crimean fir *Abies nordmanniana*

This slow-growing, densely branched tree is probably one of the most handsome and uniform-looking firs in the world. It makes a magnificent large specimen tree in parks, gardens and arboreta throughout Europe. It is also widely grown for sale as a Christmas tree, marketed as one of the "non-drop" trees because of its ability to retain its needles after it has been cut. When it is crushed, the foliage emits a fruity, citrus aroma.

Identification: The bark is grey and smooth when the tree is young and becomes cracked into small, square plates in maturity. The leaves are linear, bluntly tipped, glossy dark green above with two white bands of stomata beneath, 2.5cm/1in long and carried all around the shoot but more densely on the top side. The male flowers are red and borne beneath the shoot, the female flowers are green and borne above the shoot, both on the same tree in spring. The fruit is a broad cylindrical cone up to 15cm/6in long, green maturing to a deep red-brown.

Distribution: Caucasus, north-east Turkey.
Height: 50m/165ft
Shape: Broadly conical
Evergreen
Pollinated: Wind
Leaf shape: Linear

Left: Male flowers are red and borne beneath the shoot.

Left: Leaves are blunt and needle-like, glossy dark green above with two bands of white stomata beneath.

Right: The cone is broad, cylindrical and up to 15cm/6in long.

Himalayan Fir

Abies spectabilis

This magnificent, large, broad-shaped conifer, sometimes known as the east Himalayan fir, has a natural range from Afghanistan eastwards to Bhutan, where it grows at altitudes up to 4,000m/ 13,100ft above sea level, higher than any other Himalayan fir. It was introduced into Europe in 1822, and although it does well in mild, wet areas of Europe, it is susceptible to late spring frosts. Its species name, *spectabilis*, actually means "beautiful". It produces dark purple cones, which were at one time used to make a purple dye.

Left: A single needle-like leaf.

Above: The fruit is an attractive dark purple cone which ripens brown and is borne on top of the shoot.

Identification: The Himalayan fir has rough pink-grey bark that shreds into fine strips even when young. A distinctive feature of this tree is the way it produces low, heavy, horizontal branches, which frequently break off in maturity. The shoots are stout and reddish-brown, with a covering of hairs in the grooves between the leaf bases. The leaves are dense, and lie forward in two ranks, with the inner rank rising and the outer rank curving downwards beneath the shoot. They are up to 6cm/2¼in long, dark green above and silvery white beneath.

Right: When young, the cones exude a sticky aromatic resin which crystallizes around the cone and on the surrounding leaves.

Distribution: Himalayas.
Height: 20m/65ft
Shape: Broadly columnar
Evergreen
Pollinated: Wind
Leaf shape: Linear

Algerian Fir

Abies numidica

This handsome fir is native to Mount Babor, Algeria, where it grows in association with the Atlas cedar, *Cedrus atlantica*, at approximately 1,500m/5,000ft above sea level. It was discovered in the mid-19th century and introduced into cultivation in Europe in 1861, where it was planted in the gardens of the Natural History Museum in Paris and named by head gardener E. A. Carrière. The Algerian fir is more lime-tolerant than most firs.

Identification: The overall shape of this tree is conical with an abruptly pointed top. It has dense foliage on numerous downward-sweeping branches, which then curve upwards at their tips. The bark is purplish-grey and smooth at first, becoming fissured and flaking in maturity. The leaves are rigid, to 2.5cm/1in long, with a blunt point. They are dark green above with two conspicuous bands of white stomata on the underside. The fruit is a cylindrical upright cone up to 18cm/7in long. It is pale green at first, ripening to brown, and ending with a short "peak" at the tip.

Left: The Algerian fir produces a distinctive green cylindrical upright cone which ends in a peaked tip and matures to brown.

Below: The female flower.

Distribution: North-east Algeria.
Height: 25m/80ft
Shape: Narrowly conical
Evergreen
Pollinated: Wind
Leaf shape: Linear

Cheng Fir

Abies chengii

This uncommon, vigorous tree, found mainly in arboreta and botanic gardens, was first described by the English arboriculturalist Keith Rushforth in 1987. It is believed to have originated in north-west Yunnan in China and to have been introduced into Europe by the Scottish plant hunter George Forrest in 1931. It is closely related to the Forrest fir, *A. forrestii*, and some botanists claim it is a hybrid of this tree. It differs from that species in having longer needles and much more pointed buds.

Right: The 4cm/1.5in–long needle-like leaves are dark green above, sage green beneath and surround cylindrical upright cones.

Identification: The cheng fir has smooth grey bark when young, becoming fissured towards the base in maturity. It has shiny, mahogany-red shoots, pointed pale-brown buds and glossy, dark green needle-like leaves with sage green undersides. They are up to 4cm/1½in long, and are borne on the shoots in such a way as to create a 'V' down the centre. The fruit is an upright cylindrical cone, up to 10cm/4in tall, purple-brown in colour and disintegrating on the tree once ripe.

Distribution: Probably native to Yunnan, China.
Height: 15m/50ft
Shape: Broadly conical
Evergreen
Pollinated: Wind
Leaf shape: Linear

OTHER SPECIES OF NOTE

Momi Fir *Abies firma*
Also known as Japanese fir, this tree was introduced into Europe in 1853. It is a wide-spreading, large tree, to 30m/100ft tall. It has pink-grey bark and distinctive yellow-green, stiff leathery needles, each up to 5cm/2in long and rounded at the tips. It has a rather open appearance with well-spaced, long branches. The yellow-brown cones are 12cm/4½in long.

Faber Fir *Abies fabri*
This attractive, large tree, up to 40m/130ft tall, is native to western Sichuan, China. It was introduced into Europe in 1901. It has attractive, dark orange-brown scaly bark, deep green needles, 2.5cm/1in long, which are bright silver-white beneath, and bluish-black cones with protruding bracts.

Sicilian Fir *Abies nebrodensis*
The Sicilian fir is native to the slopes of Monte Scalone in northern Sicily where, due to deforestation, it is now very rare. It is similar to the European silver fir, *A. alba*, and it has been suggested that this tree is an island form of that species. However, it differs in having orange shredding bark and shorter needles, which are densely arranged on the top of the branchlets.

Spanish Fir *Abies pinsapo*
Also known as the hedgehog fir because of its distinctive blunt, rigid, dark green needles, which stick out from all sides of the branchlets, this Spanish, medium-size tree, 20m/65ft tall, is common in cultivation throughout Europe. It is one of the best firs for planting on chalk.

Cilician Fir

Abies cilicica

This attractive, slow-growing large tree is native to the Taurus Mountains of southern Turkey, from where its range extends southwards to Mount Lebanon. It is closely related to the Caucasian fir, *A. nordmanniana*, but can be distinguished by its thinner, narrower leaves and crown. It is a relatively rare species, both in the wild and in cultivation, but is quite often found growing in botanic gardens and arboreta. It was introduced to western Europe, including Britain, in 1855.

Identification: The bark is dark grey, smooth at first, becoming distinctively wrinkled and cracked into rings, which radiate out from the knots of old branches, in maturity; the overall appearance is not dissimilar to that of an elephant's leg. Cilician fir foliage is variable, even on the same tree, with some shoots displaying very short leaves 1cm/½in long and others densely clothed with long leaves measuring 2.5cm/1in. All the needles point forward on the shoot and are shiny dark green above and pale green beneath. The tree has upright cones, 20cm/8in long, which disintegrate on the tree once ripe, leaving behind an upright woody spike.

Distribution: Lebanon, north-west Syria and southern Turkey.
Height: 30m/100ft
Shape: Narrowly conical
Evergreen
Pollinated: Wind
Leaf shape: Linear

Below: The needles all point forward on the shoot and are dark shiny green above and pale green beneath.

SPRUCES

The spruces, Picea, are a group of hardy evergreen conifers that grow throughout most of the colder regions of the Northern Hemisphere. They differ in one significant way from firs, Abies, which allows for quick genus identification: on all spruces there is a peg-like stump at the base of every needle. When the needles fall this peg remains, creating a rough texture to the shoot. Firs have smooth shoots.

Oriental Spruce

Caucasian spruce *Picea orientalis*

This graceful tree is one of the best spruces for cultivation, being more lime-tolerant and better able to withstand drier conditions than most other spruces. It was introduced into Europe in 1839 and is common in parks, large gardens and arboreta. There are trees in the wild reputed to be around 400 years old, something obviously yet to be achieved in cultivation. The oriental spruce is easily recognized by its dense, blunt-tipped short needles and conical form.

Right: The female flowers are red.

Right: Both male and female flowers are borne on the same tree; the male flowers are bright red opening to yellow.

Identification: The bark is pinkish-brown, relatively smooth at first, flaking into small irregular plates in maturity. The needle-like leaves are up to 1cm/½in long, bluntly pointed at the tips, shiny dark green above, paler beneath and pointing forward on buff-coloured shoots. The male flowers are bright red at first, opening yellow, and the female flowers are red. Both appear on the same tree, in separate clusters, in spring. The fruit is a cylindrical drooping cone, up to 10cm/4in long, purple ripening to brown, and covered with patches of sticky aromatic resin.

Distribution: Caucasus, north-east Turkey.
Height: 50m/165ft
Shape: Narrowly conical
Evergreen
Pollinated: Wind
Leaf shape: Linear

Above: Short, shiny dark green needle-like leaves are borne on pale buff-coloured shoots.

Sitka Spruce

Coast spruce *Picea sitchensis*

Distribution: USA: narrow coastal strip from Kodiak Island, Alaska, to Mendocino County, California.
Height: 50m/165ft
Shape: Narrowly conical
Evergreen
Pollinated: Wind
Leaf shape: Linear

The largest of the North American spruces, this is a major species of north-west American forests. Valued for its timber, Sitka spruce has been widely planted across the Northern Hemisphere (including Europe) in forestry plantations. The timber is pinkish-brown, and is strong for its light weight. Originally used for aircraft frames, it is now the main species used in paper manufacture.

Far left: Male flower.

Left: Female flower.

Right: Cones are pale buff, 10cm/4in long with thin, papery scales and are pendulous in habit.

Identification: The overall shape is an open, narrow cone, with widely spaced, slender, ascending branches. Sitka spruce can easily grow more than 1m/3ft a year when young. The bark in young trees is a deep purple-brown. Older trees have large, curving cracks, which develop into plates of lifting bark. The needles are stiff with a sharp point, blue-green above with two white stomatal bands beneath, and up to 3cm/1¼in long. They are arranged all around the pale, buff-coloured shoot. The male flowers are reddish and occur in small quantities on each tree, shedding pollen in late spring. The female flowers are greenish-red and present on only the topmost shoots.

Norway Spruce

Picea abies

Norway spruce is the Christmas tree of Europe. It has a regular, symmetrical form with horizontal branching at low levels, which gradually becomes upswept towards the top of the tree. It grows naturally throughout northern Europe (except in the United Kingdom) up to altitudes of around 1,500m/4,900ft. Elsewhere it has been widely cultivated for its timber. Norway spruce is traditionally used to make the bellies of violins and other stringed instruments.

Left: The cones hang down.

Identification: The bark in young trees is a deep coppery-pink; on older trees it becomes a dark purple, with shallow round or oval plates that lift away from the trunk. The needles are a rich dark green with a faint sheen and are up to 2cm/¾in long. When crushed they emit a citrus fragrance, which has become synonymous with Christmas. The male flowers are golden, shedding copious amounts of pollen in late spring. The female flowers are purple-red, and are frequently confined to the top of the tree. The pendulous cones are cylindrical, slightly curved and up to 15cm/6in long.

Left: Male flowers occur in groups at the shoot tips.

Right: A female flower.

Distribution: Northern Europe (excluding the UK), from the Pyrenees to western Russia.
Height: 50m/165ft
Shape: Narrowly conical
Evergreen
Pollinated: Wind
Leaf shape: Linear

OTHER SPECIES OF NOTE

Tiger-tail Spruce *Picea polita*
This ornamental, pyramid-shaped, medium-size spruce originates from central and southern Japan. It is one of the most striking and attractive spruces. Consequently, it has been widely planted in parks and gardens throughout the world. It has long (up to 5cm/2in), rigid, spine-tipped needle-like leaves – probably the sharpest of any spruce – which are flattened and stand out at right angles to the chestnut-brown shoots. Its common name "tiger-tail" comes from the fact that the foliage-covered branch ends are pendulous – looking very much like a tiger's tail.

Serbian Spruce

Picea omorika

The Serbian spruce has a very small natural population and because of this is considered to be endangered in the wild. It is a beautiful, slender, spire-like tree with branches that sweep elegantly downwards, only to arch upwards at their tips. This habit means that it is able to resist damage by efficiently shedding snow rather than collecting it. It is also the spruce that is most resistant to atmospheric pollution.

Identification: The bark is orange-brown to copper, broken into irregular to square plates. The shoot is a similar colour to the bark and quite hairy. The needles are short with blunt tips, less than 2cm/¾in long, glossy dark green above and with two broad white stomatal bands underneath. The male flowers are crimson and held below the new shoots; the female flowers are also red but confined to the topmost branches. This tree's most distinctive characteristic is its spire-like form.

Left: The needles are short with blunt tips.

Right: To help shed snow the branches sweep downwards.

Left: The cone is pendulous, held on a thick curved stalk, tear-shaped, 6cm/2⅖in long and purple-brown in colour.

Distribution: Europe: confined to the Drina Valley in south-west Serbia.
Height: 30m/100ft
Shape: Very narrowly conical
Evergreen
Pollinated: Wind
Leaf shape: Linear

Dragon Spruce

Picea asperata

The dragon spruce was discovered in China in 1903 and introduced into Europe by the English plant collector Ernest Wilson in 1910. Wilson described it as being similar in form to Norway spruce, *P. abies*. It is a slow-growing tree, which begins life narrowly conical in outline but becomes progressively broader as it matures. It is common in botanic gardens and arboreta across Europe.

Below: The needle-like leaves are rigid and sharply pointed and borne on stout shoots.

Identification: The bark is purplish at first, becoming purple-brown with loosely hung scales in maturity. Where the bark is exposed to direct sunlight it may fade to pale grey. The dragon spruce has rigid, sharply pointed, needle-like leaves, which are dark bluish-green and around 2cm/¾in long, borne on stout pink-buff shoots that are rough to the touch. The cones are cylindrical, shortly tapered to a rounded end and up to 15cm/6in long. Both male and female flowers are borne on the same tree and conspicuous in spring, when clouds of pollen are released.

Left: Male and female flowers are borne on the same tree and release copious amounts of pollen in spring.

Right: The cones, which may be up to 15cm/6in long, hang in clusters from the branches.

Distribution: North-west China.
Height: 20m/65ft
Shape: Broadly conical
Evergreen
Pollinated: Wind
Leaf shape: Linear

Sargent Spruce

Picea brachytyla

This tree is one of the most ornamental of all spruces. It has two-toned, needle-like leaves, which are fresh, bright green on the top side and silver-white beneath. Each shoot is also white on the underside. It is a hardy species, growing in China at elevations in excess of 4,000m/13,000ft above sea level, and does not suffer damage from late spring frosts. It was discovered by the French missionaries Jean Marie Delavay and Paul Farges and was introduced into Europe by the English plant hunter Ernest Wilson in 1901.

Right: The young shoot tips can be used to make a tea rich in vitamin C.

Right: Cones grow to a long elongated shape.

Identification: The tree has long, gracefully ascending and spreading branches that arch downwards towards the tip. The bark on young trees is smooth, pinkish-grey and pockmarked with white resinous spots. In maturity it is pale grey and roughly fissured into irregular scales. The needle-like leaves are up to 2cm/¾in long and the purple-green cones are cylindrical, tapering to each end, up to 15cm/6in long, and held on a short stalk.

Right: The seeds mature in October and November.

Distribution: China.
Height: 30m/100ft
Shape: Broadly conical
Evergreen
Pollinated: Wind
Leaf shape: Linear

**West Himalayan
Spruce** *Picea smithiana*
The west Himalayan
spruce (also known as
the morinda spruce) has
weeping foliage, which
allows it to shed snow
easily. It is native to
Afghanistan, Kashmir
and Nepal, where it grows at altitudes in excess
of 3,500m/11,500ft. Its needles are slender, up
to 4cm/1½in long and shiny dark green.

Sikkim Spruce *Picea spinulosa*
This rare, beautiful tree is native to Sikkim,
Bhutan and the eastern Himalayas, where it may
reach 60m/200ft in height. It was introduced into
Europe as early as 1878. It is recognizable by its
open green crown and spreading branches,
draped with pendulous branchlets that have a
covering of flat, green, needle-like leaves.

Koster's Blue Spruce *Picea pungens* 'Koster'
This cultivated form of the Colorado blue spruce,
P. pungens, was raised in Holland in the late 19th
century. It is a small to medium-size conical tree,
suitable for garden use, with silvery-blue to
almost white, stiff foliage.

Creeping Spruce *Picea abies* 'Nana'
'Nana' is a dwarf form, first raised around 1855
and of irregular conical habit, with sharply
pointed, small, needle-like leaves that densely
clothe its numerous branches.

Likiang Spruce

Picea likiangensis

This is a beautiful, ornamental tree of
medium to large size, which grows naturally
from north-west Yunnan to south-east Tibet
Autonomous Region in China. The species
displays considerable variation and sat
one time split by taxonomists into
several different species. The
best-known form is the 'Yunnan'
form, which was introduced
into Europe around 1900.

Identification: Although this is a
variable species, the following
features are fairly constant. The
bark is pale grey with a few
shallow, vertical fissures. The
needle-like leaves are blue-
green above and distinctly
banded with two white
lines of stomata beneath.
They are up to 2cm/¾in
long and bluntly pointed.
The cones are cylindrical,
pale brown with red
margins to each scale.
Both male and
female flowers are
large, brilliant red and
produced in profusion. In
springtime they stand out on each branch
like burning embers.

Distribution: China.
Height: 30m/100ft
Shape: Broadly conical
Evergreen
Pollinated: Wind
Leaf shape: Linear

*Right: The
cones are up
to 13cm/
5in long*

*Below: The distinctive
feature of Likiang spruce
is its flowers.*

Siberian Spruce

Picea obovata

This hardy sub-Arctic tree has been in
cultivation in Europe since the mid-
19th century, although it did not
reach Britain until 1908. In the wild
in Scandinavia it hybridizes with
Norway spruce, *P. abies*, which it
resembles, except that it usually
has shorter, matt, needle-like
leaves and smaller cones. As
with other Arctic species,
Siberian spruce comes into
leaf early in spring in
response to increasing
light levels and
its young
foliage is
therefore at
risk from frost
damage.

Identification: In cultivation the
Siberian spruce is sometimes a
bushy, even shrubby, tree, but
more often it is conical, with a
broad base and ascending
branches with pendulous foliage
toward the tips. The bark is
purple-grey flecked with white,
becoming brown and flaking in
maturity. The needle-like leaves
are short (2cm/¾in), slender,
pointed and forward-facing on
buff to pale brown shoots. The
cones are cylindrical,
tapered at each end,
golden brown and
leathery and up to
10cm/4in long.

Distribution: From northern
Scandinavia across Russia
and Siberia to east Asia.
Height: 30m/100ft
Shape: Broadly conical
Evergreen
Pollinated: Wind
Leaf shape: Linear

*Far left to left: Short needle-like
leaves face forward on the shoot.
The cone is roughly cylindrical,
tapering at both ends and up to
10cm/4in long.*

DECIDUOUS LARCHES

This small genus of fewer than a dozen species is confined to temperate regions of the Northern Hemisphere. Deciduous larches are fast-growing conifers – several species have been widely planted for forestry purposes. Larches are some of the most seasonally attractive of all conifers, as their needles turn gold and fall in autumn, to be renewed every spring with a flush of lime-green foliage.

European Larch

Larix decidua

This attractive, hardy tree grows naturally at altitudes up to 2,500m/8,200ft above sea level. It is a long-lived conifer, with some trees in the Alps recorded at over 700 years old. European larch has been widely planted throughout Europe and North America for both forestry and ornamental purposes.

Identification: On young trees the bark is pale grey and smooth; on old trees it is dark pink and heavily fissured. Whorls of upswept branches are well spaced. The 4cm/1½in needles are soft and bright green, becoming yellow before falling in autumn. They are carried singly on main shoots and in dense whorls on side shoots. The shoots are pendulous and straw-coloured. The male flowers are pink-yellow discs, normally on the undersides of shoots. The female flowers, appearing before the leaves in early spring, are purple-pink, upright and develop quickly into immature cones.

Far right and left: Cones are 4.5cm/1¾in long.

Distribution: From the southern Alps through Switzerland, Austria and Germany to the Carpathian Mountains of Slovakia and Romania.
Height: 40m/130ft
Shape: Narrowly conical
Deciduous
Pollinated: Wind
Leaf shape: Linear

Japanese Larch

Larix kaempferi

In the wild, this larch is confined to the Japanese island of Honshu, where it grows at altitudes exceeding 2,750m/9,000ft. It was introduced to Britain in 1861 and makes up a large portion of the conifer forests of Wales where it is cultivated for timber. It is also grown as an ornamental species in Japanese temple gardens, where it is quite often trained as a bonsai.

Above: Cones are borne intermittently along the shoot among the foliage.

Distribution: Central Honshu, Japan.
Height: 30m/100ft
Shape: Broadly conical
Deciduous
Pollinated: Wind
Leaf shape: Linear

Identification: The form is broader than that of the European larch. Branches sweep upwards when young, becoming level or even slightly descending in older trees. The bark is reddish-brown and scaly. The young shoots are a distinctive purple-red, sometimes covered with a slight silver bloom. The needles are 5cm/2in long, and flatter and broader than those of European larch. They dull to grey-green in summer, then become orange before falling in autumn. The male flowers are yellow globules clustered on pendulous shoots. The female flowers, which occur all over the tree, have a pink centre and creamy-yellow margins. The bun-shaped cones are 3cm/1¼in long.

Left: Japanese larch cones have scales that turn outwards. The needles are soft, bright green when they sprout in early spring, then fade to grey-green in summer and turn orange in autumn.

Golden Larch

Pseudolarix amabilis

The golden larch is a slow-growing, deciduous conifer, but it is not actually a true larch. It differs in having cones that disintegrate on the tree and spur shoots that lengthen annually. This beautiful tree deserves to be more widely grown; it is normally found only in botanic gardens and arboreta across western Europe.

Identification: The overall shape is broadly conical with level branches that sometimes curve upwards at the tips. The bark is grey-brown, deeply fissured into thick, square plates. The shoot is pale yellow to pink-buff. The soft needles, 5cm/2in long, are set spirally around the shoots, occurring in dense whorls on side shoots and singly on leading shoots, where they face forwards. They are bright grass-green on emerging in spring and a glorious bright orange-gold in autumn just before falling. Both male and female flowers are yellow, borne in clusters at the ends of shoots on the same tree. Cones appear only after long, hot summers; they are 6cm/2½in long, with curious, triangular scales, reminiscent of a green globe artichoke. They ripen to golden brown in autumn before breaking apart on the tree.

Distribution: Provinces of Zhejiang, Anhui and Guangxi in eastern China.
Height: 40m/130ft
Shape: Broadly conical
Deciduous
Pollinated: Wind
Leaf shape: Linear

Left: Bright, new needles appear in spring. The cones ripen in autumn, then open to release their seeds.

OTHER SPECIES OF NOTE

Dahurian Larch *Larix gmelinii*
This broad, rather squat tree will, in good growing conditions, reach a height of 20m/65ft; elsewhere it may resemble a spreading bush. It grows in temperate regions of Europe where frost does not damage its early emerging new growth. The needles, which emerge bright green in mid-winter, are 4cm/1½in long and turn butter-yellow in autumn before falling. The cones are produced prolifically. They are ovoid, 2.5cm/1in long, shiny pale brown with broad scales that curve slightly outwards at the margins.

Sikkim Larch *Larix griffithiana*
This tree is native to eastern Nepal, Sikkim, Bhutan, and Tibet Autonomous Region, in China. It also grows in the Alps. A narrow, conical tree up to 20m/65ft tall, it is rare both in the wild and in cultivation. It has bark like a Corsican pine – grey-purple fissured into rough, scaly ridges. A graceful tree, it has pendulous red-brown shoots, bright green needles 5cm/2in long, and large erect cylindrical cones, 7–10cm/2¾–4in long.

Siberian Larch *Larix russica*
Sometimes referred to as *L. sibirica*, this tough, hardy, 30m/100ft tree originates from an area that extends from northern Russia east to the Yenisei River in Siberia. Its overall shape varies according to the location in which it is planted; in northern Europe it is narrow and conical with upswept branches. Further south it becomes broadly spreading with horizontal branching. This tree comes into leaf in late winter and consequently may suffer from frost damage.

Dunkeld Larch

Hybrid larch *Larix* x *eurolepis* (*L.* x *marschlinsii*)

This vigorous, beautiful tree is a hybrid between the European larch, *L. decidua*, and the Japanese larch, *L. kaempferi*. Both species were planted in close proximity to each other in the grounds of Dunkeld House, Scotland, in 1885. Seed collected from the Japanese larch in 1897 produced seedlings, which were formally identified and described as hybrids in 1919. Since then the Dunkeld larch has been widely planted as a timber-producing forestry plantation species.

Distribution: Of garden origin but now cultivated throughout Europe.
Height: 35m/115ft
Shape: Broadly conical
Deciduous
Pollinated: Wind
Leaf shape: Linear

Identification: The Dunkeld larch has reddish-brown scaly bark, orange-brown to pink-buff shoots, and egg-shaped, upright cones, as tall as those of the European larch (4cm/1½in), but with reflexed scales like the cones of the Japanese larch. The needles are soft to the touch, up to 4cm/1½in long, borne singly on leading shoots and in whorls on side shoots. They are grey-green to blue-green in summer, becoming golden-brown before falling in autumn.

Above: In early spring this tree produces pink-purple female flowers on bare branches just before the soft needle-like leaves appear.

TWO- AND THREE-NEEDLE PINES

The pines of Europe, of the family Pinaceae, are as diverse as the landscapes they inhabit. From the sprawling shrub-like pines of the Alps to the stately giants of the Mediterranean coastline, there are pines for every location. Perhaps most widespread and easily recognizable is the Scots pine, Pinus sylvestris. *It has a natural range from Scotland to Siberia and occurs as far south as the Mediterranean.*

Maritime Pine

Pinus pinaster

Distribution: Central and western Mediterranean regions including North Africa.
Height: 40m/130ft
Shape: Broadly columnar
Evergreen
Pollinated: Wind
Leaf shape: Linear

The maritime pine has been cultivated for forestry purposes since the 16th century because its timber is strong and straight-grained. It was first described in 1789 by the British botanist William Aiton. It thrives in coastal locations, in sandy soils, and is very tolerant of salt spray. In exposed conditions it becomes a twisted, irregularly-shaped tree, whereas in plantations, such as those along the southern coasts of Spain, Portugal and France, it will grow to a height of 40m/130ft with a clean, straight trunk.

Identification: Maritime pine bark is purple-brown and smooth at first, becoming ridged and deeply fissured in maturity. It has sharp, needle-like leaves, 20cm/8in long, which are grey-green to dark green and borne in pairs on stout, pale brown shoots. The yellow male and red female flowers are borne in separate clusters on the same tree in late spring to early summer. The cones are hard and woody with spines on each scale, up to 20cm/8in long. Borne in clusters, they persist on the branches for several years.

Right: Sharp, slender needle-like leaves up to 20cm/ 8in long are borne in pairs on stout shoots.

Corsican Pine

Pinus nigra subsp. *laricio*

Distribution: Southern Italy and Corsica.
Height: 40m/130ft
Shape: Broadly columnar
Evergreen
Pollinated: Wind
Leaf shape: Linear

Right: Needles are long, measuring up to 18cm/7in.

A large tree, this differs from the species, *P. nigra* (the Austrian pine) by having a more open crown with fewer, shorter branches, which are level rather than ascending. The Corsican pine is grown throughout Europe, including Britain, for its timber, which is strong and relatively free of knots.

Identification: The stiff, stout shoots are pale yellow-brown, with buds that are narrowly conical, sharply pointed and commonly covered with white resin. The needles, in pairs, are sparsely positioned on the shoot. They are pale grey-green, up to 18cm/7in long and twisted. The male flowers are golden yellow and abundant at the bases of shoots, shedding pollen from late spring to early summer. The female flowers are dull pink and positioned on the tips of growing shoots. The cone is ovoid to conical with a slight sweep and up to 8cm/3in long.

Above: The bark is light grey to pink and is fissured from an early age.

Left: Flowers appear from spring to early summer.

Lace-bark Pine *Pinus bungeana*
This is a beautiful slow-growing, broad, widely branched pine, with smooth, grey-green bark, which the tree gradually sheds to reveal patches of new bark. This is pale yellow, but slowly turns olive-brown, red and purple when exposed to light. It has dark yellow-green, needle-like leaves, which are borne in threes and are up to 8cm/3in long. Lace-bark pine was introduced into Europe

in 1846 from its native territory in central China. Since then it has been planted in gardens and arboreta, but perhaps not as widely as it should be, considering its beauty.

Identification: The bark is grey, with orange fissure lines running vertically down the trunk. The tree has a short main trunk and has branching relatively low down. The shoots are pale green, smooth and curved, with a bright chestnut-red bud, fringed with white hairs, at each shoot tip. The needles are forward pointing, in pairs, grey-green in colour, stout and up to 12cm/4½in long. The cone has a flat base but is almost round, up to 10cm/4in across, glossy brown and smooth. It is relatively heavy and can weigh up to 375g/12oz. After forming, the cones remain tightly closed for three years before opening to reveal up to 100 edible seeds.

Stone Pine

Umbrella pine *Pinus pinea*

Widely planted throughout the Mediterranean for its seeds, which are eaten as nuts, the tree is also known as the umbrella pine because of its flat-topped shape in maturity. With its long, horizontal branches and dense foliage, it is a tree of unusual and aesthetically pleasing habit, and has become a distinctive part of the Mediterranean landscape.

Distribution: Mediterranean from Portugal to Turkey.
Height: 20m/65ft
Shape: Broadly spreading
Evergreen
Pollinated: Wind
Leaf shape: Linear

Above: Female cone (left) and male cone (right).

Above: The needles are long and occur in pairs.

Right: The closed cone is almost egg-shaped.

Scots Pine

Pinus sylvestris

This is one of the temperate world's most prolific and popular trees, which most Americans would instantly recognize as their Christmas tree. The Scots pine flourishes on dry, sandy soils but will grow in wet conditions, although more slowly. It is a prolific seed producer and is able to colonize new territory quickly. It is well known as a pioneer species, establishing itself long before other trees begin to move in.

Identification: An old Scots pine has a distinctive low, broadly domed crown and large, level but snaking branches. The bark is one of its most distinctive features. It ranges from grey-green in a juvenile to a stunning orange-red in maturity. On branches this red bark peels and flakes away. On the main stem it becomes cracked and fissured with age. The paired needles are stiff, twisted, bluish green, set in an orange-brown basal sheath and up to 7cm/2¾in long. The male flowers are yellow and the females are red; they are held in separate clusters on young shoots in late spring and early summer. The cone is egg-shaped, up to 7cm/2¾in long and green, ripening to brown.

Distribution: From Scotland right across northern Europe to the Pacific coast and southwards to the Mediterranean and Turkey.
Height: 35m/115ft
Shape: Broadly spreading
Evergreen
Pollinated: Wind
Leaf shape: Linear

Left: The trunk is often branchless.

Right: Cones may occur in pairs.

Bosnian Pine

Pinus leucodermis

A medium-sized, neat, distinctive tree, this grows particularly well on sunny slopes, on dry and shallow soils overlying chalk or limestone, where it can live for more than 1,000 years. The needles are a deep black-green, giving the whole tree a sombre, dark appearance that makes this pine instantly recognizable.

Identification: The overall shape is ovoid to conical, rather narrow, regular and dense. The branches ascend slightly from the trunk. The bark is greenish-grey and smooth when young, becoming finely fissured in maturity. The shoots are pale brown and slightly hairy, and have a glaucous bloom. The male flowers are yellow and the females purple-red. Both are held at the tips of the shoots on the same plant. Clouds of pollen are often seen blowing in the breeze around the tree in late spring.

Left: Flat-bottomed cones, cobalt-blue or black when young, ripen to brown in the second year.

Above: The needles, which are in pairs, are prolific on the shoot; they are up to 9cm/3½in long and all point neatly forward at a 45° angle. They have a sharp point and are very rigid.

Distribution: Balkans, Bosnia-Herzegovina, Bulgaria, Albania into northern Greece and south-western Italy.
Height: 25m/80ft
Shape: Narrowly conical
Evergreen
Pollinated: Wind
Leaf shape: Linear

Left: The upright bundles of needles are a deep lustrous green colour. They grow on branches that are set tightly together.

Aleppo Pine

Pinus halepensis

The Aleppo pine is a medium-sized tree that has the ability to survive in hot, dry conditions, including desiccating winds, and in exposed coastal locations. Consequently, it has been widely planted in arid areas as part of afforestation schemes to help stabilize sandy soils. Due to this artificial distribution its original natural range is unknown. However, its common name is derived from the second largest city in Syria. It was introduced into Britain in 1683. In the eastern Mediterranean the timber is used for fuel.

Identification: The overall shape of mature trees is domed and rugged, with large, contorted branches. The bark on young trees is purple-brown with orange, shallow fissures. Older trees have dark red-brown bark and orange fissures. The needle-like leaves are borne in pairs; they are bright fresh green, slender, shiny and smooth, and up to 10cm/4in long. The cones are orange to red-brown, woody and up to 10cm/4in long; they are normally borne in whorls that face backwards along the shoot.

Right: The cones are orange to red-brown at first becoming woody and up to 10cm (4in) long.

Distribution: Southern Europe/Mediterranean to south-west Asia and Afghanistan.
Height: 20m/65ft
Shape: Broadly conical
Evergreen
Pollinated: Wind
Leaf shape: Linear

Canary Island Pine

Pinus canariensis

The Canary Island pine is restricted to the Canary archipelago, where it occurs naturally on all the islands except Lanzarote and Fuerteventura. It is one of the dominant tree species in the monteverde and montane cloud forests, which occur at high altitude, up to 2,500m/8,200ft above sea level, on the western and northern slopes of mountains such as Mount Teide, 3,718m/12,200ft, on Tenerife. Here, moisture-laden clouds, carried in on the winds, are "combed" for valuable moisture by the long needles of this pine. It is unlikely to survive outside in northern Europe.

Identification: The Canary Island pine has spreading branches and drooping branchlets. When young the overall form is conical, becoming broader as the tree matures. The bark is red-brown, thick, fissured and flaking. The long needle-like leaves are at first glaucous, becoming bright grass green as they mature. They are very slender and lax, up to 30cm/12in long and borne on new shoots in clusters of three. The cones are red-brown and may be up to 25cm/10in long.

Distribution: Canary Islands.
Height: 30m/100ft
Shape: Broadly conical
Evergreen
Pollinated: Wind
Leaf shape: Linear

Left: Cones are cylindrical egg-shaped and have raised scales giving a rough appearance.

OTHER SPECIES OF NOTE

Dwarf Mountain Pine *Pinus mugo*
This is a sprawling, small, but very hardy two-needled pine, which is native to the Alps and other mountainous regions of south-east Europe. In its native habitat it will crawl along the ground for great distances, but seldom attains heights in excess of 4m/13ft. It has been widely planted in Europe, both as an ornamental species in rock gardens and as a shelter species for protecting less hardy plants in exposed upland situations.

Golden Scots Pine *Pinus sylvestris* 'Aurea'
This is a popular garden cultivar of the Scots pine, which is native across Europe, from Spain to Siberia. As its name suggests, this particular cultivar has golden or yellow foliage, which is at its most vibrant in the winter months. The needle-like leaves are up to 7.5cm/3in long, borne in pairs on golden-brown shoots. It has been in cultivation since 1876 and may have been raised in Germany. It is slow-growing and seldom reaches heights in excess of 15m/50ft.

Japanese Black Pine *Pinus thunbergii*
This is a magnificent two-needled pine, which in maturity has a distinctive leaning top and numerous long, twisted branches. In its native Japan, where it is often found growing near the seashore, it may reach heights in excess of 40m/130ft, but in Europe it seldom reaches half that height. It was introduced into Europe in 1861 and is now widely grown in parks, large gardens and arboreta. It is also a favoured species for bonsai.

Gerard's Pine

Chilgoza pine *Pinus gerardiana*

This small to medium-sized rare ornamental tree inhabits dry valleys and mountainsides in the Himalayas and Afghanistan. It was discovered by Captain Gerard of the Bengal Native Infantry (hence its common name) in 1832, and was introduced into Europe seven years later. It is somewhat reminiscent of the lace-bark pine, *P. bungeana*: like that species it has exfoliating bark that creates a beautiful patchwork.

Identification: The overall appearance is of an open crown with few branches, but each one is clothed in dense, spiky foliage. The grey-pink bark flakes in papery scales to reveal patches of green, yellow and brown new bark beneath. The needle-like leaves are densely borne in spreading clusters of three all around the shoot; they are up to 10cm/4in long and dull green in colour. Gerard's pine has large, woody, oval-shaped cones, which may be up to 20cm/8in long and 10cm/4in wide.

Distribution: North-west Himalayas and Afghanistan.
Height: 20m/65ft
Shape: Broadly conical
Evergreen
Pollinated: Wind
Leaf shape: Linear

Below: Needle-like leaves are borne in threes.

FIVE-NEEDLE PINES

Five-needled pines are those pines where the needles grow in clusters of five on the shoots.
They are considered to include some of the most beautiful of all pines, quite often producing
long soft foliage, which gives the trees an elegant feathery appearance. This group includes the
ornamental Holford's pine.

Bhutan Pine

Himalayan white pine *Pinus wallichiana*

The soft, slender, pendulous appearance of this pine belies its resilience and ruggedness. In the Himalayas it is able to grow at altitudes in excess of 2,440–3,800m/ 8,000–12,470ft. It has also proved more resistant to air pollution than almost any other conifer. Although the tree is sometimes confused with *P. strobus*, its appearance has more in common with *P. ayacahuite*. The bark of young trees is grey with resin blistering. On older trees the bark becomes pinkish-orange and is lined with tiny fissures. It is common in cultivation in western Europe.

Identification: The crown is strongly whorled and relatively open. Young trees have a conical appearance; older trees become more broad and columnar. Lower branches descend gracefully from the trunk, curving upwards at their tips. Upper branches sweep skywards. The shoots are long, strong and pale grey with a purple bloom. The needles are light green, 18–20cm/7–8in long, in groups of five cupped in a red-brown basal sheath. They curve forward along the shoot, then droop at each side. The male flowers are pale yellow, ovoid, positioned at the bottom of new shoots; they shed their pollen in early summer. The female flowers also appear in early summer; they are dull purple and grow towards the tips of new shoots. The fruit is a long (up to 30cm/12in), drooping, banana-shaped, green cone covered in sticky white resin. It ripens to pale brown in its second year.

Right: After hanging for more than a year on the tree, cones open to drop their seeds.

Distribution: Himalayas, from Afghanistan to eastern Nepal and Bhutan.
Height: 40m/130ft
Shape: Broadly conical
Evergreen
Pollinated: Wind
Leaf shape: Linear

Macedonian Pine

Pinus peuce

This is a distinctively dark-crowned pine, with dense, dark green foliage that is reminiscent of yew when viewed from a distance. The dense canopy extends downwards to the lower third of the tree, even on mature specimens. This pine was introduced into cultivation in 1864 by the Greek botanist Theodoros Orphanides. Today, as well as being used as an ornamental in gardens and arboreta across Europe, it is widely planted as a timber-producing species in forestry plantations.

Identification: The bark is dark purple, with large smooth areas between vertical fissures. New shoots are bright green, maturing to orange-brown. The dark green, stiff needle-like leaves are 10cm/4in long and borne in clusters of five. Male and female flowers are borne in separate clusters on the same trees in early summer. The leathery, cylindrical cones are resinous and up to 15cm/6in long.

Above: The male flowers are yellow and the females red.

Left and right: The drooping cones are green at first, ripening to rich brown.

Distribution: Balkans, Bulgaria and northern Greece.
Height: 30m/100ft
Shape: Narrowly conical
Evergreen
Pollinated: Wind
Leaf shape: Linear

Armand's Pine

Chinese white pine *Pinus armandii*

This Asian five-needled pine is reasonably common in cultivation in Europe, particularly in botanic gardens and arboreta. It was discovered by the French Jesuit missionary Abbé Armand David in 1873 (hence its common name) and was introduced into Europe in 1895. Armand's pine is an attractive, medium-size tree with drooping foliage and large barrel-shaped cones.

Identification: The bark is a dull pink-grey, smooth at first but becoming deeply fissured into square or rectangular flaking plates. The crown is broadly conical with widely spaced whorls of horizontal branches, which give the tree an open, airy quality. Armand's pine has glaucous, blue-green, needle-like leaves that are long and lax, giving a "floppy" appearance. They are up to 15cm/6in long and gradually droop below the shoot as they mature. Each orange-brown cone is held by a thick 2.5cm/1in stalk; the cones are roughly cylindrical but broadest near the base, 15 x 7.5cm/6 x 3in with thick scales.

Left: Long lax blue-green needles are borne in drooping clusters of five.

Right: The orange-brown cones may be up to 15cm/6in long.

Distribution: China, from the west to the Tibet Autonomous Region; Korea and Taiwan.
Height: 40m/130ft
Shape: Broadly conical
Evergreen
Pollinated: Wind
Leaf shape: Linear

OTHER SPECIES OF NOTE
Mexican White Pine *Pinus ayacahuite*
This beautiful tree attains heights of up to 35m/115ft. It is extremely hardy and grows high on mountain slopes. It has graceful, drooping foliage with blue-green, slender, lax needles up to 15cm/6in long, held in fives. The cone can grow up to 45cm/18in long and is normally covered with sticky white resin. It thrives in central Europe and the Alps.

Weymouth Pine *Pinus strobus*
Sometimes known as the eastern white pine, this North American species is one of the largest pines, reaching 75m/225ft in the wild. It was cultivated in Europe from around 1705, when trees were planted in Britain at the Badminton, Gloucestershire, estate of the Duchess of Beaufort and by Lord Weymouth (hence its name) at Longleat, Wiltshire. It is a five-needled pine, each needle being blue green and up to 12cm/4¾in long.
See also page 126.

Arolla Pine

Swiss stone pine *Pinus cembra*

This is a dense, slow-growing, small to medium-size tree, and has been common in cultivation in Europe since at least the mid-18th century. It has a rather formal, neat appearance, which is favoured by some landscape architects. An unusual feature of this tree is that the cones seldom open on the tree to release the seeds inside. From two to three years after ripening, the cone begins to rot and either falls to the ground or is broken apart by birds and squirrels in search of the edible seeds inside.

Identification: The bark is grey-brown with vertical scales curling away from the trunk. The needle-like leaves are clustered in fives and densely borne on shoots covered in fine, rust-coloured hairs. The needles, up to 9cm/3½in long, are dark, shiny green on one side and bright bluish-white on the other. Male flowers are purple opening to yellow, female flowers red; both are borne on the same tree in late spring to early summer.

Distribution: Central Alps and Carpathians.
Height: 25m/80ft
Shape: Conical
Evergreen
Pollinated: Wind
Leaf shape: Linear

Above: The cones are erect, up to 7.5cm (3in) long, deep blue at first.

Korean Pine

Pinus koraiensis

This tough, hardy Asian pine inhabits mountain slopes and river valleys throughout its extensive range. In cultivation it seldom exceeds 35m/115ft in height, but in the wild it is known to exceed 50m/165ft. It was introduced into Europe by the English nurseryman James Veitch in 1861. Since then it has become a popular ornamental tree in parks, gardens and arboreta and has spawned many cultivars.

Identification: The shape is loosely conical, with a feathery appearance. On young trees the bark is smooth and dark grey; on older trees it becomes pink-grey and thick, with curling, flaking scales. The needle-like leaves are densely clustered in groups of five and face forward on young shoots. Each needle is blunt-tipped, up to 12cm/4¾in long and has two, or sometimes three, sides: the outer side is a deep shining green and the inner surface is blue-white with distinct bands of stomata. The cones are oval-shaped, purple-brown and approximately 13cm/5in long.

Above: The needles are grouped in fives, blunt-tipped and rather rough to the touch.

Distribution: North-east Asia, Japan and Korea.
Height: 50m/165ft
Shape: Broadly conical
Evergreen
Pollinated: Wind
Leaf shape: Linear

Left: The cones have short stalks, are oval-shaped and up to 13cm/5in long and up to 5cm/2in wide. They have one blunt end. Cones grow singly on the branch in groups of three.

Holford's Pine

Pinus x holfordiana

This beautiful tree is a hybrid between the Mexican white pine, *P. ayacahuite*, and the Bhutan pine, *P. wallichiana*, which initially developed by chance in Westonbirt Arboretum, Gloucestershire, England, where both parents were growing close together. In 1904 seed was collected from the Mexican white pine and propagated. The resulting progeny were planted in several locations in the arboretum and as they developed it became clear that they were different to the parent pine. The hybrid was officially recognized and named in 1933.

Right: Cones are large – up to 30cm/ 12in long and quite often covered in a sticky white resin.

Right: The needles are blue-green, lax and hang from buff-coloured shoots.

Identification: From a distance the tree has a graceful feathery appearance. The bark is grey and vertically fissured. The needle-like leaves, which are clustered in fives, are up to 18cm/7in long, slender, pointed, lax and blue-green. The cones are buff brown, covered with white sticky resin and occasionally up to 30cm/12in long. They are heavy and hang either singly or in twos and threes on the outside of the crown, creating a quite beautiful effect against the soft blue-green foliage. The tree is a vigorous hybrid.

Right: Clusters of long lax needles give the tree a feathery appearance.

Distribution: Of UK garden origin.
Height: 30m/100ft
Shape: Broadly conical
Evergreen
Pollinated: Wind
Leaf shape: Linear

Pinus x _schwerinii_
This elegant, large, five-needled tree is a hybrid between the Weymouth pine, _P. strobus_, and the Bhutan pine, _P. wallichiana_. It was found on the estate of Dr Graf von Schwerin near Berlin in 1905 and named in his honour in 1931. It differs from both parents in having densely hairy shoots and has shorter needles than the Bhutan pine.

Cerro Potosi Pinyon _Pinus culminicola_
This small five-needled pine takes its name from the mountain in north-east Mexico where it was first discovered. Since then it has been found in other mountainous locations in northern Mexico. It is a hardy, slow-growing, shrubby species with grey-green needles up to 5cm/2in long. It was introduced into Europe before 1979.

Bristlecone Pine _Pinus aristata_
This North American pine is closely related to the ancient pine, _P. longaeva_, which is also, confusingly, known as the bristlecone pine. However they are two different species. _P. aristata_ is a small tree with thick, hairy, red-brown shoots. The needle-like leaves are in clusters of five, to 5cm/2in long and spotted with white resin, unlike those of _P. longaeva_. _P. aristata_ also has longer bristle-like spines on the tip of each cone scale than _P. longaeva_. It was introduced into Europe in 1863.

Dwarf Siberian Pine

Japanese stone pine _Pinus pumila_

This hardy, dwarf five-needled pine, which rarely grows to more than 6m/20ft in height, inhabits high, exposed rocky mountain slopes from eastern Siberia to the Pacific Ocean. It thrives in the Alps. In these habitats it is usually the dominant species, forming extensive forests of scrub. It is closely related to the Arolla pine, _P. cembra_, and it is often difficult to distinguish from dwarf forms of that species.

Identification: The bark is grey-brown, smooth at first becoming shallowly fissured in maturity. The shoots are green-brown and covered with grey down. The needle-like leaves, up to 10cm/4in long, are dark green and slightly glossy on the outside and bright blue-green with bands of stomata on the inner surface. The cones are purple when young, ripening to red-brown or golden yellow-brown.

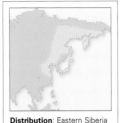

Distribution: Eastern Siberia south to north-eastern China and Japan.
Height: 6m/20ft
Shape: Broadly spreading
Evergreen
Pollinated: Wind
Leaf shape: Linear

Left: The cones are small and egg-shaped, 5cm/2in long by 3cm/1¼in wide.

Left and above left: The leaves are densely borne along the branchlets in clusters of five.

Japanese White Pine

Pinus parviflora

This is a small to medium-size hardy tree that originally inhabited mountain slopes in its native Japan. It has been so widely planted, both in Japan and around the world, that it is now difficult to ascertain its exact natural distribution. It was introduced into Europe by English nurseryman James Veitch in 1861. This tree is much favoured for bonsai because of its broadly spreading, flat-topped shape. It also provided the motif for traditional "willow pattern" ceramic decoration.

Identification: The thick trunk supports a dense crown and old trees develop a picturesque shape as the upper branches lengthen to create a flat top. The bark is grey, scaly and in maturity covered with vertical fissures. The tree has twisted, needle-like leaves that are borne in clusters of five and emerge from bright orange leaf buds. Each needle is up to 6cm/2½in long and blue-green in colour. The male flowers are purple opening yellow, and the female flowers are red; they are both borne, in separate clusters, on the same tree in late spring.

Distribution: Japan.
Height: 25m/80ft
Shape: Broadly columnar
Evergreen
Pollinated: Wind
Leaf shape: Linear

Right: The stiff, blue-green needles grow in brush-like tufts.

Left: The cones are small, to 7.5cm/3in long, and red-brown, with very few scales.

MAGNOLIAS

The Magnoliaceae family contains 12 genera and just over 200 species, of which the majority are native to North America or Asia. They include some of the most beautiful of all flowering trees. Many cultivars have been developed from the true species. There are magnolias to suit all locations – some are giants, others little more than large shrubs. They were introduced to Europe in the 1700s.

Yulan Magnolia

Lily tree *Magnolia denudata*

Distribution: Central and eastern China.
Height: 15m/50ft
Shape: Broadly spreading
Deciduous
Pollinated: Insect
Leaf shape: Ovate

Sometimes known as the lily tree, this beautiful small to medium-size tree has been cultivated in Chinese Buddhist temple gardens since about AD600. Its pure white, cup-shaped, fragrant flowers were regarded as a symbol of purity in the Tang Dynasty period and it was planted in the grounds of the emperor's palace.

Right: The beautiful white flowers are unfortunately prone to browning if subjected to frost.

Identification: The Yulan magnolia is a rather low, rounded, thickly branched tree. It has thick, bright green leaves that are ovate, 15cm/6in long and 7.5cm/3in wide. After falling they decompose to leave a skeletal form. The pure white flowers are heavily scented with a citrus-lemon fragrance. They open from early to late spring: erect and goblet-shaped at first, they gradually spread to form a water-lily shape, as each thick petal curls outwards.

Japanese Big-leaf Magnolia

White bark magnolia *Magnolia hypoleuca*

Sometimes known as *M. obovata*, this is one of the largest of all magnolias, not only in height but also in girth. In the forests of Hokkaido, Japan, girths in excess of 3m/10ft have been recorded. Japanese craftsmen prize the tree for its light but strong, easily worked timber, which is used for lacquerwork and for items such as sword sheaths and handles. In some parts of the country, the large leaves that earn this tree its name are used for wrapping food.

Identification: The bark in young trees is smooth and dark purple-brown. In maturity it becomes slate grey. The leaves are up to 45cm/18in long and 20cm/8in wide. They are thick and leathery, sage green above, with silvery blue downy undersides. They are held in whorls of five to eight, positioned at the end of each shoot. Large, cup-shaped, creamy pink flowers are produced in early summer. The flowers are up to 20cm/8in across and strongly scented. They have bright purple-red stamens, which create a distinctive central "eye" to each flower. Seeds are produced on a conspicuous red cylindrical pod, up to 20cm/8in long.

Distribution: Japan and the Pacific coast of Russia.
Height: 30m/100ft
Shape: Broadly columnar
Deciduous
Pollinated: Insect
Leaf shape: Obovate

Left: The flowers of this tree, although large, are dwarfed by its massive leaves.

Bull Bay

Magnolia grandiflora

This magnificent evergreen flowering tree is more often than not grown as a wall shrub. However, given a warm, sheltered, sunny position it will develop into a broad-canopied, short-stemmed tree. The bull bay is common throughout warmer regions of Europe in parks, gardens and arboreta. The combination of glossy, dark green, leathery leaves and creamy white flowers makes it a very popular garden tree.

Identification: The bark is grey-brown, cracking into irregular small plates. The leaves, which grow up to 25cm/10in long and 10cm/4in across, are thick and rigid, glossy dark green above and either pale green or covered in copper-coloured hairs beneath. Flowers begin to appear when the tree is only around ten years old; they are wide-brimmed and cup-shaped, creamy white to pale lemon and deliciously scented. They can be up to 30cm/12in across and stand out splendidly against the dark foliage.

Above: The spectacular flowers are like dinner plates, measuring up to 30cm/12in across.

Left: The flowers are produced in spring.

Distribution: North American south-east coastal strip, from North Carolina to Florida and west along the gulf to south-east Texas.
Height: 25m/80ft
Shape: Broadly conical
Evergreen
Pollinated: Insect
Leaf shape: Elliptic to ovate

Right: The red seed pods first appear in midsummer.

OTHER SPECIES OF NOTE
Dawson's Magnolia *Magnolia dawsoniana*
This beautiful, medium-size Chinese magnolia was discovered in western Sichuan in 1908 and was introduced into Europe in 1919. It is one of the earliest magnolias to flower, producing masses of pale pink, slightly fragrant, goblet-shaped flowers, with up to 12 lax tepals (petals) up to 13cm/5in long, in early spring.

Sargent's Magnolia *Magnolia sargentiana*
This large Chinese magnolia is named after Charles Sargent of the Arnold Arboretum, Boston, USA. It produces flowers like large pink water lilies in mid-spring, before the glossy, leathery, dark green leaves appear.

Willow-leaf Magnolia *Magnolia salicifolia*
This small and broadly conical Japanese magnolia was introduced into Europe in 1892. It has narrow, willow-like leaves (occasionally ovate), which emit a lemon fragrance when crushed. The fragrant flowers, up to 12.5cm/5in across, are white with yellow stamens, produced before the tree comes into leaf in mid-spring.

Large-leaf Magnolia *Magnolia macrophylla*
This south-eastern US tree has the largest leaves of any magnolia, up to 90cm/36in long and 30cm/12in wide, rather like tobacco leaves. Its large, creamy-yellow, fragrant flowers are borne in early to mid-summer. It was discovered by the French explorer André Michaux in 1759. See also page 137.

Umbrella Magnolia

Magnolia tripetala

This is a hardy small tree. It grows in woodland shade, quite often beside streams in valley bottoms. It has fragrant flowers and striking foliage, which make it a much planted ornamental tree. It was first identified in the 18th century and since then has been widely cultivated across the western world. It requires acid soil to grow well.

Identification: The bark is pale grey and smooth. The leaves can be up to 50cm/20in long and 25cm/10in wide, with a rich green upper surface and a sage green underside covered with soft down. They are borne in large whorls at the tips of the shoots, looking somewhat like umbrellas. The loose goblet-shaped flowers appear in late spring; they are 20cm/8in across, creamy-white and very fragrant, with up to 12 narrow, waxy, spreading tepals (petals). The fruit is a squat banana-shaped cone, up to 10cm/4in long, covered with crimson seeds.

Right: The heavily veined leaves are huge and not dissimilar to tobacco leaves.

Distribution: Eastern USA from Pennsylvania to Georgia.
Height: 12m/40ft
Shape: Broadly spreading
Deciduous
Pollinated: Insect
Leaf shape: Obovate to elliptic

Hybrid Magnolia

Magnolia x soulangeana

This hybrid between *Magnolia denudata* and *M. liliiflora* has become the most widely planted ornamental magnolia in gardens throughout Europe. It was raised in the garden of Etienne Soulange-Bodin, at Fromont, near Paris, in the early 1800s, and first flowered in 1826. Since then, scores of forms of this hybrid have been named and introduced into cultivation, including 'Alba Superba', 'Rustica Rubra' and 'Brozzonii'.

Identification: This extremely ornamental small tree has wide-spreading multiple stems and grey, smooth bark. The flowers are large, goblet-shaped and normally creamy-white with pink-purple staining at the base of each tepal (petal). The colouring varies according to the different forms. The leaves, which taper to a narrow base and a pointed tip, are dark green above, paler green beneath and up to 20cm/8in long. Seeds are produced in irregular, cylindrical pink clusters in late summer to early autumn.

Distribution: Of garden origin, France.
Height: 9m/30ft
Shape: Broadly spreading
Deciduous
Pollinated: Insect
Leaf shape: Elliptic to obovate

Below and left: The flowers appear from grey, downy buds, before the leaves, in spring.

Star Magnolia

Magnolia stellata

This beautiful, slow-growing, wide-spreading small tree or large shrub is considered by some authorities to be a variety of *M. kobus* and by others to be *M. tomentosa*. It is native to the mountains of Nagoya, Japan, from where it was introduced into Europe in around 1877. It is a perfect magnolia for planting in small gardens; it will start to flower at a young age and is more tolerant of limy soils than most other magnolias.

Identification: The bark is grey, smooth and aromatic when scratched. The flower buds, borne through winter, are covered with silver-grey down, and the star-like white flowers, which appear before the leaves in mid-spring, are fragrant. Some cultivars, such as 'Dawn', have flowers that are flushed with pink. The narrow leaves are deep green above and paler beneath.

Distribution: Japan.
Height: 3m/10ft
Shape: Broadly spreading
Deciduous
Pollinated: Insect
Leaf shape: Obovate

Right: The narrow leaves are up to 10cm/4in long.

Left: The flowers have up to 18 narrow white tepals (petals), each up to 5cm/2in long.

Delavay's Magnolia *Magnolia delavayi*
This broadly spreading, tender, Chinese evergreen, 10m/33ft tall, produces among the largest leaves of any tree grown in Europe: they are up to 35cm/14in long and 15cm/6in wide, dark glossy green and stiff to the touch. It produces cream, saucer-shape flowers in late summer to early autumn, which are up to 20cm/8in across and seldom last more than 48 hours before fading.

Magnolia liliiflora
This is an attractive, wide-spreading, deciduous small tree or large shrub. Slow-growing and shade tolerant, it is now considered to be native to China, but came to Europe from Japan in 1790. It has erect, tulip-shape flowers, which are purple-pink on the outside and creamy-white within. The flowering season is long, beginning in mid-spring and ending in early summer.

Magnolia sinensis
This elegant, small, deciduous tree, to 6m/20ft tall and wide, thrives on chalky soils. It is hardy, growing at elevations up to 2,750m/9,000ft above sea level, and has long been grown as an ornamental species in Europe. It has beautiful, pure white, nodding flowers, which are set off by bright crimson stamens. The flowers, which are strongly citrus-scented, do not open until after the leaves have appeared in early summer.

Goddess Magnolia

Magnolia sprengeri var. *diva*

Almost all the trees of this variety growing in Europe are descended from a specimen at Caerhays Castle in Cornwall, England. It was raised from a seed collected in western China by Ernest Wilson in 1900 and is a large, vigorous tree with beautiful pink, goblet-shaped flowers. (All the other seeds Wilson sent in the same batch produced white flowers.)

Identification: The bark is grey and smooth. The leaves are up to 17.5cm/7in long. The flower buds are large, up to 7.5cm/3in long, and covered in silver-grey down. The erect flowers start to appear in early spring. As they mature the colour fades to light pink and the tepals become lax, spreading out to form an open flower the size of a small plate. The ripe seed is contained in an irregular bright red cylinder about 7.5cm/3in long.

Distribution: China.
Height: 28m/90ft
Shape: Broadly conical
Deciduous
Pollinated: Insect
Leaf shape: Obovate

Above right: The flowers are deep pink and goblet-shaped.

Above: The leaves are bright green above, pale beneath.

Campbell's Magnolia

Magnolia campbellii

This majestic tree is capable of attaining a height of up to 30m/100ft in less than 60 years. It is hardy, growing at up to 3,000m/9,850ft above sea level in the Himalayas. *M. campbellii* is grown widely for its dramatic flowers, which do not appear on seedlings for 20 years. They appear as early as mid-winter and are prone to frost damage.

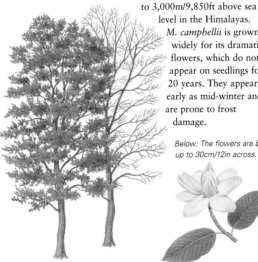

Below: The flowers are big, up to 30cm/12in across.

Identification: The bark is smooth and grey, even in old age. The leaves are up to 30cm/12in long, with a pronounced point, medium green above and sometimes faintly hairy beneath. The flower buds are large, ovoid and covered in grey hairs: they stand out dramatically on the bare branches in late winter. The flowers are even more dramatic, beginning goblet-shape but opening to a lax cup-and-saucer shape, up to 30cm/12in across. Their colour can vary from deep pink to pale pinkish-white, and they have a slight fragrance. Each flower is held upright on a smooth green stalk. The fruit is a cylindrical, cone-like pod, up to 15cm/6in long, containing bright red seed.

Right: Flowers often appear in profusion on both cultivated and wild trees.

Distribution: Himalayas from Nepal to Assam and into south-west China.
Height: 30m/100ft
Shape: Broadly conical
Deciduous
Pollinated: Insect
Leaf shape: Obovate

MAGNOLIAS AND TULIP TREES

Tulip trees are closely related to magnolias. Both represent some of the oldest flowering trees on earth. Their flowers are usually large and showy single flowers that appear all over the tree, usually in spring. Also related to magnolias and tulip trees is the beautiful evergreen Michelia doltsopa which is native to China.

Chinese Tulip Tree

Liriodendron chinense

As its name suggests, this majestic medium-size tree is native to China (and Vietnam), where it grows in mixed woodland on mountain slopes up to 2,000m/6,560ft above sea level. It is one of only two species in the genus *Liriodendron*, the other being the American tulip tree, *L. tulipifera*. It was introduced into Europe by Ernest Wilson in 1901, and some of the original introductions are still growing in the grounds of the Royal Botanic Gardens at Kew, near London.

Identification: The bark is slate grey, smooth at first, becoming fissured in maturity. The leaves are dark green above and sage green below, to 15cm/6in long with two distinct lobes at the tip and two at the side. The flowers, resembling tulips in size and shape, are pale yellow-green on the outside and banded with orange-yellow inside. They appear singly at the ends of the shoots in mid-summer.

Right: The leaves look as if their tips have been snipped off with scissors. They turn yellow in autumn.

Right: The flowers are produced on mature trees.

Distribution: China and North Vietnam.
Height: 20m/65ft
Shape: Broadly columnar
Deciduous
Pollinated: Insect
Leaf shape: Simple lobed

Tulip Tree

Yellow poplar *Liriodendron tulipifera*

This magnificent tree is one of the largest and fastest-growing deciduous trees. Fossil records show it lived in Europe before dying out in the last ice age. It stands out from the crowd for its size, its flowers, its unusual leaf shape and its ability to withstand atmospheric pollution. It is an adaptable tree, capable of growing in extreme climatic conditions.

Identification: The bark is grey-brown and smooth, becoming fissured with age. In maturity, tulip trees have clear, straight stems with broad crowns. The dark green leaves are up to 15cm/6in long and lobed on each side with a cut-off, indented leaf tip. The underside of the leaf is almost bluish-white. In autumn the leaves turn butter yellow before falling. The flowers are produced in summer once the tree reaches 12–15 years old. They are upright, 6cm/2½in long, tulip-shaped with nine petals: some are green, some are light green to yellowy-orange at the base. Inside each flower is a bright cluster of orange-yellow stamens. Unfortunately, because of the branchless stems of older trees, the flowers are very often positioned at the top of the tree, so it is difficult to admire their beauty.

Distribution: Eastern North America from Ontario to New York in the north to Florida in the south.
Height: 50m/165ft
Shape: Broadly columnar
Deciduous
Pollinated: Bee
Leaf shape: Simple

Left: As the flowers fade on the tree, the leaves change colour, giving the tulip tree a second flush of beauty.

Michelia

Michelia doltsopa

Without doubt this is one of the most beautiful of all evergreen trees and one that should be more widely planted in warmer regions of Europe. It is related to magnolias and was discovered in 1918 in western China by the Scottish plant collector George Forrest. He sent seeds to Caerhays Castle in Cornwall, England; these were propagated and the five resulting seedlings were planted in the grounds. The first seedling flowered in April 1933.

Distribution: China and the eastern Himalayas.
Height: 20m/65ft
Shape: Broadly spreading
Evergreen
Pollinated: Insect
Leaf shape: Oval to oblong

Identification: The leaves are dark green, glossy and leathery, 20cm/8in long, with rust-coloured down on the undersides. The flower buds form in autumn; they are like large magnolia flower buds, covered with fine, cinnamon-coloured hairs. They overwinter on the tree and begin to open early the following spring to reveal beautiful, multi-petalled flowers, soft lemon to white and reminiscent of water lily flowers. They have a strong, luscious fragrance that, on warm spring days, may be carried for quite some distance away from the tree.

Above: The flowers are softly fragrant.

Left: Fragrant water-lily-like flowers are produced in spring, set among dark green leathery leaves.

Right: The flowers are cup shaped.

OTHER SPECIES OF NOTE

Magnolia x loebneri 'Leonard Messel' This is a beautiful deciduous magnolia cultivar. It is a vigorous upright shrub or small tree that has lilac-pink flowers with 12 narrow lax tepals (petals). It is said to have resulted from a cross between *M. kobus* and *M. stellata* 'Rosea'. It thrives in Europe.

Cucumber Tree
Magnolia acuminata
Otherwise known as the mountain magnolia, because of its ability to grow at altitudes of up to 1,220m/4,000ft. This is a large, vigorous, deciduous tree that can grow to a height of 30m/100ft. It has elliptical, rich green leaves, 25cm/10in long, and blue-green to yellow-green cup-shaped flowers, which are reminiscent of those of its distant cousin, *Liriodendron tulipifera*. Its common name refers to the shape of the erect, cylindrical fruits, green when unripe, turning red, that contain the seed. It was introduced to Europe in the 16th century. *See also page 134.*

Wilson's Magnolia

Magnolia wilsonii

One of the loveliest of all magnolias, this was named after the English plant collector Ernest Wilson, who discovered the species in western China in 1908. It is distinctive for having drooping flowerheads, which can be seen at their best when standing directly beneath the tree.

Identification: This large spreading shrub or small tree is primarily grown for its delightful flowers, which hang from arching stems. They are cup-shaped, up to 10cm/4in across and pure white with a brilliant crimson centre. The flower bud is covered in dense grey, soft down, which is obvious from mid-winter onwards. After flowering, a purple-pink, cylindrical-ovoid seed pod is produced, which is 5–7.5cm/2–3in long and contains scarlet-coated seed. The narrow leaves are almost spear-shaped, dull green above and covered in pale-brown down beneath. This magnolia is often found growing in shade.

Distribution: Western Sichuan and Yunnan, China.
Height: 8m/26ft
Shape: Broadly spreading
Deciduous
Pollinated: Insect
Leaf shape: Elliptic-lanceolate

Above: The flowers appear in great quantities in spring.

TREE RHODODENDRONS

Commonly thought of as a genus of shrubs, there are in fact several rhododendrons that grow to tree-like proportions. Most of the species featured here attain heights in excess of 6m/20ft. In the wild they are an integral part of their native Himalayan and Chinese forests. All are widely cultivated as ornamental specimens in Europe. Some of the finest are to be found in Great Britain and Ireland.

Tree Rhododendron

Rhododendron arboreum

This was the first rhododendron to be introduced into Europe from the Himalayas, in around 1810. The first account of it came from the naturalist Thomas Hardwicke, then an army captain in India, who saw it flowering in 1796. Its natural range extends from Kashmir to Sikkim, where it grows at elevations in excess of 2,600m/8,500ft. It is now widely grown in gardens throughout northern and western Europe.

Distribution: Himalayas.
Height: 15m/50ft
Shape: Broadly columnar
Evergreen
Pollinated: Insect
Leaf shape: Oblong to lanceolate

Identification: The tree is sometimes columnar and erect, with a rounded crown on a single stem, and sometimes multi-stemmed and broadly spreading. The red-brown bark flakes in maturity. The leaves are dark green above and covered with rust-coloured hairs beneath. The flowers are normally blood red, borne in dense clusters of up to 20 in early spring.

Left: The flowers are bell-shaped and up to 5cm/2in long.

Right: The stiff, leathery leaves are up to 20cm/8in long.

Rhododendron griffithianum

This majestic tree rhododendron, one of the finest for flower, originates from the Himalayas and can be found growing from Nepal to north-eastern India. It is not particularly common in the wild anywhere. It was introduced into Europe in 1850 by Sir Joseph Hooker of the Royal Botanic Gardens at Kew, England. In the wild it will grow up to 2,750m/9,000ft above sea level, but in Europe it thrives in only the mildest climates. It is the parent of numerous hybrids.

Distribution: Himalayas.
Height: 6m/20ft
Shape: Broadly columnar
Evergreen
Pollinated: Insect
Leaf shape: Narrowly oblong

Identification: The bark, on both main stems and branches, is reddish-brown and peeling. The leaves are narrow and leathery, dark to mid-green, up to 30cm/12in long and held by a stalk that is up to 4cm/1½in long. *R. griffithianum* has possibly the most magnificent flowers of all rhododendrons. They are white, sometimes with the faintest blush of pink, and are speckled with green markings. They are bell-shaped with a wide spreading mouth, up to 7.5cm/3in long and up to 15cm/6in in diameter. They are borne in loose clusters of up to six in mid- to late spring and are deliciously fragrant.

Left: The dramatic contrast between the milk-white flowers and the dark green leaves makes this species one of the most spectactular of all rhododendrons.

Rhododendron falconeri

This is a magnificent rhododendron, which is widely cultivated in parks and gardens throughout western and northern Europe. It is a moisture-loving species, needing more than 75cm/30in of rainfall a year to perform at its best. It is native to the Himalayas, from Nepal to Bhutan, and although it was first described by Joseph Hooker in Sikkim in 1849 it had actually been introduced into Europe 20 years earlier.

Distribution: Himalayas.
Height: 10m/33ft
Shape: Broadly columnar
Evergreen
Pollinated: Insect
Leaf shape: Oval to obovate

Identification: The leaves are large, up to 30cm/12in long and 15cm/6in wide, and very thick and wrinkled with pronounced veining. The upper surface of the leaf is glossy dark green; the lower surface has a thick felting of rust-coloured indumentum, and young shoots also have a temporary covering of brown down. The flowers are borne in huge, tightly packed, dome-shaped clusters. They are bell-shaped, cream-yellow with a distinctive dark purple blotch at the base. Each flower may be 5cm/2in long and roughly the same across. They open from large pointed flower buds in mid- to late spring.

Left: The flowers emerge from large cone-shaped buds in mid- to late spring.

Left: The upper surface of the leaf is dark glossy green.

OTHER SPECIES OF NOTE

Rhododendron calophytum
One of the largest rhododendrons, this species regularly attains heights in excess of 15m/50ft. It is a hardy Chinese rhododendron, native to western Sichuan. It was discovered by the French missionary Abbé Armand David in 1869. It has large trusses of white or blush-white, bell-shaped flowers, each with a dark crimson or maroon blotch at the base.

Rhododendron sinogrande
This rhododendron has some of the finest foliage. It has magnificent, glossy, dark green, leathery leaves, which may be up to 80cm/32in long and 30cm/12in wide. The lower surface of each is covered with silver-grey or buff-coloured indumentum. The flowers are creamy-white to soft yellow, with a crimson blotch at the base. It thrives in Europe.

Rhododendron macabeanum
This large rhododendron, from northern India, is a handsome small tree, which has been widely planted in European gardens since its introduction in the 1920s. It has large, shiny, dark green leaves, covered with silver-grey indumentum beneath. The bell-shape flowers are pale yellow, purple-blotched at the base.

Rhododendron rex
This is a beautiful Chinese tree rhododendron, with bell-shape, blush-white to rose colour flowers, with crimson blotches around the base. They are borne in large trusses of up to 20 flowers in mid- to late spring. It was introduced into Europe in the 1920s.

Rhododendron barbatum

This is one of the most beautiful rhododendrons for bark colour. It has deep blood-red bark that peels to reveal patches of smooth, slate blue-grey, sometimes olive-green, bark beneath. It grows wild up to 3,700m/12,000ft above sea level in Nepal; Bhutan; southern Tibet Autonomous Region, in China; and northern India. Introduced into Europe around 1829, it has been a valued specimen for planting in woodland gardens in northern and western Europe ever since.

Distribution: Himalayas.
Height: 5m/16ft
Shape: Broadly spreading
Evergreen
Pollinated: Insect
Leaf shape: Oblong

Identification: This wide-spreading small tree or large shrub has leathery, oblong, evergreen leaves, heart-shaped at the base. They are borne in whorls at the tips of the branches and are matt dark green above, and covered with a pale felting beneath – even the leaf stalk is bristly. The flowers are bell-shaped and vivid scarlet to blood-red, and up to 20 flowers are densely packed into globular heads of about 10cm/4in across.

Left: The oblong-shaped leaves are borne on bristly stalks.

Right: The vivid red flowers appear on the tree in early spring.

BAYS AND SPICE TREES

The Lauraceae family contains more than 40 genera and 2,000 different species, most of which are tropical, originating from Asia and South America. Those that are hardier, and can survive in temperate regions of the world, tend to have several characteristics in common, including evergreen leaves and aromatic foliage or bark.

Spice Tree

Benjamin *Lindera benzoin*

Distribution: South-eastern USA.
Height: 5m/16ft
Shape: Columnar
Deciduous
Pollinated: Insect
Leaf shape: Obovate

This is a small to medium-size tree that is native to the eastern United States, from where it was introduced into Europe as early as 1683. Despite this early introduction the spice tree is relatively uncommon in cultivation, being confined to botanic gardens and arboreta across western and northern Europe. Its name is derived from the fact that when the leaves are crushed they emit a pungent, spicy odour.

Identification: *Lindera benzoin* has smooth grey bark, which becomes finely fissured in maturity. Its leaves, which are up to 12.5cm/5in long and 5cm/2in wide, are distinctly veined and taper to both the base and the tip. In autumn the leaves turn a clear bright yellow before falling. Both male and female flowers are small and yellow, or yellow-green, and are borne on separate trees in early to mid-spring. Although small, they are produced in profusion and are an attractive feature of the tree. On female trees the flowers are followed by red, oval berries.

Right: The flowers are fragrant.

Right: Red berries appear in autumn.

Spice Bush

Lindera praecox

This beautiful small tree was introduced into Europe from Japan in 1891, but has not been widely cultivated since then, and today it is mainly found in tree collections and botanical gardens in northern and western areas. It is reasonably hardy and a specimen has been flowering in the Royal Botanic Gardens at Kew, near London, since the 1930s.

Identification: The bark is grey-brown and smooth. The leaves are thin, oval to ovate, 7.5cm/3in long, and translucent in bright sunlight. They are mid-green above and glaucous beneath. In autumn they turn bright butter-yellow before falling. The male and female flowers are borne on separate trees. They are yellow-green and appear in short clusters along the bare branches in early and mid-spring. The fruit is a red-brown, oval berry, which appears in late summer into autumn.

Distribution: Japan and Korea.
Height: 8m/26ft
Shape: Columnar
Deciduous
Pollinated: Insect
Leaf shape: Ovate to oval

Right: Yellow-green flowers appear before the leaves in early spring.

Left: Butter-yellow leaves and red-brown berries appear in early autumn.

Bay Laurel

Sweet bay *Laurus nobilis*

This is the laurel used by the Greeks and Romans as a ceremonial symbol of victory; it was usually woven into crowns to be worn by champions. Fruiting sprays were also made into wreaths and given to acclaimed poets, hence the term "poet laureate". The title "bachelor", as awarded to those with university degrees, is derived from the French word *bachelier*, which means "laurel berry".

Identification: A dense small tree or shrub with aromatic leaves, which are widely used to flavour food. The bark is dark grey and smooth, even in old age. The leathery, glossy leaves are alternate, dark green above with a central lighter vein, and pale green beneath. They are 10cm/4in long, 4cm/1½in across and pointed at the tip. The male flowers, which appear in late winter, are greenish-yellow, 1cm/½in across, with many yellow stamens, positioned in the axils of the previous year's leaves.

Above: The small, male flowers open in late winter. Bay leaves are commonly harvested for use in cooking.

Distribution: Throughout Mediterranean regions.
Height: 15m/50ft
Shape: Broadly conical
Evergreen
Pollinated: Insect
Leaf shape: Elliptic

Left: The fruit is a rounded berry, 1cm/½in across, green ripening to glossy black.

OTHER SPECIES OF NOTE
Canary Island Laurel *Laurus azorica*
This handsome evergreen tree grows up to 15m/50ft in the wild and its trunk may grow to over 90cm/3ft in diameter. The young shoots emit a pleasant aroma, like that of bay laurel, *L. nobilis*, when brushed. It is an important component of the laurisilva forests of the humid northern and western slopes of the Canary Islands, and grows in parks, gardens and arboreta in the warmer regions of Europe.

Lindera megaphylla
This tender, small evergreen tree, native to southern China and Taiwan, was introduced into Europe in 1900. It has never become common and is confined to botanic gardens and arboreta. It has dark purple shoots and oblong, glossy, dark green leaves, which are pointed at the tip and rounded at the base, and when crushed emit a spicy aroma.

Willow-leaved Bay *Laurus nobilis* 'Angustifolia'
This form of the bay laurel, *L. nobilis*, is similar in all respects except for its long, narrow, pale green, pointed, wavy-edged, leathery leaves, which are reminiscent of willow leaves. It is perfectly hardy and common in cultivation across Europe.

Japanese Spicebush

Lindera obtusiloba

This beautiful small Japanese tree, which is also native to China and Korea, was introduced into Europe in 1880 and although quite often cultivated in botanic gardens and arboreta its beauty suggests it should be more widely planted. It normally produces a compact rounded shape but on occasions may develop a more erect habit. It is a two-season tree, producing greenish-yellow flowers in early spring and butter-yellow leaves in autumn.

Identification: This large shrub or small tree has waxy blue-green leaves, which are irregularly lobed and turn butter-yellow in autumn. Small fragrant yellow flowers are produced in some profusion in early to mid-spring. The fruit is a shiny reddish round berry, ripening to black, that is evident against the backdrop of clear yellow autumn foliage.

Below left: The flowers are tiny, pale greenish-yellow and are produced in clusters in the leaf axils in spring.

Below right: The fruit is an egg-shaped berry, approximately 1cm/½in long.

Distribution: China, Japan and Korea.
Height: 6m/20ft
Shape: Rounded
Deciduous
Pollinated: Insect
Leaf shape: Lobed

MYRTLES AND WINTERWOODS

Most of the trees represented here come from warmer regions of the Southern Hemisphere, such as Chile and Argentina, and as such are only cultivated in parts of Europe with a temperate mild climate. They include some of the most beautiful evergreen trees, such as the New Zealand Christmas tree, which produces intense red flowers, and the South American myrtle, which has bright cinnamon-orange bark.

Winter's Bark

Drimys winteri

This handsome Central and South American evergreen tree, with highly aromatic bark, is named after Captain William Winter, who sailed with Sir Francis Drake on his voyage round the world. Winter used the bark of the tree, which has a high vitamin C content, to treat sailors on his ship who were suffering from scurvy. It was cultivated in Europe in 1827 and is a valuable ornamental tree in parks and gardens throughout milder regions of Europe.

Right: The white flowers with yellow centres are mildly fragrant.

Above: The elongated leaves have a peppery scent.

Identification: The bark of Winter's bark is brown-grey, smooth and very aromatic when crushed or scratched. The tree has large, leathery, oblong to elliptic leaves, 20cm/8in long and 5cm/2in broad. They are a glossy dark green above and bluish-silver-green beneath, and when crushed are aromatic. The flowers are ivory white, up to 5cm/2in across and borne in branched clusters in late spring. These are followed by small, purple-black berries, also borne in branched clusters, in late summer and autumn.

Distribution: Mexico south to Chile and Argentina.
Height: 15m/50ft
Shape: Narrowly conical
Evergreen
Pollinated: Insect
Leaf shape: Oblong to elliptic

New Zealand Christmas Tree

Metrosideros robusta

When in flower this is one of the world's most beautiful trees. In New Zealand it is known as Pohutukawa, which is Maori for "drenched with salt spray". As this name suggests, it is found growing around the coast of New Zealand. As well as being tolerant of sea air, it also tolerates wind and drought. It was introduced into Europe in 1840 and is found in cultivation in warmer coastal regions. Some of the finest European specimens grow on Tresco, part of the Isles of Scilly.

Identification: This is a broadly columnar tree that may become widely spreading in maturity. The bark is grey-brown and smooth. The leaves are elliptic, dark green on top with a light green midrib, and covered with a fine silver-grey down beneath. It has dazzling, bright crimson "bottlebrush" flowers, which are made up mainly of long red stamens. In large clusters, they smother the branches in summer, almost obscuring the dark evergreen foliage.

Distribution: New Zealand.
Height: 20m/65ft
Shape: Broadly columnar
Evergreen
Pollinated: Insect
Leaf shape: Elliptic

Left: The bright crimson flowers appear in summer.

Right: Woody seed capsules are borne among the evergreen leaves.

Chilean Firebush

Embothrium coccineum

This beautiful South American small evergreen tree grows in exposed locations from the Pacific coast to high in the Andes Mountains. It was named from a specimen collected during Captain James Cook's second voyage to this region. It was introduced into Europe in 1846 by the plant collector William Lobb, and has been widely cultivated in parks, gardens and arboreta across milder regions of Europe.

Left: The flowers, which appear in late spring to early summer, are reminiscent of a large honeysuckle.

Identification: The bark is purple-brown and smooth at first, flaking in maturity. The soft leathery leaves, up to 15cm/6in long and 2.5cm/1in broad, are matt blue-green above and pale green beneath. The flowers, tubular at first, to 5cm/2in long, open into four narrow lobes that peel back to reveal a long, vivid red-orange style. They grow in clusters resembling glowing red embers along the branches. The fruit is a woody capsule, 2.5cm/1in long, which opens to release numerous winged seeds.

Distribution: Chile and Argentina.
Height: 9m/30ft
Shape: Broadly columnar
Evergreen
Pollinated: Insect
Leaf shape: Elliptic

OTHER SPECIES OF NOTE

Wheel Tree *Trochodendron aralioides*
This attractive, evergreen, Japanese tree is the sole species in the only genus in the family Trochodendraceae. Its nearest relative is believed to be *Drimys winteri*. It has shiny dark green, narrow, elliptical, leathery leaves and aromatic bark. Its most interesting feature is its wheel-like bright green flowers, 2cm/¾in across, with no petals and exposed stamens radiating outwards from a central disc. They appear on upright slender stalks in early summer.

Gutta Percha
Eucommia ulmoides
This Chinese tree is the only member of the Eucommiaceae family. It is believed to be most closely related to the elms, and is the only temperate tree that produces rubber. If the leaf is gently torn in half, the two halves will still hang together, held by thin strands of sticky latex. In China, gutta percha has been cultivated for hundreds of years for medicinal purposes. It has never been found growing wild, so its origins are unknown.

Sassafras *Sassafras albidum*
This eastern North American, medium-sized deciduous tree produces a range of leaf shapes, from those with a large lobe on each side, like a fig leaf, to entire and oval. They turn yellow and orange in autumn. It was introduced into Europe as early as 1633 and has been cultivated in gardens ever since. *See also page 138.*

Myrtle

Myrtus luma

This is one of the finest small trees for bark colour, and one that has been cultivated in warmer parts of Europe since its introduction from the temperate forests of Chile and Argentina by the English plant collector William Lobb in 1844. In some areas of Europe, such as southern Ireland, it has become naturalized, reproducing itself with ease. It may sometimes be found in gardens and arboreta labelled with its former botanical name, *Luma apiculata*.

Identification: *M. luma* has bright cinnamon-orange, soft-felted bark, which peels in patches to reveal cream-coloured fresh bark beneath. A curious feature of this tree is that the bark always feels cold to the touch, even when the tree is grown in full sun. The leaves are dark, dull green, oval to elliptic, up to 2.5cm/1in long and ending in a short point. When crushed they are pleasantly aromatic. *M. luma* has small, white, fragrant, four-petalled flowers, which are borne singly in late summer and early autumn.

Distribution: Chile and Argentina.
Height: 12m/40ft
Shape: Broadly columnar
Evergreen
Pollinated: Insect
Leaf shape: Broadly elliptic

Above: Spherical red fruits ripen to purple in autumn.

Below: The flowers stand out against the dark leaves.

OLIVES AND PITTOSPORUMS

One of the most widely recognized and cultivated trees is the olive. It has been grown for its fruits in warm regions of Europe for thousands of years. Due to recent increases in mean annual air temperatures and the popularity of domestic conservatories it is increasingly cultivated in cooler regions too. Along with the New Zealand pittosporums, the European future looks bright for these tender evergreens.

Common Olive

Olea europaea

The olive has been cultivated for its fruits and oil in the warm regions of Europe for thousands of years, to the extent that its true native distribution is now obscure. There are certainly specimens in excess of 1,000 years old growing in Italy and Greece. According to Greek mythology, the club wielded by the hero Hercules was made from the wood of a wild olive tree. Groves of olive trees have become an integral part of the Mediterranean landscape. Further north, in Britain for example, olive trees rarely produce fruit, but survive outside in warm, sheltered positions if well drained.

Distribution: South-west Asia and the Mediterranean region.
Height: 9m/30ft
Shape: Broadly spreading
Evergreen
Pollinated: Insect
Leaf shape: Narrowly obovate

Identification: The olive has a distinctive, short grey, fissured trunk, which may become very thick and hollow in maturity, and a broadly spreading crown. It has grey-green, tough, leathery, opposite, evergreen leaves, which are silver-sage beneath. Small racemes of fragrant white cruciform flowers are produced in late summer. The green oval fruits, each containing a single seed or stone, ripen to a glossy purple-black.

Left: The leaves are an instant guide to identification.
Far left: Olive oil is extracted from the fruit.

Chinese Privet

Ligustrum lucidum

Distribution: China.
Height: 12m/40ft
Shape: Broadly spreading
Evergreen
Pollinated: Insect
Leaf shape: Ovate

This handsome, medium-sized tree is the finest of all the privets and from a distance, with its lush, lustrous evergreen leaves, it resembles a tropical rainforest tree. It grows naturally in the mountains of central and western China, particularly in hillside woodland above river valleys. It was introduced into Europe by the botanist Sir Joseph Banks in 1794. It is very hardy and well suited for urban planting as it tolerates air pollution and compacted dry soils. Chinese privet will also tolerate salt spray and is therefore suitable for coastal planting.

Identification: The bark is grey and smooth, even in maturity. The leaves, which taper to a fine point, are ovate, 10cm/4in long and 5cm/2in broad, bronze when first produced, becoming glossy dark green above and paler and matt beneath as they mature. The flowers are small, creamy-white, fragrant and profusely borne in large, upright, conical panicles, 20cm/8in long, which stand proud of the surrounding foliage, from mid-summer to early autumn. The fruit is a small blue-black berry.

Right: Small blue-black berries are produced in autumn.

Phillyrea

Phillyrea latifolia

This elegant small evergreen tree, which is a
member of the olive family (Oleaceae), is
sometimes mistaken for holm oak, *Quercus
ilex*. Like holm oak, phillyrea is native to
southern Europe, especially around the
Mediterranean coastline. It has been in
cultivation in northern regions of Europe,
such as Britain, since 1597. It is widely
planted to provide shelter in exposed
locations, especially along coastal strips,
and is quite often used as a substitute for
holm oak where space is limited.

Distribution: Southern
Europe and Asia Minor.
Height: 10m/33ft
Shape: Broadly spreading
Evergreen
Pollinated: Insect
 Leaf shape: Elliptic to
 ovate

Identification: In overall
appearance, this tree resembles a
small evergreen oak, or even an
olive. Occasionally it is
clipped to form a dense
hedge. The bark is pewter-
grey, smooth even in
maturity, and relatively
thin. Each long, spreading
branch is covered with
masses of small, glossy,
dark green, opposite
leaves. These are thick and
leathery, elliptic to ovate,
5cm/2in long, have a bluntly
toothed margin and are pale green on
the underside. The flowers are small,
creamy or yellowish-white, produced in
clusters in the leaf axils in late spring.

*Below: The
elongated leaf.*

*Right: In
warm regions
the flowers are
followed
by tiny, round, blue-
black fruits.*

Fringe Tree

Chionanthus virginicus

Distribution: Eastern United
States.
Height: 10m/33ft
Shape: Rounded
Deciduous
Pollinated: Insect
Leaf shape: Elliptic

This attractive small tree inhabits moist woods and
riverbanks in its natural range. It was
introduced into Europe in 1736 and is
cultivated in parks and gardens across the
continent. It is sometimes known as old
man's beard because of its feathery,
beard-like flowers, which are borne in
early summer. It is a member of the
olive family and the connection can be
seen in its olive-like fruits.

Identification: The bark is silver-grey and
smooth becoming vertically fissured with age.
The fringe tree has untoothed, lustrous
leaves, which are elliptic, narrow, up to
20cm/8in long and 7.5cm/3in across, tapering
to a short point. They are borne on short
petioles (leaf stalks), to 2.5cm/1in long, and turn a
clear butter yellow in autumn. The feathery flowers are
creamy-white and slightly fragrant and are borne abundantly
in conical erect panicles in summer.

*Right: The fruit is a bloomy, egg-
shaped, blue-black berry, up to
2.5cm/1in long.*

ELMS

The Ulmaceae family contains about 15 genera and 140 species of mainly deciduous trees. They thrive in all but the poorest of soils and are widespread throughout most temperate regions of the Northern Hemisphere, including Europe, North America and Asia – except, that is, where they have been affected by the fungus Ophiostoma novo-ulmi, *which causes Dutch elm disease.*

European Hybrid Elm

Dutch elm *Ulmus* x *hollandica*

This is an extremely variable, naturally occurring hybrid between two European elms, the wych elm, *U. glabra*, and the smooth-leaved elm, *U. minor*. It is found throughout western Europe, including Britain, and is prevalent in France, Belgium, Holland and Germany. This hybrid has resulted in several vigorous cultivars common in western Europe, including *U.* x *hollandica* 'Vegeta', *U.* x *hollandica* 'Major', and *U.* x *hollandica* 'Belgica'.

Identification: The bark is grey-brown, becoming regularly and vertically fissured in maturity. The leaves are up to 12.5cm/5in long and 7.5cm/3in broad, rough to the touch and unequal at the leaf base, where the petiole attaches the leaf to the twig. The flowers are small and red and are produced in obvious clusters on the shoots in early spring.

Distribution: Western Europe.
Height: 30m/100ft
Shape: Broadly columnar
Deciduous
Pollinated: Wind
Leaf shape: Ovate to elliptic

Far left: The fruit is an oval-shaped, winged seed 2.5cm/1in long.

Left: The leaf.

European White Elm

Fluttering elm *Ulmus laevis*

Distribution: Central and eastern Europe to western Asia.
Height: 30m/100ft
Shape: Broadly spreading
Deciduous
Pollinated: Wind
Leaf shape: Obovate

This large, widely spreading elm is known as the fluttering elm because of its long-stalked flowers and fruit, which shiver in the slightest breeze. It is widely cultivated throughout eastern Europe, particularly in Russia, where it is planted alongside railway lines to protect them from snowdrifts. *Laevis* means "smooth" and refers to the smooth bark that this elm maintains into maturity. It has hard, durable timber, which is moisture-resistant even when in contact with water, and at one time it was favoured for use in the construction of waterwheels.

Identification: The bark is smooth, dull grey-brown and in old trees is covered in a shallow network of broad, smooth ridges. The leaves are double-toothed around the margin and distinctly oblique at the base. There may be up to 17 distinct veins on the long side of the leaf and only 14 on the short side. The winter leaf bud is a distinctive orange-brown and sharply pointed. Both flowers and fruit are held on long, pendulous stalks.

Far right: After flowering pendulous bunches of oval-shaped individual paper-like seeds are produced in summer.

Cornish Elm *Ulmus minor* var. *cornubiensis*
The Cornish elm is believed to be a smaller-leaved variety of the smooth-leaved elm, *U. minor* subsp. *minor*, and grows in isolated populations in north-west France and south-west England. It is a large tree with a dense, conical shape and sharply ascending branches. There is a suggestion that it survived the last Ice Age on land that is now submerged off the south coast of Cornwall. However, others believe it was introduced from France during the Anglo-Saxon period.

Wheatley Elm *Ulmus minor* 'Sarniensis'
This cultivar may also be a descendent of the smooth-leaved elm, *U. minor* subsp. *minor*. It has a narrower, denser crown and broader leaves than the Cornish elm. It occurs in all the Channel Islands, but Dutch elm disease has reduced it to mainly small, isolated clumps of sucker re-growth. A clone introduced from northern France has fared better and has produced narrow conical trees, ideal for roadside and coastal planting.

Ulmus laciniata
This east Asian elm is closely related to the European wych elm, *U. glabra*, and was introduced into Europe in 1905. It is a small tree in cultivation although in the wild it may reach 30m/100ft. Its large obovate leaves, up to 8in/20cm long, are rough to the touch and irregularly and sharply double-toothed. In Asia its fibrous inner bark (bast) is used to make rope and baskets.

English Elm

Ulmus minor var. *vulgaris* (formerly *U. procera*)

This magnificent, large stately tree has for centuries been an inseparable part of the English landscape. Ironically, it is now believed that it is not truly native but was introduced from north-west Spain in early Neolithic times. Nevertheless, it was for centuries considered the quintessential English tree, but in the mid-20th century it was severely affected by Dutch elm disease and populations of mature trees were virtually eradicated from western Europe.

Identification: The bark is grey-brown and regularly fissured into rectangular plates. The leaves are 5–10cm/2–4in long, unequal at the base, pointed at the tip and coarsely toothed around the margin. Each has 10–12 pairs of veins. Small clusters of red flowers appear in early spring and are followed by oval-shaped, paper-thin winged seeds.

Below: The leaves are dark green above, pale green beneath and rough to the touch.

Below right: The winged seeds are 2.5cm/1in long.

Distribution: South-west Europe.
Height: 35m/115ft
Shape: Broadly columnar
Deciduous
Pollinated: Wind
Leaf shape: Ovate to oval

Siberian Elm

Dwarf elm *Ulmus pumila*

This hardy medium-size elm has a natural range that extends from Tibet Autonomous Region, China, to eastern Siberia. The further north it grows, the shrubbier the plant's habit becomes. It was introduced into cultivation in Europe in 1870; most specimens in cultivation are derived from taller southern specimens. It has some resistance to Dutch elm disease and grows better than any other elm in cold, dry, poor soil conditions. It has therefore become very popular for planting in the prairie lands of the mid-west United States.

Identification: The bark is grey-brown and smooth at first, becoming roughly ridged with long vertical fissures. The leaves are elliptic to narrowly ovate, 5cm/2in long and 2.5cm/1in broad, almost equal at the base (which is unusual for an elm), sharply but regularly toothed around the margin, dark green and smooth on the upper side with some pubescence beneath. The flowers are small and red and are borne in clusters on the shoots in early spring. The fruit is an oval-winged seed.

Distribution: Northern Asia.
Height: 20m/65ft
Shape: Broadly columnar
Deciduous
Pollinated: Wind
Leaf shape: Elliptic to ovate

Left: The leaves are elliptic to narrowly ovate and regularly toothed.

Left: Each seed is contained in a paper-thin oval-shaped wing.

ELMS AND NETTLE TREE

The Ulmaceae family includes, in addition to elms, the North American nettle tree and several zelkovas. All tend to be large trees, perfectly hardy in Europe and quite often planted in extensive landscapes such as parkland and arboreta. In some cases they have been used as a replacement for elms lost to Dutch elm disease.

Wych Elm

Ulmus glabra

This tough medium-size tree survives particularly well in exposed coastal areas and on mountain slopes. It has strong, dense timber, which is very resistant to decay when immersed in water. For centuries, hollowed-out elm branches were used for water pipes, waterwheel paddles and boat building.

Identification: The overall shape is of a short, stocky stem surmounted by a widely spreading, open crown. The bark is grey-brown and in maturity uniformly lined with vertical fissures. The leaves are up to 20cm/8in long and 10cm/4in broad. They are coarsely and doubly toothed, with unequal sides at the base of each leaf where it joins the stalk. The upper surface of the leaf is dull green and rough textured; the lower surface is lighter in colour and heavily furred. The flowers appear in late winter before the leaves. The seed is carried in the centre of a flat, papery, hairy disc, known as a samara. The samaras are 5mm/¼in across and are borne in clusters.

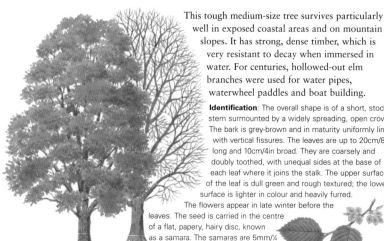

Distribution: Europe from Spain to Russia, including western Scandinavia.
Height: 30m/100ft
Shape: Broadly spreading
Deciduous
Pollinated: Wind
Leaf shape: Oval to obovate

Left and right: The male flowers have bright red anthers and are very conspicuous in early spring, when copious amounts of pollen are released.

Nettle Tree

Common hackberry *Celtis occidentalis*

Distribution: North America.
Height: 25m/82ft
Shape: Broadly columnar
Deciduous
Pollinated: Wind
Leaf shape: Ovate

This medium-size tree, which is closely related to the elm, was introduced into Europe in the 17th century. It also grows prolifically across North America. It is also known as the hackberry because it produces a profusion of purple, edible, sweet-tasting berries, which are an important food source for birds.

Identification: The bark is light grey, smooth when the tree is young, becoming rough and corky with warty blemishes in maturity. The oval leaves are up to 12cm/4¾in long and 5cm/2in across, pointed, toothed at the tip and rounded at the base, where there are three pronounced veins. They are smooth, glossy rich green on top; lighter green and slightly hairy on the veining underneath. Both the male and female flowers are held separately on the same tree in spring – they are small and green, without petals, and appear in the leaf axils. The reddish fruit, ripening to purple-black, is a rounded berry approximately 1cm/½in across, borne on a thin green stalk, 2.5cm/1in long.

Right: The nettle tree is named for its leaves, which resemble those of the stinging nettle.

Smooth-leaved Elm

Ulmus minor subsp. *minor*

As the common name suggests, this is an elm with a smooth, lustrous upper leaf surface, which easily distinguishes it from other European sub-species and varieties. It is still occasionally referred to as the European field elm, *U. carpinifolia*, which indicates the confusion that still surrounds the origins of these European elms. Much of this confusion stems from the way they were widely transported around Europe during the Bronze and Iron Ages. The leaves of this particular species were extensively used as cattle fodder.

Identification: The tree is large and broadly conical with an open habit. In later life the lower branches may become pendulous. The bark is light grey, sometimes silvery, and relatively smooth even in maturity. The narrowly oval leaves, up to 10cm/4in long, are unequal at the base, double-toothed, leathery, smooth and shiny. The flowers, which appear in early spring, are small, purple and produced in clusters over much of the tree.

Distribution: Europe, North Africa and parts of south-west Asia.
Height: 30m/100ft
Shape: Broadly conical
Deciduous
Pollinated: Wind
Leaf shape: Oval

Left: Leaves have 10–13 pairs of veins.

Right: The seed is contained in a thin, paper-like wing.

Chinese Elm *Ulmus parvifolia*
This small rounded tree, deciduous or semi-evergreen, is native to China, Japan, Taiwan and Korea, where it inhabits the lower rocky slopes of mountains. It appears to be resistant to Dutch elm disease but does not have the stature of either the English or American elm, so has not been widely planted in Europe.

Japanese Elm *Ulmus japonica*
This graceful, broadly spreading large tree, up to 30m/100ft, originates from north-east Asia, including Japan, and was introduced into Europe in 1895. It has downy twigs that sometimes develop corky wings, pale grey-brown fissured bark, obovate, double-toothed, dark green, rough leaves, 10cm/4in long, and small red flowers, which are borne in clusters in early spring.

Keaki *Zelkova serrata*
Native to China, Japan and Korea, this potentially large (40m/130ft), broadly spreading member of the elm family was introduced into Europe by the English nursery Veitch & Sons in 1862.
Since then it has been widely planted in parks, gardens and arboreta right across northern and central Europe. It has attractive brown bark, which flakes to reveal fresh orange bark beneath, and deciduous ovate to oblong leaves, up to 12cm/4½in long, which are sharply toothed and taper to a point. *See also page 141.*

Caucasian Elm

Zelkova carpinifolia

This slow-growing, long-lived forest tree has a very distinctive and pleasing shape. It is similar to hornbeam, having a short trunk and a large, almost mop-head of dense, upright branching. The overall impression is of a tree that was once pollarded but has long since been left to grow unchecked.

Identification: The smooth, grey-buff bark flakes in maturity; the trunk has pronounced fluting and a buttressed base. The flowers are small and green and are borne in the leaf axils in spring. The fruit is an insignificant-looking, small, rounded pea-like capsule with pronounced ridging.

Distribution: Caucasus Mountains and northern Iran.
Height: 30m/100ft
Shape: Rounded
Deciduous
Pollinated: Wind
Leaf shape: Elliptic to oblong

Left: The leaves are 10cm/4in long and have parallel veining.

Right: The flowers are small and easily missed.

Right: Bark.

MULBERRIES AND WALNUTS

One of the main characteristics of these two families is that they both contain trees that produce edible fruits. The mulberry family, or Moraceae, includes both mulberries and figs, while the walnut family, or Juglandaceae, includes the common walnut. There are about 800 different species of fig; the majority of them are found in tropical and subtropical regions.

Common Walnut

Juglans regia

Although the walnut is naturally widespread, it has been distributed further by humans, who have cultivated the tree for its nuts since Roman times. The Romans introduced it to Britain and it spread to the USA in colonial times.

Above: Flowers hang from the twigs.

Above: Individual leaflets have smooth edges and are up to 13cm/5in long.

Distribution: From Greece in the west to central China and Japan in the east.
Height: 30m/100ft
Shape: Broadly spreading
Deciduous
Pollinated: Wind
Leaf shape: Pinnate

Identification: The bark is light grey with black fissures, creating narrow, rough ridges. The aromatic leaves have up to nine leaflets on each leaf stalk. They are bronze-pink when young, becoming deep green with a dull sheen in maturity. When the shoot is cut lengthways, a compartmentalized pith is revealed. Both male and female flowers are green catkins, appearing in late spring. The fruit is a round green husk, 5cm/2in across, not unlike a spineless horse-chestnut husk. Inside is the familiar, brown walnut.

Japanese Walnut

Juglans ailantifolia

This attractive ornamental tree has the largest of all walnut leaves. The sticky fruit husk is poisonous but the nut inside is edible and has been a valuable food source in Japan for centuries. The timber is light and strong. It is grown in parkland across Europe for its ornamental leaves.

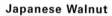

Identification: The grey-brown bark is fissured, segmenting into irregular plates in maturity. The leaves are pinnate and large, each with up to 17 slightly toothed leaflets 15cm/6in long. They are rich green and slightly hairy above; the undersides are very furry. The stout brown shoot is also hairy and very sticky. The male flowers are green, pendulous catkins, up to 30cm/12in long. Both male and female flowers appear on the same tree but are borne separately in late spring. The brown nut is contained in a green, hairy, sticky, rounded husk up to 5cm/2in across.

Distribution: Japan.
Height: 25m/82ft
Shape: Broadly spreading
Deciduous
Pollinated: Wind
Leaf shape: Pinnate

Above: The nuts are borne on the tree in clusters of up to 20 in autumn.

Right: The female flowers are red upright catkins up to 10cm/4in long.

Black mulberry

Morus nigra

King James I of England decreed in 1608 that "every Englishman should cultivate a mulberry tree" as a way of establishing a native silk industry. Many took him at his word and dutifully planted mulberries. Unfortunately they planted the black mulberry, *M. nigra*, rather than the Chinese white mulberry, *M. alba*, the only species on which silkworms will flourish. Although not a good start for the silk industry, the decree did result in a land full of delicious black mulberry fruits.

Identification: Black mulberry trees often appear older than they are. The orange bark takes on an ancient look early in life and trees often start to lean, or even fall over, when young, often growing in a prostrate position for many years. The leaves are bright green, over 12cm/4¾in long and 10cm/4in wide, rough and hairy with coarsely serrated margins. Both male and female flowers are small, green, soft, cone-like structures. They appear in early summer and are followed by raspberry-like fruits, which ripen from green to red to dark purple.

Distribution: Western Asia.
Height: 10m/33ft
Shape: Broadly spreading
Deciduous
Pollinated: Insect
Leaf shape: Ovate

Right: A mulberry fruit looks like a small raspberry and appears at the end of a twig.

OTHER SPECIES OF NOTE

Common Fig *Ficus carica*
Originally from south-west Asia, this large shrub or small spreading tree is now cultivated for its fruit throughout the temperate world. It has smooth, grey bark and distinctive, heavily lobed leaves. The flowers, which are fertilized by wasps, are small and green and borne on separate trees. The delicious fruit is heart-shaped and green, becoming purple-brown when ripe.

Paper Mulberry
Broussonetia papyrifera
This medium-size, broadly spreading tree is a close relative of the mulberries. It was introduced to Europe from Asia in 1750. It has attractive, coarsely toothed, hairy, purple-green leaves, which vary in shape from ovate to rounded and are deeply lobed. The tree's name derives from Japan, where its inner bark was traditionally used to make paper.

Osage Orange *Maclura pomifera*
This hardy North American tree, to 15m/50ft, produces large, heavy, pale yellow orange-like fruits in late summer and early autumn. It has ovate, glossy, bright green leaves, to 10cm/4in long, and orange-brown fissured bark, and was introduced into Europe in 1818. *See also page 143.*

White Mulberry

Morus alba

This medium-sized Chinese tree has long been cultivated around the world as a food source for silkworms, which eat the leaves. White mulberry is believed to have been introduced into Europe in 1596 or earlier. It does produce an edible fruit but these fruits are normally less sweet and borne in less profusion than those of its more popular cousin the black mulberry, *M. nigra*. White mulberry has spawned a number of cultivars including *M. alba* 'Pyramidalis' which has the form and appearance of a Lombardy poplar.

Identification: The bark is orange-brown and the tree's shape becomes wide-spreading and rather ungainly in maturity. The leaves are variable, ovate to rounded, 20cm/8in long, toothed around the margin, bright green, lustrous above and paler beneath, turning bright yellow in autumn. The fruit can vary in colour from white through pink to purplish-red. Although edible it is not as pleasant to eat as the fruit of the black mulberry, *M. nigra*.

Distribution: Northern China.
Height: 15m/50ft
Shape: Broadly spreading
Deciduous
Pollinated: Insect
Leaf shape: Ovate

Above: The fruit looks like an elongated raspberry.

Below: The leaves are used as cattle fodder.

WING NUTS AND HICKORIES

The Juglandaceae family contains seven genera and over 60 tree species, which grow throughout the temperate regions of North America, Europe and Asia. They include some of the fastest-growing of all deciduous trees. The leaves of all species are pinnate and the flowers are all catkins. Many of these trees produce edible fruit in the form of nuts.

Caucasian Wing Nut

Pterocarya fraxinifolia

The natural habitat of the Caucasian wing nut is damp woodland adjacent to rivers and marshland. It is a very fast-growing species, quite regularly achieving 3m/10ft of growth in a single year. Re-growth from coppiced stumps has been known to reach twice that height in a season. This tree has a habit of producing a profusion of sucker shoots around its base.

Identification: The bark is light grey, smooth in young trees and becoming fissured in maturity. The leaves are pinnate, up to 60cm/24in long and made of up to 23 slightly toothed, ovate to oblong dark green leaflets, up to 15cm/6in long. Winter buds are naked, with brown hairy bud leaves not unlike those of the wayfaring tree, *Viburnum lantana*. The small flowers, green with a red stigma, are carried in pendulous catkins up to 15cm/6in long in spring.

Distribution: Caucasus Mountains, the eastern shore of the Black Sea, southern shore of the Caspian Sea and into the northern provinces of Iran.
Height: 30m/100ft
Shape: Broadly spreading
Deciduous
Pollinated: Wind
Leaf shape: Pinnate

Above: The nut-like fruit has a pair of semicircular wings.

Left: The nuts are borne in hanging "necklaces" (far left) up to 50cm/20in long. The flowers hang in pendulous catkins.

Chinese Wing Nut

Pterocarya stenoptera

Native to damp woodland and riverbanks throughout China, the Chinese wing nut was identified by the French missionary Joseph Callery in 1844 and introduced into Europe in 1860. It is easily distinguished from the Caucasian wing nut by the serrated wings on the leaf stalk in the spaces between each pair of leaflets.

Identification: This fast-growing tree has grey-brown bark, which becomes deeply fissured as it matures. The bright green, smooth leaves are pinnate, with up to 21 slightly toothed leaflets, from 10–20cm/4–8in long. Both male and female flowers are small and green, in separate pendulous catkins, each up to 5cm/2in long, on the same tree in spring. The seed is a nut, flanked by two green-pink, narrow erect wings. Seeds occur in long pendulous catkins up to 30cm/12in long, throughout the summer.

Right: The nut-like seed is winged.

Distribution: China.
Height: 25m/80ft
Shape: Broadly spreading
Deciduous
Pollinated: Wind
Leaf shape: Pinnate

Left: Flowers are hanging catkins.

Right: Nuts occur in necklace-like structures.

Bitternut Hickory

Bitternut *Carya cordiformis*

As the name suggests, the nuts are not palatable. They do, however, have a high oil content and were once crushed to produce lamp oil. "Hickory" comes from the Native American word for nut oil, *pawcohiccora*. It was introduced into Europe from North America in 1766. It differs from mockernut by its slender, bright yellow winter buds. It is not commonly planted outside its natural range.

Distribution: East of a line from Minnesota to Texas.
Height: 30m/100ft
Shape: Broadly columnar
Deciduous
Pollinated: Wind
Leaf shape: Pinnate

Identification: The bark is grey and smooth, becoming thick and heavily ridged in maturity. The pinnate leaves have up to nine heavily serrated leaflets, which may be up to 15cm/6in long. They are deep green above and yellow-green beneath. In autumn they turn a rich golden-yellow. Both the male and female flowers are carried on catkins; the male catkins hang in threes and are up to 7.5cm/3in long; the females are short spikes at the shoot ends. They appear separately on the same tree in late spring. The thin-shelled fruit is a nut with an inedible bitter kernel.

Right: The nuts are rounded and reddish-brown, in a thin husk that splits along four ridges.

OTHER SPECIES OF NOTE

Hybrid Wing Nut *Pterocarya* x *rehderiana*
This hybrid, which was raised at the Arnold Arboretum of Harvard University, Boston, in 1879, is more vigorous than either of its parents, *P. fraxinifolia* and *P. stenoptera*. It has glossy, bright green pinnate leaves with up to 21 leaflets, which turn yellow in autumn. The bark is purple-brown and obliquely fissured. In late summer and autumn pendulous catkins, up to 45cm/18in long, contain winged seeds.

Mockernut *Carya tomentosa*
This North American hickory, sometimes called big-bud hickory, is highly valued for its timber, which has a number of uses. Because of the strength of its slender, straight trunk, and its ability to withstand impact, the wood has been used all over the world to make tool handles; it is also used for sports equipment such as hockey sticks. The wood gives off a fragrant smoke when burnt, and is used to smoke meats. The pinnate leaves also give off a pleasing aroma when crushed. See also page 144.

Kingnut *Carya laciniosa*
Also known as big shellbark, this medium-size, slow-growing, deciduous tree, growing to 20m/65ft, is native to the eastern United States, from where it was introduced into Europe in 1804. It has the largest compound leaves of any hickory, up to 60cm/24in long, and the largest nuts, up to 5cm/2in long, which are sweet and edible. The wood is much used to make tool handles. The botanical name *laciniosa* means "with flaps" and successfully describes the way the shaggy bark curls away from the trunk.

Shagbark Hickory

Carya ovata

Distribution: Eastern North America, from Quebec to Texas.
Height: 30m/100ft
Shape: Broadly columnar
Deciduous
Pollinated: Wind
Leaf shape: Pinnate

This large, vigorous tree differs from other hickories in having flaking, grey-brown bark, which curls away from the trunk in long thin strips up to 30cm/12in long, but stays attached to the tree at the centre point. This gives the whole trunk a shaggy, untidy but attractive appearance.

Identification: The leaves are pinnate, with five to seven leaflets on each leaf. Each leaflet is up to 25cm/10in long, yellowish green with a serrated edge for the top two-thirds. In autumn the leaves turn brilliant yellow. In winter, the bud scales curve away from the bud at the tip. Both the male and female flowers are small, yellowish-green and borne on pendulous catkins clustered in threes in late spring. In North America, the tree produces a profusion of nuts most years. Elsewhere crops are not so prolific. The white, sweet-tasting, kernel is contained in a green husk.

Right: Fruit occurs at twig ends.

Below: The husk has four ridges.

Right: Leaves appear finger-like before they fill out.

BEECHES

The Fagaceae family contains ten species of true beech, all of which occur in temperate regions of the world. They can be found in Asia, North America and Europe, including Britain. Beeches are some of the most majestic of all deciduous trees. They typically have smooth, thin, silver-grey bark and can attain heights in excess of 40m/130ft.

Common Beech

European beech *Fagus sylvatica*

The name "beech" comes from the Anglo-Saxon *boc* and the Germanic word *Buche*, both of which gave rise to the English word "book". In northern Europe early manuscripts were written on thin tablets of beech wood and bound in beech boards. Beech is widely used for hedging because, if trimmed, it retains its dead leaves in winter, providing extra wind protection. In summer, the leaves provide good browse for livestock.

Distribution: Europe from the Pyrenees to the Caucasus and north to Russia and Denmark.
Height: 40m/130ft
Shape: Broadly spreading
Deciduous
Pollinated: Wind
Leaf shape: Ovate to obovate

Identification: The bark is silver-grey and remains smooth in maturity. The leaves are up to 10cm/4in long and 5cm/2in wide. They have a wavy, but normally untoothed, margin and a rather blunt point at the tip. In spring, juvenile leaves have a covering of hairs and are edible, with a nutty flavour. As they mature, the leaves become tough and bitter. Beech flowers are small: the female flowers are green and the males yellow, and they are borne in separate clusters on the same tree in spring. The fruit is an edible nut. Up to three nuts are contained within a woody husk, which is covered in coarse bristles.

Right: The husks open in early autumn.

Far right: Mature leaves are smooth and have a rich colour.

Copper Beech

Fagus sylvatica 'Purpurea'

Neither a true species nor of garden origin, copper or purple beeches are "sports" or quirks of nature. They were first seen growing naturally near Buchs, Switzerland, and in the Darney forest in the Vosges of eastern France in the 1600s. Seed collected from common beech may produce one in 1,000 seedlings with purple leaves.

Identification: The copper beech is similar to common beech. It is reported that copper beech may be slightly slower-growing and not quite as spreading in maturity as the common beech, but this is likely to have more to do with local growing conditions than to be a distinct characteristic of the tree.

Distribution: Switzerland and Vosges in eastern France.
Height: 40m/130ft
Shape: Broadly spreading
Deciduous
Pollinated: Wind
Leaf shape: Ovate to obovate

Left: The greatest difference between common and copper beech is the leaf colour. The leaves are more oval in shape.

Oriental Beech

Fagus orientalis

The oriental beech is native to the forests of the Caspian Sea, the Caucasus, Asia Minor, Bulgaria and Iran. It is similar to common beech, and there is undoubtedly some hybridization between the two species on the boundary between their ranges. The oriental beech has larger leaves, with more pairs of veins, than common beech, and, given the right conditions, will develop into a larger tree. It was introduced into cultivation before 1880.

Identification: The bark is grey and smooth, occasionally becoming shallowly fissured in maturity. The leaves are elliptic to obovate, 12cm/4¾in long with up to 12 pairs of leaf veins and a wavy margin. They are dark, rich green above and paler beneath, becoming burnished gold in the autumn. Both the male and female flowers are small and yellow-green, carried in separate clusters on the same tree in spring. They are followed by woody, bristly fruit husks, containing up to three edible nuts.

Distribution: South-east Europe and south-west Asia.
Height: 30m/100ft
Shape: Broadly spreading
Deciduous
Pollinated: Wind
Leaf shape: Elliptic to obovate

Above left: The leaves of the oriental beech turn golden-yellow in autumn.

Left: The wavy-edged leaves are often obovate – at their widest near the tip.

OTHER SPECIES OF NOTE
Pendulous Beech *Fagus sylvatica* 'Pendula'
Several cultivars of common beech have weeping foliage, but 'Pendula' has to be the best. It grows into a large tree with enormous pendulous branches, which droop from the main stem rather like elephants' trunks. Where they touch the ground they sometimes take root, sending up another stem that in turn begins to weep. Over time a large tent-like canopy can develop around the original tree. Probably the best example of this is in the grounds of the old Knap Hill nursery near Woking in Surrey, England.

Dawyck Beech *Fagus sylvatica* 'Dawyck'
This delightful narrowly columnar tree, shaped like a Lombardy poplar and up to 25m/82ft tall, was discovered on the Dawyck estate in southern Scotland in 1860. It was an overnight success with gardeners and nurserymen, providing the perfect solution for those who wanted a beech tree but lacked space.

Fern-leaved Beech *Fagus sylvatica* 'Aspleniifolia'
Sometimes referred to as cut-leaved beech, this is one of the most beautiful of all beech cultivars. It is slightly smaller than the common beech in height and spread, but is not suitable for the domestic garden. However, if there is space, it is well worth growing for its handsome and variable foliage. The leaves may be long and narrow, 10cm x 6mm/4 x ¼in wide, deeply lobed, or anywhere in between. The effect is of hazy, soft green feathery foliage forming an irregular, rounded canopy.

Japanese Beech

Siebold's beech *Fagus crenata*

This species is sometimes called Siebold's beech after the 19th-century German naturalist Philipp Franz von Siebold, physician to the Governor of the Dutch East India Company's Japanese trading post at Deshima. Siebold first identified the tree in Japan, where it forms considerable forests from sea level to 1,500m/4,900ft. It was introduced to the West in 1892.

Identification: Similar to common beech, this tree differs mainly in its more obovate leaf shape and a small leaf-like structure found at the base of each seed husk in early autumn. The bark is silver-grey and smooth, even in older trees. Leaves are up to 10cm/4in long and 5cm/2in wide with a bluntly toothed margin with fine hairs. Each leaf has 7–11 pairs of veins. The leaf stalk is 1cm/½in long. Leaves turn an "old gold" colour in autumn. The seed husk is 1.5cm/⅔in long and covered in long bristles.

Right: A Japanese beech leaf and mast.

Distribution: Japan.
Height: 30m/100ft
Shape: Broadly spreading
Deciduous
Pollinated: Wind
Leaf shape: Ovate to obovate

Japanese Beech

Fagus japonica

Confusingly, the name "Japanese beech" is also applied to *F. crenata*, which is a more widespread native Japanese beech and therefore probably more worthy of the name. The actual trees are rarely confused: *F. japonica* is a smaller tree, often producing multiple stems, which give it a shrubby appearance, and its leaves are more oval and broad than those of *F. crenata*. It was introduced into Europe in 1907, when it was sent to the Royal Botanic Gardens, Kew, from the Arnold Arboretum in Boston. However, a century later it is still relatively uncommon in cultivation.

Distribution: Japan.
Height: 25m/80ft
Shape: Broadly spreading
Deciduous
Pollinated: Wind
Leaf shape: Oval to ovate

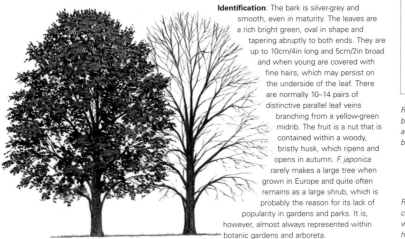

Identification: The bark is silver-grey and smooth, even in maturity. The leaves are a rich bright green, oval in shape and tapering abruptly to both ends. They are up to 10cm/4in long and 5cm/2in broad and when young are covered with fine hairs, which may persist on the underside of the leaf. There are normally 10–14 pairs of distinctive parallel leaf veins branching from a yellow-green midrib. The fruit is a nut that is contained within a woody, bristly husk, which ripens and opens in autumn. *F. japonica* rarely makes a large tree when grown in Europe and quite often remains as a large shrub, which is probably the reason for its lack of popularity in gardens and parks. It is, however, almost always represented within botanic gardens and arboreta.

Right: The leaves are bright green, oval and taper towards both ends.

Right: The seed is contained in a woody, bristly husk.

Chinese Beech

Fagus lucida

This small tree was discovered by the Irish physician and plant collector Augustine Henry, in the province of Hubei, China, in 1887. It was almost 20 years later that Ernest Wilson introduced it into Britain and Europe. It has probably the most distinctive leaf surface of any green beech, being bright glossy green on both surfaces. Examples of this species are found in most botanic gardens and arboreta but it is rarely cultivated elsewhere.

Distribution: Western China.
Height: 10m/33ft
Shape: Broadly spreading
Deciduous
Pollinated: Wind
Leaf shape: Ovate

Identification: In maturity this tree has a broad, flattened or rounded crown. The bark is smooth and light grey. The ovate leaves are up to 10cm/4in long and 5cm/2in wide, glossy green on both surfaces and with distinctive leaf veins that end in small teeth at the wavy margin. Both male and female flowers are small and yellow-green, carried in separate clusters on the same tree in spring. The fruit is contained in a woody husk, the surface of which is covered with small, blunt spines.

Right: The leaves are glossy green on both surfaces and have distinctive leaf veining.

Below: The fruit.

Engler Beech

Chinese beech *Fagus engleriana*

In the wild, in central China, this medium-sized tree almost invariably divides near the base into multiple stems, but this occurs less in cultivation. It is an attractive tree, which although uncommon in Britain and Europe deserves to be more widely planted. It was introduced into Europe in 1911. There is a fine specimen in southern England, which was planted in 1928 and is now 18m/60ft tall.

Distribution: Central China.
Height: 18m/60ft
Shape: Broadly spreading
Deciduous
Pollinated: Wind
Leaf shape: Ovate to oval

Identification: The silver-grey bark is smooth, even in maturity, and the tree is quite often multi-stemmed. The leaves are a glaucous sea-green, rounded at the base, pointed at the tip, and up to 10cm/4in long with a wavy margin. There is some hair on the leaf underside and the leaf stalk is longer than on most beeches, being up to 1.25cm/½in long. The fruits, which are nuts contained in a woody, bristly husk, are also borne on a long stalk, up to 5cm/2in long.

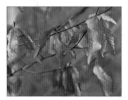

Right: The leaves of the Engler beech turn to a warm russet colour in autumn.

OTHER SPECIES OF NOTE

Fagus sylvatica 'Zlatia'
This tree was cultivated in Serbia, and its name is derived from the Serbian word for gold, *zlato*. The original tree was found growing among native beech in the 1880s. It is slow-growing, with soft yellow young leaves, which gradually turn green in summer.

Round-leaved Beech *Fagus sylvatica* 'Rotundifolia'
As its name suggests, this upright, neat-looking, medium-sized beech has dainty round leaves, 2.5cm/1in in diameter, which are borne on strongly ascending branches. Bred in England around 1872, it has remained popular in cultivation across Europe ever since.

Fagus sylvatica 'Purpurea Tricolor'
This small, rather attractive tree, developed in France in the 1880s, has purple leaves blotched with cream, with a purple-pink margin. They are smaller and narrower than in common purple beech. The variegation is most striking when the leaves are young. At one time this cultivar was considered identical to the form known as 'Roseomarginata'.

Fagus sylvatica 'Rohan Gold'
This uncommon cultivar is similar to Rohan's beech but with yellow-green leaves, which emerge from bud in spring a bright golden yellow before fading in summer. It is a relatively recent variety, having been raised in Holland in 1970. It is a vigorous small tree, which will reach a height of around 13m/42ft.

Rohan's Beech

Fagus sylvatica 'Rohanii'

This beautiful, purple, cut-leaved beech has leaves reminiscent of those of the fern-leaved beech, *F. sylvatica* 'Aspleniifolia'. It was raised at Sychrov, in Czechoslovakia, in 1888, and was commercially available in 1908. It is a popular addition to parks, gardens and arboreta throughout northern and western Europe. There are a few other purple cut-leaved beeches in cultivation, but this is the best cultivar.

Distribution: Originally raised in Czechoslovakia.
Height: 15m/50ft
Shape: Broadly spreading
Deciduous
Pollinated: Wind
Leaf shape: Ovate cut-leaved

Identification: This is a slow-growing, straight tree that will ultimately reach 15m/50ft in height. The bark, as with most beeches, is silver grey and smooth. The leaves are unlikely to be confused with those of any other tree. They are deep red-purple, sometimes tinged with green or brown; the leaf margin is deeply cut into triangular teeth, which may themselves carry serrations. The leaf veins and the leaf stalk are prominently red.

Below: The leaves are the most distinctive feature.

SOUTHERN BEECHES

This relatively little-known group of trees comes from temperate regions of the Southern Hemisphere, and is known by the genus name Nothofagus. Nothos *comes from the ancient Greek for "spurious" or "false" and* fagus *means "beech", so the name can be translated as "false beeches". Although the trees are similar to beeches there are some differences – many* Nothofagus *are evergreen and have smaller leaves.*

Roble Beech

Nothofagus obliqua

Distribution: Argentina
and Chile.
Height: 35m/115ft
Shape: Broadly columnar
Deciduous
Pollinated: Insect
Leaf shape: Ovate

*Far right: The fruit is a bristly
brown husk, similar to that of
beech, containing three nuts.*

Roble is Spanish for oak, and in some respects this large South American tree does resemble a European deciduous oak. Its timber is oak-like, tough and durable, and over the years has been used for shipbuilding, interior joinery and furniture. It is the most warmth-loving of all southern or false beeches and thrives in the Mediterranean climate.

Identification: The grey bark becomes cracked and fissured with age. The tree has dark green ovate to oval leaves; they are blue-green on the underside, roundly toothed, up to 7.5cm/3in long, and have 8–11 pairs of distinct veins. In autumn, the leaves turn golden yellow. The flowers are small and green: the males are borne singly and the females in threes, in late spring.

Rauli

Raoul *Nothofagus nervosa*

Also known as *N. procera*, this large, deciduous forest tree has upswept branching and heavily veined leaves. The name was given by early Spanish settlers who saw its grey, smooth bark and named it after the Spanish word for beech. It is a fast-growing tree that produces good quality timber and is being planted for forestry purposes in temperate regions of the Northern Hemisphere.

Identification: The dark grey bark becomes heavily fissured as the tree matures. The leaves, up to 10cm/4in long and 5cm/2in across, are easily distinguished from those of other *Nothofagus* because they have 14–18 pairs of deep veins, though they could at first glance be mistaken for hornbeam, *Carpinus* spp. The leaves are positioned alternately along the shoots; they are bronze-green above and paler beneath, with some hair on the midribs and veins. The fruit is a four-valved husk about 1cm/½in long, containing three small nuts.

Distribution: Central Chile
and western Argentina.
Height: 25m/80ft
Shape: Broadly conical
Deciduous
Pollinated: Insect
Leaf shape: Oblong to ovate

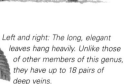

*Left and right: The long, elegant
leaves hang heavily. Unlike those
of other members of this genus,
they have up to 18 pairs of
deep veins.*

Silver Beech

Nothofagus menziesii

This slightly tender, graceful tree is native to both islands of New Zealand, where it grows on mountain slopes up to 1,000m/3,280ft above sea level. It is similar to the Australian species, *N. cunninghamii*. Both are far distant from the main populations of the *Nothofagus* genus, which are to be found in South America. Their occurrence here is evidence of the fact that the continents of Australasia and South America were both part of the ancient vast supercontinent. They are well represented in Europe.

Right: The dark green leaves are distinctively toothed around the margin.

Identification: When young the bark is like that of the *Prunus* species. It starts silvery-white and dulls to grey in maturity. The evergreen leaves are ovate to diamond shaped, doubly round toothed and up to 1cm/½in long. Both the leaf stalk and the shoot are covered in fine yellowish-brown hairs. The flowers are inconspicuous, being small and green. After flowering, four-lobed woody husk-like fruits develop. Each husk normally contains three small nuts.

Distribution: New Zealand.
Height: 30m/100ft
Shape: Broadly columnar
Evergreen
Pollinated: Insect
Leaf shape: Ovate

OTHER SPECIES OF NOTE

Dombey's Southern Beech
Nothofagus dombeyi
A native of Chile and Argentina, introduced into Europe in 1916, this vigorous, evergreen tree is one of the most elegant of all South American temperate trees. In maturity it resembles an old cedar in form, and as a juvenile its glossy, dark green leaves in combination with bright red male flowers make it extremely striking. *See also page 149.*

Antarctic Beech
Nothofagus antarctica
This elegant, fast-growing, small to medium-sized tree, to 15m/50ft, is native to South America, inhabiting mountainsides from Cape Horn to northern Chile. It is deciduous and fast-growing, with ovate, crinkly, glossy, dark green leaves which, when crushed, emit a sweet, honey-like fragrance. In autumn the leaves turn orange-red and yellow. It was introduced into Britain in 1830, though most of the specimens now growing in Europe come from seed brought from Chile at a later date. *See also page 148.*

Oval-leaved Southern Beech *Nothofagus betuloides*
This hardy, South American columnar evergreen tree, to 25m/80ft, has very ornamental, oval, shiny dark green leaves, 2.5cm/1in long, which are carried densely on multiple twisted stems and branches. It was introduced into Europe in 1830 and is fairly common in botanic gardens and arboreta. It produces inconspicuous small green flowers in spring, which are followed by woody husk-like fruits, each containing three small brown nuts.

Red Beech

Nothofagus fusca

This beautiful evergreen tree is native to both islands of New Zealand, from 37 degrees latitude southwards. It reaches large proportions in the wild. In cultivation in the Northern Hemisphere it seldom attains more than 25m/80ft in height. It is quite tender when young, being prone to frost damage, but becomes hardier with age.

Identification: The bark of red beech is smooth and dark grey when young, becoming flaky with lighter patches in maturity. The leaves are very distinctive because of their deep, sharply toothed margins. At 4cm/1½in long they are also bigger than those of any other evergreen *Nothofagus* species. They have long leaf veins, normally in three to four pairs. Although evergreen, the old leaves turn coppery-red before they eventually fall, hence the tree's common name. The leaf-stalk is covered in grey-brown hairs. The fruit is a four-lobed husk containing three nuts. The flowers are small, green and inconspicuous. Both male and female flowers are borne on the same tree in late spring.

Distribution: North and South Island, New Zealand.
Height: 30m/100ft
Shape: Broadly spreading
Evergreen
Pollinated: Insect
Leaf shape: Ovate to round

Left: The richly coloured, evergreen leaves of red beech are the largest of any southern beech species.

CHESTNUTS

The chestnut genus, Castanea, contains just 12 deciduous trees, all of which grow wild in temperate regions of the Northern Hemisphere. They are closely related to both the beech, Fagus, and oak, Quercus, genera. The majority are long-lived, large trees, which are drought-resistant and thrive on dry, shallow soils. They all have strongly serrated leaves and edible fruits in the form of nuts.

Japanese Chestnut

Castanea crenata

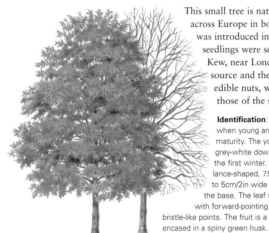

This small tree is native only to Japan but is cultivated across Europe in botanic gardens and arboreta. It was introduced into Europe in 1895, when seedlings were sent to the Royal Botanic Gardens, Kew, near London. In Japan it is a valuable food source and the tree is grown in orchards for its edible nuts, which are slightly smaller than those of the sweet chestnut, *C. sativa*.

Identification: The bark is a dull lead grey, smooth when young and becoming vertically fissured in maturity. The young shoots are covered in grey-white down, which persists well into the first winter. The leaves are oblong or lance-shaped, 7.5–17.5cm/3–7in long, up to 5cm/2in wide and heart-shaped at the base. The leaf margin is serrated, with forward-pointing small teeth with bristle-like points. The fruit is a fairly large edible nut, encased in a spiny green husk.

Distribution: Japan.
Height: 10m/33ft
Shape: Broadly spreading
Deciduous
Pollinated: Insect
Leaf shape: Oblong-lanceolate

Right: The flowers are pollinated by insects.

Left: Each husk contains two or three chestnuts.

Sweet Chestnut

Spanish chestnut *Castanea sativa*

This fast-growing ornamental tree is native to warm, temperate regions around the Mediterranean and in south-western Asia. It has also been widely cultivated elsewhere, often introduced by the Romans, who valued the tree as a source of food for themselves and their animal stock.

Identification: As a young tree the bark is smooth and grey. Older trees develop spiral fissures, which immediately distinguish the tree from oak. The leaves are oblong, up to 20cm/8in long, sharply pointed at the tip and rounded at the base. The leaf margin is edged with coarse teeth, each tooth linking to a strong vein running back to the midrib. Each catkin may be up to 25cm/10in long. The fruit is a spiny greenish-yellow husk, up to 6cm/2½in across, with up to three edible brown nuts.

Distribution: Southern Europe, North Africa and south-west Asia.
Height: 30m/100ft
Shape: Broadly columnar
Deciduous
Pollinated: Insect
Leaf shape: Oblong

Above left: The male and female flowers are borne on the same upright yellow catkin in summer, making it one of the last trees to come into flower.

Left and right: The chestnuts ripen in autumn.

OTHER SPECIES OF NOTE

American Chestnut *Castanea dentata*
This majestic tree, similar to sweet chestnut, *C. sativa*, was once widespread throughout its native North America, but since the 1930s its population has been devastated by chestnut blight. It can be found in botanic gardens in western Europe. *See also page 150.*

Golden Chestnut *Chrysolepis chrysophylla*
Sometimes referred to as the golden chinquapin, this medium-size evergreen tree is native to the USA, from where it was introduced into Europe in 1844. The description "golden" refers to the underside of the leaf, which is covered with bright golden hairs, a characteristic that distinguishes this tree from other members of the Fagaceae family. *See also page 151.*

Tanbark Oak *Lithocarpus densiflorus*
This medium-size, pyramidal, evergreen North American tree is closely related to oak and displays some of the characteristics of the oak family, such as the fruit, which is a bristly-cupped acorn. The leaves are, however, more characteristic of chestnut, as are the erect, creamy-yellow, spike-like flowers. It was introduced into Europe in 1874. *See also page 151.*

Chinquapin *Castanea pumila*
This deciduous small tree or large shrub was introduced into Europe in 1699 but is seldom grown outside botanic gardens and arboreta. It is distinguished from other chestnuts by the fact that it throws up suckers from the root system. Both the shoots and the underside of the leaves are covered with a white-grey down. The oblong leaves are coarsely toothed, up to 12cm/4¾in long. The egg-shaped nut is up to 2.5cm/1in long. *See also page 150.*

Chinese Chestnut

Castanea mollissima

This Chinese tree is common throughout its native land from Beijing westwards, where it is normally found growing in moist woodlands on lower mountain slopes. It was introduced into Europe in 1908.

Below: The nut and husk.

Distribution: China.
Height: 25m/80ft
Shape: Broadly columnar
Deciduous
Pollinated: Insect
Leaf shape: Oblong to lanceolate

Identification: The bark is dark grey and smooth, becoming deeply fissured in maturity. The leaves are up to 20cm/8in long and 7.5cm/3in broad, rounded at the base and tapering and curving to a sharp point at the tip. They have forward-pointing, coarse teeth around the leaf margin and are glossy dark green above with lighter green undersides. Both male and female flowers are erect, creamy-yellow catkins, to 20cm/8in long, which appear on the tree in mid-summer. These are followed by edible, shiny red-brown fruits, which are contained within a bristly husk.

Japanese Chinquapin

Castanopsis cuspidata

Of a genus of 120 species of evergreen trees, this is the only member that will grow outside the tropics. It is native to China, Korea and Japan, where it is common from Tokyo southwards. It is closely related to both chestnuts and oaks and displays the characteristics of both. It was introduced into Europe in 1830 but seldom attains anything like the dimensions to which it grows in its native lands. The largest specimen in Britain is growing in the grounds of Muncaster Castle, Cumbria, and is 10m/33ft tall.

Identification: The dark grey-brown bark is finely fissured from a young age. The oblong to ovate leaves are leathery, 10cm/4in long and 4cm/1½in broad, rounded at the base and drawn out into a slender, blunt tip, dark shiny green above and pale metallic green beneath. The leaf margin is sometimes bluntly toothed or wavy, more so towards the tip. The fruit is acorn-like, with the cup almost completely enclosing the seed, and borne in clusters of six to ten on the same stalk.

Right: The fruit of the Japanese chinquapin is acorn-like, but the erect catkins resemble those of a chestnut.

Distribution: Japan and China.
Height: 30m/100ft
Shape: Spreading
Evergreen
Pollinated: Insect
Leaf shape: Ovate

OAKS

There are almost 600 different species of oak, Quercus, in the world, the majority of which grow in the Northern Hemisphere. The oaks of Europe and Asia are on the whole slower growing and have less dazzling autumn leaf colour than their American cousins, but what they lose in terms of vibrancy and vigour, they more than make up for in diversity and longevity.

English Oak

Common oak *Quercus robur*

This majestic tree is one of the most familiar arboreal sights across Europe. It is usually a lowland species, growing best on damp, rich, well-drained soils. It is a long-lived tree, with many recorded veterans over 1,000 years old. In Britain it has hybridized with the sessile oak, *Q. petraea*, which is dominant in upland areas.

Identification: The bark is pale grey and smooth when young, quickly developing regular vertical fissures. The leaves, up to 10cm/4in long and 8cm/3in wide, either have no stalk or are on short stalks. The leaf margin is divided into three to six rounded lobes on each side, tapering towards the base where there are normally two smaller lobes. The upper surface is dark green, the underside glaucous. The fruit is an acorn, up to 4cm/1½in long, one-third of which is in a cup that is attached to the shoot by a long, slender stalk up to 10cm/4in long.

Distribution: Europe from Ireland to the Caucasus and north to Scandinavia.
Height: 35m/115ft
Shape: Broadly spreading
Deciduous
Pollinated: Wind
Leaf shape: Elliptic to obovate, lobed

Right: The male flowers are long catkins that appear in late spring.

Turkey Oak

Quercus cerris

The Turkey oak is a tall, vigorous, deciduous tree with a straight stem and deeply fissured bark. It is native to central and southern Europe, from France to Turkey, but has been cultivated across the rest of Europe since at least the mid-18th century and has become naturalized in many regions. It is an ornamental species, quite often used for planting in avenues. With its straight, clean stem it might be expected to yield valuable timber; in fact this is not so, as in most cases the timber cracks and splits before it reaches the sawmill.

Identification: The bark is silver-grey, thick and deeply fissured in maturity. The leaves are variable in shape, up to 12cm/4¾in long and 7.5cm/3in broad, variably and deeply lobed. They are dark glossy green, which may give the impression that they are evergreen, which they are not. The male flowers are yellow-green pendulous catkins that appear in late spring to early summer, and the seed is an acorn 2.5cm/1in long, carried in a bristly cup.

Distribution: Central and southern Europe.
Height: 40m/130ft
Shape: Broadly spreading
Deciduous
Pollinated: Wind
Leaf shape: Elliptic to oblong and lobed

Right: The leaves are a less defined version of those of Q. robur.

Sessile Oak

Durmast oak *Quercus petraea*

This valuable timber-producing tree is native right across Europe, from Ireland, Spain and Portugal to Turkey. In some countries, such as England, it grows alongside the English oak, *Q. robur*, and intermediate forms between the two species may result. Over the years its timber has been used for everything from barrels for wines and spirits to ship building.

Identification: The bark is grey with regular vertical fissures. The leaves are glossy dark green above and paler, and slightly hairy, beneath. Their shape is elliptic, to 13cm/5in long and 7.5cm/3in broad, tapering towards the base and with a margin that has rounded, untoothed lobes. Each leaf is attached to the twig by a yellow stalk up to 1.25cm/½in long. The male flowers appear in late spring and are yellow-green pendulous catkins. The seed is an unstalked acorn, one-third enclosed within a scaly cup.

Distribution: Europe.
Height: 40m/130ft
Shape: Broadly spreading
Deciduous
Pollinated: Wind
Leaf shape: Elliptic and lobed

Left: The leaves and catkins have yellow stalks.

Right: Sessile oak acorns are stalkless and directly attached to the twig by the base of the acorn cup.

OTHER SPECIES OF NOTE

Red Oak
Quercus rubra
The red oak is one of the largest and most widespread deciduous trees of eastern North America. It is found growing naturally from Nova Scotia to North Carolina and is widely planted in Europe. It has deeply cut leaves similar to those of scarlet oak, but not so glossy on the upper leaf surface. *See also page 152.*

Pin Oak *Quercus palustris*
Some specimens of this native of eastern and central North America are known to have exceeded 30m/100ft in height. The pin oak grows naturally in wet, swampy ground and is able to withstand flooding better than any other oak. It has been planted widely as a street tree, both in the USA and in Europe. Its name refers to the profusion of short side shoots that cover the lower part of the crown. The leaves are deeply cut. *See also page 152.*

Scarlet Oak *Quercus coccinea*
Scarlet oak is one of the most ornamental trees of eastern North America. It was introduced into Europe in 1691 and is common in large gardens, parks and arboreta, although it never quite colours with the intensity seen in North America. It has large, elliptic leaves, 15cm/6in long, which are cut into by angular, deep, bristle-tipped lobes. *See also page 153.*

Holm Oak

Evergreen oak *Quercus ilex*

This domed, densely branched tree is native to southern Europe and the Mediterranean, where it grows to over 1,520m/5,000ft above sea level. It has been cultivated in northern Europe since the 16th century and is important for shelter in coastal areas. It will grow on sand and can withstand prolonged drought. In colder regions up to 50 per cent of its leaves may be shed and replaced in spring.

Identification: The bark is charcoal grey, smooth at first but quickly developing shallow fissures which crack into small, square plates. The leathery, tapered leaves, to 7.5cm/3in long and 5cm/2in broad, are occasionally toothed but more often entire; they are dark green above, almost black from a distance, and sage green and covered with fine pale grey hair beneath. The seed is a small, pointed acorn, to 5mm/¼in long, one-third encased in a fawn, scaly cup.

Below: The male flowers are yellow pendulous catkins, which appear in early summer. The fruit, a nut, appears in the autumn.

Distribution: Southern Europe.
Height: 30m/100ft
Shape: Broadly spreading
Evergreen
Pollinated: Wind
Leaf shape: Elliptic to ovate

Cork Oak

Quercus suber

This medium-size evergreen tree has thick, corky bark and for centuries it has been used to make cork products such as stoppers for wine bottles. The cork oak is cultivated for this purpose in orchards, particularly in Portugal and Spain, and the outer bark is stripped from the trees on a rotation of 8–10 years. Removing it carefully does no damage to the living tissue beneath the bark, and some trees are known to be over 300 years old.

Identification: The obvious distinguishing feature of this tree is its pale grey, prominently creviced, corky bark. The leaves are similar to those of holm oak, *Q. ilex*, although far more variable. They may be anything from oblong to oval in shape, up to 7.5cm/3in long, normally with an entire margin or with occasional serration. They are glossy dark green on top and covered with a grey down underneath. Although the tree is evergreen, the older leaves are shed and replaced in early summer. The acorns are up to 3cm/1¼in long, glossy brown and half encased in their cups.

Distribution: Western Mediterranean and southern European Atlantic coast.
Height: 20m/65ft
Shape: Broadly spreading
Evergreen
Pollinated: Wind
Leaf shape: Ovate to oblong

Right: The distinctive thick bark.

Below left: The male flower is carried on a weeping yellow catkin in spring.

Above: The leaves are up to 7.5cm/3in long. The acorn is quite slender and pointed at the tip.

Pyrenean Oak

Quercus pyrenaica

Distribution: South-west Europe and North Africa.
Height: 20m/65ft
Shape: Broadly columnar
Deciduous
Pollinated: Wind
Leaf shape: Elliptic

The Pyrenean oak, as its name implies, is native to mountain woods in the Pyrenees, where it is found growing up to 1,520m/5,000ft above sea level. It also grows naturally in other parts of Spain, France, Portugal, Italy, and across the Mediterranean in Morocco. It is closely related to the Hungarian oak, *Q. frainetto*. The Pyrenean oak was introduced into cultivation in 1822 and is popular in large tree collections. The cultivar 'Pendula', which has a graceful weeping habit, is often grown in preference to the species.

Identification: The tree develops a domed, spreading crown. The bark is pale grey and roughly fissured into knobbly rectangular or square plates. The leaves are variable in size, up to 20cm/8in long and 7.5cm/3in broad, and are deeply indented with wedge-shaped, forward-pointing lobes. The upper surface of the leaf is a glossy deep green and the underside is pale green and covered in dense grey hairs. The male flowers are borne in long, attractive golden catkins, which appear in early summer.

Left: The leaves are deeply indented with wedge-shaped, forward-pointing lobes. The acorns are broad and rather squat and carried to half their length in a scaly woody cup.

Hungarian Oak

Quercus frainetto

This large, handsome, deciduous oak is native to south-eastern Europe, including Hungary, and was introduced into cultivation in 1838. It has probably the largest and most distinctive leaves of any oak growing in Europe. They are up to 20cm/8in long and 10cm/4in wide, deeply and regularly cut by many large, forward-pointing lobes. It has long been grown as an ornamental species in parks and arboreta across Europe.

Identification: The bark of the Hungarian oak is dark grey, rugged and heavily fissured in maturity. The leaves are the tree's most distinctive feature for identification purposes, and even in winter they still provide clues to its identity because they do not rot easily and persist on the ground around the base of the tree right through to the following spring. The male flowers are green-yellow pendulous catkins, which appear in late spring. The seed is a squat, egg-shaped acorn, with up to half its length encased in a cup.

Distribution: South-east Europe.
Height: 30m/100ft
Shape: Broadly spreading
Deciduous
Pollinated: Wind
Leaf shape: Obovate

Left: The large leaves have seven lobes.
Right: Male catkins.

OTHER SPECIES OF NOTE

Algerian Oak *Quercus canariensis*
Also known as Mirbeck's oak, this handsome tree is native to North Africa and south-western Europe, but it also survives well farther north, where it is regularly planted in gardens. It is columnar when young, broadening in maturity. Although not strictly evergreen, most of its neatly lobed leaves stay on the tree in winter.

Armenian Oak *Quercus pontica*
This rare, small tree or large shrub, which grows to 6m/20ft, is native to Turkey, Armenia and the land between the Black and Caspian seas into southern Russia, where it inhabits mountain woodlands. It is fully hardy and quite distinctive, with thick, large, deeply veined leaves, which are glossy and bright green, reminiscent of chestnut leaves, and borne on stout shoots.

Lucombe Oak *Quercus* x *hispanica* 'Lucombeana'
This magnificent semi-evergreen tree is a form of the hybrid Spanish oak, *Q.* x *hispanica*, which is itself a variable but natural hybrid between the cork oak, *Q. suber*, and the turkey oak, *Q. cerris*. The original Lucombe oak was found growing close to a cork oak in the Exeter nursery of William Lucombe in 1762. He propagated the tree by grafting it on to turkey oaks, and several thousand clones were distributed around Britain and Europe, some of which are still alive today. It is a large, spreading tree, resembling the turkey oak, with glossy toothed leaves, dark green above and grey beneath. The bark is pale grey and deeply fissured, with a corky texture.

Downy Oak

Quercus pubescens

This small to medium-size, sometimes shrubby-looking tree, which has a large natural range across southern and central Europe, is closely related to the sessile oak, *Q. petraea*, and the two can be quite difficult to tell apart. In general, the downy oak is smaller, with a shrubbier, more ragged outline, and the leaves and twigs tend to carry more pubescence, or down. It grows best in dry soil conditions with plenty of light and warmth. It is relatively uncommon in parks and gardens.

Distribution: Spain to the Caucasus.
Height: 20m/65ft
Shape: Broadly spreading
Deciduous
Pollinated: Wind
Leaf shape: Elliptic

Identification: The bark is dark grey and deeply fissured. The leaves are variable, elliptic to obovate, to 10cm/4in long and 5cm/2in broad. They are dark grey-green above and paler green with a covering of soft grey hair beneath, as are the leaf stalks. The leaf lobes are rounded, some ending in a small, sharp point. The male flowers are borne in pendulous, yellow-green catkins. The seed is a stalkless acorn, to 4cm/1½in long and contained, to up to half its length, in a hairy, scaly acorn cup.

Below: The fruit.

Right: The tree is named for the down on its leaves and shoots.

Turner's Oak

Quercus x turneri

This small to medium-size, semi-evergreen, compact, dense-leaved oak is the result of an artificial hybrid cross between the holm oak, *Q. ilex*, and the English oak, *Q. robur*, carried out by Turner's Nursery, Essex, England, in the early 1780s. By the early 19th century it was commonly cultivated in gardens across much of western Europe. More recently it has been planted in urban areas because it can withstand atmospheric pollution and also provides an evergreen screen in the winter.

Identification: The bark is dark grey and fissured into rectangular plates. The leaves are oblong to obovate, 13cm/5in long and 5cm/2in broad, shiny dark green above, pale green beneath, borne on hairy shoots and persisting well into winter. The leaves taper towards the base and have variable shallow and triangular lobing around the margin. The male flowers are borne in yellow-green weeping catkins in early summer. The seed is an acorn, one half of which is enclosed in a scaly cup. The acorns do not always develop into mature fruits.

Distribution: Of UK garden origin.
Height: 20m/65ft
Shape: Broadly spreading
Semi-evergreen
Pollinated: Wind
Leaf shape: Oblong to obovate

Left: The leaves take many of their characteristics from the holm oak parent. They are shallow to un-lobed and in mild areas of Europe the leaves may persist on the tree all winter.

Sawtooth Oak

Quercus acutissima

As the name suggests, this distinctive oak has leaves that are regularly edged with saw-like teeth. It is native to a broad region that runs from the eastern Himalayas through China to Japan, and it is a close relation of the Turkey oak, *Q. cerris*. The sawtooth oak was introduced into European cultivation in 1862 by an Englishman, Richard Oldham. It is said that in Japan, silkworms were at one time fed on its leaves.

Identification: The bark of the sawtooth oak is dull grey-brown, smooth at first, becoming vertically and deeply fissured in maturity. The leaves are chestnut-like, oblong, to 20cm/8in long and 5cm/2in broad, with many distinctive parallel leaf-veins running from the midrib and ending in slender-tipped teeth. They are glossy dark green above and pale green beneath. The male flowers are borne on yellowish pendulous catkins in late spring. The seed is a rounded acorn, to 2.5cm/1in long.

Distribution: South-east Asia.
Height: 15m/50ft
Shape: Broadly spreading
Deciduous
Pollinated: Wind
Leaf shape: Oblong

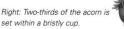

Right: Two-thirds of the acorn is set within a bristly cup.

Above and above left: The leaves persist on the tree into winter.

Golden Oak of Cyprus

Quercus alnifolia

This interesting small oak takes its name from the golden undersides of its leaves, which are covered with a dense golden- or mustard-yellow felt quite similar to the indumentum found on some Himalayan rhododendrons. In the wild, in Cyprus, the golden colouring can be extremely vibrant; it is less so in cultivation in western Europe. The tree was introduced into Europe in 1885 and, although perfectly hardy, it is not as common in cultivation as might be expected.

Identification: The bark is dark grey and smooth with pale orange flecks. The leaves are thick and leathery, rounded, up to 5cm/2in in diameter, edged with sparse small teeth, glossy deep green above and golden-brown beneath. Young leaves will also have some pubescence on the top side. The male flowers are borne in drooping, yellow-green catkins in late spring. The acorns (not always present) are elongated, broadening from the base upwards and shaped like a policeman's truncheon. When ripe these are also a rich golden colour.

Distribution: Cyprus.
Height: 8m/26ft
Shape: Broadly spreading
Evergreen
Pollinated: Wind
Leaf shape: Rounded

Left: The leaves have a distinctive golden covering to the underside. Acorns are shaped like a policeman's truncheon.

OTHER SPECIES OF NOTE
Caucasian Oak *Quercus macranthera*
This handsome, medium-size to large, rounded, deciduous tree is native to the Caucasus Mountains and northern Iran, south of the Caspian Sea. It has strongly ascending branches and verdant foliage. The leaves are large, and can be up to 15cm/6in long and 10cm/4in wide. They taper towards the base, with up to 11 rounded, forward-pointing lobes on each side.

Daimo Oak
Quercus dentata
This 20m/65ft spreading and heavily branched deciduous oak is native to Japan and mainland north-east Asia, from where it was introduced into Europe and cultivation in 1830. Its main claim to fame is that it produces some of the largest leaves of any oak: they may be anything up to 30cm/12in long and 15cm/6in broad. Each leaf has between five and nine lobes on each side.

Gall Oak *Quercus infectoria*
This small semi-evergreen tree, 6m/20ft tall, is native to the region around the Aegean Sea and Cyprus. Its twigs often bear galls, which are collected as a source of tannin for the dyeing industry. It was cultivated in western Europe from 1850 but has never been widely grown there. It has leathery, oblong to elliptic leaves, 7.5cm/3in long and 5cm/2in wide, which are serrated around the margin with sharp spines.

Portuguese Oak

Quercus faginea

At one time it was thought this broad-headed tree was native to North Africa as well as the Iberian peninsula. It was cultivated in northern Europe, including Britain, in 1824, but has never become popular, despite its ability to grow well on all soil types including shallow chalk. The leaf form is very variable and may be anything from oval to elliptic with either regular pronounced teeth around the margin, or sometimes no teeth at all. In mild winters the leaves will persist on the tree right through to the following spring.

Identification: The bark is grey-brown, smooth at first, becoming vertically cracked in maturity. The leaves are rather leathery, up to 7.5cm/3in long and 5cm/2in broad, grey-green above and covered with a dense grey felt beneath. The male flowers are borne in early summer on pendulous yellow-green catkins. The seed is a squat, rounded acorn, which is enclosed to one third of its length in an urn-shaped cup.

Distribution: Spain and Portugal.
Height: 20m/65ft
Shape: Broadly spreading
Semi-evergreen
Pollinated: Wind
Leaf shape: Oval to obovate

Right: The fruit.

Right: Up to 12 pairs of parallel leaf veins end in sharp, regular teeth.

BIRCHES

The birches, Betula, *are a group of catkin-bearing, alternate-leaved, deciduous trees, native to northern temperate regions of the world. There are more than 60 species, spread right across the region, from Japan to Spain and across North America. They are particularly well known for their attractive bark, which, depending on species, varies from pure white to red.*

White Birch

Downy birch *Betula pubescens*

Distribution: Northern Europe to northern Asia.
Height: 25m/80ft
Shape: Broadly conical
Deciduous
Pollinated: Wind
Leaf shape: Ovate to round

This common birch thrives in wet conditions and poor soils right up into the Arctic region. It is sometimes known as downy birch because of its hairy shoots. Although related to silver birch, *B. pendula*, it is distinct, and the two species rarely hybridize. White birch is not as popular as silver birch, lacking its graceful pendulous form.

Identification: The bark on young trees may be dull grey, but it matures white. Branches and shoots are glossy copper-brown. The male flowers are yellow catkins and the females green upright catkins, both borne on the same tree in early spring. When ripe, the female catkins break up on the tree, shedding copious small, papery winged seeds.

Right: The dark green leaves are 5cm/2in long and wide, with toothed edges, ending in a pointed tip.

Silver Birch

Betula pendula

The silver birch is one of the toughest of all trees, able to withstand intense cold and long periods of drought. It seeds prolifically and will quickly establish on cleared ground. Birch was one of the first trees to colonize northern Europe after the last ice age 12,000 years ago. It is just as much at home in semi-tundra regions of northern Scandinavia as it is in temperate southern France.

Identification: The bark is a distinctive white to silver colour. Mature trees develop corky black fissures between white irregular plates. The leaves are almost triangular in shape, 6cm/2½in long and 4cm/1½in across, tapering to a point. They are glossy grass green above and paler beneath, normally turning butter yellow before falling in autumn. The leaf stalk is usually red-brown, 2.5cm/1in long and attached to a slim, hairless, warty, weeping shoot. Both male and female flowers are catkins, appearing separately on the same tree in early spring. The male flower is yellow and drooping, up to 6cm/2½in long; the female flower is green, erect and smaller.

Distribution: Europe and northern Asia, from the Atlantic to the Pacific.
Height: 30m/100ft
Shape: Narrowly weeping
Deciduous
Pollinated: Wind
Leaf shape: Ovate to triangular

Above: The silver birch is often planted for the ornamental value of its distinctive bark.

Right: The catkins are thick and the leaves coarsely serrated.

Himalayan Birch

Betula utilis

The exact distribution of the Himalayan birch is difficult to define, because several other Asiatic birches occur in the same region, and cross-pollination and hybridization do occur. At one stage the Chinese red-barked birch, *B. albo-sinensis*, was considered to be a form of this birch and not a separate species. The colour of Himalayan birch bark varies from white, in the west of its natural range, to pink-brown or orange-red in the east. The tree grows in parks and arboreta all over Europe.

Identification: The variably coloured bark is paper-thin and peels off in long, ribbon-like, horizontal strips. The serrated leaves, up to 10cm/4in long and 6cm/2¼in wide, taper to a point. They have strong veining with up to 12 pairs of parallel veins, each vein ending in a sharp tooth. The leaves are shiny dark green above and paler beneath, with some hair on the midrib, and are attached to hairy shoots by a short leaf stalk, 1.25cm/½in long. The flowers are catkins: the male long, yellow and drooping, up to 12.5cm/5in; the female smaller, green and upright. Both flowers are borne on the same tree in early spring.

Distribution: Himalayas from Kashmir to Sikkim and western and central China.
Height: 25m/80ft
Shape: Broadly conical
Deciduous
Pollinated: Wind
Leaf shape: Ovate

Right: A long, yellow male catkin.

Left: The leaf is teardrop-shaped.

OTHER SPECIES OF NOTE

River Birch *Betula nigra*
Extensively grown in Europe, where it grows on river banks and swampy ground, this tree has ovate, toothed leaves up to 10cm/4in long and peeling, pink-brown bark, that becomes fissured in maturity. It regenerates from the stump and is often coppiced to encourage multiple stems, displaying the peeling effect. *See also page 158.*

Canoe Birch *Betula papyrifera*
Also known as the paper birch, this creamy white-barked large birch grows extensively across Europe and is extremely hardy. Native Americans used the timber to make canoes. It has ovate, toothed leaves that turn orange-yellow in autumn. *See also page 159.*

Erman's Birch *Betula ermanii*
This magnificent, long-lived birch, to 25m/80ft tall, has a natural range from Japan to Siberia. It was introduced into cultivation in 1890. It has creamy white to pink bark, which peels in long papery strips and then hangs from the main branches, giving the tree a ragged appearance.

Monarch Birch *Betula maximowicziana*
Also known as Japanese red birch and sometimes Maxim's birch, this magnificent large Japanese birch has long been cultivated across Europe. Its heart-shaped leaves are larger than those of any other birch, 15cm/6in long and 13cm/5in broad, and its reddish-brown bark peels to reveal greyish-yellow, or grey-pink, new bark beneath. The leaves turn yellow in autumn.

Chinese Red-barked Birch

Betula albo-sinensis

This beautiful, medium-sized birch is best known for its attractive coppery to orange-red bark, which peels to reveal cream-pink bark beneath, on both the trunk and branches. The bark and catkins make this tree a spectacular sight. It grows high in the mountains in mixed woodland on relatively impoverished, shallow soils. It was introduced into Europe in 1901 by the English plant collector Ernest Wilson and has been a favourite for planting in gardens and arboreta ever since.

Identification: The leaves are ovate, 7.5cm/3in long and 4cm/1½in across. The margin is cut by forward-pointing, sharp serrations, and the leaf ends in a long, fine, slightly curved tip. When the leaves emerge from small, slightly sticky buds, they are covered with a soft down. This quickly disappears to reveal glossy grass-green leaves, which turn golden yellow in autumn before falling. Both male and female flowers are catkins, and are very similar to those of the Himalayan birch. Fertilized female flowers develop into brown papery catkins containing hundreds of winged seeds.

Right: The male and female catkins appear on the same tree.

Distribution: Western China.
Height: 25m/80ft
Shape: Broadly conical
Deciduous
Pollinated: Wind
Leaf shape: Ovate

Japanese Cherry Birch

Betula grossa

This medium-size Japanese birch, native to the mountains of Honshu, Shikoku and Kyushu, was introduced into Europe in 1896. It is comparatively uncommon within cultivation but normally found in botanic gardens and arboreta. It is closely related to the American cherry birch, *Betula lenta*, and has similar characteristics, such as bark colouring and aromatic foliage and twigs.

Below: The leaves turn yellow in the autumn.

Identification: The bark on young trees is shiny red-brown, becoming grey-brown and flaking in maturity into horizontal strips. The leaves are ovate, heart-shaped at the base, rather like hornbeam, with prominent veins and a coarsely-toothed margin, up to 10cm/4in long and 5cm/2in broad, dark green above, paler beneath with some fine pubescence. Both male and female flowers are borne in catkins, male are yellow and pendulous, female green and upright. Female catkins ripen and break up on the tree releasing hundreds of paper-winged seed.

Left: The tree can grow to be as wide as it is tall.

Distribution: Japan.
Height: 20m/65ft
Shape: Broadly conical
Deciduous
Pollinated: Wind
Leaf shape: Ovate

Below: The bark is an attractive shiny red-brown when the tree is young, and becomes grey-brown and flaking in maturity.

Transcaucasian Birch

Betula medwediewii

The transcaucasian birch is a very hardy species native to the Caucasus Mountains, between the Black Sea and the Caspian Sea, where it grows up to sub-alpine elevations. It is a small, spreading tree or large shrub, which was introduced into cultivation in Germany and Britain around 1897. In parks and gardens it is mainly grown for the attractive bright yellow autumn colour of its large leaves, and for its handsome, prominent catkins in spring. The species is recognizable in winter by its large, glossy green sticky buds, which are borne on stout upright branches.

Identification: The bark, on what is often a multi-stemmed tree, is shiny pale grey-brown, and on older trees has a tendency to flake and peel. The leaves are ovate to rounded, up to 10cm/4in long and 7.5cm/3in wide and sometimes slightly heart-shaped at the base. They are heavily indented, almost to the point of corrugation, with 8–11 pairs of sunken veins. The top surface of the leaf is dark green and the lower surface is paler green with some hairiness along the leaf veins. The male and female flowers are borne on separate catkins, both on the same tree, in early spring.

Distribution: Caucasus.
Height: 4.5m/15ft
Shape: Broadly spreading
Deciduous
Pollinated: Wind
Leaf shape: Ovate to round

Right: The large corrugated leaves turn bright yellow in autumn.

Young's Weeping Birch

Betula pendula 'Youngii'

There are few weeping trees that surpass Young's weeping birch for sheer beauty and elegance. Consequently it is commonly planted throughout Europe just about everywhere, from shopping centre car parks to large arboreta. It was raised in a nursery at Milford, Surrey, England, in the latter part of the 19th century. The trees are seen at their very best when planted as a group, close enough to allow their domed mushroom heads to intermingle, so that the fine tracery of branches produces a hanging "curtain" of foliage.

Above: The leaves are coarsely serrated.

| Distribution: Of garden origin. |
| Height: 10m/30ft |
| Shape: Broadly spreading and weeping |
| Deciduous |
| Pollinated: Wind |
| Leaf shape: Ovate to triangular |

Identification: Young's weeping birch is relatively easy to identify because its grey-white bark instantly suggests birch (though on very young trees the bark is glossy brown), and there is no other tree with such graceful weeping branches. Mature trees invariably develop crooked trunks that have a tendency to lean to one side. The overall effect could be described as untidy but it is very charming. The leaves are the same as those of the silver birch, *B. pendula*, or slightly smaller, and are borne on fine, thin, weeping branches.

OTHER SPECIES OF NOTE

White-barked Himalayan Birch

Betula utilis var. *jacquemontii*

The Himalayan birch has a long natural range, from Afghanistan to China. Across this range its characteristics vary considerably; depending on the region in which forms have been raised, their bark colour may vary from pure white through pink to copper-brown. *Jacquemontii* has dazzling white bark and has spawned several popular cultivars, including 'Grayswood Ghost', 'Jermyns' and 'Doorenbos'.

Creamy Bark Birch *Betula costata*

This vigorous, attractive birch, of conical habit, is native to north-east Asia and deserves to be more widely planted than it is. It has been suggested that it may be a form of Erman's birch, *B. ermanii*: if not, it is certainly closely related. However, it differs in having narrower leaves, which are wedge-shaped at the base and more pointed at the tip. It has beautiful pink to creamy-fawn peeling bark and in autumn the leaves turn clear yellow.

Asian Black Birch *Betula davurica*

This medium-size hardy tree from northern China and Korea takes its common name from the American black birch, *B. nigra*, which it resembles in having the same peeling dark silver-grey bark, which gives the tree a rough, rugged, almost shaggy appearance. In the wild it may reach 30m/100ft, but is more likely to achieve 20m/65ft in cultivation. It comes into leaf earlier than most birches grown in northern Europe, and the foliage can be damaged by frost.

Swedish Birch

Betula pendula 'Dalecarlica'

This distinctive cultivar of silver birch, sometimes wrongly called *B. pendula* 'Laciniata', has slender leaves that are deeply cut, almost back to the midrib. It was found in Ornas, north of Stockholm, Sweden, in 1767, and in 1810 grafts were cultivated in the Stockholm Botanical Garden, from where it was made commercially available. Today, it is a reasonably common sight in botanic gardens and arboreta across northern and western Europe.

Identification: The bark is similar to that of the silver birch, *B. pendula*. The overall form is of an elegant, light and airy, tall, narrow tree with weeping twigs and shoots borne on ascending branches. The leaves are slenderly oval and then cut almost to the midrib. The lobes are themselves lance-shaped, finely toothed and have a long slender point. They are glossy dark green above, paler beneath and turn butter yellow in autumn. Both male and female flowers are borne on catkins in early spring.

| Distribution: Of garden origin. |
| Height: 25m/80ft |
| Shape: Narrowly conical |
| Deciduous |
| Pollinated: Wind |
| Leaf shape: Ovate and deeply cut |

Below: The deeply cut leaves give the tree a delicate appearance.

ALDERS

Alders are a group of 36 deciduous species within the Betulaceae family. They are primarily native to northern temperate regions of the world, where they grow in damp conditions, quite often alongside rivers and other watercourses. In boggy ground they can form inpenetrable thickets, and when growing in the open they have a broad open shape.

Common Alder

Black alder *Alnus glutinosa*

This tree has always been associated with water. It thrives in damp, waterlogged conditions, growing close to rivers and marshy ground, where it creates its own oxygen supply. Alder timber is waterproof and has been used to make everything from boats to water pipes, including wooden clogs. It also forms the foundations of many of the buildings in Venice, Italy.

Identification: The bark is dark grey-brown and fissured from an early age. The leaves are obovate to circular, finely toothed with up to ten pairs of pronounced leaf veins and a strong central midrib. Up to 10cm/4in long and 8cm/3in wide, they are dark green and shiny above and pale grey-green beneath, with tufts of hair in the leaf axils. Both male and female flowers are catkins: the male is greenish yellow, drooping and up to 10cm/4in long; the female is a much smaller, red, upright catkin which, after fertilization, ripens into a distinctive small brown cone. Spent cones persist right through to the following spring.

Distribution: All of Europe, extending into western Asia and south to North Africa.
Height: 25m/80ft
Shape: Broadly conical
Deciduous
Pollinated: Wind
Leaf shape: Obovate

Left: The catkins appear in early spring, before the leaves open. Alder cones begin to grow in summer, by which time the rounded leaves are thick on the branches.

Grey Alder

Alnus incana

Distribution: Europe (not Britain) to the Caucasus.
Height: 20m/65ft
Shape: Broadly conical
Deciduous
Pollinated: Wind
Leaf shape: Ovate

Right: The fruit is a woody cone-like structure containing tiny winged seeds.

This medium-size, fast-growing tree reaches elevations of up to 1,000m/3,300ft in the Caucasus Mountains, and gets its name from the dense covering of grey hairs on the undersides of the leaves. It has been in cultivation in Europe since 1780 and, due to its exceptional hardiness, is a popular tree for planting in cold, wet conditions and in areas being reclaimed following industrial activities, such as mining and landfill. It has spawned several ornamental cultivars, including the handsome, cut-leaved 'Laciniata'.

Identification: The bark is dark grey and smooth, even in maturity. The leaves are ovate, matt dark green above and paler with grey hairs beneath. They are 10cm/4in long and 5cm/2in broad, with a double-toothed margin and a pointed tip. The flowers are borne in catkins: the male catkin is 10cm/4in long, orange-yellow and pendulous, the female catkin is erect and red. Both are carried separately on the same tree in late winter. The fruit persists on the tree long after ripening.

Italian Alder

Alnus cordata

This handsome tree originated in southern Italy, parts of Albania and Corsica, where it grows at up to 1,000m/3,300ft on dry mountain slopes. It is less dependent on damp conditions than most alders, thrives on chalk, and is by far the largest of its genus, sometimes attaining heights over 30m/100ft in the wild. It was named *cordata* because of its heart-shaped leaves, and was introduced into cultivation in 1820.

Identification: The bark is dull grey, smooth at first becoming shallowly fissured with age. The 10cm/4in leaves are glossy bright green above, paler with some hairs beneath. The male catkins are yellow and pendulous, 7.5cm/3in long; the females are smaller, red and erect. Both appear on the same tree in early spring and are followed by egg-shaped, woody, cone-like fruits.

Right: Female and male catkins, and the heart-shaped leaf.

Distribution: Southern Italy and Corsica.
Height: 28m/90ft
Shape: Broadly conical
Deciduous
Pollinated: Wind
Leaf shape: Broadly ovate

OTHER SPECIES OF NOTE

Red Alder *Alnus rubra*
This pioneer species is native to the west coast of North America, where it grows on just about any available space not already colonized by other species. It was introduced to Britain in the mid-19th century. Although not a large tree, it grows particularly fast until it reaches its optimum height of 15m/50ft. Red alder has light brown-grey bark, which is rough and warty, and an ovate leaf up to 10cm/4in long with rusty-red hairs on the underside. *See also page 160.*

Oriental Alder *Alnus orientalis*
This medium-size tree, to 15m/50ft tall, is native to the eastern Mediterranean region, including Syria and Cyprus, from where it was introduced into cultivation in western Europe in 1924. It has oval to ovate, glossy green, irregularly toothed leaves, bright green sticky buds in winter, and clusters of yellow, pendulous male catkins in early spring. It is related to the Italian alder, *A. cordata*, but is distinguished from this species by its small wingless seeds.

Caucasian Alder *Alnus subcordata*
This attractive, fast-growing, medium-size tree, to 20m/65ft, is native to the Caucasus region, between the Black and Caspian Seas and south into Iran, where it grows naturally in damp woodland on flood plains. It has large, oval to ovate, heart-shaped, matt green leaves, which may be up to 15cm/6in long. It is one of the earliest alders to flower: its long, 15cm/6in, male catkins may appear as early as the beginning of winter. It was introduced into Britain in 1838 and into France in 1861.

Green Alder

Alnus viridis

This small spreading tree, or large shrub, which produces clumps of long, erect stems, is native to the central and southern European Alps, where it can be found growing naturally up to elevations around 1,000m/3,300ft. It was introduced into cultivation in 1820 but has not been widely planted as an ornamental since. However, when planted on poor soils its root system has the ability to fix nitrogen in the soil and thereby improve soil fertility, both for itself and for other plants growing around it.

Distribution: Central and south-east Europe.
Height: 6m/20ft
Shape: Broadly spreading
Deciduous
Pollinated: Wind
Leaf shape: Ovate

Identification: The bark is grey-green and smooth and the tree regularly sends up olive green, cane-like suckers. The rounded leaves, up to 10cm/4in long and 7.5cm/3in broad, end in a pointed tip. They are dark green and smooth above, paler beneath with some hair along the midrib and veins. Male and female flowers are borne in separate catkins on the same tree in spring.

Above: The woody fruit.

Right: The leaves are unevenly toothed.

Alnus firma

This alder is native to all the main islands of Japan, where it is found primarily in mountainous regions. Elsewhere, particularly in the agricultural land outside Tokyo, it has been widely cultivated along field boundaries. At one time these trees were used to support poles erected to dry freshly cut rice. The species was introduced into Europe in 1893, and although not common in cultivation it is represented in most botanic gardens and arboreta.

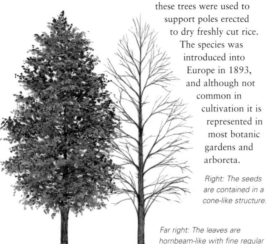

Right: The seeds are contained in a cone-like structure.

Far right: The leaves are hornbeam-like with fine regular serrations around the margin and distinctive parallel veining.

Identification: This is a small tree, clothed rather densely but gracefully in long slender branches. The leaves are similar to those of the common hornbeam, *Carpinus betulus* – rounded or wedge-shaped at the base and with a long slender tip. They are 11cm/4½in long and 5cm/2in wide, with distinctive parallel veining, and are finely toothed around the margin. The lower surface may be covered with fine hairs, as is the shoot. An interesting characteristic is that the leaves remain green until they fall in early winter.

Distribution: Japan.
Height: 9m/30ft
Shape: Broadly conical
Deciduous
Pollinated: Wind
Leaf shape: Ovate-lanceolate

Below: The catkins are lime-yellow in colour.

Manchurian Alder

Alnus hirsuta

The Manchurian alder is native to Eastern China and Japan, from where it was introduced into Europe in 1879, when propagation material was collected and sent to James Veitch. The species is closely related to the grey alder, *A. incana*, and effectively extends that tree's natural range east into Asia. *A. hirsuta* is distinguished from *A. incana* by its larger leaves, which are occasionally more round than ovate and have more pronounced indentations around the margin. It is a vigorous and handsome tree that, like many other alders, thrives in wet conditions.

Identification: The bark is dark grey-brown and smooth even in maturity. Large trees may have a trunk girth up to 1.8m/6ft. Young shoots are covered in fine hairs and the winter buds are purple and shaped like boxing gloves. The leaves are broadly ovate, rounded at the base and at the apex, with shallow lobes and double serrations around the margin. They are 12.5cm/5in long and nearly as wide, dull dark green and heavily corrugated, with between 9 and 12 pairs of leaf veins. The fruit is a large woody cone 2.5cm/1in long.

Distribution: North-east Asia and Japan.
Height: 20m/65ft
Shape: Broadly conical
Deciduous
Pollinated: Wind
Leaf shape: Ovate

Below: The leaves are ovate with shallow lobes and double serrations, and the catkins.

Japanese Alder

Alnus japonica

This is a striking large alder with a distinctive pyramidal shape and unusually narrow leaves. In maturity it makes a fine, shapely specimen. It has never been widely cultivated and is relatively rare in gardens and arboreta across Europe.

Identification: *A. japonica* has dull grey, smooth bark, and the young shoots may be covered in fine hairs. The leaves are narrowly elliptic to lanceolate, tapering at both ends, with a slender tip. They are up to 12.5cm/5in long and 5cm/2in wide, and are glossy dark green with minimal veining branching from a yellow midrib. The male flowers are borne in terminal clusters of yellow-brown catkins. The seed is borne in an oval, woody cone-like structure.

Distribution: China, Japan, Korea and Taiwan.
Height: 25m/80ft
Shape: Pyramidal
Deciduous
Pollinated: Wind
Leaf shape: Lanceolate to elliptic

Left: The leaves are glossy dark green, narrowly elliptic, tapering at both ends. The flowers are catkins.

Alnus maximowiczii

This small tree, or large shrub, with thick shoots and twigs, is native to high mountain ranges. It is closely related to the Sitka alder, *A. sinuata*, a native of north-west North America, to which 250 million years ago Asia would have been joined in the supercontinent Pangaea. *A. maximowiczii* was first cultivated in Europe just before World War I.

Far right: Clusters of short-fat yellow catkins appear in spring.

Distribution: South-east Asia and Japan.
Height: 9m/30ft
Shape: Broadly spreading
Deciduous
Pollinated: Wind
Leaf shape: Broadly ovate

Right and above left: The leaves are broadly ovate to heart-shaped and reminiscent of some lime (Tilia) species.

Identification: This is a shrubby tree with thick shoots and grey bark. The leaves are bright green on both surfaces, with a fine point and fine, slender teeth around the margin, giving a slightly ragged, fringe-like appearance. They are up to 10cm/4in long and 7.5cm/3in wide, with tufts of hair in the leaf axils on the undersides. Clusters of stout yellow male catkins are produced in spring.

OTHER SPECIES OF NOTE

Alnus glutinosa 'Imperialis'

This cultivar of the common alder, *A. glutinosa*, is one of the most distinctive and graceful alders, on a par with other cut-leaved trees for ornamentation. Its delicate leaves are cut into long slender lobes, which run right into the midrib and give a light, feathery effect. It was raised in 1859 and has been widely planted across Europe.

Alnus glutinosa 'Pyramidalis'

Sometimes referred to by its former name, 'Fastigiata', this cultivar has a rather conical shape with branches at an acute angle. It has been in cultivation since the late 1800s and is commonly planted across Europe, particularly in damp soil close to water.

Alnus x spaethii

This is a 1908 hybrid between the Caucasian alder, *A. subcordata*, and the Japanese alder, *A. japonica*. It is fast-growing, up to 20m/65ft tall, and has leaves that are purple when they first emerge in spring. It is grown in European arboreta for its outstanding display of male catkins, which appear in late winter.

Himalayan Alder *Alnus nitida*

This tall alder, to 25m/80ft, has bark that is dark brown or almost black, and thin, ovate toothed leaves up to 15cm/6in long. It is unique among alders in having male catkins that appear in autumn rather than spring. It was introduced into cultivation from the north-west Himalayas in 1882.

HORNBEAMS AND HAZELS

Hornbeams are attractive, hardy trees, which have long been cultivated in Europe. Common hornbeam is used for hedging and, as a hedge, has similar characteristics to beech, including retaining its dead leaves into winter and forming a solid windbreak. The genus Corylus includes hazel, which is widely distributed throughout Europe and west Asia.

Heartleaf Hornbeam

Carpinus cordata

This medium-sized attractive tree was introduced into Europe from Japan in 1879. In its natural habitat it grows in mixed woodland in mountainous regions. Since then it has become widely distributed in botanic gardens, but is still fairly uncommon in parks and gardens. The name *cordata* means "heart-shape" and refers to the leaves, which are heart-shaped at the base. It is a slow-growing tree and hardy in northern Europe and Great Britain.

Identification: It has a broadly columnar form, smooth charcoal-grey bark at first, becoming fluted at the base and shallowly fissured in maturity. The leaves are deeply veined, relatively broad when compared to other hornbeams, oblong to ovate, heart-shaped at the base, dark green and up to 10cm/4in long and 5cm/2in wide. Male and female flowers are borne in yellow-green catkins in spring. The fruit is a nut that is covered with several small, overlapping green bracts.

Distribution: Japan, North-east Asia, north and west China.
Height: 15m (50ft)
Shape: Broadly columnar
Deciduous
Pollinated: Wind
Leaf shape: Oblong-ovate

Left: The catkins.

Above right: The leaves are heart-shaped at the base and deeply veined.

Hornbeam

European hornbeam *Carpinus betulus*

Distribution: Central Europe, including southern Britain, to south-west Asia.
Height: 30m/100ft
Shape: Broadly spreading
Deciduous
Pollinated: Wind
Leaf shape: Ovate

Left: The fruit is a ribbed nut, which is held in a three-lobed bract.

Hornbeam is sometimes confused with beech because of its silver-grey bark and similar leaf. However, hornbeam bark is far more angular than beech bark. Hornbeam leaves also have obvious serrations around the margin, which are not present on beech. Hornbeam timber is dense and hard and has a clean, white, crisp appearance. It was traditionally used to make ox yokes and butchers' chopping blocks.

Identification: The leaves are oval to ovate, up to 10cm/4in long and 5cm/2in across, double-toothed around the margin and tapering to a long point. There are normally between 10 and 13 pairs of leaf veins. The upper leaf surface is dark green, the underside a paler green. In autumn the leaves turn rich yellow before falling. Male and female catkins are borne separately in spring on the same tree. The fruit is a distinctive three-lobed bract with a small, ribbed, brown nut at the base of the centre bract. The bract is green in summer, ripening to fawn in autumn and persisting on the tree until the following spring.

Right: The male catkins are up to 5cm/2in long. Female catkins (not shown) are much smaller.

Turkish Hazel

Corylus colurna

This magnificent tree has a very stately, symmetrical form. It normally develops a straight, short stem holding a pyramid of foliage, and is ideal for planting as an avenue tree. It was introduced into central and western Europe, including Britain, in the middle of the 16th century and has been popular in cultivation ever since. There are particularly good specimens in Hanover, Germany, and Vienna, Austria. It produces a pink-brown timber, much prized for furniture.

Identification: The bark is light grey-brown and distinctly corky in maturity. The leaves are dark green, broadly oval, heart-shaped at the base, toothed around the margin and up to 15cm/6in long and 10cm/4in broad. The male and female flowers are carried in separate catkins on the same tree. The males are yellow, pendulous and up to 7.5cm/3in long, while the females are red and small.

Above: The leaf.

Distribution: South-east Europe and western Asia.
Height: 25m/80ft
Shape: Broadly conical
Deciduous
Pollinated: Wind
Leaf shape: Broadly oval

Above left: The fruit is an edible nut, the husk of which is covered with bristles.

OTHER SPECIES OF NOTE

Japanese Hornbeam *Carpinus japonica*
This is a handsome, widely spreading Japanese tree, to 15m/50ft tall, which was first cultivated in Europe in 1895. It has narrow, ovate leaves with up to 24 pairs of prominent, parallel, leaf veins, which give the whole leaf a corrugated effect. In spring the male catkins are bright yellow and pendulous. The nut is covered with green bracts, which resemble the fruit of the ironwood, *Ostrya virginiana*.

Oriental (Caucasian) Hornbeam
Carpinus orientalis
This small tree or large shrub, to 15m/50ft tall, is native to south-east Europe, the Caucasus Mountains and south-west Asia. It grows on hot, dry sites, and was abundant on the battlefields of the Crimean War. It produces dense, almost impenetrable branches and foliage. The leaves are ovate, up to 5cm/2in long and sharply toothed, with 12–15 pairs of parallel veins.

Ironwood *Ostrya virginiana*
Otherwise known as the American hop hornbeam, this medium-sized tree, to 20m/65ft, is native to eastern and southern USA, from where it was introduced into Europe in 1692. It has ovate, heavily veined leaves, which turn a rich warm yellow in autumn. The name ironwood refers to the timber, which is very heavy and strong and is often used to make tool handles. See also page 163.

Common Hazel

European filbert *Corylus avellana*

There is much discussion about whether hazel is a tree or a shrub. In theory, a tree has 1m/3ft of clear stem before it branches or forks, and has the potential to grow to more than 6m/20ft in height. Hazel can certainly achieve the latter, but has a tendency to fork low down. Its status as a tree is not helped by the fact that for centuries, right across Europe, it has been regularly coppiced to ground level. Its ability to regrow after such harsh pruning has made it a popular plant for agricultural hedging.

Identification: The bark is smooth and silver-grey to pale brown, even in maturity. The trunk seldom exceeds 20cm/8in in diameter. The leaves are up to 10cm/4in across, with double teeth around the margin, and are thick and rough to the touch. There are coarse hairs on the leaf, bud and shoot. The male flower is a yellow catkin, up to 10cm/4in long, which ripens in early spring to release copious amounts of pollen to the wind. The female flower is a tiny red floret, which is borne on the end of what looks like a leaf bud but will develop into the fruit – a round to ovoid, matt, light brown, edible nut, which is half encased in a green calyx.

Right: Hazel catkins are a familiar sight across Britain and Europe in early spring.

Distribution: Europe, western Asia and North Africa.
Height: 6m/20ft
Shape: Broadly spreading
Deciduous
Pollinated: Wind
Leaf shape: Orbicular

Left: Hazel leaves are almost round in shape. This plant produces the popular hazelnut.

LIMES

There are about 45 species within the Tilia *genus. All are deciduous and are found in northern temperate regions. Limes, also known as lindens, are handsome trees, and many grow into large, ornamental specimens. Several species have been used for urban tree planting, as they respond well to pollarding and hard pruning in street situations. They look good planted in avenues and formal vistas.*

Small-leaved Lime

Tilia cordata

This tall, attractive column-like tree has heart-shaped leaves and fragrant yellow flowers. When found growing wild in woodland across its natural range it is a good indicator that the woodland is very old or even ancient. There are some coppiced trees in Britain that are believed to be over 2,000 years old. The inner bark (known as bast) was at one time used to make rope.

Identification: The bark is grey and smooth when young, becoming vertically fissured in maturity. The leaves are cordate, almost rounded, glossy bright green above and glaucous beneath, with some hairiness in the vein axils. In autumn they turn a rich butter-yellow. In summer, highly scented yellow flowers are borne in drooping clusters of up to ten, and are accompanied by a long, 10cm/4in, pale green bract.

Left: The heart-shaped leaf tapers abruptly to a blunt tip.

Right and left: The flowers are followed by round, hard, grey-green felted fruits.

Distribution: Europe from Portugal to the Caucasus.
Height: 30m/100ft
Shape: Broadly columnar
Deciduous
Pollinated: Insect
Leaf shape: Cordate

Weeping Silver Lime

Pendent silver lime Tilia tomentosa 'Petiolaris'

This is without doubt one of the most beautiful of all large trees growing in Britain and Europe. It is a cultivar of the silver lime, *T. tomentosa*, and was first described in Switzerland in 1864, although the original plant is believed to have been raised 20 years earlier. The structure of the tree is superb, with long arching branches creating what has been described as a "vaulted cathedral ceiling". The flowers are beloved by bees, and their humming is a characteristic feature of this tree in summer.

Distribution: Of garden origin from an eastern European species.
Height: 30m/100ft
Shape: Broadly columnar
Deciduous
Pollinated: Insect
Leaf shape: Broadly ovate to rounded

Right: The creamy-white flowers are borne in fragrant clusters in summer.

Identification: The bark is grey and vertically fissured in maturity. Quite often a graft union will be evident anywhere between 2–5m/6½–16½ft from the ground. Weeping shoots hang from arching branches and are covered with almost rounded leaves, which are dark green above and pure silvery-white beneath. Close inspection reveals that this whiteness is made up of thousands of tiny white hairs.

European Lime

Common lime *Tilia* x *europaea*

Distribution: Most of Europe.
Height: 40m/130ft
Shape: Broadly columnar
Deciduous
Pollinated: Insect
Leaf shape: Broadly ovate

The European lime is a hybrid between the small-leaved lime, *T. cordata*, and the large-leaved lime, *T. platyphyllos*, and occurs naturally wherever the ranges of the two parents overlap. It does not have the elegance of either parent, producing unsightly suckering around the base. It is also prone to aphid attack in summer, which results in a coating of sticky aphid excrement, known as honeydew, appearing on anything that lingers beneath its boughs. Surprisingly, despite all this, it is regularly planted in towns and avenues in preference to its parents.

Identification: The bark is grey to grey-brown, smooth when young and developing shallow vertical fissures in maturity. The leaves are broadly ovate and up to 10cm/4in both in length and across. They are heart-shaped at the base with a sharply toothed margin and end in a tapering point at the tip. The colour of the leaves is a rather flat green above and slightly paler beneath, and they have hairy tufts in the main vein axils. The flowers are yellow and fragrant, borne in drooping clusters of up to ten under a pale green bract in summer.

Right: The clusters of flowers hang down beneath the leaves in summer.

Left: Like that of other limes, the fruit is small and pea-like.

Large-leaved Lime

Tilia platyphyllos

This splendid, large, domed tree has a clean, straight trunk and graceful arching branches. Unlike the European lime, *T.* x *europaea*, it does not produce suckers or suffer from aphid attack, so does not shed sticky honeydew in summer.

Left: The leaves have pointed tips.

Distribution: Europe into South-west Asia.
Height: 30m/100ft
Shape: Broadly columnar
Deciduous
Pollinated: Insect
Leaf shape: Broadly ovate

Identification: The bark is light grey with shallow fissures in maturity. The large leaves are rounded, up to 15cm/6in across. They are deep green above with some hair, and light green on the underside, with dense hairs along the midrib and in the vein axils. The leaf stalk, which can be up to 5cm/2in long, is also covered in soft white down. The flowers are pale yellow, very fragrant and produced in weeping clusters of up to six in early summer. Each flower cluster is accompanied by a downy floral bract, up to 12.5cm/5in long and 1.5cm/⅔in wide. The fruit is a pale green, downy "pea", borne on a stalk in late summer and early autumn.

OTHER SPECIES OF NOTE

American Basswood *Tilia americana*
Commonly known as American lime, this attractive tree has a natural range from Maine to North Carolina and west to Missouri. It was introduced to Britain in 1752. It has rough, almost corky bark in maturity and the largest leaf of any lime, up to 25cm/10in long and almost as broad. *See also page 164.*

Crimean Lime *Tilia* x *euchlora*
This elegant tree is believed to be a hybrid cross between the small-leaved lime, *T. cordata*, and *T. dasystyla*, which occurred naturally in the wild somewhere in the Crimea region around 1860. Crimean lime is a "clean" lime, which means it does not suffer attack by aphids and so escapes their sticky "honeydew" excretions, which fall on to cars parked beneath the tree. It does, however, have yellow fragrant flowers that are extremely attractive to bees. The bees gorge on the nectar until they become intoxicated and then stumble around beneath the tree.

Oliver's Lime *Tilia oliveri*
This elegant, medium-sized, broadly spreading lime, otherwise known as Chinese white lime, was discovered in central China in 1888 by the English plant hunter Ernest Wilson, who introduced it into Europe in 1900. It has silver-grey smooth bark and heart-shaped leaves, which are dark green above and covered with fine white hairs beneath. It is a popular tree, widely cultivated across western Europe in parks, gardens and arboreta.

Begonia-leaved Lime

Tilia begoniifolia

This hardy, vigorous, medium-sized tree is native to the lands bordering the eastern side of the Caspian Sea – where it may attain heights around 25m/80ft. It is too early to say how tall it will grow in cultivation, as the tree was introduced into western Europe only in 1972. Since its introduction, specimens at the Hillier Arboretum in Hampshire, England, have already exceeded 10m/30ft in height.

Distribution: Southern Russia and Northern Iran.
Height: 25m/80ft
Shape: Broadly columnar
Deciduous
Pollinated: Insect
Leaf shape: Broadly ovate

Identification: The bark is grey and smooth when young, becoming shallowly and sparsely fissured as the tree matures. The leaves are broadly ovate, large (up to 15cm/6in long), heart-shaped at the base and regularly toothed around the margin. They are deep grass green above and paler beneath, with some hair in the leaf vein axils. In autumn, the leaves turn a strong yellow before falling. The winter shoots are orange-red and an attractive feature when caught by low winter sun.

Above: The leaves are heart-shaped at the base and regularly toothed around the margin.

Caucasian Lime

Tilia caucasica

Distribution: Northern Iran to the Caucasus.
Height: 30m/100ft
Shape: Broadly columnar
Deciduous
Pollinated: Insect
Leaf shape: Rounded to broadly ovate

Although cultivated in Europe since at least 1880, this vigorous tree from the Caucasus and northern Iran has never been widely planted in gardens or parks across Europe. This is a shame, because it is a regular-shaped, tidy-looking tree, which does well in urban areas where space is not a limiting factor. It was identified and described by the German botanist Franz Joseph Ruprecht, and is probably more widely cultivated in Germany than elsewhere in Europe.

Identification: The bark is grey and smooth; the shoots and twigs are olive green and when young are covered with fine hairs. The leaves are almost round, up to 15cm/6in across, with a sharply bristle-toothed margin running to a short point. They are glossy deep green above and pale green with tufts of cream hairs in the vein axils beneath. Clusters of fragrant, pale yellow flowers, each with a single long, narrow, pale green bract, are produced in summer, followed by rounded fruits.

Left: In autumn the leaves turn golden-brown.

Right: The flowers and fruits hang beneath a pale green bract.

Japanese Lime

Tilia japonica

There is a school of thought that suggests the Japanese lime may represent merely an eastern extension of the natural range of the small-leaved lime, *T. cordata*, to which it is closely related. In fact, there is a difference in leaf shape: the Japanese lime has larger leaves, with a distinctive pointed tip that is not so evident on the small-leaved lime. It is an attractive ornamental tree, which was introduced into Europe in 1875.

Identification: This medium-sized lime is conical in form with a densely leaved crown. Its bark is silver-grey and smooth. The leaves are broadly ovate, heart-shaped at the base and up to 7.5cm/3in long. They are regularly serrated around the margin, running to a long, pointed tip. They are bright matt green above, pale green beneath and appear relatively early in the spring. Flowering tends to be much more prolific than on the small-leaved lime, with large flower clusters appearing all over the crown in summer.

Distribution: Japan and eastern China.
Height: 20m/65ft
Shape: Broadly conical
Deciduous
Pollinated: Insect
Leaf shape: Broadly ovate

Right: Clusters of pale yellow fragrant flowers appear in summer.

Left: The heart-shaped leaves run to a long pointed tip.

OTHER SPECIES OF NOTE

Tilia insularis
This lime is native to the South Korean island of Cheju Do (Daghelet) and in the wild it may grow up to 35m/115ft tall. However, in cultivation it seldom exceeds a height of 20m/65ft. It is an attractive tree, which produces masses of fragrant pendulous flowers in summer. It has heart-shaped, coarsely toothed leaves, to 10cm/4in long.

Tilia kiusiana
On first inspection, this small tree or large shrub, which comes from southern Japan, looks more like a birch than a lime. It has fine, slender branches and small, narrowly ovate leaves, to 5cm/2in long. It produces multiple stems and is commonly grown in gardens and urban areas in some parts of central Europe. It is not cultivated so widely in Britain, where it was introduced from Japan in 1930.

Tilia mandshurica
This small to medium-sized lime is native to north-east Asia, from where it was introduced into Europe in 1860. It is related to the American lime, *T. americana*, and has similarly large, 20cm/8in long and 15cm/6in broad, coarsely toothed, heart-shaped leaves. It differs in having hair on both surfaces of the leaf and by the fact that it comes into leaf much earlier in the spring, as a result of which it is sometimes damaged by late frosts.

Mongolian Lime

Tilia mongolica

The Mongolian lime was first seen by Europeans in 1864, when the French Jesuit missionary Abbé Armand David discovered it in central China, but it was not cultivated in Europe until 1880, when specimens were planted at the Jardin des Plantes in Paris. It is a slow-growing small lime, ideal for the smaller garden, and perfectly hardy. Unusually for a lime, its new leaves are reddish-bronze on emerging in early spring.

Identification: The bark is grey and smooth becoming slightly and vertically fissured in maturity. The leaves are broadly ovate, glossy dark green above and glaucous beneath with tufts of hairs in the leaf vein axils. They are up to 7.5cm/3in long and have between three and five irregular lobes. At first glance they look like maple (*Acer*) leaves, but are not borne in opposite pairs. In autumn they turn golden yellow before falling.

Distribution: Mongolia, northern China and eastern Russia.
Height: 15m/50ft
Shape: Broadly columnar
Deciduous
Pollinated: Insect
Leaf shape: Broadly ovate

Below: The leaves are lobed and coarsely toothed.

POPLARS

The poplars, of the family Salicaceae, are a genus of over 35 species of deciduous trees found throughout the northern temperate regions of the world. They produce small male and female flowers, which are borne in catkins on separate trees and pollinated by wind. Poplars are fast-growing trees, many of which can withstand atmospheric pollution and salt spray from the ocean.

Chinese Necklace Poplar

Populus lasiocarpa

Distribution: Central China.
Height: 20m/65ft
Shape: Broadly spreading
Deciduous
Pollinated: Wind
Leaf shape: Broadly ovate

Right: The large leaves have toothed margins.

This striking, medium-sized tree has among the largest and thickest leaves of all poplars. The word "necklace" in its name refers to the long, hanging, green seed capsules that appear in mid-summer. In late summer these ripen and burst, shedding phenomenal amounts of seed over a wide area. It grows all over Europe.

Identification: The overall shape of the tree tends to be open and gangly; it can look particularly dishevelled in winter. The bark is grey-brown and fissured in maturity. The leaves are large and broadly ovate to heart-shaped; on some trees they are up to 35cm/14in long and 20cm/8in across. They have a leathery feel and are attached to the chunky shoots by red leaf stalks up to 10cm/4in long. The leaf-stalk colouring appears to "bleed" into the midrib and main veins of the leaves. In autumn the leaves turn light brown and crisp, making a distinctive sound on windy days. The male and female flowers are stiff, yellow-green catkins, borne on separate trees in spring.

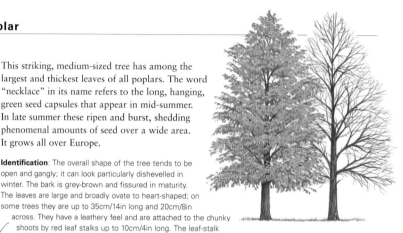

Right: The green necklaces" of seed capsules give this poplar its common name.

Black poplar

Populus nigra

This is a large, broadly spreading tree, with long heavy branches. It inhabits river valleys and damp regions right across western Asia and much of Europe, but in western Europe, including Britain, it gives way to the Atlantic sub-species *P. nigra* subsp. *betulifolia*. Black poplar has long been cultivated outside its natural range.

Identification: The bark is pale grey and when young it is covered with darker diamond-shaped fissures. In maturity it develops a characteristic craggy appearance, with deep furrows and large burrs. The leaves are glossy deep green above, pale sage green beneath, and densely covered in silver-grey down. They are 7.5cm/3in long and broad. The male and female flowers are borne in drooping catkins up to 10cm/4in long, which appear on separate trees in early spring. The female flowers are green, the males are grey with red anthers. The fruit is a small green capsule; it ripens to release hundreds of tiny seeds, which are covered in white hairs that resemble cotton wool, and are carried on the wind.

Distribution: Western Asia and Europe.
Height: 30m/100ft
Shape: Broadly spreading
Deciduous
Pollinated: Wind
Leaf shape: Triangular to ovate

Right: The leaves are ovate to triangular, sometimes rounded.

Lombardy Poplar

Populus nigra 'Italica'

The Lombardy poplar is probably one of the most easily recognizable of all trees because of its slender, columnar outline and upright branching. It is not a true species but a distinctive variety of the black poplar, *P. nigra*, which is believed to have originated beside the River Po in northern Italy in the early 1700s. Since then the Lombardy poplar has been propagated by cuttings and planted as an ornamental tree around the world.

Below: Leaves may be 10cm/4in wide. Catkins have an orange tinge.

Distribution: Originated as a 'sport' (variety) of black poplar in northern Italy.
Height: 30m/100ft
Shape: Narrowly columnar
Deciduous
Pollinated: Wind
Leaf shape: Ovate

Identification: The tree is immediately recognizable by its upright form. Strongly ascending branches grow from near ground level. The trunk, with its dark grey bark, is normally fluted and buttressed at the base. Each leaf is ovate to diamond-shaped and glossy bright green. Lombardy poplars are predominantly male trees, hence the need to propagate from cuttings. The male catkins are up to 7.5cm/3in long and borne in mid-spring. This poplar is not long-lived and is susceptible to bacterial canker and fungal diseases.

Aspen

European aspen *Populus tremula*

This tree is properly known as European aspen, so as not to confuse it with its American cousin, *P. tremuloides*. The botanical name *tremula* is derived from the fact that the leaves, which are borne on slender flattened leaf stalks, tremble and quiver in even the slightest breeze. "To tremble like an aspen leaf" is a phrase that goes back to the time of the 16th-century English poet, Edmund Spenser.

Identification: This medium-sized suckering tree has grey, smooth bark, becoming ridged at the base in maturity. The leaves are 7.5cm/3in long and equally wide. The leaf margin is edged with rounded teeth and there are three distinct, light-coloured veins at the base of each leaf. The leaves emerge a pink-bronze colour from the bud in spring, gradually turning dull green by early summer. Both male and female flowers are catkins, up to 5cm/2in long, borne in early spring before the leaves emerge. Tiny seeds carried in white, cotton wool-like hairs are released from green catkin-like capsules in late spring.

Distribution: Europe from the Atlantic to the Pacific, south to North Africa.
Height: 20m/65ft
Shape: Broadly spreading
Deciduous
Pollinated: Wind
Leaf shape: Broadly ovate

Right: Male and female catkins appear on separate trees.

Left: Leaves are rounded.

Western Black Poplar

Atlantic black poplar *Populus nigra* subsp. *betulifolia*

This fascinating and confusing sub-species of black poplar, *P. nigra*, is known as the Manchester poplar in that English city, where the entire population originated from two or three individual trees. The true sub-species is considered rare, or possibly even endangered, in the wild. This is due to the cultivation of faster and straighter-growing hybrids, which have been planted in preference, as well as years of cross-pollination and hybridization with other cultivated poplars, such as *P. x canadensis*. Most of the mature pure specimens left are male trees.

Distribution: Britain, western France, Belgium and Holland.
Height: 30m/100ft
Shape: Broadly spreading
Deciduous
Pollinated: Wind
Leaf shape: Triangular to ovate

Identification: The bark is pale grey, smooth at first, becoming deeply fissured in maturity. The leaves are triangular to ovate, 7.5cm/3in long and broad, glossy dark green above and pale green beneath. This tree differs from the typical form of *P. nigra* in that its shoots, leaf stalks, young leaves and flower stalks are all covered with a soft pubescent down. Both male and female flowers are borne in long, pendulous catkins, which appear in early spring on separate trees.

Right: Male and female catkins appear on separate trees in early spring.

Left: The leaves are almost triangular in shape.

Asian Balsam Poplar

Laurel-leaf poplar *Populus laurifolia*

This slow-growing, medium-sized tree was introduced into western Europe from Siberia around 1830. Although it has an elegant form it has never been widely planted in parks and gardens and is normally confined to arboreta and botanic gardens. It has a rather lax growth, with semi-pendulous branching and distinctive, angular, grey young shoots. It is a balsam poplar and has sticky winter buds, which emit a strong balsam-like fragrance in early spring.

Identification: The bark is silver-grey and smooth. The leaves are lanceolate, or narrowly ovate, tapering at both ends, rounded at the base and pointed at the tip with a margin that has small, fine, regular serrations. Each leaf is up to 12.5cm/5in long and 5cm/2in wide, dark green above and grey-green beneath with some down. The underside displays a fine network of leaf veins. Both the male and female flowers are borne in catkins. The male catkins are erect at first, becoming pendulous and up to 5cm/2in long when ripe.

Distribution: Eastern Siberia, Mongolia and parts of China.
Height: 21m/70ft
Shape: Broadly spreading
Deciduous
Pollinated: Wind
Leaf shape: Narrowly ovate to lanceolate

Left: Asian balsam poplar has an open, spreading crown.

Right: The leaves are narrowly ovate, rounded at the base, pointed at the tip with small serrations around the margin.

Balm of Gilead *Populus* x *candicans* 'Aurora'
This is a popular cultivar of a hybrid that is
believed to have developed naturally between
two North American species, the balsam poplar,
P. balsamifera, and the eastern cottonwood,
P. deltoides, in the 18th century. It was
introduced into Europe in 1773. It is strongly
balsam-scented when young. The cultivar
'Aurora' has been commercially available since
the 1920s and has distinctive, broadly ovate
leaves, which are strikingly marked in summer
with pink, white and cream blotches.

Populus szechuanica
This is a fast-growing, handsome, large tree,
growing to 30m/100ft, which is native to
western China, from where it was introduced
into Europe in 1908. It has dramatic, large, ovate
leaves, 30cm/12in long and 20cm/8in broad, and
a distinctive red midrib and leaf stalk, which
stand out well against the pale green-white
lower surface of the leaf.

Populus wilsonii
This attractive, medium-sized poplar takes its
species name from the English plant collector
Ernest Wilson, who introduced the species into
Europe from Central China in 1907. It is similar
to the Chinese necklace poplar, *P. lasiocarpa*,
bearing long, pendulous strings of ripe fruit in
summer, but with smaller leaves. On this tree
the ovate leaves are 20cm/8in long and 15cm/
6in wide, bright blue-green and borne on thick,
rigid shoots.

Korean Poplar

Populus koreana

This handsome poplar is native to Korea,
parts of Russia and possibly Japan, where it
naturalized in western regions of Honshu.
It was introduced to Europe in 1918 by
Ernest Wilson. It is a balsam poplar, and
emits the distinctive balsam-like fragrance in
early spring. It is one of the first trees to
come into leaf in spring.

Distribution: Korea and
southern Russia.
Height: 30m/100ft
Shape: Broadly columnar
Deciduous
Pollinated: Wind
Leaf shape: Ovate to oval

Identification: The bark is grey,
smooth at first becoming heavily
fissured in maturity. The leaves
are up to 15cm/6in long and
10cm/4in broad, ovate to oval,
borne on thick, strong shoots.
They are fresh grass-green on the
upper surface and almost white
beneath, with some down. The
central midrib is red.
The male and female
flowers are borne in
long, pendulous
catkins on separate
trees in spring.

*Right: The female
catkins may be up to
25cm/10in long.*

Hybrid Black Poplar

Populus x *canadensis*

This hybrid between the European black poplar,
P. nigra, and the North American cottonwood,
P. deltoides, occurred naturally in western Europe,
soon after the American species was introduced
in the early 18th century. It was recognized as
being superior, both in form and vigour, to
each parent, and by the 1750s was widely
planted throughout Europe. Since then,
many fast-growing and ornamental cultivars
of the original hybrid have been developed
including 'Serotina', 'Robusta' and the
glorious yellow-foliaged 'Serotina Aurea'.

Identification: The bark is grey, smooth at first, then
developing deep, vertical fissures. The leaves are
glossy green above, paler beneath, broadly triangular,
to 10cm/4in long and broad with a short point at the
tip. Both male and female flowers are borne in
pendulous catkins on separate trees in early spring.
The female flowers are green. The fruit is a small
green capsule, which ripens to release numerous
seeds coated in fluffy white hairs.

Distribution: Of garden
origin in western Europe.
Height: 35m/115ft
Shape: Broadly columnar
Deciduous
Pollinated: Wind
Leaf shape: Broadly
triangular

*Right: The male
flowers are
grey-green and
up to 10cm/
4in long.*

WILLOWS

There are more than 300 species of willow in the world, varying from large, spreading, ornamental specimens to diminutive, creeping, tundra-based alpines. The majority are native to northern temperate regions of the world. Willows are mainly deciduous, although one or two subtropical species have leaves that persist into winter. Male and female flowers are normally borne on separate trees.

Crack Willow

Salix fragilis

Distribution: Asia and Europe.
Height: 25m/80ft
Shape: Broadly spreading
Deciduous
Pollinated: Wind
Leaf shape: Lanceolate

This fast-growing riverside tree is one of the largest willows, and regularly attains heights in excess of 20m/65ft. It takes its name from the distinctive crack heard when a twig is snapped off the tree. The wood is brittle, and large branches are quite often broken off by high winds. Where such a branch touches the ground roots may grow out from the bark, keeping the branch alive and eventually making another tree genetically the same as the parent.

Identification: The bark is dull dark grey, becoming heavily fissured in maturity. Stems may be up to 2m/6½ft in diameter. The leaves are glossy dark green above and blue-green beneath, to 15cm/6in long and 2.5cm/1in broad, tapering to a fine point at the tip. Both the male and female flowers are very small and are borne in pendulous catkins, 5cm/2in long, on separate trees in spring.

Right: The leaves appear in mid-spring.

Right: The male catkins are yellow, the females green.

White Willow

Salix alba

White willow thrives in damp soils and grows naturally alongside rivers and in watermeadows. The dense coating of hairs on the leaves gives the tree an attractive silvery appearance, particularly when the leaves are stirred by the wind.

Identification: The bark is brown-grey, becoming deeply fissured in maturity. The leaves are lanceolate, tapering at both ends, and are up to 10cm/4in long and 1.25cm/½in wide. Young leaves are covered in silver hairs on both sides; mature leaves retain this pubescence on the underside but the top side becomes smooth and bright green. Both male and female flowers are catkins, borne on separate trees in spring as the leaves emerge. The fruit is a green capsule, ripening to release numerous white-haired seeds, which are dispersed by the wind.

Right: The long, slender leaves hang from the tree and move easily in the wind.

Distribution: Europe and western Asia.
Height: 25m/80ft
Shape: Broadly columnar
Deciduous
Pollinated: Insect, and occasionally wind
Leaf shape: Lanceolate

Right: Male catkins are 5cm/2in long and have yellow anthers; female catkins are green and smaller.

Goat Willow

Pussy willow *Salix caprea*

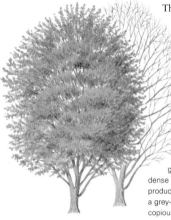

This small tree, sometimes a large shrub, of bushy habit, is common throughout Britain, Europe and western Asia. Through prolific seed dispersal it will, if left unchecked, colonize vacant or cultivated land for vast distances. Male trees produce the golden catkins known as "palm"; females produce the soft, silvery catkins called "pussy willow".

Identification: The bark is dull grey and smooth, with some shallow fissures in maturity. Young shoots are covered with fine grey down. The leaves vary from oval to obovate or lanceolate and are up to 10cm/ 4in long (usually 5–7.5cm/2–3in). They are dull green and wrinkled above and grey-green with dense hair beneath. Male and female flowers are produced in early spring on separate trees. The fruit is a grey-green capsule, covered with down, from which copious amounts of tiny seed are released to the wind.

Distribution: Europe and western Asia.
Height: 10m/33ft
Shape: Broadly spreading
Deciduous
Pollinated: Wind
Leaf shape: Variable

Left: The leaf shape varies from oval to lanceolate and the male and female flowers are produced on separate trees in early spring.

OTHER SPECIES OF NOTE

Grey Willow *Salix cinerea*
Sometimes known as grey sallow, this is a large shrub or small spreading tree, to 4.5m/15ft. It has obovate leaves, the undersides of which are covered in grey down. The grey willow is native to Europe, western Asia and parts of North Africa and is a pioneer species, meaning that it will colonize vacant land before other tree species. It grows well in wet, marshy conditions. There is a subspecies called *oleifolia*, which has slightly smaller leaves with copper-coloured down, and is more prevalent in western Europe.

Violet Willow
Salix daphnoides
Native to central Europe, this attractive small tree, to 10m/33ft tall, has long been cultivated because of its plum-coloured shoots, which when young are covered with a white bloom, and for its conspicuous male catkins in early spring. The cultivar 'Aglaia' produces masses of bright white male catkins in the late winter.

Golden Weeping Willow *Salix x sepulcralis* 'Chrysocoma'
This is the familiar ornamental weeping willow, grown alongside rivers throughout western Europe. It is a cultivar of a hybrid between the white willow, *S. alba*, and the Chinese weeping willow, *S. babylonica*, and was raised in 1888. No other weeping willow has such bright yellow twigs and young leaves. It is prone to attack by canker disease. *See also page 170.*

Bay Willow

Salix pentrandra

This is a beautiful small to medium-sized tree, with bay-like leaves that emit an attractive fragrance when crushed. In Scandinavia, bay willow is used as a culinary substitute for true bay, *Laurus nobilis*. Although widely distributed in both Europe and Asia, it prefers cooler conditions and does not grow naturally around the Mediterranean. It is grown as an ornamental tree in parks, gardens and arboreta, and is considered one of the most handsome willows in cultivation.

Distribution: Europe and Asia.
Height: 15m/50ft
Shape: Broadly spreading
Deciduous
Pollinated: Wind
Leaf shape: Elliptic to narrowly ovate

Identification: The bark is grey to grey-brown, smooth at first, becoming shallowly and vertically fissured in maturity. The leaves and shoots are a deep glossy green, up to 10cm/4in long and 5cm/2in broad. Both male and female flowers are small and borne in catkins on separate trees in late spring to early summer. The male flowers are yellow, the females are green.

Below: The leaves are finely toothed around the margin and taper to a short point.

Almond-leaved Willow

Salix triandra

This small spreading tree is unusual among willows in having grey bark, which flakes to reveal lighter brown bark beneath. It has long been cultivated right across Europe and Asia for its vigorous, strong new growth, which is used to make heavy-duty basketware. In Britain it is grown on the Somerset Levels for this purpose. The stems of *S. triandra* may grow more than 3m/10ft in one season. Over the years many cultivars, including 'Black Hollander', 'French' and 'Pomeranian', have been developed specifically for basketry.

Distribution: Europe to eastern Asia.
Height: 12m/40ft
Shape: Broadly spreading
Deciduous
Pollinated: Wind
Leaf shape: Lanceolate

Identification: Almond-leaved willow has distinctive grey bark, flaking to reveal brown patches beneath. It has lanceolate, glossy green leaves, to 10cm/4in long, with a leaf margin that is finely toothed and tapering to a long point. The lower surface of the leaf is a glaucous blue-green. Small flowers are produced in catkins in mid- to late spring. The male catkins are up to 6cm/2½in long, pendulous and yellow; the female catkins are smaller and green. Each gender is produced on separate trees.

Right and far right: The leaves are lanceolate-shaped, glossy green above and matt blue-green beneath.

Left: Yellow male catkins appear in early spring.

Kilmarnock Willow

Salix caprea 'Kilmarnock'

Distribution: Of Scottish garden origin.
Height: 3m/10ft
Shaped: Domed and pendulous
Deciduous
Pollinated: Wind
Leaf shape: Obovate

The original cultivar, called *S. caprea* 'Pendula', is said to have come from a single male tree, found by James Smith, "an old and enthusiastic Scottish botanist", growing on the banks of the River Ayr in Scotland, in the mid-1800s. By 1853 it was being sold commercially by the nurseryman Thomas Lang of Kilmarnock, hence its current name. Today, it is one of the most popular trees for growing in small gardens throughout Europe.

Identification: Unmistakable and unlikely to be confused with anything else, the Kilmarnock willow is a weeping form of the goat willow, *S. caprea*. It is a neat, umbrella-shaped tree with numerous weeping branches, covered in spring with beautiful "pussy willow" catkins that start silver-grey and gradually turn golden yellow. The catkins are borne on the tree before the obovate, wrinkled, grey-green leaves emerge from bud.

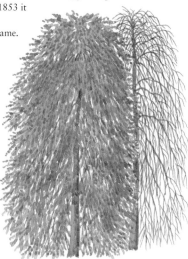

Left: The female flowers are borne in less showy green catkins.

Right: The leaves are a matt grey-green colour and quite often wrinkled.

Left: In spring the silvery male catkins develop showy yellow anthers.

Corkscrew Willow

Salix babylonica 'Tortuosa'

This very popular willow is widely planted as a curious ornamental in gardens across Europe. It is a quirk of nature that was cultivated in northern China, where it is known as the dragon's claw willow. It was introduced into France and the rest of Europe in the 1920s. Everything about this tree is contorted – branches, twigs and leaves. Cut twigs and small branches are very often used by flower arrangers.

Identification: Instantly recognizable, this tree is unlikely to be confused with anything else (other than, possibly, in winter, the corkscrew hazel, *Corylus avellana* 'Contorta'). It is a vigorous small tree of roughly columnar habit, which can normally reach a height of 10–15m/33–50ft in less than 30 years. It is relatively short-lived, with few specimens surviving beyond 50 years of age. The contortions begin with the major branches and are carried through the twigs to the leaves, which are linear, glossy grass-green above, slightly paler beneath and up to 10cm/4in long.

Distribution: China.
Height: 15m/50ft
Shape: Columnar and contorted
Deciduous
Pollinated: Wind
Leaf shape: Linear to lanceolate

Left: Both the leaves and the twigs have a distinctive twisted appearance.

Silver Willow *Salix alba* var. *sericea*
This is a smaller, more round-headed, less vigorous tree than the white willow, *S. alba*, but it is grown for its superb bright silver foliage, which is particularly striking when the whole tree is viewed from afar. This form occasionally occurs in the wild, but most trees available for sale from garden centres and nurseries have been selectively cloned in cultivation.

Coral-bark Willow *Salix alba* 'Britzensis'
This cultivar of the white willow, *S. alba*, is grown for its brilliant orange-scarlet winter shoots, which are reminiscent of the new shoots of the dogwood shrub, *Cornus alba* 'Sibirica'. The coral-bark willow has narrow, glaucous, lanceolate leaves and an upright columnar form. For best effect it should be coppiced to almost ground level every two to three years to stimulate bright new growth. It was raised at Britz, near Berlin, in 1878.

Caspian Willow
Salix acutifolia
This elegant small tree, to 10m/33ft, is native to Russia, and was first cultivated in western Europe around 1890. It is closely related to the violet willow, *S. daphnoides*, and has similar plum-red shoots, which are covered in white bloom when young. The leaves are narrowly lanceolate with a long point at the tip, rather lax and up to 15cm/6in long. The male flowers are borne in erect bright yellow catkins in spring.

Cricket Bat Willow

Salix alba var. *caerulea*

Sometimes referred to as the blue willow, this subspecies is a variant of the white willow, *S. alba*, and was discovered as a single specimen growing in Norfolk, England, around 1700. As the common name suggests, the timber of this tree is highly prized for the production of cricket bats. All the trees cultivated worldwide for this purpose have been propagated vegetatively (by cuttings), so effectively the original 1700 tree is still being grown today.

Identification: Cricket bat willow has a conical or pyramidal form with ascending branches. The grey-brown bark is smooth at first and becomes vertically fissured in maturity. The lanceolate leaves are a distinctive blue-grey-green and lose their downy covering much earlier than those of the white willow, *S. alba*. They are up to 10cm/4in long. The winter buds are long, pointed, held close to the shoot and a bright chestnut brown.

Distribution: England.
Height: 30m/100ft
Shape: Broadly conical
Deciduous
Pollinated: Wind
Leaf shape: Lanceolate

Right: The leaves are long and thin and a distinctive blue-grey-green colour.

PLANES AND WITCH HAZELS

Although the trees under this heading belong to two different genera, they have two things in common. They are all deciduous, dropping their leaves in autumn and producing replacements the following spring. And, before they lose their leaves, they all take on spectacular autumn leaf colour. Because of their beauty, many are planted as ornamental trees.

London Plane

Platanus x hispanica

Distribution: Of garden origin.
Height: 40m/130ft
Shape: Broadly columnar
Deciduous
Pollinated: Insect
Leaf shape: Palmate lobed

This tree is a hybrid between the oriental plane, *P. orientalis*, and the American buttonwood, *P. occidentalis*. It is widely planted in cities across the world as it is able to withstand atmospheric pollution and severe pruning. It is more vigorous than both its parents, its leaves have shallower lobes and it has a lighter bark, which peels to reveal cream patches.

Above: The fruits are mace-like, bristly spheres, hanging on long stalks.

Identification: The leaves are glossy bright green above and paler green beneath, with conspicuous yellow leaf veins, and are covered with rust-coloured down when young. They are 20cm/8in long and up to 25cm/10in broad, with three to five large toothed lobes. Both the yellow male and red female flowers are small and are borne in clusters on the same tree in late spring to early summer. The fruit persists well into winter after the leaves have fallen.

Oriental Plane

Platanus orientalis

The oriental plane is a majestic tree. Hippocrates, the ancient Greek "father of medicine", is said to have taught his medical students under the great oriental plane tree that still stands on the island of Cos. Another large oriental plane, beside the Bosphorus near Buyukdere, is known as "the plane of Godfrey de Bouillon", because tradition states that the French nobleman and his knights camped under it during the first Crusade in 1096.

Identification: One of the largest of all deciduous temperate trees, this plane can reach heights in excess of 30m/100ft, with a great spreading canopy and a trunk girth of up to 6m/20ft. It has attractive buff-grey bark, which flakes to reveal cream-pink patches. The leaves are palmate, 20cm/8in long and 25cm/10in across, deeply cut into five narrow lobes, shiny green above, pale green below, with brown tufts of hair along the veins. They are attached alternately to the shoots by yellow-green leaf stalks up to 7.5cm/3in long. In autumn the leaves turn clear yellow, then old gold. The fruits are globular and mace-like, 2.5cm/1in across, attached in clusters of two to six on pendulous stalks.

Right: Fruit remains on the tree through the winter.

Distribution: Albania, Greece, Crete, Cyprus, Lebanon, Syria and Israel.
Height: 30m/100ft
Shape: Broadly spreading
Deciduous
Pollinated: Insect
Leaf shape: Palmate lobed

Chinese Witch Hazel

Hamamelis mollis

This small, widely spreading ornamental tree, or large shrub, was introduced into Europe in 1879. It is prized for its bright yellow, fragrant winter flowers, and is widely cultivated in parks, gardens and arboreta. In autumn the leaves turn clear yellow before falling. Chinese witch hazel is best grown in acid soil.

Identification: The bark is dark grey and smooth, occasionally flaking to reveal lighter bark beneath. The leaves are up to 13cm/5in long (more usually 10cm/4in) matt mid-green above with some hair beneath, unequally heart-shaped at the base and shallowly toothed around the margin, which runs to an abrupt point. The fragrant yellow flowers are borne in crowded clusters, directly on the twigs, in winter.

Distribution: Western China.
Height: 4m/13ft
Shape: Broadly spreading
Deciduous
Pollinated: Wind
Leaf shape: Broadly ovate

Right: The leaves are broadly ovate to rounded,

Far right: The flowers are made up of rich sulphur-yellow, spidery petals.

Japanese Witch Hazel

Hamamelis japonica

This beautiful winter-flowering tree, or large shrub, was introduced into Europe from Japan in 1862. It is widely cultivated across Europe. It is small, spreading and sparsely branched and has smaller, more variable leaves than Chinese witch hazel, *H. mollis*. They are sometimes almost diamond-shaped and have a glossier upper surface. Japanese witch hazel also tends to flower more prolifically than its Chinese cousin.

Identification: The bark is dark grey and smooth. The leaves are variable, to 7.5cm/3in long and 5cm/2in broad. They have a wavy margin and are slightly heart-shaped at the base. The lower surface of the leaf is covered with fine grey down, which disappears by autumn, when the leaves turn bright yellow before falling. The flowers are bright yellow and fragrant, with four spidery, crimped petals.

Distribution: Japan.
Height: 4m/13ft
Shape: Broadly spreading
Deciduous
Pollinated: Wind
Leaf shape: Oval to ovate

Right: Each dark green leaf has five to eight pairs of parallel leaf veins, which run forward from the midrib.

Right: The flowers are borne directly on the bare branches in winter.

OTHER SPECIES OF NOTE
Buttonwood *Platanus occidentalis*
Sometimes called the American sycamore, this large tree occurs right across eastern North America. Specimens have been grown in Europe since the 17th century, and it is one of the parents of the London plane, *P. x hispanica*. The leaf is heart-shaped at the base, with more, but shallower, lobing than either the London plane or the oriental plane. The bark is grey-brown and has the same flaking characteristic as the other planes.

Virginian Witch Hazel
Hamamelis virginiana
This small North American deciduous tree, to 6m/20ft tall, has spreading zig-zag branches and a short, thick trunk. It is native to eastern North America, from Nova Scotia to Tennessee, from where it was introduced into Europe in 1736. It is not grown so widely as the Asian witch hazel, mainly because the beauty of its sulphur-yellow flowers is masked by it still being in full leaf when the flowers appear in autumn.

Hybrid Witch Hazel *Hamamelis x intermedia*
This is a hybrid between the Chinese and Japanese witch hazels, and is of variable nature, taking on some of the characteristics of both parents. From this hybrid many of the common cultivars commercially available today have been raised. These include 'Arnold Promise', 'Diane', which has red flowers, and 'Jelena', which has copper-coloured flowers.

SWEET GUMS AND
TREES WITH STUNNING AUTUMN FOLIAGE

The trees in this section all belong to different families, but are grouped together here because of their stunning leaf colours they produce in autumn. Because of their beauty many are planted in Europe as ornamental trees in parks.

Katsura Tree

Cercidiphyllum japonicum

The single representative of the family Cercidiphyllaceae, this graceful tree, with its attractive foliage and the unusual "sweet caramel" aroma emitted by the leaves as they begin to decompose, is a favourite for ornamental planting. Once established, growth may be anything up to 60cm/24in per year.

Identification: The bark is grey-brown, freckled with lenticels, and becoming fissured and flaking in maturity. The thin leaves are heart-shaped, slightly toothed around the margin and up to 7.5cm/3in long and wide, turning orange-apricot in late autumn. The male flowers are bright red, appearing on side shoots before the leaves emerge in early spring. Female flowers develop in late spring in clusters of four to six.

Distribution: Western China, and Hokkaido and Honshu in Japan.
Height: 30m/100ft
Shape: Broadly spreading
Deciduous
Pollinated: Insect
Leaf shape: Cordate

Right: Male and female flowers are on separate trees.

Left: Leaves fade to blue-green in summer and then vibrant shades of butter yellow to purple-pink in autumn.

Chinese Tupelo

Nyssa sinensis

Distribution: Central China.
Height: 15m/50ft
Shape: Broadly conical
Deciduous
Pollinated: Insect
Leaf shape: Oblong to lanceolate

Closely related to both the tupelo, *N. sylvatica*, and the water tupelo, *N. aquatica*, this attractive small tree grows in woodland and along stream banks in central China. It is comparatively rare in cultivation, although under the right conditions it produces superb autumn leaf colours, ranging from red to yellow. Seeds of the tree were first sent from China to Britain in 1902 by the English plant collector Ernest Wilson.

Identification: The bark is grey-brown and smooth, becoming cracked and flaking with age. The narrow, pointed leaves, up to 20cm/8in long and 6cm/2½in wide, emerge from bud a purplish-red but quickly fade to shiny deep green above and paler and matt beneath. Both the male and female flowers are small and green. They are borne in separate clusters in the leaf axils on the same tree in summer. The fruit is a purple-blue berry about 2.5cm/1in long.

Right: The narrow pointed leaves are a shiny deep green colour on the top side.

Left: In autumn the leaves turn red and yellow and a purple-blue berry is borne on the tree.

Chinese Sweet Gum

Liquidambar formosana

This large tree inhabits mountainous woodland areas, growing at altitudes of up to 2,000m/6,560ft, in Taiwan (formerly Formosa) and southern and central China. It was introduced into Europe in 1884, but in cultivation rarely attains heights in excess of 20m/65ft. It is grown mainly for its autumn colour, which in good years ranges from vibrant scarlet to burgundy. In spring, when the leaves first emerge from bud, they are bronze-purple before turning dark green.

Identification: The bark on young trees is grey-white, becoming darker and vertically fissured in maturity. The palmate leaves, to 12.5cm/5in long and 15cm/6in broad, are carried on long, purple-red stalks. They normally have three lobes but occasionally five, each being regularly toothed and running to a fine point. The male and female flowers are small and green, borne in separate rounded clusters on the same tree in spring.

Distribution: China and Taiwan.
Height: 40m/130ft
Shape: Broadly conical
Deciduous
Pollinated: Insect
Leaf shape: Palmate lobed

Left: The deep green leaves take on a range of vibrant red tints in autumn.

OTHER SPECIES OF NOTE

Tupelo *Nyssa sylvatica*
This slow-growing, medium-sized North American tree, also known as the black gum, was introduced into Europe in 1750 and has been widely cultivated, mainly for its spectacular autumn colours, which range from yellow and orange to red and burgundy. It has obovate to elliptic leaves up to 15cm/6in long.

Sweet Gum *Liquidambar styraciflua*
This giant tree, with maple-like leaves, is known to have reached 45m/150ft in height in its native eastern North America. In cultivation in Europe it rarely exceeds 30m/100ft. Sweet gum takes its name from the sweet, viscous sap it exudes when the bark is damaged. This sap dries into a gum. The tree was introduced into Europe in the 17th century. *See also page 175.*

Oriental Sweet Gum *Liquidambar orientalis*
This slow-growing, medium-sized tree, to 20m/65ft, is native to south-west Turkey, from where it was introduced into Europe around 1750. It has leaves that are similar to those of the field maple, *Acer campestre*, with leaves deeply cut into three or five lobes. In autumn the leaves turn a glorious orange-marmalade colour. *See also page 174.*

Persian Ironwood

Parrotia persica

A member of the Hamamelidaceae family, this is one of the finest trees for autumn colour, turning copper to burgundy in mid-autumn. In the wild it tends to be a broad, upright tree, but in cultivation it becomes a sprawling mass, seldom attaining a height greater than 15m/50ft. Its botanical name is derived from the German climber F. W. Parrot, who made the first ascent of Mount Ararat in 1829.

Above: Small ruby-red flowers appear in winter.

Identification: The tree is quite often seen in large gardens and arboreta as a dense low-spreading mound, which is quite difficult to penetrate because of criss-cross branching. The bark is dark brown, flaking to reveal light brown patches. The leaves are obovate, sometimes elliptic, 12cm/4¾in long and 6cm/2½in wide, becoming progressively shallowly toothed and wavy towards the tip. They are glossy bright green above and dull green with slight hairiness beneath. The flowers are tiny, clothed in soft velvet-brown casing but emerging a startling ruby-red, which stands out dramatically on the bare branches in mid-winter. The fruit is a nut-like brown capsule, 1cm/½in across.

Below: The leaves are dark and glossy on top and lighter beneath.

Distribution: Mount Ararat, eastern Caucasus to northern Iran.
Height: 20m/65ft
Shape: Broadly spreading
Deciduous
Pollinated: Insect
Leaf shape: Obovate

STRAWBERRIES, SNOWBELLS AND STEWARTIAS

Strawberries, persimmons and snowbells form part of the camellia subclass, known as Dilleniidae. They are a mixture of deciduous and evergreen, acid-loving and lime-tolerant species. They all have an ornamental appeal, which has secured their places in gardens and arboreta across the temperate world.

Strawberry Tree

Arbutus unedo

This small, attractive, evergreen tree is a member of the heather family but, unlike most heathers, it grows perfectly well on limy soil. It is sometimes called the "Killarney strawberry tree" because it is so common in that part of Ireland, where it is often used for hedging. The strawberry-like fruits, which are borne on the tree at the same time as the flowers, are edible but not enjoyable.

Identification: The young bark is a rich red-brown, fading to grey-brown and becoming rough and fissured in maturity. The tough, leathery leaves are elliptic to obovate, up to 10cm/4in long, glossy dark green above and paler beneath, with uniform serrations around the margin. The small creamy-white flowers are urn-shaped and are borne in drooping clusters in autumn. The strawberry-like fruit is a warty berry, approximately 2.5cm/1in across and ripening red in autumn from flowers borne in the previous year.

Distribution: Southern Ireland, western France, Iberian peninsula and countries bordering the Mediterranean.
Height: 10m/33ft
Shape: Broadly spreading
Evergreen
Pollinated: Insect
Leaf shape: Elliptic

Left: Drooping clusters of creamy-white flowers are borne in autumn.

Left: The fruit is a red, strawberry-like, warty berry.

Grecian Strawberry Tree

Cyprus strawberry tree *Arbutus andrachne*

This beautiful small tree has been in cultivation across warm temperate regions of Europe since 1724. It is rather tender when young but hardier in maturity. It has particularly attractive bark, which is a rich red-brown to cinnamon colour and peels to reveal bright orange or cream new bark beneath. Where it grows in the wild alongside the strawberry tree, *A. unedo*, the two species naturally cross-pollinate to produce the hybrid strawberry tree, *A. x andrachnoides*.

Distribution: South-east Europe.
Height: 10m/33ft
Shape: Broadly spreading
Evergreen
Pollinated: Insect
Leaf shape: Elliptic to obovate

Identification: This is a dome-shaped tree, very often with multiple stems growing from just above ground level. The oval leaves are thick and leathery, up to 10cm/4in long and 5cm/2in broad, glossy dark green above and pale green beneath, with no serrations around the leaf margin. The flowers are small and green, turning to white or creamy-white as they open. They are heather-like and are borne in upright clusters at the end of the shoots in late spring.

Right: The fruits are small, rounded, orange-red berries and the leaves are glossy dark green.

Japanese Snowbell Tree

Styrax japonica

This beautiful, small, spreading tree deserves to be much better known and more widely planted than it is. It was introduced to the West in 1862, when Richard Oldham collected a specimen from Japan, which was then planted in the Royal Botanic Gardens, Kew, London. Since then the tree has been grown in various botanic collections and arboreta, but is comparatively rare as a garden specimen. It is an ideal tree for a small garden: it seldom reaches more than 7m/23ft tall and is perfectly hardy even in cooler regions, although late frosts may injure the flower buds.

Identification: The bark is orange-brown, smooth at first and becoming fissured in maturity. The leaves are oval to elliptical, tapering at both ends, to 10cm/4in long and 5cm/2in across. The leaf margin is set with small, shallow teeth. The leaves are a rich shiny green above and a paler green beneath, and are normally arranged in groups of three on the shoot. The slightly fragrant, open, bell-shaped flowers are creamy white with yellow anthers, and hang, either on their own or in small clusters, all along the branches on long slender stalks in early summer. The overall effect is delightful. The fruit is an egg-shaped green-grey berry containing a single seed.

Distribution: Japan, Korea and China.
Height: 10m/33ft
Shape: Broadly spreading
Deciduous
Pollinated: Insect
Leaf shape: Oval to elliptic

Below: The leaves are reminiscent of bay. Once pollinated, the hanging flowers form green berries.

OTHER SPECIES OF NOTE
Mountain Snowdrop Tree *Halesia monticola*
This magnificent spreading tree grows wild in upland areas, reaching altitudes in excess of 1,230m/4,000ft in North Carolina, Tennessee and Georgia, USA. It is widely cultivated for its masses of hanging, bell-shaped white flowers, which appear in late spring before the leaves.

Hybrid Strawberry Tree
Arbutus x andrachnoides
This is a naturally occurring hybrid between the strawberry tree, *A. unedo*, and the Grecian strawberry tree, *A. andrachne*, which is found most commonly in Greece. It is widely planted elsewhere across Europe as an ornamental species in gardens and parks. It inherits its attractive flaking red-brown bark from one parent and its hardiness from the other.

Hemsley's Storax *Styrax hemsleyana*
This beautiful small Chinese tree, or large shrub, to 8m/26ft tall, was introduced into Europe in 1900. It has ovate to obovate leaves, to 13cm/5in long and 10cm/4in broad, and small white flowers with bright golden anthers, which are borne in upright terminal racemes in early summer.

Japanese Stewartia

Stewartia pseudocamellia

This small to medium-sized, tender Japanese tree is related to the camellia, which is reflected not only in its species name, but also in its beautiful camellia-like flowers. It was introduced into cultivation in Europe in the 1870s. It takes its generic name from John Stuart, a patron of the Royal Botanic Gardens in Kew, London.

Below: The flowers have five frilly petals and conspicuous bright orange stamens.

Below: The leaves are ovate.

Distribution: Japan.
Height: 20m/65ft
Shape: Broadly columnar
Deciduous
Pollinated: Insect
Leaf shape: Elliptic to ovate

Identification: The bark is smooth, red-brown and thinly flaking to reveal patches of cream, fawn or pink-grey fresh bark. The leaves, alternately borne on the twig, are dark green above, paler beneath with some hair, and up to 10cm/4in long. In autumn they turn orange-red to burgundy-purple before falling. The white flowers appear in mid-summer; each one falls all in one piece when it is finished.

LABURNUMS, BROOMS AND ACACIAS

The pea family, Leguminosae, contains over 15,000 species of trees, shrubs and herbaceous plants in 700 genera. They are found growing wild throughout the world, in both temperate and tropical conditions. Most have compound leaves, pea-like flowers and seed pods, and root systems that have the ability to use bacteria to absorb nitrogen from the soil.

Mount Etna Broom

Genista aetnensis

Although it is native only to Sardinia and Sicily, where it grows prolifically in volcanic ash on the slopes of Mount Etna, this hardy, spreading broom has become naturalized along much of the coastline of southern and western Europe. In mid- to late summer every shoot is usually covered with fragrant, bright yellow pea-flowers.

Identification: This elegant tree has grey-brown bark, which may be very heavily fissured around the base. The bright green leaves, sparsely borne on green shoots, are narrowly linear and small, to 1cm/½in long. By summer, when the tree comes into flower, most of the leaves have fallen.

Right: The flowers are 1.5cm/½in long, golden yellow and borne in profusion.

Distribution: Sardinia and Sicily.
Height: 15m/50ft
Shape: Broadly spreading
Deciduous
Pollinated: Insect
Leaf shape: Linear

Right: Shoots are grass-like.

Judas Tree

Cercis siliquastrum

This small, sparsely branched tree is said to be the one from which Judas Iscariot hanged himself, but the name may derive from "Judea's tree", after the region encompassing Israel and the Palestinian state, where the tree is commonplace. It has long been cultivated across Europe for its bright pink flowers. It requires a sunny position to flower well.

Identification: Mature trees may develop a pronounced lean, or even fall to the ground, but carry on growing. The leaves quite often fold in on themselves along the midrib. The flowers are borne in clusters on old wood, just as the leaves emerge.

Distribution: South-east Europe and western Asia.
Height: 10m/33ft
Shape: Broadly spreading
Deciduous
Pollinated: Insect
Leaf shape: Rounded to cordate

Above: Lilac-pink pea-like flowers appear in spring.

Right: The leaves are heart-shaped.

Mimosa

Silver wattle Acacia dealbata

This tender, temperate tree is prized by florists and
flower arrangers the world over for its delicate,
feathery foliage and fragrant yellow flowers.
It has been known to reach 30m/100ft in
height in the wild but seldom attains this
in cultivation. It is extremely popular for
planting as an ornamental street tree in
Mediterranean countries but does not
grow as well in cooler climates
further north.

Identification: The bark is green-grey to
almost glaucous with pale vertical striations.
It becomes darker in maturity. The lax leaves,
up to 12cm/4¾in long, are doubly pinnate
and have countless small, linear, blue-green
hairy leaflets, giving the whole tree a soft,
feathery effect. The small, rounded flowers are
sulphur yellow and fragrant. They are clustered
on rounded panicles up to 10cm/4in across. In
the Southern Hemisphere flowers appear in summer; in
Europe they bloom from late winter to early spring.
The fruit is a flat, blue-white seed pod, ripening to brown.
It contains several round brown seeds.

*Below: The flat seed
pod measures
up to 7.5cm/
3in long.*

Distribution: South-east
Australia and Tasmania.
Height: 25m/80ft
Shape: Broadly conical
Evergreen
Pollinated: Insect
Leaf shape: Bipinnate

*Left: The scented flowers open
in summer in the Southern
Hemisphere. North of the
Equator they appear earlier.*

Common Laburnum

Laburnum anagyroides

This beautiful tree occurs naturally in mountainous regions
of central Europe at elevations up to 2,000m/6,560ft. A
small, spreading, short-lived tree, it grows particularly well
on lime-rich soils and is best known for its profusion of
pendulous golden yellow flowers in late spring. All parts of
the tree contain an alkaloid that is poisonous if eaten; the
green, unripe seed pods are
particularly toxic.

*Below: The
seedpods hang
down from the tree
after flowering. The
leaves are trifoliate.*

*Above: The bright yellow flowers
appear in spring.*

Distribution: Central and
southern Europe from France
to Hungary and Bulgaria.
Height: 9m/30ft
Shape: Broadly spreading
Deciduous
Pollinated: Insect
Leaf shape: Trifoliate

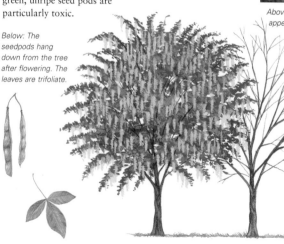

Identification: The bark is dark brown-
grey and smooth, becoming shallowly
fissured in maturity. The new shoots are
olive green and the winter buds are
covered with silver hairs. The elliptic
leaflets, borne in threes, are up to 10cm/4in
long, rich green above, grey-green beneath and
covered with silver hairs when young. The flowers are
golden yellow, pea-like, 2.5cm/1in long, in dense, hanging
sprays up to 30cm/12in long. They are followed by green,
hairy, pea-like seed pods, which ripen brown and contain
several small, round, black seeds.

CHERRIES

The cherry genus, Prunus, *contains over 400 different species of tree, the majority of which are deciduous and native to northern temperate regions of the world. They include some of the most beautiful spring-flowering trees, many of which have been cultivated in parks, gardens and arboreta for centuries. The genus is distinguished by having fruit that is always a drupe surrounding a single seed.*

Wild Cherry

Gean, Mazzard *Prunus avium*

Distribution: Europe.
Height: 25m/80ft
Shape: Broadly columnar
Deciduous
Pollinated: Insect
Leaf shape: Elliptic

This is the largest of Europe's native cherries. It has been widely grown across Europe and in western Asia and is the parent of many cultivated sweet cherries that are grown for their edible fruit. The botanical name *avium*, meaning "of the birds", is a reference to the fact that the fruit is loved by birds. The wild cherry is used as a rootstock on to which many other ornamental members of the Rosaceae family are grafted.

Right: The fruit of the wild cherry is small and shiny and may taste sweet or bitter.

Identification: The bark is rich red brown and glossy; in maturity distinctive horizontal light brown bands of lenticels, interspersed with peeling red-brown bark, ring the stem. Suckering around the base is common. The leaves are elliptic, occasionally oblong, up to 15cm/6in long and 5cm/2in broad, deep green on both sides and sharply toothed around the margin. The flowers are single, white with five petals, 2.5cm/1in across and borne in clusters in spring just as the leaves emerge from bud.

Right: The white flowers are sweetly scented.

Bird Cherry

Prunus padus

This hardy, medium-sized tree has a natural range that extends from the British Isles to Japan and grows on both acid and alkaline soils, on the edge of woodland or in small clearings. It has small, black, bitter-tasting fruits, which are relished by birds, hence its common name. The tree has long been grown in parks and gardens across Europe and has given rise to a number of ornamental cultivars, including the beautiful 'Colorata', which has dark purple stems and pink flowers.

Identification: The bark is dark grey and smooth and has a strong acrid smell when cut or scratched. The elliptic leaves are dark matt green, to 10cm/4in long, finely serrated around the leaf margin and ending in a short point. In autumn they turn red or orange before falling. The flowers, which appear in mid- to late spring, are small, white, fragrant and borne in 10–15cm/4–6in long, upright racemes, which become lax and pendulous as they mature. Small, round to egg-shaped berries, to 1cm/½in across, are produced in summer.

Distribution: Europe and northern Asia.
Height: 15m/50ft
Shape: Broadly spreading
Deciduous
Pollinated: Insect
Leaf shape: Elliptic

Right: The flowers appear in spring.

Right: The black fruits are bitter.

Cherry Laurel

Prunus laurocerasus

This common plant is widely cultivated in gardens throughout Europe. It is particularly favoured for hedging and can be clipped into a dense, windproof barrier. Despite its appetizing-sounding name, both the fruit and leaves of cherry laurel contain cyanide and are poisonous. Where it is allowed to grow to tree size little grows beneath its dense, evergreen canopy. It was introduced into western Europe at the end of the 16th century and was in cultivation in Britain early in the 17th century.

Identification: The bark of cherry laurel is dark grey-brown and smooth, even in maturity. The leaves are thick and leathery, glossy dark green above, and pale or even yellow-green beneath. They are oblong to elliptic, up to 20cm/8in long and 6cm/2½in broad, with occasional shallow teeth around the margin, which ends in a short point. The flowers are small, dull white, fragrant and borne in upright racemes to 13cm/5in long in mid- to late spring.

Distribution: South-east Europe and south-west Asia.
Height: 10m/33ft
Shape: Broadly spreading
Evergreen
Pollinated: Insect
Leaf shape: Oblong

Far left: The fruit is a shiny rounded berry 1.25cm/½in across, red becoming jet black.

OTHER SPECIES OF NOTE

Great White Cherry
Prunus 'Tai Haku'
Hundreds of ornamental garden cherries have been cultivated in Japan. Most are either forms or hybrids of two native Japanese cherries: the Oshima cherry and the mountain cherry. The great white cherry is one of the finest hybrids. It has large, pure white, single flowers, which when its bronze-pink leaves emerge from the bud. *See also page 181.*

Pissard's Purple Plum *Prunus cerasifera* 'Pissardii'
This is a well-known variety of the myrobalan or cherry plum, *P. cerasifera*. It is widely grown in parks and gardens for its shiny, deep purple leaf colour, which is very distinctive and provides great contrast with the green leaves of other trees. It has abundant, delicate, small flowers, which are pink in bud and open white, well before the leaves emerge in spring.

Tibetan Cherry *Prunus serrula*
This small, spreading cherry tree is widely grown in parks and gardens because of its striking, highly polished, deep mahogany-red bark, which becomes a real feature in winter. It originates from western China and may attain heights of around 15m/50ft, but more often 10m/33ft. The white flowers are relatively inconspicuous and are produced after the lanceolate leaves appear in mid-spring.

Japanese Cultivated Cherry

Prunus 'Kanzan'

Sometimes labelled 'Sekiyama', *Prunus* 'Kanzan' is the most popular and commonly cultivated ornamental cherry in Europe. It was introduced into Europe from Japan immediately before World War I, and since then has become a familiar springtime feature in cities, towns and parks.

Identification: The overall form of this small to medium-sized tree is vase-shaped, with ascending branches when young becoming more spreading as the tree matures. The bark is brown-pink with distinctive horizontal banding caused by the presence of light brown lenticels. The oval leaves, to 13cm/5in long, have a shallow serrated margin and end in a drawn-out point at the tip. In spring, when they appear, they are at first a beautiful bronze colour, which changes to bright green within a few days.

Below: Bright pink, frilly double flowers are densely borne throughout the canopy just as the leaves emerge in spring.

Distribution: Of Japanese garden origin.
Height: 10m/33ft
Shape: Broadly spreading
Deciduous
Pollinated: Insect
Leaf shape: Obovate

Apricot

Prunus armeniaca

The apricot was being cultivated for its edible fruit in China over 2,000 years ago. It gradually spread west into Europe and was being cultivated in Britain by at least the 16th century. It is now naturalized in many warmer parts of Europe, but it requires protection in northern Europe. The species name, *armeniaca*, indicates its possible Armenian origins. There are a number of free-fruiting cultivars that have been developed over the centuries.

Distribution: Northern China and sporadically throughout central Asia.
Height: 10m/33ft
Shape: Broadly spreading
Deciduous
Pollinated: Insect
Leaf shape: Ovate

Identification: The bark is smooth and a warm chestnut brown with a low sheen. The leaves are broadly ovate to roundish, 7.5cm/3in long and 5cm/2in wide, and abruptly pointed. They are deep lustrous green above and a similar colour beneath, but with tufts of hair in the leaf axils. There are fine, even serrations around the leaf margin and the leaf is borne on a 2.5cm/1in long stalk which may feel "warty" to the touch. The single flowers are white to very pale pink, 2.5cm/1in across and produced on the previous year's wood. The fruit is rounded, golden-yellow when ripe, 3–5cm/1¼–2in across, with sweet edible flesh surrounding a single hard, slightly flattened stone.

Left: The flowers are small and delicate.

Right: The leaves are lustrous green.

Left: The seed is within a golden yellow, sweet fruit.

Sour Cherry

Prunus cerasus

There is much discussion as to whether this is a cultivated tree of garden origin from which many orchard varieties of fruiting cherry have been raised, or a native tree of South-east Asia. Either way, it has become naturalized over much of Europe, including some parts of Britain. The tree is certainly related to the wild cherry, *P. avium* (which is native to Europe), and is one of the parents of the Morello cherry, which has been in cultivation in European orchards for centuries.

Distribution: Possibly South-east Asia.
Height: 8m/26ft
Shape: Broadly spreading
Deciduous
Pollinated: Insect
Leaf shape: Elliptic

Below: The double flowers are pure white and are borne in clusters. The fruit is a sour red cherry.

Identification: The sour cherry is a small rounded tree, quite often suckering at the base. It has purple-brown bark with horizontal, peeling orange-brown stripes. The leaves are elliptic to oval, abruptly pointed, up to 7.5cm/3in long and 5cm/2in wide. They are dark green above, slightly paler beneath and sharply, but finely, double-toothed around the margin. The flowers are double, pure white, up to 2.5cm/1in across and appear in clusters in mid-spring. The cherry fruit is red, ripening to black, and up to 2cm/¾in across. Although edible, it has a sour, acid taste.

Plum

Prunus domestica

Distribution: Unknown but probably a hybrid of garden origin.
Height: 10m/33ft
Shape: Broadly spreading
Deciduous
Pollinated: Insect
Leaf shape: Elliptic to obovate

The origins of the garden plum are lost in the mists of time. It is probably a hybrid, possibly between the sloe, *P. spinosa*, and the cherry plum, *P. cerasifera*. Both species are native to the Caucasus and known hybrids have occurred naturally here. In the future, DNA examination may be able to unravel the mystery.

Identification: There are countless cultivars of plum, all developed to enhance the quality of the fruit, which is of course not just edible, but delicious. If it were not for the fruit, it is unlikely that this tree would be planted widely for ornamental purposes. It has brown-grey bark, fissured in maturity, and bluntly serrated leaves, up to 7.5in/3in long, which are a dull grass-green. The flowers are white, slightly fragrant and about 2.5cm/1in across, and are borne in spring before the leaves emerge.

Above: The plum fruit is a succulent drupe with a single large seed.

Right: There are various plum cultivars, which produce egg-shaped fruit in a variety of different colours. Plum leaves and flowers are always the same, however.

OTHER SPECIES OF NOTE
Common Almond *Prunus dulcis*
This much planted tree, originally from Asia and North Africa, has been widely cultivated for its nuts for at least 2,000 years and has become naturalized right across southern Europe. It is a small tree with lanceolate, long-pointed leaves and beautiful pink flowers in spring.

Ground Cherry *Prunus fruticosa*
This small, mop-headed miniature tree, or large spreading shrub, is native to central and northern Europe and Siberia. It was introduced into western Europe in the 16th century and is often grown as a top-grafted plant on wild cherry, *P. avium*. It has glossy, deep green obovate leaves, small white flowers and purple red fruits about the size of a large pea.

Willow Cherry *Prunus incana*
This is a small erect-branched tree or large shrub, with slender willow-like leaves. It is native to the Caucasus, from where it was introduced into western Europe in 1815. It has deep rosy-red flowers and small red fruits.

Fuji Cherry *Prunus incisa*
This slow-growing, small flowering cherry, a native of south-west Japan, has been popular for ornamental planting in Europe since its introduction in the early 20th century. Its small, doubly and sharply toothed leaves emerge a beautiful bronze and colour up well in autumn. The flowers, which open before the leaves, are white or pale-pink and emerge from pink buds in mid-spring.

Prunus conradinae

This beautiful elegant cherry is one of the earliest trees to come into flower. It regularly produces masses of fragrant, pale pink or white flowers in late winter, and in warmer climates they may appear even earlier. The flowers are long-lasting and provide a welcome hint that spring is not far away. It is native to western Hubei, China, from where it was introduced into Europe by Ernest Wilson in 1907. Since then it has been widely cultivated in parks and gardens throughout the continent.

Distribution: China.
Height: 10m/33ft
Shape: Broadly spreading
Deciduous
Pollinated: Insect
Leaf shape: Oval

Identification: The bark is red-brown, with a sheen that is particularly evident in low winter sunshine. The serrated leaves are rounded at the base and slender-pointed, serrated around the margin, mid-green, with some hair on the underside. They are up to 11cm/4½in long and 5cm/2in wide. The 2.5cm/1in flowers, white or pale pink and fragrant, are produced in clusters. The fruit is a small, ovoid, red cherry.

Left: The leaves.

Far left: Flowers appear on bare branches.

Portugal Laurel

Laurel *Prunus lusitanica*

This is one of the most handsome and useful evergreen trees. Ideally, it should be grown as an isolated specimen in order to show off its rich green, glossy foliage and elegant form to its best. However, the Portugal laurel can be grown as a bushy, dense shrub that regrows readily after pruning, so it also makes an effective and luxuriant hedge or screen, and this is how it is mostly seen. In the wild it can grow significantly taller than the cultivated height. It has been cultivated outside its natural range since the mid-17th century. There is also a sub-species known as subsp. *azorica*, which is native only to the Azores and has larger and thicker leaves than the species, with reddish-purple shoots and red emerging leaves.

Identification: The bark is dark slate-grey to grey-brown and smooth, even in maturity. The leaves are ovate to elliptic, around 10cm/4in long and 5cm/2in across. They are a rich, glossy, deep green above and paler beneath, tapering at the point and with some shallow, round serrations along the margin. The flowers are small, creamy-white, scented (not necessarily pleasantly) and borne in long, slender racemes, 25cm/10in long, in early to mid-summer. The fruit is egg-shaped, red at first, ripening to purple-black.

Distribution: Portugal, Spain and south-west France.
Height: 10m/33ft
Shape: Broadly spreading
Evergreen
Pollinated: Insect
Leaf shape: Ovate to elliptic

Right: After flowering, long open clusters of purple-black berries are produced.

Autumn Cherry

Prunus x *subhirtella* 'Autumnalis'

As the name suggests, this beautiful small cherry has flowers that initially open in autumn and then appear intermittently through winter into early spring. It was cultivated in Japan in the late 19th century and introduced into Europe around 1900. It is a popular small tree that is commonly found in parks, gardens, town squares and precincts. It is a cultivar of the spring cherry, *P. subhirtella*, which it is believed by some may be a hybrid of two other Japanese cherries.

Identification: The bark is smooth and grey-brown, becoming horizontally banded in maturity. The leaves are elliptic to ovate, 7.5cm/3in long and 5cm/2in across, sharply toothed around the margin and running to a long, tapered point. They emerge bronzy-pink from bud in early to mid-spring and turn golden yellow before falling in autumn. The flowers are this tree's most distinctive feature, appearing in autumn rather than spring. They are white flushed with pale pink, opening from pink buds and grouped in small clusters along the bare branches, occasionally among the autumn foliage.

Distribution: Of Japanese garden origin.
Height: 6m/20ft
Shape: Broadly spreading
Deciduous
Pollinated: Insect
Leaf shape: Elliptic to ovate

Far left: The leaves are sharply toothed.

Left: The fruit is a small dark red cherry, seldom produced in great numbers upon the tree.

Hill Cherry

Prunus serrulata

This was one of the first Asian cherries to be introduced into Europe, arriving in Britain from China in 1822. Its original natural distribution is obscure, and due to the excessive natural variability of the population, it may be that this species is itself a variation of the Chinese hill cherry, *P. serrulata* var. *hupehensis*. Today it is rarely found outside botanic gardens and old collections, since its popularity has been surpassed by the Japanese 'Sato Zakura' free-flowering cherries.

Identification: The bark is grey-brown with horizontal banding. The leaves are oval to lance-shaped, up to 13cm/5in long and 5cm/2in wide, with a long tapered point and a finely serrated margin. They are bright grass-green above and blue-green beneath. The double-petalled flowers open in mid- to late spring, held in short-stalked clusters of between two and five. They are white or white flushed pink, without fragrance and up to 4cm/1½in across.

Distribution: China.
Height: 5m/16½ft
Shape: Broadly spreading
Deciduous
Pollinated: Insect
Leaf shape: Ovate to ovate-lanceolate

Left: The leaves have a long tapering point. The fruit is inconspicuous and seldom produced in any quantity.

OTHER SPECIES OF NOTE

Sargent's Cherry
Prunus sargentii
Sargent's cherry is one of the loveliest of all cherries, producing a profusion of rich pink, single flowers, coupled with bronze emerging leaves in spring, and brilliant orange-red leaves in autumn. It is named after Professor Charles Sargent, one-time director of the Arnold Arboretum, Boston, USA. It was introduced into Europe in 1890 and is now commonly cultivated. *See also page 180.*

St Lucie Cherry *Prunus mahaleb*
Native to central and southern Europe, this attractive, fast-growing cherry, to 12m/40ft tall, has been cultivated since 1714. It produces masses of small, pure white and very fragrant flowers in mid- to late spring. The wood was at one time used to make cherry-wood pipes for smoking tobacco and for walking sticks.

Peach *Prunus persica*
Probably native to China, the peach has been cultivated for its sweet, edible fruit throughout Asia and southern Europe for centuries. It has glossy deep green, narrow elliptic to lanceolate leaves, which are up to 15cm/6in long and 5cm/2in across. Flowers may vary from white, through pink to red (normally pale pink). The fruit is round, normally to 7.5cm/3in across, orange, yellow and red and surrounding a stone (pit).

Japanese Apricot

Prunus mume

This beautiful small tree with olive-green twigs and sweetly fragrant flowers has been cultivated in China for at least 1,500 years. It was introduced into Japan very early on and it rapidly found popularity there, becoming widely used for bonsai. Up to 300 cultivars have been raised in Japan. It was introduced into Europe in 1841 and is one of the earliest cherries to flower, before the leaves appear. In Japan, the fruits are used to make a sweet liqueur.

Identification: The bark is red-brown, becoming banded in maturity, and the twigs are a striking green to black-green. The leaves have a long tapering point and are up to 10cm/4in long. They are finely serrated around the margin, mid-green with some sporadic hairs along the midrib beneath. The flowers, borne either singly or in pairs, are pale pink, 2.5cm/1in across and almond-scented. The fruits are round, 2.5cm/1in across, yellow or yellow-green and bitter to the taste.

Right: The flowers are pale pink and almond scented.

Far right: A leaf.

Distribution: China and Korea but not Japan.
Height: 10m/33ft
Shape: Broadly spreading
Deciduous
Pollinated: Insect
Leaf shape: Rounded to broadly ovate

HAWTHORNS

The Hawthorns are among the hardiest and most adaptable of all trees. Many species will withstand very low temperatures, exposure, pollution and salt spray in coastal regions. They are also extremely attractive trees, particularly when in flower, and as such are widely planted as ornamental specimens throughout northern and western Europe.

Midland Hawthorn

Crataegus laevigata

This hardy small tree takes its name from an area in central England, where it is found growing in much profusion and is an accepted indicator of sites of ancient woodland. It is native to north-west and central Europe and differs from common hawthorn, *C. monogyna*, in having less deeply lobed leaves. The popular garden cultivar 'Paul's Scarlet' was raised from it in the mid-1800s. It is a common tree of hedgerows and woodland edges.

Distribution: Europe.
Height: 10m/33ft
Shape: Broadly spreading
Deciduous
Pollinated: Insect
Leaf shape: Ovate to obovate, lobed

Identification: The bark is grey-brown, smooth at first becoming cracked into small plates in maturity. The leaves are glossy dark green above, paler beneath, shallowly lobed and toothed, up to 5cm/2in across and long. The flowers are scented, white with five petals and pink-orange anthers, and occur in small clusters in late spring and early summer. They are followed by oval, glossy red fruits (haws), up to 2.5cm/1in long, each containing two hard seeds.

Left: The leaves are most attractive in summer.

Right: The fruit is a glossy red in colour.

Hungarian Hawthorn

Crataegus nigra

Although not regularly found in parks and gardens, this Hungarian native has been cultivated in other parts of Europe since 1819. Its species name, *nigra*, is derived from the fact that it has black fruits (haws) rather than red, found on most hawthorns. Another distinctive feature is that the young shoots are covered with a felt-like grey down. In maturity, the Hungarian hawthorn forms a round-headed tree made up of stiff, angular branches.

Distribution: Hungary.
Height: 6m/20ft
Shape: Broadly spreading
Deciduous
Pollinated: Insect
Leaf shape: Triangular

Right: The fruits are borne on the tree in autumn.

Right: The leaves are known in folklore for their medicinal use.

Identification: The bark is grey-brown, smooth at first becoming shallowly cracked and flaking in maturity. The leaves are quite distinctive, being triangular to ovate, almost straight across the base, with 7–11 lobes on each side and finely serrated margins. Both surfaces are a dull mid-green, covered with fine hair when young. The flowers, produced in late spring, are white, turning rosy-pink and often hidden by the leaves. After flowering, flattened globular, shiny, black, soft fruits appear.

Oriental Thorn

Crataegus laciniata

This beautiful, small, oriental tree has been widely cultivated in parks, gardens and arboreta since its introduction into western Europe in 1810. It is almost always without thorns and has a rounded, sometimes flattened and spreading, canopy of branches, which may become slightly pendulous at the tips in maturity. It is a sun-loving tree, which in the wild is most commonly found growing on woodland edges and in copses. In flower it is one of the loveliest of all hawthorns.

Identification: The leaves are deeply lobed, in some instances almost to the midrib, normally with three or four lobes on each side. They are deep green on the upper surface and grey-green with grey hair beneath. The flowers are up to 2.5cm/1in across, white with conspicuous orange-pink anthers, and are borne in much profusion all over the tree in late spring and early summer. They are followed by rounded to oblong fruits, to 2.5cm/1in across, which are bright coral-red or yellow flushed with red.

Distribution: South-east Europe and south-west Asia.
Height: 6m/20ft
Shape: Broadly spreading
Deciduous
Pollinated: Insect
Leaf shape: Triangular to diamond-shaped

Right: The leaves are deeply cut and downy.
Left: In autumn, the haws are borne in profusion.

Azarole *Crataegus azarolus*
Otherwise known as the Mediterranean medlar because of its small, pale yellow to orange edible fruits, which have the flavour of apples, the azarole is native to southern Europe, North Africa and western Asia. It has been cultivated in western Europe, since the 17th century. It grows to 9m/30ft, which produces white flowers with purple anthers in dense clusters in mid-summer.

Hybrid Cockspur Thorn *Crataegus* x *lavallei*
This attractive, small thorn, 6m/20ft tall and broad, is widely planted in parks and gardens across Europe. It is a hybrid between two American species, *C. crus-galli* and *C. mexicana*, believed to have been raised in France in 1880. It has glossy dark green, elliptic leaves, to 10cm/4in long, and white flowers with pink anthers, which appear in mid-summer. They are followed by rounded fruits that ripen to orange-red, persisting on the tree well into winter.

Cockspur Thorn *Crataegus crus-galli*
This small tree, to 8m/26ft, is distinguished by its long, ferociously sharp spines. It is native to eastern and southern North America, from where it was introduced into Europe as early as 1691. In autumn the leaves turn a bright marmalade-orange. It has bright red fruits that persist on the tree long after leaf fall. *See also page 182*.

Hawthorn

May *Crataegus monogyna*

Native throughout Europe, the hawthorn is a slow-growing, hardy tree, which can withstand exposure, strong winds and cold better than most northern temperate trees. For centuries, it has been used both to shelter animal stock and to enclose it, particularly in upland areas. A regularly clipped hawthorn hedge is a very effective windbreak and is virtually impenetrable. The other name for hawthorn, may, refers to the month of flowering in Britain, when the tree is at its most conspicuous.

Distribution: Europe.
Height: 10m/33ft
Shape: Broadly spreading
Deciduous
Pollinated: Insect
Leaf shape: Obovate

Identification: The bark is dull brown with vertical orange cracks. The leaves are deeply cut, almost to the midrib in some cases, so the outline is not obvious. They are dark green above and paler with some hairs in the vein axils beneath. The creamy white, slightly pungent flowers are produced in profusion in mid-spring.

Above: The fruit is deep red when ripe.

Right: Twigs have vicious thorns.

Siberian Hawthorn

Crataegus dahurica

This small, extremely hardy hawthorn is native to woodlands in the Transbaikalia region of south-east Siberia, from where it was introduced into western Europe in the early 20th century. It is rare in cultivation and restricted to some botanic gardens and arboreta. It is one of the first hawthorns to come into leaf and flower, regularly producing blossom from mid- to late spring. In autumn it produces attractive orange-red fruits, which persist on the tree well into winter.

Identification: The bark is brown and smooth at first, becoming finely fissured with some flaking into rectangular plates in maturity. The leaves are broadly ovate, to 5cm/2in long and across, with four or five shallow lobes on each side. They are bright mid-green with some hairs on the underside. The flowers are up to 2.5cm/1in across, white with dark pink anthers. They are slightly fragrant and are borne in clusters of up to ten.

Distribution: South-east Siberia.
Height: 6m/20ft
Shape: Broadly spreading
Deciduous
Pollinated: Insect
Leaf shape: Ovate

Below right: The leaves are a main identifying feature.

Above right: The globular orange-red fruits are 2cm/¾in across.

Crataegus dsungarica

This small, extremely hardy tree is native to much of central Russia, south-east Siberia and on into northern China from where it is believed to have been introduced into western Europe by the English plant collector Ernest Wilson, in the early years of the 20th century. There is some discussion among taxonomists that it may in fact be a hybrid between two other Asian thorns. It is a small tree with spiny branches and although ornamentally attractive it is seldom found growing outside botanic gardens and arboreta.

Identification: It is a handsome thorn with numerous spines up to 2.5cm/1in long borne on all branches. The leaves are triangular, flat at the base with three to seven lobes on each side. The flowers are white, produced in clusters in late spring. They are followed by shiny purple-black fruits, each containing between three and five seeds.

Distribution: Central Russia.
Height: 7m/23ft
Shape: Broadly spreading
Deciduous
Pollinated: Insect
Leaf shape: Ovate

Right: The fruit is a large, shiny purple-black fruit which contains between three and five seeds.

OTHER SPECIES OF NOTE
Tansy-leaved Thorn *Crataegus tanacetifolia*
This small, slow-growing tree is native to Syria and adjacent Middle Eastern countries. It was first cultivated in Europe in 1789. As the name suggests, it has variable, deeply cut leaves, which are reminiscent of some members of the *Tanacetum* genus, a group that includes the common tansy and other feathery-leaved perennials. The tree is normally thornless and produces fragrant white flowers in early summer, followed by yellow fruits, flushed red, which look (and taste) like small apples.

Crataegus wattiana
This attractive, small, often thornless, tree originates from central Asia. It has bright red-brown lustrous twigs and large oval leaves, up to 10cm/4in long, which are sharply toothed. White flowers with pale yellow anthers appear in clusters up to 7.5cm/3in across, in late spring and early summer. These are followed by globular, translucent, yellow-orange fruits, which appear in summer but fall to the ground before autumn.

***Crataegus laevigata* 'Rosea Flore Pleno'**
This is one of the oldest of all hawthorn cultivars and still one of the most popular. It is widely cultivated in towns, parks and gardens, and as a street tree. It has beautiful, double, rose-like pink flowers. It is believed to be one of the parents of Paul's scarlet thorn.

Paul's Scarlet Thorn

Craetagus laevigata 'Paul's Scarlet'

This lovely tree is a cultivar of the Midland hawthorn, *C. laevigata*. 'Paul's Scarlet' was produced as long ago as 1858 in England, and since then has become a favourite ornamental species for parks and gardens because of its spectacular, profusely borne, double red flowers.

Distribution: Of garden origin.
Height: 10m/33ft
Shape: Broadly spreading
Deciduous
Pollinated: Insect
Leaf shape: Ovate to obovate

Identification: The bark of 'Paul's Scarlet' is grey and smooth, becoming shallowly fissured in maturity. It has ovate to obovate glossy dark green leaves, which are 5cm/2in long and across with shallow lobes around the upper half of each leaf. The double, almost rose-like, flowers are the tree's main feature, being a bright deep pink colour and produced in dense clusters all over the tree in late spring and early summer. They are followed in late summer by bright red, oval-shaped fruits, up to 2.5cm/1in long, which persist long into autumn.

Right: The flowers are produced in profusion.

Right: The leaves have shallow lobes.

Glastonbury Thorn

Crataegus monogyna 'Biflora'

This interesting small tree is planted as a curiosity across western Europe. It has the unique, if rather erratic, habit of producing both new leaves and flowers around Christmas time. A legend attached to the tree suggests that after the crucifixion of Christ, Joseph of Arimathea travelled to England to found Christianity. On arriving at Glastonbury in Somerset, he sat down to rest and stuck his walking staff in the ground. It immediately took root and came into both leaf and flower, even though it was Christmas Day. The tree continued to grow there, flowering at the same time each year, until the early 19th century, when it eventually died. It was of course widely cultivated and its progeny became widespread.

Distribution: Of garden origin.
Height: 6m/20ft
Shape: Broadly spreading
Deciduous
Pollinated: Insect
Leaf shape: Ovate to obovate

Right: The fruit is a small red haw.

Right: The leaves are dark green and deeply cut.

Identification: In most respects this tree reflects its origins, being a variety of the common hawthorn, *C. monogyna*. It has the dull brown bark of that species, which fissures vertically when mature, deeply cut dark green leaves, creamy-white fragrant flowers and small, deep red fruits, which appear from late summer into autumn. Whether the legend itself is true remains open for discussion, but the ability of this tree to produce both leaves and flowers in winter as well as in spring is not in doubt.

FLOWERING CRABS AND PEARS

The flowering crab genus, Malus, contains over 25 species, mainly native to northern temperate regions.
They are hardy, small to medium-sized deciduous trees, widely grown as garden ornamentals for their
profusion of spring flowers and late summer fruit. The flowers are similar to those of cherry, except that
crab apple flowers have five styles presenting the female stigma for pollination instead of just one.

Crab Apple

Malus sylvestris

Distribution: Europe.
Height: 10m/33ft
Shape: Broadly spreading
Deciduous
Pollinated: Insect
Leaf shape: Elliptic

Far right: Crab apples produce a mass of white flowers in spring. The crab apples themselves develop through the summer.

This tree is known to many as the "sour little apple", because of its profusion of small, green, inedible apples in late summer. The wild crab apple is not regarded as an important ornamental species; however, it is one of the parents of the domestic orchard apple, *M. domestica*, and of some very attractive ornamental flowering crabs.

Identification: The overall appearance is of an uneven, low-domed tree with a head of dense twisting branches, normally weighted to one side. The bark is brown and fissured, even when the tree is relatively young. The leaves are elliptic to ovate, 4cm/1½in long, slightly rounded at the base, deep green above and grey-green beneath with some hair on the leaf veins. The leaf margin is finely, but bluntly, toothed. The flowers are white, flushed with pink, 2.5cm/1in across and carried on short spurs. The fruit is apple-like, up to 4cm/1½in across, green to yellow and sometimes flushed with red.

Common Pear

Pyrus communis

Over 1,000 cultivars of common pear are known, and it is itself believed to be a hybrid that originated in western Asia over 2,000 years ago. This has naturalized throughout Europe, making it very difficult to ascertain what the original species would have looked like. The pear has been cultivated in Europe for centuries, and many named cultivars were raised at Versailles, France, in the 17th century.

Distribution: Europe.
Height: 15m/50ft
Shape: Broadly columnar
Deciduous
Pollinated: Insect
Leaf shape: Ovate to elliptic

Identification: A tall columnar to pyramidal crown and distinctive spur shoots (rarely spines) give the tree a slightly angular appearance. The bark is dark grey, cracking into small irregular flakes in maturity. The leaves are mainly rounded at the base, up to 10cm/4in long and 5cm/2in across. The flowers are single white, with five petals and purple anthers, borne in clusters in mid-spring. The fruits are variable, rounded to pear-shaped, containing sweet, edible flesh surrounding small, hard, brown seeds.

Left: The fruits of the common pear are russet to yellow, sometimes flushed red.

Right: The leaves are a glossy dark but bright green.

Hupeh Crab

Malus hupehensis

This is one of the most beautiful of all small deciduous trees. The Hupeh crab is a hardy tree growing in the mountainous region of central China, where local people use the leaves to make a drink called "red tea". It was introduced to the West in 1900 by the plant collector Ernest Wilson.

Distribution: Central and western China.
Height: 12m/40ft
Shape: Broadly spreading
Deciduous
Pollinated: Insect
Leaf shape: Ovate to elliptic

Identification: The bark is lilac-brown with irregularly shaped plates, flaking from the trunk to reveal orange-brown fresh bark beneath. The leaves are 10cm/4in long, elliptic to ovate and finely toothed around the leaf margin. They are grass green above and pale beneath, with some hairs along the midrib and main veins. The flowers are pink in bud, opening white with a rose flush. They are 5cm/2in across and slightly fragrant. The fruit is greenish-yellow, ripening to red, and normally stays on the tree long after the leaves have fallen.

Left: The fruit is a rounded "apple" 1cm/½in across.

Left: The leaf tapers to a fine point.

Right: Flowers open in early spring.

OTHER SPECIES OF NOTE
Malus 'Golden Hornet'
This hybrid has become one of the most frequently planted of all garden crab apples. In autumn, it produces deep yellow, rounded to egg-shaped fruits, up to 2.5cm/1in long, which stay on the tree long after the leaves have fallen. The fruits shine brightly like little lanterns in winter sun. The parentage is unknown but it was developed in England in the 1940s.

Malus 'John Downie'
Numerous crab apple hybrids are raised and grown for their flowers and fruit. This is one of the most popular and it is widely grown in towns and cities right across Europe. An upright tree, becoming conical as it matures, it has delicate white flowers, which open from soft pink buds, and beautiful egg-shaped fruits, which are bright yellow to orange with a flush of red. They are edible, and when fully ripe, quite sweet-tasting.

Siberian Crab Apple *Malus baccata*
As the name suggests, this hardy, broadly spreading 15m/50ft tree is native to north-east Asia and northern China. It was first cultivated in western Europe in 1784 and is well represented in gardens and arboreta. The leaves are reminiscent of pear leaves and the flowers are single, white with yellow anthers, fragrant and borne in mid-spring. The fruits are globular, yellow turning red and borne on a long red stalk.

Weeping Silver-leaved Pear

Willow-leaved pear *Pyrus salicifolia* 'Pendula'

This tree is the most ornamental of all the pears. It was discovered in 1780 by the German botanist and explorer P. S. Pallas, who introduced it to Western cultivation. It is a firm favourite for planting where a small tree with silver foliage is required. Unfortunately, it is not a long-lived species.

Above left: Blossom appears in clusters.

Left: Mature leaves are sage green and smooth.

Distribution: Russia, the Caucasus, from the steppes south into Turkey and northern Iraq.
Height: 10m/33ft
Shape: Broadly weeping
Deciduous
Pollinated: Insect
Leaf shape: Lanceolate

Identification: The bark is pale grey, becoming vertically fissured in maturity. The leaves are narrowly lanceolate, up to 10cm/4in long and tapering at both ends. They have a characteristic twist along their length. The young leaves appear silver because they are covered with a silvery white down, which gradually wears off. They are borne on thin, horizontal branches, which become pendulous towards the tip. When young, these are also covered in silvery hairs. The flowers are 2.5cm/1in across, creamy white with purple anthers. The fruit is green, hard, pear-shaped and up to 3cm/1¼in long.

ROWANS AND WHITEBEAMS

The rose family, Rosaceae, is one of the largest of all plant families. It encompasses an incredibly diverse range of plants, including cherries, apples, quinces, loquats, cotoneasters, rowans and of course roses. It is also one of the families most commonly represented in cultivation, because of the flowering and fruiting beauty of its members. They include this diverse and beautiful group of trees.

Rowan

Mountain ash *Sorbus aucuparia*

This elegant, hardy, small to medium-sized tree grows at elevations in excess of 1,000m/ 3,300ft on some northern European mountains. Rowan berries are loved by birds and the tree has been associated with providing protection against evil spirits.

Above: The flowers are creamy-white. and fragrant.

Identification: The bark varies from silver-grey to purple-grey. It is smooth even in maturity. The pinnate leaves, to 20cm/8in long, comprise up to 15 leaflets, each 5cm/2in long, sharply toothed around the margin, bright green above and blue-green beneath. In autumn, they may turn red or yellow before falling. The flowers, which appear in late spring, are borne in soft clusters, to 15cm/6in across. They are followed in late summer by bright orange-red berries.

Above and right: The berries are 1cm/½in across, borne in large, pendulous clusters.

Distribution: Europe and Asia.
Height: 20m/65ft
Shape: Broadly conical
Deciduous
Pollinated: Insect
Leaf shape: Pinnate

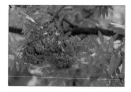

Swedish Whitebeam

Sorbus intermedia

This is an extremely hardy tree, which thrives in exposed conditions and tolerates localized pollution in city streets. It is often used to transform areas previously affected by industrial despoliation, as it is able to grow on thin, impoverished soils. Swedish whitebeam is very attractive, and makes a handsome garden tree, with its broad, even crown and arching branches, which become pendulous towards the tips.

Identification: The bark is grey, smooth at first, cracking into flakes in maturity. The leaves are ovate, sometimes broadly elliptic, glossy dark green above, much paler with grey hair beneath. They are lobed and toothed around the margin, up to 10cm/4in long and 5cm/2in broad. The flowers are individually small but borne in large clusters, up to 12.5cm/5in across.

Left: The small flowers are dull white with five petals.

Right and above left: Deep red, oval berries are borne in pendulous clusters at the end of summer.

Distribution: North-west Europe.
Height: 15m/50ft
Shape: Broadly columnar
Deciduous
Pollinated: Insect
Leaf shape: Ovate

Wild Service Tree

Chequer tree *Sorbus torminalis*

This attractive, medium-sized tree has russet-brown, edible fruits, which were at one time used to flavour beer. It has a wide natural range, which extends from northern Europe south to North Africa. Its presence within a wood is considered a good indicator that the woodland is ancient and has suffered little disturbance. At first glance, the leaves are reminiscent of maple or plane; they are stiff to the touch and turn yellow-brown in autumn.

Distribution: Europe and North Africa.
Height: 20m/65ft
Shape: Broadly columnar
Deciduous
Pollinated: Insect
Leaf shape: Broadly ovate

Identification: The bark is dark brown and smooth, becoming cracked and flaky in maturity. The winter buds are olive green. The leaves are deeply cut into sharply toothed lobes. They are glossy dark green above, paler green beneath, 10cm/4in broad and long, and held in a distinctive rigid way on the branches. The small, white flowers are borne in flattened clusters, which may be 10cm/4in across, in early summer.

Left: The fruits, which are small, warty, russet-brown berries, follow the small white flowers.

OTHER SPECIES OF NOTE

Chinese Rowan
Sorbus hupehensis
This is a beautiful small tree, native to much of temperate China and cultivated throughout the temperate world as a garden ornamental. It has ash-like, deep green leaves and delightful white berries, flushed with pink.

Service Tree of Fontainebleau *Sorbus latifolia*
This interesting medium-sized tree is believed to have originated in a small region in France which has the forest of Fontainebleau at its centre. The tree's existence there has been known since the early 18th century. It probably originally developed as a hybrid of the wild service tree, *S. torminalis,* and the whitebeam, *S. aria,* but is now considered a species in its own right and does come true from seed. Its leaves are like those of the wild service tree, *S. torminalis.*

Sorbus vilmorinii
This small, beautiful Chinese tree is one of the most attractive species of the whole *Sorbus* genus and is worthy of space in every garden. It was introduced into Europe in 1889 by Père Jean Marie Delavay, the French Jesuit missionary, and has been widely cultivated as an ornamental tree ever since. It has glaucous, fern-like, pinnate leaves and white flowers in late spring. They are followed by berries, which ripen from deep red through pink to white and persist on the branches like pendulous bunches of white grapes well into winter.

Whitebeam

Sorbus aria

Whitebeam is a tree of calcareous uplands, thriving on thin limestone and chalk soils. Its edible red fruit is collected and made into jam, jelly and wine in some parts of Europe. The timber is dense and hard and at one time was used to make wheels and cogs. In the past it was sometimes referred to as the "weather tree", for when the white underside of the leaf became visible, rain was believed to be on the way.

Distribution: North, west and central Europe.
Height: 15m/50ft
Shape: Broadly columnar
Deciduous
Pollinated: Insect
Leaf shape: Ovate

Identification: The bark is smooth silver-grey-brown, even in maturity. By far the most distinguishing feature of this tree is its two-coloured leaves. They are up to 12.5cm/5in long and 6cm/2½in wide, pale green when emerging from the bud, turning a shiny deep green above and white with hairs beneath. When the wind catches the leaves, the effect of flickering green and white over the whole tree is quite remarkable. The flowers are borne in flattened clusters in mid-spring. The fruit is slightly speckled and rough, due to surface lenticels. The leaves do not produce good autumn colour but persist beneath the tree as a grey, crisp covering right through winter.

Above: The flowers are 1cm/½in across.

Below: The fruit is a red, round berry.

Medlar

Mespilus germanica

This small, spreading tree has rather angular branching. It is grown mainly for its fruit, which is an acquired taste. When ripe, the dumpy, pear-shaped fruits have an extremely disagreeable taste and are not edible until they have been exposed to frost and "bletted" (allowed to reach the first stages of decay). Even then the taste is rather acidic. Medlars were popular in the past and were widely cultivated in orchards.

Distribution: South-west Asia and south-east Europe.
Height: 6m/20ft
Shape: Broadly spreading
Deciduous
Pollinated: Insect
Leaf shape: Elliptic to lanceolate

Identification: The bark is dull brown, smooth at first, developing fissures in maturity. The bright green, almost stalkless, elliptic leaves are up to 15cm/6in long, minutely toothed around the margin and slightly hairy on both sides. The flowers, borne singly at the end of leaf branches, are up to 5cm/2in across, white with five well-spaced petals; they appear in early summer. The fruits are russet-brown and shaped like a flattened pear. They grow to 3cm/1¼in across and have a slightly open brown top surrounded by a persistent calyx, which gives them a tasselled look.

Left: The flowers open in summer, later than those of many fruit trees.

Right: The fruit is small and brown.

Quince

Cydonia oblonga

Like many trees long cultivated for their fruit, the exact origins of the common quince are unknown. It has certainly been grown around the Mediterranean for at least 1,000 years. In the wild it commonly inhabits shallow limestone soils on mountain slopes. The golden yellow fruit is pear-shaped.

Identification: The bark is brownish purple, smooth at first but maturing into irregular plates that flake to reveal orange-brown fresh bark beneath. The leaves are ovate to elliptic, up to 10cm/4in long, dark green and smooth above with cinnamon-grey hairs beneath. The leaves persist on the branches into early winter. The flowers are white flushed with pink and up to 5cm/2in across. They are borne singly at the end of hairy leaf shoots in mid-spring. The fragrant, golden yellow, pear-shaped fruit grows up to 10cm/4in long and is quite waxy to the touch.

Distribution: South-west Asia.
Height: 5m/16ft
Shape: Broadly spreading
Deciduous
Pollinated: Insect
Leaf shape: Ovate to elliptic

Right: Quince fruit is fragrant and quite bitter. The leaves have smooth, unserrated edges and stay on the tree until the beginning of winter.

Sargent's Rowan

Sorbus sargentiana

This magnificent, large *Sorbus*, native to the mountains of Sichuan in south-west China, was collected by Ernest Wilson in 1908, for the Arnold Arboretum in Boston, USA. From there specimens were sent to Europe in 1910. It is one of the best of the genus for autumn colour: the leaves turn brilliant orange-red, it produces large, conspicuous clusters of brilliant red berries and it has large, sticky, mahogany-red winter buds.

Identification: The bark is plum-brown and smooth. The pinnate leaves are up to 35cm/14in long and are made up of 11 finely toothed and long tapered leaflets, each of which is up to 10cm/4in long and 5cm/2in broad. They are deep green above, and grey-green beneath with some hair. The flowers, which appear in early summer, are small, creamy-white and borne in large, dense clusters, up to 20cm/8in across. They are followed by large clusters of bright red berries.

Distribution: South-west China.
Height: 10m/33ft
Shape: Broadly columnar
Deciduous
Pollinated: Insect
Leaf shape: Pinnate

Left: Small white flowers are followed by bright red berries.

Right: The sticky winter buds are crimson.

Kashmir Rowan

Sorbus cashmiriana

Although described in 1901 from specimens in Kashmir, this beautiful small tree did not arrive in Europe until the 1930s. Since then it has become a valued species in botanic gardens and arboreta. Despite its warm origins it is perfectly hardy and there are few trees to surpass its splendid display of fruit in autumn and early winter, which for some reason is completely ignored by birds.

Identification: The bark is grey, sometimes red-grey, and smooth even in maturity. The leaves are pinnate, deep green above, paler with some hair beneath, up to 15cm/6in long with 15–17 leaflets, each 5cm/2in long, taper-pointed and sharply toothed. The flowers are produced in clusters, to 10cm/4in across, in late spring. They are followed by pink berries, which ripen to pure white and are borne in loose pendulous clusters, like white marbles, well into winter.

Distribution: Kashmir, western Himalayas.
Height: 8m/26ft
Shape: Broadly conical
Deciduous
Pollinated: Wind
Leaf shape: Pinnate

Left: The flowers are soft pink.

Right: The round berries are white, flushed pink.

FALSE ACACIAS, PAGODAS AND TREE OF HEAVEN

The main trees within this group are members of the pea family. Most have broad crowns, compound leaves, pea-like flowers that grow in clusters and seed pods. The species included here are all grown in Europe as ornamental specimens.

Pagoda Tree

Sophora japonica

Despite its botanical name, *japonica*, the pagoda tree is thought not to be a native of Japan. However, it has been widely cultivated there for centuries, particularly in temple gardens and places of learning. In China the flower buds were used to make a yellow dye and all parts of the tree, if taken internally, have a strong purgative effect. Flowers on trees grown from seed take anything up to 30 years to appear.

Identification: The overall shape is rounded, with branching starting low on the stem. The bark is greenish brown, becoming vertically fissured and ridged in maturity. The leaves are pinnate and up to 25cm/10in long, with up to 15 opposite, untoothed, ovate, pointed leaflets, which are dark green above and glaucous with some hair beneath. The flowers are white, pea-like and fragrant, and are borne in terminal panicles in summer. The fruit is a seed pod up to 7.5cm/3in long, containing up to six seeds. It ripens from green to brown.

Distribution: Northern China but could be more widespread.
Height: 20m/65ft
Shape: Broadly spreading
Deciduous
Pollinated: Insect
Leaf shape: Pinnate

Left: The white flowers of the pagoda tree are produced in summer in open sprays.

Tree of Heaven

Ailanthus altissima

This fast-growing Chinese tree, with large ash-like leaves, was introduced into Europe in 1751. It is extremely adaptable and copes admirably with the rigours of city life. However, it does have the habit of producing suckers, which will come up through cracks in city streets, sometimes up to 20m/65ft away from the original tree. The female tree is more commonly grown because the male tree produces flowers that emit a disagreeable odour, which can cause nausea and headaches.

Identification: The bark is ash-like – slate grey, relatively smooth at first but developing vertical shallow fissures as the tree matures. The pinnate leaves may be up to 75cm/30in long and made up of 15–20 leaflets, each up to 12.5cm/5in long and ending in a long, tapered point. Both the male and female flowers are yellow-green and are borne in large panicles on separate trees in summer. After flowering on female trees, large conspicuous bunches of attractive, ash-like winged seeds are produced. These start green and ripen to reddish-brown.

Distribution: Northern China.
Height: 30m/100ft
Shape: Broadly columnar
Deciduous
Pollinated: Insect
Leaf shape: Pinnate

Right: Each pinnate leaf has a tough texture.

Left: The conspicuous seed pods are borne in late summer.

OTHER SPECIES OF NOTE

Honey Locust *Gleditsia triacanthos*
This large, spreading tree with frond-like leaves and sharp spines is native to eastern and central North America, from Ontario to Florida. It is also naturalized in parts of southern Europe. It is sometimes known as the sweet locust, because of the sweet, edible flesh that surrounds the seeds in its glossy brown pods, which may be up to 45cm/18in long. The honey locust is extremely tolerant of atmospheric pollution and is widely planted in urban areas. *See also page 189.*

Kentucky Coffee Tree *Gymnocladus dioica*
This elegant tree is native to eastern and central USA. It is a medium-sized, slow-growing tree, with large compound, bipinnate leaves that can be up to 1m/3ft long. They emerge bronze-pink from the bud in spring, gradually turn dark green in summer and finally become butter yellow before falling in autumn. Small, star-like white flowers appear in early summer. *See also page 189.*

Takeda *Maackia chinensis*
This attractive, small to medium-sized, broad-headed Chinese tree was first cultivated in Europe in 1908. It has pinnate leaves, up to 20cm/8in long, composed of up to 13 ovate leaflets, which when young are silvery blue-green and covered with fine down. Its pea-like flowers, which are dull creamy-white and borne in erect panicles, appear in mid- to late summer.

Robinia pseudoacacia 'Frisia'

This cultivated form of the North American black locust is now one of the most popular trees for ornamental planting in Europe. It was raised at the Jansen Nursery, Zwollerkerspel, Holland, in 1935, and since then has been widely planted both in town and country. It is less vigorous and smaller than the species, but does suffer the same problem of brittle wood, and therefore branches may break in exposed conditions.

Identification: The bark is grey-brown, smooth at first becoming deeply and vertically furrowed in maturity. The leaves are pinnate, to 25cm/10in long, with up to 21 elliptic to ovate untoothed leaflets, which are an intense bright, glowing, golden yellow from spring to autumn. 'Frisia' is less floriferous than the species, and any flower that does appear is masked by the brightness of the foliage. Smaller branches carry the occasional sharp spine at the base of some leaves.

Distribution: Of Dutch garden origin.
Height: 15m/50ft
Shape: Broadly columnar
Deciduous
Pollinated: Insect
Leaf shape: Pinnate

Right: The fruits are pea-like pods.

Below: The leaves become greener in summer.

Black Locust

Robinia pseudoacacia

This is the most widespread of all the locust trees. It originated in the Appalachian Mountains, from Pennsylvania to Georgia, but it is now naturalized over most of the USA and was one of the earliest American trees to reach Europe, in the early 17th century. It was once valued for ships' masts because of its durable, straight timber, and Native Americans used the wood to make bows. Black locust has the habit of suckering from the root system, and on a mature tree suckers can occur up to 10m/33ft from the base of the trunk.

Identification: The bark is grey-brown, smooth at first, becoming deeply fissured with scaly ridges in maturity. The pinnate leaves, up to 30cm/12in long, have 11–21 ovate to elliptic, untoothed, thin leaflets, each 5cm/2in long and ending in a sharp point. Quite often there are two sharp spines at the base of each leaf. The fragrant flowers are pea-like, white, with a pea-green blotch in the throat.

Right: The leaves are grass-green above and blue-green below. The fruit is a dark brown bean pod up to 10cm/4in long.

Distribution: Eastern USA.
Height: 25m/80ft
Shape: Broadly columnar
Deciduous
Pollinated: Insect
Leaf shape: Pinnate

EUCALYPTUS

There are more than 400 species of eucalyptus, or gum trees, all native to the Southern Hemisphere.
They are abundant in Australia, Tasmania, New Guinea, the Philippines and Java. Most eucalyptus trees
are evergreen and fast-growing, with attractive bark, luxuriant foliage and white flowers. They are
widely cultivated for their ornamental qualities and timber in other warm temperate regions of the world.

Cider Gum

Eucalyptus gunnii

The cider gum is native to the island of Tasmania, where it grows in moist mountain forests up to 1,300m/4,250ft above sea level. It is one of the hardiest of all eucalyptus species and one of the most widely planted around the world. The glaucous, rounded juvenile foliage is prized by flower arrangers and florists. In order to maintain these attractive leaves, trees have to be regularly coppiced to stimulate the growth of new shoots. Wild trees grow to 30m/100ft tall.

Right: Mature cider gum leaves are long and slender, and hang down from the branches.

Identification: This potentially large, fast-growing tree has smooth, grey-green to orange bark, peeling to reveal creamy fawn patches. The juvenile leaves are round, 4cm/1½in across, glaucous to silver-blue in colour and borne opposite in pairs. The mature leaves are lanceolate, up to 10cm/4in long, sage-green to silver and borne alternately on the twigs. The flowers are white with numerous yellow stamens, and are borne in clusters of three in the leaf axils during summer. The fruit is a green, woody capsule, open at one end and containing several seeds.

Right: After pollination in summer, the flowers develop into woody fruit.

Distribution: Tasmania.
Height: 30m/100ft
Shape: Broadly columnar
Evergreen
Pollinated: Insect
Leaf shape: Juvenile leaves rounded, mature leaves lanceolate

Tasmanian Snow Gum

Mount Wellington Peppermint *Eucalyptus coccifera*

This is one of the hardiest of all eucalyptus trees. In its native land it grows on mountains up to 1,400m/4,600ft above sea level. The species was introduced into Britain around 1840, and has since been widely planted in temperate regions of Europe. It has striking glaucous foliage and beautiful bark, making it one of the most attractive eucalyptus for ornamental planting. It is a fast-growing tree and requires plenty of space. When the foliage is crushed it emits a peppermint fragrance.

Identification: The bark is smooth and grey-white, and peels in vertical strips to reveal bright creamy-white bark beneath. The juvenile leaves are round and mature leaves are lanceolate, to 5cm/2in long and 2cm/¾in broad, running to a fine, tapered tip. Both young and mature leaves are glaucous blue-green. The fruit is a woody, funnel-shaped capsule up to 1cm/½in long.

Right: The flowers are white with numerous yellow stamens, and are borne in clusters in the leaf axils in early summer.

Distribution: Tasmania.
Height: 25m/80ft
Shape: Broadly spreading
Evergreen
Pollinated: Insect
Leaf shape: Juvenile leaves round, mature leaves lanceolate

Mountain Gum

Broad-leaved kindling bark *Eucalyptus dalrympleana*

This attractive, very fast-growing eucalyptus is perfectly hardy in central and western Europe. Near the Wicklow Mountains of Ireland there are specimens that were planted in 1945 and have already reached heights greater than 33m/110ft. In its native habitat in Australasia, the tree is known to reach 45m/145ft tall. However, high in the mountains of New South Wales at 1,300m/4,250ft above sea level, this species grows to only shrub-like dimensions.

Identification: The mountain gum has beautiful patchwork bark, which is grey-brown to red-brown, peeling to reveal patches of creamy-white, or blush-white, fresh bark beneath. The juvenile leaves are rounded and borne opposite on the twigs. The mature leaves are lanceolate, to 18cm/7in long. They are bronze when young, turning glaucous as they mature. The flowers are borne in clusters of three in the leaf axils in summer; they are white with yellow stamens. The seeds are contained in a woody brown hemispherical capsule.

Distribution: Tasmania and south-east Australia.
Height: 33m/110ft
Shape: Broadly columnar
Evergreen
Pollinated: Insect
Leaf shape: Juvenile leaves rounded, mature leaves lanceolate

Left: The mature leaves are lanceolate and up to 18cm/7in long. Bronze when young turning blue-green as they mature.

OTHER SPECIES OF NOTE
Tasmanian Blue Gum *Eucalyptus globulus*
Native to Tasmania and Victoria in Australia, this fast-growing species can reach 60m/195ft tall. In Europe, it rarely reaches large proportions. However, one specimen on Jersey in the Channel Islands is supposed to have reached 35m/115ft in just 30 years. *See also page 190.*

Silver Top
Eucalyptus nitens
Also known as shining gum, this fast-growing blue gum is native to south-east Australia, from where it was introduced into Europe in the early 20th century. It is slightly tender, and although there are some specimens of up to 29m/95ft tall growing in southern Ireland, in colder regions of Europe it is unlikely to reach anywhere near this height. It has long ribbon-like, purple-grey to blue-grey leaves and smooth, silver-white bark, which peels in long vertical strips.

Silver Gum *Eucalyptus cordata*
This beautiful tree from Tasmania is one of the most tender eucalyptus to survive in Europe, and is quickly cut to the ground in regions that experience frost. It is also one of the finest for leaf colour, producing vibrant silver-blue-grey, rounded, sometimes heart-shaped, leaves. Quite often in European gardens this tree is grown as bedding and planted just for one summer; in a single season it may grow to 1m/3ft.

Urn Gum

Eucalyptus urnigera

This hardy species is native to the rocky slopes of Mount Wellington in the mountains of south-eastern Tasmania, where it is to be found at elevations of up to 1,000m/3,300ft. Outside Tasmania, including Europe, it has been widely planted as an ornamental species and also for wind protection. It is, in many respects, very similar to the cider gum, *E. gunnii*, but can be distinguished by its smaller fruit and smaller overall size.

Identification: This is a small tree or large shrub with horizontal branches that droop at the ends. The bark is pale grey to orange-yellow, shedding vertically in long strips. The juvenile leaves are rounded, up to 5cm/2in in length and width, and are silver-blue with a white bloom. The adult leaves are ovate to lanceolate, waxy to the touch, glossy green and up to 15cm/6in long. The flowers are white with several golden yellow stamens. They grow in clusters of three in the leaf axils in spring. The fruit is urn-shaped (hence the tree's name), about 1.5cm/⅔in long, woody and sharply tapered below the rim. It looks similar to a poppy seed capsule.

Distribution: South-east Tasmania.
Height: 12m/40ft
Shape: Broadly columnar
Evergreen
Pollinated: Insect
Leaf shape: Juvenile leaves rounded, adult leaves lanceolate

Above: The flowers and urn-shaped seed capsules grow from the leaf axils.

Left: The brush-like flowers are held together in clusters of three.

Red Flowering Gum

Eucalyptus ficifolia

Native to south-west Australia, this small, beautiful but tender eucalyptus was introduced into Europe around 1890. It is widely cultivated under glass for its large corymbs of bright red flowers, which are much valued by florists and flower arrangers. In southern European countries it will grow outside to a height of 12m/40ft. This is one tree which will become more popular for planting in parks and gardens if the climate of western Europe continues to warm up.

Identification: The bark is red with grey-red patches becoming stringy in maturity. The alternate mature leaves are a light sage green colour, evergreen, leathery, lanceolate, up to 10cm (4in) long and very fragrant when crushed. They are borne on reddish-brown shoots. The flowers are highly visible and distinctive being a bright red – sometimes pink – colour and carried in large clusters throughout the summer. These are followed by large oval to rounded woody seed capsules, up to 7.5cm (3in) long, which are green at first ripening to brown.

Distribution: South-west Australia.
Height: 12m/40ft
Shape: Rounded
Evergreen
Pollinated: Insect
Leaf shape: Ovate to lanceolate

Right: Each lanceolate leaf may be up to 10cm/4in long and emits a strong fragrance when crushed.

Left: This eucalyptus has showy red-pink flowers which are borne in conspicuous clusters in summer.

Small-leaved Gum

Eucalyptus parviflora

This extremely hardy, rare, small to medium-sized tree grows wild in just one location in New South Wales, at elevations in excess of 1,500m/4,900ft. Unlike many eucalyptus species, the small-leaved gum will grow well on alkaline soil. It was introduced into Europe in the 1930s and has established itself as far north as Britain, where one tree, at Windsor, west of London, is already over 21m/70ft tall.

Identification: The tree is handsome and densely leaved, with attractive smooth, grey, peeling bark. The ovate, juvenile grey-green leaves are borne opposite, in pairs, on short leaf stalks up to 2cm/¾in long. Mature leaves are carried alternately on longer leaf stalks. They are blue-green to glaucous, up to 5cm/2in long and 5mm/¼in wide. The flowers are white and are borne in clusters of four to seven on a short, common stalk in summer. The seed is contained in a woody, grey-green cylinder, which is closed at the base. The hanging seed pods are long and woody.

Distribution: New South Wales, Australia.
Height: 10m/33ft
Shape: Broadly columnar
Evergreen
Pollinated: Insect
Leaf shape: Juvenile ovate, adult lanceolate

Below: The mature leaves are lanceolate in shape.

Left and right: The creamy-white, brush-like flowers are often obscured by leaves.

Mountain Swamp Gum

Broad-leaved Sally *Eucalyptus camphora*

This small eucalyptus is able to withstand prolonged water-logging in its native region of south-east Australia. It takes its botanical name from the fact that when the leaves are crushed they emit a strong camphor-like fragrance and are rich in essential oils. The foliage of *E. camphora* is a staple part of the diet of koalas. It has been cultivated in Europe since the early 20th century, but is still an uncommon specimen in parks and gardens.

Identification: The bark is rough and dark, normally grey-brown to almost black. It is shed in long vertical ribbons. The juvenile leaves are small and round; the adult leaves are ovate to lanceolate, glaucous blue tinged with red, and up to 10cm/4in long. The flowers, which appear in summer, are small and white, or sometimes pale lemon, with masses of stamens, which give a rather fluffy appearance. They are borne in clusters of around three in the leaf axils.

Left: The grey-green leaves are broad and long.

Left: After flowering, brown woody urn-shaped seed capsules are produced.

Distribution: New South Wales, Australia.
Height: 10m/33ft
Shape: Broadly spreading Evergreen
Pollinated: Insect
Leaf shape: Ovate to lanceolate

OTHER SPECIES OF NOTE

Varnished Gum *Eucalyptus vernicosa*
This very hardy small tree, or large shrub, is native to mountains in Tasmania, where it is found at heights of up to 1,500m/4,900ft above sea level. It takes its name from its shiny leaves and shoots, which look as if they have been varnished. The juvenile leaves are rounded and thick and have a red margin. The adult leaves are lanceolate, with a red margin, and run to a sharp red point. They are borne on red shoots that point skywards in an erect manner. The tree is often found in European tree collections and botanic gardens.

Spinning Gum *Eucalyptus perriniana*
Native to south-east Australia and Tasmania, this small tree, which grows to 10m/33ft, is cultivated in arboreta and botanic gardens across southern and western Europe. It has white bark and both its juvenile and adult leaves are silver. The juvenile leaves, which are rounded, have the curious habit of being attached by the actual leaf blade all around the shoot, and they appear to "spin" in the wind.

Black Peppermint *Eucalyptus amygdalina*
As the common name suggests, this small tree has foliage that emits a strong peppermint fragrance when crushed. It is native to eastern Tasmania and, although cultivated in Europe, it is relatively tender and is seldom found in northern or central regions. It has rough, fibrous, dark grey-brown bark. The juvenile leaves are elliptic and grey-green; the adult leaves are stalked, long and narrow with a hooked point at the tip.

Lemon-scented Gum

Eucalyptus citriodora

The lemon-scented gum is native to the central and northern coastal regions of Queensland, Australia, and as such is tender and unlikely to survive in northern or central European winters. However, it is cultivated in southern Europe, particularly in Portugal and Spain, and elsewhere it is sometimes grown as a conservatory plant for its deliciously fragrant foliage. The leaves of this tree yield a lemon-scented oil that is rich in citronella. It is used in the perfume industry and as an antiseptic.

Identification: The bark is smooth, normally grey-white, and peels in thin irregular scales to reveal fresh blue-white bark beneath. In maturity the whole crown is a mass of elegant drooping foliage. The aromatic leaves are narrowly lanceolate, up to 20cm/8in long and 2.5cm/1in broad, and are a bright, fresh green. The flowers are borne on short stalks in clusters of three to five. The seeds are contained in a woody brown urn-shaped capsule.

Distribution: Queensland, Australia.
Height: 40m/130ft
Shape: Broadly columnar Evergreen
Pollinated: Insect
Leaf shape: Lanceolate

Above: The flowers are white with numerous threadlike stamens.

Above right: The leaves yield a lemon-scented oil used in the perfume industry.

DOGWOODS AND HANDKERCHIEF TREE

The trees within this section are some of the most attractive and ornamental of all the trees that grow in Britain and Europe. Consequently they are widely cultivated in parks, gardens and arboreta throughout the region. For some, such as the Japanese strawberry tree and the handkerchief tree, their most beautiful and distinguishing features are the showy white bracts that surround the flowers.

Table Dogwood

Cornus controversa

Distribution: Japan, China and Taiwan.
Height: 20m/65ft
Shape: Broadly spreading
Deciduous
Pollinated: Insect
Leaf shape: Ovate to elliptic

Right: After flowering small blue-black berries are produced.

This superb ornamental Asian tree has symmetrical, horizontal branches, which become progressively shorter towards the top of the tree in tiers, rather like a wedding cake. It was introduced into Europe before 1880, and is commonly grown in parks, gardens and arboreta throughout western Europe. It is one of only two dogwoods to have alternate leaves (the other being *C. alternifolia*); the rest are all opposite.

Identification: The bark is smooth, grey to light brown, becoming slightly fissured with age. The oval leaves are up to 15cm/6in long, dark green and glossy above and blue-green beneath with fine hairs. They are clustered together on thin stalks at the tips of the shoots. In autumn the leaves turn a rich plum-purple before falling. The flowers are small and creamy-white, borne in broad, flattened heads, 15cm/6in wide, along the horizontal branches in early summer. They are followed by small, spherical blue-black berries, also borne in clusters.

Japanese Strawberry Tree

Cornus kousa

This small Japanese tree has been widely planted as an ornamental right across Europe since its introduction in 1875. It has distinctive and decorative creamy-white bracts, sometimes tinged with pink, which surround very small greenish-white flower clusters in early summer. A Chinese variety of this tree, *C. kousa* var. *chinensis*, which was collected by Ernest Wilson in 1907, is also cultivated in Europe and is bigger in overall height, leaves and bracts.

Identification: The bark of this beautiful tree is rich brown-red, and flakes to reveal fresh cream or fawn bark beneath. The leaves are ovate, to 7.5cm/3in long, dark green and slightly shiny above, paler with tiny tufts of rust-coloured hair in the leaf vein axils beneath. They are untoothed and have a conspicuously undulating margin. The tiny flowers are surrounded by four creamy-white, or blush-white, taper-pointed bracts. They are followed by clusters of small, red, strawberry-like, edible, sweet-tasting fruit.

Distribution: Japan.
Height: 8m/26ft
Shape: Broadly columnar
Deciduous
Pollinated: Wind
Leaf shape: Ovate

Left: Small red edible fruits are produced following a hot summer.

Left: Four large white or pink-tinged bracts surround the insignificant flowers in summer.

OTHER SPECIES OF NOTE

Golden Rain Tree *Koelreuteria paniculata*
The golden rain tree is native to northern China and southern Mongolia, and was introduced into Europe in 1763. The name *Koelreuteria* commemorates the 18th-century German professor of botany, Joseph Koelreuter, who experimented with plant hybridization. It is a beautiful tree with pinnate leaves and yellow flowers, with bright orange-red stamens, in superb panicles up to 35cm/14in long, which drip from the tree in summer. *See also page 193.*

Flowering Dogwood *Cornus florida*
Native to the eastern USA and introduced into Europe as long ago as 1730, this beautiful small tree grows to 12m/40ft. Despite its name, it is cultivated not for its flowers, which are insignificant, but for the protective bracts that surround them. The bracts are 5cm/2in long and white with pink blotching around the base. Numerous cultivars have been raised from this species, including 'Cherokee Chief', which has deep rosy-red bracts. *See also page 192.*

Pacific Dogwood *Cornus nuttallii*
This west coast North American dogwood, introduced into Europe in 1835, has some of the largest bracts of any flowering dogwood. Also known as the mountain dogwood, it is a medium-sized tree, to 25m/80ft tall, and has elliptic, deciduous leaves, 15cm/6in long, which turn bright red and yellow in autumn. The insignificant flowers are surrounded by four to seven beautiful creamy-white to blush-white bracts, which may be up to 7.5cm/3in long, in late spring.

Handkerchief Tree

Dove tree, Ghost tree *Davidia involucrata*

This beautiful tree was introduced to the West from China in 1904 by Ernest Wilson, who had been commissioned by Veitch's nursery to collect propagating material for "this most wondrous of species". All of the tree's common names refer to the spectacular white hanging leaf bracts that appear in late spring.

Identification: The bark is orange-brown with vertical fissures, creating flaking, irregular plates. The leaves, up to 15cm/6in long, are sharply toothed with a drawn-out, pointed tip. They are glossy bright green above and paler with some hairs beneath. In times of drought they tend to roll up to reduce water loss. The small flowers, clustered into a ball with conspicuous lilac anthers, appear in late spring, surrounded by the showy white bracts. The fruit is a green-purple husk containing a single hard nut, inside which are up to five seeds.

Above and below: Surrounding the flowers are two large white bracts of unequal size, up to 20cm/8in long, which flutter in the breeze.

Distribution: Western China.
Height: 25m/80ft
Shape: Broadly conical
Deciduous
Pollinated: Insect
Leaf shape: Heart-shaped

Bentham's Cornel

Cornus capitata

This beautiful small tree takes its name from the Victorian botanist George Bentham. It has the reputation of being too tender for northern and western European gardens, but in a sheltered location it will survive and indeed flourish. Some of the best specimens are to be found in Cornwall, England: in the latter part of the 19th century there was an avenue of *C. capitata* on the entrance drive to the estate now known as the Lost Gardens of Heligan.

Identification: The bark is red-brown and relatively smooth. The evergreen leaves are variably elliptic, tapering at both ends, and are grey-green, leathery and covered with fine hair. They are 7.5–12.5cm/3–5in long and up to 5cm/2in broad. The flowers are very small and clustered together in the centre of four or six beautiful, sulphur-yellow bracts, up to 5cm/2in long.

Distribution: China and Himalayas.
Height: 12m/40ft
Shape: Broadly spreading
Evergreen
Pollinated: Insect
Leaf shape: Elliptic

Left: After flowering, crimson, edible, strawberry-like fruits are produced on long pendulous stalks.

HOLLIES

There are more than 400 species of evergreen and deciduous trees and shrubs in the Aquifoliaceae family; the vast majority belong to the holly, or Ilex, genus. Hollies are dioecious and berries are only produced on female trees. The leaves occur alternately on the shoot and the seed is always contained within a berry. Hollies are widely grown as ornamental trees throughout Britain and Europe.

Common Holly

Ilex aquifolium

Holly is one of the most useful and ornamental trees of the temperate world. It is extremely hardy and its dense foliage provides better shelter in exposed coastal and mountainous localities than just about any other tree. It has long been considered an integral part of Christmas celebrations and its bright berries cheer up the dullest of winter days. Holly timber is dense and hard and has been used for making just about everything from piano keys to billiard cues. The common holly has given rise to numerous attractive garden cultivars.

Identification: The bark is silver-grey and smooth even in maturity. The leaves are elliptic to ovate, up to 10cm/4in long, glossy dark green and waxy above, and pale green beneath. They are extremely variable: some leaves have strong spines around the margin; others are spineless. Both the male and female flowers are small and white with a slight fragrance; they appear on separate trees, clustered into the leaf axils in late spring and early summer. The fruits are round, shiny, red berries up to 1cm/½in across, borne in clusters along the shoots in winter.

Right: The dense foliage of holly makes it a useful hedging plant.

Distribution: Whole of Europe, western Asia and North Africa.
Height: 20m/65ft
Shape: Broadly columnar
Evergreen
Pollinated: Insect
Leaf shape: Elliptic to ovate

Right: Holly flowers are scented and appear from spring into summer.

Horned Holly

Ilex cornuta

This slow-growing, rather shrubby, small tree was discovered by the Scottish plant collector Robert Fortune in China in 1846, and sent to England shortly afterwards. In Europe it is still relatively uncommon in cultivation and is usually found in botanic gardens and arboreta. This is a shame because it is an ideal holly for small gardens, and has distinctive, handsome foliage.

Right: The rectangular leaves often have a spine in each corner and one at the tip.

Identification: The bark is grey and smooth even in old age. The leaves are almost rectangular and very stiff. They exhibit between three and five spines, but there are normally fewer spines on leaves positioned higher up the tree. The leaves are leathery, glossy dark green, up to 10cm/4in long and 5cm/2in wide. The flowers are small and dull white, and are borne in clusters in spring. The fruits are round and bright red, slightly larger than those of the common holly, *I. aquifolium*.

Distribution: China and Korea.
Height: 4m/13ft
Shape: Broadly spreading
Evergreen
Pollinated: Insect
Leaf shape: Rectangular to variable

Madeira Holly

Ilex perado

This elegant, small to medium-sized tree is similar to the common holly, *I. aquifolium*, except for its winged leaf stalks and variable leaf shapes, which may be oval to round, and with or without spines. It has been cultivated in Europe since 1760 but is tender and does not thrive in the colder northern and central regions. It is one of the parents of the ornamental garden cultivars known as the Highclere hollies, *I.* x *altaclarensis*.

Identification: The Madeira holly has leathery, flattened leaves, deep green above and paler beneath, that are up to 10cm/4in long and 5cm/2in wide. The leaves may be oval, obovate or rounded. Sometimes they have no spines at all, sometimes just spine-tipped teeth near the tip, and occasionally they are spiny all round the leaf margin. They are borne on short, winged leaf stalks. The bark is silver-grey and smooth, and the wood is creamy-white and extremely dense and hard. The flowers are small, pink in bud and dull white when open, borne in small clusters. The bright, glossy red fruits are pea-sized, egg-shaped to rounded, and are borne in linear clusters along the twigs.

Distribution: Madeira.
Height: 10m/33ft
Shape: Broadly columnar
Evergreen
Pollinated: Insect
Leaf shape: Variable

Left: The leaves may be oval or rounded and may be spined or have no spines at all.

OTHER SPECIES OF NOTE

Yellow-fruited Holly *Ilex aquifolium* 'Bacciflava'
This handsome and distinctive cultivar of the common holly, *I. aquifolium*, produces large clusters of bright golden fruits in early winter. In all other respects it is virtually indistinguishable from the species. It is sometimes named 'Fructu Luteo' in garden centres and nurseries.

Hedgehog Holly *Ilex aquifolium* 'Ferox'
Cultivated since the early 17th century, hedgehog holly was probably one of the first cultivars of the common holly. It is unmistakable and easily identified by the way its small evergreen leaves have short, sharp spines, both around the leaf margin and emanating from the flat, upper surface of the leaf. It is a male cultivar and therefore does not produce fruit.

Ilex aquifolium 'J. C. van Tol'

This is an interesting cultivar of common holly in that it produces both male and female flowers and is therefore self-pollinating, whereas most hollies are of one sex only. It is a handsome tree with large, thick, deep green matt leaves, which are conspicuously veined and normally without spines. Large, bright red berries are produced in profusion.

Highclere Holly

Ilex x *altaclarensis*

This is a hybrid between the common holly, *I. aquifolium*, and the Madeira holly, *I. perado*. It is believed to have been raised in England before 1838, and has given rise to an important group of ornamental garden cultivars, including some of the finest evergreen trees for planting in small gardens. Among them are the varieties 'Golden King', 'Camelliifolia' and 'Hodginsii'. The original hybrid is now rarely planted, having been superseded by its popular offspring.

Identification: The bark is silver-grey and smooth, even in maturity. The leaves are variable both in size and shape. They may be oval, round or even oblong and up to 12.5cm/5in long and 7.5cm/3in wide. The leaves normally have a spiny tip, but the spines around the margin may vary. Both male and female flowers are fragrant, small and white, sometimes with a dark pink blush, and are borne in clusters in the leaf axils, on separate trees, in spring. Female trees bear bright red, globular berries in autumn, which are retained into winter.

Distribution: Of garden origin.
Height: 20m/65ft
Shape: Broadly columnar
Evergreen
Pollinated: Insect
Leaf shape: Variable

Left: Attractive leaf shapes and colours, and a profusion of berries makes these cultivars some of the most ornamental hollies.

HOLLIES AND BOX

Along with hollies, members of the Buxus genus, particularly common box, have been widely grown for centuries in gardens throughout Europe. They are hardy small trees, thriving in most soil types and in sun or shade. They respond particularly well to shearing and clipping and consequently have been widely used for topiary.

Ilex corallina

Distribution: Western and south-west China.
Height: 10m/33ft
Shape: Broadly conical
Evergreen
Pollinated: Insect
Leaf shape: Ovate

This attractive Asian holly was introduced into Europe in 1900 from the province of Hubei in Western China. Since then it has been planted in botanic gardens and arboreta, but is not common in parks and gardens. In cultivation it is a slow-growing, small holly of graceful, slender habit. There are some fine young specimens planted as street trees in the Boskoop region of Holland.

Identification: The bark is smooth and light grey, sometimes silver-grey. The wood is hard and dense and a clean creamy-white. The evergreen leaves are glossy dark green above and paler beneath without a sheen. They are ovate-lanceolate, up to 15cm/6in long and 5cm/2in wide with a slender point, and are bluntly serrated around the leaf margin. The juvenile leaves may be prickly. The fruits are small, rounded, bright red berries, borne in clusters from autumn to late winter.

Right: Evergreen leaves may be up to 15cm/6in long with a slender point.

Perny's Holly

Ilex pernyi

This small tree, or occasionally large shrub, is native to central and western China, and was discovered by Abbé Paul Perny, a French Jesuit missionary, in 1858. It was another 40 years before it was introduced into Europe. Today, it is common in botanic gardens and arboreta, but still not as widely planted in gardens as might be expected for such a handsome tree.

Right: The leaves are virtually triangular.

Left: The bright red berries persist on the tree well into winter.

Identification: The tree has stiff branches and a slender, conical form. The bark is grey and smooth. The leaves, which are borne on thick leathery stalks, are distinctive in being almost triangular: they are very angular, with between three and seven ferocious spines, small (to 3cm/1¼in long) and dark glossy green. The flowers are cream to pale yellow, borne in tight clusters in the leaf axils. After flowering, clusters of pea-sized, bright red berries are produced.

Distribution: Central and western China.
Height: 10m/33ft
Shape: Broadly conical
Evergreen
Pollinated: Insect
Leaf shape: Triangular

Japanese Holly
Ilex crenata
Native to both Japan and Korea, this attractive evergreen plant is more a tall shrub than a tree, seldom attaining heights in excess of 4m/13ft. It has stiff, deep green, glossy leaves, which are 1cm/½in long and more akin to those of common box than holly. They are densely borne on reddish-brown shoots, which also carry globular, glossy black berries in winter.

Himalayan Holly *Ilex dipyrena*
This large conical tree, to 15m/50ft tall, is native to the eastern Himalayas and western China. It was introduced into Europe in 1840. It has elliptic, dark green leaves, to 10cm/4in long, which have regular, fine, forward-pointing spines around the margin. The leaves are attached to the twigs by short purple leaf stalks. The fruit is a deep red glossy berry.

Balearic Islands Box *Buxus balearica*
This slightly tender, Mediterranean evergreen tree, which grows to 10m/33ft, was introduced into western and northern Europe before 1780. It has an upright narrow habit, is densely branched and has large, leathery, matt green, oval leaves, to 5cm/2in long and 2.5cm/1in across. In addition to the Balearic Islands, it is also found growing wild in North Africa and southern Spain. In southern Europe it is used for hedging in much the same way as *B. sempervirens* in northern Europe.

Ilex x koehneana

This interesting small evergreen tree is a hybrid between the common holly, *I. aquifolium*, and the Asian tarajo holly, *I. latifolia*, which is said to have arisen in Florence, Italy, around 1890. It is named after the German botanist Bernhard Koehne, who reported its existence. It has large leaves like the tarajo holly, but takes its hardiness from common holly. It is not widely cultivated, but is found in European arboreta and botanic gardens.

Identification: *Ilex* x *koehneana* has grey smooth bark, olive green twigs and purple young shoots. When the leaves first emerge they are distinctly bronze-coloured. They are elliptic to oblong, 12.5cm/5in long, glossy mid-green above and slightly paler beneath, and they have numerous regular and relatively large spines around the margin. The male and female flowers are small, greenish-white, and borne in clusters in the leaf axils on separate trees in spring. Small clusters of pea-sized, glossy red berries are borne on female trees in winter.

Distribution: Of garden origin.
Height: 6m/20ft
Shape: Broadly conical
Evergreen
Pollinated: Insect
Leaf shape: Elliptic to oblong

Left: The leaves have numerous regular and relatively large spines around the margin.

Common Box

Buxus sempervirens

This small tree or spreading shrub has dense foliage and has been grown for centuries in gardens for hedging, screening and topiary. It is a favourite for use in defining knot gardens and parterres, and clips well. It withstands dense shade and will happily grow beneath the branches of other trees. It has hard, cream-coloured wood, which has been extensively used for wood engraving and turnery.

Identification: The bark is fawn or buff-coloured, smooth at first, then fissuring into tiny plates. The leaves are ovate to oblong, 2.5cm/1in long, rounded at the tip with a distinctive notch, glossy dark green above, pale green below and borne on angular shoots. Both male and female flowers are produced in mid-spring; they are small, pale green with yellow anthers and carried in the same clusters on the same trees.

Left: The fruit is a small woody capsule holding up to six seeds.

Right: Flowers are produced in the leaf axils, with several males surrounding one female flower.

Distribution: Europe, North Africa and western Asia.
Height: 6m/20ft
Shape: Broadly conical to spreading
Evergreen
Pollinated: Insect
Leaf shape: Ovate

HORSE CHESTNUTS

The horse chestnut genus, Aesculus, *contains some of the most popular and easily recognizable ornamental trees in the world. There are just 15 species, all native to northern temperate regions, where they are widely grown in parks, gardens and arboreta for their stately habit and attractive flowers and fruit. All horse chestnuts have compound, palmate leaves and large flowers borne in upright panicles.*

Indian Horse Chestnut

Aesculus indica

Distribution: North-western Himalayas and northern India.
Height: 30m/100ft
Shape: Broadly columnar
Deciduous
Pollinated: Insect
Leaf shape: Compound palmate

Right: The leaflets spread like fingers from the leaf stalk. Indian horse chestnut seeds are contained in a smooth husk.

This magnificent tree is not as widely known as the common horse chestnut, but equals it in stature and beauty. In the Himalayan forests where it grows wild, Indian horse chestnut regularly exceeds 30m/100ft. Tall flower spikes appear in mid-summer. For many years the white, light timber was used to make tea boxes.

Identification: The bark is grey-brown and smooth, even in maturity. The leaves are compound and palmate, with either five or seven leaflets all joining the leaf stalk at a common point. Each leaflet is obovate to broadly lanceolate and up to 25cm/10in long. They emerge bronze-coloured, gradually turning glossy grass-green in summer and then golden yellow in autumn. The white to pale pink flowers are borne in mid-summer on erect, cylindrical panicles, up to 30cm/12in long. Each flower has a yellow or red blotch at the base. The fruit is a rough (but not spiny), green, slightly pear-shaped husk containing up to three dark brown nuts, commonly known as conkers.

Right: The flowers appear on long spikes in the middle of summer, poking through the foliage like candles.

Red Horse Chestnut

Aesculus x carnea

Distribution: Of garden origin.
Height: 20m/65ft
Shape: Broadly columnar
Deciduous
Pollinated: Insect
Leaf shape: Compound palmate

This popular tree, planted in parks and gardens throughout Europe, is a hybrid between the common horse chestnut, *A. hippocastanum*, and the American red buckeye, *A. pavia*. Little is known of its origins, but it is possible that it occurred naturally in Germany in the early 1800s. There are several different clones of this hybrid in cultivation and they vary in terms of flower quality, how soon they begin to produce flowers, and their susceptibility to branch-break.

Identification: The bark is dull brown, smooth at first, becoming shallowly fissured and flaking in maturity. The leaves are palmately compound, mid-green with pronounced parallel veining. There are normally between five and seven obovate, short-stalked leaflets, each up to 25cm/10in long, joined at the base to a long leaf stalk. The flowers, which appear in late spring, range from pink to deep red and are borne in erect panicles up to 20cm/8in long. The fruit is a brown shiny single seed, which may be known as a conker, enclosed in a slightly spiny husk.

Below: The fruit.

Above: Erect panicles of red flowers cover the tree in spring.

Common Horse Chestnut

Aesculus hippocastanum

This tree is native only to Albania and Greece, but its distribution is often wrongly thought to be larger because of its popularity and widespread planting as an ornamental tree. It came into cultivation outside its natural range as early as 1650, when it was introduced into Vienna, Austria.

Identification: The bark is orange-brown to grey, smooth at first, turning shallowly fissured and scaly in maturity. The large winter buds are rich red-brown and covered in sticky resin. The leaves are large: each leaflet can be up to 30cm/12in long, and there are normally five to seven strongly veined, obovate leaflets on each leaf. The nuts are grouped in twos or threes in a husk 5cm/2in across.

Left: Horse chestnut leaf buds are covered by brown scales. The seed husks have sharp spines.

Distribution: Albania and Greece.
Height: 30m/100ft
Shape: Broadly columnar
Deciduous
Pollinated: Insect
Leaf shape: Compound palmate

Left: The flowers are creamy white, blotched with yellow and pink, and borne in large upright, conical panicles, up to 25cm/10in long, in mid-spring.

OTHER SPECIES OF NOTE
Sweet Buckeye *Aesculus flava*
Sometimes called yellow buckeye, this handsome, round-headed tree, to 30m/100ft, was introduced from North America to Europe by 1764. *Flava* means yellow and refers to the yellow flowers that are borne in upright panicles in late spring. The leaves turn orange-red in autumn. *See also page 196.*

Red Buckeye *Aesculus pavia*
Native to eastern USA, this tree grows in woods and thickets. It is a small tree with a slightly weeping, pendulous habit in the outer branches. Introduced into Europe in 1711, it is one of the parents of the hybrid red horse chestnut, *A. x carnea*, to which it gives the red flower. *See also page 197.*

Ohio Buckeye *Aesculus glabra*
This small North American horse chestnut, to 10m/33ft, was introduced into Europe around 1812. It has rough bark and palmate leaves with five leaflets. It produces yellow-green flowers in late spring and has bright autumn leaf colour. *See also page 197.*

Sunrise Horse Chestnut *Aesculus x neglecta* 'Erythroblastos'
This is a stunningly beautiful cultivar of the hybrid between *A. flava* and *A. sylvatica*. It is grown for its spectacular young leaves, which erupt in mid-spring a brilliant shrimp-pink. The leaves gradually change to pale yellow-green, but the tree is worth growing for those few splendid weeks in spring.

Japanese Horse Chestnut

Aesculus turbinata

In many ways this large tree is similar in appearance to the common horse chestnut, *A. hippocastanum*. It is widely planted in Japan as an ornamental species but is slower-growing than the common horse chestnut and its flowers are not so large or carried in such profusion. Its leaves are much larger, however, and turn bright orange in autumn.

Identification: The bark is brown and flaky in maturity. The winter buds are glossy, red-brown and sticky. The leaves are compound and palmate, with five to seven obovate, toothed leaflets all attached at the same point to a common leaf stalk. Each rich green leaflet can be up to 40cm/16in long and is heavily veined. The flowers are creamy-white with a red blotch and are borne on upright panicles up to 25cm/10in tall in late spring. The fruit is an egg-shaped, virtually spineless yellow-green husk, ripening brown to reveal two to three shiny brown seeds, or conkers, inside.

Distribution: Japan.
Height: 30m/100ft
Shape: Broadly columnar
Deciduous
Pollinated: Insect
Leaf shape: Compound palmate

Above: The husks have tiny spines.

Below: An elegant flower spike.

MAPLES

There are more than 100 species of maple, Acer, in the world and countless cultivars, particularly of the Japanese maples. Mainly deciduous, they are predominantly found throughout northern temperate regions, with a few extending into subtropical Asia. They range in size from mighty American giants to slow-growing Japanese bonsai. Many are cultivated for their attractive foliage and graceful habit.

Field Maple

Acer campestre

This small, hardy maple has a massively wide natural distribution, which runs from the Atlantic to Siberia and south to the Mediterranean. It is a small to medium-sized tree of woodland edges and hedgerows. It is widely cultivated as a hedging species throughout Europe. Field maple is a long-lived tree, and there are European specimens that are known to be more than 500 years old. It produces good golden-yellow leaf colour in autumn.

Identification: The bark is pale grey-brown, smooth at first but becoming very "corky", particularly on small twigs, which may take on a 'winged' appearance. The leaves are palmately lobed with five lobes, dark green above, paler beneath, to 7.5cm/3in long and much the same across. They are borne on a short stalk that exudes a milky liquid when crushed or broken, particularly in spring. The flowers are small and greenish-yellow, and are borne in erect clusters in spring. These develop into pendulous clusters of winged seeds.

Distribution: Europe, south-west Asia and parts of North Africa.
Height: 20m/65ft
Shape: Broadly spreading
Deciduous
Pollinated: Insect
Leaf shape: Palmately lobed

Left and right: The leaves turn red and golden brown in the autumn.

Sycamore

Acer pseudoplatanus

Sycamore is one of the most common northern temperate trees. It has an extensive natural range and has been widely planted, and subsequently naturalized, in Britain and North America. It is hardy and resistant to strong winds and exposure to salt-laden air in coastal areas.

Identification: The bark is grey and smooth when young, becoming a delightful greyish-pink in maturity with irregular-sized flaking plates. The leaf buds are lime green. They open in spring to release bronze-yellow leaves, which turn deep green within two weeks of emerging. The leaves are up to 20cm/8in across, palmate, with five coarsely toothed lobes. The small flowers are borne in dense, yellow-green, pendulous clusters as the leaves emerge in spring. The fruit is the familiar two-winged seed. Each wing is 2.5cm/1in long. The seeds are grouped in pendulous clusters from early summer; they are red-green in colour, ripening to brown in mid-autumn.

Right: Sycamore seeds are easily recognized by their paired wings. The leaves are typically maple-shaped.

Distribution: Europe, from the Pyrenees in Spain to the Carpathians in the Ukraine.
Height: 30m/100ft
Shape: Broadly columnar
Deciduous
Pollinated: Insect
Leaf shape: Palmate

Norway Maple

Acer platanoides

This fast-growing, handsome, hardy maple has been cultivated as an ornamental species for centuries. It has a large, spreading crown with upswept branches and is as much at home in parkland settings as in woodland. Recently, smaller cultivars have been developed, which are being planted in great numbers alongside roads.

Identification: The bark is grey and smooth when young, becoming vertically ridged and fissured in maturity. The leaves are rather like the leaf on the Canadian flag – palmate with five lobes, each ending in several sharp teeth and a slender point. Each leaf is bright green and up to 15cm/6in in both length and width; it is borne on a long, slender, pink-yellow leaf stalk. The flowers are bright yellow, sometimes red, and are borne in conspicuous drooping clusters in spring as the leaves emerge.

Right: Flowers may be either yellow or red.

Distribution: South-west Asia and Europe, north to southern Norway.
Height: 30m/100ft
Shape: Broadly columnar
Deciduous
Pollinated: Insect
Leaf shape: Palmate

Left: The fruit is a pair of green-yellow winged seeds, borne in clusters. Each is up to 5cm/2in long.

Right: The foliage is a fresh bright green.

OTHER SPECIES OF NOTE

Paperbark Maple
Acer griseum
This beautiful small tree was discovered in China in 1901 and almost immediately became a European garden favourite. It has cinnamon-coloured, wafer thin bark, which flakes to reveal fresh orange bark beneath. Its distinctive trifoliate leaves turn burgundy-red and orange in autumn.

Père David's Maple *Acer davidii*
This beautiful small tree, to 15m/50ft, is native to China, from where it was introduced into Europe in 1879, when it was named after the great French Jesuit missionary and plant collector. *A. davidii* is a snake-bark maple and has smooth, olive-green bark, beautifully marked with narrow, vertical white stripes. The leaves are ovate, to 15cm/6in long and 10cm/4in broad, and turn a beautiful orange-red in autumn.

Hers's Maple *Acer grosseri* var. *hersii*
This superb Chinese maple, growing to 10m/33ft and introduced into Europe around 1923, is widely planted as an ornamental. It has green bark that has beautiful long, narrow, linear white markings. The leaves are ovate, normally with three to five lobes, and turn a rich marmalade-red in autumn. The green flowers are borne in conspicuous pendulous racemes in late spring.

Cappadocian Maple

Acer cappadocicum

This stately, handsome tree was introduced into western Europe in 1838, and has since been a popular addition to parks, gardens and arboreta. It makes a relatively large, broad but round-headed tree, normally with a clean trunk of 3–4m/10–13ft, though some root suckering may occur around the base. In autumn the leaves turn a rich butter-yellow before falling. If the leaf or leaf stalk is torn, a milky, sticky sap is extruded.

Identification: The bark is similar to that of ash, light grey and quite smooth. The palmate leaves, to 10cm/4in long and 15cm/6in across, have five to seven pointed lobes. They emerge a warm red before fading to grass-green above and paler beneath, with some hair in the leaf vein axils. The small, greenish-yellow flowers appear in spring. The fruits are winged seeds carried in pairs, in clusters, turning from green to light brown as they ripen.

Distribution: Turkey, Iran, the Caucasus and into western China.
Height: 20m/65ft
Shape: Broadly spreading
Deciduous
Pollinated: Insect
Leaf shape: Palmately lobed

Above: Flowers are in erect clusters.

Right: The seeds are winged pairs.

Smooth Japanese Maple

Acer palmatum

The smooth Japanese maple was discovered in 1783 and introduced into the West in 1820. Surprisingly, however, it was almost another 80 years before it became popular and began to be widely planted. The famous Acer Glade at Westonbirt Arboretum, in Gloucestershire, England, was planted in 1875. Today there are literally hundreds of cultivars of smooth Japanese maple. In the wild the species grows within, or on the edge of, mixed broad-leaved woodland, providing dappled shade and shelter.

Identification: The overall shape of the tree is like a large natural bonsai, with horizontal, spreading, meandering branches forking from the main stem quite close to the ground. The bark is grey-brown and smooth, even in maturity. The leaves are palmate with between five and seven deep, pointed lobes that have forward-facing serrations around the margin. They are up to 10cm/4in across. The flowers are burgundy-red with yellow stamens. They are borne in upright or drooping clusters as the leaves emerge in spring. The fruits are green to red winged seeds carried in pairs; each wing is up to 1cm/½in long and up to 20 seeds are clustered together on the branch.

Below left: In autumn, the leaves turn red and gold before falling.

Distribution: China, Taiwan, Japan and Korea.
Height: 15m/50ft
Shape: Broadly spreading
Deciduous
Pollinated: Insect
Leaf shape: Palmate

Right: The new leaves emerge bright green.

Full Moon Maple

Japanese maple *Acer japonicum*

The full moon maple is native to the islands of Hokkaido and Honshu in Japan, from where it was introduced into Europe in 1864. Despite this relatively early introduction it is hardly ever seen as a species in gardens, having been superseded by a number of beautiful cultivars produced from it, including 'Vitifolium' and 'Aconitifolium'. The species has lime green foliage, which turns red, orange and yellow in autumn.

Identification: The bark is silver grey and smooth, even in maturity. The leaves are palmately rounded, to 12.5cm/5in across, with 7–11 toothed, taper-pointed lobes. The leaves have some fine hair on both their upper and lower surfaces. The flowers are small and purple-red, and are borne in conspicuous pendulous clusters, which appear before the tree comes into leaf. These are followed by winged seeds, to 2.5cm/1in long, which are borne in pairs. They are green at first, ripening to light brown in late summer.

Right: Clusters of small, reddish-purple flowers open in spring.

Distribution: Japan.
Height: 10m/33ft
Shape: Broadly spreading
Deciduous
Pollinated: Insect
Leaf shape: Palmately lobed

Below: The lobed leaves are rounded and mid-green in summer, turning red before they fall in autumn.

OTHER SPECIES OF NOTE

Silver Maple *Acer saccharinum*
This is one of the fastest-growing North American maples and is widely planted as an ornamental specimen in parks and gardens across Europe. Although at first glance it is similar in outline to sycamore, it is altogether a much more elegant tree, with a light, open crown and bi-coloured leaves that are bright green above and silver-green beneath. *See also page 199.*

Oregon Maple *Acer macrophyllum*
The specific name of this large North American tree, *macrophyllum*, translates as "large-leaved", which is an appropriate description. The dark green leaves, which are palmate with large, coarsely toothed lobes, may be up to 25cm/10in long and 30cm/12in broad, and are carried on long straw-coloured leaf stalks. They turn yellow and orange in autumn. *See also page 200.*

Ash-leaved Maple *Acer negundo*
Also known as box elder, this 20m/65ft, North American maple is not immediately recognizable as a maple, having pinnate leaves, rather like ash, with up to seven leaflets. *A. negundo* has a light airy look, with long, widely spaced branching, silver-grey bark and bright green leaves. Yellow-green flowers hang, tassel-like, from the outer twigs in spring. *See also page 198.*

Snake-bark Maple

Acer capillipes

This beautiful small tree, native to Japan, was introduced into the USA by Charles Sargent in 1892. From there saplings were sent to Kew Gardens, London, in 1894. It is now widely planted in parks and gardens right across western Europe. It is a graceful tree with arching branches and foliage that turns bright orange and red in autumn.

Identification: The bark is grey-green and marked with vertical, narrow white stripes, flushed with red when young, and carried through from the main stem to the secondary branching and twigs. The leaves are up to 15cm/6in long and 10cm/4in across, serrated around the margin and with three to five lobes. The central lobe is the largest and runs to an extended tip. The leaf, borne on a red leaf stalk, has a grass-green upper surface and is paler beneath. The flowers are small, green and carried in pendulous clusters in spring. The fruits are winged seeds, carried in pairs.

Left: The flower clusters are to 10cm/4in.

Right: The bark is marbled with vertical white stripes.

Distribution: Japan.
Height: 10m/33ft
Shape: Broadly spreading
Deciduous
Pollinated: Insect
Leaf shape: Lobed

Forrest's Maple

Acer pectinatum subsp. *forrestii*

This beautiful snake-bark maple takes its name from the plant collector George Forrest, who discovered it in south-west China in 1906. Considering its beauty it is surprising that it is not more widely cultivated in Europe. However there are two splendid specimens at Caerhays Castle, Cornwall, England, which are believed to be plants originally introduced by Forrest.

Identification: This is a beautiful maple with stem bark and young branches that are purple-red, sometimes green, striated with white. It is a sparsely and gracefully branched tree. The leaves, to 12.5cm/5in long and 5cm/2in wide, are mostly heart-shaped with three to five lobes; the central lobe is drawn out into a long slender point and the side lobes are triangular. The leaves are carried on coral-red leaf stalks. The flowers are small and purple-red, and are borne in pendulous clusters as the leaves emerge in spring. They are followed by winged seeds, carried in pairs, in clusters, in late summer to early autumn. The leaves turn bright yellow or orange-red before falling in autumn.

Distribution: China.
Height: 15m/50ft
Shape: Broadly spreading
Deciduous
Pollinated: Insect
Leaf shape: Cordate lobed

Left: Small purple-red flowers are borne in pendulous clusters in spring.

Left: Winged seeds are borne in late summer into autumn as the leaves begin to turn colour.

MAPLE CULTIVARS

Over the centuries hundreds of maple cultivars have been developed for their beauty and then grown as ornamental trees in gardens right across the world. Many of the original Japanese maple cultivars were developed in the Japanese temple gardens during the 17th and 18th centuries. The vast majority produce stunning leaf colour changes in autumn.

Vine-leaved Japanese maple

Acer japonicum 'Vitifolium'

Distribution: Of garden origin.
Height: 10m/33ft
Shape: Broadly spreading
Deciduous
Pollinated: Insect
Leaf shape: Roundly lobed

The origins of this beautiful maple cultivar have been lost in time, although it is known to have been in cultivation by around 1882. The name refers to the fact that its leaves, which are more deeply divided than those of the species, resemble the leaves of a grape vine (*Vitis*). It is one of the mainstays of autumn leaf colour displays throughout Europe, producing leaves of several colours on the same tree at the same time: the autumn foliage ranges from green to burgundy, scarlet, orange, gold and yellow.

Identification: It is a wide-spreading tree with many low horizontal branches, which sweep upwards towards the tip. The bark is grey-brown and smooth, even in maturity. The leaves are heart-shaped at the base, rounded with a serrated margin. They are up to 12.5cm/5in long and 15cm/6in wide, with 9–11 lobes, separated almost halfway to the leaf centre and ending in sharp points. The flowers are small and green to red-purple, borne in conspicuous clusters in the spring.

*Above: The leaves resemble those of the grape vine (*Vitis*).*

Acer palmatum 'Katsura'

Distribution: Of garden origin.
Height: 7m/23ft
Shape: Broadly columnar
Deciduous
Pollinated: Insect
Leaf shape: Palmately lobed

In Japan and in the USA this maple cultivar is considered a dwarf form; however, in Europe it may reach 7m/23ft in height. It is widely cultivated for its leaf shape and spring colour. New leaves, when they emerge from bud, are a beautiful apricot-yellow with a darker margin, which is usually orange. As the season progresses the leaves turn a bright golden-green.

Identification: The tree has rather shrubby, dense growth, with strongly ascending branching. The bark is grey and smooth. The leaves are small, seldom more than 5cm/2in long and broad. They have five lobes, which are lanceolate and taper to a long point, with the centre lobe being the longest. The margins are shallowly toothed and the lobes divide the leaf almost to the centre. Each leaf is attached to the twig by a 1cm/½in leaf stalk. In autumn the leaves revert from green to bright apricot-yellow and orange before falling.

Above and below: The autumn leaf and key.

Acer palmatum 'Beni komachi'

Everything about this small tree is attractive. It is one of the very best dwarf Japanese maple cultivars and probably the best of all red-leaved cultivars. Even the name is delightful, roughly translating to "the beautiful, red-haired little girl". It was raised in the USA in the 1960s and is still relatively uncommon in European gardens, although its beauty is sure to make it more popular in the future.

Identification: The leaves, which are up to 5cm/2in long and broad, are deeply divided, almost to the midrib and leaf stalk, by five long, narrow lobes. The margins of each lobe are finely toothed and taper to a blunt point. Each lobe tends to curve down and to the side. When the leaves emerge from bud in spring they are bright scarlet-red. They then fade through late spring and summer to a blue-green red and then in autumn they return to brilliant scarlet.

Distribution: Of North American garden origin.
Height: 2m/6ft
Shape: Broadly columnar
Deciduous
Pollinated: Insect
Leaf shape: Palmately lobed

Left: The leaves turn a bright scarlet colour.

OTHER SPECIES OF NOTE

Acer palmatum 'Linearilobum'
This is an elegant cultivar that is said to have been raised in the Netherlands in 1867. However, there is some suggestion that it is a natural form of *A. palmatum*, which was being grown in Japan before then. It is a very popular maple, widely cultivated across Europe. It has bright grass-green leaves, with seven very narrow lobes, often little more than broadened midribs. It is vigorous and may eventually reach 5m/16ft tall.

Acer palmatum 'Crimson Queen'
This outstanding, dissected, purple-leaved Japanese maple was raised in the USA in the 1960s, and is now very popular in gardens in Europe. It has fern-like dissected leaves, which emerge dark purple-red and stay that way throughout summer, unlike some cultivars, which turn a muddy green or bronze as they mature. In autumn the leaves turn bright red. It reaches an eventual height of around 3m/10ft.

Acer palmatum 'Burgundy Lace'
'Burgundy Lace' is an American cultivar, which was raised in Washington in the 1950s but was not introduced into Europe until 1972. It is grown in European gardens but not so widely as 'Crimson Queen'. It is a small tree, eventually attaining a height of 4–5m/13–16ft, and has deeply dissected palmate leaves, to 7.5cm/3in long and wide. Throughout spring and early summer the leaves are the colour of Burgundy wine; in late summer they turn bronze-green.

Acer palmatum 'Filigree'

This is one of the most beautiful of all dissected maples. Its delicate foliage and pendulous habit make it a real showstopper. It is a small tree, ideal for planting in a confined space, and is widely cultivated in European gardens, parks and arboreta. It is a fairly recent cultivar, having being raised by Joel Spingarn in New York, around 1955. It is very slow-growing and eventually forms a neat mushroom shape. The name refers to the lace-like quality of the dissected foliage.

Identification: The overall form resembles an overgrown bonsai specimen, with a multitude of twisted branches making the tree a striking feature in winter when the leaves have fallen. The bark is grey and smooth, becoming silvery green, with white elongated flecks on the twigs and shoots. Each leaf may be up to 10cm/4in across but is deeply dissected all the way to the centre by seven lobes; these are also deeply dissected, and up to 7.5cm/3in long.

Distribution: Of garden origin.
Height: 2m/6ft
Shape: Broadly spreading
Deciduous
Pollinated: Insect
Leaf shape: Palmately lobed

Left: The leaves are light yellow-green in spring, darkening through summer, then turning fiery gold in autumn.

Coral-barked Maple

Acer palmatum 'Sangokaku'

Sometimes referred to as 'Senkaki', this is one of the original Japanese maple cultivars and was widely cultivated in Japan in the 19th century, and probably earlier. It was introduced into Europe and was being cultivated in Britain around 1920. It is a stunning tree, grown for its brilliant red stems, which are at their most vibrant in winter. The Japanese name 'Sangokaku' translates as "coral tower".

Distribution: Of garden origin.
Height: 11m/36ft
Shape: Broadly columnar
Deciduous
Pollinated: Insect
Leaf shape: Palmately lobed

Identification: This relatively large and vigorous Japanese maple is easily identified by its striking red bark. The deepest colour is on the new growth, but even old branches and the main stem maintain a red-green colouring. The palmate leaves are 5cm/2in across and long, normally with five lobes, each serrated around the margin and ending in a sharp point. They are a fresh green, becoming a subtle but beautiful apricot colour in autumn.

Right: The bright green leaves turn yellow in autumn, creating a contrast with the reddish bark.

Fern Leaf Maple

Acer japonicum 'Aconitifolium'

This outstanding Japanese maple has been cultivated since the 1880s and is grown for its beautiful aconite-like leaves and glorious autumn colours. It can make a large tree for a Japanese maple and is often as wide as it is tall. It is a strongly structured plant, not at all thin and wispy like some *A. palmatum* cultivars. It has leaves that tend to lie in the horizontal plane, giving the tree a Far-Eastern appearance.

Distribution: Of garden origin.
Height: 8m/26ft
Shape: Broadly spreading
Deciduous
Pollinated: Insect
Leaf shape: Palmately lobed

Identification: The bark is smooth and grey-brown. The leaves are deeply cut, almost to the base, with 7–11 lobes that are themselves divided on each side with irregular cuts extending to the lobe midrib. Each lobe runs to an extended but blunt point. The leaf size is variable, from 7.5–15cm/3–6in long and broad. The foliage is deep green, becoming clear scarlet with gold, orange or purple tints in autumn.

Below: The leaves resemble those of the aconite plant and turn from rich green to scarlet and orange in autumn. The seeds appear inside keys.

OTHER SPECIES OF NOTE

Red-leaved Norway Maple *Acer platanoides* 'Crimson King'
This large, 25m/80ft, handsome tree is the best red-leaved Norway maple cultivar and is particularly attractive in spring when the leaves and flowers combine. It was raised in 1937 in a nursery in Belgium. Since then it has become a popular tree for planting in towns and cities right across Europe and North America. The flowers are bright yellow flecked with red.

***Acer platanoides* 'Drummondii'**
This striking variegated Norway maple cultivar was raised in a Scottish nursery in 1903. It is a medium-sized tree, seldom exceeding 12m/40ft tall, with a broad rounded crown, light brown bark and strongly lobed leaves, to 15cm/6in long and 17.5cm/7in broad. The leaves are deep green in the centre with a broad creamy-yellow to creamy-white margin.

***Acer pseudoplatanus* 'Brilliantissimum'**
This sycamore cultivar is like a bright star that burns itself out too soon. In spring when the leaves emerge from bud they are a glorious terracotta-orange-pink, but within days they fade through yellow to light green and the show is over. It is a compact small tree of slow growth.

***Acer palmatum* 'Seiryu'**
This is the only upright cultivar of the cut-leaved or dissected Japanese maple. That alone makes it worth growing, but it also has beautiful dissected foliage that emerges in spring with reddish flecks to the tips of each fresh green leaf. The autumn colour ranges from rich marmalade to translucent apricot.

Golden Moon Maple

Acer shirasawanum 'Aureum'

Distribution: Of garden origin.
Height: 8m/26ft
Shape: Broadly spreading
Deciduous
Pollinated: Insect
Leaf shape: Orbicular

When this graceful tree is given the right soil and moisture conditions it makes one of the finest ornamental trees for garden use, providing a glorious canopy of subtle golden foliage. It was for a long time thought of as a cultivar of *A. japonicum*, which it is not, but old labels on specimens in botanic gardens may refer to it as such. It has been in cultivation in Japan for at least 200 years, and was introduced into Europe in 1865.

Identification: The bark is grey-brown and smooth, even in maturity. The leaves are round, to 10cm/4in across, with 9–11 lobes divided a third of the way to the centre. They are a clear golden yellow, sometimes with a reddish margin. In autumn they turn old gold before falling. The flowers are small and red, and are borne in conspicuous erect spikes in spring. They are followed by winged seeds, borne in pairs, which are green ripening to brown in late summer.

Left: The leaves are a golden lime colour from spring to late summer.

Acer palmatum 'Osakazuki'

Undoubtedly the best-known Japanese maple cultivar of all and widely planted in parks, gardens and arboreta right across Europe, this maple has been listed in nursery catalogues since the 1850s. 'Osakazuki' takes on intense crimson-red autumn leaf colouring reliably every year, producing the best colour if it is planted in a sunny location. Although the tree grows rapidly in the first few years, it slows down considerably after ten years or so, and becomes a densely branched, round-topped tree reaching a maximum of 10m/33ft tall.

Distribution: Of garden origin.
Height: 10m/33ft
Shape: Broadly spreading
Deciduous
Pollinated: Insect
Leaf shape: Palmately lobed

Identification: The bark is grey-brown and smooth. The leaves are palmate, normally up to 10cm/4in long and broad, with seven ovate lobes, which are finely serrated around the margin and run to a long narrow tip. The two lobes on each side of the leaf stalk are normally much smaller than the other five. When the leaves first emerge in spring they are olive-orange; they turn slowly to bright grass-green in late spring and summer before finally changing to intense crimson in autumn.

Below: In autumn, when the leaves turn, the seeds turn scarlet, becoming part of a very showy display from this tree.

Below: The leaves will reliably turn a good crimson-red colour every autumn.

ASHES

There are about 65 species within the ash genus, Fraxinus. All have pinnate leaves and are found in temperate regions of the world, primarily North America, Europe and Asia. They are hardy, fast-growing deciduous trees that tolerate exposure, poor soils and atmospheric pollution. Included within this genus are members of the beautiful flowering ashes, which includes the manna ash from southern Europe.

Common Ash

Fraxinus excelsior

One of the largest of all European deciduous trees, the common ash is found growing wild from the Pyrenees to the Caucasus. Ash grows particularly well on calcareous limestone soils. It produces strong, white timber that has long been used where strength and durability are required, along with impact resistance, such as in coach building and for items such as ladders and tool handles.

Distribution: Europe.
Height: 40m/130ft
Shape: Broadly columnar
Deciduous
Pollinated: Insect
Leaf shape: Pinnate

Right: The leaves are pinnate and up to 30cm/12in long. Each may have up to 12 pairs of shallow toothed, rich green leaflets.

Identification: The ash has a light airy crown, with a trunk that tends to be straight and long with little branching. The bark is pale fawn when young, becoming grey and fissured with age. One distinguishing characteristic of ash is its velvet-black winter buds. The fruits, flattened, winged seeds known as "keys", 4cm/1½in long, are borne in clusters throughout the winter.

Left: Both male and female flowers are produced in profusion in early spring.

Narrow-leaved Ash

Fraxinus angustifolia

This elegant tree has, as its name suggests, the narrowest leaves of any ash. These give the tree an open, feathery look. It is a fast-growing tree, which was introduced into western Europe in 1800. There are several cultivars of *F. angustifolia*, including 'Raywood', which has leaves that turn plum-purple in autumn.

Identification: The bark is grey-brown with vertical fissures. Older trees may have been grafted on to the rather incompatible, slower-growing *F. excelsior*, which results in a prominent horizontal banding effect at the graft union. Winter buds are dark brown. The small, inconspicuous, green or purple flowers are borne on bare twigs in early spring. The fruits are flattened, winged seeds, up to 4cm/1½in long, borne in hanging fawn clusters that persist well into winter.

Above: Narrow-leaved ash is a graceful tree with well-spaced branches and light, airy foliage.

Right: The leaves are pinnate, with up to 13 lanceolate, sharply toothed, glossy dark-green leaflets, up to 10cm/4in long.

Distribution: Southern Europe, North Africa and western Asia.
Height: 25m/80ft
Shape: Broadly columnar
Deciduous
Pollinated: Insect
Leaf shape: Pinnate

American Ash *Fraxinus americana*
Otherwise known as white ash, this North American tree with rust-brown winter leaf buds and olive-green shoots was introduced into Europe in 1724. It is a fast-growing tree, which can attain heights up to 28m/94ft. It has pinnate leaves, small purple flowers and single winged seeds, which are borne in dense pendulous clusters. *See also page 202.*

Fraxinus angustifolia 'Raywood'
This is a handsome tree and one that deserves to be even more widely planted in European towns and cities than it already is. Raised in 1928, in the Raywood Gardens, Adelaide, Australia (hence its name), it is a fast-growing tree, with a compact, dense crown of upward arching branches and pinnate leaves, which turn a distinctive and handsome, vibrant plum-purple in autumn.

Fraxinus holotricha
This medium-sized ash, uncommon in cultivation, is native to the Balkan peninsula of south-eastern Europe. It was cultivated in Germany in the early 20th century, but is seldom seen growing outside botanic gardens and arboreta. It has pinnate grey-green leaves, normally with 11 or 13 narrow leaflets, and downy shoots.

Manna Ash

Fraxinus ornus

This beautiful flowering ash grows wild in south-western Asia and southern Europe and has been widely cultivated throughout central and western Europe since around 1700. It produces, rather unusually for ash, large panicles of creamy-white, fragrant flowers, which hang in fluffy clusters from the branches in late spring. Manna sugar, a form of sweetener tolerated by diabetics, is derived from the sap of this tree.

Identification: The bark is grey and smooth and the winter leaf buds are dark grey. The pinnate leaves, to 20cm/8in long, have five to nine sharply toothed and tapered leaflets, each up to 10cm/4in long and 5cm/2in broad. They are matt mid-green above and slightly paler beneath. The fruit is a single, flat, winged seed, up to 4cm/1½in long, green at first ripening to pale brown.

Below: Hanging clusters of creamy-white flowers are produced in late spring.

Distribution: Southern Europe and south-west Asia.
Height: 20m/65ft
Shape: Broadly spreading
Deciduous
Pollinated: Insect
Leaf shape: Pinnate

Chinese Flowering Ash

Fraxinus mariesii

This beautiful flowering ash, which is occasionally planted in gardens and arboreta throughout Europe, is named after the English plant collector Charles Maries, who introduced propagation material to James Veitch's nursery in 1878. It is a small, slow-growing tree, which forms a rounded, bushy head of branches in maturity. It is ideal for medium-sized gardens and should be more widely planted for its beauty.

Identification: The bark is light grey-brown and smooth, and the light grey winter leaf buds are covered with fine down, which makes them look as if they are covered with frost. The pinnate leaves, up to 17.5cm/7in long, have up to seven oval to ovate leaflets, each up to 10cm/4in long and 5cm/2in wide. They are dark green above and silver-green beneath, with a purple tinge to the leaf stalks. The flowers are creamy-white, borne in pendulous clusters, followed in late summer by attractive deep purple fruits.

Distribution: Central China.
Height: 7m/23ft
Shape: Broadly spreading
Deciduous
Pollinated: Insect
Leaf shape: Pinnate

Left: Each leaf has between five and seven leaflets.

Right: Purple-brown single-winged seeds appear in late summer.

Afghan Ash

Fraxinus xanthoxyloides

This small shrubby ash is native to dry valleys in the north-western Himalayas and Afghanistan. It was first cultivated in central and western Europe in the 1870s. It is not common in cultivation, but can be found in some botanic gardens and arboreta, where it is quite often grafted on to the common ash, *F. excelsior*. It is not immediately recognizable as an ash, having leaflets of variable shape and size.

Identification: The bark is dull grey-brown and smooth, even in maturity. The leaves, leaf stalks and young shoots may be covered in a fine white down on some trees and be entirely hairless on others. Each leaf has between five and nine leaflets – sometimes as many as 13. The leaflets are usually lanceolate or narrowly elliptic, up to 5cm/2in long and 2cm/¾in broad. The flowers are borne in short, dense clusters in the leaf axils in early spring.

Distribution: North-west Himalayas and Afghanistan.
Height: 8m/26ft
Shape: Broadly spreading
Deciduous
Pollinated: Insect
Leaf shape: Pinnate

Right: Each leaf is made up of smaller leaflets.

Chinese Ash

Fraxinus sogdiana

This small tree, a native of Turkistan, was introduced into the St Petersburg Botanic Garden in 1891, and from there into much of central, and eventually western, Europe. It is an elegant small tree, growing to 10m/33ft, with green shoots and pinnate leaves with between seven and eleven lanceolate, toothed leaflets, which are attached to the midrib by a short leaf stalk.

Distribution: Central Asia
Height: 10m/33ft
Shape: Broadly spreading
Deciduous
Pollinated: Insect
Leaf shape: Pinnate

Identification: The bark is silver-grey and smooth even in maturity. The shoots are bright green. The leaves are produced in whorls of three towards the tips of the branches. Each leaf is made up of between seven and eleven leaflets. Each leaflet is dull olive-green and bears distinctive teeth around the leaf margin. Each leaf is attached to the shoot by a short leaf stalk. The flowers are white, borne in clusters up to 5cm/2in long. In the autumn they turn rich butter yellow before falling.

Left: The leaflets are typical of the species in their size and shape.

Left: The seeds appear in the autumn.

OTHER SPECIES OF NOTE

Syrian Ash *Fraxinus angustifolia* subsp. *syriaca*
This rare small ash, first cultivated in Europe in 1880, is sometimes still referred to as *F. syriaca*. It has bright, apple-green pinnate leaves, densely borne in whorls of three. Each leaf is made up of between three and seven lanceolate, sharply toothed leaflets. This ash is recognizable from a distance by its crowded, dense foliage.

Golden Ash *Fraxinus excelsior* 'Jaspidea'
This is a fast-growing and popular cultivar of the common ash, *F. excelsior*, which was raised in the 1870s. It produces bright orange-yellow shoots, which are very conspicuous when the tree is bare of leaves in winter, and golden yellow autumn leaf colour. It is sometimes wrongly named as *F. excelsior* 'Aurea', which is, in fact, a golden-leaved dwarf ash.

Weeping Ash *Fraxinus excelsior* 'Pendula'
Originally discovered growing wild in Cambridgeshire, England, in the 18th century, this beautiful structural tree with weeping branches, which form a spreading umbrella-like canopy, is widely planted in parks and gardens throughout Europe. Most trees are grafted on to the common ash, *F. excelsior*, at 3–5m/10–16ft above the ground. It does not grow much above the point of grafting.

Griffith's Ash

Fraxinus griffithii

This handsome ash, native to northern India, Burma and south-west China, and slightly tender, was introduced into Europe in 1900 by the plant collector Ernest Wilson. It has a tidy form and bright green shiny leaves, which are evergreen in warm winter climates and semi-evergreen to deciduous in colder regions of northern and western Europe. It has a leaf that is reminiscent of Chinese privet, *Ligustrum lucidum.*

Identification: The bark is pale grey and smooth and the young shoots are angular and bright green. The leaves are pinnate, with five to eleven ovate, glossy, bright green leathery leaflets, each up to 7.5cm/3in long, and tapering to a blunt point at the tip. Griffith's ash has large, fluffy, open panicles of creamy-white, slightly fragrant flowers, which are borne in late spring. They are followed by loose clusters of single winged seeds, which ripen to brown in the autumn and persist on the tree into winter.

Distribution: Northern India and south-east Asia.
Height: 11m/36ft
Shape: Broadly spreading
Semi-evergreen
Pollinated: Insect
Leaf shape: Pinnate

Left: The shiny green leaves are smaller than typical ash.

Fraxinus paxiana

Distribution: Northern India, Himalayas and western China.
Height: 20m/65ft
Shape: Broadly spreading
Deciduous
Pollinated: Insect
Leaf shape: Pinnate

This distinctive, medium-sized Asian ash is a member of the Ornus section of the genus – the group of about 15 species that bear terminal, rather than lateral, inflorescences – also known as flowering ashes. As such, it produces large clusters of white flowers in late spring. It was introduced into Europe from western China in 1901. It has large winter buds and stiff young shoots. It is uncommon in European parks and gardens but normally represented in botanic gardens and arboreta.

Identification: The bark of *F. paxiana* is light grey and smooth. The winter leaf buds are conspicuously large and are covered with velvety brown down, resembling moleskin. The leaves are pinnate, up to 30cm/12in long, with between seven and nine toothed, lanceolate leaflets, each up to 15cm/6in long and 5cm/2in wide, and running to a slender point. Panicles of creamy-white flowers, up to 25cm/10in across, are carried on the tree in late spring and early summer.

Left: After flowering, clusters of brown single-winged seeds are produced.

Left: With each individual leaflet up to 15cm/6in long, the leaves can become huge.

SPINDLE TREES

This genus of small trees and large shrubs is extremely diverse. They thrive in almost any soil including chalk. They are widely grown as ornamental trees in European gardens for their autumn leaf colour and fruits. Spindles are found growing wild right across the Northern Hemisphere from Japan to Great Britain and are common in gardens, parks and in hedgerows.

Winged Spindle

Euonymus alatus

This distinctive, slow-growing small tree, or large shrub, has been planted throughout Europe since its introduction from China in 1860. It has conspicuous corky bark and angular branches that develop thin, corky wings. It is one of the best spindles for autumn colour, turning deep scarlet-pink.

Distribution: China and Japan.
Height: 3m/10ft
Shape: Broadly spreading
Deciduous
Pollinated: Insect
Leaf shape: Oval to obovate

Identification: Instantly recognizable by its corky winged branches, the tree has a rather stiff habit and is often wider than it is tall. It has narrow dark green leaves, finely toothed around the margin, up to 7.5cm/3in long and 2.5cm/1in broad. The flowers are small, greenish-yellow and insignificant. The fruits, which appear in late summer, are purple-red; four small pods, joined at the base, open when ripe to reveal bright orange seeds.

Left: The vividly coloured fruits ripen in autumn.

Right: The dark green leaves turn brilliant red.

Common Spindle Tree

Euonymus europaeus

This common small tree inhabits woodland edges and hedgerows throughout most of Europe. The name "spindle" comes from the fact that the tree has very hard, dense wood, which was at one time used to make spindles, skewers, charcoal and clothes pegs (pins). In the Victorian era it was commonly called skewerwood. The spindle tree is one of the best small European trees for autumn colour.

Distribution: Europe and western Asia.
Height: 6m/20ft
Shape: Broadly spreading
Deciduous
Pollinated: Insect
Leaf shape: Elliptic to ovate

Identification: The stem bark is smooth and grey. However, young twigs are angular and may have a covering of thin, corky bark. The leaves are pale green, elliptic to ovate, to 7.5cm/3in long and 2.5cm/1in wide, finely toothed and running to a short point at the tip. In autumn they turn purple-red and yellow before falling. The flowers are small and greenish-white, borne in clusters in the leaf axils in early summer. The fruits, which appear in autumn, are bright pink, and open like parasols to reveal bright orange-coated seeds.

Right: The yellow-green leaves turn purple-yellow in autumn.

Left: The seed is contained within a bright pink or pink/red capsule.

Euonymus latifolius

This small tree, or large spreading shrub, which has a rather lax crown, has been in cultivation in western Europe since 1730. It is planted in gardens and parks for its vibrant autumn displays of fruit, seeds and foliage. In many ways this is a more ornamental tree than its European cousin, *E. europaeus*, having larger fruit and a more graceful habit.

Identification: The bark is smooth and grey and the young shoots are angular. The leaves are oval, sometimes oblong, a dull grass-green, to 12.5cm/5in long and 5cm/2in broad, finely and evenly toothed and running to a short point. Their autumn colours range from wine-purple to light pink and orange. The fruits are pendulous and bright scarlet, opening to reveal bright orange-coated seeds.

Distribution: Europe, the Caucasus and northern Iran.
Height: 6m/20ft
Shape: Broadly spreading
Deciduous
Pollinated: Insect
Leaf shape: Oval to oblong

Right: The scarlet fruits have four or five winged lobes.

OTHER SPECIES OF NOTE

Euonymus verrucosus
A native of Eastern Europe and western Asia, cultivated in Austria since 1763, this small, densely branched tree, to 3m/10ft tall, has conspicuous and distinctive "warts" along the younger branches. It has ovate leaves, which turn red and lemon in autumn. The fruit capsule may be yellow or red and contains orange-coated seeds.

Euonymus oxyphyllus
This handsome, slow-growing small tree, or large shrub, which is native to Japan, Korea and China, has been widely planted in parks and gardens since its introduction into Europe in 1895. It produces wine-red leaves in autumn at the same time as rich maroon-pink pendulous fruits containing bright orange-coated seeds.

Euonymus illicifolius
This unusual euonymus has evergreen, holly-like leaves, which are thick, spined and glossy green. It is native to central China and although introduced into Europe in 1930 it has never been widely cultivated. It is rather tender and will not grow outdoors in northern Europe. It produces round, white seed capsules that contain orange-coated seeds.

Euonymus europaeus 'Red Cascade'
This popular cultivar of the common spindle was raised in England just after World War II. It is similar in size and leaf shape to the species but has graceful, long, arching branches, which in autumn weep under the weight of a profusion of bright red fruits.

Chinese Spindle Tree

Euonymus hamiltonianus

The sight of a good specimen of *E. hamiltonianus*, its branches dripping with bright fruits set against beautiful coloured foliage, is one of the joys of autumn. It is a Himalayan species, which grows in China and Japan and was introduced into Europe in the early 20th century by Ernest Wilson. There are several varieties and sub-species, some of which are now more common in cultivation than the species.

Identification: The bark is dark grey-brown and smooth. The leaves are variable in shape and anywhere between 5cm/2in and 15cm/6in long. In autumn they turn copper-red on the top side, but beneath may be pale fawn. The fruits are pale pink capsules, borne on long stalks and ripening to reveal deep pink-orange coated seeds.

Above: The pink fruits.

Right: The leaves are arranged opposite.

Distribution: Asia.
Height: 9m/30ft
Shape: Broadly spreading
Deciduous
Pollinated: Insect
Leaf shape: Variable, ovate to obovate

BEANS, FOXGLOVE AND VARNISH TREES

The catalpas make up a genus of eleven species of beautiful flowering trees. Along with the foxglove trees they produce some of the largest leaves of any temperate deciduous tree. Catalpas have a strong resistance to atmospheric pollution and are commonly planted in towns and cities across warmer regions of Europe. The genus Rhus *includes the very popular Stag's-horn sumach.*

Varnish tree

Rhus verniciflua

The sap of this handsome Asian tree is the source of the varnish used to give a high-gloss finish to Chinese and Japanese lacquerware. Oil extracted from the fruit is also used in China to make candles. However, almost all parts of the tree are poisonous and if they contact the skin they may cause irritation and blistering. *R. verniciflua* was cultivated in Europe before 1862.

Identification: This is an open-branched tree with light grey-brown bark, smooth at first, becoming vertically and shallowly fissured in maturity. The pinnate leaves, up to 60cm/24in long, are divided into 7–19 broadly ovate leaflets, each to 15cm/6in long. These are bright green above, paler beneath with some hairs. Large drooping panicles of small yellow-white flowers are produced in summer. On female trees they are followed by pea-sized yellow fruits.

Left: The flowers are pea-sized and appear in panicles in late summer.

Right: The leaves were traditionally used to extract tannin.

Distribution: China, Japan and eastern Himalayas.
Height: 20m/65ft
Shape: Broadly spreading
Deciduous
Pollinated: Insect
Leaf shape: Pinnate

Farge's Catalpa

Catalpa fargesii

This beautiful flowering Chinese tree is named after the French Jesuit missionary Paul Farges, who discovered it in western China in 1896. Since then it has been widely grown in both Europe and North America for its delicate pink flowers, which appear in early to mid-summer, several weeks earlier than its American counterpart, *C. bignonioides*. The form *duclouxii* is the most common in cultivation.

Above: Each broadly ovate leaf may be up to 15cm/6in long.

Identification: The bark is dark grey, becoming scaly and peeling to reveal grey-pink fresh bark beneath. The leaves are broadly ovate, with the occasional small side lobe (not always present), and up to 15cm/6in long and 12.5cm/5in wide. They are bronze when first emerging from buds, becoming bright green with a slight sheen by late spring. Farge's catalpa has bell-shaped flowers, which are light pink with maroon spots and a yellow blotch at the entrance to the flower throat. These are followed by pendulous seed pods, up to 45cm/18in long.

Distribution: China.
Height: 20m/65ft
Shape: Broadly columnar
Deciduous
Pollinated: Insect
Leaf shape: Broadly ovate

Right: Long brown-black pendulous seed pods appear in autumn.

Foxglove Tree

Princess tree *Paulownia tomentosa*

This beautiful flowering tree is native to central China, and is perfectly hardy in Europe. It takes its genus name from Anna Paulownia, the daughter of Tsar Paul I of Russia. The spectacular pale purple, foxglove-like flowers appear on spikes in late spring. The timber has a resinous quality and was used in China and Japan to make a stringed instrument similar to a lute. *Paulownia* is quite often coppiced to enhance its foliage, which on juvenile shoots can be up to 45cm/18in across.

Identification: The bark is rather like that of beech, being grey and smooth, even in maturity. The leaves are ovate, up to 45cm/18in wide and long, heart-shaped at the base with two large, but normally shallow, lobes on each side. They are dark green, with hair on both surfaces and shoots. The shoots are soft and pithy. Each trumpet-shaped, pale purple flower, blotched inside with dark purple and yellow, is 5cm/2in long. The flowers are on upright panicles up to 45cm/18in tall.

Distribution: Central and eastern China.
Height: 20m/65ft
Shape: Broadly columnar
Deciduous
Pollinated: Insect
Leaf shape: Ovate

Left: The fruit is a green, pointed, egg-shaped, woody capsule containing several winged seeds. The purple flowers resemble foxgloves.

OTHER SPECIES OF NOTE

Stag's-horn sumach *Rhus typhina*
This North American, spreading and sparsely branched tree, to 10m/33ft, was first cultivated in Europe as early as 1629. It is now widely planted in gardens throughout Europe. It is quite distinctive, with downy thick shoots, large pinnate leaves and upright, candle-like, red hairy fruits.

Potanin's sumach *Rhus potaninii*
This sumach, first cultivated in Europe in 1902, grows to 20m/65ft in its native China, with a neat, round-topped form. In cultivation it is usually a smaller, multi-stemmed tree. It is grown for the autumn colours of its large pinnate leaves, which may be burgundy, bright red or orange.

Rhus trichocarpa
From mountainous country in China, Japan and Korea, this is a small, broadly spreading tree, to 8m/26ft, with large pinnate leaves made up of 17 taper-pointed leaflets, each 10cm/4in long. It is widely cultivated in Europe for its beautiful autumn leaf colour, which is rich marmalade-orange.

Empress Tree *Paulownia fargesii*
This perfectly hardy, fast-growing, handsome Chinese tree, to 20m/65ft tall, produces fragrant foxglove-like white flowers, with dark purple speckles in the throat. It appears to be hardier than the foxglove tree, *P. tomentosa*, and flowers at an early age. It has large ovate leaves, which on pruned stems may be up to 60cm/24in across.

Indian Bean Tree

Catalpa bignonioides

The Indian referred to in the name is in fact the Native American who used to wear the seeds. This is one of the last trees in its region to flower, and is normally at its best in mid-summer. It is hardy throughout Europe. It tolerates atmospheric pollution well and has become a firm favourite for planting in towns and cities, despite its broadly spreading crown.

Identification: The tree has grey-brown bark, becoming loose and flaking in patches in maturity. The leaves are broadly ovate, up to 25cm/10in long and 15cm/6in wide, rarely lobed and heart-shaped at the base. On emerging from the bud they are bronze-coloured, gradually turning grass-green with some hair beneath. Each leaf is borne on a long, lax leaf stalk. The branches are quite brittle and prone to breakage in summer.

Distribution: South-east USA.
Height: 20m/65ft
Shape: Broadly spreading
Deciduous
Pollinated: Insect
Leaf shape: Ovate

Right: The seed pods are 40cm/16in long.

Below: Each of the trumpet-shaped flowers is up to 5cm/2in long.

TAMARISKS

The tamarisks are a beautiful group of small, elegant trees that thrive in warm, sunny locations. They are found growing wild throughout southern Europe and are often planted in coastal locations because they withstand exposure and salt spray extremely well. They have graceful slender branches, plume-like foliage and small pink flowers, which are often produced in profusion.

French Tamarisk

Tamarix gallica

Like most tamarisks, French tamarisk thrives in coastal locations and copes with salt spray, exposed conditions and periods of drought. Originally native to an area running from coastal north-west France southwards to North Africa, this species has become widely naturalized elsewhere in Europe, including the south coast of Britain. If regularly pruned, tamarisk makes a good windproof hedge; unpruned it soon becomes wide-spreading and straggly.

Identification: The bark on the main stems is brown; on branches and new growth it is purple-brown. The leaves are scale-like, like those of juniper. They are blue-green, without any hairs, and very small, creating an overall feathery appearance. The flowers, which are white flushed with pink on the outside, are also very small and crowded on lax, slender racemes, which may be up to 5cm/2in long. They appear in late summer on shoots from the previous year, in such profusion that the whole crown may appear to be just flowers.

Distribution: South-west Europe.
Height: 8m/26ft
Shape: Broadly spreading
Deciduous
Pollinated: Insect
Leaf shape: Scale-like

Left: The tiny leaves and flowers give the whole plant a soft, feathery look.

Left: The individual flowers are star-shaped and soft pink.

Tamarix ramosissima

Otherwise known as *T. pentandra*, this rather sprawling, multi-stemmed small tree has a wide natural distribution that runs from southern Russia south through most of temperate Asia. It has been cultivated in Europe since 1885 and is a popular garden tree, particularly in coastal locations. Pruning stems to the ground quickly stimulates new growth. There are two main cultivars that have been developed from the species and are commonly found in gardens, 'Rubra' and 'Rosea'.

Distribution: Western and central Asia.
Height: 6m/20ft
Shape: Broadly spreading
Deciduous
Pollinated: Insect
Leaf shape: Scale-like

Left: Tiny pink flowers are borne in long slender racemes throughout the summer. They are as fine as the leaves.

Identification: The bark of each mature stem is reddish-brown; it is smooth at first, becoming finely fissured in maturity. The current year's shoots are green-yellow, darkening to reddish-brown as they mature. The leaves are bright green, without any hairs. They are scale-like, like those of juniper, and very small, giving the tree an overall feathery appearance. The very small flowers, which are pink, are borne in slender racemes up to 5cm/2in long. They are carried in profusion, on the current year's shoots, in late summer.

Tamarix parviflora

This beautiful, spreading, multi-stemmed small tree is native to the coastal regions bordering the Aegean Sea, through the Balkans and possibly even in North Africa, where it thrives in dry, infertile and salty soils. It has been cultivated elsewhere in Europe, particularly in parks, since at least 1853, and has become naturalized in central and southern Europe. It differs from most other tamarisk species in that the flowers appear on the old wood in spring, rather than on the current year's growth in late summer.

Identification: The mature bark of *T. parviflora* is brown or purplish-brown. The bark on new growth is purple. The branches are long and have a graceful arching habit. Each shoot is covered in very small, bright-green, scale-like deciduous leaves. The flowers, which are small and appear in late spring, are deep pink, sometimes stained purple, and carried in much profusion, in lax racemes about 5cm/2in long, which are densely arranged along the branches.

Distribution: South-east Europe.
Height: 6m/20ft
Shape: Broadly spreading
Deciduous
Pollinated: Insect
Leaf shape: Scale-like

Right: Each shoot is covered in small, bright green scale-like leaves.

Left: The flowers of T. parviflora have only four petals.

OTHER SPECIES OF NOTE

Canary Tamarisk *Tamarix canariensis*
As its name suggests, this shrubby, small tree is native to the Canary Islands and is to be found growing wild on all the islands except El Hierro. It is multi-stemmed and has red-brown bark, small, scale-like grey-green leaves, which are arranged alternately on the branches, and thin, spike-like racemes of pink-white flowers. In the Canaries it is cultivated as a windbreak for crop protection.

Chinese Tamarisk
Tamarix chinensis
This native of eastern and central Asia has been cultivated in Europe since at least the 1830s. It is a small tree, or large shrub, of dense habit, with distinctive, very thin branches. It has small, scale-like, pale green foliage. The flowers, which are dark pink in bud, become pale pink on opening, in late spring, on the previous year's wood.

Tamarix ramosissima 'Rosea'
This beautiful tamarisk was raised in Orleans, France, around 1883, and since then has become a popular small tree for planting in parks and gardens. The flowers are a bright rosy-pink and are densely borne on slender branching racemes, to 10cm/4in long, in late summer. Such is the profusion of flower that the foliage is completely hidden.

Tamarix tetrandra

This shrubby tamarisk is native to southern Russia, the eastern Balkans and into Iran. It has been cultivated in Europe since 1821, but is not as widespread as some of the other species. Like *T. parviflora*, it flowers on the previous year's wood in late spring or early summer, rather than on new growth in late summer. In some old collections trees labelled *T. tetrandra* var. *purpurea* are in fact *T. parviflora*.

Identification: *T. tetrandra* is unique among tamarisk species in having bark that is very dark brown, almost black. This is a distinctive feature and is helpful in identifying this particular species. The overall appearance of the tree is of an open crown with lax, rather sparse, long, dark-coloured branches. The leaves are scale-like, small and bright green. The flowers are very small and light pink. They are clustered together on racemes that may be up to 7.5cm/3in long. These racemes are densely carried on the branches.

Distribution: South-east Europe and western Asia.
Height: 5m/16ft
Shape: Broadly spreading
Deciduous
Pollinated: Insect
Leaf shape: Scale-like

Below: T. tetrandra is a perfect specimen plant for a sunny spot.

Right: The light pink flowers are stunningly pretty in spring.

PALMS AND TREE FERNS

There are about 150 genera of palms in the world. Thirty years ago, the species detailed below would have only grown in southern Europe. Recent climate warming across the region means that some now survive outside as far north as the Netherlands, Estonia and Scotland. In particular, chusan palms and tree ferns are becoming increasingly popular for planting in parks and gardens.

Canary Island Date Palm

Phoenix canariensis

This is the most majestic and stately of all palms that thrive outside the tropics, and is able to withstand several degrees of frost. Although native only to the Canary Islands, it is widely planted as an ornamental species in warm temperate regions throughout the world, commonly on sea fronts and in formal avenues. Specimens over 100 years old thrive in the gardens of Tresco in the Scilly Isles.

Far right: The fruits ripen to purple-brown in autumn.

Identification: The Canary Island date palm has a long, straight golden-brown fibrous stem with reptilian scales formed by the shedding of previous fronds. It may be up to 1.5m/5ft in diameter at the base, which tends to splay out just above ground level. The leaves are evergreen, comb-like fronds, up to 5m/16ft long, which gracefully arch skywards before drooping towards the tip. Golden yellow flower spikes, up to 2m/6½ft long, are borne in spring, followed in warm climates on female trees by bunches of purple-brown fruits.

Distribution: Canary Islands.
Height: 12m/40ft
Shape: Palm-like
Evergreen
Pollinated: Insect
Leaf shape: Pectinate

Chusan palm

Chinese windmill palm *Trachycarpus fortunei*

Despite this tree's image as a tender desert island native, it does, in fact, originate from the mountains of China, and is perfectly hardy in warm regions of Europe. It was introduced into Europe in 1830 by the German botanist Philipp von Siebold, though not from China: Siebold sent seeds home from a tree he had found growing in Japan. Today, the chusan palm is commonly found as an ornamental, planted in coastal parks and gardens throughout Europe, including coastal regions of south-west Britain.

Identification: The bark is covered with grey-brown fibrous hairs and is clearly marked with discarded leaf scars. The leaves are fan-shaped, stiff, and blue-green, up to 1.2m/4ft across, and divided almost to the base into approximately 40 linear and pointed strips. They are joined to the tree by a stiff leaf stalk. The flowers are small, fragrant and golden yellow, borne in large drooping panicles in early summer.

Far left: The flowers are golden yellow and fragrant.

Left and right: The blue-green leaves are fan shaped.

Distribution: Central and southern China.
Height: 12m/40ft
Shape: Palm-like
Evergreen
Pollinated: Insect
Leaf shape: Fan-shaped

Tree Fern

Australian tree fern *Dicksonia antarctica*

Since their introduction into Europe in 1880, tree ferns have become a favourite for planting in warm, wet regions, where they thrive and bring a touch of the exotic to temperate gardens. Strictly speaking they are not trees at all but true ferns, but their interest lies in the fact that they reach tree-like proportions. The trunk is made up of the fibrous remains of old roots. New roots grow down the trunk each year, to enable the fern to produce a new set of fronds. Growth is slow, normally less than 5cm/2in in height each year. Some fronds may live for two years.

Identification: The surface of the trunk is soft, fibrous and chestnut-brown. Under this surface covering is a black, bone-like woody core. In winter the tree resembles little more than an upright log. In spring new fronds unfurl from the top of the trunk. Each frond is like a typical fern leaf but larger, up to 4m/13ft long. The upper surface of the leaf is a dark but rich green, the lower surface paler and duller, and close inspection reveals light brown spores at regular intervals along each frond.

Distribution: South-eastern Australia and Tasmania.
Height: 7m/23ft
Shape: Palm-like
Semi-evergreen
Pollinated: Wind
Leaf shape: Fern-like

Right: Each leaf is like a fern frond but may be up to 4m/13ft long.

Jelly Palm *Butia capitata*
Otherwise known as *Cocos capitata*, and also commonly known as the pindo palm, this beautiful, small palm is native to Brazil, but has been widely cultivated in southern coastal areas of the USA, and is planted in south-west Europe. It has grey-green to silver arching fronds and fragrant yellow flowers, which are tinged with purple. These are followed by yellow or orange round fruits, with a flavour reminiscent of apricots, pineapple and bananas, which can be used to make jelly or wine.

Cabbage Palm *Cordyline australis*
This slow-growing, palm-like tree, to 10m/33ft tall, is in fact a member of the lily family. It is native to New Zealand and has been grown in Europe since 1823. New Zealand Maoris used to eat the tender tips of the shoots, hence its common name. It is widely cultivated right across the warmer coastal regions of Europe, including south-western Britain. In early summer the tree produces masses of fragrant, creamy-white flowers.

Cabbage Palmetto *Sabal palmetto*
This tall palm, to 25m/80ft, is native to south-eastern USA and the West Indies, but has been widely cultivated in parks and gardens across the Mediterranean region of Europe. It has fan-shaped leaves that are palmately divided and may be up to 3m/10ft long, with a prominently arching midrib. Creamy to yellowish-white flowers are borne in drooping clusters in summer.

Dwarf Fan Palm

European fan palm *Chamaerops humilis*

This is the only member of the palm family that is truly native to mainland Europe. It is found growing wild in Spain, Gibraltar, Italy, Sardinia, Sicily, Algeria and Morocco, where it inhabits mountainsides in coastal regions. It is widely cultivated in mild coastal regions in other parts of Europe, including southern and western Britain, but is not as hardy as the chusan palm, *Trachycarpus fortunei*. It has been in cultivation since 1731. Most specimens do not exceed 2m/6½ft tall.

Identification: The overall appearance of this palm tree is of a dense semicircular mass of stiff, grey-green, fan-shaped leaves on a short trunk, which is covered with stiff dark grey-brown fibres towards the top. The large fan-shaped leaves are green to grey-green. They can measure up to 90cm/36in across, and are divided nearly to the base into stiff, pointed segments, which may be up to 45cm/18in long. Each leaf is attached to the trunk by a thick leaf stalk, of variable length, which is armed with sharp, forward-pointing spines. The flowers are small and yellow and are borne in a stiff upright panicle, to 15cm/6in long.

Distribution: Southern Europe and North Africa.
Height: 2.5m/8ft
Shape: Palm-like
Evergreen
Pollinated: Insect
Leaf shape: Fan-shaped

Above: The yellow flowers are stiff upright panicles.

Below: The pointed leaf segments.

TREES OF AFRICA, ASIA AND AUSTRALASIA

Within the tropical, subtropical and temperate areas of Africa, Asia and Australia is a very wide range of diverse habitats. These include ferociously hot dry deserts, humid and windless lowland forests, cool temperate-like montane areas and coastal mangrove swamps.

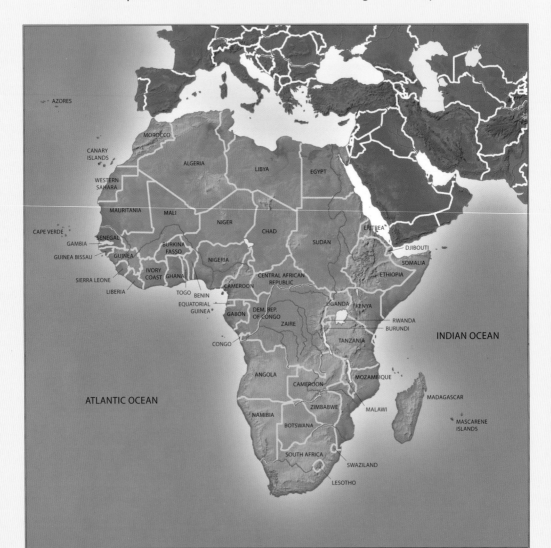

Constant factors are the high light intensity and day length, which
fluctuates around 12 hours throughout the year, and the resulting weak
seasonality. Trees receive plenty of light, and the majority are evergreen.
Within these pages there are many stunning tree specimens, from the
Australian Flame Tree and the Cape Chestnut tree to the Burmese Fish-
tail Palm and the Tropical Almond Tree. Many tropical trees demonstrate
cauliflory, whereby flowers and fruit emerge directly from the trunk,
enabling easier access for pollination by wind, insects, bats and birds.

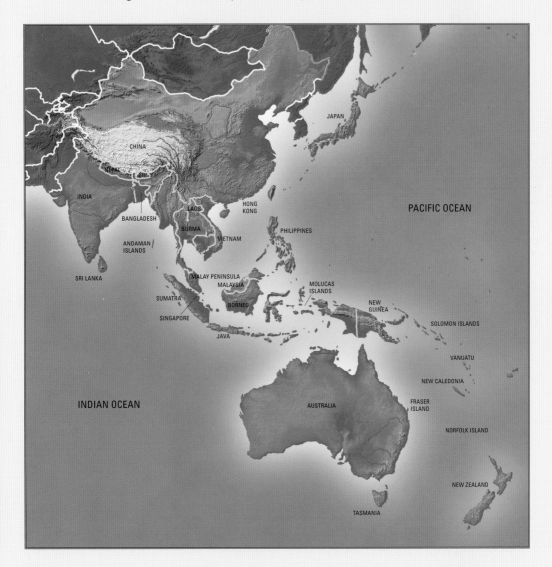

CONIFERS

*Gymnosperms include all of the plants known as conifers, in which the naked seeds
are held within a cone. The majority are evergreen trees with leaves reduced to needles or scales.
Many of them live to a great age. Incredibly, for such a large and ancient group, they are
relatively rare in the tropics.*

Hoop Pine

Araucaria cunninghamii

This species occurs naturally in drier rainforests, although most wild
trees have been cut down for timber. The hoop pine is incredibly slow
growing and long lived, growing at only 2–3mm (⅛in) a year when
mature and living for up to 450 years. The tight clusters of foliage
around the branches give the tree the appearance of having soft,
fluffy protruding arms.

Identification: The young bark is coppery but matures to become rough and then
peels horizontally, resulting in lines or "hoops". The short horizontal branches carry
branchlets in dense tufts at their tips. The juvenile leaves are 1–2cm (⅜–¾in) long,
bright green and have a sharp tip. When mature, the leaves become tiny, pointed,
inward-curving scales. Hoop pines may not produce cones until they are 200 years
old. The male cones are spike shaped and 5–8cm (2–3in) long. The female cones
are 10cm (4in) long x 8cm (3in) wide and appear through the
winter. When ripe, cones fall apart
releasing winged seed.

*Far left: The female cone
contains naked seeds.*

*Left: A branchlet of
tiny scale leaves.*

Distribution: New South
Wales and Queensland,
Australia and New Guinea.
Height: 60m (200ft)
Shape: Columnar
Evergreen
Pollinated: Wind
Leaf shape: Lanceolate,
curved

Queensland Kauri

Agathis robusta

Distribution: South
Queensland and Frasier
Island, Australia.
Height: 45m (150ft)
Shape: Conical
Evergreen
Pollinated: Wind
Leaf shape: Ovate

*Far right: The unusual broad
foliage of the Queensland kauri.*

Right: A hard female cone.

An emergent tree of subtropical rainforest, the
Queensland kauri is also found at the bottom of valleys
and in small clearings. The thick trunk, reaching 4m/13ft
in girth, tapers very little and is often free of branches
for two-thirds of its height. Consequently, the timber is
knot free with a straight grain. It is also strong and
durable, making it valuable, and this species is now
under threat.

Identification: The trunk is coated in highly
resinous, thick, rough, flaky, brown bark. The whorled
horizontal side branches remain short while the tree is
young. They carry spirally arranged leaves, which will
persist on the tree for many years. The immature leaves
are a reddish colour. When mature they are ovate,
10–15cm (4–6in) long, 9–10cm (3½–4in) wide, dark green,
thick and leathery with longitudinal lines on the upper
surface, and paler green below. The male catkins emerge
singly from the leaf axils and are 3–5cm (1¼–2in) long. The woody
female cones are ovoid, 10–13cm (4–5in) long, 9–10cm (3½–4in) wide
and covered in 2.5cm (1in-wide) scales.

Bunya-Bunya

Araucaria bidwillii

This slow-growing, distinctive tree
has a symmetrical form. The
long, horizontal, whorled
branches and foliage are sparse
low down the trunk, whereas
in the crown they are dense
with the foliage clustering
to the ends of the twigs.
The seed-bearing cones
are an impressive sight,
weighing up to 8kg
(18lbs) and looking
remarkably like large,
green pineapples.
The seeds are eaten
by Australia's
aboriginal people.

Distribution: Coastal south-
east Queensland, Australia.
Height: 45m (150ft)
Shape: Domed
Evergreen
Pollinated: Wind
Leaf shape: Lanceolate,
curved

*Right: The male
cones release
pollen.*

Identification: The thick, pale bark is resinous and
peels off the trunk. The leaves are arranged spirally
and densely clustered at the end of the branches.
Each leaf is 5cm (2in) long, 1cm (½in) wide,
lanceolate, curved, bright to dark green and leathery
with a stiff, prickly point at the tip. The male cones
are 15–18cm (6–7in) long and 1.5cm (½in) wide. The
female cones are 30cm (12in) long and 23cm (9in)
wide, and carry up to 150 seeds.

*Below: The foliage
is spiny to the
touch.*

OTHER SPECIES OF NOTE

Norfolk Island Pine *Araucaria heterophylla*
From Norfolk Island but not a pine, this beautiful, fast-growing
conifer reaches 60m (200ft) and grows successfully throughout
the tropics. In Hawaii, plantations provide timber for ships' masts.
The Norfolk Island pine is a very symmetrical, formal looking tree.
It stands upright and has a conical shape with a regular branching
pattern. The soft, curved leaves are bright green and glossy. This
tree will thrive in deep sand and is wind tolerant, and as a result,
is often seen planted in coastal locations. Due to its tolerance of
low light levels when young, it is sold as a houseplant in
temperate climates.

Amboina Pine *Agathis dammara*
Agathis is an ancient plant genus very closely allied to *Araucaria*.
All parts of these trees spontaneously exude a resin called
dammar (or damar), which is collected and used commercially in
varnishes and the making of linoleum. The amboina pine grows
in dense clumps in the rainforests of Sumatra and peninsular
Malaysia. It grows to 55m (180ft) tall, has grey or black bark and
ovate, dark green, 6–12cm (2½–5in) long leaves. The male cones
are 4–7cm (1½–3in) long spikes, the female cones are ovoid,
6–8.5cm (2½–3in) long.

Blue Kauri *Agathis atropurpurea*
This tree grows in the montane rainforest of northern
Queensland, where it is protected from over-exploitation across
large areas. It reaches 60m (200ft) tall and has a purplish-brown or
black bark which usually peels into irregular flakes that become
thicker on more mature trees. The leaves are oblong to elliptic
with a blunt notched tip, 4cm (1½in) long and tightly arranged.
The male cones are 1.5cm (½in) long. The female cones are olive
green, round and 3.5–5.5cm (1½–2in) across.

Dacrydium elatum
This interesting conifer has leaves of two forms, some are tiny
and triangular, packed tightly together to form green stems, while
others are four-sided, needle-like and up to 2cm (¾in) long. The
fine foliage is greyish green. The tree grows from India through to
mainland Malaysia in highland forested areas. It is particularly
prevalent in Malaysia where it is scattered in moist rainforest,
growing mostly in open situations. It reaches an average height of
24m (80ft) and has a dark, fissured, scaly bark, and dense, domed
crown. The flowers of the male tree are tiny catkins, while those
of the female tree form in short spikes, producing black seeds in
a shallow, fleshy cup.

THE ANNONA FAMILY

The Annonaceae family consists mostly of tropical trees, shrubs and climbers. Annonas have a distinctive odour and smooth, simple leaves arranged alternately, or spirally in paired ranks. Flowers have both male and female organs, three sepals and two whorls of three petals. Beetles are the major pollinators. Fruit often consists of a cluster of units, sometimes fused together, and contains large, hard, smooth seeds.

Keppel Tree

Stelechocarpus burahol

Distribution: South-east Asia.
Height: Small
Evergreen
Pollinated: Beetle
Leaf shape: Narrowly oblong

Right: Keppel fruit is 8cm (3in) across and emerges directly from the trunk, a common characteristic of tropical fruit.

This endangered tree is rare both wild and cultivated. It is grown in a small area of Java for its fruit, which hangs in masses directly from the lower trunk. The fruit has a spicy, mango-like flavour. Indonesian people once believed that eating the fruit gave one's bodily secretions a pleasant aroma.

Identification: The dark green, glossy leaves alternate on the twigs and form a dense crown. When young, the leaves are deep red. The flowers are small and appear in clusters directly from the trunk. The fruit is eye-catching with rough, pale orange to cinnamon-brown skin and a pointed tip. The flesh of the fruit is orange and contains reddish-brown seeds.

Left: Smooth surfaces and pointed tips of the leaves help excess water run off.

Ylang-Ylang

Cananga odorata

This well-known tree produces fragrant flowers from which an oil (ilang-ilang) is distilled for use in the perfume industry. Ylang-ylang flowers are sold locally in markets for perfuming rooms, as temple offerings, for leis (in Hawaii) and for scenting coconut oil. The tree is fast growing on moist soil and has long, pendulous, rather brittle branches.

Identification: The glossy green leaves are 10–35cm (4–14in) long, vary in shape from oblong to elliptic and may be slightly wavy along the margins. Flowers appear in clusters throughout the year and are particularly abundant in autumn. The flowers are green when they open and gradually become yellow. They are spidery with six long, twisted, hanging petals, each 4–9cm (1½ –3½in) long. The clusters of fruit, each 1–2cm (½–1in) across, are rounded and black when ripe.

Distribution: Tropical Asia, Pacific Islands, India.
Height: 25m (80ft)
Shape: Oval crown
Evergreen
Pollinated: Beetle
Leaf shape: Oblong to elliptic

Above left: The smooth, pale grey trunk is often hidden behind awkward, drooping branches.

Left: The fragrance of the flowers is variable, and wild specimens may smell quite rank.

Indian Mast Tree

Polyalthia longifolia

This is a popular tree in parks and avenues throughout Asia. It thrives in monsoon areas but is also found next to rivers in drier regions. Indian mast trees very in their width. Some grow into upright poles of greenery, while other have a somewhat greener shape. The more columnar forms have been selected for cultivation, but many loose thier tightform when they mature, with their lower branches spreading wider.

Identification: The drooping branches have dark grey bark and clothe the trunk almost entirely to the ground with swathes of glossy green, wavy edged leaves, 15cm (6in) long. The small flower clusters appear in the leaf axils on older branchesin summer but are often hidden on the lower partof the tree by dense foliage. Each tiny star-like flower is greenish yellow and less than 1cm (½in) across. The round to oval fruit is 2 cm (¾in) long and ripens from yellow through red to black.

Above: Leaves are yellowish underneath, have wavy edges and may curl under at the tip.

Distribution: Sri Lanka.
Height: 15m (50ft)
Shape: Narrowly columnar
Evergreen
Pollinated: Insect
Leaf shape: Lanceolate

Left: Each flower results in a bunch of five to thirteen fruits which are eaten by bats.

Canary Beech *Polyalthia nitidissima*
Grown in gardens for its dark glossy foliage and bright red and yellow, inedible fruits, the canary beech grows wild in dry rainforests and damp riverside locations in the Australian states of New South Wales and Queensland, and in New Caledonia. The alternate leaves are glossy, smooth, and bright green, on short leaf stems. It grows to 18m (60ft) tall and produces small green flowers in the summer. The clustered fruit does not ripen simultaneously, so black, red, orange, yellow and green fruit may be seen together through the summer and autumn.

Yellow Lacewood *Polyalthia oblongifolia*
Found in New Guinea, it is grown for its timber, which is used in marquetry and varies from a light cream to mid-brown. It has smooth, leathery, 25cm- (10in-) long, broadly oblong, alternate leaves with prominent veins. Flower clusters form opposite or between leaves. They are 3cm (1¼in) long and have a rusty pubescence on the sepals. Small one-seeded fruit forms in clusters. Each is egg shaped, smooth and 1.5cm (½in) long.

Anaxagorea javanica
Common in Malaysia's rainforests, this small evergreen tree has beautifully scented flowers similar to ylang-ylang. The tree reaches 6m (20ft), or may grow as a shrub. Leaves are elliptic to oblong, 10–25cm (4–10in) long, light green, and blunt-ended. The 2.5cm (1in) flowers have thick, fleshy, green or cream petals and are followed by 2.5–5cm- (1–2in-) long, thin, dark green fruit. Ripe fruit fires its two small, smooth, black seeds 2–3m (3–6ft) from the tree.

African Nutmeg

Monodora myristica

This beautiful, very tropical-looking tree produces fleshy seeds high in an aromatic oil similar to nutmeg. Historically the fruit was exported from Africa to the West Indies, where the oil was extracted. The African nutmeg tree has a straight trunk and large, horizontal branches. It prefers moist ground and if grown in drier conditions may become deciduous.

Identification: The drooping leaves are bright, shining green with a prominent paler midrib and reach 60cm (24in) long. The flowers hang from the branches and are 25cm (10in) long x 15cm (6in) wide and fragrant. They have three large, frilled petals, which are bright yellow or white and fringed with purple or red and green spots. The outsides of the flowers are downy and the insides shiny. The fruits are round, dark brown and 8–20cm (3–8in) across. They have a very hard shell and hang on strong, 60cm- (24in-) long stems. The flesh and seeds of the fruit are very like true nutmeg.

Distribution: Tropical Africa, Senegal through Nigeria to Kenya.
Height: 23m (75ft)
Evergreen
Pollinated: Beetle
Leaf shape: Elliptic to obovate

Below: These beautiful and unusual flowers are thought to trap beetles inside them before they are ready to release their pollen.

THE LAUREL FAMILY

The Lauraceae family is made up mostly of aromatic, evergreen, tropical and sub-tropical trees and shrubs. The leaves are often irregularly spaced and clustered at branch tips. They are simple, generally elliptical and glossy with smooth margins – typical rainforest leaves. The six-petalled flowers are small, greenish or yellow and arranged singly along stalks in racemes. The fruit is a one-seeded berry or drupe.

Camphor Tree

Cinnamomum camphorum

Some camphor trees bear camphor oil, others solid camphor. Camphor is used in the manufacture of plastics, lacquers, explosives and film. It is also used as an insect repellent and has medicinal properties. Camphor is extracted by distilling the wood, roots, twigs and leaves of the tree in water. This fast-growing species can be an invasive pest. It has a dense crown up to 21m (70ft) in diameter and low heavy branches on the short trunk. In some cities, camphor is grown along streets as a shade tree.

Right: The heavily fissured bark of a mature camphor tree.

Identification: The bark is coppery on young wood and ages to become grey brown and heavily fissured. The young leaves are a pinkish coppery colour, maturing through pale to deep, glossy green. They are 13cm (5in) long, ovate, have three veins, are leathery and smell of camphor, if crushed. The flowers are tiny and greenish yellow. The fruit is a small black berry.

Distribution: China, Taiwan and south Japan.
Height: 30m (100ft)
Shape: Rounded spreading crown
Evergreen
Pollinated: Insect
Leaf shape: Ovate

Right: The flowers and fruit of the camphor tree are insignificant. The leaves are distilled to extract camphor.

Cinnamon

Cinnamomum zeylanicum

Cinnamon spice is obtained by peeling the bark from young trunks and branches and drying it into quills. To ensure a regular supply of young bark the trees are often grown as coppiced specimens. All parts of the tree above ground are highly aromatic. Cinnamon is grown on a large scale in its native Sri Lanka but has become an invasive weed in the Seychelles, where it has spread rapidly.

Identification: The bark is light brown and papery when mature, and cinnamon-coloured when young. The smooth leaves are eye-catching; they are bright red and droopy for a few days when young and gradually mature to become glossy green with three distinctive white parallel veins. Pale below, they grow to 18cm (7in) long. The insignificant but numerous, tiny flowers are found in loose racemes and are off-white or pale yellow. The very dark purple to black fruit is less than 1cm (½in) across and equally easy to miss.

Above: Cinnamon bark is harvested at 2–3 years old and 3cm (1¼in) in diameter for cinnamon production.

Distribution: Malaysia, Sri Lanka and southern India.
Height: 10m (33ft)
Shape: Domed
Evergreen
Pollinated: Insect
Leaf shape: Oblong

Right: The beautiful leaves have distinctive parallel veins.

Above: Large numbers of the tiny flowers form into loose racemes.

THE NUTMEG AND MAGNOLIA FAMILIES

The families Myristicaceae and Magnoliaceae are closely related to the annona family within the
Magnoliales order. The nutmeg family is made up of tropical trees and shrubs throughout Asia, Africa
and South America. They usually have aromatic wood and foliage, and seeds wrapped in a coloured aril.
The magnolia family contains trees, shrubs and climbers of temperate and subtropical regions.

Nutmeg

Myristica fragrans

Naturally found in coastal regions in the humid tropics,
nutmegs are grown commercially in Indonesia, Sri Lanka
and on the Caribbean island of Grenada. They are famed
for their hard seed containing richly scented oil and for the
bright red tissue that surrounds the seed, the spice mace.
This pretty tree has a dense, formal canopy of close set
whorls of branches. Both nutmegs and mace are used in
cooking, while nutmeg oil is used medicinally.

Identification: This slender, slow-growing tree has smooth, grey bark.
The leaves alternate on each side of the stem and are aromatic, 12cm
(4½in) long, smooth and have smooth margins. When new, they are
covered in small, silver scales, which persist on the lower
surface throughout the life of the leaf. The flowers are
produced throughout the year. They have pale yellow
sepals but no petals, and are found individually,
hanging like small bells 1cm (½in) long. Nutmeg trees are
either male or female, and only female trees produce fruit.
The fruit takes five to six months to develop; it is pear
shaped, 8cm (3in) long, pale yellow and fleshy. Each fruit
contains one brown seed (the nutmeg itself) 3–4cm (1–1¼in) long.

Distribution: Moluccas
islands of Indonesia.
Height: 15m (50ft)
Shape: Columnar
Evergreen
Pollinated: Insect
Leaf shape: Oblong-elliptic

Above: The seed has a hard
brown case and a bright red
laced aril.
Left: The simple leaves are silvery
on their lower surface.

Orange Chempaka

Michelia champaca

This tree has highly scented blossoms,
which appear all year round in truly
tropical conditions, filling the air with
their perfume. In cooler, less humid areas
it flowers only in summer. Throughout
its range, the blossoms are used as
temple offerings. The orange
chempaka is a fast-growing tree.
Conical at first, it soon becomes
oblong with horizontal branches.

Identification: The mature bark is
pale grey and smooth, whereas
the twigs are covered with short,
soft, downy hair. The light green,
silky smooth leaves droop from
the branches. They have soft hair
below and measure 28cm (11in)
long x 10cm (4in) wide. The
flowers vary in colour from white
through yellow to orange. They
have twelve long, narrow, twisted
petals, are cup shaped and sit
upright on the branch tips. Each
flower is 10–13cm (4–5in) wide
with a very sweet scent during
the day that becomes foul
smelling at night.

Distribution: India, Java,
lower Himalayas.
Height: 30m (100ft)
Shape: Oblong
Evergreen
Pollinated: Beetle
Leaf shape: Ovate-lanceolate

Above: The simple leaves
are little to go by when
identifying this tree.

Left and right: The beautifully
scented flowers often form out of
sight, high in the canopy, but their
perfume penetrates the air.

THE MULBERRY FAMILY

The diverse family Moraceae includes mostly tropical trees, shrubs, herbs, climbers and stranglers. All members have milky sap and distinctive conical caps that cover the growing tips of twigs. The leaves are simple and often large. Flowers are of one sex, generally small and clustered in spikes, discs or hollow receptacles. The fruits are fleshy with a single, hard stone, and often many are grouped into one body.

Paper Mulberry

Broussonetia papyrifera

Easy to grow, this tree is widely cultivated in eastern Asia and has naturalized in the Pacific Islands. It is a fast-growing, untidy, sprawling, sparse tree or large shrub with a rounded crown. The paper mulberry is grown primarily for the fine, smooth fibres of its inner bark. These silky fibres are extracted and made into paper and cloth.

Identification: The trunk is dark with an uneven surface. The shoots and leaves have a thick woolly surface. The alternate leaves are generally dull green, although they may vary in colour, and vary greatly in shape. Juvenile leaves may be 30cm (12in) long with two or three lobes. Mature leaves are thin, rarely lobed and have a toothed margin. They are 8–20cm (3–8in) long and nearly as wide. The male flowers are twisted catkins 4–8cm (1½–3in) long, and the female flowers have globular heads 1cm (½in) wide. The fruit appears in groups. It is 1cm (½in) across, round, red, dry and unpalatable.

Distribution: Eastern Asia, China and Japan.
Height: 15m (50ft)
Shape: Domed
Deciduous
Pollinated: Wind
Leaf shape: Ovate

Left to right: This unkempt tree has rough serrated leaves, small globular female flowers, catkins as male flowers and rounded, fuzzy fruit.

Breadfruit

Artocarpus altilis

It was the lavish attention received by breadfruit saplings that caused the infamous mutiny on the Bounty. The trees now thrive in the West Indies and are grown throughout the humid tropics for their valuable and plentiful fruit. The fruit is rich in carbohydrate, and tastes and is cooked like potato. The cooked seeds are also eaten and taste like chestnuts.

Identification: These fast-growing trees have smooth bark, ascending branches and a dense bushy crown. The leaves are very dramatic looking. They are 60–90cm (24–36in) long, ovate and deeply cut into six to nine lobes. Deep glossy green above, they have a rougher texture and are paler below. The minute green flowers are found on a round organ, which looks like a developing young fruit. The compound fruit is round or ovoid, 10–20cm (4–8in) long, weighs up to 5kg (10lbs) and is green with a bumpy surface. Breadfruit does not usually have seeds – those that do produce seeded fruit are called breadnuts.

Left: Breadfruit leaves are huge and glossy green.

Distribution: Malaysia, Indonesia, Pacific Islands.
Height: 20m (66ft)
Shape: Columnar to domed
Evergreen
Pollinated: Wind and insect
Leaf shape: Ovate

Above: The compound fruit oozes white sticky latex when cut but is a popular tropical staple.

Jackfruit

Artocarpus heterophyllus

Jackfruit trees are grown for their gigantic compound fruit, which measures up to 90cm (36in) long x 50cm (20in) across and weighs up to 18kg (40lbs). The fruit varies enormously between trees. It is full of starches – 23 per cent of the sticky, pink to golden yellow, waxy flesh is carbohydrate. Jackfruit flesh has a strong, unpleasant smell but a sweet taste. The seeds within the flesh are also eaten. These fast-growing trees are cultivated throughout the wet tropics, particularly in South-east Asia.

Identification: The reddish brown, straight trunk carries a dense crown. Juvenile leaves are often lobed, whereas mature leaves are oblong to egg shaped with the leaf stalk at the narrow end, dark green, leathery, 10–20cm (4–8in) long and downy beneath. The flowers are minute, green and emerge directly from the trunk and older branches. The fruit contains numerous 3cm- (1¼in-) long seeds with a gelatinous covering.

Distribution: India to Malaysia.
Height: 20m (66ft)
Shape: Domed, columnar
Evergreen
Pollinated: Wind and insect
Leaf shape: Obovate

Left: The yellowish green fruit has short fleshy spines and hangs from the trunk.

OTHER SPECIES OF NOTE

Common Cluster Fig *Ficus sycomorus*
This is the biblical "Sycamore Fig" that Zacchaeus the tax collector climbed to see Jesus. This species originated in the area from Egypt to Syria and is now widespread throughout Africa. It has a huge, spreading crown held up by a very thick trunk with narrow buttresses. The large leaves are ovate and smooth or slightly rough. The young leaves and leaf stalks are slightly hairy. This species' figs are found in clusters on the trunk, branches and twigs. They are 5cm (2in) wide, yellowish red, often produced abundantly. The fruits are edible and used as animal fodder.

Iroko *Milicia excelsa*
Iroko wood is very valuable because it is hard, termite resistant and durable. It is used around the world for furniture, doors, panelling, flooring and outdoor products such as garden furniture. It grows quickly for a hardwood and is a popular choice for plantations, although it often proves difficult to establish. In the wild it grows in lowland and riverine forests throughout tropical Africa, reaching heights of 50m (164ft). It is a deciduous tree and has leathery leaves up to 20cm (8in) long and 10cm (4in) wide. The mature leaves are elliptic to oblong with a notched margin; when young, they are hairy. The male flowers are 15cm (6in) spikes and hang from the branches. The female flowers are upright spikes of 5cm (2in) long by 2cm (¾in) wide. The fruit is fleshy, elliptic, 3mm (⅛in) across, soft when ripe and popular with bats and squirrels.

Bo Tree

Ficus religiosa

It is said that the Buddha was sitting beneath a bo tree when he attained enlightenment. This type of fig is incredibly long lived, with specimens thought to be more than 2,000 years old. It is sacred to Buddhists and Hindus and is regularly seen growing in the grounds of temples. A strangling climber, it may start its life on house roofs or gutters. Despite the problems this can cause, it is rarely removed, because of its sacred status.

Identification: The great trunk has slight buttressing and dark brown bark. Most mature specimens have only a few aerial roots and some surface roots. The open crown, which is as wide as the tree is tall, consists of heart-shaped leaves with long elegant tails. Each leaf is 20cm (8in) long x 15cm (6in) wide and blue-green with a pale midrib. The leaves have long stalks on which they move in the slightest breeze, and drop briefly in late winter. The tiny dark purple or brown figs grow in pairs in leaf axils along the branches.

Distribution: India, Burma, Thailand and South-east Asia.
Height: 30m (100ft)
Shape: Spreading
Deciduous
Pollinated: Wasp
Leaf shape: Cordate (deltoid)

Left: The elegant, wispy-tailed leaves of the bo tree are used in arts and crafts in the West.

FIGS

This large genus of plants, in the mulberry family, has around 750 species growing predominantly in the tropics and subtropics. Figs are enormously varied and range from small-leafed climbers to huge trees and epiphytes (plants that grow on others). The infamous "strangling" figs begin their lives as small epiphytes. Fig flowers are tiny and enclosed within a fleshy receptacle. This receptacle is the fig itself.

Banyan Tree

Ficus benghalensis

Distribution: South Asia, India, Burma, South China, Thailand.
Height: 30m (100ft)
Shape: Very low and spreading
Evergreen
Pollinated: Wasp
Leaf shape: Broadly ovate to elliptic, blunt ended

Banyans are awe-inspiring trees of often grandiose proportions. They include the largest trees in the world in terms of spread, some covering many acres. Banyans may start as epiphytes, strangling their host. The pale grey or tan trunk carries immense, low, spreading branches from which grow reddish brown aerial roots. Some of these will stiffen and thicken, forming secondary trunks. In this way, the tree spreads over huge areas. Ancient writings suggest that there may be trees now living that are more than 5,000 years old. Banyans are planted widely throughout the tropics as shade and avenue trees.

Identification: The leaves are thick, leathery, blunt ended and may reach 25cm (10in) long. Dark green with a pronounced pale yellow midrib and veins, they are used in some parts of Asia to hold food in place of plates. The figs grow in pairs in the leaf axils along the branches. Spherical, they are up to 2cm (¾in) in diameter and turn scarlet when ripe.

Above and left: The dense foliage of the banyan casts deep shade.

Fiddleleaf Fig

Ficus lyrata

A small, attractive and formal-looking tree, the fiddleleaf fig is found in tropical forests, and is sometimes planted for ornamental purposes or shade. It occasionally begins life as an epiphyte but rarely produces aerial roots.

Identification: The trunk is very dark, brown, grey or black, with deep vertical fissures. The leathery leaves are widest at their far end and reach 45cm (18in) long and 30cm (12in) wide. Dark green, glossy, and strongly marked with veins, particularly on the underside, they have wavy margins, a puckered top and may be somewhat brittle. The twigs carry dark brown, pointed, boat-shaped sheaths at the leaf bases, and the figs grow in the leaf axils near the tips of twigs, either singly or in pairs.

Distribution: Tropical west and central Africa.
Height: 12m (40ft)
Shape: Narrow
Evergreen
Pollinated: Wasp
Leaf shape: Fiddle-like

Above: The tree has an upright, stiff habit and dense canopy.

Right: The tree was named after its fiddle-shaped leaves.

Below: When ripe, the figs are round, brownish green with white specks, fleshy and 3–5cm (1–2in) in diameter.

Weeping Fig

Ficus benjamina

A graceful tree that, when mature, is wider than it is tall, the weeping fig has strongly ascending branches that weep at the tips. It grows as an epiphyte and strangler fig in forests, rocky places and by streams. The pale grey bark of the trunk, sometimes almost white, is latticed with aerial roots, which form a dense mass around the trunk but rarely fall away from it. The invasive roots can disrupt building foundations – nevertheless this tree is often planted on streets. Various varieties with dark, variegated or twisted foliage are grown as house plants in temperate regions.

Identification: The 10cm- (4in-) long alternate leaves are smooth, pale green and glossy. They are delightful shimmering in a breeze. The figs are produced throughout the year and grow in pairs in leaf axils near the end of twigs. They are attractive in their own right, changing from green through to pink, red, scarlet and deep purplish black as they ripen.

Distribution: South and South-east Asia, north Australia and south-west Pacific.
Height: 30m (100ft)
Shape: Spreading and domed
Evergreen
Pollinated: Wasp
Leaf shape: Ovate-elliptic

Left: Leaves are elegant, thin and tough.

OTHER SPECIES OF NOTE

Moreton Bay Fig *Ficus macrophylla*
This strangler from tropical Australia reaches 60m (200ft) high and has an even greater spread. The light brown or grey trunk is heavily buttressed, reaching up to 3m (10ft) in circumference. The Moreton Bay fig produces few prop roots but does have many wide, pale surface roots. The 25cm- (10in-) long leaves are glossy and leathery with bright pink persistent sheaths. The 2cm- (¾in-) wide figs occur along the twigs and are purplish brown specked with white or yellow.

Java Fig *Ficus virens*
A deciduous fig from India to the Solomon Islands and Northern Australia, this species reaches 15m (50ft) in height and has ascending branches that droop at the ends. The leaves, up to 17cm- (6½in) long, have wavy margins and long tails. The 1cm- (½in-) wide figs are white with red spots when ripe. In the northern Indian state of Sikkim the young shoots are pickled and eaten.

Rusty-leaf Fig *Ficus rubiginosa*
This fig from tropical Australia prefers moist conditions and grows to 18m (60ft) tall with a slightly wider spread. The dark grey or black trunk sometimes forms buttress roots near its base. The rusty-leaf fig gets its name from the soft, rust-coloured hairs on young cinnamon-coloured young leaves and leaf stems. Young bark is cinnamon coloured and the figs, in pairs towards twig tips, vary from yellowish green to cinnamon.

Indian Rubber Tree

Ficus elastica

A mature specimen is an impressive sight. Curtains of aerial roots form a veritable forest of high buttressed trunks, while the surface roots swarm over the soil. The tree lives wild in tropical and subtropical forests but is grown throughout Asia for shade and ornament. In temperate countries this species is known as the rubber plant and grown in pots indoors. The milky latex tapped from the trunk was the traditional rubber of commerce until *Hevea* rubber was discovered.

Identification: Each leaf measures over 30cm (12in) long and 15cm (6in) wide and has a single, prominent midrib. Young leaves are tinged pink, and a long pink or red sheath protects the growing tip. The leaves form a dense crown at the end of clear branches. The oval, 2cm- (¾in-) long, greenish-yellow figs are crowded in pairs in the leaf axils towards the ends of twigs on trees over 20 years old. Figs are produced all year round.

Right: The spirally arranged foliage is simple, dark green, very smooth, thick and leathery.

Distribution: East Himalayas, north-east India, Burma, north Malay Peninsula, Java, Sumatra.
Height: 60m (200ft)
Shape: Spreading
Evergreen
Pollinated: Wasp
Leaf shape: Oblong to elliptic, tip pointed

THE NETTLE AND CASUARINA FAMILIES

The nettle family, Urticaceae, and casuarina family, Casuarinaceae, are closely linked to the mulberry family. The nettle family is mainly tropical and includes only a few trees. Many of these plants have stinging hairs. Their small flowers are usually green, and when the pollen is ripe, it is released when the anthers suddenly uncoil. The casuarina family contains only the one genus featured below.

Upas Tree

Antiaris toxicaria

The upas tree is famous for being poisonous and has an unwarranted reputation for killing anyone unlucky enough to fall asleep under it. The sap is poisonous and used on arrow-tips; the dense inner bark is also used by forest people. Once beaten to remove the sap, it is made into a thick fibrous material for clothing, ropes and sacking. This tree towers above other trees in its native evergreen forests.

Identification: The upas tree has a buttressed trunk. Its young shoots, leaf stems and midribs are velvety. The smooth, pointed leaves are 8–20cm (3–8in) long, and some have toothed margins. The flowers appear in September and October. The male flowers are crowded on to flat mushroom-shaped organs in the leaf axils, while the female flowers are enclosed inside a pear-shaped receptacle. The elliptical, ripe fruit is 2–4.5cm (¾–1¾in) long, velvety and red or purple.

Distribution: Sri Lanka, Malaysia, Philippines, Burma, northern India and Fiji.
Height: 75m (250ft)
Shape: Domed
Evergreen
Pollinated: Wind
Leaf shape: Oblong-elliptic

Right: In Polynesia the tree is grown for its edible fruit. The leaves contain thin white poisonous latex that turns brown on contact with air.

Australian Pine

Casuarina equisetifolia

This elegant, wispy tree looks to all intents and purposes like a pine, hence its common name. However, it is not a true pine. Fast growing, this species has the ability to fix nitrogen by its roots and is tolerant of wind and some salinity. The Australian pine is used for windbreaks, soil stabilization and dune reclamation in coastal regions. It is also grown for its timber, which is used for making boats, furniture and houses. This species may live for several hundred years.

Identification: The short trunk has thick, brown, peeling bark, while the long, weeping branches are silvery grey. From the branches arise 10–20cm- (4–8in-) long, extremely narrow, downy branchlets. These branchlets resemble long pine needles and are coated in minuscule triangular leaves. The flowers appear in May and June. Male flowers are red, tufted, catkin-like and measure 4cm (1½in) long x 5mm (¼in) wide. Female flowers are greyish brown and globular, and measure 2cm (¾in) across. The cone-like fruit takes five months to develop. It is greenish grey, 2.5cm (1in) long and contains winged seeds.

Distribution: Coastal regions of north-east Australia, South-east Asia and Polynesia.
Height: 35m (115ft)
Shape: Columnar
Evergreen
Pollinated: Wind
Leaf shape: Reduced to tiny scales

Right and far right: The tiny scale leaves are highly adapted to coastal conditions.

Left: The compound, cone-like fruit is highly misleading as an identifying feature, as this tree is not a conifer.

THE CECROPIA FAMILY

These plants have prominent stilt roots and sheaths or caps protecting their growing tip. They often have palmate, lobed leaves and produce brown latex in the shoot tips. The cecropia family, Cecropiaceae, is very closely related to the fig family, Moraceae, and is considered by some to be a sub-division of it. It is also related to the nettle family, Urticaceae.

Guarumo

Cecropia insignis

This fast-growing, softwood species inhabits wet lowland rainforest and is a pioneer species, colonizing open or recently disturbed places with plenty of light. The guarumo grows into a large, open-crowned tree with branches radiating in tiers. Its trunk and thick branches are hollow, providing a home for ants. The large, umbrella-like leaves of this species are very eye-catching. It is a popular tree in arboretums across the tropical world.

Identification: The trunk is pale in colour and produces milky sap: the twigs are reddish brown. Each of the dramatic leaves is round, up to 1m (3ft) across and heavily lobed, usually with seven separate lobes. Lobes are oblong to egg shaped with the narrow end nearest the leaf stalk. The tiny flowers are densely clustered on to spikes: the male and female flower spikes are similar, 6–12cm (2½–4½in) long by 1cm (½in) wide, initially enveloped in a pink to brownish-red spathe (a modified leaf), pale green and generally erect. The tiny, green fruit is a dry, single-seeded nut, held on a spike up to 22cm (8½in) long x 1cm (½in) wide.

Left: The leaves are rough on the upper surface.

Distribution: Costa Rica.
Height: 25m (80ft)
Shape: Irregularly domed
Deciduous
Pollinated: Insect
Leaf shape: Orbicular, deeply lobed

Right: Each spike carries numerous tiny seeds, which are popular with birds.

OTHER SPECIES OF NOTE

Amazon Grape *Pourouma cecropifolia*
The amazon grape is grown for its enormous, majestic leaves and for the fruit that it produces prolifically over three months in the wet season. It can be seen in many arboretums across the world. This fast-growing tree may produce fruit from the age of three years. The fruit has a sweet, white pulp beneath an inedible skin that is easily removed. It is eaten fresh and used to make sweet wine, jams and jellies. The amazon grape grows on damp ground, exploiting the light from gaps in the forest canopy.
This tree has a light tan-coloured trunk, characteristic stilt roots and short, very wrinkly branches, often containing brown latex. The beautiful circular leaves consist of 10–13 lobes, each broader and rounded at the tip and tapering at the base. When young, the leaves are burgundy in colour and droop, but they flatten out as they mature. Each mature leaf is 60cm (24in) long x 80cm (28in) wide and held on a bright green, 60cm (24in) long leaf stalk. The leaf is wavy edged, mid-green and rough above with strongly marked veins. There may be a woolly down on the underside. The young leaf stems are covered with a dark rusty brown velvet. The flowers form in a dense branched structure 10cm (4in) long. The yellowish-green fruit is ovoid, 2cm (1in) long and covered in a dense hair. Each fruit contains a large seed and sweet, juicy pulp with a gummy, sticky texture.

Monkeyfruit *Myrianthus abroreus*
From tropical West Africa, this 20m (66ft) evergreen tree is used in numerous medicinal preparations. The leaves, sap, roots, fruit and bark are all used in many different preparations to treat disorders as varied as headaches, chest complaints, dysentery, boils, and difficulties in pregnancy. The young leaves and shoots are eaten, and are said to make good soup. The fruit pulp, which may be sweet or acidic, depending on the tree, is eaten fresh, while the seeds, which are rich in oil, are eaten once cooked. The pale, fibrous wood from this tree is of poor quality and used for burning.
The tree grows in secondary rainforest and particularly favours damp or riverside positions. The trunk is often short, branching close to the ground, and reaches 1m (3ft) in diameter with many aerial stilt roots. The bark is variable in colour, generally pale and sometimes greenish. The huge leaves can be 70cm (28in) wide and are divided into seven to nine leaflets. Each leaflet has a coarsely toothed margin, and the largest may be 50cm (20in) long. The flowers form towards the end of the dry season. The small, yellow male flowers form in panicles, while the female flowers are green and grow in clusters. The fruit is composed of many four- or five-sided fused fruits. It is soft and yellow when ripe, 10–15cm (4–6in) across, and generally heart shaped. The fruit contains 5–15 seeds.

THE DIPTEROCARP FAMILY

Dipterocarpaceae are tall forest trees found predominantly in Asia, where they dominate the forest. They are mostly evergreen, resinous and buttressed. The name "dipterocarp" means two-winged-fruit, but the seeds may actually have up to five wings, and some have none. These trees are grown and harvested from the wild for their hard timber. Many species also secrete valuable resin and camphor.

Sal

Shorea robusta

Distribution: Northern and central-eastern India, Burma, Thailand, Indo-China.
Height: 35m (115ft)
Shape: Flattened to domed
Semi-evergreen
Pollinated: Insect
Leaf shape: Broadly ovate

Right: Shuttlecock-like fruit spins away from the parent tree.

This tree's heavy, durable wood has been used in India for more than 2,000 years. Sal has many other uses: butter is made from its fat rich seeds; plates are fashioned from its leaves; tannins are extracted from its bark; dammar resin is taken from it for incense and torch fuel; and it produces another, more oily resin, which is used in inks, varnishes, for fixing perfume, as flavouring, and in medicine. Sal is a slow-growing, upright, dry forest tree with thick, fire resistant bark. Wherever it is found, this tree is normally the dominant species.

Identification: The bark is dark brown with longitudinal fissures. The smooth, shiny, leathery leaves are 10–25cm (4–10in) long. The small flowers are pale grey and velvety on the outside and orange inside. They appear early in summer in large branched structures, which appear from the axils and the ends of twigs and branches. The hard, brown fruit has two or three wings and appears early in summer. The fruit is 5–8cm (2–3in) long and often germinates while still hanging on the tree.

Left: These leaves are hard to identify, and only an expert may recognize different Shorea species.

Thingham

Hopea odorata

This highly variable species occurs in the middle layer of moist dipterocarp forests, often near to streams. Its wood is light yellowish brown with a tight, even grain. It is easy to work and used mostly for joinery. Thingham trees also produce dammar resin, and the leaves are harvested for their tannins, which are used to strengthen leather.

Identification: The trunk is straight with small buttresses. The bark is a dark grey brown but fissured with orange-brown marks. The ascending branches form a dense crown. The leaves are dark green above and bright olive green below. They measure 15cm (6in) long by 6cm (2½in) wide. The flowers are small and pale and have frilled petals. Fragrant, grey and velvety, they appear in spring and are borne on branched structures, growing from the leaf axils. The conical fruit appears in early summer. It measures 5cm (2in) long, including the pair of brown wings.

Above: Thinghams are reminiscent of the European beech (Fagus sylvatica).

Distribution: India, Bangladesh, Burma, Thailand, Malaysia.
Height: 37m (122ft)
Shape: Conical
Evergreen
Pollinated: Insect
Leaf shape: Ovate-lanceolate

Left: When fruiting, the dark green leaves are obscured by pale green fruit.

Kapur

Dryobalanops lanceolata

This extremely large tree has a very long, straight trunk with no branches for its first 15–30m (50–100ft) and large buttresses up to 4m (13ft) high. It is found away from wet areas in mixed dipterocarp forests, and is an emergent species with its crown above the forest canopy. The timber is reddish brown with a very straight, even grain and a camphorous odour. Fungus resistant, it polishes to a high shine and is used for flooring, joinery, construction and boat-building. Kapur is currently being planted in secondary (regrown) rainforest in northern Borneo as part of a forest enrichment programme.

Left: Dipterocarps have an erratic fruiting habit. In a fruiting year, trees will be smothered in flowers and yield heavily, while in other years they yield no fruit.

Identification: The bark varies from dark brown to grey with a purplish tinge and has vertical fissures. The smooth leaves have short leaf stems and measure 7–20cm (2¾–8in) long. The white flowers vary in size and have 27–33 stamens. The fruit measures 2.5 x 2.5cm (1 x 1in) and has four or five wings each 7–10cm (2¾–4in) long x 1–2cm (½–¾in) wide.

Distribution: Borneo, Malay Peninsula and East Indian Islands.
Height: 60m (200ft)
Shape: Domed
Evergreen
Pollinated: Bee
Leaf shape: Ovate-lanceolate

OTHER SPECIES OF NOTE
Shorea macrophylla This tree has a long, clear trunk up to 24m (80ft) in length and 1.5m (5ft) wide. The wood has a cedar-like aroma and is moderately hard, although not as durable as the wood of other dipterocarps. Even so, it is grown in plantations in Malaysia. The tree flowers in early summer and bears fruit in late summer and autumn. The two winged seeds each weigh 30g (1oz).

Camphor Kapur *Dryobalanops aromaticum* This 60m- (200ft-) tall tree was recorded by Marco Polo in 1299 and has been used as a source of camphor in Arabia since the sixth century. In recent times the majority of camphor has been extracted from *Cinnamomum camphorum* or produced synthetically instead. The camphor kapur tree also yields aromatic, volatile, oily resins, which are used in medicine. It grows in western Malaysia and northern and eastern Sumatra. The bark is light brown and comes away in large scaly flakes. The branches are held erect and carry an elegant, light, airy, columnar crown. Once the tree reaches 20 years old it produces its first attractive, white, fragrant flowers. It continues to produce these every three or four years for the rest of its life.

Dipterocarpus alatus This tree is from Bangladesh, Burma and the Andaman Islands. The timber is used for making canoes and housing, while the bark is used medicinally. The tree is also a source of oily resin. The leaves are ovate to elliptic and 10–15cm (4–6in) long. This species flowers in April and produces large pink flowers on short branched structures from the axils. The seeds are produced in May, measure 3 x 4cm (1¼ x 1½in) and have five wings.

Nawada

Shorea stipularis

This tree grows in wet lowland evergreen rainforest. It is harvested for timber for construction, as a source of incense resin and for its bark, which is used to halt fermentation. The wood is pale yellow and resinous. The tree has low, thick, rounded buttresses and carries a dense, rounded crown.

Identification: The very straight trunk measures up to 1.2m (47in) diameter and has deeply fissured, flaky, pale reddish-brown to dark brown bark. The young twigs have conspicuous, 1.5cm- (½-in) long stipules (paired leaf-like appendages) at the base of each axil. The leaves are 11c- (/4½in) long and have strongly marked veins. The sparsely flowered panicles (branched flowerheads) arise from the leaf axils and are 10cm (4in) long. Each flower is 1cm (½in) across, cream and has five twisted, pointed petals. The fruit measures 1 x 2cm (½ x ¾in) and has five flat oblong wings, two 5cm (2in) long and three 10cm (4in) long.

Distribution: Sri Lanka.
Height: 45m (150ft)
Shape: Rounded
Evergreen
Pollinated: Insect
Leaf shape: Ovate-elliptic

Above: Large stipules at the base of the leaf stems give rise to the species name.

Above left: This dipterocarp fruit has wings of different sizes.

THE DILLENIA FAMILY

Dilleniaceae is a small family, encompassing only 20 or so genera and about 500 species from the tropics. It includes trees, shrubs, climbers and herbs. They often have pinkish or orange bark and have hard reddish wood. The leaves are usually serrated with a rough surface, and in some plants the leaf stems are winged. The five-petalled flowers have numerous stamens and are short lived.

Simpoh Air

Dillenia suffruticosa

This fast-growing pioneer species grows as wide as it is tall and may become shrub-like. It grows in scrubby areas or disturbed forest. It is planted as a shade tree, being particularly attractive when in flower, and for the fleshy fruit which is used in jellies, preserves and curries.

Identification: The trunk of the tree has pale, grey to brown, smooth marked bark and carries branches with thick branchlets. The 25cm- (10in-) long leathery leaves are wavy through their length, have rounded tips and wide, short, wing-shaped leaf stems. They have faintly toothed margins and conspicuous parallel veins. The five-petalled flowers are bright yellow and 10cm (4in) across.

Distribution: Peninsular Malaysia.
Height: 9m (30ft)
Shape: Spreading
Evergreen
Pollinated: Insect
Leaf shape: Oblong

Above: The large, scented flowers are found in racemes of 5–15 flowers.

Right: The leaves are clustered at the branch tips.

Below: The fruit is round, surrounded by enlarged sepals, and opens to become star shaped, revealing a red lining and seeds within a thin red aril.

Elephant Apple

Dillenia indica

This spectacular tree is common in cultivation. It is grown for the combination of stunning unusual foliage, beautiful scented flowers and large edible fruit. The fruit is, in fact, heavily swollen overlapping sepals, rolled into a ball containing a sticky green mass of seeds. It is musk scented, tasting like an unripe apple, and is apparently popular with elephants. The fruit it used to make cooling drinks and jellies. The tree has an open broad crown above a short dark trunk, with leaves concentrated towards the branch tips.

Identification: The trunk carries rich orange-brown bark and few branches. The leaves are heavily corrugated, up to 75cm (30in) long, toothed, leathery, smooth on the upper surface but rough below. The flowers appear in late spring and early summer, and are fragrant, 20cm (8in) across, creamy yellow to pure white with a mass of central golden stamens. The fruit reaches 15cm (6in) across and is green.

Distribution: East India and South-east Asia.
Height: 18m (60ft)
Shape: Domed
Semi-evergreen
Pollinated: Insect
Leaf shape: Elliptic-oblong

Left: The enormous solitary flowers face downwards; they are the largest of all Malaysian flowers and last only a day.

THE ELAEOCARPUS AND LIME FAMILIES

The Elaeocarpaceae and the lime family, Tiliaceae, are related to the sterculia, bombax, mallow and lecythis
families. Most Elaeocarpaceae are trees and shrubs from India to New Zealand. They were once included
with the lime family, to which they are similar. Members of the variable lime family are found worldwide.
They have simple leaves and flowers with five or occasionally no petals, and berry- or nut-like fruit.

Blueberry Ash

Elaeocarpus cyaneus

Blueberry ash is naturally found in a wide range of habitats, including forested
areas, wooded gullies, rocky ridges and in coastal scrub. This very tough tree
withstands salt-laden air, wind, sun, shade, poor soil, and has even been
known to survive temperatures below freezing. In Australian gardens it is
often grown as a large shrub for its pretty aniseed-scented flowers and vivid
blue fruit, which is popular with birds.

Identification: The trunk may have a slightly buttressed base and carries a
dense, bushy crown. The 10–15cm- (4–6in-) long leaves are shiny, leathery,
toothed, with prominent net veining. Over a long period, from spring to
autumn, the 1cm- (½in-) long, creamy white to pink, fringed, bell-shaped
flowers appear in lax, axillary racemes up to 15cm (6in) long.
The attractive fruit appears from autumn, lasting for many months. It is
1cm (½in) long, round and deep to bright blue. The flowers and fruit
are sometimes seen simultaneously.

Distribution: East coast
Australia to Tasmania and
Frasier Island.
Height: 15m (50ft)
Shape: Columnar-conical
Evergreen
Pollinated: Insect
Leaf shape: Oblong-
lanceolate

Right: The edible fruit is not blue due to pigments; the skin is
actually green, but it is designed to reflect blue light.

Corkwood

Entelea arborescens

The wood of this fast-growing tree is incredibly light, half
the weight of cork. It is used by the Maoris to
make fishing-net floats and
frameworks for small boats. The
tree is the only species of
its genus and naturally
grows as a pioneer species
and in young woodland.
It is highly tolerant of
salt-laden wind and used
in sand dune restoration.
In addition, it is planted
as windbreaks and hedging.
When young it has an upright oval
form and may be grown as a shrub.
It can survive in areas
with light frosts.

Identification: The alternate
leaves are 10–23cm (4–9in) long
with similar length leaf stalks and
a heart-shaped base. They may
be inconspicuously lobed
and have a double-
toothed margin. All the
leaves, shoots and
flowers are covered in
short soft hair. The
white flowers with
central yellow stamens
form in spring and
summer. They are
2.5cm (1in) wide and in
terminal cymes 7–13cm (2¾
–5in) long. The autumn fruit is in
clusters, each is round, 2.5cm
(1in) diameter and covered in long
rigid bristles.

Distribution: New Zealand
North Island.
Height: 6m (20ft)
Shape: Wide spreading
Evergreen
Leaf shape: Ovate

Right: Sweetly scented flowers
in erect panicles are followed
by brown, bristly fruit composed
of four to six sections.

Right: The large, bright to light
green leaves are soft and felt-like.

THE ST JOHN'S WORT FAMILY

The trees in the Guttiferaceae family have oil glands and ducts on their leaves, which give a clear spot effect. Many also yield resins. Most are tropical trees or shrubs, and some are semi-epiphytic, using other plants to support them. They often produce latex, which may be white, yellow or even orange, and many have stilt roots. This family includes several useful timber trees and some species grown for their fruit.

Alexandrian Laurel

Calophyllum inophyllum

Alexandrian laurels are tolerant of harsh coastal climates, forming natural shelter belts in coastal areas, and are often planted along seashores where no natural shelter exists. With low branches, dense foliage and a spreading habit, they make ideal shade trees. They are also highly valued for the dark green, thick, strongly scented "domba oil" yielded by their nuts. This oil is collected under licence in Sri Lanka and exported to India, where it is used in medicines and for burning.

Identification: The bark is smooth and light brown. Deep green, smooth and highly glossy, the leaves have a fine yellow line around the margin and veining perpendicular to a yellow midrib. Thick, leathery and blunt-ended, they are 23cm (9in) long and oppositely arranged along round, succulent stems. The loose clusters of highly scented 2.5cm- (1in-) wide flowers appear in summer.

Distribution: Coastal, north Australia, South-east Asia, India and Africa.
Height: 15m (50ft)
Shape: Spreading
Evergreen
Pollinated: Insect
Leaf shape: Oblong to obovate

Far left: The fruit has a single seed and is 1.5–3.5cm (½–1½ in) long with a smooth yellowish brown or reddish skin.

Right: The genus name Calophyllum means beautiful leaf.

Ceylon Iron Wood

Mesua ferrea

This handsome, slow-growing tree, with a dense crown, grows in forests and is widely planted. In India the tree is sacred, and in Sri Lanka it is planted by Buddhist temples. In the wet seasons the new, young foliage creates an impressive sight as it hangs in limp red-pink tassels. In drier spells the scented flowers appear.

Identification: The trunk has flaky grey to reddish bark, and has small buttresses. Mature leaves are dark green above and pale below, resulting in an overall effect of grey-green. The 10–15cm (4–6in) across, solitary flowers have a cluster of bright yellow stamens. The fruit is round or oval to cone shaped, hard, brown, 2.5–5cm (1–2in) across and contains one to four dry, flattened, shiny seeds.

Above: The tree begins life with a conical habit, which broadens with maturity.

Distribution: Sri Lanka, India, Himalayas to Malaysia.
Height: 25m (82ft)
Shape: Oval to columnar
Evergreen
Pollinated: Insect
Leaf shape: Lanceolate

Right: The leaves have a pale waxy bloom below.

Far right: The beautifully scented flowers last only for a day.

THE STERCULIA FAMILY

*The Sterculiaceae family is found mainly in the tropics and includes trees, shrubs, climbers and herbs.
The plants are not easy to recognize, they have simple leaves that alternate on each side of the stem and
which may be divided. The flowers have three to five sepals and may have either five or no petals. The
fruit may be fleshy, leathery or woody, and the seed may or may not have an outer covering.*

Australian Flame Tree

Brachychiton acerifolius

This rather variable species is stunning when in flower. The profuse, foamy sprays of wide,
bell-shaped flowers are vibrant red and may develop in large numbers in late spring to early
summer. The distinctive swollen trunk stores water even though the tree occurs naturally in
wet coastal rainforests. Aborigines use the fibres
from the bark for weaving, and the seeds are a
source of dye.

Identification: The trunk is greenish and bottle
shaped. The leaves occur alternately on each side of
the twigs and have three to
seven lobes, which are particularly
obvious when they are young.
Mature leaves are mid-green,
glossy, 9–25cm (3½–10in) long
and held on an 8–23cm- (3–9in-)
long stem. The flowers appear in
sprays 30cm (12in) long and are
all the more stunning as they
occur when the tree is leafless.
The fruit is 9–12cm (3½–4½in) long.

Distribution: Queensland
and New South Wales,
Australia
Height: 30m (100ft)
Shape: Conical or oblong
Deciduous
Pollinated: Bird
Leaf shape: Palmate

*Left: The variable leaves often
have far fewer incisions as the tree
matures. The flower "petals" are
the sepals. The woody fruit splits
to release edible seeds.*

Java Olive

Sterculia foetida

Distribution: Central Africa,
Madagascar, India to Malaysia
and northern Australia.
Height: 30m (100ft)
Shape: Spreading
Semi-evergreen
Pollinated: Insect
Leaf shape: Compound
palmate

*Right: The leaf stems and
twigs of young plants are
coated in sticky hairs.*

A fast-growing tree found in rocky and sandy coastal
locations. The species name refers to foul-smelling
flowers, which are enough to deter anyone from
planting it. Even so, flowering is short lived and it
is grown as a shade tree becoming as wide as it is
tall. The fruit is botanically remarkable as it splits
soon after pollination, and the seeds finish
development completely exposed.

Identification: The smooth grey to orange-brown trunk carries
horizontal branches. The elegant leaves are 10–30cm (4–12in) long
and have between five and eleven narrow, pointed, lanceolate lobes.
Each lobe is deep olive green with a very prominent yellowish midrib.
The flowers, which are held on branched structures, occur on deciduous
trees in early spring before the leaves appear, but can be
seen year round on evergreen trees. Each flower is 2.5–5cm
(1–2in) wide, has fleshy orange or red sepals with yellow
markings and is woolly inside. The pear-shaped fruit
develops quickly. Red, woody and 7–13cm (2¾–5in) long,
the fruit splits to reveal red cavities containing the 10–15
blue-black seeds.

*Left: These seeds can
be roasted and eaten.*

Cola Nut

Cola acuminata

"Cola" is a world-renowned drink, yet few people know that it is also a tree. The "nuts" (really seeds) of this tree are two per cent caffeine and were originally used in the cola drink. The tree is cultivated in Sri Lanka, the West Indies, Malaysia and West Africa. In the tropics its seeds are chewed for medicinal purposes, for their stimulating effects and to enable people to undertake feats of endurance. They are no longer used in the drink to which they gave their name and are now little used in the West. The tree grows in humid lowlands.

Distribution: Tropical West Africa.
Height: 12m (40ft)
Shape: Spreading
Evergreen
Pollinated: Insect
Leaf shape: Oblong-ovate

Above: The long-lived cola tree may yield fruit for 100 years.

Identification: The leaves are leathery, dark green and 10–15cm (4–6in) long. The flowers are found in the axils and at the ends of twigs in branched clusters of 15 throughout the year, or, on some trees, only in winter. The flowers are 1.5cm (½in) across and have no petals. However, they do have five pale yellow sepals, each with central purple markings. The green, warty fruit is a 13–18cm- (5–7in-) long pod containing between six and ten pink, purple or white seeds. The seeds may be dried, before consumption, becoming dark brown.

Below: The ugly cola fruit contains the "cola nuts" White nuts are the most popular for chewing and demand the best price.

African Mallow

Dombeya wallichii

This tree is grown for its large, eye-catching flowers and its large, soft, felty leaves. It often takes the form of a large shrub with numerous trunks and has a very dense crown.

Identification: The bright green, heart- to diamond-shaped leaves have three lobes with jagged edges and are large, measuring 30cm (12in) long and an even greater distance across. The flowers are 2.5cm (1in) wide, fragrant, have overlapping petals and are cup shaped. Ranging from deep pink to red, they are crowded on to round, hanging heads 15cm (6in) across and appear from midsummer into winter. The flower petals turn brown and remain on the tree after they have died, giving the African mallow a rather scruffy look as its small fruit develops.

Distribution: Madagascar.
Height: 9m (30ft)
Shape: Domed
Evergreen
Pollinated: Insect
Leaf shape: Broadly elliptic, variable

Left: The dried flowers remain hanging on the tree while the fruit develops inside.

Queensland Bottle Tree

Brachychiton rupestris

This tree develops a massive, bulbous, branchless, bottle-shaped, water-storing trunk and is often planted as a novelty in parks and gardens. It is also planted on farms and streets. Unless well watered, this species is slow growing at first and does not form the characteristic swollen trunk until it is about ten years old. In the wild, the Queensland bottle tree is found inland in fertile valleys and along low ridges. The moist, fibrous, inner bark can be eaten.

Distribution: South-east Queensland
Height: 9–12m (30–40ft)
Shape: Irregularly domed
Semi-evergreen
Leaf shape: Variable

Identification: The slightly fissured bark is greyish green. The leaves are deep green and form a dense crown but are liable to drop in prolonged dry spells. They vary in shape from narrow and elliptical to wide and divided. The small, yellowish clusters of bell-shaped flowers appear from late spring to early summer towards the tips of the branches, where they are hidden among the foliage. The short, boat-shaped fruit is woody and produced in late summer.

Left: The mature foliage is long and slender, whereas the juvenile foliage may be wide and lobed.

Right: This bottle tree grows on fertile soil and can be surprisingly fast growing when well watered.

OTHER SPECIES OF NOTE

Dombeya spectabilis
This deciduous tree grows to 12m (40ft) in height and comes from Madagascar and north-eastern South Africa. Its 20cm- (8in-)wide leaves may be heart shaped, broadly oblong or even round. They are rough and covered with soft hairs above and white or rusty-coloured hair below. The large, round clusters of flowers appear during the spring dry season while the tree is leafless. Each flower is small, white or cream and sometimes has a hint of pink.

Triplochiton sceleroxylon
The pale-coloured wood of this West African tree became popular during World War II because it is strong and easy to work. *Triplochiton sceleroxylon* is an evergreen tree to 55m (180ft) of humid lowland forests and waterways. It is a fast-growing pioneer species, often found grouped in patches, and is a popular choice for reforestation programmes. Its only downside is that it is unreliable in its flowering and fruiting.
   The smooth, pale brown trunk has buttresses up to 6m (20ft) tall. It is topped with a small, sparse crown of smooth, narrow, mid-green leaves. Each leaf is 30cm (12in) across and divided into seven lobes with pale veining. The conspicuous, pretty flowers appear throughout the winter and spring. They are red or purple with paler, sometimes white, margins, 2.5–3cm (1¼in) across, and are found in dense clusters. The brown, leathery fruit is winged, carries one or two seeds and appears from early spring.

Cola nitida
This handsome, evergreen, African tree grows to 18m (60ft) in height. It produces seeds that are high in caffeine and chewed or used in drinks. The seeds taste bitter at first but have a lingering, sweet flavour that remains in the mouth after eating. This tree produces more caffeine than any other cola species, and its nuts are both collected wild and grown in West Africa for the local and export markets. The tree has greyish-brown bark and tough, glossy, elliptic leaves 30cm (12in) long.

Looking-glass Mangrove *Heritiera littoralis*
Found from East Africa to Australia on the landward side of mangroves and in riverine areas where there is less saline influence. When mature, this 25m (80ft) tree forms impressive ribbon-like buttress roots. The pale reverse side of the looking-glass mangrove's leaves appears reflective. The starchy seeds are edible once the tannins have been removed. The hard, dark red wood, which sinks in water, is used in construction, and boat- and furniture-making.
   The evergreen trees are densely branched. The bark is smooth, becoming furrowed and flaking when mature, and is white, pale grey or pinkish. The 12–25cm- (4½–10in-) long leaves are leathery, dark green above and silver below. Tiny, bell-shaped, summer flowers form in lax, branched, axillary panicles, and each is pinkish or green and downy. The 8cm- (3in-) long fruit is pale brown and ovoid with a small keel along one side, and is very hard and smooth.

THE BOMBAX FAMILY

The bombax family of tropical trees is especially well represented in South America, and includes some outstanding
species. Many have thick or swollen trunks for water storage and spectacular flat-topped, spreading crowns. Their
leaves are often lobed and clustered towards the tips of the thick branches. Bombacaceae flowers, with five petals
and many stamens, are usually large and showy. The fruit capsule is sometimes winged and contains fine hairs.

Baobab

Adansonia digitata

This incredible tree can grow to a very great age. The trunk becomes grossly swollen and may be as much as 30m (100ft) in circumference, making the baobab one of the widest trees in the world. In extremely old specimens the trunk becomes hollow and may hold up to 1,200 litres (2,540 pints) of water. The inner bark also provides fibre for ropes.

Identification: The bark is pale, and the dark green, glossy leaves are divided into between five and nine leaflets, each 15cm (6in) long with a pale midrib. The flowers appear before or with the new foliage. They hang singly from branches on cords, are 15cm (6in) wide, have fleshy, crinkled, off-white petals with numerous purple or yellow stamens, and open at night. The brown fruit hangs on long stalks. Each is 30cm (12in) long by 10cm (4in) wide and holds 30 seeds in sour pulp.

Distribution: Throughout tropical Africa.
Height: 24m (80ft)
Shape: Sparsely domed
Deciduous
Pollinated: Bat
Leaf shape: Orbicular and divided

Left: The flowers have a strong melon-like scent.

Left: One myth suggests the baobab was cursed, pulled from the ground and replanted upside down.

Right: The fruit contains an edible acidic dry pulp.

Kapok

Ceiba pentandra

This tree was sacred to the ancient Maya of Central America and today is often seen in market places. It probably originated in South America but has become so widespread that it is difficult to be certain of this. The kapok has a distinctive outline; its huge, thick trunk is heavily buttressed and often covered with thick spines. The thick, heavy branches are held at right angles to the trunk, and the tree eventually becomes as wide as it is tall. Kapok fruit yields fine silky filaments, which are used to stuff pillows and life vests.

Distribution: Throughout tropics (America, Africa and Asia).
Height: 60m (200ft)
Shape: Conical
Semi-evergreen
Pollinated: Bat
Leaf shape: Orbicular and divided

Right: Mature trees yield up to 900 fruits. These are harvested and laid out in the sun until they open.

Identification: The bark is grey. The leaves are 30cm (12in) wide and divided into between five and seven mid-green leaflets, each lanceolate and 15cm (6in) long. The fragrant flowers appear in spring, when the tree is leafless (if deciduous). They are 15cm (6in) across, woolly and white, creamy pink or yellow. The fruit pod is 15cm (6in) long, narrowly elliptical, leathery and dark.

Durian

Durio zibethinus

The durian is known as the "king of the fruits". These rainforest trees have been cultivated for hundreds of years in Malaysia, where the fruit is a delicacy. To the uninitiated, the pungent, putrid smell of the fruit is nauseating. However, the smooth flesh tastes delicious. Full of energy, it may be eaten as a vegetable if cooked before ripe. When ripe, it may be eaten raw or cooked to make cake, sweets or cookies. The distinctive smelling fruit is also very popular with large forest animals such as elephants.

Distribution: Malaysia and the East Indies.
Height: 36m (120ft)
Shape: Rounded and irregular
Evergreen
Pollinated: Insect and bat
Leaf shape: Elliptic

Identification: The tree has a straight brown trunk, broad base and almost horizontal branches. The leaves are dark green above, silvery with brown scales below and 20cm (8in) long. The flowers are greenish white or pinkish and emerge directly from the trunk and older branches in clusters between 3–30. The fruit is round, up to 38cm (15in) across, yellowish green and has coarse hard spines covering the surface. It divides into four or five segments, each containing 5cm (2in) long seeds.

Above: During the day, insects pollinate the flowers, while at night fruit bats may pollinate or eat them.

Left: The sombre-looking foliage is distinctive in Malaysia.

Right: The fruit takes up to twelve weeks to form and is only ripe when it drops to the ground.

OTHER SPECIES OF NOTE

Dead Rat Tree *Adansonia gregorii*
This 18m (60ft)-tall tree comes from a small region in north-western Australia. Outside its native home it is grown for its novelty value in arboretums, parks and public gardens. The pale, rough-barked trunk grows to enormous proportions and is used by the tree to store water. The leaves are divided, and the hanging flowers are like those of the better-known baobab. The fruits, which look like dead rats hanging from the tree, contain sour, edible pulp.

Gold Coast Bombax *Bombax buonopozense*
This deciduous tree occurs from Sierra Leone to Gabon in savannah and forests. It has large, conspicuous, deep red flowers, which appear in winter and spring when the tree is leafless. The Gold Coast bombax grows to 36m (120ft) tall and has buttress roots. The thick, corky bark is fissured and has thick, conical spines. The leaves are divided into six or seven leaflets, each

15cm (6in) long. The solitary flowers have five hairy, leathery petals, each of which is 10cm (4in) long. The fruit contains up to 1,800 tiny seeds in silky floss.

Wild Kapok *Bombax valetonii*
This tree is very similar in appearance to the kapok tree, *Ceiba pentandra* which grows throughout the tropics. The wild kapok, however, is native to Malaysia, Indonesia and Java where it is occasionally found in the forest. It grows to a maximum height of 30m (100ft) and develops a dense flattened crown in maturity. The leaves are divided into five to nine blunt-ended, elliptical leaflets, each up to 38cm (15in) long, which become smaller on mature trees. The flowers appear in the winter on leafless branches. They are 9cm (3½in) long with pale-green petals and numerous pale white stamens. They are thought to be pollinated by bats. The dark brown fruit is a hard, round, narrow pod up to 23cm (9in) long and contains silky floss.

THE MALLOW FAMILY

Most members of the Malvaceae family are herbaceous shrubs, many from temperate areas. The trees are fast growing and have soft wood. They all have palmate, lobed leaves, which are serrated along the margins. Mallow flowers have five petals, are usually asymmetrical and are often showy; many of the family are grown as garden ornamentals. In all but one species the fruit is a collection of dry seeds.

Mahoe

Hibiscus tiliaceus

Growing in lowlands, swampy and coastal areas and forming impenetrable thickets and scrub, this tree or large shrub varies enormously in shape and size. The branches are thick and drooping with dense foliage, and the trunk may be contorted. The mahoe is adapted to salty coastal air and sandy soil, and is sometimes grown in gardens as a trimmed hedge.

Distribution: Coastal old world tropics (Africa through to Asia).
Height: 15m (50ft)
Shape: Spreading
Evergreen
Pollinated: Insect
Leaf shape: Orbicular to heart shaped and lobed

Identification: The leaves are 13–20cm (5–8in) wide, leathery and covered in fine hair below. They are deep green in colour, have prominent light green to red veining and are pale underneath. The trumpet-shaped flowers appear throughout the year and last only a day. Solitary with overlapping petals each 4–7cm (1½–2¾in) long, they occur in the leaf axils near branch tips and are yellow or white with a red centre and deep red stigma. After dropping from the tree, the flowers fade to pink or maroon. The fruit capsule is ovoid, velvety, greyish green and 1.5cm (⅝in) long.

Right: The mahoe flower opens in the morning, closes around 4pm and drops off the tree by the next morning.

Portia Tree

Thespesia populnae

This tree is often confused with the mahoe, and there are numerous similarities between them. The portia tree is very salt tolerant, growing on seashores and in sandy places, and has a dense, spreading crown. The trunk, although sometimes contorted, has good, hard timber with chocolate-brown-coloured heartwood, which is used for furniture.

Identification: The trunk is short and dark, and the leaves dull deep green with prominent lighter veining. Leathery and dotted with glands above, the leaves are 6–12cm (2½–4½in) long and have a nectar zone at the base. The solitary, yellow flowers are produced throughout the year. They are tightly trumpet shaped with overlapping petals 5cm (2in) long. The fruit is a leathery, dark grey or brown, cup-shaped capsule, 2.5–5cm (1–2in) wide with woolly seeds.

Distribution: Coastal throughout all tropics.
Height: 20m (66ft)
Shape: Rounded spreading
Evergreen
Pollinated: Insect
Leaf shape: Heart to ovate

Above: A portia can be mistaken for a mahoe but has rugged bark and yellow flower stigmas.

Above and left: The flowers open in the evening attracting night-flying moths. From daybreak they fade to orange, pink or maroon to attract day-flying insects, and stay on the tree for a few days.

MISCELLANEOUS DILLENIIDAE

These families (caper family, Capparidaceae; moringa family, Moringaceae; flacourtia family, Flacourtiaceae; ebony family, Ebenaceae; and carica family, Caricaeae) are all related within the class Dilleniidae. They are generally small families or are poorly represented in the tropics. Indeed the moringa family has only the one genus, encompassing only three species.

Spider Tree

Crataeva religiosa

As the Latin name suggests, this tree is sacred to people in its native South-east Asia. It has several medicinal uses, for example, the leaves and bark are used to treat stomach upsets. The spider tree grows naturally in shady places, often along streams, but may be seen in drier areas too. The yellowish-white wood is smooth and even grained.

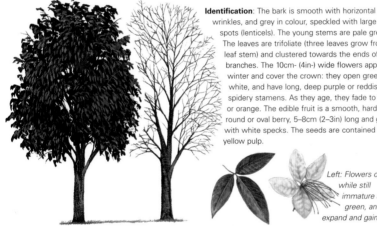

Identification: The bark is smooth with horizontal wrinkles, and grey in colour, speckled with large white spots (lenticels). The young stems are pale green. The leaves are trifoliate (three leaves grow from one leaf stem) and clustered towards the ends of the branches. The 10cm- (4in-) wide flowers appear in winter and cover the crown: they open green or white, and have long, deep purple or reddish, spidery stamens. As they age, they fade to yellow or orange. The edible fruit is a smooth, hard, round or oval berry, 5–8cm (2–3in) long and green with white specks. The seeds are contained within yellow pulp.

Distribution: South-east Asia, Pacific and northern Australia.
Height: 6m (20ft)
Shape: Domed
Deciduous
Pollinated: Insect
Leaf shape: Trifoliate

Below: Each leaflet is deep green and measures 15cm (6in) long.

Left: Flowers open while still immature and green, and then expand and gain colour.

Ebony

Diospyros ebenum

Many trees are commercially labelled as "ebony" but this species, with its jet black heartwood, is considered the best. In the wild, it grows as a middle storey tree in dry, evergreen forests. The wood, which is heavy and may have yellow or brown streaking, is a luxury product used for carving, turnery and making furniture. The value of its wood means the species is now rare.

Identification: The bark is dark grey and peels off in rectangular pieces. The leaves, held on short leaf stems, are bright green with large, darkish glands on the underside. The foliage is very dense and somewhat gloomy in appearance. The young shoots are covered in soft down. Ebony has separate male and female flowers, which are small and off-white. The female flowers are produced singly, while the male flowers appear in clusters of three to fifteen. The fruit is round, 1–2cm (½–¾in) across and green, ripening to black.

Right: The thick, glossy leaves alternate on the stem and are 5–18cm (2–7in) long, smooth and have wavy edges.

Distribution: India and Sri Lanka.
Height: 18m (60ft)
Evergreen
Pollinated: Insect
Leaf shape: Oblong-elliptic

Left: The fruit is held in a woody green cup, which is the old flower sepal.

THE MIMOSA SUBFAMILY

Mimosas, cassias and beans are all sub-divisions of the very large pea family, sometimes called "legumes".
Mimosoideae are well known for their finely divided, bipinnate leaves, although not all members of the
subfamily have leaves with this structure. Mimosa flowers have small petals, extended stamens and
appear in eye-catching clusters. Parts of these plants give off a distinctive, bean-like smell when crushed.

Knob Tree

Acacia nigrescens

This plant has fearsome curved spines on its trunk and branches to deter herbivores, yet goats and giraffes still manage to browse on it. The tree grows naturally on heavy, black soil in lowland deciduous bush and lightly wooded grassland. The leaves and pods of this species make valuable fodder for livestock, and the twigs and branches are collected for firewood.

Identification: The trunk has soft, thick, pale bark and is covered with large, knobbly spines. The spines grow in pairs below each leaf node and remain on the tree throughout its lifetime. The leaves are divided into between one and four pinnae, each carrying one or two pairs of leaflets. The leaflets are ovate to elliptical, 1–2.5cm (½–1in) long and mid-green. The flowers form in spikes in late winter and are cream or white. The straight, dark brown pods are oblong, 7–15cm (2¾–6in) long and 1.5–2.5cm (½–1in) wide. They contain 1–1.5cm (½–⅔in-wide) seeds.

Distribution: Tanzania, Botswana, northern South Africa and Lesotho.
Height: 25m (83ft)
Shape: Domed
Deciduous
Pollinated: Insect
Leaf shape: Bipinnate

Far left: The scented flowers form in 10cm- (4in-) long spikes.

Bead Tree

Adenanthera pavonina

Seeds of this tree are bright scarlet and reportedly edible if roasted but are more often used as beads after softening in boiling water. In Asia they are used by chemists and jewellers as weights. The wood is strong, durable, red and often called "red sandalwood" as it is frequently substituted for the real thing. The tree is upright with a light open canopy and fine, feathery foliage. It is grown throughout the tropics and has established itself in the wild in Florida.

Identification: The bark is smooth and grey. The leaves are mid-green, up to 40cm (16in) long and divided into between one and six pairs of side stalks, each with 5–20 pairs of leaflets. The leaflets are 2.5–5cm (1–2in) long, oblong and have blunt ends. The orange-blossom scented white, cream and yellow flowers appear in spring, tightly packed into narrow clusters up to 25cm (10in) long and growing from the leaf axils. The pods are 10–23cm (4–9in) long, 1.5cm (⅔in) wide, flat and curved. As the pods open they twist to reveal the shiny seeds.

Distribution: Sri Lanka.
Height: 18m (60ft)
Shape: Domed
Deciduous
Pollinated: Insect
Leaf shape: Bipinnate

Left: The pods ripen from green to brown.

Right: The flower petals fade to dull orange after opening.

Above: The "beads" are revealed as the pod twists open.

African Locust Bean

Parkia javanica

This fast-growing tree is both visually attractive and useful. The straight, smooth trunk is heavily buttressed, and the foliage is fine and feathery. The tree is used locally as a source of dye, soap and foodstuffs, including the white, powdery contents of the fruit pod. It is found growing in moist lowland forests and is cultivated in parks and gardens in tropical and subtropical regions.

Identification: The trunk is clear of branches for much of its height. Each leaf has 20–30 pairs of side stalks, each of which in turn carries 40–80 pairs of leaflets. Each leaflet is 1cm (½in) long, narrow and pointed. The numerous cream flowers form in winter in large globular heads on long hanging stems. The flower heads appear singly and in groups in the leaf axils and on the ends of the twigs and branches. The flowers produce a large quantity of thin nectar to attract fruit bats. The fruit is a smooth, tough, dark brown, twisted pod 38–51cm (15–20in) long and 4cm (1½in) wide. The fruits often form groups, which may be seen hanging from the branches in early spring.

Distribution: Malaysia through Burma to India.
Height: 46m (150ft)
Shape: Spreading
Evergreen
Pollinated: Bat
Leaf shape: Bipinnate

Below: The flowers attract fruit bats.

Right: The boiled beans may be eaten as a vegetable.

OTHER SPECIES OF NOTE

Mangium Wattle *Acacia mangium.*
This fast-growing tree from the rainforests of northern Queensland, Australia, may reach 30m (100ft) tall. It has a pyramidal crown atop a straight trunk and is grown in plantations for its hard, durable wood, which is used in building and for wood pulp. In South-east Asia the tree is a problem, as it is spreading rapidly outside plantations. The leaves are typically bipinnate in seedlings, but as the tree matures, the leaf stems and stems between the leaflets start to form into flattened, leaf-like, parallel-veined structures called "phyllodes". These are up to 30cm (12in) long and pale green. Through the year pale yellow flowers appear, crammed into soft spikes 8–10cm (3–4in) long and 1–2cm (½–¾in) wide. The seed pods are dark brown and twist together to form spiral clusters.

Koa *Acacia koa*
Native to Hawaii, this tree is found on slopes throughout the island in all except the driest locations. It can be seen in many tropical arboretums around the world. The wood is red and was once used for war canoes. The koa grows quickly and reaches 30m (100ft) tall with an open, spreading crown of thick, contorted, horizontal branches. In ideal conditions, the trunk may reach 3m (10ft) in diameter. The koa is tolerant of salty air and soil and on coasts forms a smaller, more contorted tree.

The leaf stems are expanded into evergreen phyllodes (*see A. mangium*), sickle shaped and 15cm (6in) long. The spring flowers are pale yellow and form spherical clusters.

Petai *Parkia speciosa*
This slow-growing evergreen tree from Malaysia can reach heights of 45m (150ft) tall and has a domed or flattened crown. In good conditions it will branch low and makes a handsome, shapely tree. It is also grown for its edible seeds, which are collected while the pods are immature and still green. The dark green leaves are bipinnate with 10–20 pairs of side stalks carrying oblong leaflets. The flowers grow on long hanging stems with a globular body at the end. This body contains many cream flowers, which have a pungent, sickly scent that attracts pollinating bats. Six to ten dark brown or black pods develop from the globular body, each up to 50cm (20in) long and 6cm/2½in wide.

African Locust *Parkia filicoidea*
The African locust is a useful tree to the savannah farmers of eastern central Africa. The husk and pulp of the seed pods are a staple food for people, and most parts of the tree have medicinal properties. The foliage is used as fodder for cattle, and the flowers are so nectar-rich that beehives are put into the tree branches by the local farmers. The African locust grows to 20m (66ft) tall and forms a dense, spreading crown. The bark is grey-brown and fissured and the bipinnate leaves composed of up to 40 pairs of side stalks, each with up to 65 pairs of oblong leaflets. The entire leaf is up to 40cm (16in) long. The brilliant red or orange flowers are clustered into hanging heads 6cm (2½in) in diameter. The pods are brown and up to 30cm (12in) long.

THE CASSIA SUBFAMILY

The legumes include well over 400 genera spread across the globe, and they are particularly common in the tropics. The family includes annuals, herbaceous plants, shrubs, trees and climbers. The trees play an important role in the forests of South America and Africa. The Caesalpinioideae subfamily is distinguished by flowers with five petals, and one odd-sized petal is enclosed by the others.

Hong Kong Bauhinia

Bauhinia x *blakeana*

Leaves of orchid trees, such as the Hong Kong bauhinia, are quite unmistakable – they are shaped like a camel's hoof. This fast-growing tree was discovered as a naturally occurring hybrid in 1908 and is thought to be a cross between *B. variegata* and *B. purpurea*. As it is sterile, the Hong Kong bauhinia does not produce seed pods, making it popular for street plantings. In 1965 this tree was chosen as the emblem of Hong Kong. It is generally considered the most beautiful of the orchid trees.

Identification: The smooth trunk is often multi-stemmed and carries a dense crown with slightly hanging branches. The deep olive green leaves are thick, tough and 20cm (8in) across. The 15cm- (6in-) wide flowers are profuse from late autumn until early spring and have a unique fragrance. Their petals are deep pink, purple or red with darker streaks on one odd petal.

Distribution: China and Hong Kong.
Height: 10m (33ft)
Shape: Domed
Evergreen
Pollinated: Sterile
Leaf shape: Orbicular and two lobed

Left: The thick leaves have raised yellowish veins.

Flame of the Forest

Flamboyant tree *Delonix regia*

Also called the flamboyant tree, the flame of the forest flowers in late spring and early summer, when it becomes one mass of intense vermilion blossoms, completely obliterating from sight any foliage across its incredibly wide, flat-topped crown. The tree is also eye-catching in fruit, when hundreds of long pods hang from its horizontal branches. Even when only in leaf the tree has a pleasant, airy appearance. It has been planted in considerable numbers throughout the tropics, but with its spreading, shallow roots and eventual buttresses, it has not proved popular as a street tree.

Identification: The smooth bark is light brown or grey, and the trunk carries thick branches, which are never straight. The leaves are delicate, 60cm (24in) long, bright green above and lighter below. The flowers have four red petals and one larger white petal with yellow and red streaks. The dark brown, flattened seed pods are up to 60cm (24in) long.

Distribution: Madagascar.
Height: 20m (66ft)
Shape: Spreading
Deciduous
Pollinated: Bird
Leaf shape: Bipinnate

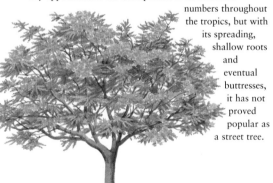

Right: This fast-growing tree may grow to 7.5m (25ft) in four years.

Above: Profuse, beautiful flowers give rise to masses of hard woody pods, which remain on the tree even when splitting open.

Tamarind

Tamarindus indica

The sweet yet tart pulp surrounding the seeds of this tree is cooked and used in Worcestershire sauce, chutneys and drinks. It is also regularly used as a raw ingredient in Asian cooking. The tree also has various local medicinal uses and, although slow growing, yields beautiful red timber. Well adapted to dry conditions and tolerant of wind, it makes a good street tree and is planted throughout the tropics. Originally from Africa, the tamarind has become naturalized throughout Asia and the Caribbean.

Identification: The thick trunk has heavily fissured, greyish-brown bark. The leaves are up to 25cm (10in) long and divided into 20–40 blunt-ended, oblong leaflets. They are a dull green and smooth. The flowers appear in early summer in loose, drooping clusters at the branch tips. The individual flowers are 1.5cm (⅔in) long, creamy yellow and have red markings. The plump fruit, which ripens in late winter, is an 18cm- (7in-) long, rich brown, rough skinned pod. The pulp inside is brown.

Above and right: The tamarind pods contain sticky, brown, sweet-sour pulp with little scent, but high acid content.

Distribution: Africa.
Height: 21m (69ft)
Shape: Rounded spreading
Evergreen
Pollinated: Insect
Leaf shape: Pinnate

OTHER SPECIES OF NOTE

Peachwood *Haematoxylon brasiletto*
The peachwood is the source of haematoxylin dye, which is extracted from the red-brown heartwood. This evergreen, South American tree has spines and grows in arid areas. It has pinnate leaves with just a few blunt-ended, egg-shaped leaflets. The small flowers are yellow, and the little pods split open to release seed, which is dispersed by the wind.

Pride of Burma *Amherstia nobilis*
This incredibly beautiful flowering tree comes from Burma and India, where the flowers are offered by Buddhists at their temples. The flowers are 10cm (4in) wide, deep pink or vermilion with one petal marked yellow and white. The pride of Burma is difficult to grow but when mature reaches 13m (43ft) in height. Its bipinnate leaves are 1m (3ft) long.

Yellow Flame Tree *Peltophorum pterocarpum*
The yellow flame tree is grown for the deep shade cast by its wide crown, its profusion of strongly scented, glowing golden flowers and its velvety, copper-coloured pods. This species occurs from northern Australia to India. It grows to heights of 66m (100ft) and has pinnate leaves, 60cm (24in) long, branched flower clusters and 10cm- (4in-) long pods.

Pink Shower Tree *Cassia grandis*
The thick canopy of coral pink flowers this tree produces falls quickly in early spring to form a pink carpet below. This species comes from Central America. It has a spreading crown and grows to 18m (60ft) tall. The leaves are pinnate, 30cm (12in) long and mid-green. The black, cylindrical pods may be up to 38cm (15in) long and contain flat yellow seeds.

THE ROSE FAMILY

Rosaceae is a well-known family of herbs, shrubs and trees and is poorly represented in the tropics. It includes many fruiting and ornamental plants of commercial importance. Roses and their relatives have alternate leaves and are often thorny. The flowers have five petals, which overlap in bud and are held equidistant in racemes, or open one after another on their own stalks in cymes. The fruits vary enormously.

Indian Cherry

Prunus cerasoides

This is a fast-growing tree, found in mixed pine and broadleaf forests, and often in disturbed areas in mountainous regions. It is also planted in gardens as an ornamental tree. The fine wood is used for furniture, panelling and floors. The fruit is edible but acidic and is said to have medicinal properties.

Identification: The trunk is narrow, reaching only 38cm (15in) in circumference. It has grey to reddish-brown bark, which peels horizontally when mature. The shiny leaves are a deep green above, pale green below, have finely toothed edges and a long tapering point. They measure 9–12cm (3½–4½in) long and 3–5cm (1¼–2in) across. Young leaves are maroon. The racemes usually appear while the tree is leafless. Each flower is 2cm (¾in) long and turns from deep pink while in bud to mid-pink upon opening. The smooth, oval fruit is 1.5cm (½in) long, bright red when ripe and contains one large seed.

Distribution: Northern Thailand, eastern Himalayas and western China.
Height: 16m (50ft)
Shape: Rounded
Deciduous
Pollinated: Insect
Leaf shape: Ovate to oblong

Above left: The flowers appear in the spring.
Left: The leaves yield a green dye, and the fruit yields a grey-green dye.

Red Stinkwood

Prunus africana

Distribution: Africa.
Height: 36m (120ft)
Shape: Rounded
Evergreen
Pollinated: Insect
Leaf shape: Elliptic

This slow-growing tree is found in humid and semi-humid highland rainforest. It is grown for timber and fuel by foresters and planted on farms for ornament, shade or protection from wind. The hard wood is used in construction and furniture-making but is not durable if used in the ground. This species is also currently being grown for its bark, which appears to have potential as a treatment for prostate cancer. Illegal over-collection of the medicinal bark is threatening this tree's survival. In 1994 it was registered as endangered.

Identification: The bark is brown and slightly fissured. The leaves are dark green, smooth, have toothed margins and reach up to 15cm (6in) long and 4.5cm (1¾in) across. The flowers appear throughout the year but peak in the winter months; they are small, off-white and found in groups of 7–15. The fruit appears mostly in the summer; it is dark brown when mature, 5mm (¼in) long and 1cm (½in) wide. The fruit contains reddish-brown pulp surrounding one or two delicate seeds and is very popular with birds and monkeys.

Right: When damaged the glossy leaves smell of almonds.

THE PROTEA FAMILY

The Proteaceae are found in warm regions of the southern hemisphere and are well represented in Australia and South Africa. Many species produce showy, long-lasting flowers used in the cut-flower industry. The flowers' petals and sepals are combined into a structure known as a "perianth" which is often curled. The leaves are often thick and waxy or hairy – adaptations for water retention.

Rewa-Rewa

Knightia excelsa

The beautiful red and brown wood of this tree is highly regarded by woodworkers and used for fine work such as inlay. The tree is easily recognizable in its native bush and woodland habitats as the only columnar tree one is likely to see. It has been planted in California and, until the severe frosts of 1947, was naturalized in the far south-west of England.

Identification: The leaves are 10–15cm (4–6in) long, 3–4cm (1–1½in) wide, have toothed margins and are very hard. When young, they are coated in fine, soft hairs. The tree does not produce many flowers, and those that it does are usually hidden by foliage. They have a spidery appearance with the stigma emerging on long styles and are held in 5–10cm- (2–3in-) long clusters, which emerge from the branches in pairs. Thick maroon velvet covers the outside of the perianth and the stigma and stamens are creamy yellow.

Above: The winter flowers produce an exceptional amount of nectar, which may be collected.

Distribution: New Zealand North Island.
Height: 30m (100ft)
Shape: Columnar
Evergreen
Pollinated: Bee
Leaf shape: Narrowly oblong-obovate

Macadamia Nut

Macadamia integrifolia

The delicious nuts for which this species is famous are found inside the fruit. Macadamia nut trees are grown throughout the tropics, particularly in Australia and Hawaii, where they were introduced in 1890. The trees grow naturally in eastern Australia's rainforests but most grown commercially are selected grafted varieties. The wild tree is handsome with a dense, wide crown.

Identification: The leaves are leathery, glossy, dark green and up to 30cm (12in) long. They appear in whorls, have wavy-toothed margins and yellowish midribs. The tiny flowers form dangling tassels, 10–30cm (4–12in) long in winter and spring. Each flower is white, cream or pale pink. The fruit is usually ready in late summer, when it hangs in long clusters. Each fruit is spherical, 2.5cm (1in) across and green with a broad scar revealing the inner husk. The shell and husk are hard to break and poisonous.

Distribution: Queensland and northern New South Wales, Australia.
Height: 21m (70ft)
Shape: Domed
Evergreen
Pollinated: Insect
Leaf shape: Oblanceolate

Above: The fruit takes up to nine months to mature.

OTHER SPECIES OF NOTE

Silky Oak *Grevillea robusta*
This fast-growing, showy, evergreen tree from the tropical rainforests of Australia's eastern coast reaches 30m (100ft) tall. It is grown on farms for fodder, firewood, timber, shading, marking boundaries and protection from wind. It is also grown as an ornamental tree in tropical and warm temperate regions for its masses of long, spidery, golden yellow and orange flowers, which appear in spring. The 15–23cm (6–9in) long leaves are pinnate with lobed leaflets and greyish- or yellowish-green. The fruit is a yellow-brown capsule and contains two winged seeds.

See also page 253.

THE MYRTLE FAMILY

Many Myrtaceae are evergreen trees and shrubs having leaves with a distinctive spicy scent. They usually have smooth margins and grow opposite one another on the stem. The bark is often papery, peeling or splotched with pale and reddish patches. The flowers are arranged in various ways but often have many stamens, giving them a "powder-puff" look.

Clove

Syzygium aromaticum

Although most members of this genus are grown for their tasty fruit, this species is not. Instead, it yields cloves – immature flower buds, which are collected and dried in the sun for use in cooking, medicine and perfumery. Another product, clove oil, is extracted from the leaves and unripe fruit. The fruit of this tree tastes quite repugnant, having an overwhelmingly bitter flavour. Cloves are widely cultivated throughout the tropics and are particularly important to the economy of Zanzibar. In the wild this handsome tree is a rainforest species. It has a dense canopy and pretty, pink young leaves.

Identification: The short trunk has smooth, pale brown bark. The highly glossy, scented leaves are dark green above, paler below, heavily dotted with glands, have undulating margins and are 8–12cm (3–4½in) long. The scented flowers are produced in threes on a short panicle. Each is pale pink, yellow or green and 2cm (¾in) across. The fruit is oblong, red or purple when ripe and 2.5cm (1in) long.

Distribution: Maluku islands.
Height: 15m (50ft)
Shape: Conical
Evergreen
Pollinated: Insect
Leaf shape: Elliptical

Left: Clove leaves yield oil traditionally used in dentistry.

Right: Flower buds ready for harvest.

Malay Apple

Syzgium malaccense

Once seen, this tree is unforgettable; throughout the year cerise pink, shaving brush-like flowers explode from the trunk and mature branches, wherever there are no leaves. As well as being grown for its fruit, the Malay apple is sometimes cultivated in tropical parks and gardens as an ornamental plant or grown as a windbreak. The fruit has an apple-like taste, sweet yet slightly tart. It is eaten raw and also made into preserves and wine.

Identification: The short, buttressed trunk has fissured flaky bark that is light to reddish-brown. The handsome, bright green leaves are smooth, glossy and thick – almost succulent. They measure 15–30cm (6–12in) long and tend to hang under their own weight. Young leaves are pink. The flowers are held in clusters on short stems. Each is 5–7.5cm (2–3in) wide and has a multitude of stamens. The fruit is pear-shaped, smooth, 5–7.5cm (2–3in) long and changes from pale pink to purple as it ripens.

Distribution: Malaysia
Height: 23m (75ft)
Shape: Oblong
Evergreen
Pollinated: Insect
Leaf shape: Ovate

Right: The tree's showy flowers may be eaten in salads, and the youngest leaves and shoots may be eaten raw or cooked.

Golden Penda

Xanthostemon chrysanthus

This handsome, upright tree is regularly planted in tropical and subtropical gardens in Australia. It is grown for its fine foliage, which contrasts well with the sprays of golden yellow, showy flowers produced in winter or after heavy rain.

Identification: The bark is a light cinnamon-brown colour. The smooth, glossy leaves have long tapering points, are leathery, 20cm (8in) long and 4cm (1½in) wide. The upper surface of a mature leaf is dark green with a bright green midrib, and the lower surface is bright green. When young, leaves are reddish-bronze. The flowers are densely packed at the branch ends in cymes, each with five to ten individual blossoms. The flowers have masses of long stamens, making them look like shaving brushes. The round fruit is dark, almost black, and 1cm (½in) across.

Left: Fine specimens of the golden penda are found all over Cairns in Australia, where it is the city's floral emblem.

Distribution: North-east Australia and New Caledonia to Malaysia.
Height: 16m (52ft)
Shape: Rounded to columnar
Evergreen
Pollinated: Insect
Leaf shape: Narrowly elliptic-obovate

OTHER SPECIES OF NOTE

Mindanao Gum *Eucalyptus deglupta*
This tree has wonderful, colourful, flaky bark which peels off longitudinally to reveal smooth striations of green, cream, brown and pinkish brown below. Native to the Philippines, the Mindanao gum is widely planted in the tropics as a fast-growing timber tree, reaching at least 20m (66ft). The ovate leaves are 8–18cm (3–7in) long, and the 1cm (½in-) long flowers are white with many stamens. The fruit is woody, cup shaped and 5mm (¼in) across.

Rose Apple *Syzygium jambos*
The rose-water-scented fruits of this tree are eaten raw and used in confectionery and preserves. The tree is from South-east Asia. A 12m- (40ft-) tall tree, the rose apple has a dense, evergreen, rounded crown of 20cm (8in), lanceolate, glossy green leaves. It produces clusters of 6–8cm- (2½–3in-) wide, white, pale yellow or green shaving brush-like flowers at the branch tips. The fruit is round, 4cm (1⅝in) across, pale green, yellow or pink with white flesh.

Weeping Paperbark *Melaleuca quinquenervia*
The thick, shaggy, peeling bark is pale cinnamon-brown to white. The tree emits volatile oils that deter insects. The smooth, shiny, hard leaves are a bluish grey green, flat, 4–10cm (1½–4in) long and have parallel veins. The leaves are harvested and distilled to produce an essential oil that has numerous uses. The flowers occur throughout the year and are particularly abundant in spring. The fruits, which persist for many years, are 5mm- (¼in-wide), woody capsules packed tightly along the stem. *See also page 254.*

Crimson Bottlebrush

Callistemon citrinus

This aptly named tree is stunning in late spring and summer when covered in its glowing crimson flowers. It is often seen pruned into a dense shrub in tropical, subtropical and temperate gardens. If left to its own devices, it will branch close to the ground and form an arching crown of lax branches. From a seedling it grows quickly to 3m (10ft) tall then slows down. This species can tolerate light frost. In the wild in Australia it is seen in coastal localities.

Identification: The leaves are 4–9cm (1½–3½in) long, dark green and very tough. The young shoots are silky soft and downy, and the cylindrical flower spikes 10cm (4in) long and erect. The round fruit is a woody capsule 1cm (½in) wide and contains many minute seeds.

Distribution: Eastern Australia.
Height: 4.5m (15ft)
Shape: Spreading rounded
Evergreen
Pollinated: Birds
Leaf shape: Lanceolate

Right: The flowers have long stamens creating a fluffy impression. The plant stem continues to grow through the top of the flower spike, resulting in the fruit capsules developing away from the branch tip.

THE LOOSESTRIFE FAMILY

The Lythraceae family includes herbaceous plants, trees and shrubs but only a few are well known, and only a handful are used in horticulture. The trees have simple, smooth-edged leaves positioned opposite one another on the stem. The star-shaped flowers have petals that are crumpled up when in bud and appear in panicles, racemes or cymes. The fruit is a capsule or berry containing many seeds.

Queen's Crepe Myrtle

Pride of India *Lagerstromia speciosa*

This tree is grown as an ornamental plant for its large panicles of showy, pink flowers – the name "speciosa" actually means "showy". It grows wild in humid forests and along forested waterways. The queen's crepe myrtle has a dense crown that loses its leaves in the cooler winter months. The tree flowers in summer.

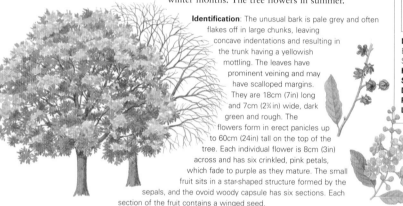

Identification: The unusual bark is pale grey and often flakes off in large chunks, leaving concave indentations and resulting in the trunk having a yellowish mottling. The leaves have prominent veining and may have scalloped margins. They are 18cm (7in) long and 7cm (2¾ in) wide, dark green and rough. The flowers form in erect panicles up to 60cm (24in) tall on the top of the tree. Each individual flower is 8cm (3in) across and has six crinkled, pink petals, which fade to purple as they mature. The small fruit sits in a star-shaped structure formed by the sepals, and the ovoid woody capsule has six sections. Each section of the fruit contains a winged seed.

Distribution: India, Sri Lanka, Burma, southern China and South-east Asia.
Height: 24m (80ft)
Shape: Spreading and round
Deciduous
Pollinated: Insect
Leaf shape: Elliptic

Above left: Leaves turn bright red before dropping.

Left: Cultivated forms have flowers in different shades of pink or mauve.

Henna

Lawsonia inerma

Henna dye is used to temporarily colour hair, skin, nails and teeth a rich, burnt orange colour. In Indian marriage ceremonies, for example, the bride has intricate henna patterns painted on her hands, arms and feet. Henna dye is made from a paste of the crushed and powdered leaves of the henna tree. The tree is heavily cultivated (and is naturalized) in India for its dye and is widely grown as a shrub or hedging plant. In Western countries henna is used as an ingredient in cosmetics.

Identification: The heavily branching twigs are grey and may carry spines. The leaves are greyish green, 4–6cm (1½–2½ in) long and 4cm (1½ in) wide. The flowers may be white, cream, greenish-yellow, pink or red and appear throughout the year. They are sweetly scented, 1cm (½ in) wide and held in panicles 20–25cm (8–10in) long. The 5mm (¼ in), round fruit contains numerous seeds and is reddish.

Distribution: North-east Africa (Egypt, Sudan, Ethiopia) through the Middle East to northern India.
Height: 8m (26ft)
Shape: Bushy
Evergreen
Leaf shape: Elliptic

Left: The flowers are heavily scented.

Far left: Henna trees are grown throughout the tropics. India and Pakistan export the dried leaves.

THE RED MANGROVE FAMILY

Many of the trees and shrubs in the Rhizophoraceae family are mangroves, living in brackish and salty
water along tropical coasts. Several allow their seeds to germinate while still attached to the branches,
giving them a better chance of getting established in-between tides. Leaf shape and size varies
considerably, but flowers are star shaped, and either solitary or produced in groups in the axils.

Red Mangrove

Rhizophora mangle

Distribution: Coastal tropical America and West Africa.
Height: 30m (100ft)
Shape: Domed or irregular
Evergreen
Pollinated: Wind or self
Leaf shape: Elliptic

Right: The thick waxy leaves are well adapted to harsh coastal conditions.

The red mangrove is an important species, ecologically speaking. Able to withstand truly saline conditions, it grows right down to the low tide mark, forming dense, often storm-proof thickets along coastlines and providing shelter for young fish and nest sites for birds. The red mangrove is able to survive where it does by excreting excess salt and by having pores on its roots that allow gaseous exchange when exposed to the air. This species is very slow growing and forms distinctive branching stilt roots. As time passes, the main trunk dies until eventually the aerial roots alone support the plant.

Identification: The bark is pinkish-red when young and grey when mature. The leaves sit opposite one another on the branch and are deep green with a prominent paler midrib. Thick, succulent and glossy, they may be up to 20cm (8in) long. The flowers appear throughout the year in groups in the axils. They are cream, 2cm (¾in) wide and have four thick petals. The fruit is 2.5cm (1in) long, brown and contains a single seed. The seedling may grow to 30cm (12in) before dropping from the tree.

Asiatic Mangrove

Rhizophora mucronata

Mangrove swamps, if they can be penetrated, make good locations for rearing fish for food. The calm waters around these trees provide a protective habitat for a rich diversity of fish, crustaceans and molluscs. The Asiatic mangrove grows from a seedling already developed on the branch before dropping. If it is unable to secure a footing in the soft mud when it lands, it may float around for up to a year and still grow upon contact with soil. It is harvested for its wood and bark, which provide an extract used for dyeing and tanning.

Identification: The leaves are bright green above and pale green dotted with red specks below. They have a sharp pointed tip and are 11–18cm (4½–7in) long. The white to pale yellow flowers are produced in bunches of three to five in the axils near the growing tips. The pendulous fruit is 4–5cm (1½–2in) long, ovoid to conical. The seedling may reach up to 75cm (30in) long before it drops.

Distribution: Coastal tropics India to Australia.
Height: 25m (82ft)
Shape: Spreading
Evergreen
Pollinated: Wind or self
Leaf shape: Elliptic

Left: The seedling may reach up to 75cm (30in) long before it drops.

THE SOAPBERRY FAMILY

The Sapindaceae family contains a large number of very diverse but mostly tropical trees, shrubs and climbers. The leaves may be simple, pinnate, bipinnate or even tripinnate. The small flowers, normally with three to five petals, form in branched clusters or in bunches with each flower on an individual stem. The fruit is also highly variable but is always composed of three sections.

Soap-nut

Sapindus emarginatus

The inedible fruit of this tree contains a substance called saponin, which lathers up in water. It is used in the manufacture of soap, or used whole, either fresh or dried, as a soap substitute. The fruit and roots also have medicinal value, and the flowers are a valuable source of nectar for honey production. Soap-nut trees grow naturally in dry, open areas of lowland monsoon forest and may be seen planted as ornamental trees in parks and gardens.

Identification: The trunk has rough, off-white bark and carries an open crown made up of numerous branches. The leaves are 10–20cm (4–8in) long and have four to six opposite or almost opposite leaflets. Each leaflet is 5–18cm (2–7in) long, elliptic to egg shaped and blunt ended or has a notched tip. The flowers are greenish white with rusty coloured down on the outside and occur in large, spreading clusters at the ends of twigs and branches. The spherical, 1.5–2.5cm- (⅔–1in-) wide fruit has thick flesh and is clustered in pairs or threes.

Distribution: Sri Lanka, India and Burma.
Height: 40m (130ft)
Shape: Domed
Deciduous
Pollinated: Bee
Leaf shape: Pinnate

Left: The fruit may be used as a soap substitute.

Fern Tree

Filicium decipiens

This slow-growing and long-lived tree is highly valued for its fine foliage and dense crown. It is tolerant of a wide range of growing conditions and is particularly prevalent in India where it is often seen planted along roadsides. The fern tree has hard, heavy, reddish-coloured timber, which is used in construction and the making of cartwheels and cabinetry.

Identification: The short trunk has rough, dark, reddish-grey bark and highly visible large leaf scars. The 30–40cm- (12–16in-) long leaves are made up of anything from 12–25 closely spaced, stemless, glossy leaflets. Between each leaflet the stem is flattened and wing-like at the edges. Each leaflet is 10–15cm (4–6in) long, narrowly oblong with a pronounced notch at the tip, has undulating margins and is deep dark green. The flowers appear in the winter – each is tiny and inconspicuous and has cream petals. They form into 15cm- (6in-) long branched clusters, which sprout from the leaf axils. The oval, fleshy fruit is purple, shiny and 1.5cm (⅔in) long.

Distribution: Southern India and Sri Lanka.
Height: 25m (80ft)
Shape: Domed
Evergreen
Leaf shape: Pinnate

Left and above: The tree is often multi-stemmed. It carries tiny resinous spots on the leaves, stems and flowers.

Right: The impressive spirally-arranged foliage of the fern tree. When very young the foliage gives the plant the look of a fern.

Ackee

Blighia sapida

The tasty fruit of the ackee is a popular ingredient in West Indian cooking, but extreme care must be exercised when preparing it. The thick, creamy flesh can be fried or boiled as a vegetable but contains highly poisonous seeds, which must be removed before cooking.

Identification: The tree is fast growing and forms a handsome, dense crown. The trunk is short and thick with grey bark. The leaves consist of three to ten egg-shaped to oblong leaflets, each of which is glossy, mid-green above and paler below, 15–30cm (6–12in) long with prominent veining. The scented flowers are hairy, white and hang from the tree. The smooth-skinned fruit is spherical to pear shaped and triangular with rounded corners in cross section. When ripe, it turns rosy pink, apricot, or red and measures 7.5–10cm (3–4in) long. The fruit divides into three sections, each containing a shiny black seed surrounded by white flesh.

Distribution: West Africa.
Height: 15m (50ft)
Shape: Rounded
Evergreen
Pollinated: Insect
Leaf shape: Pinnate

Left: The ackee fruit are deadly both before ripening and soon after bursting open.

Rambutan

Nephelium lappaceum

Rambutan fruits are particularly popular in Malaysia and parts of China. The translucent white flesh is firm, sweet and juicy, and where it is not available fresh, it is often sold in canned form. "Rambut" means "hair" in Malay, and this aptly describes the fruit, which is covered in thick, curled, soft, fleshy spines.

Identification: The tree has smooth brown bark and mid-green leaves, each 18cm (7in) long and divided into between two and six pairs of opposite leaflets. Each leaflet is oblong-elliptic, smooth, shiny and has a prominent midrib. The flowers appear in spring in large, spreading branched clusters. The fruit, which is ovoid, 5–6cm (2–2½in) long, yellowish, pinkish or orangey red, hangs in great bunches in late summer. Its hairy skin peels easily away to reveal white flesh enclosing a single large black seed.

Distribution: South-east Asia.
Height: 20m (66ft)
Shape: Spreading
Evergreen
Pollinated: Insect
Leaf shape: Pinnate

Above: The profuse flowers are small and white.

Below: In wild plants the fruit may lack the sweet, juicy white flesh for which rambutan are renowned.

OTHER SPECIES OF NOTE

Litchi *Litchi chinensis*
The litchi or lychee produces wonderfully tasty fruit. The litchi is related to the rambutan and similar in taste. It originates from southern China, where it is now under threat as the result of over-exploitation for its beautiful timber. It is grown across the warmer regions of Asia, but attempts to introduce it to other parts of the world have been mostly unsuccessful. The litchi grows slowly into a 15m- (50ft-) tall, rounded, evergreen tree with a dense crown and narrow trunk. The attractive pinnate leaves are 30cm (12in) long and divided into two to eight pairs of elliptic, deep green leaflets. The plentiful spring flowers are small, greenish white and hang in 30cm- (12in-) long branched clusters. The fruit appears in summer, is 4cm (1½in) long, ovoid and has brown, warty, hard skin. Inside the white fragrant flesh surrounds a single large seed.

Longan *Dimocarpus longan*
An evergreen fruit tree from the forests of south China, the longan is similar in appearance to the litchi apart from its bark, which is brown and fissured vertically. This species usually lives for over 100 years, with a few specimens reaching more than 1,000. Leaves are identical to the litchi, but the flowers are in erect branched clusters and provide a rich source of nectar for honey production in spring. The fruit is smooth, round and brown and tastes similar to watery litchis.

THE CASHEW FAMILY

The Anacardiaceae family includes a number of economically important tropical trees. It also contains shrubs and some temperate plants. Many members of the family have resinous bark and poisonous leaves with a white spirit-like odour. Leaves are pinnate or simple and arranged alternately or in whorls. Flowers are five-petalled stars, held in branched clusters, while the fruit has firm flesh surrounding a single seed.

Mango

Mangifera indica

Possibly the best known and most popular of all tropical fruit, the mango is thought to have been cultivated for more than 4,000 years. Mangoes are most widely grown in India, where legends surround the tree, and numerous varieties have been developed. The genus name comes from a mixture of Hindi and Latin; "mango" is the original Hindi name for the tree and "fera" is the Latin verb "to bear". The fruit of the mango tree is juicy.

Distribution: India to Malaysia.
Height: 30m (100ft)
Shape: Domed
Evergreen
Pollinated: Insect
Leaf shape: Lanceolate

Right: The fruit appears in late summer and varies greatly in shape, size and colour.

Identification: The trunk is buttressed when mature and carries a dense crown. The drooping leaves are red when young and deep green and glossy when mature. The flowers appear at the ends of twigs and branches in late winter in loose, branched clusters. Each cluster contains thousands of tiny individual blossoms, which may be pink, yellow, green, brown or white.

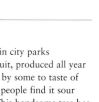

Right: The leaves reach up to 30cm (12in) long.

Golden Apple

Spondias dulcis

This fast-growing tree is seen in rural areas, gardens and occasionally in city parks throughout South-east Asia. It is grown for its large green to yellow fruit, produced all year round but particularly abundant in winter. When ripe, the fruit is said by some to taste of pineapple, but many people find it sour and unpleasant. This handsome tree has an open structure with few branches, large leaves and a beautiful trunk.

Identification: The trunk has smooth, almost white bark. The leaves are generally clustered towards the branch tips; they are up to 75cm (30in) long and have between 9–27 lanceolate leaflets, each of which is 10cm (4in) long, deep green, glossy and may have toothed margins. The tiny flowers are yellowish or greenish-white, fragrant and appear in large branched clusters, particularly in the spring. The fruit is oval, 7.5cm (3in) long, suffused with maroon and is soft and juicy when ripe.

Distribution: Indonesia and Polynesia.
Height: 20m (66ft)
Shape: Spreading
Semi-evergreen
Pollinated: Insect
Leaf shape: Pinnate

Right: Fruit often drops while still hard and green and is stored before turning golden.

Left: Young leaves are occasionally eaten raw or steamed.

THE MAHOGANY FAMILY

This family includes many important timber trees, some with sweetly scented timber. It also contains trees and shrubs with edible fruit or valuable seeds. The Meliaceae are tropical or subtropical trees and shrubs with pinnate or bipinnate leaves. The flowers have four or five petals and appear in branched clusters. The leathery-skinned fruit often contains seeds with wings.

Neem

Azadirachta indica

This fast-growing tree has a multitude of uses. Every part of it is used – its timber is termite resistant, its fruit produces medicinal oil, while its leaves and bark are collected and ground up for their insecticidal properties. Neem is planted throughout the arid and semi-arid tropics and is popular in India as an ornamental, shade, street or reforestation tree.

Identification: The erect, straight trunk supports an open crown. The glossy, mid-green leaves are up to 60cm (24in) long and have pairs of toothed, sickle-shaped, 7cm (2¾in) long leaflets. The star-shaped flowers are small, pale green, yellow or white and form airy, branched clusters from the leaf axils in spring. Flower clusters are usually partially hidden by foliage. The fruit is small, smooth-skinned, oblong and develops in the autumn. When ripe, it is orange, yellow or green-yellow.

Right: The fruit is up to 2cm (¾in) long, and contains one stone in a thin, sweet pulp.

Far right: Leaves are placed in books to deter insects.

Distribution: Sri Lanka, India and Burma.
Height: 20m (66ft)
Shape: Spreading
Evergreen
Pollinated: Insect
Leaf shape: Pinnate

Chinaberry

Bead tree *Melia azedarach*

In India this tree is venerated and grown for its pretty, honey-scented flowers, which are used as temple offerings. It is often called the "bead tree", as its poisonous seeds have a hole through them, making them ideal for threading. It was once grown in Italy specifically for the making of rosaries. The chinaberry is a short-lived tree that grows quickly and easily in dry tropical and subtropical areas. In some places it is considered a weed.

Identification: The trunk has smooth, thin, dark purplish or greyish-brown bark and carries brittle branches crowded with 50cm- (20in-) long leaves. The leaves have three to five pairs of pinnae, each with three to five pairs of leaflets. The leaflets are mid- to light green, ovate and have toothed margins. The flowers appear in large, branched clusters, which sprout from the leaf axils in spring. Each flower is pale pink with a dark purple tube at the centre and up to 2cm (¾in) wide. The abundant fruit appears in autumn; it is oval, pale yellow or orange and 2.5cm (1in) long.

Distribution: From Iraq to Japan down to Australia.
Height: 12m (40ft)
Shape: Spreading
Deciduous
Pollinated: Bee
Leaf shape: Bipinnate or tripinnate

Right: The chinaberry may produce its fragrant flowers all year round, and from a very young age, even when the tree is still a seedling.

THE RUE FAMILY

Many of these plants are strongly scented, often with a citrus-like aroma, and yield valuable oils. The oils are found in translucent glands, often visible in the flowers, fruit, leaves and bark. The Rutaceae family is comprised mostly of trees and shrubs and is well represented in Australia and South Africa. A number of the trees and shrubs have thorns, but throughout the family botanical features are highly variable.

Cape Chestnut

Calodendrum capense

This beautiful slow-growing tree is abundant in forests in its native range, where it is also an important timber source. Although preferring the company of other trees and plenty of moisture, it is planted throughout Africa and sub-tropical regions. The Latin name is translated as "beautiful tree of the cape" and each year huge clusters of pale pink scented flowers clothe the canopy.

Right: In some localities the foliage drops briefly in the autumn.

Identification: The smooth, grey trunk reaches 1m (3ft) in diameter. The leaves are deep green, 15cm (6in) long, 7.5cm (3in) wide and have many parallel veins. Terminal flowers appear in spring or summer; each is 9cm (3½in) across, has five pink petals, five pink stamens and five stamens impersonating petals. The autumn seed pods are brown, hard, round, 4cm (1½in) long and covered in blunt spines. When ripe they split into a five-petalled star and release black, triangular seeds.

Distribution: South Africa through to Kenya, not coastal.
Height: 18m (60ft)
Shape: Domed
Semi-evergreen
Pollinated: Insect
Leaf shape: Ovate

Right: The flowers appear in clusters of 8–12.

Curry Leaf

Murraya koenigii

The warm, strong, spicy, and slightly bitter flavour and aroma of the leaves of this plant have been exploited as a flavouring for curries in Indian cuisine. The distinctive scent cannot be substituted with any other spice. Although often found in mulligatawny soup and Madras curry mixes it does not play a major role in most curries. Additionally the bark, leaves and roots are used as a tonic, and the berries are edible, having a peppery flavour. The plant grows as a dense shrub or small tree in drier areas of its range.

Identification: The trunk remains narrow and carries a dense crown of foliage. Each leaf is composed of 10–20 leaflets up to 5cm (2in) long. Leaflets may be hairy, are bright green and paler below. The small, fragrant yellowish white flowers are found in loose panicles in summer. The small berries are black.

Distribution: Sri Lanka, India and Pakistan.
Height: 6m (20ft)
Shape: Round-headed
Evergreen
Pollinated: Insect
Leaf shape: Pinnate

Left: Fresh leaves are preferred for cooking. These are oven dried immediately prior to using.

Right: The 1cm (½in) flowers form panicles of up to 90 flowers.

Orange Jessamine

Murraya paniculata (L.) Jack.

This beautifully scented plant has its leaves and bark powdered to make the sweetly scented Thanaka powder. This is a famous scent in Asia and widely used by Burmese and Thai women. The small, scented, white flowers, reminiscent of orange blossom, are also used for perfumery in Java and make popular offerings in temples. This lovely dense plant is grown throughout the tropics. It may be grown as a bush and is often seen as a houseplant in temperate zones.

Identification: This tree is often multi-stemmed and carries a dense crown of dark green glossy foliage. Each 20cm- (8in-) long leaf is composed of six to nine elliptic 4cm- (1½in-) long leaflets. The flowers form in spring, summer and autumn. They are in dense clusters over the crown of the tree. Each flower is 2cm (¾in) across with four or five thick creamy white petals. The fruit is a red berry 1cm (½in) across. This plant is grown as hedging, a shrub, a tree, topiary, and may even be treated as a bonsai.

Distribution: Burma, Thailand and northern Malay Peninsula.
Height: 6m (20ft)
Shape: Round-headed
Evergreen
Pollinated: Insect
Leaf shape: Pinnate

Left: The scent from these waxy flowers fills the air in tropical gardens.

OTHER SPECIES OF NOTE

Mountain Pride *Spathelia sorbifolia*
An unusual tree from the West Indies with an elegant stem to 15m (50ft) and no branches. The crown consists of a tuft of large feathery evergreen pinnate leaves, each with 20–40 pairs of oblong to lanceolate-shaped leaflets. The huge terminal flower panicle may reach several metres in length and carries large red to purple flowers. The fruit has two wings.

African Cherry Orange *Citropsis schweinfurthii*
This small tree from central Africa occurring from Sudan to Congo is related to *Citrus*. It has spines, leathery pinnate leaves with winged midribs, white flowers and clusters of small, orange, sweetly flavoured fruit. The leaflets are narrowly lanceolate, the flowers are large and the 4cm (1½in) fruit has three or four segments to it.

Caffre Lime *Citrus hystrix*
This citrus grows only to 5m (16ft). It is grown in tropical Asia through to Sri Lanka for the very warty, 10cm- (4in-) long, pear-shaped fruit. The yellow fruit has little juice and is used in medicine, as food flavouring and in shampoos but is not eaten. The bright green leaves are also used as a curry spice.

Tetradium ruticarpum
From the valleys of the Himalayas through India to Taiwan comes this small evergreen tree with dense foliage. The branches are clothed with pinnate leaves and flowers with a soft velvety down. The small flowers are carried in panicles 7–10cm (2¾–4in) across.

Calamondin

x *Citrofortunella microcarpa*

This plant is a result of a rare natural cross between two closely related genera, in this case *Citrus* and *Fortunella*. It carries characteristics of both parents. The *Fortunella* parent, kumquat, lends a dense shrubby habit, small leaves and a hardy constitution, whereas the *Citrus reticulata*, mandarin orange, lends thorns, tasty fruit and ease of peeling. So the calamondin has smallish, easy to peel fruit with an acidic flavour. It grows well in truly tropical areas through to those with very occasional mild frosts. With its upright habit, dark glossy foliage and multitude of small brightly coloured fruits the calamondin makes a fine ornamental and is well suited to growing in containers.

Identification: The glossy leaves are about 7cm (2¾in) long and paler green below. Flowers are in clusters, each is 2.5cm (1in) wide, and white with an intoxicating scent. The orange fruit is up to 6cm (2½in) across and round.

Right: The attractive calamondin is grown as a houseplant in temperate zones.

Distribution: Laos and Vietnam.
Height: 7.5m (25ft)
Shape: Columnar
Evergreen
Pollinated: Insect
Leaf shape: Elliptic

MISCELLANEOUS ROSIDAE

These small families are all related within the class Rosidae. The mistletoe family, Loranthaceae, are
semi-parasitic plants. The torchwood family, Bursuraceae, is a small tropical family often producing
resins. The caltrop family, Zygophyllaceae, includes few trees, while the wood sorrel family, Oxalidaceae,
is composed almost entirely of herbaceous plants.

Brush Box

West Australian Christmas tree *Nuytsia floribunda*

Distribution: Western
Australia.
Height: 9m (30ft)
Shape: Domed, spreading
Evergreen
Pollinated: Bird
Leaf shape: Linear

Right: The sheer weight of the
flowers often breaks the
branches.

This tree is a sinister parasite that saps resources from other
plants. Unlike many parasites, it is terrestrial, attacking plants
underground. Underground stems travel more than 100m
(328ft) from the trunk, and on contact with another
plant's root their own roots encircle the host and pierce
it to absorb foods. Seeds and seedlings are rare, instead
the plant sends up suckers from underground stems,
resulting in clusters of the trees in the sandy damp
areas it likes. The trees are awkward and heavy-set
with brittle, lightweight branches. At Christmas
time though, they become smothered in
vibrant, golden-orange, honey-scented
flowers.

Identification: The mid-brown to
grey trunk can reach 1.2m (4ft) in
diameter. The rigid leaves are up to 7.5cm (3in)
long and 5mm (¼in) wide. The six-petalled flowers
are packed into dense racemes 10–15cm (4–6in)
long, crowded at the end of the branches. The fruit is
a nut 1cm (½in) long.

Java Almond

Canarium luzonicum

In its native home this fast-growing tree has many local uses. A
gum with a fresh lemony scent, known as brea gum or elemi, is
extracted from the trunk. The gum is used in healing
ointments, for soothing muscles and as a dietary
supplement. The gum provides a valuable volatile oil
thought to have anti-ageing properties. The flowers are
popular with bees and useful in bee keeping. The fruit
has an edible kernel, somewhat similar in taste to an
almond, from which oil is also extracted. The oil is
used for cooking and burning in lamps. The tree also
makes a fine ornamental specimen and works well as an
avenue. It is particularly popular in Java as a shade tree.

Distribution: Philippines.
Height: Large
Shape: Domed
Evergreen
Pollinated: Insect
Leaf shape: Pinnate

Identification: The trunk has enormous buttresses, which are nearly
uniform in thickness throughout. Leaves measure up to
45cm (18in) long and have seven to nine small ovate to
oblong leaflets. Leaflets vary from 7cm (2¾in) to 20cm (8in)
in length. The small, scented white flowers have three petals
and are clustered into terminal panicles. The fruit forms in large
hanging clusters in summer. Each fruit is oval, 4cm (1½in)
long and dark purple when ripe.

Below: The fruit contains one
hard, pointed stone, which has
an edible kernel inside it.

THE BEAN SUBFAMILY

Within the legumes many species have leaves that close up during stress or at night and which may be moved by the plant through the day. The bean subfamily, Faboideae, has flowers with five irregular petals: a large upper petal covers the others while the flower is in bud; two side petals form wings upon opening; and the two lower petals, often fused, form a keel.

Burmese Rosewood

Pterocarpus indicus

This tree is famous for its fine, termite-resistant timber, which is hard, yellow to brick red in colour, has an interlocking wavy grain and is rose scented. Burmese rosewood commands a high price and polishes to a high shine: it is used in furniture-making, turnery and for panelling and flooring. A red dye may be extracted from the wood, and red gum exuded from it is used locally for medicinal purposes.

Distribution: East Indies.
Height: 40m (130ft)
Shape: Spreading and domed
Semi-evergreen
Pollinated: Bee
Leaf shape: Pinnate

Identification: The trunk has finely fissured, light brown bark with well developed, large, flat, spreading buttresses in mature trees. The branches are wide spreading, elegantly arched and may trail to the ground. The leaves are pinnate, 50cm (20in) long, deep green and have seven to eleven ovate, pointed leaflets. Found in racemes, which protrude from the axils, each is 1.5cm (⅝in) across.

Right: "Pterocarpus" means "winged-fruit". The seed pods are 3–5cm (1¼–2in) across, flat and brown with a circular wing.

Far right: The golden-yellow flowers are produced in summer.

Tahiti Chestnut

Inocarpus edulis

Distribution: Tahiti and neighbouring islands.
Height: 20m (66ft)
Evergreen
Pollinated: Bird
Leaf shape: Oblong

Right: The leaves, flowers and fruit of this tree are not typically bean-like.

The large fleshy seeds of the Tahiti chestnut are eaten in its native island home; they are boiled and roasted while still unripe and said by some to taste as good as roasted almonds. The foliage is also very appetizing to livestock. The Tahiti chestnut grows in humid valleys and damp swampy locations. It grows quickly into a handsome tree with straight, heavily fluted, buttressed trunks. This species has clear sap that turns scarlet upon contact with the air. The sap is used as a dye and also medicinally.

Identification: The alternate leaves are large, glossy and leathery, measure about 40cm (16in) long and have short leaf stems. The leaves are bright green when young and mature to a dark green. The winter flowers are small and fragrant, and in axillary spikes, white with the five petals fused into a short tube. The fibrous pods are pale orange, tough skinned, 5cm (2in) across, roundish but lumpy, and contain one or occasionally two seeds.

THE EUPHORBIA FAMILY

A large family of over 200 genera, the Euphorbiaceae includes herbs, climbers, shrubs and trees, many with white poisonous sap. The leaves are highly variable, and the small flowers are often without petals. The flowers are either male or female and occur on individual stalks in bunched clusters called cymes or on branched structures known as panicles. The fruit is usually split into three sections.

Candleberry Tree

Aleurites moluccana

This fast-growing native of hillside forests has been cultivated for hundreds of years and is now naturalized throughout the tropics. Annually each tree produces up to 46kg (100lbs) of poisonous nuts, which are 50 per cent oil and burnt for light, hence the tree's common name. The nutshells are used as beads and yield a dye, while the timber is a popular choice for canoe and house-building.

Identification: The thick, straight trunk has relatively smooth grey bark. Leaves are clustered towards the branch tips, have oil glands and are slightly scented if crushed. Each leaf is 10–20cm (4–8in) long, divided into three or five lobes and has pale rusty down on the underside. Young leaves and shoots are coated in fine white down. Tiny, white, bell-shaped flowers are produced throughout the year in long, terminal panicles. The rough skinned, hard, pale green fruit is a 5cm- (2in-) wide ball.

Left: The fruit contains one seed and is poisonous when raw but can be eaten cooked.

Left and right: The juvenile and mature leaves differ in shape.

Distribution: Maluku and South Pacific Islands.
Height: 18m (60ft)
Shape: Domed
Evergreen
Pollinated: Insect
Leaf shape: Broadly ovate

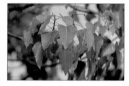

OTHER SPECIES OF NOTE

Common Tree Euphorbia *Euphorbia ingens*
This is a spiny, succulent tree species. It reaches 12m (40ft) in height and comes from the Natal area of eastern South Africa. The common tree euphorbia has a stout, fissured, brown trunk with many erect branches reaching up to form the crown. Each branch is formed from a stacked series of green segments shaped like upside-down hearts. The edges to the segments may have paired, dark brown spines along them. The flowers appear in summer and are yellowish green.

Mahang *Macaranga gigantae*
This 18m (60ft), short-lived, soft-wooded tree is common in Malaysia. It is grown for its unusually large leaves which reach 80cm (32in) long and across. Leaves are divided into three or five large lobes and are hairy on the underside. The minute male and female flowers are found in separate panicles up to 30cm (12in) long.

Peregrina

Jatropha integerrima

This tree is grown for its continuous display of vibrant, intense cerise pink or scarlet flowers. In the wild it often grows as a multi-stemmed tree, but may be trained in gardens to retain its young, shrub-like habit or force it to grow as a single-stemmed specimen. It has been successfully introduced into areas of Australasia and in temperate countries it is sold as a houseplant.

Identification: The bark is brown and fissured. The glossy leaves are deep green with paler veining. They are 4–15cm (1½–6in) long, vary from elliptic to egg shaped, have smooth margins and may be partially and irregularly lobed with a long point. Each flower is either male or female, 2.5–5cm (1–2in) wide and has five petals; the male flowers have yellow anthers. The fruit is round in shape, 1–1.5cm (½–⅔in) wide and split into three sections when ripe.

Distribution: Cuba, West Indies and Peru.
Height: 6m (20ft)
Shape: Columnar
Evergreen
Pollinated: Insect
Leaf shape: Irregular

Below: The flower cymes bear many more male than female flowers.

THE DOGBANE FAMILY

This family is renowned for its toxic properties. Plants contain a large quantity of poisonous, milky latex, which in some species is of value to humans. The family is also valuable for its contribution to ornamental horticulture. Most of the Apocynaceae are tropical, and many are shrubs. The simple leaves are usually opposite, the five-petalled flowers are funnel shaped and the fruit is usually dry and in pairs.

Dita Bark

Alstonia scholaris

Distribution: Throughout the tropical regions of Asia, Africa and northern Australia.
Height: 30m (100ft)
Shape: Oblong
Evergreen
Leaf shape: Narrowly oblong

A drug is sourced from the bark of this tree to treat malaria, the white sap can be extracted as rubber and the soft, pale lightweight timber has many uses, including for coffins and as plyboard, but it must not be used in contact with food. The timber was used historically in southern India for writing-tablets in schools, and this application explains the species name "scholaris". It is a fast-growing tree from monsoon regions and rainforests.

Identification: The straight trunk has pale, smooth bark and branches radiating out in horizontal tiers from its upper two thirds. The whorls of glossy, leathery leaves are clustered towards the branch tips, and each is deep green, paler and heavily veined below and 15–23cm (6–9in) long. In summer the terminal clusters of beautifully scented tiny greenish-white to cream flowers appear. The fruit is a 60cm- (24in-) long, deep blue pod that splits open to release many seeds.

Far right: The tiny scented flowers form in clusters 8–13cm (3–5in) wide all over the tree's crown.

Pong Pong

Sea mango *Cerbera odollam*

Naturally found in coastal forests and mangrove areas, this plant has been cultivated successfully in gardens in swampy areas, with saline soil or salty air. In addition to the attractive tropical foliage it has large, colourful fruit. The fruit is reminiscent of mango in appearance, which has resulted in its other common name of "sea mango". However, the fruit is poisonous. The tree is closely related to the frangipanis with which it shares a number of characteristics.

Identification: The sturdy grey trunk carries a dense crown. The deep green, shiny, leathery leaves with pale midribs are 15cm (6in) long and cluster at the branch tips. The scented flowers are 8cm (3in) wide, white with a yellow or red eye and form in terminal clusters all year around. The smooth round fruit is 10cm (4in) across and ripens from green through pink and red to black.

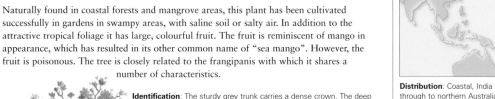

Distribution: Coastal, India through to northern Australia.
Height: 15m (50ft)
Shape: Rounded to oblong
Evergreen
Pollinated: Insect
Leaf shape: Narrowly obovate

Left: The pong pong flowers appear throughout the year. They have a sweet scent but are shortlived and last only for a day or two.

Right: The large poisonous seed contained within the fruit has been used as a rat poison.

THE IVY FAMILY

The ivy family, Araliaceae, spans temperate and tropical regions and encompasses trees, shrubs, climbers and herbs. Some are prickly and in tropical countries may be epiphytic or semi-epiphytic. They are grown for their foliage yet often have an unpleasant scent. Their alternate leaves vary immensely, whereas flowers are more distinctive, small and usually arranged in umbels. The fruit is often a small black berry.

Snowflake Tree

Trevesia palmata

'Micholitzii' is the most commonly grown form of this jungle tree. The extraordinary leaves are large and complex. They are shaped like a snowflake, though with many more points. The leaf is also coated with a snowy woolly pubescence and white speckles, giving an additional snowy feel. The plant makes few branches, many specimens have no branches at all, and is sometimes grown as a large shrub.

Identification: The trunk and stems are covered in short sharp spines. The hanging branches are white with pubescence. The leaf stems reach over 60cm (24in) in length. The leathery leaves are virtually round and 60cm (24in) across. They are mid-green with white markings and have central webbing and 7–11 lobed sections with toothed edges. The spring flowers are pale green to cream, 2cm (1in) across, have 8–12 petals and are clustered into umbels arranged on 45cm- (18in-) long terminal panicles. The fruits are fleshy, oval and 1cm (½in) across.

Distribution: Northern India eastward to Vietnam and southern China and southward into peninsular Malaysia.

Height: 6m (20ft)
Shape: Oblong
Evergreen
Leaf shape: Palmate

Left: The youngest leaves and growing tips are eaten in Thailand.

Left: The flower and fruit-bearing stems arch heavily away from the plant.

OTHER SPECIES OF NOTE

Umbrella Tree *Schefflera actinopylla*
In its native forests of Queensland and New South Wales, Australia, the 18m (60ft) evergreen umbrella tree may start life as an epiphyte, eventually strangling the host plant. It is popular for its fast-growing nature, unusual, colourful flowers and fruit, and thick glossy foliage. It is columnar while young, developing a multi-stemmed oblong crown with age. It has been very widely planted throughout the tropics as an ornamental, but in many countries has become a weed. In cooler climates it is successful as a houseplant. It often has many slender, soft-wooded, brown trunks carrying few branches but a dense canopy. Individual trunks will become quite sturdy with age. In humid climates plants may send down aerial roots from mature branches. The leaves are thick, glossy, dark green, 60cm (24in) across and divided into 9–15 oblong leaflets. The red flowers are 5mm (¼in) across and clustered into umbels along 1m/1yd-long terminal spikes in summer. The tiny flower petals fall off as they open. The flowers are pollinated by insects, resulting in long spikes carrying the fruit, which is deep red to black, round and 1.5cm (½in) wide.

Puka *Mertya denhamii*
From New Caledonia comes this impressive 6m (20ft), slender, round-headed tree. On mature trees the immense leaves reach 1.2m (4ft) in length and are clustered at the tips of the branches. Each leaf is

leathery, oblanceolate and has toothed margins. The tiny, pale green flowers cluster in panicles in spring and summer. The black fruit is 1.5cm (½in) long.

Rice Paper Tree *Tetrapanax papyrifer*
Originating from Taiwan, this moderately hardy, fast-growing, suckering tree or shrub reaches 6m (20ft). The lightweight trunks contain white pith used in Asia to make a type of Chinese rice paper. These narrow trunks rarely branch but carry enormous palmate leaves, each up to 75cm (30in) across. The tiny, cream, autumnal flowers are packed into round umbels, arranged in panicles. The small fruit is round and black.

False Aralia *Schefflera elegantissima*
This evergreen plant is common in cool temperate areas as a beautiful, low-maintenance, foliage houseplant. In this form it is unrecognizable as the same plant found growing in the under-storey of tropical rainforests. The habit and leaves of a mature plant are very different to those of a young one. The juvenile leaves are fine, elegant and delicate with dark colouring, light midribs and toothed and wavy edges. A juvenile plant has many narrow, straight unbranched stems, whereas mature plants have branches, and the foliage is much larger. The trunks are pale with no branches close to the ground. The leaves are divided into 6–10 leaflets.

Mallet Flower

Schefflera pueckleri

Incredibly, this beautiful, densely-crowned tree was only brought into cultivation in the 1960s. This tree naturally occurs in damp forested areas and prefers shady conditions. In the wild it normally grows with multiple trunks, but as it ages it may take on climbing characteristics and become a huge forest liana. In cultivation, it may be grown as a large shrub, wide spreading tree or narrow specimen. In temperate zones, it is becoming widely available as a fast-growing houseplant and is also successfully included in interior planting schemes.

Identification: The deep green, smooth, leathery, glossy leaves are composed of seven to ten pendulous leaflets, each 10–18cm (4–7in) long, narrowly oblong with a pronounced midrib. The leaf and leaflet stems are often red. The odd, greenish, mallet-shaped flowers are up to 3cm (1¼in) across. They have thick, fleshy, leathery petals, which drop off as a cap, and numerous crowded white stamens. In the wild, three to seven flowers form into short, stout, spreading, terminal panicles directly from the main stem or older wood, but these are rare in cultivation. The rounded, fleshy fruit can have a diameter of up to 4cm (1½in).

Distribution: Northern India through to Vietnam.
Height: 12m (40ft)
Shape: Oblong
Evergreen
Leaf shape: Palmate

Left: The leaves are thick, tough, smooth and shiny. Each leaflet hangs down creating an umbrella-like shape to the entire leaf.

Ming Aralia

Polyscias fruticosa

This popular and fast-growing tropical garden plant is often seen as a large shrub or hedge, for which it is well suited. If grown as a tree, the columnar habit makes it a useful "architectural" feature. It makes a fine, graceful specimen, often with multiple trunks. The elegantly cut foliage tends to form in rounded tiers up the trunks. It is also grown as an attractive houseplant in temperate zones, where many different varieties have been developed through the houseplant industry.

Identification: The leaves are variable but most often tripinnate. Each is up to 75cm (30in) long with dark green speckled stems. The leaflets are up to 10cm (4in) long, ovate, smooth, leathery, dark green and heavily toothed on the margins. The insignificant flowers form throughout the year in umbels, arranged in terminal panicles 15–20cm (6–8in) long. Up to 40 tiny, off-white flowers form each umbel. The fruit is ovoid and may reach up to 2.5cm (1in) in length.

Distribution: India through to Polynesia (Burma, Vietnam, Indonesia).
Height: 8m (26ft)
Shape: Columnar
Evergreen
Leaf shape: Pinnate, bipinnate and tripinnate

Left: There are different forms of the ming aralia. Some forms have finely divided foliage, others have congested, twisted leaflets similar to parsley.

THE COMBRETUM FAMILY

The Combretaceae family includes trees, climbers and shrubs. Its members vary significantly and have few consistent features. Many of the trees have large yet narrow buttresses and yellow inner bark, and the flowers usually have greatly reduced petals and protruding anthers. The fruit, which is dry, is dispersed by water or wind, and has wing-like structures protruding from it.

Leadwood

Combretum imberbe

This tree, a protected species in its native South Africa, may live more than 2,000 years, and may remain standing for an equally long time after death. Its leaves are popular with browsing animals, such as giraffes, elephants and impala. It also produces an edible gum. The leadwood tree is named after its exceptionally hard and heavy wood. Ash produced from burning the wood is sometimes used as toothpaste.

Identification: The trunk has silvery grey bark fissured into rectangular pieces and carries a dense network of branches. The leaves have undulate margins. They are 5cm (2in) long, 1.5cm (⅔in) wide, dull green and heavily spotted with tiny white glands on both surfaces. Young leaves are bright green and develop from pinkish-brown shoots. The creamy yellow, orange or red flowers appear in winter on long spikes. The fruit is leathery and contains a single seed.

Distribution: Tanzania to northern South Africa.
Height: 20m (66ft)
Semi-evergreen
Leaf shape: Elliptic-oblong

Left: The fruit forms in spring and summer, and is dispersed by the wind on four papery wings.

Left: A flower spike.

Tropical Almond

Terminalia catappa

The nuts of this tree are incredibly hard and popular with humans and animals. The tree is highly tolerant of salt and is often grown along beaches to provide shade and help stabilize the soil. Its reddish timber is used for boat construction. The tropical almond is a good-looking tree with horizontal tiers of foliage that spread out to make it wider than it is tall.

Identification: The trunk is short and dark, and the smooth, glossy leaves cluster towards the branch tips. The leaves are deep green turning bright orange, red or purple before dropping at any time of year. The flowers occur mostly in summer on 23cm- (9in-) long spikes, produced near the branch tips. The fruit is greenish-yellow or red, almond shaped and 5cm (2in) long.

Distribution: Tropical coastal Asia.
Height: 24m (80ft)
Shape: Spreading
Deciduous
Pollinated: Insect
Leaf shape: Obovate

Above: The inconspicuous but fragrant flowers are greenish white to cream.

Left and right: Leaves are leathery and 30cm (12in) long.

THE VERBENA FAMILY

This large family contains well known and useful plants. It is found mostly in the southern hemisphere and includes herbs, climbers, shrubs and trees, some of which are aromatic. Verbenaceae often have square-shaped twigs, and flowers with a long tube divided into five petals. The fruit is a hard capsule or fleshy with a hard stone, divided into four sections, each with one seed.

Teak

Tectona grandis

The wonderful hard timber of the teak tree was first brought to Europe in the early 1800s. It has remained a constantly popular choice for quality furniture production ever since. As a result, the monsoon forests of which it is native have been stripped of their specimens, and now few wild trees remain. Originally elephants would have been used to extract the timber before it was floated downriver out of the forest. Now, the fast-growing teak is planted in large plantations across its indigenous area.

Identification: The straight trunk carries many tiered branches and has pale grey, soft, fissured, peeling bark. The leaves are of colossal size, up to 80cm (32in) long and 40cm (16in) wide with undulating margins and prominent veining. They are rough and leathery, mid-green above and covered in soft white hairs below. The tiny cream flowers are found in large panicles 45cm (18in) long in early summer. The fleshy fruit is round, 2cm (¾in) across and purplish red or brown.

Right: The old bark peels off in small, thin, oblong pieces, revealing the yellow inner bark.

Left: The flowers appear after the tree has put on its new leaves in the wet season.

Distribution: Tropical India to Vietnam.
Height: 35m (115ft)
Shape: Oblong
Deciduous
Pollinated: Insect
Leaf shape: Widely elliptical

Meru Oak

Vitex keniensis

This tree is native to the moist evergreen mountain forests and rocky hillsides of Kenya and Tanzania but has a wide distribution including deciduous woodland, savannah, coastal and upland regions. It has valuable, hard teak-like timber used for furniture, boat-making and building poles. It is valuable to farmers because it has the ability to fix nitrogen in the soil.

Identification: The trunk has thin, lightly fissured bark and is clear of branches at the base. The leaves are divided into five obovate leaflets, each 5 x 8cm (2 x 3in), leathery, deep green above and paler below. The flowers form in the spring in a 15cm (6in) cyme. Each is less than 1cm (½in) long and white and mauve. The elliptic, fleshy fruit takes five months to develop. When ripe it is soft, black, 1.5cm (⅝in) long and has a tough leathery skin.

Right: The ripe fruit is popular with birds and monkeys. The leaves are coated on both surfaces with soft hairs and glands.

Distribution: Central and southern Africa.
Height: 40m (130ft)
Shape: Rounded
Deciduous
Pollinated: Insect
Leaf shape: Palmate

THE BIGNONIA FAMILY

Bignoniaceae is one of the more readily recognized families. They are native to the tropics and subtropics and include trees, shrubs, a few herbs and many climbing plants. Their funnel-shaped flowers are usually found in panicles or racemes and are some of the most flamboyant. Their compound leaves are opposite. The fruit is normally long, splitting into two to release numerous flat winged seeds.

Sausage Tree

Kigelia africana

The huge brown, sausage-shaped fruit hanging on long cords has given this tree its name. Originally a forest tree, it is now grown for curiosity and shade throughout the tropics. Although the hanging flower panicles reach 2m (6ft) in length, the tree is not noted for its floral display. Only one or two flowers open at any one time on a panicle, and they open overnight and have an unpleasant scent. In central Africa the tree is considered sacred, and the fruit is used medicinally and to flavour beer but is not eaten.

Identification: The smooth, grey barked trunk carries a dense head of spreading branches. The 30cm- (12in-) long leaves cluster near branch tips; they comprise 7–13 leaflets, deep green, oblong, glossy, and 4–18cm (1½–7in) long. The early summer, trumpet-like flowers are dark red or purple and 9–13cm (3½–5in) long. Smooth, woody fruit, up to 60cm (24in) long, hangs for many months and contains large seeds in pulp.

Distribution: Tropical Africa (Sudan to Senegal to Swaziland).
Height: 18m (60ft)
Shape: Rounded spreading
Evergreen
Pollinated: Bat
Leaf shape: Pinnate

Left: The fruit weighs up to 4kg (9lb). Atypically for this family it does not split open and the seeds do not have wings.
Right: The sausage tree is tolerant of arid conditions and is planted in India. When young, the foliage has a reddish hue.

African Tulip Tree

Spathodea campanulata

This outstanding tree is easy to spot and to recognize. It is grown throughout the tropics for its spectacular display of intense orange-red flowers radiating against the dark foliage. A pure yellow form is occasionally seen, too. In some places these fast-growing trees are used to mark land ownership boundaries. Their soft wood is brittle, often resulting in damage in windy conditions.

Identification: The pale trunk carries only a few thick branches but a dense crown. The 60cm (24in), dark green leaves are composed of 9–21 ovate leaflets, each about 10cm (4in) long. The terminal flowers appear throughout the yea. Domes of tightly packed buds open in succession over many weeks. Each tulip-shaped flower is 10–15cm (4–6in) long, yellow inside, and red outside with a frilly golden edge to the petals and an unusual scent. The smooth, woody pods are 20cm (8in) long, 5cm (2in) wide and split open to release hundreds of winged seeds.

Distribution: Uganda.
Height: 25m (82ft)
Shape: Oblong
Evergreen
Pollinated: Bat
Leaf shape: Pinnate

Left and right: The finger-like flower buds are full of water and when squeezed will squirt water.

THE SAPODILLA FAMILY

These tropical and subtropical trees and shrubs of the Sapotaceae family are an ecologically important part of the South American rainforest. They all have milky sap and leaves with smooth margins. The small flowers are whitish, greenish or tan and have four to eight petals fused into a tube at the base. The often edible fruit is fleshy, and the seeds are big, shiny and dark brown with a lighter coloured scar.

Chicle Tree

Manilkara zapota

The sweet fruit of this tree is very popular in tropical America, where it is eaten raw and made into syrups and preserves. The trunk produces a gum, which may be tapped every two or three years. Called "chicle", this was the original base for chewing gum, but it is now rarely used. Chicle trees are grown in plantations in tropical America and the Far East. The thick branches, closely set in tiers, have incredibly dense foliage.

Distribution: Mexico, Belize, Guatemala, northern Colombia.
Height: 35m (115ft)
Shape: Domed
Evergreen
Pollinated: Insect
Leaf shape: Elliptic

Identification: The bark is grey to brown and made up of small interlocking plates. The 13–15cm- (5–6in-) long, leathery leaves are glossy dark green with a prominent midrib and clustered towards the branch tip. The flowers are small, greenish or creamy white, tubular and found in the leaf axils, while the 8cm- (3in-) wide fruit is spherical to egg shaped and has rough, matt brown skin. The flesh varies from cream to yellowish or even reddish brown.

Left: The leaves are glossy and attractive.
Right: The fruits are produced all year and have a grainy (pear-like) texture.

Gutta Percha

Palaquium gutta

This tree is the main source of gutta-percha, a rubber-like latex, which is elastic and soft when heated and sets hard when cooled. Gutta-percha is used in moulds and for insulating underwater cables and wires. It was originally extracted by cutting the trees down and slashing the bark. Recently this species has become protected, so now the latex is tapped. Each tree may be tapped only once every year, or it stops yielding. Gutta-percha may also be extracted from the leaves, if required. As with many other plant products, gutta-percha has been largely replaced by synthetic alternatives, and the market for the natural product has reduced.

Above: These trees were once common in lowland forest areas but are now a protected species.

Distribution: Malaysia, Sumatra, Borneo.
Height: 12m (40ft)
Shape: Conical
Evergreen
Leaf shape: Obovate-oblong

Identification: The dark green leaves are 10cm (4in) long, leathery with shining golden to cinnamon-coloured velvety hairs below. Young branches are also coated in these hairs. The green, strongly-scented flowers form in clusters in the leaf axils. The fruit is an egg-shaped berry, 2–4cm (¾–1¼ in) with one or two seeds.

Left: The fruit has six thin cavities within.

Left: The leaves' lower golden surface is exposed when they shimmer in a breeze.

THE MADDER FAMILY

This is an important and virtually wholly tropical family of trees, shrubs, climbers and herbaceous plants. A number of the family Rubiaceae have economic and/or ornamental value. The family is easy to recognize. Leaves always have smooth margins, are most often oppositely arranged and simple. Flowers are usually tubular with four or five flared petals, and the fruit is usually divided into two sections.

Quinine Tree

Cinchona officinalis

Distribution: Ecuador and Peru.
Height: 10m (33ft)
Shape: Oblong to rounded
Evergreen
Pollinated: Insect and hummingbird
Leaf shape: Ovate-lanceolate

One of the most important medicinal discoveries of all time was the quinine tree. The bark of *Cinchona* plants has provided the anti-malarial drug quinine since at least 1638, when it cured the Countess of Cinchon in Peru. Commercial plantations were not developed though until the 1800s in Asia. After World War II synthetic anti-malarial drugs were developed, but due to a build-up of resistance, quinine continues, to some extent, to be used. The trees can be seen in tropical arboretums around the world.

Identification: There is great variation within each *Cinchona* species, and hybrids are readily produced. The leaves of *C. officinalis* are generally smooth, shiny, mid-green and 7.5–15cm (3–6in) long. The tubular flowers vary from red to pale pink. They are covered in fine silky hair, are often heavily fragrant, and found in terminal and axillary panicles. The ovoid fruit is 1.5cm (⅝in) long, and splits into two to release numerous winged seeds.

Right: The cinchona bark is usually harvested by either coppicing the trees every six years or by carefully shaving the bark off two sides of the trunk at any one time, without damaging the cambium.

Leichhardt Tree

Nauclea orientalis

This tree is naturally found growing in coastal locations, alongside rivers, in swamps and in boggy areas of rainforest. It is useful for stabilizing river banks. Traditionally, the tree has been used by Aborigines: the trunk was carved into canoes, the leaves and bark were used as fish poison, pain relief and medicine, while the fruit is edible and the bark also yields a yellow dye. The tree is grown for shade.

Identification: The light brown or grey trunk is deeply furrowed and carries an attractive, stately, well balanced crown with spreading branches. The foliage is thick, smooth and glossy. Leaves are 13cm (5in) long and bright green with paler veins. The tiny, delicate yellow fragrant flowers are arranged in attractive, softly spiky balls, 5cm (2in) in diameter. The flowers arise from the leaf axils in late spring and summer. The fruit is a round, soft, red berry containing black seeds.

Distribution: Coastal areas of Queensland, Australia; New Guinea and Indonesia.
Height: 20m (66ft)
Shape: Conical
Evergreen
Pollinated: Insect
Leaf shape: Ovate to obovate

Left: The fruit is composed of numerous tiny capsules, each splitting into four and containing minute black seeds.

Indian Mulberry

Morinda citrifolia

This small, fast-growing tree is grown commercially in India and Burma for the red dye in its root. Historically, the tree provided dyes of many colours from its different parts, to the Polynesians. Every part has medicinal properties. The putrid-smelling, yet edible, fruit was only eaten by indigenous people when food was scarce. The name *Morinda* is derived from *Morus* and *indica*, meaning "Indian mulberry".

Identification: The pale yellowish trunk and stout four-angled branches carry a deep green, glossy crown of foliage. Each smooth leaf is 15–25cm (6–10in) long with prominent paler veins and midrib. Small white tubular flowers form clusters in the leaf axils throughout the year. They develop from a globular head, which progresses to form the lumpy compound fruit. The fruit is ovoid, soft and 8cm (3in) long.

Distribution: Pacific islands, north Australia, New Guinea, Indonesia, Malaysia.
Height: 9m (30ft)
Shape: Domed
Evergreen
Pollinated: Insect
Leaf shape: Elliptic

Rght: The fleshy and juicy fruit is green when immature, grey to creamy yellow when ripe.

Right: Indian mulberry leaves have traditionally been used in poultices and to treat wounds.

Robusta Coffee

Coffea canephora

Beans from this species account for about a quarter of traded coffee. It is used primarily in espresso and cheaper instant coffee, as it has a poorer flavour yet higher caffeine content. The plants grow more vigorously and yield more abundantly than *C. arabica*. They are tolerant of poor growing conditions and are disease resistant. Breeding programmes are under way to introduce this resistance into other coffee species. Two different strains are apparent: an upright form and the more widely planted spreading form. Commercial plants are pruned to 3m (10ft) to facilitate harvesting of the beans.

Identification: The handsome, deep green, slightly hanging leaves are 20cm (8in) long. The pungently sweet-scented, white star-like flowers appear in clusters along the branches. The smooth, ovoid fruit forms in dense clusters, takes about ten months to ripen, and is 2cm (¾in) long and red when ripe.

Distribution: Congo, Gabon, Zaire, Angola, Uganda.
Height: 10m (33ft)
Shape: Variable
Evergreen
Pollinated: Insect
Leaf shape: Ovate

Left: The leaves have wavy margins and deeply set veins.

Left and right: The fruit contains two pale brown, flattened seeds, which are the coffee beans.

THE PALM FAMILY

The palms, Arecaceae, are monocotyledons. There are about 150 genera, the majority of which come from tropical and subtropical regions where they are a common feature in wild and cultivated areas. Most palms have a hard, woody upright stem or stems, and recognizable arching leaf fronts. Many provide invaluable products including foodstuffs, cordage, timbers, waxes and oils.

Burmese Fish-tail Palm

Caryota mitis

The aptly named fish-tail palms have unusual and distinctive foliage, each leaflet representing a fish tail. This species is an under-storey plant from humid rainforests, and a popular garden plant throughout the tropics. It is multi-stemmed. When each stem reaches its full height it commences flowering, and subsequently fruits.

Flowers appear from the top, successively opening down the length of the stem to the ground.

Identification: Each stem may reach 10cm (4in) in diameter. The suckering habit ensures that fronds are found along the entire height of the plant. The erect fronds are overall triangular in shape, reaching 2.4m (8ft) in length, with deep green, shiny leaflets. Leaflets are triangular, have a ragged distal edge and measure up to 18cm (7in) long. The tightly packed inflorescences produce masses of hanging stems clothed with white flowers followed by fruit.

Distribution: Burma to Philippines.
Height: 9m (30ft)
Shape: Multi-stemmed, palm
Evergreen
Pollinated: Insect and/or wind
Leaf shape: Bipinnate

Above: This palm puts a huge amount of energy into an enormous number of fruits. When the fruit is ripe, the fruiting stem dies.

Right: Fruits ripen to dark red or black, and they each measure 1.5cm (⅔in).

Sealing Wax Palm

Lipstick palm *Cyrtostachys lakka*

One of the most memorable plants from a first trip to the tropics will surely be this palm. The deep glossy red frond bases clasping the stems are a unique feature, satisfying its descriptive common names of "sealing wax" and "lipstick" palm. It is native to damp humid forests and coastal swamps but can prove problematic in cultivation. Nonetheless it is such a garden-worthy plant that it is persistently cultivated throughout the tropics.

Identification: The palm is multi-stemmed with narrow, grey to brown stems, reaching 15cm (6in) wide, marked with white leaf scar rings. The sparse upright arching fronds are found throughout the plant's height, due to its suckering nature. Each frond is 1.2m (4ft) long, has a red midrib and smooth, dark green, 45cm (18in) long leaflets. The flower inflorescence also has a red stem and numerous small flowers. The fruit is round, red or black when ripe and contains one seed.

Distribution: Thailand, Malaysia and Borneo.
Height: 9m (30ft)
Shape: Multi-stemmed, palm
Evergreen
Pollinated: Insect and/or wind
Leaf shape: Pinnate

Right: The elegant arching, deep green fronds and fine red stems are a striking sight.

Loyak

Licuala grandis

This diminutive palm is a popular choice for gardens throughout the tropics and is an unusual houseplant in temperate zones. The broad distinctive leaves, pleated like corrugated cardboard, are most unusual and striking. They form on long spiny stems creating an elegant yet compact head above the fine stem. This under-storey palm is found in isolated patches in forests.

Left: The yellowish flowers are 1cm (½ in) long and in 1m- (1yd-) long narrow panicles.

Identification: The 8cm- (3in-) thick stem retains the previous fronds' bases and is covered in a dense mat of tightly woven brown fibres. The crown is composed of approximately 20 leaves, which arch away from the plant on their 90cm- (3ft-) long upright stems. The leaves are smooth, bright green, heavily toothed around the margin, and undulating. Each leaf is up to 75cm (30in) long. The attractive round fruit is 1cm (½ in) across and red when ripe.

Distribution: Solomon and Vanuatu (New Britain) islands (south and east of Papua New Guinea).
Height: 3m (10ft)
Shape: Single-stemmed, palm
Evergreen
Pollinated: Insect and/or wind
Leaf shape: Orbicular to diamond (fan)

OTHER SPECIES OF NOTE

Nibung *Oncosperma tigillarium*
This is a multi-stemmed palm from the coastal areas of South-east Asia. It may have up to 40 very slender, pale grey stems, which grow to 20m (66ft) high. These are covered in long, ferocious, black spines. The small crowns of feathery palm fronds hang elegantly on top of the stems. The fruit of this palm is purple to black.

Senegal Date Palm *Phoenix reclinata*
Native to a wide area of tropical Africa and Madagascar, this multi-stemmed palm is found in open woodland, scrub thickets and beside rivers. Plants consist of up to 25 thick, yet gracefully curving stems reaching 9m (30ft). Stems are topped with a dense crown of arching fronds up to 4m (13ft) long, with vicious spines at the base. Female plants produce eye-catching fruit which is bright orange and found in large clusters. This fruit is eaten raw or cooked and used to make wine. In addition, the seeds may be roasted and ground to make a coffee substitute.

Coco de Mer *Lodoicea maldivica*
This impressive giant palm from the isolated Seychelles islands is highly endangered. It produces the largest single seeded fruit of any known plant, weighing in at up to 20kg (44lbs). The seed is like two large coconuts fused together. These characteristics led to the seeds being over-collected and sold to tourists in the 1970s. The plants are now heavily protected, but due to their incredibly slow growth, and the fact that each seed takes many years to ripen, recovery will be indeterminately slow. The palm grows to 30m (100ft) and carries a crown of colossal deep green fan-shaped leaves.

Bismarck Palm

Bismarckia nobilis

This magnificent palm is the only species in its genus and has become rare in the wild. It is incredibly beautiful, and is grown for its huge leaves held in a dense crown above a straight trunk. The leaves vary in colour between plants from blue-green to grey-green; the most highly prized are those with steely blue-grey foliage. It is highly adaptable, growing well in tropical and subtropical conditions, and is drought-tolerant. Although slow growing, it is popular and widely planted.

Identification: The rough stem reaches up to 30cm (12in) in diameter and is mid-brown. The thick leaves measure up to 2.5m (8ft) across and are very heavy. They are folded and divided into long tapering points. When young, they may have a reddish margin. The flowers form on a 1.2m (4ft) inflorescence and produce hanging clusters of large, ovoid, shiny dark brown fruit that contains large seeds.

Distribution: Madagascar.
Height: 25m (82ft)
Shape: Single-stemmed, palm
Evergreen
Pollinated: Insect and/or wind
Leaf shape: Palmate (fan)

Left: The huge silver leaves are adapted to dry conditions and held rigidly away from the trunk.

Foxtail Palm

Wodyetia bifurcata

Only discovered in the early 1980s, this species is named after the Aborigine, Wodyeti, who died in the 1970s. It made a rapid entry into the horticultural world and is now popular throughout tropical and subtropical regions. Initially fears were raised over the future of wild populations. However, the plants proved to be fast growing, highly adaptable, tolerant of garden conditions, and produced a large quantity of seed; so there was no incentive to poachers to collect from the wild. They are grown for their fluffy, plume-like, heavily arching fronds.

Identification: The grey or tan stem is slightly bottle-shaped. The long clasping leaf bases are pale green. The crown consists of only about a dozen fronds, each up to 3m (10ft) long. The leaflets are dark green and extend from the midrib in every direction to form the foxtail. The large, branched inflorescences give rise to a mass of attractive, 6cm- (2½in-) long, oval, orange or red fruit.

Distribution: Northern Queensland, Australia.
Height: 12m (40ft)
Shape: Single-stemmed, palm
Evergreen
Pollinated: Insect and/or wind
Leaf shape: Pinnate

Left: At one time there was a black market in the sale of this fruit.

Left: Considering its origin, this palm is tolerant of both drought and frost. It is becoming a very popular landscaping subject in tropical and subtropical zones.

OTHER SPECIES OF NOTE

Piccabeen Palm *Archontophoenix cunninghamiana*
An elegant palm from Australia's subtropical east-coast rainforests. *A. alexandrae* is very similar in appearance. It grows to 15m (50ft) with a straight, smooth stem and fine, upright, arching deep green leaves. The small, pale lilac flowers and bright red fruit grow in pendulous panicles. It is a popular landscaping plant although more suited to sheltered areas than exposed sites.

Manila Palm *Veitchia merrillii*
Native to the humid rainforests of the Philippines, this single-stemmed palm grows to 6m (20ft). It is a neat little palm that resembles a dwarf version of the royal palm *Roystonea regia*. It has a compact crown of stiff, bright green, arched fronds carrying upright leaflets. Often a number of seeds may be sown together, giving rise to an apparent multi-stemmed specimen.

Solitaire Palm *Ptychosperma elegans*
This graceful palm originates from the humid rainforests of north-east Queensland. It grows to 12m (40ft) with a slender stem reaching only 15cm (6in) in diameter. The few stiffly arching fronds carry broad olive-green leaflets. The flowers and subsequent orange-red fruit appear on large, dense, many-branched inflorescences. Although best suited to tropical conditions, it will survive in sheltered warm temperate sites.

Ruffle Palm *Aiphanes caryotifolia*
From northern South America, this palm's widespread habitat includes deciduous and rainforests. It is common in disturbed areas and is cultivated locally for the edible red fruit and seeds. It grows to 9m (30ft), with a single stem clothed in long black spines. The softly arching fronds have roughly triangular leaflets with jagged edges.

Toddy Palm *Borassus flabellifer* .
An impressive palm reaching 21m (70ft) with a massive trunk over 1m (3ft) in diameter and a crown of fan-shaped, blue-green leaves, each to 3m (10ft) in diameter. In its native India through to Indonesia and southern China this palm is valuable in every part. The immature seeds are canned and exported as toddy palms. The palms are also often tapped for their sap which is used to make palm sugar.

Jaggery Palm *Caryota urens*
This popular but short-lived, single-stemmed palm, native from India to Malaysia, grows to 20m (66ft). The 6m- (20ft-) long bipinnate fronds have fish-tail-like leaflets. When flower stems are cut off, a sweet sap, or toddy, is collected from the wound. One tree can yield about 800lt (176 gallons) a year, which when boiled becomes like brown sugar and is called "jaggery". The palm also yields tasty sago from its pith.

Bottle Palm

Hyophorbe lagenicaulis

This incredibly slow-growing palm found in the fertile volcanic soils of Round Island in the Mascarenes is facing extinction in the wild. The specimens which were once collected from the wild, depleting the numbers, are now found growing in gardens throughout the tropics. Ironically, these will ensure its survival. It is grown for the novelty value of its distinctive and architectural form. The sparse crown is also architectural, each arching frond held rigidly in place.

Identification: The bulging stem is grey and smooth with closely-spaced rings. The crown consists of about six fronds. The deep green fronds have heavy-duty midribs, and the two rows of rigidly held leaflets form a V-shape in cross section above it. Tiny flowers form in densely branched inflorescences around the top of the trunk.

Distribution: Mascarene Islands.
Height: 4.5m (15ft)
Shape: Single-stemmed, palm
Evergreen
Pollinated: Insect and/or wind
Leaf shape: Pinnate

Right: Fruits blacken when ripe.

Left: When mature, the trunk is swollen into a short fat bottle shape.

Left: Each frond is about 2m (7ft) long.

Triangle Palm

Dypsis decaryi

This striking palm, native to the drier forested area of Madagascar, has been successfully grown in tropical and Mediterranean regions of the world. The short, sturdy stem is topped by clasping leaf bases arranged in threes, one above the other, and thus is triangular in cross section, a feature unique within the palm family. The large, upright fronds elegantly arch at the tips and arise in a triangular shape. They are bluish-green and have long elegant threads hanging from them to the ground.

Identification: The trunk is grey with rings. The clasping frond bases may be covered in blue-grey felt. The fronds are up to 3.5m (12ft) long and carry very narrow, bluish leaflets held upright, forming a V-shape in cross section. The leaflets nearest the stem extend into long threads. The small cream flowers are found on short panicles in and around the leaf bases. The small oval fruit is green or yellow when ripe.

Distribution: Southern Madagascar.
Height: 6m (20ft)
Shape: Single-stemmed, palm
Evergreen
Pollinated: Insect and/or wind
Leaf shape: Pinnate

Below: In the wild, this palm is an endangered species because the fruit is collected and eaten.

Left: The leaves are used for thatching in Madagascar.

Coconut

Cocos nucifera

Tropical beaches would be incomplete without coconut palms arching towards the ocean. They can grow in sand and are incredibly tolerant of windy, salty conditions. Every part of this palm can be used: the leaves for thatch, the growing tip for palm cabbage, the flower for a local drink called toddy, the fruit for food, drink and oil, the fruit husk for matting and fuel, and the trunk for construction. The origins of the coconut are uncertain; it was cultivated long before records began. It is grown inland and in coastal areas throughout the tropics.

Distribution: Unknown.
Height: 30m (100ft)
Shape: Single-stemmed, palm
Evergreen
Pollinated: Insect
Leaf shape: Pinnate

Below and below left: The tough leaves can withstand strong coastal winds. Older leaves turn yellow before dropping off.

Identification: Slender, often curved trunks are swollen at the base, where new roots emerge. The lightly arching fronds grow to 6m (20ft) with long, hanging, deep green leaflets. The 1m- (1yd-) long branched inflorescence carries small, cream flowers. The fruit is a hard, triangular sphere, 30cm (12in) long and green or yellow.

Left: A coconut fruit may float at sea for many months and still be viable to germinate.

Betel Nut

Areca catechu

Distribution: Malaysia, Philippines, Indonesia.
Height: 20m (66ft)
Shape: Single-stemmed, palm
Evergreen
Pollinated: Insect
Leaf shape: Pinnate

This fast-growing forest palm is cultivated throughout humid areas of Asia. Commonly, the seeds are sliced and a tobacco leaf and a little lime added, then this is wrapped inside betel pepper leaves and chewed as a mild narcotic. The red juice stains the mouth and rots the teeth. The fruit is also said to reduce hunger, stimulate digestion, prevent indigestion and have medicinal properties. Each mature tree yields 200–250 nuts a year and they bear from 6–8 years, until they are about 35 years old.

Identification: The straight, smooth, green stem carries 2.5m- (8ft-) long deep green, glossy, erect fronds. The closely-spaced leaflets are 50cm (20in) long and 5cm (2in) wide, forming a dense crown. The small pale yellow flowers are found on a 1m- (3ft-) long weeping inflorescence. The fruit is egg-like in size and shape, with white flesh and a yellow, orange or red husk.

Left and right: The fruits each contain a seed. Seeds are brown, 2.5cm (1in) long and vaguely cone shaped.

Above: The leaves form a compact crown.

Assai

Euterpe edulis

Large stands of this fast-growing graceful palm dominate damp areas of rainforest in the Amazon basin. The fruit is edible and can be used to make a nutritious drink, assai, by soaking in water. The palm hearts are also popular, although their harvest kills the palm. The heart is harvested from the young growing tip when the palm is four years old. It is a fast growing tolerant palm and has been introduced into cities and coastal areas across the tropics. Other species of *Euterpe* are multi-stemmed and so need not be killed during the harvest of the heart.

Identification: The smooth trunk is slender, reaching about 15cm (6in) in diameter. It is grey with long green clasping leaf bases at the top. The deep green fronds are up to 3m (10ft) long and elegantly arching. Fronds consist of narrow weeping leaflets up to 90cm (36in) long. The small white flowers on erect panicles produce large quantities of purple or black fruit, 5mm (¼in) across.

Distribution: Amazon basin, Brazil.
Height: 30m (100ft)
Shape: Single-stemmed, palm
Evergreen
Pollinated: Insect
Leaf shape: Pinnate

Right: The fruit is popular with forest birds and mammals.

Left and far left: Assai foliage is particularly elegant.

African Oil Palm

Elaeis guineensis

An immensely important commercial palm product is palm oil, derived from the fruit of this palm. Vast areas of Malaysian tropical rainforest have been cleared to grow monocultures of the lucrative oil palm, but it has not been exploited in Africa, where it originated. Palm oil is used in cooking oil, lubricants, waxes, soaps and detergents. In Africa this particular species of palm is tapped for toddy (a drink made from sap). It is native to swampy and riverside locations where it tolerates flooding.

Distribution: Wet tropical West Africa (Senegal to Congo).
Height: 20m (66ft)
Shape: Single-stemmed, palm
Evergreen
Pollinated: Wind and weevil
Leaf shape: Pinnate

Identification: The trunk is thick and lumpy. The crown is dense with hanging fronds, each 4.5m (15ft) long. The fronds consist of 50–60 dark green, hanging leaflets, each 60cm (24in) long. The leaf stems carry thick, sharp spines. Male and female flowers occur on separate inflorescences. Male flowers resemble tight clusters of long, fat cream catkins. Female flowers are cream and in dense, short-stemmed clusters. The dense bunches of fruit may weigh up to 70kg (150lb); each is 5cm (2in) long and black to red-brown when ripe.

Above and left: The fruit occurs in large spiny clusters. It yields yellow to red palm oil from the fibrous flesh, and white palm kernel oil from the seed.

MISCELLANEOUS MONOCOTS

Monocotyledons are often recognized by having parallel veins, although this is not always the case, and when young, by their single seed leaf. Very few monocotyledons, except for the palms, grow into trees. The stems (trunks) of these plants tend to be pithy and fibrous with a woody surface and do not branch as readily as dicotyledons. Leaves grow from the compact growing points at the tips of the stems.

Common Screw Pine

Pandanus utilis

Planted throughout the tropics, this fine looking plant, with a strong upright form, is tolerant of coastal conditions. The common name derives from the distinctive spiral arrangement of the leaves, and the fruit that resembles a large pine cone. The fibrous leaves are used for thatching, making Manila hats and to make bags to line sacks of sugar for export.

Identification: The cylindrical stem becomes thinner towards the base of thick stilt roots. These roots grow straight down into the soil. The stem is marked with lines where leaves were previously attached. It branches in tiers and carries dense heads of 1m- (3ft-) long, 8cm- (3in-) wide, thick, leathery, green leaves at the tips. The leaves have fine red teeth along the edge. Plants are either male or female. Male flowers are found in long branched spikes and female flowers in compact heads. The hanging compound fruit is yellow to red when ripe, 15cm (6in) long and composed of about 100 separate fruits.

Distribution: Madagascar.
Height: 18m (60ft)
Shape: Conical, spreading
Evergreen
Pollinated: Wind and insect
Leaf shape: Sword

Left: The hard edible fruit has a small amount of pulp in it and is attractive to mammals. Leaves and fruit are used in tropical floral arrangements.

Traveller's Palm

Ravenala madagascariensis

The magnificent traveller's palm graces the entrance of many prestigious buildings in the tropics. Its striking, formal, two-dimensional silhouette is a result of the leaf stems growing in an east to west orientation. It is believed that lost and thirsty travellers may find their way from this plant and also find water in the base of each cup-shaped leaf stem. The plant is not a palm, but more closely related to bananas and the bird-of-paradise flowers of florists; it is the only species in its genus.

Above: Green bracts contain the pale flowers.

Identification: The straight, pale brown trunk is topped by immense 3m- (10ft-) long leaves. The long leaf stems arise very closely from the crown. The bright green leaves are often shredded by the wind. From between the leaf stems emerge dense, often congested, large green bracts holding the inconspicuous white flowers. Flowers appear year round and particularly in the winter. The bracts become hard and woody and enclose the large black seeds, coated in an extremely unnatural looking blue aril.

Distribution: Madagascar.
Height: 25m (82ft)
Shape: Fan-like
Evergreen
Pollinated: Lemur
Leaf shape: Oblong

Above: The often ragged leaves are carried on a 3m (10ft-) long stem.

Left: The leaf stems form a distinctive pattern as they emerge from the trunk.

Rhodesian Tree Aloe

Aloe excelsa

A number of aloes grow very slowly into "trees" of a few metres. They are stunning plants, with their bold form, distinctive succulent foliage and prominent winter flowers, and are a valuable addition to cactus gardens. They originate from drier regions and dislike wet winters but are very tolerant of drought conditions.

Above: The dense spires of flowers open in succession from bottom to top.

Identification: The brown stem rarely branches, and it is rough with the remains of old leaf bases. The 75cm (30in-) long leaves form a rosette at the top of the stem, emerging close to one another. They are very thick and succulent, green and arched. Each leaf is concave on the upper surface and keeled below with short spines along the edges. Older leaves become brown and withered but hang on the stem for some time. Each small tubular flower is yellow, orange or red. They are closely packed into tight spikes on the top of an upright, many-branched, 1m- (3ft-) tall stem.

Right: The fruit is densely packed along the panicles.

Distribution: Zimbabwe.
Height: 8m (26ft)
Shape: Like single-stemmed palm
Evergreen
Leaf shape: Sword

OTHER SPECIES OF NOTE

Quiver Tree *Aloe dichotoma*
Native to incredibly dry areas of Namibia and southern South Africa, this slow-growing tree may eventually reach 9m (30ft), with a massive smooth-barked trunk. The trunk divides into many thick branches, producing a dense flat-topped crown. The thick leaves are grey-green with minute yellow spines along their margins. The tiny yellow flowers appear in winter, packed on to branched spikes 30cm (12in) high.

Pandanus odoratissimus
This particularly useful plant is widely grown in the Pacific islands. Large fruiting varieties have edible seeds and flesh, and the leaf fibres are utilized in clothing, bags and mats. In India it is grown for a perfume, obtained from the tiny male flowers. From southern Asia, the Pacific islands and northern Australia, it grows to 6m (20ft) with a heavily divided trunk, many stilt roots and clusters of spiny sword-shaped green leaves. Compact female flower heads produce 30cm- (12in-) long, hard, ovoid, compound fruit.

Banana *Musa* spp.
Bananas are not really trees at all. They are gigantic herbaceous plants, the "trunk" being composed of many layers of leaves. They provide fruit, vegetable, fibre and ornamental flowers to tropical countries. Each water-filled green stem is topped with huge oblong bright green leaves. The whitish flowers are enclosed within a massive red, yellow or green flower bud. Many fruits develop simultaneously on an arching stem. When the fruit has ripened the banana stem dies while a new one grows.

Dragon Tree

Dracaena draco

The genus name *Dracaena* means "female dragon" and *draco* means "dragon". The infamous dragon tree is so named due to its deep red sap, once thought in European legend to be dragon's blood. The sap is used as a dye. This impressive, stout tree is very slow growing and lives for hundreds of years. An enormous old specimen in northern Tenerife is now quite a tourist attraction. In Mediterranean regions it thrives in coastal locations and is tolerant of drought. It is also grown as a houseplant in temperate regions.

Identification: The short wide trunk is pale brown with a rough surface and divides repeatedly into short sturdy branches. Each branch is topped by a small compact rosette of stiff, blue-green leaves. Each leaf is up to 60cm (24in) long and 5cm (2in) wide. The small, insignificant greenish white flowers are in large panicles and are followed by small orange berries.

Far right: The seed from the fleshy fruit does not germinate easily, and as a result, there are only a few dragon tree specimens growing in the dry mountainous regions of their homeland.

Distribution: Canary Islands
Height: 15m (50ft)
Shape: Spreading
Evergreen
Leaf shape: Sword

GLOSSARY

Anther The terminal part of the stamen in which the pollen matures.
Aril A fleshy and colourful appendage to the seed capsule.
Axil The upper angle between the stalk and the leaf.

Bast The outer fibrous part of the trunk.
Bipinnate (of leaves). Having leaflets which are also divided in pinnate manner.
Bract A small leaf or scale placed below the calyx.

Cambium A layer of cells just within the outer coating of the trunk of the tree from which annual growth of bark and wood occurs.
Catkin A cylindrical cluster of male or female flowers. Catkins usually hang down from the tree.
Chlorophyll. Green colouring matter of plants.
Chloroplast Part of the tree cell containing chlorophyll.
Class A collection of orders of trees containing a common characteristic.
Columnar Refers to a tall, thin upright tree shape.
Compound (of leaves). With leaf divided into leaflets.
Conical Cone-like shape of a tree.

Below: Canadian yew, Taxus canadensis.

Above: Chinese tulip tree, Liriodendron chinensis.

Conifer Cone-bearing tree. Can be evergreen or deciduous.
Cordate (of leaves). Heart-shaped.
Cotyledon The first leaf or leaf-pair within seed.
Cultivar A variety of tree produced from a natural species and maintained in existence by cultivation.
Cuticle The protective surface film on leaves.
Cutting A tree propagated from part of original tree. The cut edge of the twig may form roots and grow into a small tree once potted in suitable compost.

Deciduous Shedding leaves annually or seasonally.
Dicotyledon Plant with double leaf or leaf-pair within seed.
Dioecious Having male and female cones or flowers on separate trees.
Drupe Fleshy fruit containing stony seed-cover, for example plum.

Elliptic (of leaves). Oval in shape, with widest point at midsection.
Epidermis Protective layer of cells on leaves and stalks.
Evergreen Bearing leaves all year round, although each leaf has a limited life span.

"False" (of species). Trees that have characteristics that superficially resemble a specific species.
Family A collection of genera of trees sharing a common characteristic.
Fastigiate (of trees). Having a conical or tapering outline.
Fissure Splits, cracks and grooves, usually in the surface of the bark.
Form A group of trees distinguished from other trees by a single characteristic.

Genera Plural of genus.
Genus A taxonomic group into which a family is divided and usually containing one or more species.
Glaucous (of leaves). Blue-green colouring.
Graft A plant produced by joining dissimilar plant materials.
Gymnosperm A plant bearing seed that is unprotected by seed vessels, for example conifer.

Hardwood Deciduous trees.
Heartwood Dense wood within inner core of tree trunk.
Hybrid A new species of plant that results from a cross between two genetically dissimilar plants, often growing in close vicinity.

Below: Cedar of Lebanon, Cedrus libani.

Above: Silver maple, Acer saccharinum.

Indumentum The outer coating of down or hair on the surface of a leaf.
Inflorescence The arrangement of flowers on the flower-bearing stalks.

Lanceolate (of leaves). Narrow oval shape, tapering to point.
Layer (of propagation). A shoot or branch that grows roots while still attached to the parent plant.
Lenticel An aeration pore in bark.
Linear (of leaves). Having a narrow, elongated shape.
Lobed (of leaves). Having rounded indentations around the leaf edge.

Meristem Growing tissue in trees.
Monocotyledon A plant with a single leaf or leaf-pair within a seed.
Monoecious Having male and female flowers on the same tree.
Monotypic A tree that is the only species in the genus. These are quite unusual.

Needle A slender, elongated leaf.

Oblong (of leaves). Being longer than broad, with parallel sides.
Obovate (of leaves). Egg-shaped, with the broadest end growing furthest from the stem.
Orbicular (of leaves). Round.
Osmosis Transfer of solutions between porous partitions; process whereby liquid moves from one cell to another.
Ovate (of leaves). Egg-shaped, with the broadest end nearest the stem.

Ovoid (of flowers). Egg-shaped.
Ovule Female reproductive structure which develops into a seed after being fertilized.

Palmate (of leaves). With three or more leaflets arising from the same point.
Panicle A head of stalked flowers.
Petiole Leaf stalk.
Phloem Soft tissue within the tree trunk.
Photosynthesis Use of sunlight to create nutrients within leaves.
Phreatophyte Tree or other plant with long taproots.
Pinna(e) Primary division of pinnate leaf.
Pinnate (of leaves). Having leaflets in pairs on either side of petiole.
Primates An order of mammals typically with flexible hands and feet, a highly developed brain and good eyesight.
Prostrate With a trunk that grows along the ground. Could be caused by adverse weather.
Pubescence; pubescent. A layer of short, fine hairs; downy.

Raceme A flowerstem from which flowerheads grow, with the oldest flowers closest to the base.

Samara A winged fruit, for example ash key.
Sapwood Soft wood between heartwood and bark.
Scale Small, modified leaf.

Left: Temple juniper, Juniperus rigida.

Above: Prunus 'Tai Haku'

Scale-like Plate-like covering.
Sessile (of leaves). Without stalks.
Simple (of leaves). Leaves which are not divided into leaflets.
Softwood Coniferous trees.
Species A group into which the members of a genus are divided. Can contain forms, varieties and subspecies.
Stomata Pores in the epidermis of leaves.
Subclass A subdivision of a class.
Subspecies A subdivision of a species.

Tepal The outer part of the flower that is clearly not part of the corolla and the calyx.
Terminal inflorescence The final flowerhead on the stem.
Transpiration Loss of moisture through evaporation.
Trifoliate (of leaves). Having three leaflets to make up one leaf.
Tripinnate (of leaves). Having three or more pinnae.

Variety A group of trees with distinct characteristics, but insufficiently different from the true species to be recognized as a true species of its own.

Xerophyte Tree or other plant capable of conserving and storing water.
Xylem Woody tissue within tree trunk.

INDEX

Publisher: Joanna Lorenz
Editorial Director: Helen Sudell
Editor: Simona Hill
Designer: Nigel Partridge
Tree Illustrators: Peter Barrett, Penny Brown, Stuart Carter, Stuart Lafford, David More
Map Illustrators: Anthony Duke, Sebastian Quigley
Photographers: Peter Anderson, Sidney Teo
Consultant on the Tropical Trees of America directory: Clive Kin
Production Controller: Pirong Wang

ISBN 978-1-4351-5597-8

Manufactured in China.

2 4 6 8 10 9 7 5 3 1

Previously published in three separate volumes: *The World Encyclopedia of Trees*; *The Illustrated Encyclopedia of Trees of the Americas*;
The Illustrated Encyclopedia of Trees of Britain & Europe

PUBLISHER'S NOTE
Although the information in this book is believed to be accurate and true at the time of going to press, neither the authors nor the publisher can
accept any legal responsibility or liability for any errors or omissions that may have been made.

Page 1: Pong Pong (Sea mango) *Cerbera odollam*
Page 2: Giant Redwood *Sequoiadendron giganteum*
Page 3: English Oak *Quercus robur*

Picture Acknowledgements
The publisher would like to thank the following picture libraries for permission to use their photographs:
Ardea: p65b p310b, p364tr. **Edward Parker:** p10–11, p17tl and bc, p18 bl, p30 bl, p31 tr, p32 t, p33 tl, p34, p38 bl, p39 t, p43 tr, p44 tr, p49 all, p86,
p87 bl and b. **The Garden Picture Library:** p52 tr, p53 tl, p54 br, p55 bl, and bc, p57 bl and br, p58 bl, p59 tr, p61 all, p296b, 306b, p315tl, p327tr,
p422tr. **Garden World Images:** p 320b, p356br, p370bl, p374bl, p415tr. **Oxford Scientific Films:** p47 br, p67 all, p71, p77. **Peter Anderson:** p33b, p75t.
Tony Russell: p36 tr, p53 bl, p281 both, p283b, p333bl, p420tr, p421tl, p423.
Key: b= bottom, t = top, r = right, c = centre, l = left

Publisher's Acknowledgements
The publishers would like to thank Daniel Luscombe and Bedgebury Pinetum, Kent; Westonbirt, The National Arboretum, Gloucestershire;
Kew Gardens, Surrey; Tortworth Park, Gloucestershire; Batsford Arboretum, Gloucestershire; RHS Garden, Wisley, Surrey,
and RHS Garden, Rosemoor, North Devon.